International Dispute Resolution

International Dispute Resolution

Cases and Materials

Second Edition

Mary Ellen O'Connell
Robert and Marion Short Chair in Law & Research Professor
of International Dispute Resolution—Kroc Institute,
University of Notre Dame Law School

Carolina Academic Press
Durham, North Carolina

ISBN: 978-1-59460-904-6
LCCN: 2011943159

Carolina Academic Press
700 Kent Street
Durham, North Carolina 27701
Telephone (919) 489-7486
Fax (919) 493-5668
www.cap-press.com

Printed in the United States of America

This book is dedicated to

Sir Elihu Lauterpacht, C.B.E., Q.C.,

an extraordinary teacher and practitioner of international dispute resolution.

Contents

II. Binding Methods

B. Judicial Settlement

2. National Courts

Table of Cases

Acknowledgments

In preparing this second edition, I am very grateful for the exceptional research assistance of Emily Follas and Jolie Schwarz and the invaluable office assistance of Leslie Berg, Nicole Bourbon, and Regina Gesicki. Mary Cowsert and Patti Ogden of the Kresge Law Library provided, as always, great support.

I also gratefully acknowledge permission for the use of excerpts from the following books, periodicals, and other documents: Richard Bilder, An Overview of the International Dispute Settlement, 1986, Journal of International Dispute Resolution; Charles Manga Fombad, Consultation and Negotiation in the Pacific Settlement of International Disputes, 1989, African Journal of International and Comparative Law (707) Journals (Reprints), Edinburgh University Press; Sir Robert Jennings, The Proliferation of Adjudicatory Bodies: Dangers and Possible Answers, 1995, 9 ASIL Bulletin; Jan Klabbers, An Introduction to International Institutional Law, 2002, Cambridge University Press; Sven M.G. Koopmans, The Use of Inter-State Conciliation, Diplomatic Dispute Settlement 1–3 2008, Cambridge University Press/The Hague; Barbara Kwiatkowska, The Ireland v. United Kingdom Case: Applying to the Doctrine of Treaty Parallelism, 2003, Volume 18, International Journal of Marine and Coastal Law, Brill Academic Publishers; reprinted from International Litigation and Arbitration, 2nd Edition, 2002, pp. 339–343; Andreas Lowenfeld, with permission of the West Group; Ruth MacKenzie, Introduction, in the Role of International Courts, 2010, Carl Baudenbacher and Erhard Busek eds., German Law Publishers (GLP) Prof. Dr. Thomas Wegerich; The Prospects for Enforcing Monetary Judgments of the International Court of Justice, 1990, The Virginia Journal of International Law, ME O'Connell; Claire Palley, An International Relations Debacle, The UN Secretary General's Mission of Good Offices in Cyprus 1999–2004, 2005, Hart Publishing Limited; Thomas Princen, International Mediation—The View from the Vatican, 1987, Volume 3, Negotiation Journal, Blackwell Publishing; B. G. Ramcharan, The Good Offices of the United Nations Secretary-General in the Field of Human Rights, 1982, American Journal of International Law; August Reinisch, Avoidance Techniques, International Organizations Before National Courts, 2002; pp 35–37; J.M. Ruda, Intervention before the International Court of Justice, Fifty Years of the International Court of Justice: Essays in Honour of Sir Robert Jennings 487, 1996, Vaughan Lowe and Malgosia Fitzmaurice eds.; Anna Spain, Integration Matters: Rethinking the Architecture of International Dispute Resolution, 2010, University of Pennsylvania Journal of International Law vol 32; David P. Stewart, Samantar v. Yousef: Foreign Official Immunity Under Common Law, ASIL Insights, 2010; William Wang, International Arbitration: The Need for Uniform Interim Measures of Relief, 2003, Volume 28, Brooklyn Journal of International Law; and Teresa Whitfield, Good Offices and "Groups of Friends" in Secretary or General? The UN Secretary-General in World Politics, 2007, Cambridge University Press.

International Dispute Resolution

Chapter One

The Study of International Dispute Resolution

Introduction*

A primary, if not the primary, purpose of all law is to prevent and resolve society's disputes. Law can prevent disputes by supplying substantive rules that clarify and assign rights and duties, and, when prevention fails, law can provide procedures to resolve disputes peacefully without resort to violence. The study of international dispute resolution is the study of the law and procedures for resolving disputes in international society, especially law and procedures designed to prevent the resort to the ultimate form of violence, namely, armed conflict or war.

The mechanisms for the peaceful resolution of international disputes have been around as long as international law itself. The standard mechanisms are codified in the United Nations Charter, a multilateral treaty binding today on basically all sovereign states, the core members of international society. Article 33(1) of the Charter provides:

> The parties to any dispute, the continuance of which is likely to endanger the maintenance of international peace and security, shall, first of all, seek a solution by negotiation, enquiry, mediation, conciliation, arbitration, judicial settlement, resort to regional agencies or arrangements, or other peaceful means of their own choice.

Of these mechanisms, negotiation and mediation are probably the oldest. We have evidence of their use from earliest times and in the formation of the very agreement credited with launching the inter-state system, a set of treaties known as the Peace of Westphalia of 1648. The Peace of Westphalia in turn specifies arbitration as a dispute settlement mechanism. Arbitration continued to be used frequently by states in the 18th and 19th Centuries, until the establishment of permanent international courts in the 20th Century. With the end of the Cold War at the close of the 20th Century, obstacles to cooperation among international actors receded and the pressing demands of globalization became a driving force for the establishment of new courts, new commitments to arbitrate, the revival of inquiry and conciliation, and new uses of national courts for the resolution of international disputes. The September 11, 2001, attacks on the United States, however, have slowed the pace of development. The United States has certainly not played the same leadership role in promoting international law and institutions for peaceful settlement as it had previously. Indeed, as this second edition goes to press the United States is involved in armed conflicts in Afghanistan, Iraq, and Libya. Moreover, the United States

* This introduction draws on *Introduction*, INTERNATIONAL DISPUTE SETTLEMENT (Mary Ellen O'Connell ed., 2003 ed.).

argues that it is involved in a worldwide "armed conflict against al Qaeda, the Taliban, and associated forces."[1]

Yet, the history of international dispute resolution shows that after periods of intense inter-state violence, national leaders will tend to commit again to resolving conflict through non-violent means.[2] At the transnational level, resort to peaceful means has not abated. On the contrary, with international society's ever-expanding interactions around the globe from commerce to culture, the need to resolve disputes through the use of mechanisms of peaceful settlement will also continue to expand. Lawyers will practice their profession in this area of the law in ever-greater numbers. The purpose of this book is to prepare them for that practice.

What Is International Dispute Resolution?

The phrase "international dispute resolution" (IDR) is generally used synonymously with "international dispute settlement" and "peaceful settlement of disputes." All three phrases refer to peacefully ending "disputes." International disputes are disagreements on the international plane concerning matters of "fact, law or policy in which a claim or assertion of one party is met with refusal, counter-claim or denial by another."[3] The disagreement must rise to the level of inviting a counter-claim or denial. Mere differences of opinion are not disputes. As the International Court of Justice pointed out in the *Headquarters Agreement Case*,[4] the meaning of "dispute" is important because the obligations in the area of IDR revolve around disputes rather than lesser or greater sorts of issues between states. Thus, the UN Charter, Article 33, refers to the obligation on all member states to settle *disputes* peacefully. If faced with a more serious challenge, such as a significant armed attack, however, states may have the right to use armed force in response. At the opposite extreme, a mere difference of opinion will not trigger binding commitments to enter into dispute resolution.

The disputes of interest here are "international" disputes. An international dispute can involve any dispute in which an international boundary is relevant. Such disputes may involve sovereign states; inter-governmental organizations like the United Nations or the World Trade Organization; non-governmental organizations like the International Committee of the Red Cross or the World Wide Fund for Nature; and natural or juridical persons like Nelson Mandela or Google. The range of potential disputes and the law relevant to resolving them for such a large and diverse group of actors cannot be studied in one course. These materials focus on disputes involving states and/or international organizations. A few cases of so-called "mixed disputes" (involving individuals and states) are also included. Some cases of mixed disputes are included in the book to illustrate certain legal principles that also apply to inter-state and international organization disputes, but for which we have no case illustrating the point for our selected set of actors.

---

1. *See* Harold Hongju Koh, *The Obama Administration and International Law*, Annual Meeting ASIL, U.S. Department of State (Mar. 25, 2010), http://www.state.gov/s/l/releases/remarks/139119.htm. For a discussion of whether the policy of "armed conflict against al Qaeda et al." differs from the Bush administration's "global war on terror" and how both policies are assessed under international law, *see*, Mary Ellen O'Connell, *Choice of Law Against Terrorism*, 7 J. Nat'l Sec. Law & Pol'y 343 (2010).

2. *See infra*, pp. 7–13.

3. J.G. Merrills, International Dispute Settlement 1 (5th ed. 2011).

4. Applicability of the Obligation to Arbitrate under Section 21 of the United Nations Headquarters Agreement of 26 June 1947, 1988 I.C.J. Rep. 12 (Advisory Opinion of April 26).

The book's particular focus was chosen because it constitutes the classic area of concern in the law of international dispute resolution and because, despite that fact, we have relatively few books on this subject. There are several treatises on international dispute resolution, but this book may well offer the first set of cases and materials on the subject. By contrast, we have quite a few collections of cases and materials on related subjects. For example, a number of student casebooks deal with private international dispute settlement.[5] Private international law refers to the law governing transnational relations of individuals, such as international commercial transactions and international family relations. We also have a number of casebooks that deal with accountability of individuals for violating international law, also known as international criminal law,[6] and we have many casebooks dealing with the international rights of individuals or human rights law.[7] This book will not deal directly with international private law, international criminal law, or human rights law. Some references to these bodies of rules will be relevant, however, as no area of international law can be hermetically sealed from another. Still, in the interest of time and space, as well as the need to fill a gap in the literature, the focus here will be on states and international organizations.[8]

As the materials will reveal, the disputes among states and international organizations cover a wide range of topics. Three important classes of disputes will be followed through the book: 1) disputes over state boundaries and shared resources; 2) disputes in the area of diplomatic law, especially consular rights; and 3) disputes in the area of international dispute resolution law. In the first two thematic areas you will learn a good deal of substantive law, along with the law governing the procedures for peacefully resolving such highly important disputes.

Related Fields of Inquiry

These materials are designed for law students. They are concerned with the law governing international disputes. Students should be aware, however, that international dispute resolution is commonly associated with two separate streams of scholarship. In addition to the one represented here, which is squarely within international law and concerns the rules and procedures of dispute settlement, there is another area of scholarship more closely connected to the study of international relations and is also known as peace studies, the study of conflict prevention, or conflict resolution. The focus of peace studies scholars is on effectiveness rather than rules. Scholars ask such questions as whether a particular conflict is "ripe" for negotiation or mediation, whether a particular mediator has the trust of two disputing parties to effectively resolve a dispute, or what will sustain a peace settlement.[9] International lawyers tend to focus on whether parties have an

5. *See, e.g.*, Russell J. Weintraub, International Litigation and Arbitration, Practice and Planning (6th ed. 2011); Gary B. Born, International Commercial Arbitration (vols. 1 & 2 2009), and Gary B. Born and Peter B. Rutledge, International Civil Litigation in United States Courts, Commentary and Materials (4th ed. 2007).

6. *See, e.g.*, Jordan J. Paust et al., International Criminal Law: Cases and Materials (3d ed. 2007).

7. *See, e.g.*, Louis Henkin et al., Human Rights (2d ed. 2009).

8. Regional dispute settlement, such as through the European Union or the North America Free Trade Agreement, is plainly an important topic that cannot be wholly segregated from international dispute settlement. However, this topic is also beyond the scope of this book.

9. *See* Strategies of Peace, Transforming Conflict in a Violent World (Daniel Philpott and Gerard F. Powers eds., 2010); Peacemaking in International Conflict: Methods & Tech-

obligation to resort to dispute resolution, to obey the outcome of a dispute resolution process, or to conduct themselves in a certain fashion during dispute resolution. The two streams have always had some overlap and mutual interest; this overlap has grown along with the prominence of dispute resolution in international relations.

Nevertheless, the two streams developed separately and remain largely distinct from one another. One of the classic works in the field of international dispute resolution is an interdisciplinary study of conflict resolution looking at both the mechanisms available in international law and case studies of actual attempts at conflict prevention. The study appears in two separate volumes, one edited by international relations scholars and the other edited by an international law scholar: M.D. Donelan and F.S. Northedge, *International Disputes: The Political Aspects* (London 1971) and C.M.H. Waldock, *International Disputes: The Legal Aspects* (London 1972). Apparently no more recent book has overcome the division between international legal and international relations analysis. Yet, as ever more work is done on the same international social phenomena by international lawyers and international relations specialists, the integration of the two fields is bound to increase.[10]

Another trend in international dispute resolution is toward greater integration with domestic, particularly American, dispute resolution. The force and dynamism of American legal culture has meant that areas such as arbitration, once developed wholly within international law, are being influenced by developments in American arbitration.[11] Christine Chinkin presents a picture of hybridization of international dispute resolution and American alternative dispute resolution (ADR).[12] Interestingly, American ADR has long combined both a rules approach and, like international relations, an effectiveness approach. Fisher and Ury's *Getting to Yes* (2d ed. 1991) is a staple of the American law school curriculum on negotiation. The study of negotiation, mediation, or arbitration in the U.S. typically involves rules but also statistical studies about the circumstances surrounding successful outcomes. Interestingly, *Getting to Yes* was co-written by a scholar of international law, Roger Fisher.[13] It is a standard in conflict prevention training courses offered by schools of international affairs and international organizations. It finds only brief mention, if any at all, in classic treatments of dispute settlement in international law, like those by Merrills or Collier and Lowe.[14]

This book approaches international law from a classical perspective: it relies on positive international law, modified in some important respects by normative or natural law principles.[15] Positive law develops from positive acts: treaties, customary international law, and general principles. With the plethora of treaties and actions by states, interna-

---

NIQUES (I. William Zartman & J. Lewis Rasmussen eds., 1997), and I. WILLIAM ZARTMAN, RIPE FOR RESOLUTION: CONFLICT AND INTERVENTION IN AFRICA (1989).

10. STRATEGIES OF PEACE, *supra* note 9, includes two respected international law scholars, Simon Chesterman and Naomi Roht-Arriaza, and one respected international relations specialist, Robert Johansen, whose chapter concerns international judicial settlement in peace processes.

11. *See* Symposium: *The Americanization of International Dispute Resolution*, 19 OHIO ST. J. ON DISP. RESOL. 1 (2003).

12. *See* Christine Chinkin, *Alternative Dispute Resolution Under International Law*, REMEDIES IN INTERNATIONAL LAW: THE INSTITUTIONAL DILEMMA (Malcolm D. Evans ed., 1998).

13. *See, e.g.*, ROGER FISHER, IMPROVING COMPLIANCE WITH INTERNATIONAL LAW (1981).

14. *See* MERRILLS, *supra* note 3; JOHN COLLIER & VAUGHAN LOWE, THE SETTLEMENT OF DISPUTES IN INTERNATIONAL LAW: INSTITUTIONS AND PROCEDURES (1999); UNITED NATIONS HANDBOOK ON THE PEACEFUL SETTLEMENT OF DISPUTES BETWEEN STATES (1992).

15. For more on international legal theory, see, MARY ELLEN O'CONNELL, THE POWER AND PURPOSE OF INTERNATIONAL LAW, INSIGHTS FROM THE THEORY AND PRACTICE OF ENFORCEMENT (2008).

tional organizations, and courts, the book cannot cover all the important aspects of the law on international dispute resolution. It does provide the basic principles of this law, equipping students with the ability to research and teach themselves the answers to the questions they will confront in practice. To further help students think about this law from a practical perspective, the book has a series of problems accompanying each section of the book. These problems are drawn from actual incidents. They are problems that daily confront foreign office lawyers, lawyers for international organizations, judges, arbitrators, mediators, and others. The materials aim at preparing students for careers in the practice of international dispute resolution.

The book is designed for those who already have a basic knowledge of international law. For those who have not had a basic course—which is highly recommended—reading a good introduction to international law will be essential.

The History of International Dispute Settlement

As mentioned above, several of the classic methods of dispute settlement are associated with the Peace of Westphalia, the founding instrument of the international state system. These methods were likely not studied as a branch of international law until the middle of the 19th Century, when the use of arbitration was becoming increasingly sophisticated. The law of international dispute resolution then came into its own by 1899, the year states adopted the First Hague Convention on the Pacific Settlement of Disputes.[16] The Convention aimed at developing alternatives to war, as well as humanizing the conduct of war. The 1899 Conference marked the beginning of a new period of endeavor in the formal study and promotion of peaceful means of dispute settlement. Between 1899 and 1928, all of the peaceful means mentioned in Article 33 of the UN Charter had been developed and codified in a formal, multilateral agreement.[17] The last of the major techniques to be included in a treaty was conciliation.

The achievements of 1899–1928 grew out of centuries-long efforts. Of the contemporary dispute settlement mechanisms, the more informal ones—negotiation, good offices, and mediation—have, in one version or another, always been with us. Arbitration, on the other hand, is easier to trace to its starting point in international relations and international law. Arbitration was the first method with sophisticated procedural rules.[18] In the 17th Century, Grotius, considered the father of international law, advocated the use of arbitration in his seminal work, *The Law of War and Peace* (1625). Grotius cited the Greek war strategist, Thucydides, for the point that "[i]t is not lawful to proceed against one who offers arbitration just as against a wrongdoer."[19]

16. *See* The Final Act of the Peace Conference of 1899, July 29, 1899 in 2 James Brown Scott, The Hague Peace Conferences 1899 and 1907, 61 (1909); *see also*, Symposium, *The Hague Peace Conferences*, 94 Am. J. Int'l L. 1 (2000); The Centennial of the First International Peace Conference (F. Kalshoven ed., 2000); Arthur Eyffinger, The 1899 Hague Peace Conference (1999).

17. Merrills, *supra* note 3, at 1–2.

18. *See* VIII J.H.W. Verzijl, International Law in Historical Perspective: Inter-State Disputes and Their Settlement 52 (1976); Wilhelm G. Grewe, The Epochs of International Law 104 (Michael Byers trans. & ed., 2000).

19. Hugo Grotius, I De Jure Belli ac pacis Libri Tres 562, 560–61 (Francis W. Kelsey trans., 1964). The Ancient Greeks, according to Born, "frequently resorted to international arbitration to resolve disputes among the city-states." Born, *supra* note 5, at p. 9.

Grotian ideas are reflected in the Peace of Westphalia of 1648, which marked the end of the Holy Roman Empire and gave rise to the state system. The Peace was itself produced in part through mediation: "Among the most famous instances of mediation I cite that of Venice and the Pope between France and the Empire ... and of Denmark between the Empire and Sweden ... prior to and during the Congress of Westphalia of 1648."[20] But, as advocated by Grotius, parties to the Peace of Westphalia agreed to resolve disputes by "amicable settlement of legal discussion."[21] Such a provision in peace treaties would have been in keeping with the practice of the time:

> After an apparent decline in usage under late Roman practice, international arbitration between state-like entities in Europe experienced a revival during the Middle Ages. Although historical records are incomplete, scholars conclude that international arbitration "existed on a widespread scale" during the Middle Ages, that "the constant disputes that arose in those warlike days were very frequently terminated by some kind of arbitration," and that "it is surprising to learn of the great number of arbitral decisions, of their importance and of the prevalence of the '*clause compromissoire*.'" The states of the Swiss Confederation and the Hanseatic League, as well as German and Italian principalities, turned with particular frequency to arbitration to settle their differences, often pursuant to agreements to resolve all future disputes by arbitration.
>
> Determining the precise scope and extent of international arbitration between states or state-like entities during the medieval era is difficult, in part because a distinction was not always drawn between judges, arbitrators, mediators and *amiable compositeurs*. Indeed, one of the most famous "arbitrations" of the age—Pope Alexander VI's division of the discoveries of the New World—appears not to have been an arbitration at all, but rather a negotiation or mediation. On the other hand, numerous treaties throughout this period drew quite clear distinctions between arbitration (in the sense of an adjudicative, binding process) and conciliation or mediation (in the sense of a non-binding procedure).[22]

Vattel, the influential 18th Century international law scholar, also advocated the use of arbitration. His treatise on international law includes a number of 17th Century arbitrations as examples for states of his day to follow.[23] Vattel was particularly influential in the United States. It is not surprising, therefore, that the U.S. and Britain included a commitment to arbitrate in the Jay Treaty of 1794. The two countries conducted a number of arbitrations under that treaty starting with the St. Croix River Arbitration of 1798, in which arbitrators decided on much of the boundary between present-day Canada and the U.S.[24] Claims commissions to settle property disputes between the U.S. and Britain

---

20. VERZIJL, *supra* note 18, at 52.

21. The Articles of the Treaty of Peace, signed and sealed at Münster, in Westphalia, October 24, 1648, art. 73, PARRY'S CONSOLIDATED TREATY SERIES 319; Treaty of Peace between the Empires and Sweden, concluded and signed at Osnabrück, Oct. 24, 1648, PARRY'S CONSOLIDATED TREATY SERIES 198. *See also* ARTHUR NUSSBAUM, A CONCISE HISTORY OF THE LAW OF NATIONS (rev. ed. 1954).

22. BORN, *supra* note 5, at 11–12 (footnotes omitted).

23. EMMERICH DE VATTEL, THE LAW OF NATIONS OR THE PRINCIPLES OF NATURAL LAW, APPLIED TO THE CONDUCT AND TO THE AFFAIRS OF NATIONS AND OF SOVEREIGNS 189–92 (Charles G. Fenwick trans. of 1758 ed., 1916); *see also* Christine Gray and Benedict Kingsbury, *Developments in Dispute Settlement: Inter-State Arbitration Since 1945*, 63 BRIT. YBK. INT'L L. 97 (1992).

24. GREWE, *supra* note 18, at 366.

were also established under the Jay Treaty, but without as much success.[25] Nevertheless, the idea of arbitration saw resurgence with the Jay Treaty. Arbitration was very popular among Latin American states.[26] Then the U.S. and Britain used arbitration to settle a dispute growing out of Britain's role in failing to stop warships from reaching the American South during the U.S. Civil War. The *Alabama Claims Arbitration* engendered great enthusiasm for arbitration. The following excerpt describes the dispute that gave rise to the arbitration:

Howard N. Meyer, *The World Court in Action**

Before the Civil War the United States had fought two wars with England. Then, during that bitterly fought conflict, a grievance against England arose that threatened yet another.

In 1862, the Union was in danger; its only real victories were General Grant's in the west. There slid down the ways at Liverpool an armed frigate built in England and manned by British seamen. The ship flew the Confederate flag, yet it was never to enter a rebel-held port.

Ship No. 290, the British shipbuilder Laird called her; at sea she was christened the *Alabama*. She entered a career unlike any in the history of warfare: during a two-year period, resupplying only in English and French ports, she conducted a series of attacks on U.S. merchant ships that can be compared only with the Kaiser's unrestricted submarine attacks on allied and U.S. merchant vessels that drew the United States into World War I.

She attacked seventy ships, burning most of them down to the water's edge. Other roving ships, all from English shipyards, joined in the attacks, the total of which numbered 270.

"We shall have a day of reckoning for these wrongs," wrote Gideon Welles, Lincoln's Secretary of the Navy, in his diary, "and I sometimes think I care not how or in what manner that reckoning comes."

How severe the damage and how outraged the U.S. public were reflected in Welles's entry in July 1864, when the USS *Kearsage* engaged and sank the *Alabama*:

> Our *Alabama* news comes in opportunely to encourage and sustain the nation's heart. It does them as well as me good to dwell on the subject and the discomfiture of the British and the Rebels. The perfidy of the former is as infamous as the treason of the latter.

Five years later, Britain's day of reckoning seemed to be on hand. One topic that was receiving serious debate was whether the United States should take over British North America—Canada as we know it now. In his final observation on the subject, Welles tells us, "the English are fully conscious of the great wrong they have done us. They are more apprehensive of war than they are willing to confess, and hostilities may be nearer than our people suppose."

That there was no war can be credited to the determination of President Grant and the skill of Secretary of State Hamilton Fish. In accordance with a treaty that they nego-

25. *Id.* at 365–66.
26. Born, *supra* note 5, at 14.
* Rowan & Littlefield Publishers, Inc. pp. 1–2 (2002).

tiated, the *Alabama* claims were submitted to a board of arbitrators with neutral members selected by the heads of state of Brazil, Italy, and Switzerland. They sat and heard evidence and rendered their decision in Geneva, inaugurating that city's modern role in international affairs.

The verdict was an award of $15.5 million, a sum quite commensurate with the dollar value of the destroyed ships. "The greater victory," as admiral and historian Samuel Eliot Morrison has written, "was for peace and arbitration."

Following the *Alabama Claims*, the U.S. took the lead in promoting arbitration. By the 1890s the U.S. was working toward a standing arrangement with Britain that would require arbitration of certain disputes without the need to reach a formal agreement by treaty to arbitrate each dispute. President William McKinley had supported the standing arrangement in the U.S. Senate, but it was ultimately defeated. Senators were unwilling to give up the power to control each decision to arbitrate through their ability to withhold consent from any particular arbitration treaty.

The idea of a standing arrangement was certainly a progressive one. Given McKinley's support of it and of arbitration in general, his willingness to declare war on Spain in 1898 without first trying arbitration came as a shock to many in the American peace movement. The U.S. and Spain waged a bloody conflict in which Spain lost most of its remaining overseas colonies to the United States. The popular view of the day was that the war began due to a mistaken belief that Spanish agents had sunk a U.S. naval vessel, the *Maine*, in the Port of Havana.[27] The American peace movement believed mechanisms of peaceful settlement could have clarified the true cause of the *Maine* disaster, avoiding the war.

The peace movement redoubled its efforts of promoting peaceful settlement of disputes following the conflict. The lobbying by the peace movement for greater commitment to peaceful settlement reached the Russian Tsar who had called for a peace conference to be held in The Hague in 1899. He added peaceful settlement to the agenda, which already included arms limitations and regulation of the conduct of conflict. The Tsar was interested in pursuing ways to avoid war, not only to gain the benefits of peace, but in the interest of Russian security. The Tsar realized Russia was not keeping pace with other world powers in acquiring the new technology of war, so Russia sought alternatives to wars it feared it could not win.[28]

During the 1899 conference, delegates from 26 countries drafted a convention defining and setting out rules and procedures for good offices, mediation, inquiry, and arbitration. Just a few years later, Britain and Russia used inquiry to resolve the 1906 Dogger Bank dispute. That successful case encouraged further development of dispute settlement procedures and another peace conference was held in The Hague in 1907. At the Second Hague Peace Conference further rules were developed for inquiry and the arbitration rules agreed to in 1899 were modified and improved.

Already in 1899, the British delegation had formally proposed an international court for the settlement of disputes which was being called "the American plan." No agreement on a court was reached at the first conference. Rather, the delegates formed something they

---

27. David Caron, *War and International Adjudication: Reflections on the 1899 Peace Conference*, 94 AM. J. INT'L L. 4, 7 (2000).

28. Leila Nadya Sadat, *The Establishment of the International Criminal Court: From The Hague to Rome and Back Again*, 8 J. INT'L L. & PRAC. 97 (1999) (*citing*, WILLIAM I. HULL, THE TWO HAGUE CONFERENCES AND THEIR CONTRIBUTIONS TO INTERNATIONAL LAW 3 (1908)).

called the Permanent Court of Arbitration (PCA), which continues to exist. The PCA is not a court, however, but rather a list of available arbitrators, a set of arbitration rules, and a small secretariat in The Hague.[29] No state is bound to resort to it.

Nevertheless, the idea of creating a court persisted. The U.S. delegation, in particular, had been inspired in 1899 by the proposals for a court of compulsory jurisdiction. At the Second Hague Peace Conference, the U.S. and others renewed the effort to get a permanent international court. They failed, largely owing to German opposition. The delegates in 1907 did agree to the first multilateral treaty outlawing the use of force for a particular class of disputes: The Convention of 1907 Respecting the Limitation of the Employment of Force for the Recovery of Contract Debts.[30] The delegates also agreed to form a permanent prize court, though that court was never established.[31]

Nevertheless, U.S. Secretary of State (and first president of the American Society of International Law) Elihu Root left The Hague ever more committed to the idea of judicial settlement of disputes. He promoted the idea in Central America, where governments succeeded in establishing the Central American Court of Justice in 1911.[32] The Central American Court was the first permanent court for the settlement of inter-state disputes.[33] It existed for ten years and might have gone on longer if the U.S. had taken a greater interest in promoting its survival. In addition to the Central American Court, Root oversaw the establishment of the International Joint Commission (IJC) with Canada. The IJC was founded as a permanent institution for the regulation of joint resources and the resolution of boundary-related disputes. It continues to this day. The U.S. also promoted the commitment to binding dispute resolution through bilateral agreements with South American and European states.

Despite all of these efforts at peaceful settlement, Europe erupted into war in 1914. The First World War came as a major blow to proponents of peaceful settlement of disputes. Still, some in the international peace movement worked to keep the U.S. out of the war and to reach a speedy conclusion to the conflict through mediation. Mediation was the basis of the platform of the Woman's Peace Party (WPP) formed by Carrie Chapman Catt and Jane Addams in 1915. Addams had worked for peace and theorized about peace throughout her long career in social work in Chicago. After the war, she campaigned for the U.S. to join the League of Nations. The Covenant of the League mandated that states-members first try arbitration before resorting to war.

The U.S. did not join the League or the Permanent Court of International Justice (PCIJ) formed in 1920. The world was finally ready for an international court following the shock of the War. Ten distinguished international jurists, including Elihu Root of the United States, drafted the Statute of the Permanent Court of International Justice, the first permanent global court for the peaceful settlement of international disputes. Elihu Root and his British colleague Lord Phillimore were responsible for the breakthrough in selecting judges. At the time of the 1907 Hague Conference, all states wanted to have a judge on the court. In 1920, the Root-Phillimore plan guaranteed that the great powers

---

29. *See* the website of the Permanent Court of Arbitration, *at* http://www.pca-cpa.org. *See also* P. Hamilton et al., The Permanent Court of Arbitration: International Arbitration and Dispute Settlement, Summaries of Awards, Settlement Agreements and Reports (1999).

30. 1907 Stat. 36: 2241, Malloy's T.S. 2:2248.

31. Hans-Jürgen Schlochauer, *Permanent Court of International Justice, in* 1 Encyclopedia of Public International Law 163–164 (Rudolf Bernhardt ed., 1981) [hereinafter EPIL].

32. 2 Philip C. Jessup, Elihu Root 50 (1937); *see also* Nobel Peace Prize 1912, Elihu Root Biography, www.nobel.se/peace/laureates/1912/root-bio.html.

33. Humphrey M. Hill, *Central American Court of Justice, in* EPIL, *supra* note 31, at 41–44.

would always have judges and all other countries could fill openings on a rotating basis. Root also played a key role in determining the PCIJ's jurisdiction. Root always felt strongly that when states seek out judicial or arbitral settlement, they want an outcome based on law, not the personal views of the judges on what would be a good outcome. The PCIJ decided cases on the basis of international law.

Another major issue concerned whether the court would have compulsory jurisdiction. Some of the delegates to the drafting conference passionately supported a court with compulsory jurisdiction. Others were adamant that states would not accept such a court. The Brazilian delegate, Fernandez, proposed the possibility of states accepting compulsory jurisdiction at their option, on the basis of reciprocity with other states accepting the same obligation. Many states did accept compulsory jurisdiction on the basis of reciprocity. Many others brought cases by special agreement. The PCIJ was able to compile an impressive record, deciding 21 contentious cases and giving 26 advisory opinions in a period of less than 20 years.[34] It was a terrible disappointment to Root that the United States never joined.

Along with international courts, conciliation also originated at the beginning of the 20th Century. After a number of bilateral agreements for conciliation, including the Locarno Agreements of 1925, conciliation was included in a general, multilateral treaty, the General Act for the Peaceful Settlement of Disputes in 1928. Finally, this was a time of great activity for claims commissions dealing in particular with claims arising from Mexico's civil unrest and the First World War.[35]

Thus, by the outbreak of the Second World War, the world had a variety of means to settle disputes. The failure to prevent another world cataclysm challenged international lawyers once again to strengthen the core obligation of peaceful settlement and the general prohibition on the use of armed force to settle disputes. States worked to create a more robust organization for the preservation of the peace. The Charter of the United Nations contains clear mandates to settle disputes peacefully and to forego the use of force except in self-defense to an armed attack. The Security Council was established to ensure the peace, and a successor for the PCIJ, the International Court of Justice (ICJ), was also established, though basically on the same model as the PCIJ. Interest in dispute settlement continued to grow during the years following the adoption of the Charter. The use of international tribunals to try major war criminals at Nuremberg and Tokyo aroused great interest. A number of important international treaties containing binding dispute settlement provisions were made. The Europeans established a very successful court for the resolution of human rights claims, the European Court of Human Rights, in 1950. The attempt to establish a general international criminal court on the model of the Nuremberg Tribunal or to finally develop an international court system with compulsory jurisdiction did not occur in the years after the War. The Soviets were highly protective of their domestic sphere, generally opposing the development of international courts; Americans were divided, some supporting and some opposing courts.[36]

The UN Convention on the Law of the Sea was completed in 1982. It includes a sophisticated dispute settlement part that includes all the mechanisms of Article 33 of the charter. By the late 1980s/early 1990s, with the Cold War over and the pressing demands of globalization, several new international courts were established, new commitments

---

34. Hans-Jürgen Schlochauer, *supra* note 31, at 167.

35. *See* Nussbaum, *supra* note 21, at 274–75.

36. *See generally* Thomas M. Franck & Jerome M. Lehrman, *Messianism and Chauvinism in America's Commitment to Peace Through Law*, *in* The International Court of Justice at a Crossroads 3 (Lori F. Damrosch ed., 1987).

were made to arbitrate, new procedures for dispute resolution were created, and new use was made of national courts for the resolution of international disputes.[37] Post-Cold War international commercial disputes among states and multinational corporations are now regularly resolved in arbitration, either under the terms of the Convention for the Settlement of Investment Disputes[38] or in *ad hoc* arbitration. Trade disputes are resolved through compulsory dispute settlement at the World Trade Organization (WTO). The Permanent Court of Arbitration has had more cases as the docket at the ICJ has heated up. Judge Sir Robert Jennings launched a new scholarly concern with a short essay on the proliferation of international courts.[39] In stark contrast to the beginning of the last century, the new century began with the concern that international law will develop inconsistently or even contradictorily as a result of uncoordinated decisions from many new courts and tribunals.[40] In 2002, a new journal devoted solely to international courts and tribunals was launched.[41] This is a development that could scarcely have occurred to Root or Phillimore.

The September 11, 2001, terrorist attacks on the U.S. have apparently shaken American commitment to the non-use of force in international relations. While the U.S. continued to participate in cases at the WTO and ICJ, it announced in 2002 a policy of using force preemptively against potential threats.[42] This policy of preemptive use of force conflicts with the UN Charter prohibition on the use of force and the requirement to settle disputes peacefully.[43] The U.S. has advocated a policy of war in just those cases where international lawyers hoped dispute settlement mechanisms would play an ever-more effective role. The policy of preemptive force challenges the international legal community once again to explain why peaceful means of dispute settlement can be an alternative to war, even in an age of terrorism.

---

37. Mary Ellen O'Connell, *The Role of Soft Law in a Global Order*, *in* COMMITMENT AND COMPLIANCE, THE ROLE OF NON-BINDING NORMS IN THE INTERNATIONAL LEGAL SYSTEM 100 (Dinah Shelton ed., 2000).

38. Mar. 18, 1965, 17 U.S.T. 1270, 575, 159.

39. Sir Robert Y. Jennings, *The Proliferation of Adjudicatory Bodies: Dangers and Possible Answers*, 9 AMERICAN SOC'Y OF INT'L L. BULL. 2 (1995).

40. Jonathan I. Charney, *Is International Law Threatened by Multiple International Tribunals?*, 271 RECUEIL DES COURS 101 (1998).

41. *See* THE LAW & PRACTICE OF INTERNATIONAL COURTS AND TRIBUNALS (Kluwer Law International).

42. WHITE HOUSE, THE NATIONAL SECURITY STRATEGY OF THE UNITED STATES OF AMERICA 12–14 (2002), *at* http://www.whitehouse.gov/nsc/nss.pdf.

43. Mary Ellen O'Connell, *The Myth of Preemptive Self-Defense* (Aug. 2002), *at* http://www.asil.org/taskforce/oconnell.pdf.

Richard B. Bilder, *An Overview of International Dispute Settlement**

* * *

I. What Is an International Dispute?

In the *Mavromattis* case, the Permanent Court of International Justice defined a dispute as "a disagreement on a point of law or fact, a conflict of legal views or interests between two persons." More specifically, J.G. Merrills suggests that:

> A dispute may be defined as a specific disagreement concerning a matter of fact, law or policy in which a claim or assertion of one party is met with refusal, counter-claim or denial by another. In the broadest sense, an international dispute can be said to exist whenever such a disagreement involves governments, institutions, juristic persons (corporations) or private individuals in different parts of the world. However, the disputes with which the present work is primarily concerned are those in which the parties are two or more of the one hundred and sixty or so sovereign states into which the world is currently divided.

The significant elements of the concept of "dispute" are that:

1. The disagreement must be *specific.* That is, it must have a reasonably well-defined subject-matter, so that one can say what the dispute, at least nominally, is "about."

2. The disagreement must involve *conflicting claims or assertions.* That is, one party must actually assert or manifest what it wants or believes itself entitled to with respect to the other, and the other party must manifest its refusal or its conflicting claim. Such a manifestation may be through statements, diplomatic notes, specific actions or otherwise.

Thus, a "dispute" is something more than general attitudes of mutual dislike or hostility. Two nations may have general feelings of antagonism towards each other, yet not have any *specific* or *particular* disagreement one can identify as a dispute; conversely, two nations may be on friendly terms, yet have a particular disagreement which can be considered a dispute. Moreover, a "dispute" means something more than a situation in which one nation feels a sense of injury or grievance towards another; until that sense of grievance is formulated into a specific claim or assertion which is resisted by the other, there is no "dispute" between them.

The concept of "dispute" is useful for several reasons. First, it serves to distinguish a disagreement which has reached a level of active assertion and intensity potentially threatening the relations between the parties or the social order more generally, from lower-level and less threatening types of complaints, grievances or disagreements. Second, it serves as a way of indicating that a disagreement has reached a point of sufficient definition and concreteness where the use of certain established methods of dispute resolution may be appropriate. That is, from the perspective of the international legal system, an international dispute can be viewed as a disagreement between or among nations which international dispute-settlement techniques, such as adjudication, may be useful in resolving. Indeed, the jurisdiction of international judicial institutions, such as the International Court of Justice, typically extends only to cases involving international "disputes."

II. Do We Need to Settle International Disputes?

* * *

* Burrus-Bascom Professor of Law, University of Wisconsin-Madison. B.A. Williams College 1949, J.D. Harvard Law School 1956. 1 Emory J. Int'l Dis. Res. 1 (1986) (footnotes omitted).

As indicated, disputes are a by-product of energetic social interaction and not in themselves necessarily a "bad thing." Certainly, they need not imply a failure or breakdown of social order; indeed, a society without disputes would likely be a static society, without change and development. And, in practice, most disputes do not pose significant social problems and can be left to work themselves out, either (as is usually the case) through informal and routine low-level negotiations between the parties, by fading away over time, or otherwise. Disputes become a social problem only when and to the extent they disrupt, or threaten to disrupt, useful social relations or the more general social order—that is, when they may lead to conflict or when their social costs become excessive.

Thus, every political system must find ways to identify and try to deal with disputes that *do* pose significant social risks. In most domestic legal orders, complex and sophisticated techniques have been developed for identifying and resolving disputes that are considered to warrant or require public attention or intervention. Typically, either party acting on its own may seek state intervention, or the state under certain circumstances may intervene at its own discretion; and there are few kinds of disputes in which the state cannot if it wishes so intervene. In international society, on the other hand, the discretion of the international community or third parties to intervene in disputes is much more limited. In most cases, third-party or community intervention is considered appropriate or permissible only when *both or all* parties to the dispute have consented, or where the dispute has escalated to a point threatening general international peace and security.

It is worth noting that there may be some cases where even a significant dispute is best left unresolved. Thus, if any conceivable settlement or even attempt of settlement is likely only to exacerbate the sense of grievance of one or another party and increase tensions, it may be wisest simply to leave the dispute to simmer, hoping that someday, somehow, it will go away. The success of the Antarctic Treaty System, for example, is based largely on the parties' decision to bypass or "freeze" the very difficult and potentially troublesome issue of disputed claims to territory in Antarctica.

The timing of dispute settlement efforts may also be crucial; such efforts, or the use of a particular technique, may be helpful at one stage of a dispute but not at another. Diplomats and international lawyers need to learn more about *when*, as well as *how*, to try to settle international disputes.

III. Do States Have an Obligation to Settle Their Disputes Peacefully?

The prevailing view is that, in the absence of special agreement, states are under no international legal obligation to settle, or even to try to settle, their disputes. It is well established in particular that, absent special agreement, they have no obligation to submit their disputes to third parties for impartial settlement.

However, those states that are parties to the U.N. Charter (which means, in effect, almost all of the world's nations) have assumed at least certain broad treaty obligations in this respect. Article 1(1) of the Charter provides that the first of the purposes of the United Nations organization shall be:

> to maintain international peace and security, and to that end: ... to bring about by peaceful means, and in conformity with the principles of justice and international law, adjustment or settlement of international disputes or situations which might lead to a breach of the peace.

Article 2(3) of the Charter provides:

> All Members shall settle their international disputes by peaceful means in such a manner that international peace and security, and justice, are not endangered.

Article 33 of the Charter provides:

> 1. The parties to any dispute, the continuance of which is likely to endanger the maintenance of international peace and security, shall, first of all, seek a solution by negotiation, enquiry, mediation, conciliation, arbitration, judicial settlement, resort to regional agencies or arrangements, or other peaceful means of their own choice.
>
> 2. The Security Council shall, when it deems necessary, call upon the parties to settle their dispute by such means.

It may be noted that, while Article 2(3) establishes an essentially negative obligation—that Member nations *not* settle disputes by means that might endanger international peace, Article 33 affirmatively requires that Member nations actively seek to settle by peaceful means any dispute the continuance of which is likely to endanger international peace....

Under Article 35, any state may bring any dispute to the attention of the Security Council or General Assembly. Under Article 36, the Security Council may, at any stage of a dispute the continuance of which is likely to endanger the maintenance of international peace or security, recommend appropriate procedures or methods of adjustment; in doing so, the Council should take into consideration that legal disputes should as a general rule be referred by the parties to the International Court of Justice. Article 37 provides that, should the parties to a dispute of the nature referred to in Article 33 fail to settle it by the means indicated in Article 33, they shall refer it to the Security Council which, if it deems that the continuance of the dispute is in fact likely to endanger the maintenance of international peace and security, shall decide whether to take action under Article 36 or to recommend such terms of settlement as it may consider appropriate. Article 38 provides that:

> Without prejudice to the provisions of Article 33 to 37, the Security Council may, if all the parties to any dispute so request, make recommendations to the parties with a view to a pacific settlement of the dispute.

Other articles of the Charter authorize the General Assembly and Secretary General to make recommendations or take certain action with respect to disputes, and encourage the development of pacific settlement through regional arrangements.

It is apparent that the U.N. Charter establishes international obligations of the parties and interventionary powers of the Organization principally with respect to a particular category of disputes—those whose continuation "is likely to endanger the maintenance of international peace and security." It is less clear whether Member nations are also under an obligation to seek to settle *all* disputes—even those which are *not* likely to threaten international peace and security. Perhaps Article 2(3) could be read as establishing such a broader duty," as might also the relevant sections of the General Assembly's authoritative 1970 Declaration of Principles regarding Friendly Relations and the 1982 Manila Declaration on the Peaceful Settlement of International Disputes. Such an interpretation would place the emphasis on the word "settle" in Article 2(3), rather than on "peaceful means"; certainly, this reading would have been strengthened had there been a comma after the word "disputes." However, Articles 1(1), 33, and 38 seem more persuasively to suggest a narrower construction, under which the Charter's obligation to seek to settle disputes does *not* apply to those disputes *not* likely to threaten international peace and security. Certainly, Article 38 makes clear that, absent consent of all parties to the dispute, the Organization has no general authority to intervene to bring about a settlement of international disputes which do not involve either coercion or a threat to international peace and security.

The obligation that any settlement of disputes must be accomplished peacefully is, of course, buttressed by the prohibition on the use of force contained in Article 2(4) of the Charter and by the authority of the Security Council under Chapter VII of the Charter to intervene when it determines that any situation or dispute involves a "threat to the peace, breach of the peace, or act of aggression." It is an interesting question whether the Security Council's authority to "decide what measures shall be taken in accordance with Articles 41 and 42, to maintain or restore international peace and security" (which "decisions" are binding on all Members under Article 25 of the Charter) could include a "decision" requiring the parties to a dispute to adopt particular peaceful settlement procedures; arguably, such authority might be included by implication in the Council's far more drastic authority to employ economic or even military coercion under Articles 41 and 42.

* * *

It is debatable whether contemporary customary international law is moving to wards carrying the obligation to seek to settle disputes somewhat further than the Charter requires. It is difficult to argue that customary law requires states to try to settle or actually settle *all* of their disputes. Each nation may have many disputes with other nations, most of which are probably minor and some of which may perhaps best be left unresolved; to require states to actively pursue the settlement of *all* of these would be unreasonable, burdensome and unnecessary. Moreover, there does not seem to be any practical way in which the international legal order could implement or enforce such a broad requirement. There is some evidence, however, that a principle of customary law is gradually emerging requiring parties to at least *significant* disputes to negotiate in good faith respecting settlement, if not to actually reach a settlement. This principle finds support in provisions to this effect in many bilateral and multilateral treaties, the Declaration on Friendly Relations, a variety of other resolutions of international organizations, and various international judicial decisions such as the International Court's opinion in the *Fisheries* case. Certainly, a state which deliberately refuses to take part in good faith negotiations to settle a significant dispute incurs the risk that the international community may not only condemn its unwillingness to seek peaceful settlement but will draw adverse inferences as to the merits of its position with respect to the dispute.

It is, of course, open to nations to enter into international agreements with each other which include "compromissory clauses" or other obligations to settle their disputes peacefully, and a great number of such agreements are in effect. Frequently, such agreements will not only include general obligations of peaceful settlement, but will require, recommend, or provide procedures for the use of specific dispute settlement techniques, such as negotiation, conciliation, arbitration or adjudication.

* * *

VI. What Techniques Are Available for Settling International Disputes?

Disputes can be disposed of in various ways. While international lawyers are primarily concerned with certain traditional techniques of peaceful settlement, it is worth at least briefly noting some other ways in which disputes can be resolved:

1. *Coercion.* The use of force or other forms of coercion as a means of securing a favorable outcome of a dispute is as old as history and, unfortunately, still an all-too-

frequent occurrence in contemporary international affairs. As has been suggested, since coercive settlement poses a threat to social order, every legal system, including the international legal system, seeks to induce or in some cases require the parties to resolve their disputes through peaceful means rather than coercion. However, it is not always easy or perhaps realistic to eliminate the element of power entirely from the dispute settlement process; it may reemerge under the guise of "bargaining power" in negotiations or "practical considerations" in a judicial decision. Arguably, a "settlement" which ignores the realities of power may prove unstable over the long run and the dispute may bubble to the surface again in some other shape or form.

2. *Voluntary relinquishment.* A party might decide voluntarily to relinquish its claim because, for example, the circumstances or particular perceptions giving rise to its sense of grievance change or disappear, because the other party succeeds in persuading it that the claim has no merit, or because it becomes discouraged or bored with the futility of continuing to pursue its claim over a long period and decides to simply give up or "lump it."

3. *Chance.* Minor private differences are often resolved by the laws of chance—a flip of the coin. But since chance is not considered a "principled" method of dispute resolution, most legal systems reject it as a legitimate technique of settlement. However, at least with respect to some minor international disputes in which the equities are evenly balanced, chance may in some situations be as "rational" a technique as any other. Indeed, in cases where the law is uncertain, the equities are evenly balanced, and the judges' attitudes and biases unknown, any confident prediction of how third parties are likely to decide the dispute may be impossible and resort to adjudication in practice simply a gamble.

4. *Voting.* In democratic societies, the members of the community or their representatives may decide certain disputes—at least those involving broad issues of social policy, in contrast to disputes between particular individuals—by majority vote. Since the representative organs of international organizations, such as the U.N. General Assembly, do not normally have legislative powers, there is little direct use of such techniques in the international social order. However analogies may perhaps be found in a few cases such as the 1947 General Assembly resolution on the partition of Palestine, and U.N.-administered plebiscites such as those in the trust territories of Togoland and the Cameroons.

The more usual and accepted methods of peaceful settlement of international disputes are those listed in Article 33 of the U.N. Charter—negotiation, inquiry, mediation, conciliation, arbitration, judicial settlement, resort to regional agencies or arrangements and resort to the U.N. or other international organization dispute settlement procedures. In essence, this list of methods reflects a spectrum of techniques ranging from so-called "diplomatic means," which give control of the outcome primarily to the parties themselves, to so-called "legal means" which give control of the outcome primarily to a third party or parties. That is, the principal difference among these techniques is in the extent to which third parties can legitimately participate in helping to bring about or determining the settlement and, conversely, the extent to which the parties can reject a settlement proposed by the third party. In practice, distinctions between these techniques may be more theoretical than real, and a particular process of dispute settlement may combine elements of various techniques. For example, international arbitration or adjudication may often embody compromises reflecting strong elements of negotiation or mediation among the arbitrators or judges, at least some of whom may see their role as safeguarding the interests or representing the point of view of one or the other party.

The more traditional methods of peaceful settlement, and their distinctive characteristics; are briefly as follows:

1. *Negotiation.* Negotiation is a process whereby the parties directly communicate and bargain with each other in an attempt to agree on a settlement of the issue. By choosing to use this technique, the parties retain maximum control of the process and outcome.

Negotiation is clearly the predominant, usual and preferred method of resolving international disputes. Except in cases where the dispute is submitted directly to settlement by binding adjudication or conciliation, or where settlement is otherwise imposed by a third party, negotiation is normally an essential component of any dispute settlement process. Indeed, the use of other techniques, including adjudication, is usually preceded, accompanied by and arranged through some kind of negotiation process.

2. *Good offices and mediation.* Good offices and mediation are techniques in which the parties, unable to resolve a dispute by negotiation, request or agree to limited intervention by a third party to help them break the impasse. In the case of good offices, the role of the third party is usually limited to simply bringing the parties into communication and facilitating their negotiations. In the case of mediation, the mediator usually plays a more active part in facilitating communications and negotiations between the parties, and is sometimes permitted or expected to advance informal and nonbinding proposals of his or her own.

3. *Fact-finding, inquiry and conciliation.* These are methods of settlement in which the parties request or agree to the intervention of a third party, usually on a more formal basis, for the purpose of determining particular facts or otherwise conducting an impartial examination of the dispute and, if the parties so agree, attempting to suggest or define the terms of a mutually acceptable settlement. Like mediation, the report of a fact-finding body or conciliation commission is normally non-binding, although the third party finding or recommendation may, of course exercise an important influence on the settlement.

4. *Arbitration.* This method involves the reference of a dispute or series of disputes, by the agreement of the parties, to an *ad hoc* tribunal for binding decision, usually on the basis of international law. The parties by agreement establish the issue to be arbitrated and the machinery and procedure of the tribunal, including the method of selection of the arbitrator or arbitrators. While arbitration is normally binding, it is open to the parties to provide that the tribunal's opinion will be only advisory.

5. *Judicial settlement.* This method involves the reference of the dispute, by the agreement or consent of the parties, to the International Court of Justice or some other standing and permanent judicial body for binding decision, usually on the basis of international law. Again, if the rules establishing the court so allow, the parties may agree to an advisory or nonbinding opinion rather than a binding decision, or to a declaratory judgment specifying the principles which the parties should apply in the settlement of their dispute, as the parties did in the *North Sea Continental Shelf* case and *Continental Shelf (Tunisia/Libyan Arab Jamahiriya)* case.

6. *Settlement through the United Nations or other global or regional international organizations or agencies.* In some circumstances, the parties may request the assistance of the U.N., a regional organization, or another international organization in settling their dispute, or the U.N. or another organization (for example, a regional organization) may on

its own motion legitimately intervene in the dispute, at least for the purposes of trying to bring about a peaceful settlement. Sometimes a third party may ask for the organization's intervention.

* * *

VII. When Is a Dispute Settled?

As a legal matter, a dispute is settled when either (1) the parties formally agree to a particular settlement, either on their own or by accepting the proposal of a mediator or a conciliation commission, or (2) an international arbitral or judicial tribunal, with jurisdiction over the parties and the dispute, delivers a legally binding judgment respecting it.

As a practical matter, of course, the question is more complex. Presumably, a dispute is *really* settled only when each of the parties ceases to have a continuing sense of grievance, or at least ceases to continue actively to assert its claim. That is, a settlement, whether reached through negotiated agreement or third-party decision, must be subjectively accepted by both parties as a fair and legitimate resolution of the matter if the dispute is really to be ended and put to rest.

Certainly, one element in the acceptability of a settlement will be each party's sense of the inherent fairness of the settlement, in terms of the parties' respective claims and interests. Thus, a settlement which contains elements of compromise, giving something to each of the parties (but also taking something from each), is in many cases more likely to be regarded as acceptable and complied with than an all-or-nothing outcome. Another element will be the parties' sense of the fairness and legitimacy of the procedures through which the settlement was reached. Perhaps a third element may be the parties' sense of the extent to which the settlement bears some relation to the practical realities of their relative power with respect to the dispute—what each nation thinks it could have obtained if it had *not* agreed to peaceful settlement of the dispute. A nation may be willing to give up something, but could be very unhappy at having lost all, by resorting to peaceful settlement. Recent research by social psychologists in the field of "equity theory" may offer useful and interesting insights into the kinds of factors that affect the parties' perceptions of the fairness of a particular settlement.

Certainly, one thing it would be useful to know more about is what happens after a dispute has legally been settled by agreement or adjudication—whether such settlements are real solutions which are in fact carried out and complied with by the parties and leave both parties satisfied.

* * *

IX. What Is the Relevance of Law to Dispute Settlement?

The international legal order is relevant to dispute settlement in many ways. First, the international legal system, explicitly and implicitly, establishes the general principle that international disputes should be settled peacefully, crystallizing each state's national interest in the maintenance of international order.

Second, the legal system more specifically establishes norms, procedures and a variety of formal and informal institutions which can facilitate both the avoidance and resolution of international disputes. In particular, international law provides salient rules and principles which generally shape the parties perceptions of legitimacy and guide their efforts to reach agreement. To the extent rules and relevant expectations are clear, nations are less likely to behave in ways which give rise to disputes and, should disputes nevertheless arise, will be able to settle them more easily on the basis of the relevant rules. Even when, as is usually the case, the parties to a dispute seek to achieve their own negotiated settlement without the intervention of third parties or international courts, they will still typically bargain "in the shadow of the law."

Finally, international agreements provide a technique through which nations can both commit themselves to the principle of peaceful settlement and establish specific methods for resolving their disputes, including the reaching of legally-binding settlement agreements.

Notes and Questions on the Study of International Dispute Resolution

1. In 1907, it was the United States that pushed for an international court for the peaceful settlement of disputes, and Germany which resisted. A century later, Germany is a leading champion of international courts and the U.S. resists. (Note the negative U.S. government attitude toward the International Criminal Court and steady withdrawal from commitments to go to the International Court of Justice.) Why the change in positions? *See* William A. Schabas, *United States Hostility to the International Criminal Court: It's All About the Security Council*, 15 EUR. J. INT'L L. 701 (2004). Are we beginning to see another change in the U.S. attitude—back to greater support for courts? See a description of U.S. participation in the ICC Review conference at Kampala, Uganda, in May 2010, at the Website of the American NGO Coalition for the International Criminal Court, www.amicc.org. What might account for a state's changing attitude toward international courts over time? *See* THE SWORD AND THE SCALES: THE UNITED STATES AND INTERNATIONAL COURTS AND TRIBUNALS (Cesare Romano ed. 2009).

2. What is a dispute? What are the obligations on states with respect to disputes under the UN Charter? What do these obligations tell you about the sophistication of the international legal system? Are you favorably impressed by those obligations? Why or why not?

3. Despite the work of peace activists and scholars of dispute resolution, the world is probably experiencing more significant inter-group violent conflict than ever before. Why do you think that is? What are the causes of contemporary violence? Both the historical essay and the excerpt from Bilder describe all the means of dispute resolution known in international relations today: negotiation, good offices, mediation, inquiry, conciliation, arbitration, and adjudication. As you study these means, consider what may be missing. Reflect on what methods could be added to realize greater success in the resolution of conflicts that result in violence. Greater success in resolving conflict could well result in a more successful system of international law. What is missing from the current collection of means for the peaceful settlement of international disputes? Will progress require fundamental changes in the current structure of international relations, as might be implied in the first question above?

For a discussion of the causes of violent conflict in international relations, *see* 5 THE CARNEGIE COMMISSION ON PREVENTING DEADLY CONFLICT, PREVENTING DEADLY CONFLICT (1997).

4. Anne Peters argues that from simple good faith we have moved to a general international duty to cooperate in dispute settlement:

> [A] general (but context bound) duty to cooperate with a view to a settlement is inherent in the customary law obligation to settle disputes peacefully, because resolution of a dispute would otherwise be impossible. This general obligation comprises the duty at least to negotiate, as it would otherwise be meaningless. On the other hand, there is no customary law obligation to negotiate first, if the other party is willing to resort to another means of settlement, in particular to adjudication. Good faith relates to all stages of the settlement procedure, and it obviously becomes more important as the procedures become more flexible and the parties' respective duties of cooperation become less concrete....
>
> The failure to fulfill a concrete obligation to cooperate is normally a breach of an international obligation and triggers the state's international responsibility. If, as in the case of the ICTY and the ICC, the court is entitled to make a judicial finding on a failure to cooperate, this is the formal establishment of an internationally wrongful act. In sum, we can safely speak of an international law of cooperation in dispute settlement.

Anne Peters, *International Dispute Settlement: A Network of Cooperational Duties,* 14 EJIL 1, 29-3 (2003) (footnotes omitted).

5. As you proceed through these materials consider the many obligations on states and international organizations to resolve disputes peacefully. Do these obligations provide additional support for Peters' argument of a customary law duty to cooperate?

Also consider whether Stéphane Beaulac is correct that international law is too deficient in the area of courts to really provide the rule of law to international relations.

Beaulac defines the rule of law as including these three elements: "(1) the existence of principle normative rules, (2) adequately created and equally applicable to all legal subjects and (3) enforced by accessible courts of general jurisdiction." Stéphane Beaulac, *The Rule of Law in International Law Today, in Relocating the Rule of Law* 203–05 (Ganluigi Palombella and Neil Walker eds., 2009). Are courts necessarily the only way that law gets enforced? When you complete the book come back to this Note and reflect on whether the international legal system has "what it takes" to provide enforcement of the law. By the end of the book, you should have a firm understanding of how international law gets enforced. The international law of dispute settlement is about the many means and mechanisms available for enforcing international rights and duties.

6. In addition to the sources cited in the notes above and in footnotes throughout the chapter, here is additional reading on international dispute resolution in general:

Cesare Romano, *International Dispute Settlement, in* Oxford Handbook of International Environmental Law 1038 (Daniel Bodansky et al. eds., 2007).

Dispute Settlement in Public International Law, Texts and Materials (Karin Oellers-Frahm & Andreas Zimmermann eds., 2d ed. 2001).

Francisco Orrego Vicuna & Christopher Pinto, Peaceful Settlement of Disputes, Prospects for the 21st Century, *in* The Centennial of the First International Peace Conference 261 (Fritz Kalshoven ed., 2000).

Marcel M.T.A. Brus, Third Party Dispute Settlement in an Interdependent World (1995).

Ian Brownlie, *The Peaceful Settlement of International Disputes in Practice,* 7 Pace Int'l L. Rev. 257 (1995).

United Nations Handbook on the Peaceful Settlement of Disputes Between States (1992).

Elihu Lauterpacht, Aspects of the Administration of International Justice (1991).

Christine Chinkin & Romana Sadurska, *The Anatomy of International Dispute Resolution,* Ohio St. J. on Disp. Resol. 39 (1991).

Ion Diaconu, *Peaceful Settlement of Disputes Between States: History and Prospects in* The Structure and Process of International Law: Essays in Legal Philosophy Doctrine and Theory 1095 (Ronald St. J. Macdonald & Douglas M. Johnston eds. 1983).

Louis Sohn, *The Future of Dispute Settlement in* The Structure and Process of International Law: Essays in Legal Philosophy Doctrine and Theory 1121 (Ronald St. J. Macdonald & Douglas M. Johnston eds. 1983).

I. Non-Binding Methods

Chapter Two

Negotiation and Consultation

Introduction

Negotiation is direct communication to resolve an issue or dispute. Disputing parties commonly try negotiation to resolve their disputes before moving on to other more—or less—sophisticated methods. Negotiation is a straightforward method, easy to organize because it involves no other parties than the disputants and few rules of procedure. Negotiation is easily the most commonly used and most useful of all international dispute resolution methods. Its one obvious drawback is that parties in a dispute may be unable to overcome their differences to the point where they can negotiate. One party may refuse to recognize that another party even has a point of contention, or the animosity between parties might be so great they refuse to talk. International law's response to this key drawback is to obligate parties to negotiate. A central concern of this chapter is the international legal obligation to negotiate found in both treaties and customary international law. The chapter also examines what it takes to fulfill the obligation to negotiate. What interaction among states is adequate to satisfy an obligation to negotiate—resolution of the dispute, good faith discussion, or just showing up for the talks?

The following introductory essay discusses these central questions in more detail and provides a useful overview of the full range of issues related to negotiation in international law.

Charles Manga Fombad, *Consultation and Negotiation in the Pacific Settlement of International Disputes**

* * *

I—THE NATURE OF THE OBLIGATION TO CONSULT AND NEGOTIATE

The Concepts of Consultation and Negotiation

The terms "negotiations" and "consultations" are often used interchangeably. This usage is correct in many instances where these two concepts constitute part of a unified process. There however exists a distinction between the two concepts which is of great practical importance, especially with regards to their role in the pacific settlement of international disputes.

"Negotiation" is a broad complex notion which at first sight appears easy to define and understand but on detail analysis will reveal its multiple dimensions. For our purposes

* 1 AFRICAN J. INT'L & COMP. L. 707 (1989) (most footnotes omitted).

and in the context of pacific settlement of international disputes, the most satisfactory definition is that stated in the dissenting opinion of Judge MOORE in the *Mavrommatis Palestine Concessions* case, where he said:

> "... in the international sphere and in the sense of International Law, negotiation is the legal and orderly administrative process by which Governments, in the exercise of their unquestionable powers conduct, their relations with another and discuss, adjust, and settle their differences."

This definition brings out three important features of negotiation:

(i) It makes it clear that negotiations are a legal process and as such must operate and function within the general framework of International Law.

(ii) From the broad formulation, it covers both "ad hoc" and permanent or institutional negotiations, as well as bilateral and multilateral negotiations, and

(iii) The fact that negotiations provide a medium both for general discussions and affecting adjustments which help towards both preventing, or avoiding potential disputes and resolving actual disputes that have arisen.

The effectiveness of negotiations in any particular dispute will therefore depend on the interaction of these three factors. But, negotiation, defined in these broad terms, also covers and incorporates the notion of "consultation".

"Consultation" per se is a rather complex legal notion that eludes a precise definition. It could however be described as consisting of the formal or informal, "ad hoc" or permanent, bilateral or multilateral discussions and conversations between states aimed at resolving their differences although it is more often to avoid or prevent potential rather than actual disputes. Consultation as such, unlike negotiation *stricto sensu,* relates more to situations and issues of potential controversy rather than actual disputes.

But the distinction between these two concepts, whilst widely recognized and accepted need not be stretched too far, inasmuch as there is no clear-cut and well marked borderline which separates the two. Not only are the two terms often correctly used interchangeably, but may even have the same legal effect. Thus where a consultation clause is designed to or operates to facilitate the settlement of an actual dispute that has arisen, then it becomes indistinguishable from the operation of a negotiation clause. Even when this is not so, the consultation and negotiation process could be operated concurrently, with the former gradually merging into the latter where the discussions and conversations expose underlying differences of view between the parties. Perhaps the fundamental point here is that the existence of a dispute is not a condition *sine qua non,* nor an essential for the invocation of the consultation process generally, as it is for the negotiation process.

The Legal Nature of the Obligation to Consult and Negotiate

It is generally agreed that where there is an express stipulation or where it could be reasonably inferred from the dispute settlement clause that forms the basis of jurisdiction, that preliminary negotiations are a condition. Then an international tribunal seized is bound to satisfy itself that this obligation had been fulfilled.

A controversy has for sometime persisted over the legal nature of the obligation to negotiate in the absence of an express or implied stipulation to that effect. To one school of thought, the obligation to undertake preliminary negotiations in respect of all international disputes is considered to be a well established rule of Customary International Law or may even arise as a general principle of International Law to be complied with before any international tribunal can be seized. This view is strongly opposed by others who argue that there is neither a principle nor a rule of International Law which justifies the concept of compulsory preliminary negotiations in the absence of an express or implied stipulation to that effect. This latter view is more consistent with International Jurisprudence and the unfettered freedom of states to specifically define the method of dispute settlement procedures they will pursue when a dispute arises.

A rather broad formulation was adopted by the Permanent Court in the *Mavrommatis Palestine Concessions* case, where it stated:

> The court realizes to the full, the importance of the rule laying down that only disputes which cannot be settled by negotiation should be brought before it. It recognizes in fact that before a dispute can be made the subject of an action of law, its subject matter should have been clearly defined by means of diplomatic negotiation.

Although this judgement has frequently been relied upon by proponents of the view that there is a binding international obligation to undertake preliminary negotiations prior to the commencement of proceedings before an international tribunal. It would seem that the court rather than attempting to state a general principle, was referring specifically to the precise wordings of the clauses in the mandate on which its jurisdiction was founded. Nevertheless, subsequent decisions have been more unequivocal.

In the *Interpretation of Judgements Nos 7 and 8* (the *Chorzów Factory* case) the court pointed out that although it would no doubt be desirable that a state before proceeding to take as serious a step as summoning another state to appear before it, should have attempted to settle the matter through negotiations. It however reaffirmed the views it had expressed in the *German Interests in Polish Upper Silesia* case that, in the absence of specific stipulations in the jurisdictional clause rendering diplomatic negotiations a condition precedent, its jurisdiction could not be ousted on that ground.

It also follows that there is no general duty in International Law to consult in the absence of an express or implied provision in the relevant agreement or dispute settlement clause to this effect.

* * *

III—The Conduct of Consultations and Negotiations

The Role of Law

It has sometimes been debated whether the processes of consultations and negotiations should be subject to any strictly defined legal principles. Although the very rationale of this method of dispute settlement as contrasted with arbitral and judicial procedures could be undermined by any rigid adherence to laid down rules and procedures. Nevertheless compliance with and conformity with well established principles of International Law in the conduct of consultations and negotiations is an important factor which determines the durability and effectiveness of any settlement reached by the parties.

Perhaps the most fundamental principle that regulates the whole process is that of good faith. And as Bin Cheng points out:

> The law of treaties is closely bound with the principle of good faith, if indeed not based on it, for this principle governs treaties from the time of their formation to the time of their extinction.[25]

---

25. Bin Cheng, *General Principles of law as applied by International Courts and Tribunals*, London, Stevens & Sons (1953), at p. 106.

And in the *Nuclear Test* cases, the International Court noted:

> One of the basic principles governing the creation and performance of legal obligations, whatever their source, is the principle of good faith. Trust and confidence are inherent in international co-operation, in particular in an age when this co-operation in many fields is becoming increasingly essential.[26]

Good faith in this respect is a rather vague legal principle with no *a priori* precise legal definition and is often left to illustration and description. In the context of consultation and negotiation, a state would be in breach of the requisite good faith if it is guilty of "an unjustified breaking off of discussions, abnormal delays, disregard of agreed procedures, or systematic refusals to take into consideration adverse proposals or interests."[28] A recent illustration of this occurred during the futile efforts of the United Nations to negotiate with the United States over their dispute over the interpretation of Sect. 21 of the United Nations Headquarters Agreements of 1947 prior to the proceedings before the International Court. Here, it is submitted that the US was in breach of its duty of good faith, when it deliberately refused to engage in consultations and negotiations as contemplated by the dispute settlement procedure under Art 21 of the Headquarters Agreement, preferring to restrict itself to informal contacts and consultations outside the dispute settlement procedure.[29] For good faith not only applies to the conduct but also the invocation of, and implementation of solutions reached, during the consultation and negotiation process.

A breach of good faith, like the breach of any other international obligation involves international responsibility on the guilty party. Since it amounts to a failure to apply the agreement, a state may claim damages for any losses suffered as a result of abnormal delays caused by a systematic and deliberate refusal to implement or conduct consultations and negotiations in good faith as long as such damages are not too remote.

Compliance with the Obligation to Consult and Negotiate

Substantive Aspect

There is no laid down general rule governing the actual nature of complying with the obligation to consult and negotiate. Its very flexibility and informality militates against stringent procedural requirements. But it remains a matter of fact to be determined objectively by an international tribunal seized whether there have been adequate consultations and negotiations to justify the conclusion that this precondition has been fulfilled. In doing so, it has often been emphasized that it is not so much the form that such consultations and negotiations may have taken, as the attitude and views of the parties concerned on the substantive issues involved.

Generally, international consultations and negotiations frequently commence with the actors directly involved in the dispute before the issue is taken up at a higher level between the protecting states when no solution is reached. There is an obvious advantage in attempting to resolve issues at their lowest possible level and with the least possible publicity. Such lower-level solutions tend to be simpler, quicker and cheaper and in general, keep a controversy from being enmeshed in broader political issues or engaging national sensitivities. Subsequent discussions at state level will merely proceed at the point where the previous discussions left off, as it may well happen that the nature of the ear-

26. The *Nuclear Test* cases, ICJ Reports (1974), p. 253 at 268.

28. The *Lake Lanoux Arbitration*, 24 ILR (1959), at p. 128

29. The *Applicability of the obligation to arbitrate under Sect. 21 of the UN Headquarters Agreement case*, ICJ Reports (1988), p. 12.

lier talks will render superfluous a renewal of all the opposing contentions from which the dispute originated....

Compliance with the mandatory obligation to engage in preliminary negotiations does not necessarily require prolonged and extensive discussions. In the *Mavrommatis Palestine Concessions* case, Britain had argued that there was no dispute which could not "be settled by negotiations" under the terms of the mandate. The very small number and brevity of the communications with the idea of negotiation *stricto sensu*. In rejecting this argument, the Permanent Court stated:

> Negotiations do not always of necessity presuppose a more or less lengthy series of notes and dispatches; it may suffice that a discussion should have been, and this discussion may have been very short; this will be the case if a deadlock is reached, or if finally a point is reached at which one of the parties definitely declares himself unable, or refuses, to give way and there can therefore be no doubt that the dispute cannot be settled by diplomatic negotiation ...

The court also considered the question whether negotiations stood any chance of success or were deadlock, a relative one which could not be determined without regard to, amongst other considerations, the views of the states concerned, who are usually in the best position to judge as to the political or other reasons which could prevent a negotiated settlement.

Even where the dispute settlement clauses provide a specified duration for consultations and negotiations, probably as a safeguard against obstructionist tactics, an international tribunal would not allow a recalcitrant party to exploit this in urgent cases to delay a prompt settlement. Thus, although such a time limit may not have expired, a tribunal would in an appropriate case in accepting jurisdiction hold that a deadlock had been reached and any further delays within such a time limit would only cause unnecessary hardship.

An important objective of consultations and negotiations being that it enables the parties to express their views and for the issues in dispute to be clearly defined and agreed upon, it goes without saying that only such issues previously raised and discussed can form the subject of subsequent proceedings before an international tribunal. The mere fact that a party threatened to invoke the legal procedure provided for in the dispute settlement clause does not render such an issue one that could not be resolved through negotiations. And as Judge CHENG put it in the *Phosphates in Morocco* case:

> ... warning is not the same thing as negotiation. It is the essence of negotiation to discuss some question with a view to settling it, whereas warning is merely the intimation of a will to do certain things (...) on certain contingencies.

This injunction has often been applied to issues that were never mentioned during consultations and negotiations, to which the principle that they were not issues that could not be settled through negotiations applies with full force. Thus in the *Electricity Company of Sofia and Bulgaria* case, one of the complaints raised by Belgium in its application was rejected as being an entirely fresh issue over which there was no evidence that it had been the subject of the prior diplomatic negotiations between the parties.

On the other hand, where the issue raised is closely and intricately linked with matters that had formed the subject of previous consultations and negotiations, then the general injunction may not apply. In the *France/US Air Transport Arbitration* of 1978 one of the preliminary jurisdictional objections raised by the US was the fact that the issue concerning the application of Part 213 Order of the CAB Economic Regulations, unlike the dispute over the change of gauge, had not been raised during its preliminary negotiations with France. The tribunal in rejecting this argument pointed out that even if the discussions on the particular issue had not been specific or extensive, the two issues were in fact closely interrelated.

An important question also raised in the above arbitration is the legitimacy of threatening or actually using retaliatory measures as a means to expedite the recourse to the consultations and negotiations procedures and ultimately other third party procedures provided under the dispute settlement clause. The tribunal took the view that retaliatory measures were neither prohibited under the general principles of International Law nor inconsistent with the US obligations under the relevant air transport agreement inasmuch as they were accompanied by an offer for an accelerated procedure for resolving the dispute. This, it is submitted, is an unsatisfactory authority for the view that retaliatory measures could be legitimate when used in a genuine effort towards speeding up a negotiated settlement of a dispute. Obviously, a policy of negotiation under the threat of retaliation is the antithesis of the good faith and mutual understanding that should prevail prior to, during and after consultations and negotiations. And besides an obligation to consult and negotiate does not imply any obligation on the parties to reach a settlement of their differences. Nevertheless, good faith requires the parties at least to make a determined effort towards reaching an amicable compromise and not merely to reduce the whole process into a meaningless formality.[43]

Two other forms of consultation and negotiation are of sufficient interest to merit separate consideration here in view of their potential significance to the general process of pacific settlement of disputes.

Conference or Parliamentary Diplomacy

Conference or parliamentary diplomacy is a legal concept of relatively recent birth developed since 1945 within the proceedings of the General Assembly of the United Nations. As an extension of traditional consultations and negotiations, it could in appropriate instances constitute a substitute or an alternative to the latter not only within the framework of the United Nations but also within other international forums.

The issue whether the discussion of an issue within an international organization such as the United Nations could be considered a sufficient compliance with the requirement of direct consultations and negotiations was raised in the *South West Africa* cases. South Africa had raised as one of its preliminary objections to the court's jurisdiction, the argument that there had been no direct negotiation between itself and either Liberia or Ethiopia as was envisaged under the terms of the mandate. The court in rejecting this, held it was irrelevant that the negotiations that had taken place had not been directly between South Africa and the two applicants. It went further to expound the concept of conference or parliamentary diplomacy which is considered applicable to the case thus;

> In cases where the disputed questions are of common interest to a group of states on one side or the other in an organized body, parliamentary or conference diplomacy has often been found to be the most practical form of negotiation ... If it is one of mutual interest to many states, whether in an organized body or not, there is no reason why each of them should go through the formality and pretence of direct negotiations with the common adversary state after they have already fully participated in the collective negotiations with the same state in opposition.

43. The *North Sea Continental Shelf cases*. ICJ Reports (1969) p. 3, at 47.

But whatever its merits, this concept is not without its critics. In fact, Judges Spender and Fitzmaurice in a joint dissenting opinion expressed the views that discussions at an international organization could never be regarded as a substitute for direct negotiations nor justify the conclusion that attempts had been made at settlement at the state or diplomatic level. Judge Fitzmaurice was to repeat his views in the *Northern Cameroons* case when he observed that "negotiations" did not mean "a couple of states arguing with each other across the floor of an international assembly, or circulating statements of their complaints or contentions to its member states." This he declared was "disputation, not negotiation."

Although the concept of conference or parliamentary diplomacy is now fairly well established and provides a very important technique particularly suitable for resolving certain types of disputes which concerns a multitude of states. Certain checks seem necessary for such a collective process to be assimilated to or even substitute direct consultations and negotiations. Two conditions are essential, and these conditions will also apply in cases of intervention under the statute of the International Court as pointed out above.

(i) The issues raised in the proceedings before the tribunal or in the application to intervene must be substantially the same as those previously discussed, such as to render further direct negotiations superfluous.

(ii) The tribunal must be satisfied that there is no reasonable chance that further direct negotiation between the parties would lead to a settlement or substantially narrow down the issues raised.

Subject to such control, the concept of conference or parliamentary diplomacy offers an attractive means through which attempts could be made to resolve certain types of disputes before ultimate recourse to international litigation. International Law is not so rich in methods for pacific settlement of disputes that it can afford to ignore some of the obvious advantages that such a procedure can offer especially within the framework of an international organization like the United Nations or any of the other specialized agencies. Whilst its exact scope and potential is still uncertain, it is perhaps too early to draw any definite conclusions.

The Concept of "Judicial Negotiation"

Another dimension to the art of consultation and negotiation appears to have been added in what may appropriately be referred to as "judicial negotiation." This concept, applicable under the ICAO Council Rules for the Settlement of Differences requires the council to initiate, and encourage or actively direct a negotiated settlement between the disputants, as an integral but complimentary part of its essentially adjudicatory role under chapter XVIII of the Chicago Convention of 1944. It is only a discretionary function subject to the consent of the parties to dispute and may be undertaken at any stage of the proceedings but prior to the meeting at which the final decision is to be rendered. As such, it is not an independent, distinct, or autonomous method of resolving such disputes but remains incidental to adjudication. Although used only once since its formulation, it breaks new frontiers in the approach to international adjudication and the role of consultation and negotiation can still play at that stage.

The concept of judicial negotiation has more wider application even within the strict confines of traditional adjudication. Some ramifications of this can be seen in the practice of the International Court. In the *Aegean Sea Continental Shelf* case, the court rejected any suggestion that the existence of active negotiations constituted a legal impediment to the exercise of jurisdiction. Referring to earlier jurisprudence on this point, it observed however that whilst negotiations and judicial proceedings could be pursued *pari passu*, the latter may be discontinued if the negotiations succeeded.

In general, both the present court and its predecessor have always stressed the fact that their judicial role is simply an alternative to direct and friendly settlement through negotiations. They have on various occasions tried to facilitate such direct and friendly settlements as far as it was compatible with their statute in the *Fisheries Jurisdiction (UK v Iceland)* case, the International Court after observing that the obligation to negotiate flows from the very nature of the respective rights of the parties, considered that to direct them to negotiate was a proper exercise of its judicial functions in the circumstances.

Judicial negotiation in this respect is a promising legal development which might go some way towards encouraging recourse to the International Court if its procedures are clearly defined.

World Trade Organization, Understanding on Rules and Procedures Governing the Settlement of Dispute

Article 4
Consultation

See Annex

United Nations Convention on the Law of the Sea

Part XV Dispute Settlement
Section 1. General Provisions

Articles 279–283

See Annex

Applicability of the Obligation to Arbitrate Under Section 21 of the United Nations Headquarters Agreement of 26 June 1947

Advisory Opinion
1988 ICJ 12 (April 26)

* * *

7. The question upon which the opinion of the Court has been requested is whether the United States of America (hereafter referred to as "the United States"), as a party to the United Nations Headquarters Agreement, is under an obligation to enter into arbitration. The Headquarters Agreement of 26 June 1947 came into force in accordance with its terms on 21 November 1947 by exchange of letters between the Secretary-General and the United States Permanent Representative. The Agreement was registered the same day with the United Nations Secretariat, in accordance with Article 102 of the Charter. In section 21, paragraph *(a)*, it provides as follows:

> "Any dispute between the United Nations and the United States concerning the interpretation or application of this agreement or of any supplemental agreement, which is not settled by negotiation or other agreed mode of settlement, shall be referred for final decision to a tribunal of three arbitrators, one to be named

by the Secretary-General, one to be named by the Secretary of State of the United States, and the third to be chosen by the two, or, if they should fail to agree upon a third, then by the President of the International Court of Justice."

There is no question but that the Headquarters Agreement is a treaty in force binding the parties thereto. What the Court has therefore to determine, in order to answer the question put to it, is whether there exists a dispute between the United Nations and the United States of the kind contemplated by section 21 of the Agreement. For this purpose the Court will first set out the sequence of events, preceding the adoption of resolutions 42/229 A and 42/229 B, which led first the Secretary-General and subsequently the General Assembly of the United Nations to conclude that such a dispute existed.

8. The events in question centered round the Permanent Observer Mission of the Palestine Liberation Organization (referred hereafter as "the PLO") to the United Nations in New York. The PLO has enjoyed in relation to the United Nations the status of an observer since 1974; by General Assembly resolution 3237 (XXIX) of 22 November 1974, the Organization was invited to "participate in the sessions and the work of the General Assembly in the capacity of observer". Following this invitation, the PLO established an Observer Mission in 1974, and maintains an office, entitled office of the PLO Observer Mission, at 115 East 65th Street, in New York City, outside the United Nations Headquarters District. Recognized observers are listed as such in official United Nations publications: the PLO appears in such publications in a category of "organizations which have received a standing invitation from the General Assembly to participate in the sessions and the work of the General Assembly as observers".

9. In May 1987 a bill (S.1203) was introduced into the Senate of the United States, the purpose of which was stated in its title to be "to make unlawful the establishment or maintenance within the United States of an office of the Palestine Liberation Organization".

* * *

11. On 22 October, 1987, the view of the Secretary-General was summed up in the following statement made by the Spokesman for the Secretary-General (subsequently endorsed by the General Assembly in resolution 42/210 B):

> "The members of the PLO Observer Mission are, by virtue of resolution 3237 (XXIX), invitees to the United Nations. As such, they are covered by sections 11, 12 and 13 of the Headquarters Agreement of 26 June 1947. There is therefore a treaty obligation on the host country to permit PLO personnel to enter and remain in the United States to carry out their official functions at United Nations Headquarters."

In this respect, it may be noted that section 11 of the Headquarters Agreement provides that

> "The federal, state or local authorities of the United States shall not impose any impediments to transit to or from the headquarters district of: (1) representatives of Members ... or the families of such representatives ... ; (5) other persons invited to the headquarters district by the United Nations ... on official business ..."
>
> Section 12 provides that "The provisions of Section 11 shall be applicable irrespective of the relations existing between the Governments of the persons referred to in that section and the Government of the United States". Section 13 provides, *inter alia*, that "Laws and regulations in force in the United States re-

garding the entry of aliens shall not be applied in such manner as to interfere with the privileges referred to in Section 11."

* * *

15. On 22 December 1987, the Foreign Relations Authorization Act, Fiscal Years 1988 and 1989, was signed into law by the President of the United States. Title X thereof, the Anti-Terrorism Act of 1987, was, according to its terms, to take effect 90 days after that date. On 5 January 1988 the Acting Permanent Representative of the United States to the United Nations, Ambassador Herbert Okun, in a reply to the Secretary-General's letters of 7 and 21 December 1987, informed the Secretary-General of this. The letter went on to say that

> "Because the provisions concerning the PLO Observer Mission may infringe on the President's constitutional authority and, if implemented, would be contrary to our international legal obligations under the United Nations Headquarters Agreement, the Administration intends, during the ninety-day period before this provision is to take effect, to engage in consultations with the Congress in an effort to resolve this matter."

16. On 14 January 1988 the Secretary-General again wrote to Ambassador Walters. After welcoming the intention expressed in Ambassador Okun's letter to use the ninety-day period to engage in consultations with the Congress, the Secretary-General went on to say:

> "As you will recall, I had, by my letter of 7 December, informed you that, in the view of the United Nations, the United States is under a legal obligation under the Headquarters Agreement of 1947 to maintain the current arrangements for the PLO Observer Mission, which have been in effect for the past 13 years. I had therefore asked you to confirm that if this legislative proposal became law, the present arrangements for the PLO Observer Mission would not be curtailed or otherwise affected, for without such assurance, a dispute between the United Nations and the United States concerning the interpretation and application of the Headquarters Agreement would exist ..."

Then, referring to the letter of January 5, 1988 from the Permanent Representative and to declarations by the Legal Adviser to the State Department, he observed that neither that letter nor those declarations

> "constitute the assurance that I had sought in my letter of 7 December 1987 nor do they ensure that full respect for the Headquarters Agreement can be assumed. Under these circumstances, a dispute exists between the Organization and the United States concerning the interpretation and application of the Headquarters Agreement and I hereby invoke the dispute settlement procedure set out in Section 21 of the said Agreement.
>
> According to Section 21 *(a)*, an attempt has to be made at first to solve the dispute through negotiations, and I would like to propose that the first round of the negotiating phase be convened on Wednesday, 20 January 1988 ..."

17. Beginning on 7 January 1988, a series of consultations were held; from the account of these consultations presented to the General Assembly by the Secretary-General in the report referred to in the request for advisory opinion, it appears that the positions of the parties thereto were as follows:

> "the [United Nations] Legal Counsel was informed that the United States was not in a position and not willing to enter formally into the dispute settlement

> procedure under section 21 of the Headquarters Agreement; the United States was still evaluating the situation and had not yet concluded that a dispute existed between the United Nations and the United States at the present time because the legislation in question had not yet been implemented. The Executive Branch was still examining the possibility of interpreting the law in conformity with the United States obligations under the Headquarters Agreement regarding the PLO Observer Mission, as reflected in the arrangements currently made for that Mission, or alternatively of providing assurances that would set aside the ninety-day period for the coming into force of the legislation." (A/42/915, para. 6.)

18. The United Nations Legal Counsel stated that for the Organization the question was one of compliance with international law. The Headquarters Agreement was a binding international instrument the obligations of the United States under which were, in the view of the Secretary-General and the General Assembly, being violated by the legislation in question. Section 21 of the Agreement set out the procedure to be followed in the event of a dispute as to the interpretation or application of the Agreement and the United Nations had every intention of defending its rights under that Agreement. He insisted, therefore, that if the PLO Observer Mission was not to be exempted from the application of the law, the procedure provided for in Section 21 be implemented and also that technical discussions regarding the establishment of an arbitral tribunal take place immediately. The United States agreed to such discussions but only on an informal basis. Technical discussions were commenced on 28 January 1988. Among the matters discussed were the costs of the arbitration, its location, its secretariat, languages, rules of procedure and the form of the *compromis* between the two sides (*ibid.*, paras. 7–8).

* * *

24. On 11 March 1988 the Acting Permanent Representative of the United States to the United Nations wrote to the Secretary-General, referring to General Assembly resolution 42/229 A and 42/229 B and stating as follows:

> "I wish to inform you that the Attorney General of the United States has determined that he is required by the Anti-Terrorism Act of 1987 to close the office of the Palestine Liberation Organization Observer Mission to the United Nations in New York, irrespective of any obligations the United States may have under the Agreement between the United Nations and the United States regarding the Headquarters of the United Nations. If the PLO does not comply with the Act, the Attorney General will initiate legal action to close the PLO Observer Mission on or about March 21, 1988, the effective date of the Act. This course of action will allow the orderly enforcement of the Act. The United States will not take other actions to close the Observer Mission pending a decision in such litigation. Under the circumstances, the United States believes that submission of this matter to arbitration would not serve a useful purpose."

This letter was delivered by hand to the Secretary-General by the Acting Permanent Representative of the United States on 11 March 1988. On receiving the letter, the Secretary-General protested to the Acting Permanent Representative and stated that the decision taken by the United States Government as outlined in the letter was a clear violation of the Headquarters Agreement between the United Nations and the United States.

25. On the same day, the United States Attorney General wrote to the Permanent Observer of the PLO to the United Nations to the following effect:

> "I am writing to notify you that on March 21, 1988, the provisions of the 'Anti-Terrorism Act of 1987' (Title X of the Foreign Relations Authorization Act of 1988–89; Pub. L. No. 100-204, enacted by the Congress of the United States and approved Dec. 22, 1987 (the 'Act')) will become effective. The Act prohibits, among other things, the Palestine Liberation Organization ('PLO') from establishing or maintaining an office within the jurisdiction of the United States. Accordingly, as of March 21, 1988, maintaining the PLO Observer Mission to the United Nations in the United States will be unlawful.
>
> The legislation charges the Attorney General with the responsibility of enforcing the Act. To that end, please be advised that, should you fail to comply with the requirements of the Act, the Department of Justice will forthwith take action in United States federal court to ensure your compliance."

26. Finally, on the same day, in the course of a press briefing held by the United States Department of Justice, the Assistant Attorney General in charge of the Office of Legal Counsel said as follows, in reply to a question:

> "We have determined that we would not participate in any forum, either the arbitral tribunal that might be constituted under Article XXI, as I understand it, of the UN Headquarters Agreement, or the International Court of Justice. As I said earlier, the statute [i.e., the Anti-Terrorism Act of 1987] has superseded the requirements of the UN Headquarters Agreement to the extent that those requirements are inconsistent with the statute, and therefore, participation in any of these tribunals that you cite would be to no useful end. The statute's mandate governs, and we have no choice but to enforce it."

* * *

30. On 23 March 1988, the General Assembly, at its reconvened forty-second session, adopted resolution 42/230 by 148 votes to 2, by which reaffirmed *(inter alia)* that

> "a dispute exists between the United Nations and the United States of America, the host country, concerning the interpretation or application of the Headquarters Agreement, and that the dispute settlement procedure provided for under section 21 of the Agreement, which constitutes the only legal remedy to solve the dispute, should be set in operation"

and requested "the host country to name its arbitrator to the arbitral tribunal".

31. The representative of the United States, who voted against the resolution, said *(inter alia)* the following in explanation of the vote. Referring to the proceedings instituted in the United States courts, he said:

> "The United States will take no further steps to close the PLO office until the [United States] Court has reached a decision on the Attorney General's position that the Act requires closure ... Until the United States courts have determined whether that law requires closure of the PLO Observer Mission the United States Government believes that it would be premature to consider the appropriateness of arbitration." (A/42/PV.109, pp. 13–15.)

He also urged:

> "Let us not be diverted from the important and historic goal of peace in the Middle East by the current dispute over the status of the PLO Observer Mission." (*Ibid.*, p. 16.)

32. At the hearing, the United Nations Legal Counsel, representing the Secretary-General, stated to the Court that he had informed the United States District Court Judge

seised of the proceedings referred to in paragraph 29 above that it was the wish of the United Nations to submit an *amicus curiae* brief in those proceedings.

33. In the present case, the Court is not called upon to decide whether the measures adopted by the United States in regard to the Observer Mission of the PLO to the United Nations do or do not run counter to the Headquarters Agreement. The question put to the Court is not about either the alleged violations of the provisions of the Headquarters Agreement applicable to that Mission or the interpretation of those provisions. The request for an opinion is here directed solely to the determination whether under section 21 of the Headquarters Agreement the United Nations was entitled to call for arbitration, and the United States was obliged to enter into this procedure. Hence the request for an opinion concerns solely the applicability to the alleged dispute of the arbitration procedure provided for by the Headquarters Agreement. It is a legal question within the meaning of Article 65, paragraph 1, of the Statute. There is in this case no reason why the Court should not answer that question.

34. In order to answer the question put to it, the Court has to determine whether there exists a dispute between the United Nations and the United States, and if so whether or not that dispute is one "concerning the interpretation or application of" the Headquarters Agreement within the meaning of section 21 thereof. If it finds that there is such a dispute it must also, pursuant to that section, satisfy itself that it is one "not settled by negotiation or other agreed mode of settlement".

35. As the Court observed in the case concerning *Interpretation of Peace Treaties with Bulgaria, Hungary and Romania*, "whether there exists an international dispute is a matter for objective determination" (*I.C.J. Reports 1950*, p. 74). In this respect the Permanent Court of International Justice, in the case concerning *Mavrommatis Palestine Concessions*, had defined a dispute as "a disagreement on a point of law or fact, a conflict of legal views or of interests between two persons" (*P.C.I.J., Series A, No. 2*, p. 11). This definition has since been applied and clarified on a number of occasions. In the Advisory Opinion of 30 March 1950 the Court, after examining the diplomatic exchanges between the States concerned, noted that "the two sides hold clearly opposite views concerning the question of the performance or non-performance of certain treaty obligations" and concluded that "international disputes have arisen" (*Interpretation of Peace Treaties with Bulgaria, Hungary and Romania, First Phase, I.C.J. Reports 1950*, p. 74). Furthermore, in its Judgment of 21 December 1962 in the *South West Africa* cases, the Court made it clear that in order to prove the existence of a dispute

> "it is not sufficient for one party to a contentious case to assert that a dispute exists with the other party. A mere assertion is not sufficient to prove the existence of a dispute any more than a mere denial of the existence of the dispute proves its non-existence. Nor is it adequate to show that the interests of the two parties to such a case are in conflict. It must be shown that the claim of one party is positively opposed by the other." (*I.C.J. Reports 1962*, p. 328).

The Court found that the opposing attitudes of the parties clearly established the existence of a dispute (*Ibid.*; see also *Northern Cameroons, I.C.J. Reports 1963*, p. 27).

36. In the present case, the Secretary-General informed the Court that, in his opinion, a dispute within the meaning of section 21 of the Headquarters Agreement existed between the United Nations and the United States from the moment the Anti-Terrorism Act was signed into law by the President of the United States and in the absence of adequate assurances to the Organization that the Act would not be applied to the PLO Observer Mission to the United Nations. By his letter of 14 January 1988 to the Permanent Representative

of the United States, the Secretary-General formally contested the consistency of the Act with the Headquarters Agreement (paragraph 16 above). The Secretary-General confirmed and clarified that point of view in a letter of 15 March 1988 (paragraph 28 above) to the Acting Permanent Representative of the United States in which he told him that the determination made by the Attorney General of the United States on 11 March 1988 was a "clear violation of the Headquarters Agreement". In that same letter he once more asked that the matter be submitted to arbitration.

37. The United States has never expressly contradicted the view expounded by the Secretary-General and endorsed by the General Assembly regarding the sense of the Headquarters Agreement. Certain United States authorities have even expressed the same view, but the United States has nevertheless taken measures against the PLO Mission to the United Nations. It has indicated those measures were being taken "irrespective of any obligations the United States may have under the [Headquarters] Agreement" (paragraph 24 above).

38. In the view of the Court, where one party to a treaty protests against the behaviour or a decision of another party, and claims that such behaviour or decision constitutes a breach of the treaty, the mere fact that the party accused does not advance any argument to justify its conduct under international law does not prevent the opposing attitudes of the parties from giving rise to a dispute concerning the interpretation or application of the treaty. In the case concerning *United States Diplomatic and Consular Staff in Tehran*, the jurisdiction of the Court was asserted principally on the basis of the Optional Protocols concerning the Compulsory Settlement of Disputes accompanying the Vienna Conventions of 1961 on Diplomatic Relations and of 1963 on Consular Relations, which defined the disputes to which they applied as "Disputes arising out of the interpretation or application of" the relevant Convention. Iran, which did not appear in the proceedings before the Court, had acted in such a way as, in the view of the United States, to commit breaches of the Conventions, but, so far as the Court was informed, Iran had at no time claimed to justify it actions by advancing an alternative interpretation of the Conventions, on the basis of which such actions would not constitute such a breach. The Court saw no need to enquire into the attitude of Iran in order to establish the existence of a "dispute"; in order to determine whether it had jurisdiction, it stated:

> "The United States' claims here in question concern alleged violations by Iran of its obligations under several articles of the Vienna Conventions of 1961 and 1963 with respect to the privileges and immunities of the personnel, the inviolability of the premises and archives, and the provision of facilities for the performance of the functions of the United States Embassy and Consulates in Iran ... By their very nature all these claims concern the interpretation or application of one or other of the two Vienna Conventions." (*I.C.J. Reports 1980*, pp. 24–25, para. 46.)

39. In the present case, the United States in its public statements has not referred to the matter as a "dispute" (save for a passing reference on 23 March 1988 to "the current dispute over the status of the PLO Observer Mission" (paragraph 31 above)), and it has expressed the view that arbitration would be "premature". According to the report of the Secretary-General to the General Assembly (A/42/915, para. 6), the position taken by the United States during the consultations in January 1988 was that it "had not yet concluded that a dispute existed between the United Nations and the United States" at that time "because the legislation in question had not yet been implemented". Finally, the Government of the United States, in its written statement of 25 March 1988, told the Court that:

"The United States will take no action to close the Mission pending a decision in that litigation. Since the matter is still pending in our courts, we do not believe arbitration would be appropriate or timely."

40. The Court could not allow considerations as to what might be "appropriate" to prevail over the obligations which derive from section 21 of the Headquarters Agreement, as "the Court, being a Court of justice, cannot disregard rights recognized by it, and base its decision on considerations of pure expediency" (*Free Zones of Upper Savoy and the District of Gex, Order of 6 December 1930, P.C.I.J., Series A, No. 24,* p. 15).

41. The Court must further point out that the alleged dispute relates solely to what the United Nations considers to be its rights under the Headquarters Agreement. The purpose of the arbitration procedure envisaged by that Agreement is precisely the settlement of such disputes as may arise between the Organization and the host country without any prior recourse to municipal courts, and it would be against both the letter and the spirit of the Agreement for the implementation of that procedure to be subjected to such prior recourse. It is evident that a provision of the nature of section 21 of the Headquarters Agreement cannot require the exhaustion of local remedies as a condition of its implementation.

42. The United States in its written statement might be implying that neither the signing into law of the Anti-Terrorism Act, nor its entry into force, nor the Attorney General's decision to apply it, nor his resort to court proceedings to close the PLO Mission to the United Nations, would have been sufficient to bring about a dispute between the United Nations and the United States, since the case was still pending before an American court and, until the decision of that court, the United States, according to the Acting Permanent Representative's letter of 11 March 1988, "will not take other actions to close" the Mission. The Court cannot accept such an argument. While the existence of a dispute does presuppose a claim arising out of the behaviour of or a decision by one of the parties, it in no way requires that any contested decision must already have been carried into effect. What is more, a dispute may arise even if the party in question gives an assurance that no measure of execution will be taken until ordered by decision of the domestic courts.

43. The Anti-Terrorism Act was signed into law on 22 December 1987. It was automatically to take effect 90 days later. Although the Act extends to every PLO office situated within the jurisdiction of the United States and contains no express reference to the office of the PLO Mission to the United Nations in New York, its chief, if not its sole, objective was the closure of that office. On 11 March 1988, the United States Attorney General considered that he was under an obligation to effect such a closure; he notified the Mission of this, and applied to the United States courts for an injunction prohibiting those concerned "from continuing violations of" the Act. As noted above, the Secretary-General, acting both on his own behalf and on instructions from the General Assembly, has consistently challenged the decisions contemplated and then taken by the United States Congress and the Administration. Under those circumstances, the Court is obliged to find that the opposing attitudes of the United Nations and the United States show the existence of a dispute between the two parties to the Headquarters Agreement.

44. For the purposes of the present advisory opinion there is no need to seek to determine the date at which the dispute came into existence, once the Court has reached the conclusion that there is such a dispute at the date on which its opinion is given.

45. The Court has next to consider whether the dispute is one which concerns the interpretation or application of the Headquarters Agreement. It is not however the task of

the Court to say whether the enactment, or the enforcement, of the United States Anti-Terrorism Act would or would not constitute a breach of the provisions of the Headquarters Agreement; that question is reserved for the arbitral tribunal which the Secretary-General seeks to have established under section 21 of the Agreement.

46. In the present case, the Secretary-General and the General Assembly of the United Nations have constantly pointed out that the PLO was invited "to participate in the sessions and the work of the General Assembly in the capacity of Observer" (resolution 3237 (XXIX)). In their view, therefore, the PLO Observer Mission to the United Nations was, as such, covered by the provisions of sections 11, 12 and 13 of the Headquarters Agreement; it should therefore "be enabled to establish and maintain premises and adequate functional facilities" (General Assembly resolution 42/229 A, para. 2). The Secretary-General and the General Assembly have accordingly concluded that the various measures envisaged and then taken by the United States Congress and Administration would be incompatible with the Agreement if they were to be applied to that Mission, and that the adoption of those measures gave rise to a dispute between the United Nations Organization and the United States with regard to the interpretation and application of the Headquarters Agreement.

* * *

49. To conclude, the United States has taken a number of measures against the PLO Observer Mission to the United Nations in New York. The Secretary-General regarded these as contrary to the Headquarters Agreement. Without expressly disputing that point, the United States stated that the measures in question were taken "irrespective of any obligations the United States may have under the Agreement". Such conduct cannot be reconciled with the position of the Secretary-General. There thus exists a dispute between the United Nations and the United States concerning the application of the Headquarters Agreement, falling within the terms of section 21 thereof.

50. The question might of course be raised whether in United States domestic law the decisions taken on 11 and 21 March 1988 by the Attorney General brought about the application of the Anti-Terrorism Act, or whether the Act can only be regarded as having received effective application when or if, on completion of the current judicial proceedings, the PLO Mission is in fact closed. This is however not decisive as regards section 21 of the Headquarters Agreement, which refers to any dispute "concerning the interpretation or application" of the Agreement, and not concerning the application of the measures taken in the municipal law of the United States. The Court therefore sees no reason not to find that a dispute exists between the United Nations and the United States concerning the "interpretation or application" of the Headquarters Agreement.

51. The Court now turns to the question of whether the dispute between the United Nations and the United States is one "not settled by negotiation or other agreed mode of settlement", in the terms of section 21, paragraph *(a)* of the Headquarters Agreement.

52. In his written statement, the Secretary-General interprets this provision as requiring a two-stage process.

> "In the first stage the parties attempt to settle their difference through negotiation or some other agreed mode of settlement ... If they are unable to reach a settlement through these means, the second stage of the process, compulsory arbitration, becomes applicable." (Para. 17.)

The Secretary-General accordingly concludes that

> "In order to find that the United States is under an obligation to enter into arbitration, it is necessary to show that the United Nations has made a good faith

attempt to resolve the dispute through negotiations or some other agreed mode of settlement and that such negotiations have not resolved the dispute." (Para. 42.)

53. In his letter to the United States Permanent Representative dated 14 January 1988, the Secretary-General not only formally invoked the dispute settlement procedure set out in section 21 of the Headquarters Agreement, but also noted that "According to section 21 *(a)*, an attempt has to be made at first to solve the dispute through negotiations" and proposed that the negotiations phase of the procedure commence on 20 January 1988. According to the Secretary-General's report to the General Assembly, a series of consultations had already begun on 7 January 1988 (A/42/915, para. 6) and continued until 10 February 1988 (*ibid.*, para. 10). Technical discussions, on an informal basis, on procedural matters relating to the arbitration contemplated by the Secretary-General, were held between 28 January 1988 and 2 February 1988 (*ibid.*, paras. 8–9). On 2 March 1988, the Acting Permanent Representative of the United States stated in the General Assembly that

> "we have been in regular and frequent contact with the United Nations Secretariat over the past several months concerning an appropriate resolution of this matter" (A/42/PV.104, p. 59).

54. The Secretary-General recognizes that "The United States did not consider these contacts and consultations to be formally within the framework of section 21 *(a)* of the Headquarters Agreement" (written statement, para. 44), and in a letter to the United States Permanent Representative dated 2 February 1988, the Secretary-General noted that the United States was taking the position that, pending its evaluation of the situation which would arise from application of the Anti-Terrorism Act, "it cannot enter into the dispute settlement procedure outlined in section 21 of the Headquarters Agreement."

55. The Court considers that, taking into account the United States attitude, the Secretary-General has in the circumstances exhausted such possibilities of negotiation as were open to him. The Court would recall in this connection the dictum of the Permanent Court of International Justice in the *Mavrommatis Palestine Concessions* case that

> "the question of the importance and chances of success of diplomatic negotiations is essentially a relative one. Negotiations do not of necessity always presuppose a more or less lengthy series of notes and despatches; it may suffice that a discussion should have been commenced, and this discussion may have been very short; this will be the case if a deadlock is reached, or if finally a point is reached at which one of the Parties definitely declares himself unable, or refuses, to give way, and there can therefore be no doubt that *the dispute cannot be settled by diplomatic negotiation*" (*P.C.I.J., Series A, No. 2*, p. 13).

When in the case concerning *United States Diplomatic and Consular Staff in Tehran* the attempts of the United States to negotiate with Iran "had reached a deadlock, owing to the refusal of the Iranian Government to enter into any discussion of the matter", the Court concluded that "In consequence, there existed at that date not only a dispute but, beyond any doubt, a 'dispute ... not satisfactorily adjusted by diplomacy' within the meaning of" relevant jurisdictional text (*I.C.J. Reports* 1980, p. 27, para. 51). In the present case, the Court regards it as similarly beyond any doubt that the dispute between the United Nations and the United States is one "not settled by negotiation" within the meaning of section 21, paragraph *(a)* of the Headquarters Agreement.

56. Nor was any "other agreed mode of settlement" of their dispute contemplated by the United Nations and the United States. In this connection the Court should observe that current proceedings brought by the United States Attorney General before the United States courts cannot be an "agreed mode of settlement" within the meaning of section 21

of the Headquarters Agreement. The purpose of these proceedings is to enforce the Anti-Terrorism Act of 1987; it is not directed to settling the dispute, concerning the application of the Headquarters Agreement, which has come into existence between the United Nations and the United States. Furthermore, the United Nations has never agreed to settlement of the dispute in the American courts; it has taken care to make it clear that it wishes to be admitted only as *amicus curiae* before the District Court for the Southern District of New York.

57. The Court must therefore conclude that the United States is bound to respect the obligation to have recourse to arbitration under section 21 of the Headquarters Agreement. The fact remains however that, as the Court has already observed, the United States has declared (letter from the Permanent Representative, 11 March 1988) that its measures against the PLO Observer Mission were taken "irrespective of any obligations the United States may have under the [Headquarters] Agreement". If it were necessary to interpret that statement as intended to refer not only to the substantive obligations laid down in, for example, sections 11, 12 and 13, but also to the obligation to arbitrate provided for in section 21, this conclusion would remain intact. It would be sufficient to recall the fundamental principle of international law that international law prevails over domestic law. This principle was endorsed by judicial decision as long ago as the arbitral award of 14 September 1872 in the *Alabama* case between Great Britain and the United States, and has frequently been recalled since, for example in the case concerning the *Greco-Bulgarian "Communities"* in which the Permanent Court of International Justice laid it down that

> "it is a generally accepted principle of international law that in the relations between Powers who are contracting Parties to a treaty, the provisions of municipal law cannot prevail over those of the treaty" (*P.C.I.J., Series B, No. 17*, p. 32).

58. For these reasons,

THE COURT,

Unanimously,

Is of the opinion that the United States of America, as a party to the Agreement between the United Nations and the United States of America regarding the Headquarters of the United Nations of 26 June 1947, is under an obligation, in accordance with section 21 of that Agreement, to enter into arbitration for the settlement of the dispute between itself and the United Nations.

For the disposition of the issues in the *Headquarters* case in United States courts, see Chapter Fifteen.

Introductory Note to the Fisheries Jurisdiction Case

If you check the Website of the International Court of Justice and the Permanent Court of Arbitration, you will see that the greater share of the cases concern land and maritime boundary disputes. One reason for this growing attention to boundaries in the world is the increased interest in controlling resources. Certain resources are declining even as the world's population grows. Disputes over such resources—oil, water, fish, minerals, and the like—have been among the most difficult to settle peacefully, and have often erupted in armed conflict. In the 1960s, world fish stocks began a dramatic decline. Iceland sought to conserve the stocks near its shores by unilaterally establishing a conservation zone.

The case that follows arose when Iceland sought to exclude British and German fishing vessels from the zone. These states argued they could only be excluded from Iceland's three-mile territorial sea. Iceland, nevertheless, fired upon their fishing vessels to enforce the conservation zone. The British and German navies then accompanied their nationals on fishing voyages near Iceland. The dispute became know as the "Cod Wars." Finally, the U.K. and Germany brought a case against Iceland in the International Court of Justice (ICJ). The Court discussed the parties' dispute settlement obligations under customary international law—obligations on states sharing scarce resources to resort to dispute settlement even in the absence of a treaty commitment. Eventually, the 1982 United Nations Convention on the Law of the Sea provided to each state an exclusive economic zone of up to two hundred nautical miles—many times the size of Iceland's original zone.

Fisheries Jurisdiction Case
(*United Kingdom of Great Britain and Northern Ireland v. Iceland*)

1974 ICJ Rep. 3 (Judgment of 25 July)

* * *

73. The most appropriate method for the solution of the dispute is clearly that of negotiation. Its objective should be the delimitation of the rights and interests of the Parties, the preferential rights of the coastal State on the one hand and the rights of the Applicant on the other, to balance and regulate equitably questions such as those of catch-limitation, share allocations and "related restrictions concerning areas closed to fishing, number and type of vessels allowed and forms of control of the agreed provisions" (*Fisheries Jurisdiction (United Kingdom v. Iceland), Interim Measures, Order of 12 July 1973, I.C.J. Reports 1973*, p. 303, para. 7). This necessitates detailed scientific knowledge of the fishing grounds. It is obvious that the relevant information and expertise would be mainly in the possession of the Parties. The Court would, for this reason, meet with difficulties if it were itself to attempt to lay down a precise scheme for an equitable adjustment of the rights involved. It is thus obvious that both in regard to merits and to jurisdiction the Court only pronounces on the case which is before it and not on any hypothetical situation which might arise in the future.

74. It is implicit in the concept of preferential rights that negotiations are required in order to define or delimit the extent of those rights, as was already recognized in the 1958 Geneva Resolution on Special Situations relating to Coastal Fisheries, which constituted the starting point of the law on the subject. This Resolution provides for the establishment, through collaboration between the coastal State and any other State fishing in the area, of agreed measures to secure just treatment of the special situation.

75. The obligation to negotiate thus flows from the very nature of the respective rights of the Parties; to direct them to negotiate is therefore a proper exercise of the judicial function in this case. This also corresponds to the Principles and provisions of the Charter of the United Nations concerning peaceful settlement of disputes. As the Court stated in the *North Sea Continental Shelf* cases:

> "... this obligation merely constitutes a special application of a principle which underlies all international relations, and which is moreover recognized in Article 33 of the Charter of the United Nations as one of the methods for the peaceful settlement of international disputes" (*I.C.J. Reports* 1969, p. 47, para. 86).

76. In this case negotiations were initiated by the Parties from the date when Iceland gave notice of its intention to extend its fisheries jurisdiction, but these negotiations reached an early deadlock, and could not come to any conclusion; subsequently, further negotiations were directed to the conclusion of the interim agreement of 13 November 1973. The obligation to seek a solution of the dispute by peaceful means, among which negotiations are the most appropriate to this case, has not been eliminated by that interim agreement. The question has been raised, however, on the basis of the deletion of a sentence which had been proposed by the United Kingdom in the process of elaboration of the text, whether the parties agreed to wait for the expiration of the term provided for in the interim agreement without entering into further negotiations. The deleted sentence, which would have appeared in paragraph 7 of the 1973 Exchange of Notes, read: "The Governments will reconsider the position before that term expires unless they have in the meantime agreed to a settlement of the substantive dispute."

77. The Court cannot accept the view that the deletion of this sentence which concerned renegotiation of the interim regime warrants the inference that the common intention of the Parties was to be released from negotiating in respect of the basic dispute over Iceland's extension to a 50-mile limit throughout the whole period covered by the interim agreement. Such an intention would not correspond to the attitude taken up by the Applicant in these proceedings, in which it has asked the Court to adjudge and declare that the Parties are under a duty to negotiate a régime for the fisheries in the area. Nor would an interpretation of this kind, in relation to Iceland's intention, correspond to the clearly stated policy of the Icelandic authorities to continue negotiations on the basic problems relating to the dispute, as emphasized by paragraph 3 of the Althing Resolution of 15 February 1972, referred to earlier, which reads: "That efforts to reach a solution of the problems connected with the extension be continued through discussions with the Governments of the United Kingdom and the Federal Republic of Germany." Taking into account that the interim agreement contains a definite date for its expiration, and in the light of what has been stated in paragraph 75 above, it would seem difficult to attribute to the Parties an intention to wait for that date and for the reactivation of the dispute, with all the possible friction it might engender, before one of them might require the other to attempt a peaceful settlement through negotiations. At the same time, the Court must add that its Judgment obviously cannot preclude the Parties from benefiting from any subsequent developments in the pertinent rules of international law.

78. In the fresh negotiations which are to take place on the basis of the present Judgment, the Parties will have the benefit of the above appraisal of their respective rights, and of certain guidelines defining their scope. The task before them will be to conduct their negotiations on the basis that each must in good faith pay reasonable regard to the legal rights of the other in the waters around Iceland outside the 12-mile limit, thus bringing about an equitable apportionment of the fishing resources based on the facts of the particular situation, and having regard to the interests of other States which have established fishing rights in the area. It is not a matter of finding simply an equitable solution, but an equitable solution derived from the applicable law. As the Court stated in the *North Sea Continental Shelf* cases:

> "... it is not a question of applying equity simply as a matter of abstract justice, but of applying a rule of law which itself requires the application of equitable principles" (*I.C.J. Reports* 1969, p. 47, para. 85).

In the *Gabčíkovo-Nagymaros Project* case, (also known as the *Danube Dam* case), Hungary terminated a treaty with Slovakia (successor state to Czechoslovakia as party to the treaty) to build a series of barrages on the Danube river. The purpose of the project was to realize greater economic benefits for both states in terms of electricity generation, flood control, navigation, and the like. Hungary became concerned about potential negative environmental impacts and sought to end the agreement. When Slovakia refused, Hungary terminated.

Gabčíkovo-Nagymaros Project Case
(*Hungary v. Slovakia*)

1997 ICJ 7 (Judgment of 25 September)

* * *

109. ... Both Parties agree that Articles 65 to 67 of the Vienna Convention on the Law of Treaties, if not codifying customary law, at least generally reflect customary international law and contain certain procedural principles which are based on an obligation to act in good faith. As the Court stated in its Advisory Opinion on the *Interpretation of the Agreement of 25 March 1951 between the WHO and Egypt* (in which case the Vienna Convention did not apply):

> "Precisely what periods of time may be involved in the observance of the duties to consult and negotiate, and what period of notice of termination should be given, are matters which necessarily vary according to the requirements of the particular case. In principle, therefore, it is for the parties in each case to determine the length of those periods by consultation and negotiation in good faith." (*I.C.J. Reports 1980*, p. 96, para. 49.)

The termination of the Treaty by Hungary was to take effect six days after its notification. On neither of these dates had Hungary suffered injury resulting from acts of Czechoslovakia. The Court must therefore confirm its conclusion that Hungary's termination of the Treaty was premature.

110. Nor can the Court overlook that Czechoslovakia committed the internationally wrongful act of putting into operation Variant C as a result of Hungary's own prior wrongful conduct. As was stated by the Permanent Court of International Justice:

> "It is, moreover, a principle generally accepted in the jurisprudence of international arbitration, as well as by municipal courts, that one Party cannot avail himself of the fact that the other has not fulfilled some obligation or has not had recourse to some means of redress if the former Party has, by some illegal act, prevented the latter from fulfilling the obligation in question, or from having recourse to the tribunal which would have been open to him." (*Factory at Chorzów, Jurisdiction, Judgment* No. 8, 1927, P.C.I.J., Series A, No. 9, p. 31.)

Hungary, by its own conduct, had prejudiced its right to terminate the Treaty; this would still have been the case even if Czechoslovakia, by the time of the purported termination, had violated a provision essential to the accomplishment of the object or purpose of the Treaty.

* * *

140. ... For the purposes of the present case, this means that the Parties together should look afresh at the effects on the environment of the operation of the Gabčíkovo power plant. In particular they must find a satisfactory solution for the volume of water to be released into the old bed of the Danube and into the side-arms on both sides of the river.

141. It is not for the Court to determine what shall be the final result of these negotiations to be conducted by the Parties. It is for the Parties themselves to find an agreed solution that takes account of the objectives of the Treaty, which must be pursued in a joint and integrated way, as well as the norms of international environmental law and the principles of the laws of international watercourses. The Court will recall in this context that, as it said in the *North Sea Continental Shelf* cases:

> "[the Parties] are under an obligation so to conduct themselves that the negotiations are meaningful, which will not be the case when either of them insists upon its own position without contemplating any modification of it" (*I.C.J. Reports 1969,* p. 47, para. 85).

142. What is required in the present case by the rule *pacta sunt servanda,* as reflected in Article 26 of the Vienna Convention of 1969 on the Law of Treaties, is that the Parties find an agreed solution within the cooperative context of the Treaty.

Article 26 combines two elements, which are of equal importance. It provides that "Every treaty in force is binding upon the parties to it and must be performed by them in good faith." This latter element, in the Court's view, implies that, in this case, it is the purpose of the Treaty, and the intentions of the parties in concluding it, which should prevail over its literal application. The principle of good faith obliges the Parties to apply it in a reasonable way and in such a manner that its purpose can be realized.

For more on the aftermath of the case, still pending in 2011, see, CESARE P.R. ROMANO, THE PEACEFUL SETTLEMENT OF INTERNATIONAL ENVIRONMENTAL DISPUTES, A PRAGMATIC APPROACH 257–260 (2000).

Notes and Questions on Negotiation and Consultation

1. What makes negotiation a "legal process" deserving of inclusion with arbitration and courts? Can you argue that it is both the most and the least important of IDR procedures?

2. Fombad says mere notice is not negotiation. Consider the following:

> Today, most of the important environmental treaties have a prior negotiation or consultation requirement. The principle still appears in varied forms, from the requirement to give notice to the requirement to negotiate. At their core all formulas result in an obligation to negotiate. The International Law Association concludes, for example, that a requirement to give notice or provide information before carrying out an activity includes a negotiation requirement because "it would be of no use for a potentially affected State to be given prior notice if the informing State proceeds with its plans no matter what the informed State has objected."

Mary Ellen O'Connell, *Enforcing the New International Law of the Environment,* 35 GER. YBK. INT'L L. 293, 325 (1992).

3. In the *Fisheries* and *Gabčíkovo-Nagymaros* cases, the ICJ told the parties to negotiate in good faith. O'Connor defines good faith in international law as:

> [D]irectly related to honesty, fairness and reasonableness ... and it is determined at any particular time by the compelling standards of honesty, fairness and reasonableness prevailing in the international community at that time.

J.F. O'Connor, Good Faith in International Law 121 (1991). Is this definition consistent with the understanding of good faith you find in the two ICJ cases?

4. Is bad faith an easier concept to apply than good faith? In the arbitration between Peru and Chile to settle a territorial dispute following the Pacific War, Peru alleged that Chile was acting in bad faith. The arbitrator found "the record fails to show that Chile has ever arbitrarily refused to negotiate with Peru ... Such causes of delay as a cabinet crisis, a revolution, the illness of a minister, the death of a president—political contingencies which did not lie beyond the contemplation of the Parties—cannot be charged to either side as constituting a willful refusal to proceed with negotiations." Tacna-Arica Arbitration (*Peru v. Chile*), 2 R.I.A.A. 921, 929–33 (1925). Can you think of other examples of bad faith that might arise in multilateral or bilateral negotiation? What remedies are appropriate?

5. Peters argues that the general dispute settlement obligation is cooperation. Discuss what obligations might be entailed in cooperation that would go beyond good faith. Anne Peters, *International Dispute Settlement: A Network of Cooperational Duties,* 14 EJIL 1 (2003).

Issues of good faith in dispute resolution are considered again in the arbitration context.

6. Compare bilateral negotiations, like the negotiation of the Headquarters Agreement between the U.S. and the UN, and multilateral negotiations, like the negotiations that resulted in the World Trade Organization (WTO) or the United Nations Convention on the Law of the Sea (UNCLOS). Multilateral negotiation aimed at drafting a treaty is known as "conference negotiation." Can you argue that conference negotiation is not negotiation but rather a different procedure, maybe even a new category of procedure? The UNCLOS negotiations lasted from 1973–1982 and involved almost all states in the international community. To reach a decision, new methods were employed like package deals and consensus decision-making. Decision-making at the UNCLOS negotiations and the nature of conference negotiation in general will be discussed further in Chapter Three in a reading on Ambassador Tommy Koh's role at the negotiations.

7. The UNCLOS negotiations pioneered the use of consensus decision-making. It is now standard in conference negotiations. Consensus means:

> [g]eneral agreement or collective opinion by those most interested in the matter. In common use, the term can range in meaning from unanimity to a simple majority vote. In public policy facilitation and multilateral international negotiations, however, the term refers to a general agreement reached after discussions and consultations, usually without voting. Unanimity is required only to the extent that it means an absence of major objections.

Douglas H. Yarn, Dictionary of Conflict Resolution 122 (1999).

> For detailed descriptions of two multilateral conference negotiations see: The International Criminal Court, The Making of the Rome Statute, Issues, Negotiations, Results (Roy S. Lee, ed. 1999) and Richard Elliot Benedick, Ozone Diplomacy: New Directions in Safeguarding the Planet (2d ed. 1998).

8. Both Fombad's article and the ICJ decision in the *UN Headquarters* case cite the Permanent Court of International Justice (the ICJ's predecessor) decision *Mavrommatis Palestine Concessions.* The case involved claims by a Greek national, Mavrommatis, against Great Britain, a sovereign state. After trying to proceed directly against Britain, Mavrommatis turned to his own state to take up his claim. Greece adopted its national's case. In the words of the PCIJ:

> A dispute is a disagreement on a point of law or fact, a conflict of legal views or of interests between two persons. The present suit between Great Britain and

> Greece certainly possesses these characteristics. The latter Power is asserting its own rights by claiming from His Britannic Majesty's Government an indemnity on the ground that M. Mavrommatis, one of its subjects, has been treated by the Palestine or British authorities in a manner incompatible with certain international obligations which they were bound to observe.
>
> In the case of the Mavrommatis concessions it is true that the dispute was at first between a private person and a State—i.e., between M. Mavrommatis and Great Britain. Subsequently, the Greek Government took up the case. The dispute then entered upon a new phase; it entered the domain of international law, and became a dispute between two States. Henceforward therefore it is a dispute which may or may not fall under the jurisdiction of the Permanent Court of International Justice.

Typically, before a state can make a claim against another state on behalf of a national, the national must have exhausted whatever local remedies are available. The ICJ dismissed a case brought by Switzerland on behalf of its national against the U.S. because the national had not exhausted all the judicial remedies available in the U.S.—it had not appealed to the Supreme Court. The ICJ said, "the State where the violation occurred should have an opportunity to redress it by its own means, within the framework of its own domestic legal system." Interhandel (Switz. v. U.S.), 1959 ICJ 6, 27 (Mar. 21).

The practice of adopting a national's claim and the doctrine of exhaustion of local remedies are two important concepts in understanding how international dispute resolution operates. We will encounter both again in these materials.

9. Further reading on negotiation includes:

Alain Plantey, International Negotiation in the Twenty-First Century (2008).

Martin Rogoff, *The Obligation to Negotiate in International Law: Rules and Realities,* 16 Mich. J. Int'l L. 141 (1994).

Frederic L. Kirgis, Jr., Prior Consultation in International Law, A Study of State Practice (1983).

The Grand Lake Problem

Two states, Northland and the Union of Columbia (UC), border on Grand Lake. The Lake is divided equally between them. Several years ago, a Northland businessman went to a Northland provincial administrative office and requested a license to pump water from Grand Lake. His plan was to fill ocean tankers with water for sale in the Middle East. The license was granted. Do Northland and the UC have a dispute at this point? Why or why not?

The Northland federal government subsequently canceled the license. Assume Northland then proposed negotiations with the UC to reach agreement on water-sharing issues that might arise in the future. Do Northland and the UC have a dispute now? If the UC refuses to negotiate, would the two states have a dispute? Is the UC obligated to enter into negotiations with Northland? If the UC and Northland enter into negotiations, would the UC have to reveal that several of its cities plan to build water pipelines from Grand Lake?

The negotiations continue for three years. A number of issues related to water-sharing have been identified, and some agreements have been reached. The parties have agreed not to allow commercial pumping of water for sale to third states, but they cannot agree regarding municipal water pipelines to cities outside the Grand Lake Drainage Basin. Must the negotiations continue until they reach agreement on all disputed issues? When is a dispute resolved?

Chapter Three

Good Offices and Mediation

Introduction

Everyone can name famous mediators in international disputes: Jimmy Carter, the United Nations Secretary General, the Pope, or Nelson Mandela. Mediation may be the method most often mentioned in the news, and yet mediation is the method least discussed by legal scholars. The methods of good offices and mediation introduce a third party to assist in the settlement of a dispute. Good offices generally means that a third party brings the disputants together, helping them to get negotiations underway. Mediation, on the other hand, generally involves more, including helping parties develop proposals. If the mediator proposes a solution of her own, the mediation begins to meld into conciliation, discussed in the next chapter.[1] Good offices and mediation are offered by international organizations, governments, and individuals—often prominent individuals like those named above.[2]

Good offices and mediation are the least developed of all dispute settlement methods in terms of applicable law. While both appear in most lists of dispute resolution mechanisms, in treaties, and elsewhere, we have no cases concerning either method from any international court. And, indeed, these methods have rarely been the subject of legal scholarship.

Both good offices and mediation differ significantly in a technical sense from negotiation because both introduce a third party into the dispute. One rule clearly applies to their use—all parties must expressly consent to the third party's participation. Even when mediation is provided for in a treaty (*see e.g.*, Article 5 of the World Trade Organization (WTO) Dispute Settlement Understanding, in the Annex) the parties need to participate in choosing the mediator. Mediation has never worked in an "automatic" way where the parties have simply had to accept the appointment of a mediator, in contrast to other methods, especially adjudication.

---

1. Public international law has long made a clear distinction between mediation and conciliation, but the distinction is breaking down in private international law. Some documents define mediation and conciliation as the same process. Once the terms become inter-mixed in private international law, the clear distinction may break down in public international law, as well. *Cf.* Model Law on International Commercial Conciliation of the United Nations Commission on International Trade Law, UN Doc. A/RES/57/18 and the United Nations Model Rules for the Conciliation of Disputes Between States, UN Doc. A/RES/50/50. *See* Annex.

2. The term "mediator" will be used for an individual conducting mediation or offering good offices. We have no term "good officer." Indeed, some subsume good offices completely within mediation. *See generally* John Collier & Vaughn Lowe, The Settlement of Disputes in International Law 27–29 (1999); H.G. Darwin *Mediation and Good Offices, in* International Disputes, The Legal Aspects 83–93 (Report of a Study Group of the David Davies Memorial Institute of International Relations, Sir Humphrey Waldock, Chair, 1972).

Still, because of the close links among negotiation, good offices, and mediation, we can argue that good faith applies to parties to mediation as it does to a negotiation. This makes sense regarding state parties to mediation, but we have no authority as to whether it applies to an individual mediator. In the many studies of mediation effectiveness, writers stress the need for a mediator to gain the trust of the disputing parties. Acting in good faith, being honest, and keeping the confidences of the parties should help develop trust. Nevertheless, we cannot point to a positive rule of international law requiring such conduct.

World Trade Organization, Understanding on Rules and Procedures Governing the Settlement of Disputes

Article 5
Good Offices, Conciliation and Mediation

See Annex

Claire Palley, *The "Good Offices" Framework for Secretariat Action**

"Good offices" are an old diplomatic institution, carrying overtones of benevolence by the offeror of such services, who facilitates discussions and, if possible, negotiations between disputing parties. Successive UN Secretaries-General (and their Special Representatives) have found the institution useful to defuse threatening situations.[1] In Cyprus "good offices" were on offer from the time in early 1964 when the first Special Representative was appointed. The Secretary-General offered his own services in late 1967 and this institution facilitated inter-communal talks from June 1968. After Turkey's 1974 invasion of the Republic of Cyprus (or, as Turkey prefers to word it, her "intervention") there was a new and more extensive mission of good offices. But at no time would either Cyprus party countenance more than facilitation of discussion and production of constructive ideas, because they did not consider that any outsider, however benevolent, was the best final judge of the parties' vital interests.[2] Accordingly, until the recent negotiations, no extension of the good offices function had been acceptable in Cyprus. Elsewhere, in a more activist world of UN involvement in situations in Africa, Latin America and Asia, the Secretary-General's good offices became more extensive in character, often going well beyond mere facilitation of negotiation, with the Secretary-General (in fact Secretariat) ending up as arbiter. However, in such situations the enlarged functions had either been

---

* *In An International Relations Debacle*, THE UN SECRETARY GENERAL'S MISSION OF GOOD OFFICES IN CYPRUS 1999–2004, 5–12 (2005) (some footnotes omitted).

1. Under Mr. J P de Cuéllar, the distinction between "good offices" and "mediation" became "tenuous." He believed the distinction to be one of nuance—depending, he claims in relation to Cyprus, "largely on whether one side or the other disliked a suggestion I put forward": *Pilgrimage for Peace, A Secretary-General's Memoir* (St Martin's Press, New York, 1997), 219–20. This fusion of the concepts was useful in affording the Secretary-General greater scope to insert his own ideas of what was appropriate, but was unacceptable to parties who did not want an arbitrator and had not agreed to the appointment of one.

2. Production of constructive ideas is a small scale activity involving making suggestions intermittently. It is very different from coming forward with a major, let alone a comprehensive, plan.

agreed by the parties concerned or been conferred by the Security Council under Chapter VI or VII of the Charter.

* * *

This important UN function had been shaped by the first holders of the Secretary-Generalship. Distance is said to lend enchantment, but the actions of earlier Secretaries-General and their senior aides, looked at in historical perspective, reveal that their caution in doing nothing likely to lead to their being perceived as protagonists firmly established an invaluable international relations mechanism. At worst, that caution could lead to stabilization without settlement, but it could sometimes lead over time to a settlement, and it did nothing to hamper reaching one.

The developments in the course of the Cyprus mission of good offices, as exercised since September 2002, show the adverse effect of alterations in the character of the institution of good offices. Once the member of the Secretariat exercising good offices becomes "a party" rather than a simple facilitator, one or other side will inevitably become aggrieved, so that the conduct of the Secretariat, now itself a party, will become an issue. In so far as is possible, the Secretariat, if it is ultimately to be effective, needs to remain above the fray, without acting in such manner as to become identified with particular view-points and interests, or so as to position itself that it will inescapably be perceived as deliberately promoting those interests. Mediation and arbitration, or "bridging proposals," "completing the gaps," or "addressing the key outstanding concerns of the sides" by "improvements" by way of exercise of discretion—as the Secretariat has referred to its recent Cyprus efforts—are activities in which, despite its will to assist the parties in every way it can, and even if invited by them so to involve itself, the Secretariat is unwise to engage. Had the Secretariat refrained from embarking on activities of this kind in relation to Cyprus, it would not have ended up repeatedly regretting the loss of "unique," "historic" and "extraordinary" opportunities for reaching a settlement (in April 2003 and in May 2004). Nor would it have characterized rejection of its Plan by Greek Cypriot voters as "a major setback," or as a "watershed peace activities in Cyprus". Regret for missing "a unique and historic chance" is in any event misguided, because, in international relations and in all political affairs, opportunities and the desire to seize them both go and come intermittently.

United Nations
S/1999/707
22 June 1999
ORIGINAL: ENGLISH

Report of the Secretary-General on His Mission of Good Offices in Cyprus

1. The present report is submitted pursuant to the Security Council's request in paragraph 7 of its resolution 1218 (1998) of 22 December 1998. My report on those aspects of the resolution that relate to the United Nations Peacekeeping Force in Cyprus (UNFICYP) was submitted to the Council on 8 June (S/1999/657). Meanwhile, I have informed the Council of my intention to appoint Ann Hercus as my Special Representative as of 1 July 1999.

2. As reported in my letter dated 14 December 1998 (S/1998/1166) addressed to the President of the Security Council, on 30 September 1998, following meetings with Glafcos

Clerides and Rauf Denktash, I asked my Deputy Special Representative for Cyprus, Ann Hercus, to begin a process of on-island talks with both parties with a view to reducing tension and promoting progress towards a just and lasting settlement. In its resolution 1218 (1998), the Council expressed appreciation for the spirit of cooperation and constructive approach the two sides demonstrated in working with my Deputy Special Representative.

3. In accordance with Security Council resolution 1218 (1998) and in continuation of my initiative of 30 September 1998, my Deputy Special Representative has held numerous meetings with both leaders during the past six months. The substance of these "shuttle talks," as they have come to be known, has remained confidential, and both Mr. Clerides and Mr. Denktash continued to engage in them in a constructive manner.

4. Apart from their confidentiality, the specific agreed methodology of the shuttle talks is that, at this point, neither side is aware of the views expressed to my Deputy Special Representative by the other side. While this format allows me to assess to what extent there is convergence of views on the various aspects, it also has its limitations, as a formal agreement can only be achieved in comprehensive negotiations directly involving both leaders.

5. The discussions involving my Deputy Special Representative have reconfirmed the importance of the issue of political equality. In pursuing the Secretary-General's mission of good offices, my predecessors and I have dealt with the two sides on an equal footing and, together with our representatives, have conducted our work on an equal and even-handed basis. However, the Turkish Cypriot contention is that other aspects of their situation place them at a disadvantage and undermine the commitment to political equality. A major challenge for the negotiations is how to translate this commitment into clear, practical provisions to be agreed upon by both sides. I hope that both sides will approach any resumption of negotiations in that spirit. I am confident that the international community would support any solution upon which both sides can mutually agree.

6. Cyprus is fortunate that, despite the long-running dispute and continuing tension, there has been no resumption of fighting between the two sides for the past 25 years. However, the absence of a settlement, comfortable as the status quo may appear to some, remains a source of instability and tension. Neither side has anything to gain from waiting any longer. The young generations on both sides deserve to be given the opportunity to live peacefully and in prosperity. It should be understood by all concerned that a lasting settlement can only be reached in negotiations.

7. In the decades during which it has resisted efforts at settlement, the Cyprus problem has become overlain with legalistic abstractions and artificial labels, which are more and more difficult to disentangle and which would appear increasingly removed from the actual needs of both communities. It is now time to focus on the core issues.

8. Over the years, many elements that would make up a solution have been identified. Based on past and current discussions and negotiations with and between the two leaders, the remaining core issues, in my view, put simply, are: (a) security, (b) distribution of powers, (c) property and (d) territory. A compromise on these issues would remove the remaining obstacles towards a peaceful settlement. It is essential, however, that these core issues be addressed without preconditions in a practical, realistic and straightforward manner in comprehensive negotiations.

9. I appreciate the support expressed by the Heads of State of the "G-8" countries, five of whom are members of the Security Council, at their summit held in Cologne, Germany, from 18 to 20 June for holding "a comprehensive negotiation covering all relevant issues".

Their statement highlights the continuing interest of the international community in a solution of the Cyprus problem, a solution which would have a positive effect on peace and stability in the entire region. In particular, the members of the G-8 have urged me "in accordance with relevant Security Council resolutions to invite the leaders of the two parties to negotiations in the fall of 1999."

10. In light of the above, and subject to the Security Council's guidance, I am ready to invite both leaders to enter into a process of comprehensive negotiations without preconditions and in a spirit of compromise and cooperation. While each leader faces the responsibility of representing the views and aspirations of his side, they have the joint responsibility for achieving a concrete, mutually acceptable and forward-looking solution. I will ask my Special Representative designate to continue the process of dialogue with the parties to that end.

United Nations
S/2004/437
28 May 2004

ORIGINAL: ENGLISH

Report of the Secretary-General on His Mission of Good Offices in Cyprus

1. I last comprehensively reported to the Security Council on my mission of good offices on 1 April 2003 (S/2003/398), although on 16 April 2004 (see S/2004/302) I submitted certain matters to the Security Council for its decision pursuant to the process that was then in train. The present report covers the period since April 2003, culminating in the referenda of 24 April 2004, when the proposed Foundation Agreement in the finalized "Comprehensive Settlement of the Cyprus Problem" was submitted for approval on each side. The Greek Cypriot electorate, by a margin of three to one, rejected the settlement proposal; on the Turkish Cypriot side, it was approved by a margin of two to one. Since the plan required approval on both sides, the Cyprus problem remains unsettled.

2. The referenda mark a watershed in the history of United Nations efforts in Cyprus. They are the first time that the people have been asked directly for their views on a settlement proposal. I fully respect the outcome on each side, and I have been reflecting on what they mean. The present report is the outcome of that reflection. It describes the effort recently completed and contains a series of observations about the opportunity missed, the implications of the vote on each side, and the way ahead.

The 13 February 2004 Agreement

3. After the failure of the previous effort at The Hague on 10 and 11 March 2003, I informed the Security Council that I did not propose to take a new initiative unless and until there was solid reason to believe that the political will existed necessary for a successful outcome. To that end, I sought "an unequivocally stated preparedness on the part of the leaders of both sides, fully and determinedly backed at the highest political level in both motherlands, to commit themselves (a) to finalize the plan (without reopening its basic principles or essential trade-offs) by a specific date with United Nations assistance, and (b) to put it to separate simultaneous referenda as provided for in the plan on a date certain soon thereafter"(S/2003/398, para. 148).

4. These procedures were fully consistent with the position taken by the Greek Cypriot leader, Tassos Papadopoulos, at The Hague. Mr. Papadopoulos was at that time prepared

to submit the plan to referendum provided certain procedural conditions were met (ibid., para. 56), and told me that he would want to support it. I was conscious that success could not be assured in any renewed effort, but I was sure that there was little prospect of success without the commitments of all concerned to the procedure set out above.

5. The Security Council in resolution 1475 (2003) of 14 April 2003 gave its strong support to my "carefully balanced plan"—namely, the "Basis for Agreement on a Comprehensive Settlement of the Cyprus Problem" dated 26 February 2003—as a "unique basis for further negotiations", and it called on all concerned to negotiate within the framework of my good offices, using the plan to reach a comprehensive settlement as set forth in paragraphs 144 to 151 of my report.

6. Most of 2003 was a fallow period in terms of my good offices. But I continued to follow developments closely, including the lifting of restrictions on crossings of the buffer zone in April, and the December vote in the north of the island, which brought to the fore a new Turkish Cypriot leadership.

7. For its part, the Government of Turkey was putting together the elements of a new policy on Cyprus, which was conveyed to me by Prime Minister Recep Tayyip Erdoğan when we met in Davos on 24 January 2004. He told me that Turkey supported a resumption of negotiations. He expressed preferences for dealing with the main issues by 1 May 2004, and for a political figure to handle the negotiations, but was open to discussion on these points. He added that, as far as Turkey was concerned, it had no objection to my "filling in the blanks" in the plan should the parties not be able to agree on all issues. He assured me that, henceforth, the Turkish side, including the Turkish Cypriots, would be "one step ahead" in the effort.

8. Already in December, I had received from the Greek Cypriot leader a letter calling for the resumption of substantive negotiations on the basis of the plan. When I met him in Brussels on 29 January 2004, he reiterated this call, stressing categorically that he sought a solution before 1 May 2004. He told me that if a divided Cyprus joined the European Union, he did not know how many problems that would entail. He reassured me that he did not seek "forty or fifty" changes to the plan, and that all the changes he would seek would be within the parameters of the plan. We discussed his view that it would be better for negotiations to resume first before a decision was taken about going to referendum, and he said he would get back to me on his idea that there should be parameters to guide me should it fall to me to finalize the plan.

9. I also discussed the matter with the Government and the Leader of the Opposition of Greece. Both supported a renewal of my efforts, notwithstanding the prospect of a general election in Greece. The European Union, strongly preferring the accession of a reunited Cyprus on 1 May 2004, supported a resumption of the effort.

10. After weighing the situation, on 4 February 2004, I wrote to Mr. Papadopoulos and to Rauf Denktash, the Turkish Cypriot leader, inviting them to come to New York to begin negotiations on 10 February 2004. I wrote in similar terms to the Prime Ministers of the guarantor Powers—Greece, Turkey and the United Kingdom—inviting them to have a representative on hand for the resumption of negotiations. I suggested modalities which could give effect to the procedure contained in my 1 April 2003 report, so as to ensure that negotiations would be completed and the plan finalized by 31 March 2004, that the guarantors would be fully committed to meeting their obligations, and that referenda would be conducted on a fixed date in advance of 1 May 2004. My invitation was accepted by all parties.

11. On 10 February 2004, each leader put forward, at my request, an overview of the changes his side sought to the plan. However, at the initiative of Mr. Papadopoulos, he

and Mr. Denktash agreed that they could not accept the procedure I had suggested, either relating to the finalization of the plan or the commitment to hold a referendum.

12. After I asked the parties to reflect overnight, Mr. Denktash changed his position on 11 February. He proposed a three-stage procedure which he informed me had the support of Turkey and which conformed broadly with the parameters I had proposed. The procedure enlarged the role foreseen for me, from completing any unfinished parts of the plan ("filling in the blanks") to resolving any continuing and persistent deadlocks in the negotiations—thus ruling out the possibility, which each side regarded as unacceptable, of the plan going to referendum unchanged. After studying the proposal, Mr. Papadopoulos sought certain clarifications. To facilitate agreement, I then proposed a draft press statement which retained the core elements of Mr. Denktash's proposal, incorporated the clarifications sought by Mr. Papadopoulos, and built in other elements contained in my 4 February letter.

13. The final terms of this statement were negotiated over the course of the next 48 hours, culminating in a late-night shuttle on 12 and 13 February by my Special Adviser, Alvaro de Soto, between the leaders, as well as the representatives of Greece and Turkey. The main issues dividing the parties at the end were whether there should be an institutional participation in the negotiations by organizations other than the United Nations, and the way in which the role of Greece and Turkey in the culminating phases of the process would be presented.

14. On 13 February, I sent to all parties a final proposal to resolve these issues, to which all agreed. Accordingly, I was pleased to announce the terms of what became known as the 13 February agreement, which committed the parties to a three-phase process leading to referendum on a finalized plan before 1 May 2004 (see annex I).

The First Phase of the Process in Cyprus between 19 February and 22 March 2004

15. The negotiations reconvened in Cyprus on 19 February 2004, in the United Nations Protected Area, with meetings at the political level between the leaders accompanied by their delegations in the presence of my Special Adviser and his delegation. On the Turkish Cypriot side, in addition to Rauf Denktash, the delegation included Mehmet Ali Talat and Serdar Denktash. In New York and during the first phase, the United Nations dealt with them as a triumvirate who together spoke for the Turkish Cypriot side.

16. Following the opening meeting on 19 February 2004, at the invitation of my Special Adviser, the European Commissioner for Enlargement, Günter Verheugen, briefed the leaders jointly on the European Union position concerning accommodation of a settlement, underlining also the Union's strong desire for a positive outcome.

17. In the initial meetings on the island, the leaders elaborated on the changes they had presented to me in New York on 10 February. The Greek Cypriot side stated that its primary objective was to improve what it called the workability of the plan, so as to render more functional, and therefore more viable, the United Cyprus Republic (which was to be the end result of the negotiation). The Turkish Cypriot side stated that its primary objective was to strengthen what it called bizonality, by which it meant the Turkish Cypriot character of the Turkish Cypriot State, and the maintenance of political equality over time, within the United Cyprus Republic.

18. After initial discussions, my Special Adviser clustered the issues for consideration, and asked the parties to explain in specific terms, including proposed textual amendments, the changes they sought to the plan, with a view to facilitating negotiation.

19. The Turkish Cypriot side submitted on 24 February 2004 a list of proposed textual changes to the plan, covering all issues. While that paper had the virtue of concision and of making clear the shape of the Turkish Cypriot side's demands in a single package, it proposed far-reaching changes, a number of which would have substantially altered key parameters of the plan. My Special Adviser explained this to the Turkish Cypriot side and to Turkey, and informed the Greek Cypriot side that he had done so. In suggesting agendas for meetings, and in pursuing discussions of the items clustered for consideration, my Special Adviser left aside Turkish Cypriot demands which were clearly outside the parameters of the plan. Despite United Nations requests, it was not until mid-March that the Turkish Cypriot side replaced their initial paper with a less far-reaching set of proposed textual amendments, described as a priority list. Also, despite the interest expressed by the Turkish Cypriot side in straightening the boundary between the constituent states, it failed to produce a territorial proposal, or to propose a way for the issue to be discussed.

20. The Greek Cypriot side, by contrast, took each issue in turn, and produced dense and lengthy papers, one after another, explaining the changes sought and annexing proposed textual amendments. They argued that piecemeal presentation of positions for discussion following the clusters suggested by the United Nations would assist in producing, down the line, more refined proposals. As they continued to present papers, it became apparent that the 10 February paper summary of Greek Cypriot demands was far from exhaustive. The Greek Cypriot side declined to provide a comprehensive paper of all the textual amendments it sought until mid-way through Phase 2 (in Bürgenstock, Switzerland), and declined to prioritize its demands, despite my Special Adviser's request of 15 March to both sides to do so.

21. The Greek Cypriot side stated that none of its proposed changes took away any rights from Turkish Cypriots, and therefore that few, if any, of its amendments should require trade-offs on subjects of interest to the Turkish Cypriots, notwithstanding the perception of those amendments on the Turkish Cypriot side. By contrast, the Turkish Cypriot side was generally prepared to engage on Greek Cypriot proposals and to discuss matters on a realistic basis, and sought to make counter-offers and compromise proposals.

22. The Greek Cypriot side regularly insisted on full satisfaction of its demands, while arguing that the Turkish Cypriot paper of 24 February was outside the parameters of the plan and thus precluded engagement with Turkish Cypriot proposals. When the Turkish Cypriot side produced a priority list on 18 March, this did not alter the Greek Cypriot attitude to Turkish Cypriot concerns. (That paper, together with the letter of transmittal from the United Nations to the Greek Cypriot side, found its way into the press.) The Turkish Cypriot side argued that the Greek Cypriot delay in exposing the extent of their demands was preventing the beginning of real negotiation, and amounted to filibustering. The Greek Cypriot side countered that the Turkish Cypriot failure to produce a territorial proposal left a hole at the centre of Turkish Cypriot demands, and left the Greek Cypriot side in the dark. While the discussions were therefore far less fruitful than they might have been, at least, by mid-March, the vast bulk of the material was on the table.

23. An additional factor inhibiting frank discussions at the table was the regular public disclosure of the contents of the negotiations, usually with a negative spin, either by Greek Cypriot leakage, or by the daily oral briefings of Mr. Denktash to the press, ostensibly for the Turkish Cypriot public.

24. With little progress being made at the table, the United Nations sought to have regular working-level contacts with members of the delegations on each side to elicit greater frankness and float possible areas of compromise. The Turkish Cypriot side was

relatively open in such consultations, the Greek Cypriot side less so. An additional difficulty was that accounts of bilateral meetings between my Special Adviser and the Greek Cypriot leader, at least when teams were present, often turned up in the press presented in a negative light. The Greek Cypriot leader told my Special Adviser that he deplored such leaks.

25. Since it was proving difficult to make progress through either face-to-face meetings or working-level bilateral consultations, my Special Adviser suggested that the direct meetings be halted and that, beginning on 15 March, he shuttle between the leaders in an effort to narrow differences and facilitate give and take in the run-up to Phase 2 of the process—a format to which each side readily agreed. He put to each side a framework to allow for trade-offs, and sought to elicit from them the clear identification of priorities, reaffirming that the package of overall changes to the plan would have to be balanced across all issues.

26. The Greek Cypriot side was critical of the framework suggested, while the Turkish Cypriot side responded more positively. The asymmetry of the response, together with the mini-crisis provoked by Mr. Rauf Denktash's decision not to attend Phase 2 of the process, prevented the United Nations from proposing trade-offs on the major issues in the time that remained during Phase 1. However, the United Nations focused on at least clearing away some of the secondary issues in the negotiation before the end of Phase 1. For this purpose, the leaders were brought together for one last meeting on the island on 22 March 2004. This was the last occasion on which Mr. Rauf Denktash participated in the process.

27. During this first phase, representatives of Greece and Turkey also met in Athens on 17 March 2004, at the invitation of the United Nations, to discuss security. In these talks, a number of issues were ironed out, but others were deferred until Bürgenstock.

28. I myself kept a close eye on the effort under way, being regularly briefed by my Special Adviser, and sending the Under-Secretary-General for Political Affairs, Kieran Prendergast, to the island twice to review developments with Mr. de Soto and his team and the leadership on both sides.

* * *

Conclusion

94. I wish to thank the Security Council for its strong support of my efforts; the many Member States who provided diplomatic assistance, material resources, technical expertise or conference support; the European Union, including the European Commission, for the truly exemplary assistance and support it provided, in what was a model of European Union/United Nations cooperation; and the many international organizations, including those of the United Nations system, which rolled up their sleeves and joined in this team effort.

95. I could not close without expressing my warmest thanks to my Special Adviser, Mr. Alvaro de Soto, and his team, for the outstanding dedication which they brought to a difficult task. Their careful and creative peacemaking effort offered the Cypriots the best chance they have ever had to reunify their country.

96. I know that the failure of this effort, twice now in little over a year, is a source of sadness and confusion for Cypriots, Greek Cypriots and Turkish Cypriots alike, not to mention many in Greece and Turkey, in the European Union, and throughout the international community. Many Cypriots from all walks of life worked with courage and determination to achieve a settlement. I am confident they will continue these efforts. Indeed, they

must. The prospects for the reunification of their country now rest primarily in their hands[.]

Teresa Whitfield, *Good Offices and "Groups of Friends"**

* * *

The concept of good offices is not itself mentioned in the UN Charter. It is, perhaps, implied within Article 33(1), which lists "other peaceful means of their own choice" among measures available to states to achieve the peaceful settlement of disputes, especially if read in conjunction with Article 99, which gives the Secretary-General a measure of discretion in areas of peace and security. As the phrase has come to be used within the United Nations, it can, however, very helpfully mean almost anything. A Secretary-General can undertake good offices with or without a specific mandate, on the basis of the moral authority he derives from the Charter and with the somewhat ephemeral legitimacy of the United Nations behind him. His public advocacy may bring attention to neglected conflicts and crises; his quiet diplomacy may breach differences between conflicting parties and build consensus among external actors on a path forward. While he may represent a powerful voice when acting with the support of a united Security Council, however, he is otherwise left to work, as Kofi Annan put it in 1999, "only with tools of his own making."[1]

Commanding none of the obvious sources of leverage represented by military force or ready access to financial resources, successive Secretaries-General have relied instead on two principal sets of "tools": senior officials designated to act as their envoys or representatives, and states motivated to provide backing and encouragement to their efforts. The advantages of the former are obvious: trusted officials acting on behalf of the Secretary-General can be charged with tasks that vary from the conveying of a targeted message to full-fledged negotiation or the management of a complex peace operation. The use of such officials enables the United Nations to project its diplomacy across the globe while simultaneously providing a degree of protection of the authority vested in the person and office of the Secretary-General. But without the implicit or explicit support of the latter a Secretary-General and those who act on his behalf will be able to achieve little.

The use of groups, rather than well-disposed individual states or friendly ambassadors, as a deliberate "resource" to strengthen the Secretary-General's weak hand can be traced back to Dag Hammarskjöld's use of advisory committees to support him in the creation and management of the first peacekeeping operations.[2] Such committees were put in place for both the United Nations Emergency Force (UNEF), established in 1956 to help stabilize the situation in the wake of the Suez Crisis, and the much larger and more complex United Nations Operation in the Congo (ONUC). They represented a deliberate

---

* *In* Secretary or General? The UN Secretary-General in World Politics (Simon Chesterman, ed. 2007) (some footnotes omitted).

1. Kofi Annan, Address to the Council on Foreign Relations, UN Press Release SG/SM/6865 (19 January 1999).

2. See Hammarskjöld's discussion of permanent missions and the advisory committees as "means and resources": Dag Hammarskjöld, "The International Civil Servant in Law and in Fact (Lecture Delivered to Congregation at Oxford University, 30 May 1961)," in Wilder Foote (ed.), *Servant of Peace: A Selection of the Speeches and Statements of Dag Hammarskjöld, Secretary-General of the United Nations 1953–1961* (New York: Harper & Row, 1962), pp. 346–347.

effort by Hammarskjöld to gather like-minded states around him to improve his ability to steer controversial operations through the General Assembly, in the case of UNEF, and the Cold War rivalries in the Council over the Congo. But unlike the groups of friends developed in the 1990s, created to support the Secretary-General's peacemaking, the creation of the advisory committees included consultation with the General Assembly and Security Council and, in the case of UNEF, was mandated by a resolution.[3] They were, moreover, made up of troop contributors to the operations rather than states selected for their political or other leverage over a particular issue; in addition, although their meetings were private, records of the meetings were kept, circulated, and—perhaps inevitably—leaked to the parties concerned.

Groups of states to support the Secretary-General's good offices and peacemaking occurred more frequently following the end of the Cold War, when cooperation between Russia and the United States allowed the five permanent members of the Security Council to act on the basis of consensus. This facilitated the work of the United Nations in helping to bring an end to conflicts in southern Africa, south-east Asia, and Central America, but also removed barriers to other configurations of states, evident in the proliferation of groups of all kind. These took shape as friends "of Secretary-General," friends of particular conflicts or peace processes, as well as in a variety of "core" and "contact" groups. Indeed, as many different actors—other international and regional organizations, individual states, ad hoc groups, and NGOs—became involved in conflict management, a central challenge for the Secretary-General. It also led to the emergence of new roles for the Secretary-General and his officials and new relationships to the wide variety of group mechanisms with which they were faced.

Friends of the Secretary-General: Early Days

The first "friends" of the Secretary-General to use the name, those formed for El Salvador, emerged as a brainchild of Secretary-General Javier Pérez de Cuéllar's personal representative, Alvaro de Soto, in part as a means to maintain the engagement of countries (Colombia, Mexico, Spain, and Venezuela) that were like-minded in their concern to reach a negotiated settlement of the conflict but had no direct stake in its outcome. Each had a history of engagement in attempts to end the conflict—the three Latin American states within the context of the Contadora Group, established by foreign ministers from these countries and Panama in 1983—and good contacts with the conflict parties. Nevertheless, all were inclined to favour a leading role for the United Nations. Pérez de Cuéllar was directly involved at key moments of negotiations that ran from 1990–1992 and found support and encouragement from the friends at the head of state level, as well as from their ambassadors in New York. The friends themselves, meanwhile, developed relationships of solidarity and even complicity with de Soto that helped ensure their commitment to the process.[4]

The El Salvador group exemplified the functional benefits that can be derived from a group of friends. It brought leverage over the parties to the Secretary-General and his representatives; legitimacy to a privileged involvement in the peace process to the friends themselves; a measure of equilibrium to the parties to the conflict (the Salvadoran insurgents saw in the friends a counterweight to a US-dominated Security Council while the government came to appreciate the friends as a "cushion" between itself and the UN Sec-

3. See, e.g., UN Doc. A/1001 (7 November 1956).

4. Alvaro de Soto, "Ending Violent Conflict in El Salvador," in Chester A. Crocker, Fen Osler Hampson, and Pamela Aall (eds.), *Herding Cats: Multiparty Mediation in a Complex World* (Washington, DC: United States Institute of Peace Press, 1999).

retariat); and coordination, resources, and informal guarantees to the process as a whole.[5] During implementation of the agreements reached in early 1992 the involvement of the friends—now reconstituted as a group of "four plus one" to include the United States—ranged from the provision of security to guerrilla leaders and diplomatic support to successive heads of the United Nations mission in El Salvador, to the funding of peace-related programmes and the management of the issue of El Salvador within the Security Council and General Assembly. Quite properly, the contribution made by the friends to the peace process in El Salvador was formally acknowledged by Kofi Annan as he closed the door on verification of the agreements in December 2002.[6]

The success of the group of friends in El Salvador and the utility of core groups of ambassadors in the implementation of peace agreements in Cambodia and Mozambique led to the mechanism's rapid multiplication. Between 1992 and 1995 groups of friends were mobilized in Haiti, Georgia, Western Sahara, Guatemala, and Tajikistan.[7] With the exception of the group on Tajikistan, the groups were—as in El Salvador—small in number (four-six), and both closed and informal in their working practices. They met variously in New York, their members' capitals, and in the field, and fulfilled very different functions.

Less auspicious circumstances than those in El Salvador contributed to the mixed performance of these groups, but were not the only factor. The powerful group on Haiti, for example, at first worked closely with the Secretary-General but was dominated, and at times divided, by positions taken by the United States. The Haitian process as a whole failed to sow the seeds of anything resembling a sustainable democracy; over a long engagement the Secretary-General's capacity to provide effective leadership gradually diminished and the group revealed itself to be more effective in influencing the United Nations than it was the authorities in Port-au-Prince. The groups on Guatemala and Tajikistan, formed by the parties and the Secretariat, respectively, were largely positive in the support they provided to the Secretary-General and his representatives and their contribution to the respective peace processes. Other groups formed on the initiative of member states, however, prioritized their own relationship with the parties over the settlement pursued by the Secretary-General. Indeed, positions taken by members of both the friends of Western Sahara and the friends of Georgia actively contributed to the stalemate in which these conflicts remained mired.

In the case of Western Sahara, the group of friends was formed to preserve interests of the key external actors in the region: the United States, France, and Spain. Each prioritized their bilateral relations with Morocco and Algeria, which were clearly separate from the goal pursued by the United Nations: the implementation of a referendum to give effect to the population's right to self-determination. Suspicion of the incompatibility of the two approaches perhaps lay behind Boutros Boutros-Ghali's decision to turn down a suggestion from the United States that the group be constituted as friends "of the Secretary-General".[8] However, as Boutros-Ghali's own view—made clear to the Security

5. See Michael Doyle, "War Making, Peace Making and the United Nations," in Chester A. Crocker, Fen Osler Hampson, and Pamela Aall (eds.), *Turbulent Peace: The Challenges of Managing International Conflict* (Washington, DC: United States Institute of Peace Press, 2001), p. 541.

6. Report of the Secretary-General, The Situation in Central America, UN Doc. A/57/384/Add.1 (17 December 2002).

7. Only the Haiti group was constituted as friends "of the Secretary-General" from the outset.

8. Telephone interview, Edward Walker, 2 August 2004.

Council in informal consultations in December 1995—was that he had never believed that a referendum would happen, it is unlikely that the constitution of the friends as "his" would have made much difference.[9]

Meanwhile, progress towards settlement of the conflict between Georgia and Abkhazia was not helped by divisions among the friends. Although the Secretariat worked hard to ensure the utility of the group—in this instance, pushing it to reconstitute itself as friends "of the Secretary-General" for Georgia in 1997—Western states (Britain, France, Germany, and the United States) were indeed friends of Georgia, staunchly opposed to the aspirations of Abkhaz forces one "friend" would describe as a "repellent secessionist regime.[10] Although Russia itself was both a friend and "facilitator" of the peace process, it was primarily a regional hegemon with complex and abiding interests of its own. These contributed to its role as the protector of Abkhazia and proved largely resistant to the influence of both Boutros-Ghali and Annan.

Among those working closely with the Secretary-General, by the mid-1990s concern had begun to grow that friends' groups had their drawbacks. Frustrated with being "bossed about" by the United States on Haiti, and with friends of Georgia whose interests undermined any hope of impartiality on the conflict in Abkhazia, officials within the Secretariat began to wonder whether, in some instances, groups of friends were not themselves part of the problem. In early 1995, in the *Supplement to An Agenda for Peace,* written with the credibility of the United Nations battered by the failures on Somalia, the Balkans and Rwanda, Boutros-Ghali assumed a headmasterly tone. In establishing such a group, he advised, it is necessary to "maintain a clear understanding of who is responsible for what... The members of the 'Friends' group have agreed to support the Secretary-General there is a risk of duplication or overlapping of efforts which can be exploited by recalcitrant parties."[11]

In many respects, it was a little too late to regain control of the phenomenon that "friends" represented, but the attempt reflected a change in relations between the Secretary-General and the Security Council as well as differences in the personalities of Pérez de Cuéllar and Boutros-Ghali. Caution on the future of friends would find an echo in a suggestion submitted by the departing Under-Secretary-General for Political Affairs, Marrack Goulding to the incoming Secretary-General, Kofi Annan, in 1997. He recommended that a clear distinction be made between friends selected by the Secretary-General and self-appointed contact groups, in effect dropping any pretence that the Secretary-General was "in charge" of the latter mechanism, and with it the idea that the states engaged in it were, in a reliable sense, "friends."[12] The suggestion was not acted on. But the extraordinary proliferation of peace efforts in the years that followed contributed to the creation of new groups of all kinds.

---

9. Interview, UN official, 12 November 2002. Boutros-Ghali hoped that the conflict could be resolved through some form of autonomy arrangement.

10. Interview, 13 May 2003.

11. Supplement to An Agenda for Peace: Position Paper of the Secretary-General on the Occasion of the Fiftieth Anniversary of the United Nations, UN Doc. A/50/60-S/1995/1 (3 January 1995), paras. 83–84.

12. Marrack Goulding, Internal Report to the Secretary-General on "Enhancing the United Nations' Effectiveness in Peace and Security," June 1997, mimeo.

B.G. Ramcharan, *The Good Offices of the United Nations Secretary-General in the Field of Human Rights**

* * *

In contemporary practice the term "good offices" is usually employed to refer to humanitarian intercessions by the Secretary-General. But good offices traditionally developed in the area of the settlement of international disputes, and the extension of the term to the humanitarian field has not been without challenge. Thus, at the 35th session of the United Nations General Assembly, in 1980, when a wide-ranging debate took place on good offices in the field of human rights, it was contended that good offices were properly used by the Secretary-General "only when his action had a bearing on international peace and security" and that "good offices constituted a means for the settlement of disputes and presupposed at least two parties agreeing to their use."

On the other hand, it was pointed out that in the field of human rights the good offices role of the Secretary-General had generally been recognized for a long time, and reference was made to a UN press release issued on April 29, 1967 announcing that the Permanent Representatives of Poland and Czechoslovakia, on behalf of a group of socialist countries, had requested that the Secretary-General use his "good offices" with a view to ending persecutions in Greece and to preventing the possible execution of political leaders who had been detained. This debate took place over a draft resolution submitted by the delegation of Canada, which was aimed at developing the full potential of the good offices role of the Secretary-General to enable the United Nations system to cope more adequately with situations of mass and flagrant violations of human rights. Eventually, the Third Committee of the General Assembly decided, on a procedural motion, not to vote on the draft resolution. The general view in the committee was that the Secretary-General should be left free to decide on the manner and modalities of the exercise of good offices in the field of human rights and that the function should not be restricted or regulated in any way.

In view of this reluctance of some states to "legislate" on the subject, it follows necessarily that the nature and characteristics of the concept of good offices in the field of human rights must be determined by reference to the relevant international practice and to such rules or principles of international customary law as may have emerged from that practice. An examination of the relevant rules and practice will be attempted in the following pages. It will be submitted that the exercise by the Secretary-General of good offices in the field of human rights has become part of international customary law.

I. The Nature of Good Offices Regarding Human Rights

In their traditional meaning, good offices "consist in a third party—Government, international organization, individual—attempting to bring conflicting parties to a negotiating table without interfering in the negotiation themselves." Good offices as a means of settling international disputes have a long history among the instruments of diplomacy. In more recent times the concept may be traced to Articles 2 and 3 of the Hague Conventions of 1899 and 1907 on the Pacific Settlement of Disputes.

As a method for furthering peaceful solutions of international disputes, the good offices of the Secretary-General have been defined by Pechota as "the informal contacts and friendly suggestions made as far as circumstances allow by the Secretary-General, which

* 76 Am. J. Int'l L. 130, 130–36 (1982) (footnotes omitted).

are designed to facilitate the settlement of a dispute between two or several of the Organization's Member States." The same writer classifies the good offices of the Secretary-General into: (1) forms of diplomatic assistance such as informal contacts and consultations with parties to a dispute; (2) diplomatic action designed to express international concern, to induce the parties into talks before a favorable atmosphere fades away or before they reach a point of no return, and to assist them in finding a suitable framework for settlement; (3) mediation, conciliation, and coordination; and (4) inquiries, fact finding, the supervision of plebiscites, elections, or referenda, and the determination of legal rights and duties in a specific situation. Within the third category, namely mediation, conciliation, and coordination, the author includes "various activities aimed at assisting the parties in alleviating human sufferings or easing other burdens such as refugee problems entailed in certain conflicts" but adds that "such activities can hardly be described as good offices in the usual meaning of the term." Perhaps he meant the "traditional" rather than the "usual" meaning of the term, for he himself acknowledges among the categories of involvement by the Secretary-General in the exercise of good offices, "humanitarian problems," including the situation of minorities within some states.

In the League of Nations system for the international protection of minorities, resolutions of the League Council provided for the handling of "exceptional and extremely urgent cases," and stipulated that in such cases the Secretary-General of the League should simultaneously inform the state concerned and the members of the Council of the matter. Minorities Committees, for their part, made it their practice to try to settle questions raised in communications by means of informal negotiations with the state concerned.

The exercise of good offices with respect to human rights or humanitarian matters is quite extensive in present-day international organizations, such as the United Nations, the United Nations High Commissioner for Refugees (UNHCR), the International Labour Organisation (ILO), the United Nations Educational, Scientific and Cultural Organization (UNESCO), and the International Committee of the Red Cross (ICRC). In many of these organizations, good offices with respect to human rights or humanitarian matters are exercised at various levels: by the head or by other members of the secretariat; by organs, as well as by their presidents, chairmen, or members. In some instances there are express mandates to exercise such good offices, while in others they are based on the concept of inherent or implied competence.

* * *

II. Legal Bases

For the United Nations Secretary-General to exercise good offices in the field of human rights, there may be several bases. He may be exercising a power conferred upon him by the Charter, the General Assembly, the Security Council, or some other authoritative organ such as the Economic and Social Council or, under its authority, the Commission on Human Rights. Good offices may be exercised at the request of the government concerned; in other instances they may be exercised without an invitation by, or even against the wishes of, the government concerned. In practice, whatever the legal basis, the methods and modalities do not vary greatly.

In the following section, there will be set out some of the legal bases which may be invoked either separately or cumulatively, depending on the case or situation in question, to support the exercise of good offices in the field of human rights. In the first place, the Secretariat, as a principal organ of the United Nations, is enjoined in the Charter to foster international cooperation for the promotion and encouragement of respect for human rights. Secondly, the good offices functions of the Secretary-General in the field of human rights could also be based on Article 97 of the Charter, which makes the Secretary-General the chief administrative officer of the Organization. Administration may be perceived in both procedural and substantive terms. Procedurally, it is to service the Organization and to implement the resolutions and decisions of United Nations organs. Substantively, however, the Secretary-General, as chief administrative officer, is also under a duty to promote the implementation of the purposes and principles of the Organization. If, therefore, it happens—as is constantly the case—that none of the relevant human rights organs is in session and that they have no arrangements for intersessional activity, would it not be appropriate for the Secretary-General to intercede provisionally, in order to seek to provide interim relief until one of the organs concerned becomes seized of the matter? Such an "emergency response" has developed in practice as an acknowledged and essential function of the administrative heads of the European and Inter-American Commissions on Human Rights (their respective Secretaries). The concept of interim measures or provisional measures is also one that is well known in international jurisprudence.

Thirdly, good offices may be exercised in the context of the novel powers of the Secretary-General under Article 99 of the Charter, which states that the Secretary-General of the United Nations may bring to the attention of the Security Council any matter which, in his opinion, may threaten the maintenance of international peace and security. Professor Hersch Lauterpacht was of the view "that Article 99 presents considerable potentialities for bringing to the Security Council's attention violations of human rights so grave that they threaten the maintenance of international peace and security." Moreover, he felt, "[t]he clause of domestic jurisdiction of Article 2, paragraph 7, presents no impediment in the way of the exercise of this particular function of the Secretary-General. The matters referred to in Article 99 are not, by definition, essentially within the domestic jurisdiction of any State."

In a recent instance, the question was raised whether the Secretary-General should invoke Article 99 of the Charter in situations involving serious violations of human rights. On April 8, 1979, Martin Ennals, Secretary-General of Amnesty International, addressed a telegram to the United Nations Secretary-General requesting that he use his authority under Article 99 to convene a meeting of the Security Council to consider urgent measures to stop current waves of political executions and murders across the world. On April 10, 1979, the Secretary-General replied that despite the seriousness of the problem and his distress at the increased number of executions, "invocation of Article 99 is not the most appropriate way to deal with the problem since that article deals explicitly and exclusively with matters involving international peace and security."

It has long been recognized in international law that serious violations of human rights could involve threats to the maintenance of international peace and security. They could therefore be proper grounds for the invocation of Article 99 by the Secretary-General; whether the violations do actually give rise to a threat to international peace and security is a matter of fact to be determined in each case. For present purposes, however, it is submitted that in the context of exercising his competence under Article 99, the Secretary-General could engage in exercises akin to good offices with respect to situations of massive and flagrant violations of human rights.

Fourthly, the doctrine of inherent or implied powers has frequently been invoked as a basis for the exercise of good offices. Indeed, the practice is so extensive that it may be said that the competence of the Secretary-General to exercise good offices has concretized into a rule of customary law within the United Nations. It could be argued that the Secretary-General has powers inherent in his office to undertake all kinds of conceivable good offices. Secretary-General Hammarskjöld felt that action on his part, without any mandate from an organ of the United Nations, was justified "should this appear to him necessary in order to help in filling any vacuum that may appear in the systems which the Charter and traditional diplomacy provide for the safeguard of peace and security."

An inherent or implied competence of the Secretary-General is supported by the practice of many policy-making organs, including the General Assembly, the Economic and Social Council, and the Commission on Human Rights. Thus, United Nations human rights organs have expressly recognized and appreciated the good offices of the Secretary-General in the field of human rights (see Resolution 1979/36 of the Economic and Social Council, Resolution 34/175 of the General Assembly, and Resolution 27 (XXXVI) of the Commission on Human Rights). The latter resolution, for example, "requested the Secretary-General to continue and intensify the good offices envisaged in the Charter of the United Nations in the field of human rights." The above-mentioned resolutions, together with the related practice, lend strong support to the doctrine of implied powers as well as to the view that the competence of the Secretary-General to exercise good offices in the field of human rights is now a part of international customary law.

* * *

Anna Spain, *Integration Matters: Rethinking the Architecture of International Dispute Resolution**

There is a lack of institutional capacity at the international level for mediation. There is no standing body equivalent to the ICJ to provide mediation services to states for international disputes. Although the PCA and ICSID provide conciliation, they do not offer mediation. The use of mediation for international disputes, in both the legal and armed conflict contexts, remains ad hoc.[81]

* * *

There are no universally accepted procedural rules governing the use and practice of mediation. Private mediation providers such as the American Arbitration Association and the International Mediation Institute have developed protocols for certifying mediators in the practice of international mediation.[83] But, to date, there is no venue for determining standards or qualifying international mediators that is generally accepted by the international community or recognized under international law.

This is important because states prefer mediation to adjudication for resolving disputes that arise in the context of interstate armed conflicts. Two empirical studies support this claim. The first study conducted by Bercovitch and Fretter surveyed the use of dispute resolution methods in 343 international conflicts occurring between 1945 and 2003, and found that states' preference for mediation was the highest, followed by nego-

---

* 32 U. PA. J. INT'L L. 1 (2010).

81. Christine Chinkin, *Alternative Dispute Resolution Under International Law*, *in* REMEDIES IN INTERNATIONAL LAW: THE INSTITUTIONAL DILEMMA 123, 124–25 (Malcolm D. Evans ed., 1998) (stating that mediation and other forms of dispute resolution were used for the most part on an ad hoc basis, resulting in underutilization during the Cold War).

83. *See e.g.*, *How to become IMI Certified*, INT'L MEDIATION INST., http://www.imimediation.org/how-to-become-imi-certified (last visited Oct. 25, 2010) (providing general information on International Mediation Institute certification).

tiation, with arbitration coming in last.[84] A second empirical study supports these findings, showing that mediation, categorized as a diplomatic method, is the most prevalent form of third-party conflict management.

One critique is that in encouraging parties to be forward-looking, the mediation process does not treat the need to establish facts and determine attribution for past harms.[93] Without adequate safeguards, mediation may fail to deal with important power imbalances and intensify a conflict. The mediation effort in Rwanda prior to the 1994 genocide is one costly example of this.[94] Mediation can empower spoilers in cases where one or more parties are not participating in good faith. In prioritizing the interests of the parties present, there is a concern that mediation agreements that violate interests of public importance may be permitted and may inhibit long-term peace. For example, when parties in mediation prioritize short-term security goals[95] or the mediator pursues a cease-fire agreement, these priorities often detract from, or ignore altogether, underlying causes of the dispute.[96] It may be the case that mediation is not effective in certain contexts. Failure rates linked to geographic indicators illustrate that efforts to mediate regional conflicts in Latin America have generally not been successful.[97]

Finally, the ad hoc and confidential nature of mediation makes documenting its use and lessons learned difficult. The absence of empirical information about international mediation discredits its validity as a field of scholarly study. Until recently, most sources on the subject came from narrative accounts of individual success stories.[98]

Thomas Princen, *International Mediation— The View from the Vatican: Lessons from Mediating the Beagle Channel Dispute**

In late 1978, Argentina and Chile were on the verge of war. At issue were three barren, windswept islands in the Beagle Channel, a narrow passageway at the tip of South America.

An 1881 boundary treaty had not clearly specified the islands' rightful owner and, for nearly a century, the two countries had squabbled, occasionally negotiated, but for the most

84. *See* Bercovitch & Fretter, *supra* note 15, at 29 fig. 2 (illustrating that in a study of 343 registered conflicts, 59.3% used mediation while only 0.6% resorted to arbitration).

93. *See* Carrie Mekel-Meadow, *From Legal Disputes to Conflict Resolution and Human Problem Solving: Legal Dispute Resolution in a Multidisciplinary Context,* 54 J. Legal Educ. 7 (2004) (identifying the different components necessary for successful dispute resolution).

94. *See* Melanie Greenberg, *Mediating Massacres: When "Neutral, Low-Power" Models of Mediation Cannot and Should Not Work,* 19 Ohio St. J. Disp. Resol. 185, 200–05 (2004) (explaining the failure of mediation prior to the ethnic cleansing that occurred in Rwanda in 1994).

95. *See* Jerome Delli Priscoli & Aaron T. Wolf, Managing and Transforming Water Conflicts 33–49 (2009) (discussing alternative dispute resolution in the context of water resources disputes).

96. *See* E. Franklin Dukes, *What We Know About Environmental Conflict Resolution: An Analysis Based on Research,* 22 Conflict Resol. Q. 191, 192–93 (2004) (analyzing and comparing the characteristics of environmental conflict resolution with other procedures).

97. *See* Carolyn M. Shaw, *Conflict Management in Latin America, in* Regional Conflict Management 123, 149 (Paul F. Diehl & Joseph Lepgold eds., 2003) ("[T]he guerrilla insurgencies and drug war in Columbia and Peru ... are far from ideal for achieving a diplomatic settlement.").

98. *See* Jacob Bercovitch, *Introduction: Putting Mediation in Context, in* Studies in International Mediation 3, 22 (Jacob Bercovitch ed., 2002) (stating that until recent decades, scholarly research into human conflict and their manner of resolution was rare and marginal).

* 3 Negotiation J. 347, 347–48 (Oct. 1987).

part ignored the matter. By the early-1970s, however, both countries seemed more inclined to settle the matter due to changes in international law, increased hopes for resource exploitation in the region, and domestic upheavals. But diplomacy proved inadequate, and in 1971 the dispute was submitted to arbitration by a panel of International Court jurists appointed by the Queen of England. The result, in which Chile was awarded the islands, was rejected by Argentina. The two countries then set up a formal negotiation process, but that collapsed in late 1978. With tensions mounting and troops and ships being deployed to the south, war looked imminent. At the last minute, Pope John Paul II announced he was sending his personal representative, Cardinal Antonio Samoré, a career Vatican diplomat, to both Argentina and Chile. The escalation stopped, and after two weeks of shuttle diplomacy by the papal envoy, the two countries agreed to submit the matter to mediation at the Vatican under the auspices of the Pope.

The Pope, the official mediator, appointed a special mediation team headed by Cardinal Samoré to conduct the day-to-day mediation of the Beagle Channel dispute. Beginning in May, 1979, this team spent six months gathering information and hearing out both sides' positions. In September, the Pope received the Argentine and Chilean delegations and put forth his conception of how the negotiation should proceed. After reminding them of their commitment not to resort to force during the course of the mediation, he suggested they start with those issues they had previously agreed upon and then explore a wide range of issues both inside and outside those of the Beagle Channel dispute. Finally, he requested that all statements regarding the progress of the mediation be issued jointly and through the mediation team, and he called upon the press to use prudence in its coverage.

For the next few months, the mediation team met separately with the two delegations, building an agenda, requesting position papers, and working on points of previous agreement. Only in mid-1980 did they turn their full attention to the central issues in dispute—the demarcation of territorial and maritime boundaries in the Beagle Channel. Draft solutions from each side were requested and received but as they were so far apart, the Pope delivered his own proposal for a solution in December, 1980. Granting the three islands to Chile and certain maritime concessions to Argentina, not to mention a common zone for the joint exploitation of natural resources, the papal proposal was accepted by Chile but never accepted—nor rejected—by Argentina. Due to Argentina's lack of response, the negotiations were at a standstill for much of 1981, even though the mediation team persisted in its attempts to resolve the impasse. In addition, renewed tensions between the two countries due to the detention of citizens along the border sidetracked the Vatican mediation.

Negotiations resumed in 1982, but soon stalled again: first when Argentina renounced a 1972 dispute settlement with Chile, and then when war broke out between Argentina and Great Britain over the Falklands/Malvinas Islands. Even so, the Pope and mediation team persisted in their efforts. While little progress was made on the Beagle Channel issues, by the end of the year the Pope did get the two sides to agree to an extension of the 1972 treaty and to accept, at least implicitly, the Pope's proposal as a basis for discussion.

As a result, active negotiations resumed in late 1982 and continued into 1983. But with the death of Cardinal Samoré in February, 1983, and Argentina's preparations to return to democratic rule, negotiations, once again lapsed into impasse. During this time, several diplomats from the two sides began to meet informally outside the Vatican. These "parallel negotiations," plus continued efforts in Rome, paved the way for renewed negotiations, the signing of a final treaty in 1984, and the ratification in 1985. In the end, Chile received the three islands, Argentina retained most of the maritime rights in the region, the common zone idea was abandoned, and several issues outside the Beagle Channel were settled.

United Nations General Assembly: 65th Session, Agenda Item 33

Prevention of armed conflict

Austria, Australia, Azerbaijan, Belgium, Belize, Burkina Faso, Costa Rica, Denmark, Dominican Republic, Estonia, Finland, Gabon, Georgia, Germany, Hungary, Iceland, Ireland, Italy, Japan, Latvia, Lithuania, Luxembourg, Malaysia, Mexico, Morocco, Nepal, New Zealand, Norway, Philippines, Poland, Portugal, Qatar, Republic of Moldova, Romania, Spain, Slovenia, Sweden, Switzerland, the former Yugoslav Republic of Macedonia, Turkey, Uganda and the United Republic of Tanzania: draft resolution

Strengthening the role of mediation in the peaceful settlement of disputes, conflict prevention and resolution

The General Assembly,

* * *

Recognizing the growing interest in and the provision of mediation, and its use as a promising and cost-effective tool in the peaceful settlement of disputes, conflict prevention and resolution, without prejudice to other means mentioned in Chapter VI of the Charter of the United Nations, including the use of arbitration and the roles and functions of the International Court of Justice,

Recognizing also the useful role that mediation can play in preventing disputes from escalating into conflicts and conflicts from escalating further, as well as in advancing the resolution of conflicts and thus preventing and/or reducing human suffering and creating conditions conducive to lasting peace and sustainable development, and in this regard, recognizing that peace and development are mutually reinforcing,

Emphasizing that justice is a fundamental building block of sustainable peace,

Reaffirming its commitment to the purposes and principles of the Charter of the United Nations and international law, which are indispensable foundations of a more peaceful, prosperous and just world, and reiterating its determination to foster strict respect for them and to establish a just and lasting peace all over the world.

Recalling that the peaceful settlement of disputes, conflict prevention and resolution, in accordance with the Charter of the United Nations and international law, including through mediation, remain a primary responsibility of Member States without prejudice to Article 36 of the Charter of the United Nations,

3. *Welcomes* the contributions of Member States to mediation efforts, as appropriate, and encourages them, where appropriate, to develop national mediation capacities, as applicable, in order to ensure coherent mediation and responsiveness;

6. *Invites* all Member States to consider providing timely and adequate resources for mediation, in order to assure its success, as well as for mediation capacity-building activities of the United Nations and of regional and subregional organizations, with a view to ensuring the sustainability and predictability of all catalytic resources;

7. *Requests* the Secretary-General to continue to offer good offices, in accordance with the Charter of the United Nations and of relevant United Nations resolutions, and to continue to provide mediation support, where appropriate, to special representatives and

envoys of the United Nations and to enhance partnerships with regional and subregional organizations, as well as Member States;

8. *Stresses* the importance of well-trained, impartial, experienced and geographically diverse mediation process and substance experts at all levels to ensure the timely and highest quality support to mediation efforts, supports the efforts of the Secretary-General in maintaining an updated roster of mediators, and encourages the continuing efforts to improve its gender balance and equitable geographical representation;

9. *Encourages* the Secretary-General to appoint women as chief or lead mediators in United Nations-sponsored peace processes, as well as to ensure adequate gender expertise for all United Nations processes;

10. *Recommends* that the Secretary-General, in accordance with mandates agreed upon by Member States, continue to strengthen the mediation capacities of the United Nations system, in particular the Mediation Support Unit of the Department of Political Affairs, and its responsiveness, in accordance with agreed mandates and fully taking into account existing United Nations activities and structures, including in the fields of rule of law and accountability, so as to avoid duplication....

Notes and Questions on Good Offices and Mediation

1. What are the advantages and disadvantages of good offices or mediation as a dispute settlement mechanism compared with negotiation? Why do disputants turn to mediators? Why do third parties offer to act as mediators or offer good offices? When would a third party offer good offices? When would a third party offer to act as mediator?

2. Palley argues that the Secretary General overstepped his role of good officer in the Cyprus situation. What is the role of the good officer? Do you see indications that she is correct or incorrect?

3. Mediation is occurring constantly in international relations. Think of some well known mediations. Can you think of any reason why mediation has been less subject to legal standards and is characterized by few, if any, formal procedures? Should it be subject to more regulation?

4. Do you accept the argument that mediation should at least be subject to the obligation of good faith? Why or why not? If mediation were subject to good faith, what would that mean? What specific obligation would be implied? A duty to keep confidences? A duty on the mediator to be neutral? What does neutrality in mediation mean? Can international law impose an obligation of neutrality on a mediator, for example Jimmy Carter or Nelson Mandela, acting in his personal capacity?

5. Consider the draft UN General Assembly Resolution on Strengthening the Role of Mediation included in the text above. Research whether the Resolution was adopted at the General Assembly's 66th Session. If so, find the Annex and look for any practical steps toward promoting mediation, practicing mediation, or regulating mediation. Will these steps have a positive impact in your view toward fulfilling the aims of the draft resolution?

Note 3 above indicates that mediation is the least well regulated of the standard dispute settlement mechanisms. Why do you think this is? Will the draft resolution—even as a draft—help develop any rules specific to mediation? If you think it might, explain how and indicate what rules might develop.

6. The American Bar Association adopted the Uniform Mediation Act in 2002. Do you think any of the following provisions of the Act would be useful additions to public international law?

> Section 8. Confidentiality
>
> Unless subject to the (insert statutory references to open meetings act and open records act), mediation communications are confidential to the extent agreed by the parties or provided by other law or rule of this State.
>
> Section 9. Mediator's Disclosure of Conflicts of Interest; Background
>
> (a) Before accepting a mediation, an individual who is requested to serve as a mediator shall:
>
> (1) make an inquiry that is reasonable under the circumstances to determine whether there are any known facts that a reasonable individual would consider likely to affect the impartiality of the mediator, including a financial or personal interest in the outcome of the mediation and an existing or past relationship with a mediation party or foreseeable participant in the mediation; and
>
> (2) disclose any such known fact to the mediation parties as soon as is practical before accepting a mediation.
>
> (b) If a mediator learns any fact described in subsection (a)(1) after accepting a mediation, the mediator shall disclose it as soon as is practicable.
>
> (c) At the request of a mediation party, an individual who is requested to serve as a mediator shall disclose the mediator's qualifications to mediate a dispute....
>
> (f) This (Act) does not require that a mediator have a special qualification by background or profession.
>
> ((g) A mediator must be impartial, unless after disclosure of the facts required in subsections (a) and (b) to be disclosed, the parties agree otherwise.)

Excerpts from the Uniform Mediation Act, approved by the United States National Conference of Commissioners on Uniform State Laws, Aug. 2001.

See also, Commission of the European Communities, Proposal for a Directive of the European Parliament and of the Council on Certain Aspects of Mediation in Civil and Commercial Matters (October 22, 2004) *available at* www.ejtn.net/www.en/resources/5_1095_1230_file.458.pdf.

7. Yale Law School Professor Lea Brilmayer has written critically of attempts by the U.S. government in the 1990s to mediate disputes. She concluded:

> That there are serious moral problems with the way that mediation is conducted is not an argument against mediation as an approach to international disputes. Mediation is sometimes better than the other alternatives; and that ultimately is the best that can be said about it.
>
> The serious moral problems that arise with mediation do, however, give good reason for critical examination of particular United States mediation efforts. Mediation is an exercise of coercive power just like other military power or economic pressure. The peacemakers of the world need to take a cold look in the mirror and ask themselves to what degree they are simply reflecting their own self-interest, and to what extent this is justifiable.

Lea Brilmayer, *America: The World's Mediator? Daniel J. Meador Lecture*, 51 Ala. L. Rev. 715–731 (1999).

8. Ramcharan discusses whether a government's violation of its citizens' human rights is an issue of international peace. He concludes that peace is implicated in such cases. Recall that the Secretary General is authorized to act to ensure international peace and security, but he has no specific authority regarding human rights. Thus, if human rights were not linked to peace, the Secretary General might act *ultra vires*—beyond the authority given him in the UN Charter. International organizations and their organs and officers are required to respect the limits of their authority under the treaty establishing the organization. According to Bernhardt:

> The existence and the competences of international organizations are based on legal norms, as a rule on a treaty concluded by States. The relevant treaty always attributes limited competences to the organization and its organs. Theoretically, one could imagine a treaty which leaves an organization entirely free to determine its own jurisdiction, but this does not occur in reality, and it would be hardly compatible with State sovereignty. No government and no national parliament would probably accept a treaty which gives an international entity unlimited regularity powers. International organizations are and remain for the foreseeable future legal persons with limited competences.
>
> * * *
>
> II
>
> When are acts of an international organization *ultra vires*? A simple answer: When they fall outside the competence of the organization as determined by the constituent treaty (the "constitution") of the organization concerned. The general rules of treaty interpretation are applicable when one tries to delimit the competences under the treaty. These rules are codified in the Vienna conventions on the law of treaties, but it must also be taken into account that treaties and among them especially "constitutions" of organizations are "living instruments" under which the organs develop the law of the organization beyond the original intentions of the authors. The greater the consensus among the member States of an organization, the easier is an evolutive interpretation of the constituent treaty. Much depends on the concrete circumstances.

Ultra Vires Activities of International Organizations, in Theory of International Law at the Threshold of the 21st Century, Essays in Honour of Krzysztof Skubiszewski 599, 599–602 (1996).

The *ultra vires* doctrine will be considered again, in particular in relation to the action of arbitrators in making decisions that may extend beyond what the parties to an arbitration agreed.

9. In discussing potential limits on the Secretary General's authority to act in the area of human rights, Ramcharan draws attention to a related issue for IDR. Do human rights violations by a government fall within the category of the international disputes that comprise the subject of this book: namely, disputes involving states and international organizations. Recall the definition of dispute provided by the ICJ in the *Headquarters Agreement* Case. Do human rights violations meet the definition? What is your view? Would it make a difference to you if the states involved were party to a human rights treaty and one state accused another of violating the terms of the treaty by violating the rights of its citizens? *See, e.g.*, a case before the European Court of Human Rights: *Ireland v. UK*, 25 Eur. Ct.

H.R. (Ser. A) (1978), and a case before the European Human Rights Commission: *The Greek Case*, Denmark, Norway, Sweden, and the Netherlands v. Greece, Report of the Commission Vol. II (Eur. Com. H.R., Nov. 5, 1969).

10. The UN Secretary General did not succeed after years of trying to settle the Thai-Cambodia dispute. His attempt followed a judgment by the ICJ, which had also failed to resolve matters. *See Temple of Preah Vihear* (Cambodia v. Thailand), 1962 I.C.J. 6 (June 15.) In April 2009, the Thai prime minister referred the dispute to the summit of South East Asian Nations (ASEAN). *Thai PM to Refer Thai-Cambodian Border Dispute to ASEAN Summit,* The Nation (April 5, 2009) http://www.nationmultimedia.com/2009/04/05/national/national_30099692.php.

Why do you suspect that border disputes have a history of leading to armed conflict? Most boundary judgments by the ICJ have led to peaceful settlement—the Thailand and Cambodia case is an exception. The problem appears to be that while the ICJ determined on which side of the border an ancient and revered temple stood, it was not asked to make a full determination of the boundary. Should it have provided it anyway? The issue has returned to ICJ.

In May 2011, Cambodia filed an application requesting interpretation of the judgment in the *Temple of Preah Vihear* asked Cambodia for the urgent indication of provisional measures. See http://www.icj-cij.org/docket/files/151/16480.pdf.

11. Formal mediation is increasingly being used in international commercial disputes. What impact might this have on inter-state mediation or mixed state and private mediation? *See* Harold I. Abramson, *Time to Try Mediation of International Commercial Disputes,* 4 ILSA J. Int'l & Comp. L. 323 (1998); David Plant, *Mediation in International Commercial Arbitration: Some Practical Aspects,* 4 ILSA J. Int'l & Comp. L. 329 (1998).

12. Further reading on good offices and mediation includes:

Amitzur Ilan, Bernadotte in Palestine, 1948: A Story in Contemporary Humanitarian Knight-Errantry (1989).

Raymond G. Helmick, S.J., Negotiating Outside the Law, Why Camp David Failed (2004).

The Refugee Camp Problem

Beth'sda and Hamrabi are two states in the Middle East involved in a seventy-five-year-long armed conflict. As a result of the conflict, Hamrabi has large refugee camps overseen by the UN. At one point, Beth'sda sends troops into one of these camps to find irregular fighters who have been carrying out suicide bombings against its civilians. When the troops leave, Hamrabi officials accuse Beth'sda of carrying out a massacre in the camp, killing hundreds of civilians itself. The UN Secretary General offers to send a team to determine if a massacre has indeed occurred. At first, Beth'sda agrees, but when the team members are announced, Beth'sda objects saying that the members are not forensic scientists, persons experienced in armed conflict, or otherwise appropriate to determine whether a massacre occurred in the camp.

To get an agreement on the personnel for the team, the Director General of the WTO invites the UN Secretary General and high-ranking Hamrabi and Beth'sda officials to meet secretly at the WTO headquarters in Geneva. All three parties accept the invitation and begin talking about who should be on the team. After three hours, however, they reach deadlock. The Director General decides to take some creative action to pressure the parties to reach agreement. He informs the press of the meeting and suggests that they question why an agreement has not been reached. He then invites the delegates to dinner. As the group leaves the WTO headquarters, they are deluged by reporters. The Beth'sda delegation and the UN Secretary General leave abruptly. Has anyone done anything questionable as a matter of the law of international dispute resolution?

Chapter Four

Inquiry and Conciliation

Introduction

In the late 19th and early 20th Centuries, states began developing new formal procedures for dispute resolution—commissions of inquiry and conciliation. Inquiry, also called fact-finding, is a process that aims to resolve disputes by settling issues of fact. It is a process more typically found in international than national law. Conciliation processes grew out of inquiry and,

> . . . combines elements of both INQUIRY and MEDIATION. . . . Created in the twentieth century under various bilateral and multilateral treaties and approved in the UN charter (art. 33, para. 1), conciliation has two basic functions: to investigate and clarify the facts in dispute, and to attempt to bring the parties into agreement by suggesting mutually acceptable solutions to the problem.[1]

Both procedures typically employ a commission of persons, often subject-matter experts to investigate and report. The Institute of International Law even includes the commission as an element of its definition of conciliation:

> A method for the settlement of international disputes of any nature according to which a Commission set up by the Parties, either on a permanent basis or an ad hoc basis to deal with a dispute, proceeds to the impartial examination of the dispute and attempts to define the terms of a settlement susceptible of being accepted by them or of affording the Parties, with a view to its settlement, such aid as they may have requested.[2]

Inquiry and conciliation commissions typically conduct themselves quite like an arbitral tribunal, hearing witness testimony, reviewing documents, and making site inspections. At the close of proceedings, a non-binding report is issued. It is this report that distinguishes inquiry and conciliation from mediation and arbitration. In mediation, no report is issued, and, in arbitration, the decision is typically binding.

---

1. Dictionary of Conflict Resolution 106–07 (Douglas H. Yarn ed., 1999); *see also* Sven M.G. Koopmans, Diplomatic Dispute Settlement, The Use of Inter-State Conciliation (2008); J.G. Merrills, International Dispute Settlement, Chap. 4, (5th ed. 2011); United Nations Handbook on the Peaceful Settlement of Disputes Between States, Chap. 2E (1992); Nissim Bar-Yaacov, The Handling of International Disputes by Means of Inquiry, Chap. 5 & 7 (1974); H. Fox, *Conciliation* 93, *in* International Disputes: The Legal Aspects, (C.M.H. Waldock ed., 1972); Jean-Pierre Cot, International Conciliation (R. Myers Trans., 1972).

2. Regulations on the Procedure of International Conciliation Institute of International Law, art. 1, 49 Annuaire 385, 386 (1961).

Thus, commissions offer more formality than mediation but do not require the full commitment by the disputing parties to accept a binding decision of the third-party intervener. By the 1920s, conciliation commissions had become quite popular—a number of standing conciliation commissions were established by multilateral and bilateral treaties in both Europe and the Americas. The multilateral 1899 Hague Convention for the Pacific Settlement of International Disputes contains provisions for commissions of inquiry. In 1906, inquiry was used by the United Kingdom and Russia to resolve the dangerous Dogger Bank dispute. Russian naval vessels had opened fire on six British fishing vessels. The incident nearly sparked a war, but the Commission reported that the Russians mistook the vessels for submarines. This success led to further development of inquiry in the 1907 Hague Convention.[3]

According to J. G. Merrills, the first treaty to provide for conciliation was between Sweden and Chile in 1920.[4] In 1921, Germany and Switzerland also agreed to use conciliation to settle disputes. France and Switzerland did so as well, establishing a permanent conciliation commission in 1925. Also in 1925, in the Locarno Treaties, Germany agreed to settle disputes by means of permanent commissions with Belgium, France, Czechoslovakia, and Poland. In 1928, states adopted the General Act for the Pacific Settlement of Disputes, which made conciliation compulsory in the absence of a commitment to go to the Permanent Court of International Justice. In the Treaty of Washington in 1923, sixteen U.S. states agreed to use conciliation to settle disputes. The Inter-American Convention of Conciliation was agreed to in 1929, and permanent conciliation commissions were established under the Inter-American Convention in 1933.

Despite these many commitments, states rarely use commissions. Following this introduction are excerpts from rare reports of a commission of inquiry and conciliation. The inquiry excerpt is from the *Case of the Red Crusader*. In May 1961, a British fishing vessel was suspected of fishing in restricted waters off the Faroes Islands. A Danish fisheries protection vessel attempted to arrest the Red Crusader. After successfully putting an officer on board, the Red Crusader tried to escape. The Danes fired, doing considerable damage to the trawler. Britain and Denmark agreed to the formation of a commission of inquiry to resolve the factual disputes connected with the incident. The Commission had three neutral commissioners, all international lawyers, from Belgium, France, and the Netherlands. The Commission was to investigate whether the Red Crusader had been fishing inside the blue line on a map annexed to the Agreement, on the circumstances of the arrest, and on other incidents prior to the Red Crusader reaching port.[5]

The Red Crusader incident occurred in the 1960s. The next formal use of inter-state conciliation or inquiry was not until 1980. Iceland and Norway formed a conciliation commission to suggest solutions for the maritime boundary area in the vicinity of Jan Mayen Island. The Commission recommended a joint development zone[6] rather than a

3. *See* Richard Ned Lebow, *Accidents and Crises: The Dogger Bank Affair*, 31 Nav. War. Col. Rev. 66–75 (1978).

4. Merrills, *supra* note 1, at 62.

5. *Id.*, at 52–55.

6. Report and Recommendations to the Governments of Iceland and Norway of the Conciliation Commission on the Continental Shelf Area between Iceland and Jan Mayen (May 1981), 62 I.L.R. 108, 20 ILM 797 (1981) [hereinafter Report and Recommendations]; *see also* Jonathan I. Charney, *Progress in International Maritime Boundary Delimitation*, 88 Am. J. Int'l L. 227, 256, n. 56 (1994).

strict division of the area. The case is excerpted below. It reveals both the strength and weakness of conciliation. The conciliations suggested a creative solution, but the next maritime boundary in the area of Jan Mayen Island was settled by the ICJ,[7] which could provide a binding decision. The Taba conciliation between Egypt and Israel indicates even more directly that while states may be attracted to the flexibility and creativity offered by conciliation, binding decisions on the basis of law are preferred to conciliators' recommendations.

In 1990, the U.S. and Chile settled a dispute over payment of damages growing out of the murder of a former Chilean ambassador, Orlando Letelier, and his assistant, Ronni Moffit. The two were killed in the U.S. by agents of General Pinochet.[8] A U.S. Court had found Chile liable for the killing, but Chile refused to pay damages to the families of the victims.[9] The U.S. and Chile had signed one of the so-called "Bryan" treaties in 1914 requiring them to use a commission of inquiry in case of a dispute.[10] The U.S. suggested establishing such a commission. Chile denied it was liable, but recognized its obligation to have an inquiry. Chile agreed that the commission could decide what Chile would owe, *were* it liable. A commission was established and made a determination, and Chile paid more than $2.6 million.[11]

The *Letelier* Case was an inquiry, and while inquiry is still relatively rare, it is returning to popularity. The Notes and Questions that follow the case excerpts describe a number of commissions of inquiry to investigate uses of armed force, labor rights violations, and other concerns. Conciliation, on the other hand, is almost never used these days. It has been included in recent treaties, including the Organization for Security and Cooperation in Europe's Stockholm Convention on Conciliation and Arbitration,[12] the WTO Dispute Settlement Understanding,[13] the UN Convention on the Law of the Sea (UNCLOS),[14] and the North America Free Trade Agreement.[15] Yet the conciliation provisions in these treaties are not being invoked. In 2003, the UN Commission on International Trade Law (UNCITRAL) introduced a model law on international commercial mediation that defines mediation as synonymous with conciliation. It even titles the document *The UNCITRAL Model Law on International Commercial Conciliation* (2002).[16] If UNCITRAL's terminology enters into common use, conciliation, which basically exists today in name only, may well fade even from discussion as a procedure separate from mediation and inquiry. Koopmans discusses the obscenity of conciliation and the terminological confusion.

---

7. Report and recommendations, *supra* note 6. Maritime Delimitation in the Area Between Greenland and Jan Mayen (Denmark v. Norway), 1993 I.C.J. 38 (Judgment of June 14).

8. *See Letelier v. Republic of Chile*, 502 F. Supp. 259 (D.D.C. 1980).

9. *See* Barbara Crossette, *$2.6 Million Awarded Families in Letelier Case*, N.Y. Times, Jan. 13, 1992, at A11.

10. Marian Nash Leich, *United States-Chile: Invocation of Disputes Treaty*, 83 Am. J. Int'l L. 352 (1989); Merrills, *supra* note 1, at 56–57.

11. Crossette, *supra* note 9.

12. 32 I.L.M. 557 (1993).

13. *See infra.*

14. *See infra.*

15. North American Free Trade Agreement, Dec. 17, 1992, Can.-Mex.-U.S., Ch. 20, art. 2007, 32 I.L.M. 693 (1993).

16. *Available at* www.uncitral.org/english/texts/arbitration/ml-conc-e.pdf.

Sven M.G. Koopmans,
*The Use of Inter-State Conciliation**

Inter-State conciliation is at the same time a common element in international dispute settlement and an unknown quantity. There are many provisions in international agreements naming conciliation as one of the options by which to settle disputes. Nevertheless, little is known about what conciliation is and what contributions it can make. The lack of knowledge is due largely to the rarity of its application. It is therefore also forgotten that at some time in the 20th century, conciliation was widely considered to be an outstanding method to resolve otherwise insoluble disputes, and thereby even to eradicate war.

* * *

The lack of knowledge of conciliation is also partly due to international lawyers, who have traditionally focused on international courts as the centre of international legal practice. While this limited view is increasingly broadened to include diplomacy, custom and legal and political thought, conciliation still remains little studied. Further, it is to be assessed whether international lawyers may also have directly contributed to the neglect of conciliation by frequently treating it, both in writings and in practice, as resembling adjudication, only without binding force. Following one such case, Suzanne Bastid wondered whether inter-State conciliation had yet found its distinctive and definitive form. Fifty years later, the identity of conciliation remains in question.

* * *

The problem of nomenclature is one both of lawyers and of laymen, rooted in everyday conversation. In 1994 the World Trade Organisation created the official settlement method of mediation, conciliation and good offices, which is in fact only one procedure, and one that international lawyers would recognize as a form of mediation. It may also be related to the fact that in various national jurisdictions no distinction is made between mediation and conciliation. Equally, in the press the peaceful settlement work of the United Nations Secretary-General is often called conciliation, whereas ... his activities in this field would often legally be classified as 'good offices' or 'mediation'.

Here, however, in order to assess the use of inter-State conciliation as it originated in public international law early last century, it is necessary to return to the procedure as a distinct method. Concentrating on the distinct identity of inter-State conciliation will produce a better perspective on the special traits of mediation and of other conciliation-like methods. Lastly, a focus on the distinct nature of conciliation can help to assess whether the confusion over its identity was also reason for the relative lack of its application.

Looking back, conciliation can be associated with anti-war idealism prior to WWII, but also with the legal and political culture clashes of the 1960s, when provisions for compulsory conciliation were found to be the ultimate compromise between two opposing camps on dispute settlement, one demanding binding adjudication, another insisting on non-legal

---

* S.M.G. Koopmans, Diplomatic Dispute Settlement 1–3 (2008) (Some footnotes omitted).

amicable settlement.[17] One of the questions on conciliation is therefore how it could obtain such different connotations.

United Nations Model Rules for the Conciliation of Disputes between States

CHAPTER I
APPLICATION OF THE RULES

Article 1

1. These rules apply to the conciliation of disputes between States where those States have expressly agreed in writing to their application.

2. The States which agree to apply these rules may at any time, through mutual agreement, exclude or amend any of their provisions.

CHAPTER II
INITIATION OF THE CONCILIATION PROCEEDINGS

Article 2

1. The conciliation proceedings shall begin as soon as the States concerned (henceforth: the parties) have agreed in writing to the application of the present rules, with or without amendments, as well as on a definition of the subject of the dispute, the number and emoluments of members of the conciliation commission, its seat and the maximum duration of the proceedings....

2. If the States cannot reach agreement on the definition of the subject of the dispute, they may by mutual agreement request the assistance of the Secretary-General of the United Nations to resolve the difficulty. They may also by mutual agreement request his assistance to resolve any other difficulty that they may encounter in reaching an agreement on the modalities of the conciliation proceedings.

CHAPTER III
NUMBER AND APPOINTMENT OF CONCILIATORS

Article 3

There may be three conciliators or five conciliators. In either case the conciliators shall form a commission.

* * *

CHAPTER IV
FUNDAMENTAL PRINCIPLES

Article 7

The commission, acting independently and impartially, shall endeavour to assist the parties in reaching an amicable settlement of the dispute. If no settlement is reached during the consideration of the dispute, the commission may draw up and submit appropriate recommendations to the parties for consideration.

---

17. As in the negotiations on the Vienna Convention on the Law of Treaties ((23 May 1969), 115 *UNTS* 331): I. Sinclair, *The Vienna Convention on the Law of Treaties* (2nd ed. 1984) 226–233.

* * *

World Trade Organization, Understanding on Rules and Procedures Governing the Settlement of Disputes

Article 5

Good Offices, Conciliation and Mediation

See Annex

United Nations Convention on the Law of the Sea

Part XV

Section 1. General Provisions

Article 284

Conciliation

See Annex

ICSID Convention
Convention on the Settlement of Investment Disputes between States and National of Other States

Chapter III

Conciliation

See Annex

The Red Crusader

Commission of Enquiry (Den-UK) Mar. 23, 1962*

The Facts.—On May 29, 1961, the British trawler *Red Crusader* was arrested by the Danish authorities off the coast of the Faroe Islands. A Commission of Enquiry was set up by an Exchange of Notes of November 15, 1961, between the Governments of Denmark and the United Kingdom to investigate certain incidents relating to this arrest and to subsequent events.

The Exchange of Notes requested the Commission to investigate and report to the two Governments:

> "(I) the facts leading up to the arrest of the British trawler, 'Red Crusader', on the night of the 29th of May, 1961, including the question whether the 'Red Crusader' was fishing, or with her fishing gear not stowed, inside the blue line on the map annexed to the Agreement between the two Governments concerning the Regulation of Fishing around the Faroe Islands constituted by the Exchange of Notes of the 27th of April, 1959;

* 35 I.L.R. 485 (1967) (footnotes omitted).

"(2) the circumstances of the arrest; and

"(3) the facts and incidents that occurred thereafter before the 'Red Crusader' reached Aberdeen."

The Commission was constituted on November 21, 1961, in The Hague, with Professor Charles De Visscher as President, and Professor André Gros and Captain C. Moolenburgh as Members.

At the first meeting of the Commission, on November 21, 1961, it was agreed, in the presence of the Agents for the Danish Government and for the United Kingdom Government, that Memorials would be exchanged in London and deposited in The Hague on December 5, with one copy to each Member of the Commission and to the Court of Arbitration Registry, and that Counter-Memorials would be exchanged and deposited in the same manner on January 16, 1962. It was then decided that oral proceedings would begin on March 5 in the following order: Danish evidence, British evidence, Danish oral statements, and British oral statements—followed by Danish and British replies, if required. Each witness would be examined, cross-examined and, if necessary, re-examined. The statements should be made upon an "engagement of honour", oaths not being administered. The written procedure would be in English; additional documents would be admitted upon reasonable notice. The Danish witnesses and experts would have the possibility of expressing themselves in Danish; simultaneous translation would be provided for and, if necessary, consecutive translation.

The Commission heard the Danish witnesses and experts at the meetings held on March 5–9. After examination by the Danish Agent the witnesses were cross-examined by British Counsel and, in some cases, re-examined. From March 10, the British witnesses and one expert were heard by the Commission. After examination by the British Counsel the witnesses and the expert were cross-examined by the Danish Agent and, in some cases, re-examined. From March 14–16 the Commission heard the oral statements and replies.

THE REPORT.—the following is the text of the operative part of the Report:

"The Commission decided to divide the presentation of evidence into three Chapters, to facilitate its work:

"(a) facts leading up to the arrest of the *Red Crusader*;

"(b) events between the arrest of the *Red Crusader* and the meeting with the British naval vessels;

"(c) facts and incidents from that moment up to the arrival of the *Red Crusader* in Aberdeen."

The same division is followed in the present report.

"Chapter One

"*Facts leading up to the arrest of the* Red Crusader *and circumstances of the arrest. . . .*

* * *

"2. *Movements.*—About one hour after the Commanding Officer of *Niels Ebbesen* received a signal from Faroe Island Naval District that four British fishing vessels had been reported by Myggenaes Lighthouse-keeper at 4–7 miles distance on the fishing grounds at 17.25 hours on May 29, 1961, his ship left Thorshavn to investigate the report.

"Steaming through Vestmannasund, *Neils Ebbesen* passed Sydregjov at 20.34 hours and came into the open between Mulen and Slettenaes at about 20.55 hours, flying her ensign and fishery pennant.

"The first echoes she saw on the radar 293 screen at bearings 292–298 were at 9 miles distance. Without correction this would mean that the vessels which caused the echoes were certainly inside the blue line.

"Taking into account the necessity of the fixed correction of plus 0.35 miles and a plus or minus 5 per cent correction of the maximum range on the scale in use, the Commission is unable, on the basis of this information only, to say with certainty that these vessels were inside at that time.

"A few moments later, the nearest echo was reported at 8.6 miles distance, bearing 294. The same that has been said above applies to this observation on the radar 293 screen.

"In the meantime, *Niels Ebbesen* was heading for the ships on the horizon in bearing ± 294 degrees, steering a course of 292 degrees, which after some time was changed to 299 degrees and later to 308 degrees, when the bearing to the nearest ship became more northerly.

"The positions of *Niels Ebbesen* were fixed by the double-angle method and by taking radar distances and bearings on the Decca 12 radar to conspicuous corners and headlands on the coast.

"The distances and bearings from *Niels Ebbesen* to the nearest vessel were measured on the radar sets and plotted on the Danish Chart No. 81 and the plotting table.

"As has been mentioned in this Chapter, with regard to the positions, the Commission is certain that at 21.14 hours the nearest echo on the Decca radar screen indicates the position of a vessel most probably inside the blue line, possibly just on or just outside that line.

"Combining this finding with the data on the original Exhibits Nos. 6 and 8, the Commission fully understands and shares the view of the Commanding Officer of *Niels Ebbesen* that the nearest fishing vessel had been inside.

"The Commission has noticed in the tape-recording (Exhibit 16) that on board *Red Crusader* between about 21.55 hours and 22.09 hours the gear came up and the trawl-net was taken in. As shown on the radar plot (Exhibit 8) the speed of the trawler from, at the latest, 21.09 hours to 21.48 hours was constantly too great to stream the net and the boards, *i.e.* to lower the net and the boards into the water, but not too great to proceed with the trawl in the water. This means that at least during the period from 21.09 hours until 21.14 hours *Red Crusader* was with her gear in the water inside the blue line.

"With regard to the signals, *Niels Ebbesen* gave from 21.39 hours onwards several stop-signals, by siren and searchlight, to which the trawler paid no attention until a blank 40 mm. shot was fired across her bows.

"Though Skipper Wood agreed that naval signalmen are properly trained, he stated that he had been unable to understand the signals given by the Danish frigate. Skipper Wood's evidence with regard to signals showed that he was not at all certain of the signals that must be given in circumstances which often occur at sea.

"Therefore the Commission is unable to accept the Skipper's statements with regard to the siren signals given by *Niels Ebbesen.*

"His statement that he was unable to read the flash signal given to him by searchlight, as the searchlight was not properly trained, is not in agreement with other evidence. On the tape-recording it can be seen that *Niels Ebbesen* changed course to starboard before the signal by searchlight was sent. This brought the trawler on 2 points on the port bow. It is therefore logical that the searchlight on the port side was used, and the evidence given by Skipper Wood, that he would have seen the searchlight signals from starboard much better than those from port, is not justified.

"Skipper Wood's suggestion that these signals were meant for *Millwood* is unfounded. The searchlight was trained by an experienced Chief Petty Officer, who had to aim the apparatus on 'the blue trawler', which proved to be *Red Crusader*. The Commission is unable to accept that this experienced naval man trained the searchlight at the black hull of the *Millwood,* when the dark blue *Red Crusader* was nearer to his ship.

"During the proceedings it was submitted that if the *Red Crusader* had been inside the blue line for a certain period, this was unintentional and caused by drifting in a south-easterly direction during a necessary repair of the trawl.

"In view of the evidence submitted, the Commission cannot accept that an accident to the trawl has been established as a fact.

* * *

"As a result of its investigation in Chapter One, the Commission finds:

"(1) that no proof of fishing inside the blue line has been established, in spite of the fact that the trawl was in the water inside the blue line from about 21.00 hours until 21.14 hours on May 29, 1961;

"(2) that the *Red Crusader* was with her gear not stowed inside the blue line from about 21.00 hours until 21.14 hours on May 29, 1961;

"(3) that the first signal to stop was given by *Niels Ebbesen* at 21.39 hours and that this signal and the later stop-signals were all given outside the blue line.

"*Chapter Two*

"*Events between the arrest of the* Red Crusader *and the meeting with the British naval vessels.*—It will not be necessary to deal at great length with some parts of this period, the facts of which have been agreed upon by both Parties.

"The Captain of *Niels Ebbesen* sent Lieutenant Bech, Fishery Officer, and Corporal Kropp, Signalman, on board the *Red Crusader* by a boat launched at about 22.I9 hours. Lieutenant Bech stayed aboard the *Red Crusader* for approximately twenty minutes (arriving back on *Niels Ebbesen* at about 22.40 hours), during which time the distance of the *Red Crusader* to Baret Head was checked on the radar of the trawler. Lieutenant Bech measured 8.95 miles and the Skipper 8.9 miles. At the same time, 22.28 hours, Lieutenant Anderson checked both radars on board *Niels Ebbesen* and observed 8.4 miles on the display unit of Decca 12 and 8.0 miles on that of radar 293. By a double-angle fix taken at 22.29 hours the distance was found to be 8.6 miles on Chart No. 81 (Exhibit 6); confirmation of the distance was requested from *Red Crusader* and the reply was the same, 8.9 miles to Baret Head. At the time, on Skipper Wood's chart no positions or indications relevant to the incident of May 29 were plotted.

"Immediately after the arrival of Skipper Wood and Lieutenant Bech on board *Niels Ebbesen* a conference was held in Captain Sølling's cabin, which lasted until just before 23.20 hours, when the Skipper was taken back to *Red Crusader.*

"During that conference Captain Sølling informed Skipper Wood that his trawler was under arrest and gave the reasons which, in his view, justified such arrest. Skipper Wood denied that he had ever been fishing inside the blue line.

"There cannot have been any doubt left in Skipper Wood's mind at the end of this conference: he was ordered to follow the *Niels Ebbesen* and to go to Thorshavn to be examined and tried by a Faroese Court immediately on arrival there. The Skipper did not refuse to accept the order but, on the contrary, obeyed it by receiving on board the *Red Crusader* an officer and rating of the *Niels Ebbesen*, in accordance with the normal procedure which he knew to be used by Danish Fishery Protection vessels in similar cases; there could not be any misunderstanding concerning the significance of the presence on board the trawler of the Danish officer and rating.

"Skipper Wood, having returned to his trawler at 23.22 hours with Lieutenant Bech and Corporal Kropp, followed the *Niels Ebbesen* towards Thorshavn at full speed, about one mile astern. Radio-telephone communication was established between *Niels Ebbesen* and Lieutenant Bech on *Red Crusader* and it was agreed to call every half-hour.

"There can be no other explanation of Skipper Wood's change of mind than his own. He thought that he had not been fishing illegally and that a trial at Thorshavn would not give him a fair chance.

"At 02.58 hours Skipper Wood asked Lieutenant Bech to send a message to *Niels Ebbesen* reporting that he was not going to enter Thorshavn, and at 03.05 hours Lieutenant Bech sent another message to the *Niels Ebbesen* saying that he was locked up. Both these messages indicate the time when Skipper Wood decided to put his plan into operation.

"The Commission will examine successively two matters: *(a)* the situation of the Danish officer and rating on board the *Red Crusader;* and *(b)* the firing.

"*(a)* The Commission finds that the situation of Lieutenant Bech and Corporal Kropp on the *Red Crusader* was as follows:

"On his own admission, Skipper Wood wanted to keep Lieutenant Bech off the bridge to avoid not only any interference in the direction of the trawler but also any altercation with him, at the very moment when he attempted to escape from the *Niels Ebbesen*. This could only be achieved by an effective seclusion and not by an illusory or apparent one.

"Skipper Wood has admitted his intention to break away and to proceed back to Aberdeen, discussing it with his crew out of the hearing of Lieutenant Bech and Corporal Kropp and making plans accordingly.

"There is, therefore, neither any reason whatsoever to think that, having locked the door leading from the passage outside the Skipper's cabin into the wheelhouse, to achieve the two purposes mentioned above, Skipper Wood left open the other exit from his quarters, nor to believe that Lieutenant Bech, if he had found that exit open, would not have taken the opportunity of regaining his freedom.

"The Commission finds that Lieutenant Bech was thus kept effectively locked up inside the Skipper's quarters in *Red Crusader* for about an hour before 04.08 hours, when the Skipper reopened the door from the wheelhouse to his quarters and let him out.

"The measures taken against Corporal Kropp were different. It was not necessary for Skipper Wood, in order to realize his double purpose, to lock him up. Neither his rank, nor his age, made the same degree of coercion necessary. But it is quite clear that the 'invitation' to go down aft, where he was escorted by members of the crew, was equivalent to an order. He was kept there for a period of about an hour under the courteous but efficient guard of some members of the crew.

"*(b)* The facts concerning the firing are as follows:

"At 03.22 hours one round of 127 mm. gunshot was fired astern and to the right of the trawler, at a distance estimated at 2.100 metres with the elevation 24/r25.

"At 03.23 hours the first stop signals were given by steam whistle-signal K.

"At 03.25 hours one round of 127 mm. gun-shot was fired ahead and to the left, at the same estimated distance with the elevation 24/1 20.

"At 03.26 hours the signal K was repeated by steam whistle.

"It is established that no signal by radio, steam whistle, blank shot or otherwise was attempted earlier than 03.23 hours, and it is also clear that these two shots, as well as the first two machine-gun shots astern, fired at 03.40 hours, were intended to be warning shots to stop and were not aimed to hit the *Red Crusader.*

"The distance between the two ships had decreased to 0.9 miles at 03.30 hours and to 0.45 miles at 03.38 hours, when the Captain of *Niels Ebbesen* gave the order to fire at the *Red Crusader.*

"At 03.40 hours a warning was given by portable loud-hailer to the *Red Crusader,* as well as the order to stop, which appear in full in the tape-recording (Exhibit 16), with the indication of the firing of two shots in the middle of the recording (the two machine-gun shots referred to above).

"It was from this time only that firing was directed at the *Red Crusader* in the following manner:

03.40 hours	8 machine-gun shots at the *Red Crusader's* scanner, by single shot (Exhibit 16 to the Danish Memorial, p. 20). Two hits verified later.
03.4I hours	New hailing to *Red Crusader* and order to stop.
03.42 hours	21 machine-gun shots at *Red Crusader's* mast, also by single shot—no hits found later.
03.44 hours	1 round of 40 mm. gun at masthead light—no hit.
03.47 hours	1 round of 40 mm. gun at mast—no hit.
03.47 hours	New hailing to *Red Crusader*: "Stop, or I have to shoot you in your hull."
03.5I hours	2 rounds of 40 mm. gun at stem—one hit a little abaft of name-plate.
03.53 hours	1 round of 40 mm. gun at stem—no hit.

"The firing, which took place in Danish territorial waters, then ceased by order of Captain Sølling's. It is agreed that the gun-shots fired were solid shots and not explosive shells.

"No slowing down of the *Red Crusader* is indicated in any evidence and the trawler did not stop before the meeting with the British naval vessels.

* * *

"As a result of its investigation in Chapter Two, the Commission finds:

"(1) The *Red Crusader* was arrested. This conclusion is established by Captain Sølling's declarations as well as by the evidence given by Skipper Wood. Even if the Skipper formally denied his guilt, his answers clearly implied that he considered at the time that he had been duly arrested for illegal fishing. Notes made in the Skipper's red pocket-book and the *Red Crusader's* log-book also leave no doubt on that point.

"(2) Skipper Wood, after having obeyed for a certain time the order given him by Captain Sølling, changed his mind during the trip to Thorshavn and put into effect a plan, concerted with his crew, whereby he attempted to escape and to evade the jurisdiction of an authority which he had at first, rightly, accepted.

"(3) During this attempt to escape, the Skipper of the *Red Crusader* took steps to seclude Lieutenant Bech and Corporal Kropp during a certain period and had the intention to take them to Aberdeen.

"(4) In opening fire at 03.22 hours up to 03.53 hours, the Commanding Officer of the *Niels Ebbesen* exceeded legitimate use of armed force on two counts: (*a*) firing without warning of solid gun-shot; (*b*) creating danger to human life on board the *Red Crusader* without proved necessity, by the effective firing at the Red Crusader after 03.40 hours.

"The escape of the *Red Crusader* in flagrant violation of the order received and obeyed, the seclusion on board the trawler of an officer and rating of the crew of *Niels Ebbesen*, and Skipper Wood's refusal to stop may explain some resentment on the part of Captain Sølling. Those circumstances, however, cannot justify such violent action.

"The Commission is of the opinion that other means should have been attempted, which, if duly persisted in, might have finally persuaded Skipper Wood to stop and revert to the normal procedure which he himself had previously followed.

"(5) The cost of the repair of the damage caused by the firing at and hitting of the Red Crusader submitted by the British Government has been considered reasonable by the Danish Agent.

"*Chapter Three*

"*Events after the meeting with the British naval vessels.*—In an Aide-Mémoire of the Danish Government dated June 2, 1961, as well as in the Danish Counter-Memorial, certain naval officers of Her Majesty's Navy were criticized for interfering with the lawful authority exercised by the *Niels Ebbesen* over a trawler legally arrested by that vessel. The imputations related first to the circumstances of the return to the *Niels Ebbesen* of the boarding party put on the *Red Crusader* and secondly to the question of interference by H.M.S. *Troubridge* with an attempt by the *Niels Ebbesen* to return the boarding party to the *Red Crusader.* On both points the Commission notes that the Danish Counter-Memorial had reserved final conclusions until presentation of evidence during the oral proceedings.

"The Commission has taken note of the withdrawal by the Danish Delegation of any charges concerning the question of the return of Lieutenant Bech and Corporal Kropp to the *Niels Ebbesen* and of any implication which could, at a certain moment in the proceedings, have resulted from these charges. It will simply be recorded that some misunderstanding arose on board the *Red Crusader* at the moment of embarking in H.M.S. *Troubridge's* boat. The reasons for this misunderstanding are somewhat difficult and in any case useless to define, taking into consideration the declarations made by the Danish Delegation at the meetings of March 13, 15 and 16, 1962.

"Moreover, the Commission feels that the return of the boarding party to *Niels Ebbesen,* whatever its cause, was in fact the best solution; nothing would have been gained by the taking to Aberdeen of a Danish naval officer and a Danish rating on board a British trawler which had escaped from the jurisdiction of Danish and Faroese authorities.

"The second imputation was the existence or non-existence of interference by H.M.S. *Troubridge* with a possible attempt by the *Niels Ebbesen* to put back the boarding party on *Red Crusader.* The Commission on this second point also has only to take note of the withdrawal of any allegation by the Danish Government relating to that question.

* * *

"As a result of the proceedings in connection with Chapter Three, the Commission finds: that Commander Griffiths and the other officers of the British Royal Navy made every effort to avoid any recourse to violence between *Niels Ebbesen* and *Red Crusader.* Such an attitude and conduct were impeccable."

[Unreported.]

NOTE.—On April 4, 1962, the Lord Privy Seal, a Minister in the British Government, said in the House of Commons:

> "In accordance with the Agreement for reference to the Commission, Her Majesty's Government accepts its findings as final." *House of Commons Debates,* Vol. 657, Written Answers, col. 43.

On January 23, 1963, the Joint Under-Secretary of State for Foreign Affairs made the following statement in the House of Commons:

> "Her Majesty's Government and the Danish Government have now completed their consultation about the Report of the Commission of Enquiry into the incidents affecting the Scottish trawler 'Red Crusader' at the end of May 1961. In their desire to remove a source of disagreement between them, the two Governments have decided that the incident should be settled by a mutual waiver of all claims and charges arising out of the incident. These waivers enter into effect forthwith. The owners of the trawler have concurred in this settlement.
>
> "As a result Skipper Wood and the 'Red Crusader' are free to enter Danish waters without fear of arrest in relation to the events of May 1961, and the owners' claim for compensation has been dropped. The two Governments consider that the incident can now be considered closed, though without prejudice to the view on points of law maintained by each Government." *House of Commons Debates,* Vol. 670, Written Answers, cols. 77–78.

* * *

Conciliation Commission on the Continental Shelf Area between Iceland and Jan Mayen: Report and Recommendations to the Governments of Iceland and Norway*

Commission

The Honorable Elliot L. Richardson, Chairman

H.E. Hans G. Andersen, Conciliator for Iceland

H.E. Jens Evensen, Conciliator for Norway

Washington, D.C., 1981

Section 1

Brief Examination of the Agreement between
Iceland and Norway of May 28, 1980.

On May 28, 1980 the Governments of Iceland and Norway concluded an Agreement concerning fishery and continental shelf questions. Articles 1–8 of this Agreement deal with fishery questions.

In the preamble of the Agreement it was recognized that Iceland should have an economic zone of 200 miles pursuant to the Icelandic Law on Territorial Sea, Continental Shelf and Economic Zone of June 1, 1979. The shortest distance between Iceland and Jan Mayen is about 290 nautical miles. During the negotiations of the aforementioned agreement the Icelandic Government advanced the view that Iceland was entitled to a continental shelf area extending beyond the 200-mile economic zone. Since no agreement was reached on this question during the negotiations, the parties agreed to refer it to a Conciliation Commission to be established in accordance with Article 9 of the agreement.

Article 9 reads:

> "The question of the dividing line for the shelf in the area between Iceland and Jan Mayen shall be the subject of continued negotiations.
>
> For this purpose the Parties agree to appoint at the earliest opportunity a Conciliation Commission composed of three members, of which each Party appoints one national member. The Chairman of the Commission shall be appointed by the Parties jointly.
>
> The Commission shall have as its mandate the submission of recommendations with regard to the dividing line for the shelf area between Iceland and Jan Mayen. In preparing such recommendations the Commission shall take into account Iceland's strong economic interests in these sea areas, the existing geographical and geological factors and other special circumstances.
>
> The Commission shall adopt its own rules of procedure. The unanimous recommendations of the Commission shall be submitted to the two Governments at the earliest opportunity. The parties envisage the presentation of the recommendations within five months of the appointment of the Commission.
>
> These recommendations of the Commission are not binding on the Parties; but during their further negotiations the Parties will pay reasonable regard to them."

---

* 20 I.L.M. 797 (1981) (Note in ILM: "Reproduced from the text provided to *International Legal Materials* by the Embassy of Iceland at Washington, D.C. I.L.M. page numbers have been substituted where appropriate.")

* * *

Section III

Jan Mayen: Geography and Geology

Jan Mayen is an island situated at the Northern end of the Jan Mayen Ridge

....

Jan Mayen is an entirely volcanic island. It was formed during the last 10–12 million years. The rocks are lava (alkali basalt) and other volcanic material. The island is volcanically active to-day, with frequent earthquakes. The most recent volcanic eruption was in 1970, when lava, ash, smoke and steam flowed out through a 6 km long fracture on the northeastern side of Beerensburg. The lava flowed to the coast where a coastal terrace of $4km^2$ was built. Volcanic eruptions have also been reported by whalers in 1732 and 1818.

The Norwegian Meteorological Institute established a meteorological station on Jan Mayen in 1912. The station has been permanently staffed since that time except for one year when the Second World War broke out. Several other permanent stations have been added since that time for LORAN A and C, CONSOL, Coast-radio, etc. Most of these stations are under the administration of the Ministry of Defense. Between thirty and forty people live throughout the winter on the eastern coast in the central part of the island. This is also where the stations and the airport are located. Roads connect the installations and living quarters.

Section IV

Status of Islands

Article 121 of the Draft Convention on the Law of the Sea (Informal Text) of August 27, 1980 reads as follows:

Article 121

Regime of Islands

1. An island is a naturally formed area of land surrounded by water, which is above water at high tide.
2. Except as provided for in paragraph 3, the territorial sea, the contiguous zone, the exclusive economic zone and the continental shelf of an island are determined in accordance with the provisions of this Convention applicable to other land territory.
3. Rocks which cannot sustain human habitation or economic life of their own shall have no exclusive economic zone or continental shelf.

In the opinion on of the Conciliation Commission this article reflects the present status of international law on this subject. It follows from the brief description of Jan Mayen in Section III of this report that Jan Mayen must be considered as an island. Paragraphs 1 and 2 of Article 121 are thus applicable to it.

Therefore, Jan Mayen is entitled to a territorial sea, an economic zone and a continental shelf. On the other hand, it must be kept in mind that Articles 74 and 83 concerning delimitation are also applicable. The first paragraphs of these articles read as follows:

Article 74

Delimitation of the exclusive economic zone between States with opposite or adjacent coasts

1. The delimitation of the exclusive economic zone between States with opposite or adjacent coasts shall be effected by agreement in conformity with international

law. Such an agreement shall be in accordance with equitable principles, employing the median or equidistance line, where appropriate, and taking account of all circumstances prevailing in the area concerned.

Article 83
Delimitation of the continental shelf between States with opposite or adjacent coasts

1. The delimitation of the continental shelf between States with opposite or adjacent coasts shall be effected by agreement in conformity with international law. Such an agreement shall be in accordance with equitable principles, employing the median or equidistance line, where appropriate, and taking account of all circumstances prevailing in the area concerned.

According to these provisions such delimitation shall be effected *by agreement* between the parties in conformity with international law. The parties have concluded such agreement on May 28, 1980 implicitly recognizing that Iceland shall have a full economic zone of 200 nautical miles in areas where the distance between Iceland and Jan Mayen is less than 400 miles. The agreement also provides that Norway will establish a fishing zone around Jan Mayen. Such a zone of 200 nautical miles was established around Jan Mayen by Norwegian Royal Decree of May 23, 1980, with effect from May 29, 1980. The Royal Decree provides that the boundaries with neighboring countries shall be affected by agreement.

The Conciliation Commission will consider the continental shelf problems involved in the remaining sections of this report.

* * *

Section VI
Possible Methods and Approaches

* * *

As mentioned in Section IV, Jan Mayen, as an island, is in principle entitled to its own territorial sea, contiguous zone, exclusive economic zone and continental shelf (Article 121 of the Draft Convention). On the other hand, where boundary questions arise with neighboring states, the principles pertaining to delimitation are applicable to Jan Mayen (Articles 15, 74, and 83 of the Draft Convention).

In state practice a wide variety of solutions have been used in regard to drawing boundary lines. Frequently the median line has been chosen as providing an equitable solution. In other cases account has been taken of special circumstances leading to a great diversity of solutions in order to accommodate the relevant factors of each case.

Islands belonging to a state and lying in the vicinity of its coasts are ordinarily given full weight for delimitation purposes. Where both coastal states have islands along their coasts, examples are found where a "trade-off" takes place by ignoring the islands on both sides when drawing the boundary line. Where islands are situated within the 200-mile economic zone of another state, the "enclave principle" has sometimes been utilized to give them territorial seas. There are other examples in which islands have been given limited weight, particularly in straits and other narrow areas.

Finally, there are examples of agreements for joint development and cooperation in overlapping areas of continental shelves between neighboring countries.

In its judgment of February 20, 1969 in the North Sea Continental Shelf Case, the International Court of Justice emphasized the wide variety of situations as follows:

> "93. In fact there is no legal limit to the considerations which States may take account of for the purpose of making sure that they apply equitable procedures, and more often than not it is the balancing-up of all such considerations that will produce this result rather than one to the exclusion of all others. The problem of the relative weight to be accorded to different considerations naturally varies with the circumstances of the case." (I.C.J. Reports 1969 p. 51.)

Having in view the broad scope of the considerations that may appropriately be recognized in formulating its recommendations, the Commission concluded that an approach should be used which takes into account both the fact that agreement by Iceland and Norway on Iceland's 200-mile economic zone has already given Iceland a considerable area beyond the median line and the fact that the uncertainties with respect to the resource potential of the area create a need for further research and exploration. Rather, therefor, than propose a demarcation line for the continental shelf different from the economic zone line, the Commission recommends adoption of a joint development agreement covering substantially all of the area offering any significant prospect of hydrocarbon production. The Commission's reasons for this recommendation include the desire to further promote cooperation and friendly relations between Iceland and Norway. Special consideration has also been given to the following factors:

(a) Iceland is totally dependent on imports of hydrocarbon products.

(b) The shelf surrounding Iceland is considered by scientists to have very low hydrocarbon potential.

(c) The Jan Mayen Ridge between Jan Mayen and the 200-mile economic zone of Iceland is the only area which is considered to have the possibility of finding hydrocarbons. The experts consider, however, the whole area to be a high geological risk.

(d) The water depths overlying the Jan Mayen Ridge are too great to permit exploration using present technology. The distances from the natural markets for hydrocarbons—especially gas—are great. Consequently, very large hydrocarbon discoveries would seem necessary in order to make such finds commercial.

The Report goes on to propose details for a joint development scheme involving the two governments and oil companies.

Sven M.G. Koopmans, *Diplomatic Dispute Settlement: The Use of Inter-State Conciliation**

A substantially different conciliation was undertaken in the mid-1980s between Egypt and Israel. The Camp David accords of 1979, which brought peace between Egypt and Israel, required the two countries to demarcate the boundary between them.[287] There were disagreements on the location of the border in the Sinai desert, largely resulting

* (2008).

287. G. Lagergren, 'The Taba Tribunal, 1986–89,' (1989) I *RADIC* 525; p. Weil, 'Some Observations on the Arbitral Award in the Taba Case,' (1989) 23 *Israel Law Review* 1; R. Lapidoth, 'Some Reflections on the Taba Award,' (1992) 35 *GYIL* 224; P.D. Trooboff, H. Ding and S. Koenig, 'Boundary Dispute Concerning the Taba Area', (1989) 83 *AJIL* 590; D.W. Bowett, 'The Taba Award of 29 September 1988,' (1989) 23 *Israel Law Review* 429; E. Lauterpacht, 'The Taba Case; Some Recollections and Reflections,' (1989) 23 *Israel Law Review* 443.

from unclear demarcation exercises in the early 20th century, when the border divided English—and Turkish—controlled area. In 1986, the parties agreed to put the dispute to an arbitration tribunal, consisting of five members, including one national of each party. The mandate of the tribunal was limited: it would have to choose from among the border pillar positions put forward by the parties. At the same time, the president of the tribunal had to select some of his fellow arbitrators to form a separate body, to attempt conciliation *during* the arbitration proceedings.[288]

* * *

Judge Bellet was chosen as chairman of the conciliation chamber, of which the respective Egyptian and Israeli arbitrators, sultan and Lapidoth, were also members. It appears that the conciliators assumed functions resembling those of a mediator rather than a conciliator, in that they did not present the parties with a report of the issues in dispute. Nevertheless, as the conciliation phase took place towards the end of the written stage of the proceedings, the conciliatory work was necessarily based on a thorough investigation of the dispute.

The Compromis provided that the conciliation mandate expired at completion of the written proceedings. The conciliators decided, however, that they wished to take into consideration the arguments contained in the final written submissions. Therefore, bending the rules somewhat, it was agreed that the deadline for these submissions in the arbitral proceedings was extended with one month, while they would nevertheless be 'informally submitted' to the conciliators at the original date. The commission did however only meet once, two days after the 'informal submission'. Further work was done by Judge Bellet, acting alone. Four weeks later, at the expiry of the commission's mandate, Judge Bellet reported that the Chamber had not been able to make any recommendation for settlement.[289]

Insiders have given sparse comments on the precise reasons for the conciliation's failure.[290] Israel's arbitrator/conciliator Lapidoth considered it preferable that the conciliation and arbitration stage would not have been concurrent, but did not see this as the reason for the failure. On the other hand, Bowett, counsel to Egypt, recommends the option for future occasions.[291] It is noted that a concurrent mediation conducted by a US State Department official was also unsuccessful. Israel's counsel Elihu Lauterpacht reasons that in the light of the pending arbitration neither side was prepared to give the impression that it was willing to concede any points. The basis of the failure may of course have essentially been intransigence of the parties, and the fact that, unlike Belgium and Denmark in the *Gorm and Svava* Case, Egypt and Israel were not on equally friendly footing, and that the issue of demarcating Israel's borders was not an isolated matter. Lapidoth hints that over time the positions of the parties became more entrenched, and that in the advanced stages of arbitration, acceptance of a compromise may be seen by the national audiences as an admission of failure.

---

288. Agreement to Arbitrate the Boundary Dispute concerning the Taba Beachfront (Egypt-Israel) (11 September 1986), (1987) 26 *ILM* 1 Annex Art. 9.

289. Ibid., Art. 10; G. Lagergren, 'The Taba Tribunal, 1986–89,' (1989) 1 *RADIC* 525, 528.

290. E. Lauterpacht, 'The Taba Case; Some Recollections and Reflections,' (1989) 23 *Israel Law Review* 443; D.W. Bowett, 'The Taba Award of 29 September 1988,' 23 *Israel Law Review* 429; R. Lapidoth, 'Some Reflections on the Taba Award,' (1992) 35 *GYIL* 224, 237–40.

291. D.W. Bowett, 'The Taba Award of 29 September 1988,' (1989) 23 *Israel Law Review* 429.

Notes and Questions on Inquiry and Conciliation

1. Compare mediation, inquiry, and conciliation. What are the advantages and disadvantages of mediation compared with inquiry and conciliation? What are the advantages and disadvantages of inquiry compared with conciliation?

2. Inquiry appears to be making a return, especially in the area of armed conflict. Although the several inquiries described below do not mention the Geneva Conventions, the Conventions provide for just such commissions in the case of a dispute over the conduct of armed conflict. *See* Geneva Convention IV Relative to the Protection of Civilian Persons in Time of War art. 149, Aug. 12, 1949, 75 U.N.T.S. 287:

> At the request of a Party to the conflict, an inquiry shall be instituted, in a manner to be decided between the interested Parties, concerning any alleged violation of the Convention.
>
> If agreement has not been reached concerning the procedure for the inquiry, the Parties should agree on the choice of an umpire who will decide upon the procedure to be followed.
>
> Once the violation has been established, the Parties to the conflict shall put an end to it and shall repress it with the least possible delay.

See also, Geneva Convention III Relative to the Treatment of Prisoners of War art. 132, Aug. 12, 1949, 75 U.N.T.S. 135.

3. During 2000–2002, two commissions of inquiry were formed to investigate conflict in the Middle East. One was the Mitchell Commission, formed in November 2000 to investigate the origins of the violence which broke out in September 2000 between Palestinians and Israelis. Matthew Less, *U.S. Names Panel to Probe Mideast Violence Ahead of White House Talks,* Agence France-Presse, Nov. 7, 2000. The Commission issued its report in April 2001. *See* Report of the Sharm el Sheikh Fact-Finding Committee, http://www.consilium.europa.eu/uedocs/cms_data/docs/pressdata/en/reports/acf319.pdf.

A year later, the UN Secretary-General Kofi Annan formed a fact-finding commission to look into claims of a massacre by Israeli troops in the Jenin Palestinian Refugee Camp. John Lancaster, *Israel Sets Conditions for Jenin Camp Probe; UN Team to Investigate Circumstances of Assault,* Wash. Post, Apr. 21, 2002, at A16. Eventually, Israel refused to cooperate with the inquiry.... [A]n Israeli official said Sharon objected to the makeup of the fact-finding team, to be led by former Finnish president Martti Ahtisaari. The other members are Sadako Ogata, the former U.N. high commissioner for refugees, and Cornelio Sommaruga, a former president of the International Committee of the Red Cross.... Israel has a long history of contentious dealings with the Red Cross.... The Israeli leader also apparently believes the team's mandate is overly broad and is skeptical of the team's ability to fairly evaluate the challenge faced by Israeli troops fighting house to house in a dense urban neighborhood, the official added. Sharon fears, he said, that a critical finding could be used as a pretext for introducing international peacekeeping forces, which Israel has long resisted.... "You don't want to set yourself up for a trap," the official said. "We don't want an open-ended probe that could extend to massive and open-ended U.N. intervention."

> Following a meeting tonight with Israel's U.N. Ambassador, Yehuda Lancry, Annan agreed to briefly postpone the mission in order to hear Israel's concerns, but said he expected the team to arrive in the Middle East by Saturday. Lancry said that an Israeli delegation would travel to New York on Thursday to discuss the composition and scope of the mission. "The team should be more balanced

> and should include military and counter terrorism experts," Lancry said. "The mandate of the fact-finding mission should cover not only the military operation of Israel, but the terrorist network which has flourished in the Jenin refugee camps."

John Lancaster and Craig Whitlock, *Israel Reverses Position on Probe of Jenin Assault; U.N. Inquiry Delayed Over U.S. Urging,* Wash. Post, Apr. 24, 2002, at A01 (some paragraph breaks eliminated).

4. In April 2009, the United Nations Human Rights Council (UNHRC) formed a fact-finding mission into Israel's use of force in the Palestinian Occupied Territory of Gaza. The Israeli incursion called Operation Cast Lead was a response to indiscriminate, occasional rocket fire that originated in Gaza. Operation Cost Lead began on December 27, 2008 and lasted about three weeks. Between 1200 and 1400 Palestinians were killed, while 13 Israelis died. A prominent Jewish South African Supreme Court Justice and prosecutor of the International Criminal Tribunal for the former Yugoslavia, Richard Goldstone led the mission. Israel again refused to cooperate. The "Goldstone Report" was issued anyway finding that both sides had violated the law of armed conflict and human rights law. After a campaign of harsh criticism against Goldstone by Israel and Israeli supporters worldwide, Goldstone wrote an op-ed in 2011 saying he no longer believed that Israel had intentionally targeted civilians. Richard Goldstone, *Reconsidering the Goldstone Report on Israel and War Crimes*, Washington Post (April 1, 2011), http://www.washingtonpost.com/opinions/reconsidering-the-goldstone-report-on-israwl-and-war-crimes/2011/04/01/AFg111JCstory.html. The other members of the fact-finding mission, Hina Jilani, Christine Chinkin, and Desmond Travers stood by their earlier findings. Hina Jilani, et al., *Goldstone Report: Statement Issued by Members of UN Mission on Gaza War*, Guardian (Apr. 14, 2011), http://www.guardian.co.uk/commentisfree/2011/apr/14/goldstone-report-statement-un-gaza.

What was the purpose of the UNHRC fact-finding mission to Gaza? Was it dispute settlement? What was the purpose of the Jewish mission described in the previous note?

What impact might these two experiences of fact-finding have on the future of this method of dispute resolution?

5. In 2002, the U.S. and Canada instituted commissions to look into a friendly fire incident in Afghanistan.

> Two American pilots who mistakenly bombed and killed Canadian troops in Afghanistan were charged with manslaughter and assault last night in a case that has strained relations between the United States and Canada. Majors Harry "Psycho" Schmidt and William Umbach bombed Canadian soldiers on the night of April 18 this year, killing four and injuring eight more. A joint US-Canadian inquiry found that the pilots had failed to exercise caution or follow procedures.

Kathy Kay & Richard Cleroux, *US Pilots Charged Over Friendly Fire Deaths,* Times (London), Sept. 14, 2002, at 16. A similar inquiry was agreed in a case arising in the U.S.-led invasion of Iraq between the U.S. and Turkey in which U.S. soldiers arrested Turkish soldiers, although Turkey was on the same side as the U.S.

> US Ambassador to Turkey Robert Pearson said on Tuesday [8 July] that the USA provided preliminary information to Turkey about detention of Turkish soldiers on 4 July in Sulaymaniyah ...

> Pearson said that the mentioned information would also constitute a part of the issues to be taken up by the joint commission to be founded by Turkish and American officials, adding: "We wanted to provide this information to Turkish government and Turkish Armed Forces so that they could understand better the basis of the 4 July incident."

Turkish-US Probe into N. Iraq Arrests Will Bring "Objective Results"—ENVOY, BBC MONITORING EUROPEAN, Jul. 9, 2003.

6. Who should be a member of an *ad hoc* fact-finding commission or commission of inquiry? In the materials above, can you argue any particular rule exists regarding who can be a commissioner? Should there be such rules? What about good faith and/or confidentiality and neutrality? What about rules requiring qualifications? And what about the all-important rule governing arbitration and litigation: *audi alteram partem* (hear both sides)? What if one side refuses to co-operate and it is not possible to hear its side?

7. Are any general rules regarding conciliation commissions applicable to *ad hoc* conciliation commissions? What rules would you suggest in comparing the successful Jan Mayen conciliation with the unsuccessful Taba conciliation?

8. In 1992, the Organization for Security and Co-operation in Europe adopted the Stockholm Convention on Conciliation and Arbitration within the CSCE, *available at* http://www.osce.org.

The Convention came in to force in 1994 but after 17 years has not been used. Why do you think formal conciliation, unlike formal inquiry, is so rarely used? Can you argue that *informal* conciliation is, by contrast, used very frequently? Consider the difference between mediation and conciliation. Can you think of some dispute settlement attempts that were labeled "mediation" but really better fit the category "conciliation"?

9. Commissions of Inquiry are used by the ILO to address violations of certain fundamental Conventions. Two commissions have been set up in the last 10 years to address violations by Belarus and Zimbabwe of the Right to Organize and Collective Bargaining conventions: *See* ILO website: http://www.ilo.org/ilolex/english/INQUIRY.htm; and Keri Tapiola, Lee Swepston, *The ILO and the Impact of Labor Standards: Working on the Ground after an ILO Commission of Inquiry*, 21 STAN. L. & POL'Y REV. 513 (2010).

10. The UN Commission on International Trade Law (UNCITRAL), which develops rules and model laws for use in private international commercial transactions, has developed both conciliation rules and a Model Law on Conciliation. *Available at* http://www.uncitral.org/pdf/english/texts/arbitration/MI-conc-e.pdf. Both the rules and the model law state, in contrast to international law authorities, that mediation and conciliation are synonymous. Mediation is becoming a common practice in international commerce. If parties begin to use the terms mediation and conciliation synonymously in that robust field, can you predict the impact on conciliation in international law? Is the potential elimination of conciliation as a separate procedure important? See Koopmans comment above on the terminological confusion.

11. The International Centre for the Settlement of Investment Disputes (ICSID) is part of the World Bank and is located, like the Bank, in Washington, D.C. The Centre seeks to settle "mixed" investment disputes, disputes between states and private parties. The primary method used at ICSID is arbitration, but ICSID also provides conciliation. As in other contexts mentioned in this Chapter, resort to conciliation is infrequent. Of about 225 concluded cases as of mid-2011, only six were requests for conciliation.

*About ICSID**

On a number of occasions in the past, the World Bank as an institution and the President of the Bank in his personal capacity have assisted in mediation or conciliation of investment disputes between governments and private foreign investors. The creation of the International Centre for the Settlement of Investment Disputes (ICSID) in 1966 was in part intended to relieve the President and the staff of the burden of becoming involved in such disputes. But the Bank's overriding consideration in creating ICSID was the belief that an institution specially designed to facilitate the settlement of investment disputes between governments and foreign investors could help to promote increased flows of international investment.

* * *

Pursuant to the Convention, ICSID provides facilities for the conciliation and arbitration of disputes between member countries and investors who qualify as nationals of other member countries. Recourse to ICSID conciliation and arbitration is entirely voluntary.

* * *

ICSID conciliations are found on the ICSID Website: http://icsid.worldbank.org/ICSID/Index.jsp and include:

—Shareholders of SESAM v. Central African Republic (CONC/07/1), Report issued 13 August 2008.

—Togo Electricité v. Republic of Togo (CONC/05/1), Report issued 6 April 2006 (Parties entered into arbitration immediately after the report issued (ARB/06/7).)

—TG World Petroleum Ltd. v. Republic of Niger (CONC/03/1) (The parties settled before a commission was constituted.)

—SEDITEX Engineering v. Madagascar (CONC/94/1), Report issued 19 July 1996 (These parties were also engaged in CONC/82/1, but that dispute settled before a commission was constituted.)

—Tesoro Petroleum Corp. v. Trinidad & Tobago (CONC/83/1) (Settled; report issued 27 November 1985.)

On the first conciliation, see, Lester Nurick and Stephen J. Schnably, The First ICSID Conciliation: Tesoro Petroleum Corporation v. Trinidad and Tobago, ICSID Review-Foreign Investment Review 340–53 (1986).

The Warn Territory Dispute

Xanadu and Yarow are nations that share a common border. In 1960, both Xanadu and Yarow won independence from the Kingdom of Unity (K.U.), which borders both states to the north. Along this common border is a disputed territory, Warn, which both Xanadu and Yarow claim, but where most people identify with the common cultural and ethnic traditions of Yarow and K.U. After 20 years of escalating tensions, both Xanadu and Yarow invade the area and an armed conflict, lasting 5 years, ensues. In 1985, Yarow, whose forces had almost completely overrun Xanadu, demanded that

* http://www.worldbank.org/icsid/about/main.htm.

Xanadu sign a treaty conveying most of Warn to Yarow. Under the treaty the new border was to be along the Elin river that flows south from K.U. Under the terms of the treaty:

> Any future disputes regarding the borders of Warn must be referred to arbitration, with the King of K.U. as the sole arbitrator, after a period of formal discussions that must be carried on in the good offices of our common and neutral neighbor to the north, K.U.

In 2009, a drought hits the area and the Elin river dries up. Xanadu immediately invades, claiming the treaty was no longer valid, since the river was no longer in existence, and that Xanadu had title to all of Warn all along under the doctrine of *uti possidetis*. Yarow has requested K.U. to begin the "good offices" process by inviting Xanadu to a neutral forum in which discussions can proceed. Xanadu responds with a statement saying it refuses to participate in negotiations with Yarow, but would consider going forward with arbitration as long as K.U. did not appoint an arbitrator to the tribunal.

1) Can Xanadu and Yarow submit their dispute to arbitration? What is required before they do so—negotiation, good offices, or something else?
2) Do Xanadu and Yarow have duties of good faith or confidentiality in their discussions over the Warn territory?
3) If the UN Secretary-General offers assistance and Xanadu and Yarrow accept but the dispute is still not resolved, may Yarrow then demand arbitration by the King of K.U.?

II. Binding Methods

A. Arbitration

Chapter Five

Arbitration

Introduction

Arbitration, in contrast to formal inquiry and conciliation, is a long-established method of international dispute resolution. As the history in Chapter One describes, formal arbitration was included as a method of dispute resolution in the very treaty that gave rise to modern international law, the Peace of Westphalia of 1648. Like inquiry and conciliation, however, arbitration is not often used in inter-state dispute resolution. Rather, it is the method of choice to resolve international commercial disputes; indeed, international commercial arbitration is booming. This trend portends that arbitration may begin to challenge the primacy of negotiation, and adjudication as the dominant methods of inter-state dispute resolution. Still, more and more inter-state disputes, especially boundary and resource-sharing issues are coming to arbitral tribunals.

International arbitration refers to a process of dispute resolution where a third party reaches a binding decision (usually called an award) to resolve the dispute. The International Law Commission defines arbitration as "the procedure for the settlement of disputes between states by a binding award on the basis of law and as the result of an undertaking voluntarily accepted."[1] Most arbitrations involving states and international organizations are *ad hoc*, organized especially for the purposes of resolving one dispute. The parties choose the arbitrators, the law applicable—including equitable principles—the procedural rules, the location, and other details. This control by the parties over the design of the procedure distinguishes arbitration from judicial settlement.

In any particular case, disputants may decide to use arbitration or they may be obligated to arbitrate under the terms of a pre-existing treaty, as was the case in the *Headquarters Agreement Case* studied in Chapter Two. The Iran-U.S. Claims Tribunal is an *ad hoc* arbitral tribunal, but one in existence for decades. It is a sort of semi-permanent arbitral tribunal. Several permanent institutions also exist to organize arbitrations—the Permanent Court of Arbitration (PCA), for example, is a secretariat with a set of procedural rules, a list of potential arbitrators, and space to conduct arbitrations in the Peace Palace in The Hague.[2] Parties conduct arbitrations under the PCA's auspices for convenience and to ensure a professional arbitration.

Many treaties not only require arbitration, but also provide detailed provisions for the procedure itself. The WTO and North America Free Trade Agreement (NAFTA) both

1. Report of the International Law Commission, Official Records of the General Assembly, Eighth Session, Supp. No. 9, ¶ 16, *cited in* J.L. Simpson & Hazel Fox, International Arbitration, Law and Practice 1 (1959).

2. *See* www.pca-cpa.org. *See also*, *Permanent Court of Arbitration, Summaries of Awards*, 1999–2009 (Belinda Mcmahon and Fedelma Claire Smith eds. 2010).

provide for arbitration as aspects of their comprehensive dispute settlement systems. The UN Convention on the Law of the Sea has special provisions for arbitration. Finally, it would be possible for states and international organizations to use the facilities of arbitration institutions that more typically deal with international commercial arbitration, such as the International Chamber of Commerce in Paris. In the last chapter we saw ICSID's facility for mixed conciliation and arbitration.

These elaborate institutions and provisions for arbitration exist because the outcome of arbitration is binding, unlike other procedures we have studied so far. This fact adds a new dimension to the discussion. In addition to the focus on resolving the dispute, we now have the issue of getting compliance with the binding decision of the arbitrators. Before a party can be held to a binding decision, the party must consent to arbitration in the first place and the arbitration must proceed according to accepted rules. In this chapter, we will discuss the all-important agreement to arbitrate. This agreement contains the parties' consent to abide by the outcome of the arbitration[3] and establishes what exactly the parties have consented to in terms of the scope of the arbitration. The Southern Blue Fin Tuna (SBT) Arbitration, the first excerpt, concerns whether parties have in fact given their consent to arbitrate. The arbitrators place a heavy emphasis on finding specific consent before holding that parties have agreed to arbitration. The second excerpt, from the U.S.-France Air Services Arbitration, is a case in which the states clearly agreed to arbitrate, but one party believes the other is hesitating to do so.

The agreement to arbitrate contains the assent or consent to arbitrate. It is this consent that in turn gives rise to an obligation to resolve the dispute in arbitration and to abide by the outcome. It also obligates the parties to comply with the orders of the tribunal during the pendency of the arbitration. Chapter Six considers the agreement to arbitrate in addition to cases in which arbitral tribunals have made rather extensive orders to parties during the course of a proceeding in order to prevent a party's action from undermining the arbitration. International courts routinely issue such orders; it is recognized that their authority flows from their inherent power as judicial bodies. It is not so certain, however, whether arbitral tribunals have such inherent power. Arbitral tribunals are not courts. A court may establish the scope of a given adjudication, but it is the parties involved that control this question in their agreement to arbitrate or in a specialized agreement providing the details for the arbitration, called the *compromis*. If the arbitrators make a decision that reaches beyond the *compromis*, the losing party may well challenge its obligation to comply on the basis of the doctrine of *excès de pouvoir*—the exercise of excessive power by the tribunal. Arbitral awards may also be challenged if the arbitration was not conducted according to the rules of arbitral procedure. A variety of such issues that can arise in the course of an arbitration are presented in Chapter Seven.

Finally, Chapter Eight takes up the last topic in our discussion of arbitration—compliance with and enforcement of arbitral awards. This topic is of central importance for all binding methods of dispute resolution. While it is widely accepted that the success of international commercial arbitration is due largely to the impact of the New York Convention on the Recognition and Enforcement of Foreign Arbitral Awards,[4] this Convention is of only limited usefulness in arbitrations involving states and/or international organizations. The Convention opened the way for straightforward enforcement of arbitral awards by national courts. National courts tend to control assets

---

3. Hazel Fox, *States and the Undertaking to Arbitrate*, 37 INT'L & COMP. L. Q. 1, 6 (1988).

4. 7 ILM 1046 (1968); *see* A.J. VAN DEN BERG, THE NEW YORK ARBITRATION CONVENTION OF 1958 (1981).

and, thus, can satisfy monetary awards. This ability to actually get an award enforced made arbitration an attractive option for parties wishing to protect their interests in major international commercial agreements. International public law arbitrations involving boundary disputes, aviation rights, fishing rights, and so on are not so easily enforced by national courts, even if states agree to give the role to a national court. The *Rainbow Warrior* case, demonstrates the difficulty of getting an arbitral award enforced.

One avenue that a number of states have used when facing a recalcitrant award creditor is to return to the tribunal or the International Court of Justice to get the award "clarified." Following clarification, parties will often comply—certainly when the ICJ acts as a court of review for major international arbitrations. The ICJ's prestige has tended to induce compliance with most of its decisions. Even the ICJ, however, has limited means of enforcing its decisions. Indeed, it may have been the realization of how difficult it would be to get France to comply with the arbitral award in Rainbow Warrior that led the arbitrators to reach their controversial decision that France had in fact complied.

The countermeasure is the ultimate means of enforcing an arbitral award—or any rule of international law. Countermeasures are discussed in the Air Services Arbitration excerpt in the second part of this chapter. The Air Services arbitrators set out the rules for using countermeasures to induce a party to comply with the parties' agreement to arbitrate. Countermeasures are also available to induce a party to comply with a final award. The right to use countermeasures to enforce rules and agreements in international law is part of why we can say that agreements to arbitrate are binding, arbitral awards are binding, and international legal rules in general are binding.[5]

International Law Commission

Annex

Model Rules on Arbitral Procedure*

Article 1

1. Any undertaking to have recourse to arbitration in order to settle a dispute between States constitutes a legal obligation which must be carried out in good faith.

2. Such an undertaking results from agreement between the parties and may apply to existing disputes (arbitration ad hoc) or to disputes arising in the future (arbitration treaties—arbitration clauses).

3. The undertaking shall result from a written instrument, whatever the form of the instrument may be.

4. The procedures offered to States Parties to a dispute by this draft shall not be compulsory unless the States concerned have agreed, either in the compromis or in some other undertaking, to have recourse thereto.

---

5. *See*, Mary Ellen O'Connell, The Power and Purpose of International Law, Insights from the Theory and Practice of Enforcement, Ch. 6 (2008).

* Documents of the Tenth Session, Including the Report of the Commission to the General Assembly, Arbitral Procedure [Agenda item 2], Document A/CN.4/113, II Y.B. Int'l L. Comm'n (1958).

Article 2

Unless there are earlier agreements which suffice for the purpose, for example in the undertaking to arbitrate itself, the parties having recourse to arbitration shall conclude a compromis which shall specify, as a minimum:

(a) The undertaking to arbitrate under which the dispute shall be submitted to the arbitrators;

(b) The subject-matter of the dispute and, if possible, the points on which the parties are or are not agreed;

(c) The method of constituting the tribunal and the number of arbitrators.

The compromis shall likewise include any other provisions deemed desirable by the Parties, such as:

(1) The rules of law and the principles, to be applied by the tribunal, and the right, if any, conferred on it to decide ex aequo et bono as though it had legislative functions in the matter;

(2) The power, if any, of the tribunal to make recommendations to the parties;

(3) Such power as may be conferred on the tribunal to make its own rules of procedure;

(4) The procedure to be followed by the tribunal, on condition that, once constituted, the tribunal shall remain free to override any provisions of the compromis which may prevent it from rendering its award;

(5) the number of members constituting a quorum for the conduct of the proceedings;

(6) The majority required for the award;

(7) The time-limit within which the award shall be rendered;

(8) The right of members of the tribunal to attach or not to attach dissenting opinions to the award;

(9) The languages to be employed in the proceedings before the tribunal;

(10) The manner in which the costs shall be divided;

(11) The services which the International Court of Justice may be asked to render.

This enumeration is not intended to be exhaustive.

Article 3

1. If, before the constitution of an arbitral tribunal, the parties to an undertaking to arbitrate disagree as to the existence of a dispute, or as to whether the existing dispute is wholly or partly within the scope of the obligation to arbitrate, such preliminary question shall, failing agreement between the parties upon the adoption of another procedure, be brought by them within three months either before the Permanent Court of Arbitration for summary judgement, or, preferably, before the International Court of Justice, likewise for summary judgement or for an advisory opinion.

2. In its decision on the question, either Court may prescribe the provisional measures to be taken for the protection of the respective interests of the parties. The decision shall be final.

3. If the arbitral tribunal has already been constituted, any dispute concerning arbitrability shall be referred to it.

Article 4

1. Immediately after the request made by one of the Governments parties to the dispute for the submission of the dispute to arbitration or after the decision on the arbitrability of the dispute, the parties to an undertaking to arbitrate shall take the necessary steps, either in the compromis or by special agreement, in order to arrive at the constitution of the arbitral tribunal.

2. If the tribunal is not constituted within three months from the date of the request made for the submission of the dispute to arbitration, or from the date of the decision on arbitrability, the President of the International Court of Justice shall at the request of either party appoint the arbitrators not yet designated. If the President is prevented from acting or is a national of one of the parties, the appointments shall be made by the Vice-President. If the Vice-President is prevented from acting or is a national of one of the parties, the appointments shall be made by the oldest member of the Court who is not a national of either party....

[The full text of the Model Rules is found in the Annex.]

United Nations Convention on the Law of the Sea

Part XV
Dispute Settlement

Section 1. General Provisions

Articles 279–285

Section 2. Compulsory Procedures Entailing Binding Decisions

Articles 286–296

Section 3. Limitations and Exceptions to Applicability of Section 2

Articles 297

Annex VII. Arbitration

Articles 1–13

See Annex

Southern Bluefin Tuna Case
(*Australia and New Zealand v. Japan*)

Award on Jurisdiction and Admissibility
August 4, 2000
rendered by the Arbitral Tribunal constituted under Annex VII of the United Nations Convention on the Law of the Sea*

the Arbitral Tribunal being composed of:

---

* International Centre for Settlement of Investment Disputes (ICSID) http://www.worldbank.org/icsid/index.html.

Judge Stephen M. Schwebel, President
H.E. Judge Florentino Feliciano
The Rt. Hon. Justice Sir Kenneth Keith, KBE
H.E. Judge Per Tresselt
Professor Chusei Yamada

* * *

II. Background to the Current Proceedings

21. Southern Bluefin Tuna (... "SBT") is a migratory species of pelagic fish that is included in the list of highly migratory species set out in Annex I of the United Nations Convention on the Law of the Sea. Southern Bluefin Tuna range widely through the oceans of the Southern Hemisphere, principally the high seas, but they also traverse the exclusive economic zones and territorial waters of some States, notably Australia, New Zealand and South Africa. They spawn in the waters south of Indonesia. The main market for the sale of Southern Bluefin Tuna is in Japan, where the fish is prized as a delicacy for sashimi.

22. It is common ground between the Parties that commercial harvest of Southern Bluefin Tuna began in the early 1950s and that, in 1961, the global catch peaked at 81,000 metric tons ("mt"). By the early 1980s, the SBT stock had been severely overfished; it was estimated that the parental stock had declined to 23–30% of its 1960 level. In 1982, Australia, New Zealand and Japan began informally to manage the catching of SBT. Japan joined with Australia and New Zealand in 1985 to introduce a global total allowable catch (hereafter, "TAC") for SBT, initially set at 38,650 mt. In 1989, a TAC of 11,750 tons was agreed, with national allocations of 6,065 tons to Japan, 5,265 tons to Australia and 420 tons to New Zealand; Japan, as the largest harvester of SBT, sustained the greatest cut. But the SBT stock continued to decline. In 1997, it was estimated to be in the order of 7–15% of its 1960 level. Recruitment of SBT stock—the entry of new fish into the fishery—was estimated in 1998 to be about one third of the 1960 level. The institution of total allowable catch restrictions by Japan, Australia and New Zealand to some extent has been offset by the entry into the SBT fishery of fishermen from the Republic of Korea, Taiwan and Indonesia, and some flag-of-convenience States. Whether, in response to TAC restrictions, the stock has in fact begun to recover is at the core of the dispute between Australia and New Zealand, on the one hand, and Japan, on the other. They differ over the current state and recovery prospects of SBT stock and the means by which scientific uncertainty in respect of those matters can best be reduced.

23. In 1993, Australia, Japan and New Zealand concluded the Convention for the Conservation of Southern Bluefin Tuna (hereafter, the "1993 Convention" or "CCSBT"). The provisions most pertinent to these proceedings are the following:

> "Recalling that Australia, Japan and New Zealand have already taken certain measures for the conservation and management of southern bluefin tuna;
>
> "Paying due regard to the rights and obligations of the Parties under relevant principles of international law;
>
> "Noting the adoption of the United Nations Convention on the Law of the Sea in 1982;
>
> "Noting that States have established exclusive economic or fishery zones within which they exercise, in accordance with international law, sovereign rights or jurisdiction for the purpose of exploring and exploiting, conserving and managing the living resources;

"Recognising that southern bluefin tuna is a highly migratory species which migrates through such zones;

"... Recognising that it is essential that they cooperate to ensure the conservation and optimum utilization of southern bluefin tuna;"

The Parties agreed inter alia that:

Article 3

The objective of this Convention is to ensure, through appropriate management, the conservation and optimum utilisation of southern bluefin tuna.

Article 4

Nothing in this Convention nor any measures adopted pursuant to it shall be deemed to prejudice the positions or views of any Party with respect to its rights and obligations under treaties and other international agreements to which it is party or its positions or views with respect to the law of the sea.

Article 5

1. Each Party shall take all action necessary to ensure the enforcement of this Convention and compliance with measures which become binding under paragraph 7 of Article 8.

2. The Parties shall expeditiously provide to the Commission for the Conservation of Southern Bluefin Tuna scientific information, fishing catch and effort statistics and other data relevant to the conservation of southern bluefin tuna and, as appropriate, ecologically related species.

3. The Parties shall cooperate in collection and direct exchange, when appropriate, of fisheries data, biological samples and other information relevant for scientific research on southern bluefin tuna and ecologically related species.

4. The Parties shall cooperate in the exchange of information regarding any fishing for southern bluefin tuna by nationals, residents and vessels of any State or entity not party to this Convention.

Article 6

1. The Parties hereby establish and agree to maintain the Commission for the Conservation of Southern Bluefin Tuna (hereinafter referred to as "the Commission").

Article 7

Each Party shall have one vote in the Commission. Decisions of the Commission shall be taken by a unanimous vote of the Parties present at the Commission meeting.

Article 8

1. The Commission shall collect and accumulate information described below.

* * *

3. For the conservation, management and optimum utilisation of southern bluefin tuna:

a. the Commission shall decide upon a total allowable catch and its allocation among the Parties unless the Commission decides upon other appropriate measures on the basis of the report and recommendations of the Scientific Committee.

* * *

7. All measures decided upon under paragraph 3 above shall be binding on the Parties.

* * *

Article 16

1. If any dispute arises between two or more of the Parties concerning the interpretation or implementation of this Convention, those Parties shall consult among themselves with a view to having the dispute resolved by negotiation, inquiry, mediation, conciliation, arbitration, judicial settlement or other peaceful means of their own choice.

2. Any dispute of this character not so resolved shall, with the consent in each case of all parties to the dispute, be referred for settlement to the International Court of Justice or to arbitration; but failure to reach agreement on reference to the International Court of Justice or to arbitration shall not absolve parties to the dispute from the responsibility of continuing to seek to resolve it by any of the various peaceful means referred to in paragraph 1 above.

3. In cases where the dispute is referred to arbitration, the arbitral tribunal shall be constituted as provided in the Annex to this Convention. The Annex forms an integral part of this Convention.

* * *

Article 20

Any Party may withdraw from this Convention twelve months after the date on which it formally notifies the Depositary of its intention to withdraw.

24. In May 1994, the Commission established by the 1993 Convention set a TAC at 11,750 tons, with the national allocations among Japan, Australia and New Zealand set out above. There has been no agreement in the Commission thereafter to change the TAC level or allotments. Japan from 1994 sought an increase in the TAC and in its allotment but any increase has been opposed by New Zealand and Australia. While the Commission initially maintained the TAC at existing levels due to this impasse, since 1998 it has been unable to agree upon any TAC. In the absence of a Commission decision, the Parties in practice have maintained their TAC as set in 1994. At the same time, Japan pressed in the Commission not only for a TAC increase, initially of 6000 tons and then of 3000 tons in its allotment, but also for agreement upon a joint Experimental Fishing Program ("EFP"), whose particular object would be to gather data in those areas where fishing for SBT no longer took place, with a view to reducing scientific uncertainty about recovery of the stock. Japan sought agreement upon its catching 6000 EFP tons annually, for three years, for experimental fishing, in addition to its commercial allotment; it subsequently reduced that request to 3000 tons, also the same amount that it sought by way of increase in its TAC. While the Commission in 1996 adopted a set of "Objectives and principles for the design and implementation of an experimental fishing program," it proved unable to agree upon the size of the catch that would be allowed under the EFP and on modalities of its execution. However, Australia, Japan and New Zealand are agreed on the objective of restoring the parental stock of Southern Bluefin Tuna to its 1980 level by the year 2020.

25. At a Commission meeting in 1998 Japan stated that, while it would voluntarily adhere to its previous quota for commercial SBT fishing, it would commence a unilateral, three-year EFP as of the summer of 1998. Despite vigorous protests by Australia and New Zealand over pursuance of any unilateral EFP, Japan conducted a pilot program with an estimated catch of 1,464 mt. in the summer of 1998.

26. In response, Australia and New Zealand formally requested urgent consultations and negotiations under Article 16(1) of the 1993 Convention. Despite intensive efforts within this framework to reach agreement on an experimental fishing program for 1999, an accord was not achieved. At a meeting in Canberra May 26–28, 1999, Australia was advised that, unless it accepted Japan's proposal for a 1999 joint experimental fishing program, Japan would recommence unilateral experimental fishing on June 1; and New Zealand was similarly so informed. Neither Australia nor New Zealand found Japan's proposal acceptable. While differences about the dimension of EFP tonnage had narrowed, they maintained that Japan's EFP was misdirected and that its design and analysis were fundamentally flawed. In their view, Japan's EFP did not justify what they saw as the significant increased risk to the SBT stock. They informed Japan that, if it recommenced unilateral experimental fishing on June 1, 1999 or thereafter, they would regard such action as a termination by Japan of negotiations under Article 16(1) of the 1993 Convention. Japan, which resumed its EFP on June 1, 1999, replied that it had no intention of terminating those negotiations. It maintained that independent scientific opinion had advised the Commission that Japan's EFP proposals were soundly conceived.

27. On June 23, 1999, Australia restated its position that the dispute did not relate solely to Japan's obligations under the 1993 Convention, but also involved its obligations under UNCLOS and customary international law. It considered that there had been a full exchange of views on the dispute for the purposes of Article 283(1) of UNCLOS, which provides that, "When a dispute arises between States Parties concerning the interpretation or application of this Convention, the parties to the dispute shall proceed expeditiously to an exchange of views regarding its settlement by negotiation or other peaceful means."

28. Also on June 23, 1999, Japan stated that it was ready to have the dispute resolved by mediation under the provisions of the 1993 Convention. Australia replied that it was willing to submit the dispute to mediation, provided that Japan agreed to cease its unilateral experimental fishing and that the mediation was expeditious. Japan responded that the question of its unilateral EFP could be discussed in the framework of mediation. On July 14, 1999, Japan reiterated its position that its experimental fishing was consistent with the 1993 Convention and that it could not accept the condition of its cessation in order for mediation to proceed. Japan declared that it was ready to have the dispute resolved by arbitration pursuant to Article 16(2) of the 1993 Convention, indicating however that it was not prepared to halt its unilateral EFP during its pendency though it was prepared to resume consultations about it. Thereafter Australia notified Japan that it viewed Japan's position as a rejection of Australia's conditional acceptance of mediation, and that Australia had decided to commence compulsory dispute resolution under Part XV of UNCLOS. It followed that it did not accept Japan's proposal for arbitration pursuant to Article 16(2) of the Convention. Australia emphasized the centrality of Japan's obligations under UNCLOS and under customary international law to the dispute and the need for those obligations to be addressed if the dispute were to be resolved. Australia reiterated its view that the conduct of Japan under the 1993 Convention was relevant to the issue of its compliance with UNCLOS obligations and may be taken into account in dispute settlement under Part XV of UNCLOS. Pending the constitution of the arbitral tribunal to which the dispute was being submitted under UNCLOS's Annex VII, Australia announced its intention to seek prescription of provisional measures under Article 290(5) of UNCLOS, including the immediate cessation of unilateral experimental fishing by Japan.

29. As the preambular references in the 1993 Convention quoted above confirm, the 1993 Convention was prepared in light of the provisions of the 1982 United Nations Convention on the Law of the Sea and the relevant principles of international law. UNCLOS

had not come into force in 1993, and in fact did not come into force for the three Parties to the instant dispute until 1996, but the Parties to the 1993 Convention regarded UNCLOS as an umbrella or framework Convention to be implemented in respect of Southern Bluefin Tuna by the adoption of the 1993 Convention.

30. In reliance upon provisions of UNCLOS and of general international law, including UNCLOS provisions for settlement of disputes (Part XV of UNCLOS), Australia and New Zealand thus sought in 1999 to interdict pursuance of Japan's unilateral EFP. They requested the establishment of an arbitral tribunal pursuant to Annex VII of UNCLOS, and sought provisional measures under Article 290(5) of UNCLOS, which provides:

> "Pending constitution of an arbitral tribunal to which a dispute is being submitted under this section, any court or tribunal agreed upon by the parties or, failing such agreement within two weeks from the date of the request for provisional measures, the International Tribunal for the Law of the Sea ... may prescribe ... provisional measures if it considers that prima facie the tribunal which is to be constituted would have jurisdiction and that the urgency of the situation so requires. Once constituted, the tribunal to which the dispute has been submitted may modify, revoke or affirm those provisional measures ..."

31. The Applicants' Statement of Claim filed in invoking arbitration under UNCLOS Annex VII maintained that the dispute turned on what the Applicants described as Japan's failure to conserve, and to cooperate in the conservation of, the SBT stock, as manifested, inter alia, by its unilateral experimental fishing for SBT in 1998 and 1999. The Applicants stated that the dispute concerned the interpretation and application of certain provisions of UNCLOS, and that the arbitral tribunal will be asked to take into account provisions of the 1993 Convention and the Parties' practice thereunder, as well as their obligations under general international law, "in particular the precautionary principle."

32. The provisions of UNCLOS centrally invoked by Australia and New Zealand were the following:

Article 64
Highly migratory species

1. The coastal State and other States whose nationals fish in the region for the highly migratory species listed in Annex I shall cooperate directly or through appropriate international organizations with a view to ensuring conservation and promoting the objective of optimum utilization of such species throughout the region, both within and beyond the exclusive economic zone. In regions for which no appropriate international organization exists, the coastal State and other States whose nationals harvest these species in the region shall cooperate to establish such an organization and participate in its work.

2. The provisions of paragraph 1 apply in addition to the other provisions of this Part.

Article 116
Right to fish on the high seas

All States have the right for their nationals to engage in fishing on the high seas subject to:

(a) their treaty obligations;

(b) the rights and duties as well as the interests of coastal States provided for, inter alia, in article 63, paragraph 2, and articles 64 to 67; and

(c) the provisions of this section.

Article 117
Duty of States to adopt with respect to their nationals measures for the conservation of the living resources of the high seas

All States have the duty to take, or to cooperate with other States in taking, such measures for their respective nationals as may be necessary for the conservation of the living resources of the high seas.

Article 118
Cooperation of States in the conservation and management of living resources

States shall cooperate with each other in the conservation and management of living resources in the areas of the high seas. States whose nationals exploit identical living resources, or different living resources in the same area, shall enter into negotiations with a view to taking the measures necessary for the conservation of the living resources concerned. They shall, as appropriate, cooperate to establish subregional or regional fisheries organizations to this end.

Article 119
Conservation of the living resources of the high seas

1. In determining the allowable catch and establishing other conservation measures for the living resources in the high seas, States shall:

(a) take measures which are designed, on the best scientific evidence available to the States concerned, to maintain or restore populations of harvested species at levels which can produce the maximum sustainable yield.

* * *

33. In seeking provisional measures, Australia and New Zealand among other contentions argued that Article 64, read in conjunction with other provisions of UNCLOS, imposes an obligation on Japan, as a distant water State whose nationals fish for SBT, to cooperate with Australia and New Zealand, as coastal States, in the conservation of SBT. The Commission established under the 1993 Convention is "the appropriate international organization" for the purposes of Article 64. Japan's unilateral actions defeat the object and purpose of the 1993 Convention. In such a case, the underlying obligations of UNCLOS remain. While the 1993 Convention was intended as a means of implementing the obligations imposed by UNCLOS in respect of highly migratory fish species, it is not a means of escaping those obligations. Australia and New Zealand contended that Japan's conduct also placed it in violation of Articles 116, 117, 118, and 119, inter alia by failing to adopt necessary conservation measures for its nationals so as to maintain or restore SBT stock to levels which can produce the maximum sustainable yield, by ignoring credible scientific evidence presented by Australia and New Zealand and by pursuing a course of unilateral action in its exclusive interest contrary to their rights as coastal States while enjoying the benefits of restraint by Australia and New Zealand, with discriminatory effect upon nationals of the Applicants. They requested the prescription of provisional measures requiring that Japan immediately cease experimental fishing for SBT; that Japan restrict its SBT catch to its national allocation as last agreed in the Commission, subject to reduction by the amount of catch taken in pursuance of its unilateral EFP; that the Parties act consistently with the precautionary principle pending a final settlement of the dispute; and that the Parties ensure that no action is taken to aggravate their dispute or prejudice the carrying out of any decision on the merits.

* * *

III. Provisional Measures Prescribed by ITLOS

35. Australia and New Zealand requested provisional measures on July 30, 1999. The International Tribunal for the Law of the Sea held initial deliberations on August 16 and 17 and noted points and issues that it wished the Parties specially to address; oral hearings were conducted at five public sittings on August 18, 19 and 20. On August 27, 1999, ITLOS issued an Order prescribing provisional measures.

* * *

36. It should be observed that, while the Order of ITLOS was not unanimous, no Member of the Tribunal disputed "the view of the Tribunal" that "the provisions of the Convention on the Law of the Sea invoked by Australia and New Zealand appear to afford a basis on which the jurisdiction of the arbitral tribunal might be founded" (paragraph 52). It so held despite Japan's contention that recourse to the arbitral tribunal "is excluded because the Convention of 1993 provides for a dispute settlement procedure" (paragraph 53). It noted the position of Australia and New Zealand "that they are not precluded from having recourse to the arbitral tribunal since the Convention of 1993 does not provide for a compulsory dispute settlement procedure entailing a binding decision as required under article 282 of the Convention on the Law of the Sea" (paragraph 54). It held that, "in the view of the Tribunal, the fact that the Convention of 1993 applies between the parties does not preclude recourse to the procedures in Part XV, section 2 of the Convention on the Law of the Sea" (paragraph 55). For the above and other reasons quoted, "the Tribunal finds that the arbitral tribunal would prima facie have jurisdiction over the disputes" (paragraph 62).

37. It is these holdings of the International Tribunal for the Law of the Sea that were the particular focus of controversy in these proceedings. The Agents and counsel of Australia, New Zealand and Japan plumbed the depths of these holdings with a profundity that the time pressures of the ITLOS processes did not permit. In any event, the ITLOS holdings upheld no more than the jurisdiction prima facie of this Tribunal. It remains for it to decide whether it has jurisdiction to pass upon the merits of the dispute.

* * *

VII. The Paramount Questions and the Answers of the Tribunal

44. The Preliminary Objections raised by Japan and the arguments advanced in support of them, and the rejection of those Preliminary Objections by Australia and New Zealand and the arguments advanced in support of that rejection present this Tribunal with questions of singular complexity and significance. The Tribunal is conscious of its position as the first arbitral tribunal to be constituted under Part XV ("Settlement of Disputes"), Annex VII ("Arbitration") of the United Nations Convention on the Law of the Sea. The Parties, through their written pleadings and the oral arguments so ably presented on their behalf by their distinguished Agents and counsel, have furnished the Tribunal with a comprehensive and searching analysis of issues that are of high importance not only for the dispute that divides them but for the understanding and evolution of the processes of peaceful settlement of disputes embodied in UNCLOS and in treaties implementing or relating to provisions of that great law-making treaty.

45. Having regard to the final Submissions of the Parties, the Tribunal will initially address the contention that the case has become moot and should be discontinued. The relevant arguments of the Parties have been set forth above (in paragraphs 40(c), 41(m)). In short, Japan maintains that the essence of the dispute turns on its pursuance of a uni-

lateral experimental fishing program; that the contentious element of that program is its proposal to fish 1800 mt. of Southern Bluefin Tuna; that in the course of exchanges between the Parties in that regard, Australia had in 1999 proposed an EFP limit of 1500 mt.; that Japan is now prepared to limit its EFP catch to 1500 mt.; hence that the Parties are in accord on what had been the focus of their dispute, with the result that it has been rendered moot. Australia and New Zealand reply that the proposed acceptance of an EFP of 1500 tons of tuna was an offer made in the course of negotiations which is no longer on the table; and that in any event their dispute with Japan over a unilateral EFP is not limited to the quantity of the tonnage to be fished but includes the quality of the program, i.e., the design and modalities for its execution, which they maintain is flawed.

46. In the view of the Tribunal, the case is not moot. If the Parties could agree on an experimental fishing program, an element of which would be to limit catch beyond the de facto TAC limits to 1500 mt., that salient aspect of their dispute would indeed have been resolved; but Australia and New Zealand do not now accept such an offer or limitation by Japan. Even if that offer were today accepted, it would not be sufficient to dispose of their dispute, which concerns the quality as well as the quantity of the EFP, and perhaps other elements of difference as well, such as the assertion of a right to fish beyond TAC limits that were last agreed. Japan now proposes experimentally to fish for no more than 1500 mt., but it has not undertaken for the future to forego or restrict what it regards as a right to fish on the high seas for Southern Bluefin Tuna in the absence of a decision by the Commission for the Conservation of Southern Bluefin Tuna upon a total allowable catch and its allocation among the Parties.

47. The Tribunal will now turn to the fundamental and multifaceted issues of jurisdiction that divide the Parties. Putting aside the question of mootness, it is common ground that there is a dispute, and that the core of that dispute relates to differences about the level of a total allowable catch and to Japan's insistence on conducting, and its conduct of, a unilateral experimental fishing program. What profoundly divides the Parties is whether the dispute arises solely under the 1993 Convention, or whether it also arises under UNCLOS.

48. ...[T]he Applicants maintain, and the Respondent denies, that the dispute involves the interpretation and application of UNCLOS does not of itself constitute a dispute over the interpretation of UNCLOS over which the Tribunal has jurisdiction. In the words of the International Court of Justice in like circumstances, "in order to answer that question, the Court cannot limit itself to noting that one of the Parties maintains that such a dispute exists, and the other denies it. It must ascertain whether the violations of the Treaty ... pleaded ... do or do not fall within the provisions of the Treaty and whether, as a consequence, the dispute is one which the Court has jurisdiction ratione materiae to entertain ..." (Case Concerning Oil Platforms (*Islamic Republic of Iran v. United States of America*), Preliminary Objections, Judgment, I.C.J. Reports 1996, para. 16.) In this and in any other case invoking the compromissory clause of a treaty, the claims made, to sustain jurisdiction, must reasonably relate to, or be capable of being evaluated in relation to, the legal standards of the treaty in point, as determined by the court or tribunal whose jurisdiction is at issue. "It is for the Court itself, while giving particular attention to the formulation of the dispute chosen by the Applicant, to determine on an objective basis the dispute dividing the parties, by examining the position of both Parties ... The Court will itself determine the real dispute that has been submitted to it ... It will base itself not only on the Application and final submissions, but on diplomatic exchanges, public statements and other pertinent evidence ..." (Fisheries Jurisdiction Case (*Spain v. Canada*), I.C.J. Reports 1998, paragraphs 30–31.) In the instant case, it is for this Tribunal to decide

whether the "real dispute" between the Parties does or does not reasonably (and not just remotely) relate to the obligations set forth in the treaties whose breach is alleged.

49. From the record placed before the Tribunal by both Parties, it is clear that the most acute elements of the dispute between the Parties turn on their inability to agree on a revised total allowable catch and the related conduct by Japan of unilateral experimental fishing in 1998 and 1999, as well as Japan's announced plans for such fishing thereafter. Those elements of the dispute were clearly within the mandate of the Commission for the Conservation of Southern Bluefin Tuna. It was there that the Parties failed to agree on a TAC. It was there that Japan announced in 1998 that it would launch a unilateral experimental fishing program; it was there that that announcement was protested by Australia and New Zealand; and the higher level protests and the diplomatic exchanges that followed refer to the Convention for the Conservation of Southern Bluefin Tuna and to the proceedings in the Commission. The Applicants requested urgent consultations with Japan pursuant to Article 16(1) of the Convention, which provides that, "if any dispute arises between two or more of the Parties concerning the interpretation or implementation of this Convention, those Parties shall consult among themselves with a view to having the dispute resolved ..." Those consultations took place in 1998, and they were pursued in 1999 in the Commission in an effort to reach agreement on a joint EFP. It was in the Commission in 1999 that a proposal by Japan to limit its catch to 1800 mt. under the 1999 EFP was made, and it was in the Commission that Australia indicated that it was prepared to accept a limit of 1500 mt. It was in the Commission that Japan stated, on May 26 and 28, 1999 that, unless Australia and New Zealand accepted its proposals for a joint EFP, it would launch a unilateral program on June 1. Proposals for mediation and arbitration made by Japan were made in pursuance of provisions of Article 16 of the CCSBT. In short, it is plain that all the main elements of the dispute between the Parties had been addressed within the Commission for the Conservation of Southern Bluefin Tuna and that the contentions of the Parties in respect of that dispute related to the implementation of their obligations under the 1993 Convention. They related particularly to Article 8(3) of the Convention, which provides that, "For the conservation, management and optimum utilization of southern bluefin tuna: (a) the Commission shall decide upon a total allowable catch and its allocation among the Parties ..." and to the powers of a Party in a circumstance where the Commission found itself unable so to decide.

50. There is in fact no disagreement between the Parties over whether the dispute falls within the provisions of the 1993 Convention. The issue rather is, does it also fall within the provisions of UNCLOS? The Applicants maintain that Japan has failed to conserve and to cooperate in the conservation of the SBT stock, particularly by its unilateral experimental fishing for SBT in 1998 and 1999. They find a certain tension between cooperation and unilateralism. They contend that Japan's unilateral EFP has placed it in breach of its obligations under Articles 64, 116, 117, 118 and 119 of UNCLOS, for the specific reasons indicated earlier in this Award (in paragraphs 33 and 41). Those provisions, they maintain, lay down applicable norms by which the lawfulness of Japan's conduct can be evaluated. They point out that, once the dispute had ripened, their diplomatic notes and other demarches to Japan made repeated reference to Japan's obligations not only under the 1993 Convention but also under UNCLOS and customary international law.

51. Japan for its part maintains that such references were belated and were made for the purpose of permitting a request to ITLOS for provisional measures. It contends that the invoked articles of UNCLOS are general and do not govern the particular dispute between the Parties. More than that, Japan argues that UNCLOS is a framework or umbrella convention that looks to implementing conventions to give it effect; that Article 64

provides for cooperation "through appropriate international organizations" of which the Commission is an exemplar; that any relevant principles and provisions of UNCLOS have been implemented by the establishment of the Commission and the Parties' participation in its work; and that the lex specialis of the 1993 Convention and its institutional expression have subsumed, discharged and eclipsed any provisions of UNCLOS that bear on the conservation and optimum utilization of Southern Bluefin Tuna. Thus Japan argues that the dispute falls solely within the provisions of the 1993 Convention and in no measure also within the reach of UNCLOS.

52. The Tribunal does not accept this central contention of Japan. It recognizes that there is support in international law and in the legal systems of States for the application of a lex specialis that governs general provisions of an antecedent treaty or statute. But the Tribunal recognizes as well that it is a commonplace of international law and State practice for more than one treaty to bear upon a particular dispute. There is no reason why a given act of a State may not violate its obligations under more than one treaty. There is frequently a parallelism of treaties, both in their substantive content and in their provisions for settlement of disputes arising thereunder. The current range of international legal obligations benefits from a process of accretion and cumulation; in the practice of States, the conclusion of an implementing convention does not necessarily vacate the obligations imposed by the framework convention upon the parties to the implementing convention. The broad provisions for the promotion of universal respect for and observance of human rights, and the international obligation to co-operate for the achievement of those purposes, found in Articles 1, 55 and 56 of the Charter of the United Nations, have not been discharged for States Parties by their ratification of the Human Rights Covenants and other human rights treaties. Moreover, if the 1993 Convention were to be regarded as having fulfilled and eclipsed the obligations of UNCLOS that bear on the conservation of SBT, would those obligations revive for a Party to the CCSBT that exercises its right under Article 20 to withdraw from the Convention on twelve months notice? Can it really be the case that the obligations of UNCLOS in respect of a migratory species of fish do not run between the Parties to the 1993 Convention but do run to third States that are Parties to UNCLOS but not to the 1993 Convention? Nor is it clear that the particular provisions of the 1993 Convention exhaust the extent of the relevant obligations of UNCLOS. In some respects, UNCLOS may be viewed as extending beyond the reach of the CCSBT. UNCLOS imposes obligations on each State to take action in relation to its own nationals: "All States have the duty to take ... such measures for their respective nationals as may be necessary for the conservation of the living resources of the high seas" (Article 117). It debars discrimination "in form or fact against the fishermen of any State" (Article 119). These provisions are not found in the CCSBT; they are operative even where no TAC has been agreed in the CCSBT and where co-operation in the Commission has broken down. Article 5(1) of the CCSBT provides that, "Each Party shall take all action necessary to ensure the enforcement of this Convention and compliance with measures which become binding ..." But UNCLOS obligations may be viewed not only as going beyond this general obligation in the foregoing respects but as in force even where "measures" being considered under the 1993 Convention have not become binding thereunder. Moreover, a dispute concerning the interpretation and implementation of the CCSBT will not be completely alien to the interpretation and application of UNCLOS for the very reason that the CCSBT was designed to implement broad principles set out in UNCLOS. For all these reasons, the Tribunal concludes that the dispute between Australia and New Zealand, on the one hand, and Japan on the other, over Japan's role in the management of SBT stocks and particularly its unilateral experimental fishing program, while centered in

the 1993 Convention, also arises under the United Nations Convention on the Law of the Sea. In its view, this conclusion is consistent with the terms of UNCLOS Article 311(2) and (5), and with the law of treaties, in particular Article 30(3) of the Vienna Convention on the Law of Treaties.[15]

53. This holding, however, while critical to the case of the Applicants, is not dispositive of this case. It is necessary to examine a number of articles of Part XV of UNCLOS. Article 286 introduces section 2 of Part XV, a section entitled, "Compulsory Procedures Entailing Binding Decisions". Article 286 provides that, "Subject to section 3, any dispute concerning the interpretation or application of this Convention shall, where no settlement has been reached by recourse to section 1, be submitted at the request of any party to the dispute to the court or tribunal having jurisdiction under this section". Article 286 must be read in context, and that qualifying context includes Article 281(1) as well as Articles 279 and 280. Under Article 281(1), if the States which are parties to a dispute concerning the interpretation or application of UNCLOS (and the Tribunal has just held that this is such a dispute) have agreed to seek settlement of the dispute "by a peaceful means of their own choice", the procedures provided for in Part XV of UNCLOS apply only (a) where no settlement has been reached by recourse to such means and (b) the agreement between the parties "does not exclude any further procedure."

54. The Tribunal accepts Article 16 of the 1993 Convention as an agreement by the Parties to seek settlement of the instant dispute by peaceful means of their own choice. It so concludes even though it has held that this dispute, while centered in the 1993 Convention, also implicates obligations under UNCLOS. It does so because the Parties to this dispute—the real terms of which have been defined above—are the same Parties grappling not with two separate disputes but with what in fact is a single dispute arising under both Conventions. To find that, in this case, there is a dispute actually arising under UNCLOS which is distinct from the dispute that arose under the CCSBT would be artificial.

55. Article 16 is not "a" peaceful means; it provides a list of various named procedures of peaceful settlement, adding "or other peaceful means of their own choice." No particular procedure in this list has thus far been chosen by the Parties for settlement of the instant dispute. Nevertheless—bearing in mind the reasoning of the preceding paragraph—the Tribunal is of the view that Article 16 falls within the terms and intent of Article 281(1), as well as Article 280. That being so, the Tribunal is satisfied about fulfillment of condition (a) of Article 281(1). The Parties have had recourse to means set out in Article 16 of the CCSBT. Negotiations have been prolonged, intense and serious. Since in the course of those negotiations, the Applicants invoked UNCLOS and relied upon provisions of it, while Japan denied the relevance of UNCLOS and its provisions, those negotiations may also be regarded as fulfilling another condition of UNCLOS, that of Article 283, which requires that, when a dispute arises between States Parties concerning UNCLOS' interpretation or application, the parties to the dispute shall proceed expeditiously to an exchange of views regarding its settlement by negotiation or other peaceful means. Manifestly, no settlement has been reached by recourse to such negotiations, at any rate, as yet. It is true that every means listed in Article 16 has not been tried; indeed, the Applicants have not accepted proposals of Japan for mediation and for arbitration under the CCSBT, essentially, it seems, because Japan was unwilling to suspend pursuance of its

15. Article 30(3) of the Vienna Convention on the Law of Treaties provides: When all the parties to an earlier treaty are parties also to the later treaty but the earlier treaty is not terminated or suspended in operation under article 59, the earlier treaty applies only to the extent that its provisions are compatible with those of the later treaty.

unilateral EFP during the pendency of such recourse. It is also true that Article 16(2) provides that failure to reach agreement on reference of a dispute to the International Court of Justice or to arbitration "shall not absolve parties to the dispute from the responsibility of continuing to seek to resolve it by any of the various peaceful means referred to in paragraph 1 above". But in the view of the Tribunal, this provision does not require the Parties to negotiate indefinitely while denying a Party the option of concluding, for purposes of both Articles 281(1) and 283, that no settlement has been reached. To read Article 16 otherwise would not be reasonable.

56. The Tribunal now turns to the second requirement of Article 281(1): that the agreement between the parties "does not exclude any further procedure." This is a requirement, it should be recalled, for applicability of "the procedures provided for in this Part," that is to say, the "compulsory procedures entailing binding decisions" dealt with in section 2 of UNCLOS Part XV. The terms of Article 16 of the 1993 Convention do not expressly and in so many words exclude the applicability of any procedure, including the procedures of section 2 of Part XV of UNCLOS.

57. Nevertheless, in the view of the Tribunal, the absence of an express exclusion of any procedure in Article 16 is not decisive. Article 16(1) requires the parties to "consult among themselves with a view to having the dispute resolved by negotiation, inquiry, mediation, conciliation, arbitration, judicial settlement or other peaceful means of their own choice." Article 16(2), in its first clause, directs the referral of a dispute not resolved by any of the above-listed means of the parties' "own choice" for settlement "to the International Court of Justice or to arbitration" but "with the consent in each case of all parties to the dispute." The ordinary meaning of these terms of Article 16 makes it clear that the dispute is not referable to adjudication by the International Court of Justice (or, for that matter, ITLOS), or to arbitration, "at the request of any party to the dispute" (in the words of UNCLOS Article 286). The consent in each case of all parties to the dispute is required. Moreover, the second clause of Article 16(2) provides that "failure to reach agreement on reference to the International Court of Justice or to arbitration shall not absolve the parties to the dispute from the responsibility of continuing to seek to resolve it by any of the various peaceful means referred to in paragraph 1 above." The effect of this express obligation to continue to seek resolution of the dispute by the listed means of Article 16(1) is not only to stress the consensual nature of any reference of a dispute to either judicial settlement or arbitration. That express obligation equally imports, in the Tribunal's view, that the intent of Article 16 is to remove proceedings under that Article from the reach of the compulsory procedures of section 2 of Part XV of UNCLOS, that is, to exclude the application to a specific dispute of any procedure of dispute resolution that is not accepted by all parties to the dispute. Article 16(3) reinforces that intent by specifying that, in cases where the dispute is referred to arbitration, the arbitral tribunal shall be constituted as provided for in an annex to the 1993 Convention, which is to say that arbitration contemplated by Article 16 is not compulsory arbitration under section 2 of Part XV of UNCLOS but rather autonomous and consensual arbitration provided for in that CCSBT annex.

58. It is plain that the wording of Article 16(1) and (2) has its essential origins in the terms of Article XI of the Antarctic Treaty; the provisions are virtually identical. In view of the States that concluded the Antarctic Treaty—divided as they were between some States that adhered to international adjudication and arbitration and a Great Power that then ideologically opposed it—it is obvious that these provisions are meant to exclude compulsory jurisdiction.

59. For all these reasons, the Tribunal concludes that Article 16 of the 1993 Convention "exclude[s] any further procedure" within the contemplation of Article 281(1) of UNCLOS.

60. There are two other considerations that, to the mind of the Tribunal, sustain this conclusion. The first consideration is the extent to which compulsory procedures entailing binding decisions have in fact been prescribed by Part XV of UNCLOS for all States Parties to UNCLOS. Article 286, in providing that disputes concerning the interpretation or application of UNCLOS "shall ... where no settlement has been reached by recourse to section 1, be submitted at the request of any party to the dispute to the court or tribunal having jurisdiction under [Article 287]", states that that apparently broad provision is "subject to section 3" of Part XV. Examination of the provisions comprising section 3 (and constituting interpretive context for sections 1 and 2 of Part XV) reveals that they establish important limitations and exceptions to the applicability of the compulsory procedures of section 2.

61. Article 297 of UNCLOS is of particular importance in this connection for it provides significant limitations on the applicability of compulsory procedures insofar as coastal States are concerned. Paragraph 1 of Article 297 limits the application of such procedures to disputes concerning the exercise by a coastal State of its sovereign rights or jurisdiction in certain identified cases only, i.e.: (a) cases involving rights of navigation, overflight, laying of submarine cables and pipelines or other internationally lawful uses of the sea associated therewith; and (b) cases involving the protection and preservation of the marine environment. Paragraph 2 of Article 297, while providing for the application of section 2 compulsory procedures to disputes concerning marine scientific research, exempts coastal States from the obligation of submitting to such procedures in cases involving exercise by a coastal State of its rights or discretionary authority in its exclusive economic zone (EEZ) or its continental shelf, and cases of termination or suspension by the coastal State of a research project in accordance with article 253. Disputes between the researching State and the coastal State concerning a specific research project are subject to conciliation under annex V of UNCLOS. Under paragraph 3 of Article 297, section 2 procedures are applicable to disputes concerning fisheries but, and this is an important "but", the coastal State is not obliged to submit to such procedures where the dispute relates to its sovereign rights or their exercise with respect to the living resources in its EEZ, including determination of allowable catch, harvesting capacity, allocation of surpluses to other States, and application of its own conservation and management laws and regulations. Complementing the limitative provisions of Article 297 of UNCLOS, Article 298 establishes certain optional exceptions to the applicability of compulsory section 2 procedures and authorizes a State (whether coastal or not), at any time, to declare that it does not accept any one or more of such compulsory procedures in respect of: (a) disputes concerning Articles 15, 74 and 83 relating to sea boundary delimitations or historic bays or titles; (b) disputes concerning military activities, including military activities by government vessels and aircraft engaged in non-commercial service, and disputes concerning law enforcement activities by a coastal State. Finally, Article 299 of UNCLOS provides that disputes excluded by Article 297 or exempted by Article 298 from application of compulsory section 2 procedures may be submitted to such procedures "only by agreement of the parties to the dispute".

62. It thus appears to the Tribunal that UNCLOS falls significantly short of establishing a truly comprehensive regime of compulsory jurisdiction entailing binding decisions. This general consideration supports the conclusion, based on the language used in Article 281(1), that States Parties that have agreed to seek settlement of disputes concerning the interpretation or application of UNCLOS by "peaceful means of their own choice"

are permitted by Article 281(1) to confine the applicability of compulsory procedures of section 2 of Part XV to cases where all parties to the dispute have agreed upon submission of their dispute to such compulsory procedures. In the Tribunal's view, Article 281(1), when so read, provides a certain balance in the rights and obligations of coastal and non-coastal States in respect of settlement of disputes arising from events occurring within their respective Exclusive Economic Zones and on the high seas, a balance that the Tribunal must assume was deliberately established by the States Parties to UNCLOS.

63. The second consideration of a general character that the Tribunal has taken into account is the fact that a significant number of international agreements with maritime elements, entered into after the adoption of UNCLOS, exclude with varying degrees of explicitness unilateral reference of a dispute to compulsory adjudicative or arbitral procedures. Many of these agreements effect such exclusion by expressly requiring disputes to be resolved by mutually agreed procedures, whether by negotiation and consultation or other method acceptable to the parties to the dispute or by arbitration or recourse to the International Court of Justice by common agreement of the parties to the dispute. Other agreements preclude unilateral submission of a dispute to compulsory binding adjudication or arbitration, not only by explicitly requiring disputes to be settled by mutually agreed procedures, but also, as in Article 16 of the 1993 Convention, by requiring the parties to continue to seek to resolve the dispute by any of the various peaceful means of their own choice. The Tribunal is of the view that the existence of such a body of treaty practice—postdating as well as antedating the conclusion of UNCLOS—tends to confirm the conclusion that States Parties to UNCLOS may, by agreement, preclude subjection of their disputes to section 2 procedures in accordance with Article 281(1). To hold that disputes implicating obligations under both UNCLOS and an implementing treaty such as the 1993 Convention—as such disputes typically may—must be brought within the reach of section 2 of Part XV of UNCLOS would be effectively to deprive of substantial effect the dispute settlement provisions of those implementing agreements which prescribe dispute resolution by means of the parties' choice.

64. The Tribunal does not exclude the possibility that there might be instances in which the conduct of a State Party to UNCLOS and to a fisheries treaty implementing it would be so egregious, and risk consequences of such gravity, that a Tribunal might find that the obligations of UNCLOS provide a basis for jurisdiction, having particular regard to the provisions of Article 300 of UNCLOS. While Australia and New Zealand in the proceedings before ITLOS invoked Article 300, in the proceedings before this Tribunal they made clear that they do not hold Japan to any independent breach of an obligation to act in good faith.

65. It follows from the foregoing analysis that this Tribunal lacks jurisdiction to entertain the merits of the dispute brought by Australia and New Zealand against Japan. Having reached this conclusion, the Tribunal does not find it necessary to pass upon questions of the admissibility of the dispute, although it may be observed that its analysis of provisions of UNCLOS that bring the dispute within the substantive reach of UNCLOS suggests that the dispute is not one that is confined to matters of scientific judgment only. It may be added that this Tribunal does not find the proceedings brought before ITLOS and before this Tribunal to be an abuse of process; on the contrary, as explained below, the proceedings have been constructive.

66. In view of this Tribunal's conclusion that it lacks jurisdiction to deal with the merits of the dispute, and in view of the terms of Article 290(5) of UNCLOS providing that, "Once constituted, the tribunal to which the dispute has been submitted may modify, revoke or affirm those provisional measures ...", the Order of the International Tribunal for the Law of the Sea of August 27, 1999, prescribing provisional measures, shall cease to have effect as of the date of the signing of this Award.

67. However, revocation of the Order prescribing provisional measures does not mean that the Parties may disregard the effects of that Order or their own decisions made in conformity with it. The Order and those decisions—and the recourse to ITLOS that gave rise to them—as well as the consequential proceedings before this Tribunal, have had an impact: not merely in the suspension of Japan's unilateral experimental fishing program during the period that the Order was in force, but on the perspectives and actions of the Parties.

68. As the Parties recognized during the oral hearings before this Tribunal, they have increasingly manifested flexibility of approach to the problems that divide them; as the Agent of Japan put it, "strenuous efforts which both sides have made in the context of the CCSBT have already succeeded in narrowing the gap between the Parties." An agreement on the principle of having an experimental fishing program and on the tonnage of that program appears to be within reach. The possibility of renewed negotiations on other elements of their differences is real. Japan's counsel, in the course of these hearings, emphasized that Japan remained prepared to submit the differences between the Parties to arbitration under Article 16 of the 1993 Convention; Japan's Agent observed that, "That would allow the Parties to set up procedures best suited to the nature and the characteristics of the case." Japan's counsel affirmed Japan's willingness to work with Australia and New Zealand on the formulation of questions to be put to a CCSBT Arbitration Tribunal, and on the procedure that it should adopt in dealing with those questions. He restated Japan's willingness to agree on the simultaneous establishment of a mechanism in which experts and scientists can resume consultation on a joint EFP and related issues. The agent of Japan stated that, not only is its proposal to cap its EFP at 1500 mt. on the negotiating table; negotiations on the appropriate design for the EFP are already underway.

69. Counsel for Australia pointed out that the ITLOS Order already had played a significant role in encouraging the Parties to make progress on the issue of third-party fishing. The Agents of Australia and of New Zealand declared that progress in settling the dispute between the Parties had been made. They expressed the hope that progress would continue and stated that they will make every attempt to ensure that it does; they "remain ready to explore all productive ways of finding solutions."

70. The Tribunal recalls that Article 16(2) prescribes that failure to reach agreement on reference to arbitration shall not absolve the parties to the dispute from the responsibility of continuing to seek to resolve it by any of the various peaceful means referred to in paragraph 1; and among those means are negotiation, mediation and arbitration. The Tribunal further observes that, to the extent that the search for resolution of the dispute were to resort to third-party procedures, those listed in Article 16 are labels that conform to traditional diplomatic precedent. Their content and modus operandi can be refined and developed by the Parties to meet their specific needs. There are many ways in which an independent body can be configured to interact with the States party to a dispute. For example, there may be a combination or alternation of direct negotiations, advice from expert panels, benevolent supervision and good offices extended by a third-party body, and recourse to a third party for step-by-step aid in decision-making and for mediation, quite apart from third-party binding settlement rendered in the form of an arbitral award. Whatever the mode or modes of peaceful settlement chosen by the Parties, the Tribunal emphasizes that the prospects for a successful settlement of their dispute will be promoted by the Parties' abstaining from any unilateral act that may aggravate the dispute while its solution has not been achieved.

71. Finally, the Tribunal observes that, when it comes into force, the Agreement for the Implementation of the Provisions of the United Nations Convention on the Law of the Sea of 10 December 1982 Relating to the Conservation and Management of Straddling

Fish Stocks and Highly Migratory Fish Stocks, which was adopted on August 4, 1995 and opened for signature December 4, 1995 (and signed by Australia, Japan and New Zealand), should, for States Parties to it, not only go far towards resolving procedural problems that have come before this Tribunal but, if the Convention is faithfully and effectively implemented, ameliorate the substantive problems that have divided the Parties. The substantive provisions of the Straddling Stocks Agreement are more detailed and far-reaching than the pertinent provisions of UNCLOS or even of the CCSBT. The articles relating to peaceful settlement of disputes specify that the provisions relating to the settlement of disputes set out in Part XV of UNCLOS apply mutatis mutandis to any dispute between States Parties to the Agreement concerning its interpretation or application. They further specify that the provisions relating to settlement of disputes set out in Part XV of UNCLOS apply mutatis mutandis to any dispute between States Parties to the Agreement concerning the interpretation or application of a subregional, regional or global fisheries agreement relating to straddling fish stocks or highly migratory fish stocks to which they are parties, including any dispute concerning the conservation and management of such stocks.

72. FOR THESE REASONS

The Arbitral Tribunal

By vote of 4 to 1,

1. Decides that it is without jurisdiction to rule on the merits of the dispute; and,

Unanimously,

2. Decides, in accordance with Article 290(5) of the United Nations Convention on the Law of the Sea, that provisional measures in force by Order of the International Tribunal for the Law of the Sea prescribed on August 27, 1999 are revoked from the day of the signature of this Award.

73. Justice Sir Kenneth Keith appends a Separate Opinion.

Signed:

Stephen M. Schwebel
President of the Arbitral Tribunal

Margrete L. Stevens
Co-Secretary of the Arbitral Tribunal

Washington, D.C.
August 4, 2000

Case Concerning the Air Services Agreement of 27 March 1946 (*United States v. France*)*

Arbitral Tribunal established by the *Compromis* of 11 July 1978
9 December 1978
(Riphagen, President; Ehrlich and Reuter, Arbitrators)

* * *

II. THE FACTS

1. An Exchange of Notes of 5 April 1960 relating to the Air Services Agreement concluded between the United States of America and France on 27 March 1946 authorises air

* XVIII R.I.A.A. 417 (1978).

carriers designated by the United States to operate to Paris via London (without traffic rights between London and Paris) services to and from United States West Coast points.[56] A carrier so designated, Pan American World Airways (hereinafter referred to as Pan Am) intermittently operated services over this route until 2 March 1975.

2. On 20 February 1978, pursuant to French legislation requiring flight schedules to be filed thirty days in advance, Pan Am informed the competent French authority, the *Direction gènèrale de l'Aviation civile* (hereinafter referred to as *D.G.A.C.),* of its plan to resume its West Coast—London—Paris service (without traffic rights between London and Paris) on 1 May 1978 with six weekly flights in each direction. The operation of this service was to involve a change of gauge, in London, from a Boeing 747 aircraft to a smaller Boeing 727 on the outward journey and from a Boeing 727 to a larger Boeing 747 on the return journey.

3. On 14 March 1978, the *D.G.A.C.* refused to approve Pan Am's plan on the ground that it called for a change of gauge in the territory of a third State and thus was contrary to Section VI of the Annex to the 1946 Air Services Agreement, which deals with changes of gauge in the territory of the Contracting Parties only.[57] The United States Embassy in Paris having, on 22 March 1978, requested the French Foreign Ministry to re-consider the decision of the *D.G.A.C.*, the matter then became the subject of discussions and of diplomatic exchanges between the two Parties, the United States arguing that Pan Am's proposed change of gauge in London was consistent with the 1946 Air Services Agreement and France contending that it was not and reserving its right to take appropriate measures.

4. On 1 and 2 May 1978, when Pan Am operated for the first time its renewed West Coast—London—Paris service with a change of gauge in London, the French police confined themselves to drawing up reports of what they considered to be unlawful flights. Another flight having taken place on 3 May, Pan Am's Boeing 727 aircraft was surrounded by French police upon arrival at Paris Orly Airport, and its captain was instructed to return to London without having disembarked the passengers or freight. Thereupon Pan Am's flights were suspended.

5. On 4 May, the United States proposed that the issue be submitted to binding arbitration, on the understanding that Pan Am would be permitted to continue its flights pending the arbitral award. On 9 May, the United States Civil Aeronautics Board (hereinafter referred to as C.A.B.) issued a first Order putting into operation phase 1 of Part 213 of its Economic Regulations by requiring the French companies Air France and Union de transports aèriens (U.T.A.) to file, within prescribed time-limits, all their existing flight schedules to and from the United States as well as any new schedules. After having unsuccessfully attempted to have this Order stayed and revised by the C.A.B. or the United States courts, the two companies complied with it on 30 May 1978 by filing their schedules.

6. In a Note dated 13 May 1978, the French Embassy in Washington had in the meantime acknowledged Pan Am's Suspension of its flights to Paris and had informed the United States Department of State of France's agreement "to the principle of recourse to arbitration." At the same time, the Embassy had objected to the unilateral measure decreed by the Order of the C.A.B. prior to the exhaustion of the means of direct negotiations; it had proposed that such negotiations be held and had noted that French local remedies had not been exhausted; finally, it had warned the Department of State that the pursuit

56. Part of this Exchange of Notes is reproduced below, para 50, n. 20.
57. For the full text of this provision, see below, para 45.

of a course of unilateral measures "would have damaging consequences for the French airline companies and create an additional dispute regarding legality and compensation."

7. On 18 May 1978, Pan Am requested the Administrative Tribunal of Paris to annul as being *ultra vires* the decision taken by the *D.G.A.C.* on 14 March 1978 to disapprove Pan Am's flight schedule. This request is still pending. In a motion filed on 31 May, Pan Am asked that the decision of 14 March 1978 be stayed. This motion was denied on 11 July on the ground that implementation of that decision would not cause irreparable harm.

8. In the meantime, on 31 May 1978, the C.A.B. issued a second Order under Part 213 of its Economic Regulations. This Order, which was subject to stay or disapproval by the President of the United States within ten days and which was to be implemented on 12 July, was to prevent Air France from operating its thrice-weekly flights to and from Los Angeles and Paris via Montreal for the period during which Pan Am would be barred from operating its West Coast-London-Paris service with change of gauge in London.

9. The second Part 213 Order was not implemented, however. Legal experts of both Parties having met on 1 and 2 June in Washington, on 28 and 29 June in Paris, and on 10 and 11 July in Washington, a *Compromis* of Arbitration was signed between the United States and France on 11 July 1978. This *Compromis* reads as follows:

* * *

V. QUESTION (A)

43. The first question to be decided by the Tribunal is as follows:

> Does a United States-designated carrier have the right to operate West Coast—Paris service under the Air Services Agreement between the United States and France with a change of gauge in London (transshipment to a smaller aircraft on the outward journey and to a larger aircraft on the return journey)?

On this question, the decision of the Tribunal shall be binding.

44. To answer Question (A), the Tribunal first examined the terms of the Agreement itself as they refer specifically to change of gauge. In the absence of a clear answer based solely on those terms, the Tribunal next referred to other provisions of the Agreement as a whole. This analysis led to a tentative judgment on a response to Question (A). The Tribunal then tested that judgment in the light of both the overall context of international civil aviation in which the Agreement was negotiated and the practice of the Parties as they operated under the Agreement. The analysis indicates that neither the overall context nor the practice of the Parties is inconsistent with the tentative judgment based on the text of the Agreement as a whole. Finally, the Tribunal undertook a limited examination of practice under air services agreements similar to the France—United States one, for the sole purpose of ensuring that this practice did not suggest a wholly dissimilar approach from the Tribunal's tentative judgment. Having taken these steps, the Tribunal concluded that the judgment referred to is valid and should properly serve as the basis for its response to Question (A). Each of the steps is discussed in some detail below.

1. *The Text of the Agreement Relating to Change of Gauge*

45. The only specific provision concerning change of gauge in the Agreement is in Section VI of the Annex.[65] 16 Section VI provides:

65. Throughout this Award, the Tribunal uses the terms "change of gauge" and "*rupture de charge*" to mean a change in the size of the aircraft.

(a) For the purpose of the present Section, the term 'transshipment' shall mean the transportation by the same carrier of traffic beyond a certain point on a given route by different aircraft from those employed on the earlier stages of the same route.

(b) Transshipment when justified by economy of operation will be permitted at all points mentioned in the attached Schedules in territory of the two Contracting Parties.

(c) However, no transshipments will be made if the territory of either Contracting Party which would alter the long range characteristics of the operation or which would be inconsistent with the standards set forth in this Agreement and its Annex and particularly Section IV of this Annex.

46. By its terms, therefore, Section VI covers only a change of gauge (or other forms of transshipment) within the territory of one of the Parties. It does not apply to situations, such as the one referred to in Question (A), when a carrier seeks to change gauge in the territory of a third country along one of the routes covered by the Agreement. What implications may be drawn from the absence of any reference in the Agreement to change of gauge in third countries?

47. The French Government has argued that this silence should be interpreted to preclude any change of gauge in third countries by a carrier of one Party unless specifically approved by the Government of the other Party. The French Government contends that no grant of authority to change gauge in third countries may be implied, particularly since only one type of situation involving change of gauge is expressly covered by Section VI. The United States Government takes the opposite position. A change of gauge in third countries is always permitted, it argues, and no prohibition may be implied from the Agreement. Rather, the United States Government urges, the implication of Section VI is that the only restrictions on change of gauge are those that relate to the territories of the Parties. Outside those territories, it claims, the Parties are permitted to change gauge without limitation.

48. In the view of the Tribunal, neither of these extreme positions may be properly derived on the basis of Section VI, viewed in isolation from the other terms of the Agreement. It is necessary, instead, to turn to the text of the Agreement as a whole. As stated by the Permanent Court of International Justice in its Advisory Opinion of 12 August 1922 regarding the *Competence of the International Labour Organisation,* it is obvious that the Treaty must be read as a whole and that its meaning is not to be determined merely upon particular phrases which, if detached from the context, may be interpreted in more than one sense (Publications of the P.C.I.J., Series B, No.2, p. 23); see also the *United States-France Air Arbitration,* 1963 (United Nations, Reports of International Arbitral Awards, vol. XVI, pp. 46–47).

2. *The Text of the Agreement as a Whole*

49. The Agreement states in Article I that the Contracting Parties grant to each other the rights specified in the Annex hereto for the establishment of the international air services set forth in that Annex ...

It is the terms of the Annex, therefore, that must be examined for a consideration of the rights of the Parties and any limitation on those rights.

50. In Sections I and II of the Annex, the two Parties grant each other "the right to conduct air transport services" on the routes designated in the attached Schedules. In the present case, the relevant texts are Schedule II and the Exchange of Notes dated 5 April 1960.

51. In Section III, each Party provides limited rights on its own territory to the other Party—"rights of transit, of stops for nontraffic purposes and of commercial entry and departure for international traffic ...".

52. Section IV establishes basic guidelines for regulating capacity on the authorised routes. It states that both Parties wish to encourage air travel "for the general good of mankind at the cheapest rates consistent with sound economic principles"; that each Party shall take into account the interests of the carrier of the other Party in regard to services on the same routes; that services should "bear a close relation to the requirements of the public for such services and, perhaps most important, that services "shall retain as their primary objective the provision of capacity adequate to the traffic demands between the country of which such air carrier is a national and the country of ultimate destination of the traffic." Finally, the rights of carriers of either Party to embark or disembark passengers in the territory of the other Party are subject to an additional set of guiding principles.

53. Section V deals with rates to be charged by carriers of the Parties. Section VI, of course, has already been discussed. Section VII permits route changes by one Party in the territory of third countries—but not in the territory of the other Party—with a requirement only of prompt notice and an opportunity to consult if requested. Lastly, Section VIII calls for the prompt exchange of information by the Parties.

54. The text of the entire Agreement is as significant for what it omits as for what it specifies. It is silent concerning most of the major operational issues facing an air carrier-types of plane, number of crew members, and the like. When jet planes were first developed, for example, one unfamiliar with the Agreement might have assumed that a new accord would be necessary. In fact, however, the 1946 Agreement was not modified at the time this remarkable technological innovation was introduced. Similarly, recent objections to supersonic planes were not based on the terms of the Agreement but solely on environmental concerns. The point is that the Agreement leaves to the Parties—and, if a Party chooses, to its designated air carriers—the right to decide a wide range of key issues concerning almost every aspect of service on designated routes apart from those regarding rates and capacity.

55. Exceptions to this basic approach are made in the Agreement, but in the main they concern regulation by a Party of activities in that Party's territory. Section VII of the Annex provides, for example, that one Party may make changes in the routes described—with notice and the option of consultation—in the territory of third countries, but not in the territory of the other Party.

56. Section VI of the Annex refers, as has been discussed, solely to change of gauge in the territory of one of the Parties. This in itself is understandable when the Agreement is viewed as a whole. It is entirely reasonable to draw a distinction between activities within the territory of a Party and activities within the territories of third countries. Each Party is naturally more concerned about what happens on its own territory than what happens elsewhere. Within a network of bilateral air services agreements throughout the world, this approach assures that activities in each territory are primarily regulated by the countries most directly concerned.

57. What insights on Question (A) emerge from this examination of the text of the Agreement as a whole? First, it seems evident to the Tribunal that neither extreme position on the change-of-gauge issue may be accepted. On the one hand, some gauge changes in third countries must be permitted. When a plane has a mechanical failure, for example, a transshipment is plainly required, and no plane of the same size may be available.

Similarly, carriers on routes that involve extremely long distances—including, most obviously, routes around the world—must change planes at some point or points, and there seems to be no reason why the same size aircraft must be used on every segment of such routes.

58. On the other hand, the Agreement includes a variety of conditions concerning services by carriers of the Parties. The route descriptions in the Schedules are one set of conditions. The capacity provisions in Section IV of the Annex are another. It would undercut the terms of the Agreement to permit a change of gauge for the *sole* purpose of enabling a carrier to act inconsistently with one or more of these conditions.

59. The issue that must be resolved, therefore, is how to distinguish between permitted and prohibited gauge changes in third countries. On this issue, the terms of the Agreement referred to above are of considerable assistance. Most important, they refer to designated routes and to services on those routes. Passengers may embark and disembark at various points, but the Agreement consistently reflects a concept of continuous service scheduled from a point of origin on a route to a point of termination on that route. This concept is not stated expressly in the Agreement, but it emerges from the text when read as a whole—particularly Section I of the Annex and the Schedules.

60. On this basis, the Tribunal tentatively concluded that change of gauge is authorised in the territory of a third country when the service involved is continuous—when the change of gauge is not simply a basis for providing a series of separate services.

61. Under this approach, change of gauge cannot be used as an excuse for acting inconsistently with provisions of the Agreement, most obviously those relating to capacity. At the same time, change of gauge may be the most appropriate means to ensure compliance with certain provisions. Traffic demands may diminish, for example, over the course of an extended route. This is plainly the case when, as in the particular situation at issue, so-called fifth freedom traffic is precluded. United States carriers are prohibited from embarking passengers in London on the route to Paris via London from United States West Coast points. It is virtually certain, therefore, that the traffic demands on the route will be less on the London to Paris segment than on the preceding segment.

62. Although Section VI is not by its terms applicable to the situation raised in Question (A), its text may properly be taken into account, and seems appropriately to reflect the Tribunal's tentative judgment. That text refers specifically to three criteria: first, a change of gauge within the territory of a Party must be justified by "economy of operation"; second, it must not "alter the long range characteristics of the operation"; and third, it must not be inconsistent with other provisions of the Agreement, particularly Section IV of the Annex regarding capacity.

63. The focus of the Tribunal on a concept of continuous service appears related to these criteria, when interpreted broadly. Economy of operation would naturally be a guiding principle for gauge changes that are consistent with the concept of continuous service; the "long range characteristics of the operation" (i.e. characteristics of a service as opposed to a particular aircraft) reflect a sense of that concept; and, as already stated, a change of gauge may not be used simply as a basis for action inconsistent with provisions in the Agreement—most obviously the capacity provisions in Section IV of the Annex.

64. Drawing on Section VI for appropriate guidance thus further confirms the judgment that a concept of continuous service is the key to a resolution of Question (A). A change of gauge that is consistent with that concept is authorised; a change of gauge that is designed to establish essentially separate services is precluded.

65. At a point on a route where fifth-freedom rights are allowed, therefore, a scheduled change of gauge from a smaller to a larger plane is not permitted if experience has shown that the purpose of the change is solely to accommodate more fifth-freedom traffic than is allowed under the capacity principles in Section IV. Even if—as in the situation involved in Question (A)—no fifth-freedom rights are permitted at a point, change of gauge must not be used as an excuse for a significant delay in service—in effect to change a continuous service into a series of separate services.

3. *The Context in which the Agreement was Negotiated*

66. Although no negotiating history of the Agreement concerning the specific question at issue was uncovered by the Parties, the broader context in which the Agreement was negotiated is relevant. There is no need to dwell at length on the Convention on International Civil Aviation concluded at Chicago on 7 December 1944, the basic instrument that set the stage for the rapid expansion of international civil aviation. It is considered in some detail in the *Italy-United States Air Arbitration,* 1964 (United Nations, Reports of International Arbitral Awards, vol. XVI, pp. 96–98). Most important, the Convention established the structure for an international règime for civil air services that was remarkably open and unregulated except in terms of routes, rates, and capacity, and certain activities that may be regulated by the government of a country within its own territory. Taken as a whole, the Chicago Convention reflects neither the concept of "freedom of the air" nor a concept of national sovereignty of a State over the airspace above its territory as would permit that State to impose on the use of that airspace by foreign air carriers *any* condition whatsoever relating to conduct of that air carrier prior to or after such use. This context supports, therefore, the distinction that has been drawn above between activities relating to the territories of the Parties, which generally require specific authorisation, and activities on the territories of third countries, which are generally permitted absent a specific prohibition.

67. The 1946 Bermuda Agreement between the United Kingdom and the United States, which preceded the France—United States Agreement by only a few months, is also a part of the relevant context, although France is clearly not bound by the Bermuda Agreement, let alone its negotiating history, for it was not a Party to the Agreement.

68. The negotiating history of the Bermuda Agreement does indicate, however, a compromise between an initial United Kingdom position that was opposed to any change of gauge by a carrier of one Party without specific authorisation by the other Party, and an initial United States position favouring completely unrestricted change of gauge. The change-of-gauge provision that was finally adopted and the negotiating history make clear that the Bermuda Agreement embodies a position on change of gauge consistent with the judgment expressed in this Award.

4. *The Practice of the Parties*

69. The activities of the Parties under an international agreement over a period of time may, of course, be relevant—occasionally even decisive—in interpreting the text. In this case, a number of changes of gauge in third countries by United States carriers on routes specified in the Schedules occurred during the years that the Agreement has been in force. Not surprisingly, the Parties differ on the weight to be given to this practice. In the circumstances of this case, the Tribunal believes that all that can be fairly concluded from the entire course of practice by the Parties is that it does not lead to a different conclusion from the one tentatively adopted on the basis of the text of the Agreement and supported by the overall context in which the Agreement was negotiated.

70. The United States has also referred to thousands of gauge changes under other international air services agreements to which it was or is a Party. Some of these agreements contain provisions similar to those in the France—United States Agreement; others are substantially different.

71. The Tribunal would be extremely hesitant to draw firm conclusions from this practice, at least without detailed examination of each agreement and the relevant practice of the Parties—an examination that has not been possible in the limited time available to the Tribunal. On this basis, it is possible to say no more than that this practice also does not appear inconsistent with the approach adopted by the Tribunal.

VI. QUESTION (B)

* * *

80. The Tribunal will consider, in turn, the principle of the legitimacy of "counter-measures" and the limits on these measures in the light either of the existence of a machinery of negotiations or of a mechanism of arbitration or judicial settlement.

81. Under the rules of present-day international law, and unless the contrary results from special obligations arising under particular treaties, notably from mechanisms created within the framework of international organisations, each State establishes for itself its legal situation vis-à-vis other States. If a situation arises which, in one State's view, results in the violation of an international obligation by another State, the first State is entitled, within the limits set by the general rules of international law pertaining to the use of armed force, to affirm its rights through "counter-measures."

82. At this point, one could introduce various doctrinal distinctions and adopt a diversified terminology dependent on various criteria, in particular whether it is the obligation allegedly breached which is the subject of the counter-measures or whether the latter involve another obligation, and whether or not all the obligations under consideration pertain to the same convention. The Tribunal, however, does not think it necessary to go into these distinctions for the purposes of the present case. Indeed, in the present case, both the alleged violation and the counter-measure directly affect the operation of air services provided for in the Agreement and the Exchange of Notes of 5 April 1960.

83. It is generally agreed that all counter-measures must, in the first instance, have some degree of equivalence with the alleged breach; this is a well-known rule. In the course of the present proceedings, both Parties have recognised that the rule applies to this case, and they both have invoked it. It has been observed, generally, that judging the "proportionality" of counter-measures is not an easy task and can at best be accomplished by approximation. In the Tribunal's view, it is essential, in a dispute between States, to take into account not only the injuries suffered by the companies concerned but also the importance of the questions of principle arising from the alleged breach. The Tribunal thinks that it will not suffice, in the present case, to compare the losses suffered by Pan Am on account of the suspension of the projected services with the losses which the French companies would have suffered as a result of the counter-measures; it will also be necessary to take into account the importance of the positions of principle which were taken when the French authorities prohibited changes of gauge in third countries. If the importance of the issue is viewed within the framework of the general air transport policy adopted by the United States Government and implemented by the conclusion of a large number of international agreements with countries other than France, the measures taken by the United States do not appear to be clearly disproportionate when compared to those taken by France. Neither Party has provided the Tribunal with evidence that would be suffi-

cient to affirm or reject the existence of proportionality in these terms, and the Tribunal must be satisfied with a very approximative appreciation.

84. Can it be said that the resort to such counter-measures which are contrary to international law but justified by a violation of international law allegedly committed by the State against which they are directed, is restricted if it is found that the Parties previously accepted a duty to negotiate or an obligation to have their dispute settled through a procedure of arbitration or of judicial settlement?

85. It is tempting to assert that when Parties enter into negotiations, they are under a general duty not to aggravate the dispute, this general duty being a kind of emanation of the principle of good faith.

86. Though it is far from rejecting such an assertion, the Tribunal is of the view that, when attempting to define more precisely such a principle, several essential considerations must be examined.

87. First, the duty to negotiate may, in present times, take several forms and thus have a greater or lesser significance. There is the very general obligation to negotiate which is set forth by Article 33 of the Charter of the United Nations and the content of which can be stated in some quite basic terms. But there are other, more precise obligations.

88. The Tribunal recalls the terms of Article VIII of the 1946 Agreement, which reads as follows:

> In a spirit of close collaboration, the aeronautical authorities of the two Contracting Parties will consult regularly with a view to assuring the observance of the principles and the implementation of the provisions outlined in the present Agreement and its Annex.
>
> This Article provides for an obligation of continuing consultation between the Parties. In the context of this general duty, the Agreement establishes a clear mandate to the Parties to make good faith efforts to negotiate on issues of potential controversy. Several other provisions of the Agreement and the Annex state requirements to consult in specific circumstances, when the possibility of a dispute might be particularly acute. Finally, Article X imposes on the Parties a special consultation requirement when, in spite of previous efforts, a dispute has arisen.

89. But the present problem is whether, on the basis of the abovementioned texts, counter-measures are prohibited. The Tribunal does not consider that either general international law or the provisions of the Agreement allow it to go that far.

90. Indeed, it is necessary carefully to assess the meaning of counter-measures in the framework of proportionality. Their aim is to restore equality between the Parties and to encourage them to continue negotiations with mutual desire to reach an acceptable solution. In the present case, the United States of America holds that a change of gauge is permissible in third countries; that conviction defined its position before the French refusal came into play; the United States counter-measures restore in a negative way the symmetry of the initial positions.

91. It goes without saying that recourse to counter-measures involves the great risk of giving rise, in turn, to a further reaction, thereby causing an escalation which will lead to a worsening of the conflict. Counter-measures therefore should be a wager on the wisdom, not on the weakness of the other Party. They should be used with a spirit of great moderation and be accompanied by a genuine effort at resolving the dispute. But the Arbitral Tribunal does not believe that it is possible, in the present state of international re-

lations, to lay down a rule prohibiting the use of counter-measures during negotiations, especially where such counter-measures are accompanied by an offer for a procedure affording the possibility of accelerating the solution of the dispute.

92. That last consideration is particularly relevant in disputes concerning air service operations: the network of air services is in fact an extremely sensitive system, disturbances of which can have wide and unforeseeable consequences.

93. With regard to the machinery of negotiations, the actions by the United States Government do not appear, therefore, to run counter to the international obligations of that Government.

94. However, the lawfulness of such counter-measures has to be considered still from another viewpoint. It may indeed be asked whether they are valid in general, in the case of a dispute concerning a point of law, where there is arbitral or judicial machinery which can settle the dispute. Many jurists have felt that while arbitral or judicial proceedings were in progress, recourse to counter-measures, even if limited by the proportionality rule, was prohibited. Such an assertion deserves sympathy but requires further elaboration. If the proceedings form part of an institutional framework ensuring some degree of enforcement of obligations, the justification of countermeasures will undoubtedly disappear, but owing to the existence of that framework rather than solely on account of the existence of arbitral or judicial proceedings as such.

95. Besides, the situation during the period in which a case is not yet before a tribunal is not the same as the situation during the period in which that case is *sub judice.* So long as a dispute has not been brought before the tribunal, in particular because an agreement between the Parties is needed to set the procedure in motion, the period of negotiation is not over and the rules mentioned above remain applicable. This may be a regrettable solution, as the Parties in principle did agree to resort to arbitration or judicial settlement, but it must be conceded that under present-day international law States have not renounced their right to take counter-measures in such situations. In fact, however, this solution may be preferable as it facilitates States' acceptance of arbitration or judicial settlement procedures.

96. The situation changes once the tribunal is in a position to act. To the extent that the tribunal has the necessary means to achieve the objectives justifying the counter-measures, it must be admitted that the right of the Parties to initiate such measures disappears. In other words, the power of a tribunal to decide on interim measures of protection, regardless of whether this power is expressly mentioned or implied in its statute (at least as the power to formulate recommendations to this effect), leads to the disappearance of the power to initiate counter-measures and may lead to an elimination of existing counter-measures to the extent that the tribunal so provides as an interim measure of protection. As the object and scope of the power of the tribunal to decide on interim measures of protection may be defined quite narrowly, however, the power of the Parties to initiate or maintain counter-measures, too, may not disappear completely.

97. In a case under the terms of a provision like Article X of the Air Services Agreement of 1946, as amended by the Exchange of Notes of 19 March 1951, the arbitration may be set in motion unilaterally. Although the arbitration need not be binding, the Parties are obliged to "use their best efforts under the powers available to them to put into effect the opinion expressed" by the Tribunal. In the present case, the Parties concluded a *Compromis* that provides for a binding decision on Question (A) and expressly authorises the Tribunal to decide on interim measures.

98. As far as the action undertaken by the United States Government in the present case is concerned, the situation is quite simple. Even if arbitration under Article X of the Agreement is set in motion unilaterally, implementation may take time, and during this period counter-measures are not excluded; a State resorting to such measures, however, must do everything in its power to expedite the arbitration. This is exactly what the Government of the United States has done.

99. The Tribunal's Reply to Question (B) consists of the above observations as a whole. These observations lead to the conclusion that, under the circumstances in question, the Government of the United States had the right to undertake the action that it undertook under Part 213 of the Economic Regulations of the C.A.B.

VII. DISPOSITIF

For these reasons,

The Arbitral Tribunal replies as follows to the questions submitted to it:

Question (A)

Considering that under the sixth preambular paragraph of the *Compromis* of Arbitration, the French Government,

> in agreeing to resort to arbitration with respect to change of gauge ... reserves its right to argue before the tribunal that all means of internal recourse must be exhausted before a State may invoke arbitration under the Agreement.

Considering that the question asked is the following:

Does a United States-designated carrier have the right to operate West Coast—Paris service under the Air Services Agreement between the United States and France with a change of gauge in London (transshipment to a smaller aircraft on the outward journey and to a larger aircraft on the return journey)?

Considering that the Arbitral Tribunal is therefore called upon to pronounce on two points,

The Arbitral Tribunal,

With regard to the first point,

Decides, unanimously, that it is able to decide on Question (A);

With regard to the second point,

Decides, by two votes to one, that the answer to be given on this point is that a United States designated carrier *has* the right to operate West Coast—Paris service under the Air Services Agreement between the United States and France with a change of gauge in London (transshipment to a smaller aircraft on the outward journey and to a larger aircraft on the return journey), provided that the service is continuous and does not constitute separate services.

Question (B)

Considering that, under the seventh preambular paragraph of the *Compromis* of Arbitration, the United States Government,

> in agreeing to resort to arbitration with respect to Part 213 ... reserves its right to argue before the tribunal that under the circumstances the issue is not appropriate for consideration by an arbitral tribunal.

Considering that the question asked is the following:

> Under the circumstances in question, did the United States have the right to undertake such action as it undertook under Part 213 of the Civil Aeronautics Board's Economic Regulations?

Considering that the Arbitral Tribunal is therefore called upon to pronounce on two points,

> The Arbitral Tribunal,
>
> With respect to the first point,
>
> *Decides,* unanimously, to pronounce on Question (B);
>
> With respect to the second point,
>
> *Decides,* unanimously, that the answer to be given on this point is that, under the circumstances in question, the Government of the United States had the right to undertake the action that it undertook under Part 213 of the Economic Regulations of the C.A.B.

Done in English and French at the Graduate Institute of International Studies, Geneva, this 9th day of December 1978, both texts being equally authoritative, in three original copies, one of which will be placed in the archives of the Arbitral Tribunal, and the two others transmitted to the Government of the United States of America and to the Government of the French Republic, respectively.

M. Paul Reuter appends to the Arbitral Award a statement of his dissenting opinion.

* * *

Notes and Questions on Arbitration

1. Consider the differences and similarities of conciliation and arbitration. Consider the advantages and disadvantages of each.

2. In the previous chapter we learned conciliation is almost never used, but arbitration, by contrast, is increasing in use. The excerpt above explains that international commercial arbitration is booming partly because of the improved chance of getting enforcement through the New York Convention on Recognition and Enforcement of Foreign Arbitral Awards. Does this help you predict how international commercial mediation or conciliation will fare in the future?

3. The ICJ is the natural alternative to inter-state arbitration, but it is so busy that parties may wait several years to get a final judgment. Particularly contentious cases require speedier outcomes. Parties in several recent cases explained that they chose arbitration over the ICJ because of speed. See, e.g., the case of the Ethiopia-Eritrea Boundary Arbitration. *Ethiopia, Eritrea at Odds Over Border Ruling; Both Sides Claim International Commission's Support for Their Land Claims,* WASH. POST, Apr. 14, 2002, at A21.

On the other hand, the speedy outcome of this arbitration has been compromised by Ethiopia's refusal to comply with it. Eritrea, frustrated with Ethiopia's stance and perceived inaction on the part of international peacekeepers, began to thwart the efforts of peacekeepers in the area. The UN withdrew its peacekeepers in 2008, and both Ethiopia and Eritrea deployed troops into the Temporary Security Zone established between the parties. Eritrea considers that a final decision has been reached but not respected, and Ethiopia considers the boundary still not finally determined.

The outcome of this dispute raises the question of whether Ethiopia would have responded similarly to a decision of the International Court of Justice, or whether the arbitral nature of the decision made compliance seem less necessary.

4. The UN Commission on International Trade Law (UNCITRAL) has developed model rules for use in arbitration. They are very popular and are used in *ad hoc* and semi-permanent arbitrations like the Iran-U.S. Claims Tribunal. Find the rules at www.uncitral.org.

5. The basis of authority in arbitration is that it is voluntary: Consent is key. Clearly the majority of arbitrators took this principle seriously in the *SBT* arbitration. But did they take it too far? Their decision was at variance with twenty judges of the International Tribunal of the Law of the Sea who found *prima facie* jurisdiction (two did not). What is *SBT*'s likely impact on future disputes over protection of ocean space?

6. Will the *SBT* arbitration result in some unusual outcomes? Under the Tribunal's reasoning, any dispute settlement provision can oust the binding mechanisms of the Law of the Sea Convention of Part XV. Parties could, for example, include a one-week negotiation requirement to resolve disputes. Those parties would then be free of Part XV. Parties that include nothing in their treaty are, however, bound by Part XV to have resort to binding settlement. Did the drafters intend such disparate outcomes? *See* Louis B. Sohn, *Settlement of Disputes Arising Out of the Law of the Sea Convention,* 12 San Diego L. Rev. 495 (1975).

7. Four arbitrators in *SBT* indicate they think it was really too much to believe that states had committed to widespread compulsory dispute settlement in a major issue area like the oceans. The International Law Commission certainly did not think the world was ready for widespread dispute settlement in the contentious area of countermeasures:

> ... In the mid-1990s, the ILC seriously considered adding a requirement of prior dispute settlement as a pre-requisite to using countermeasures, not unlike the dispute settlement requirement developed for trade disputes ...
>
> Governments, including the United States government, were not willing to accept [prior dispute settlement]. Rosenstock points out that a requirement of dispute settlement prior to the imposition of countermeasures is tantamount to imposing general, universal, compulsory dispute settlement on States. Self-help would assume the place it has in domestic legal systems—the exceptional method when the law enforcement system cannot react quickly enough. The Commissioners deemed international society was not ready for so much. Now that the Articles are completed, however, it is difficult to foresee the next opportunity for significant progress in the area of self-help.

Mary Ellen O'Connell, *The Impact of Sanctions on the Development of New International Law, Report of the Economic Sanctions Committee,* 2001–2002 Proc. Am. Branch Int'l L. Assoc. 86, 93.

8. In the arbitrations excerpted above, four of the five parties believed they had an agreement to arbitrate. In the Air Services case, France believed the agreement to arbitrate was the remedy for any dispute arising under the air services agreement with the U.S. The Tribunal found that despite the arbitration provision, and pending the formation of the tribunal, countermeasures were lawful. Do you agree with this reasoning? Was France entitled to take counter-countermeasures?

9. The Articles on State Responsibility completed years after the *Air Services* case, includes this provision on dispute settlement and countermeasures:

> The wrongfulness of an act of a State not in conformity with an international obligation towards another State is precluded if and to the extent that the act constitutes a countermeasure taken against the latter State in accordance with chapter II of part three.
>
> Article 50
> Obligations not affected by countermeasures
>
> * * *
>
> 2. A State taking countermeasures is not relieved from fulfilling its obligations:
>
> (a) Under any dispute settlement procedure applicable between it and the responsible State....

International Law Commission, Responsibility of States for Internationally Wrongful Acts, G.A. Res. 56/83, U.N. Doc. A/RES/56/83 (2002). Does this provision coincide with the decision?

10. In order to address another kind of situation in which arbitration could be useful, the Permanent Court of Arbitration has issued Optional Rules for Arbitrating Disputes Between Two Parties of Which Only One is a State. These are available online at http://www.pca-cpa.org/upload/files/1STATENG.pdf. *See* Arbitration between Sudan and Sudan People's Liberation Movement, Final Award (July 22, 2009), *available at* http://pca-cpa.org/showpage.asp?pay_id=1306. The Abyei case is discussed in Chapter Seven.

11. In addition to the sources cited in the notes above, for further reading on international dispute resolution in general, see,

International Mass Claims Processes: Legal and Practical Perspectives (Howard & Edda Kristjánsdóttir eds., 2007).

The UNCITRAL Arbitration Rules: A Commentary (David D. Caron et al. eds., 2006).

Wayne Mapp, The Iran-United States Claims Tribunal, The First Ten Years 1981–1991 (1993).

W. Michael Reisman, Systems of Control in International Adjudication and International Arbitration: Break-Down and Repair (1992).

Stephen M. Schwebel, International Arbitration: Three Salient Problems (1987).

Resolving Transnational Disputes Through International Arbitration (Thomas E. Carbonneau ed., 1984).

J. Gillis Wetter, The International Arbitration Process: Public and Private (1979).

Alexander M. Stuyt, Survey of International Arbitrations, 1794–1970 (1972).

Chapter Six

Interim Orders in Arbitration

Introduction

As discussed in Chapter Five, international arbitral tribunals and international courts generally lack the authority typical of national courts over people and assets. These bodies must rely far more on the goodwill of participants. When goodwill is lacking, problems may arise at several phases: at the commencement of the arbitration, during enforcement of final decisions, and during the course of the procedure prior to the final decision. This chapter concerns the use of interim orders to address issues in the course of arbitration.

Courts and tribunals generally lack control at each phase, but in some respects the challenges of control during the pendency of a case have been greater. Until recently, it was unclear whether courts and tribunals could even make binding orders—as opposed to recommendations—during the pendency of a case. International court statutes or arbitration conventions make clear that final judgments or awards are binding. These same documents sometimes provide for tribunals to indicate interim relief, but rarely do the documents provide expressly that these measures are binding on the parties. In 2000, the International Court of Justice held in the *LaGrand* case that court-ordered interim or provisional measures are binding. The ICJ Statute does not state this expressly—it was a matter of interpretation for the ICJ. Similarly, with regard to this issue in arbitration, it will be a matter for the arbitral tribunal itself to decide and for any court asked to interpret the agreement to arbitrate or enforce the interim measures or final award.[1] Consider the two cases that follow. What can you conclude regarding interim orders in international arbitration?

Consider first the discussion of theoretical and practical problems in the excerpt relating to commercial arbitration and interim orders. Note that the ILC's Model Arbitral Rules presented in Chapter Five (and the Annex) do not include provisions for interim relief.

William Wang, *International Arbitration: The Need for Uniform Interim Measures of Relief**

In arbitral proceedings, the need often arises for provisional remedies or other interim measures of relief. These measures are often needed because, in reality, arbitral proceedings are no less adversarial than litigation in public courts. The idea that provisional remedies are unnecessary or inadequate in arbitral proceedings is to confuse arbitration with

---

1. *LaGrand* Case (Ger. v. U.S.), 2001 I.C.J. 466, ¶ 11 (June 27).

* 28 Brook. J. L. Int'l 1059, 1072–83 (2003) (footnotes omitted).

conciliation. These interim measures take on different forms and are often called different names. In the UNCITRAL M.L. and UNCITRAL Rules, they are called 'interim measures of protection.' In the English version of the ICC Rules, they are known as 'interim or conservatory measures,' in the French version as 'mesures provisoires ou conservatoires,' and in the Swiss law governing international arbitration they are referred to as 'provisional or protective measures.'

Provisional remedies and interim relief come in many forms, depending on the parties involved and context of the dispute. However, most often these remedies entail either the seizure of property, often called attachments or holding orders, or interim orders, also known as injunctions. In attachment proceedings, the intention of the petitioner is to preserve the assets representing the subject matter or being necessary for enforcement of the arbitration award. These orders are designed to prevent dissipation of the property or to preserve the condition of the property for future inspection. Alternatively, a litigant may be ordered to deposit property into the custody of a third party.

Another type of interim measure is an order to preserve the status quo between the parties pending the resolution of the merits of their dispute. For example, a party may be ordered not to take certain steps, such as terminating an agreement, disclosing trade secrets, or using disputed intellectual property or other rights, pending a decision on the merits. In the interest of preserving the status quo, ICC tribunals have been willing to order a contract to be performed for a limited period, even though one party claims that the contract was rescinded. The provisional relief of preserving the status quo can be provided either by the arbitrator or by the public courts, during the course of, and in conjunction with, the arbitral proceedings. Issues often arise as to whether arbitral tribunals or national courts have the power to order such relief. The arbitral tribunal must look to the set of arbitration rules under which it is operating to determine if such jurisdiction is granted. The courts, on the other hand, may have the power to act, but must determine whether it would be appropriate to do so.

Parties may also seek orders requiring adverse parties to post security for satisfying the final judgment in the case. Orders for security may be for either the amount in dispute in the underlying controversy or for the fees of legal representation and other costs to be incurred while resolving the dispute. In ICC arbitration, security for costs is usually not granted, but nevertheless, the power exists and in some circumstances may be justified. Other interim measures of relief may include: orders for payment of part of the claim, orders to comply with the arbitration rules, orders to a party to act or omit, or orders and recommendations of holding measures.

Interim measures are incredibly controversial in international arbitration because of the inherent risks involved in granting such orders. First, there is a risk that the issuance of an interim order will represent factual victory in the main proceeding for the petitioner. Even though the decision is only interlocutory, its consequences can often be irreparable. Additionally, there is a risk that the petitioner is being abusive in its use of the request for an interim order. Parties often do not use proceedings for provisional remedies solely to secure later enforcement of an award, but in reality use a petition for an interim order as an offensive weapon. The interim order can be used to exert pressure on the opponent by threatening the seizure of its assets abroad. Moreover, interim proceedings may also be used as dilatory tactics to stay the general progress of the arbitration. Thus, the proper determination of the issue of interim measures of relief is critical to any successful international arbitration.

* * *

While the different sets of rules of each arbitral institution are fairly similar, the problem of interim measures of protection is not effectively addressed by any of the various institutional rules. Although arbitration rules may provide for the issuance of interim measures of relief, there has been no uniform practice among arbitral tribunals in granting or denying such relief. Instead, some arbitral tribunals grant interim measures, others explicitly do not, and some tribunals direct parties to national courts for resolution of interim awards. Tribunals refer parties to courts because arbitral tribunals possess no coercive power for enforcement of their interim orders, and because provisional remedies can only be properly enforced through the court system. Although interim measures can be coercively enforced through the courts, presenting arbitral orders to courts is often problematic.

1. The UNCITRAL

The UNCITRAL Arbitration Rules contain a single provision that expressly permits arbitral tribunals, as well as courts, to order interim measures of protection. While the UNCITRAL Rules allow for both direct arbitral awarding of interim relief as well as court awarded relief, the Rules provide no guidance as to the enforcement of measures. The Rules provide no coercive power to the arbitral tribunal for enforcement of any interim measures of relief

2. The ICC

The ICC Rules also do not effectively address the problem. The ICC Rules were amended in 1998 to add that, 'at the request of a party, (the tribunal should) order interim or conservatory measures it deems appropriate.' While this provision permits the arbitral tribunal to grant interim measures, the ICC Rules possess no enforcement mechanism. Although parties may be reluctant to disregard arbitral tribunal decisions, the ICC Rules do not provide for sanctions against parties who remain recalcitrant and do not follow such orders....

U.S. courts have also disagreed over the effect of national legislation on the authority of national courts to grant provisional relief in aid of international arbitration. The U.S. Court of Appeals for the Second Circuit has explicitly allowed courts to attach property in international arbitrations. In *Borden Inc. v. Meiji Milk Products Co.*, the court held that "entertaining an application for a preliminary injunction in aid of arbitration is consistent with the court's power under Chapter 2 of the Federal Arbitration Act." On the other hand, some courts have held that court-ordered provisional measures are not available under the FAA. The U.S. Court of Appeals for the Eighth Circuit, in *Merrill Lynch, Pierce, Fenner & Smith, Inc. v. Hovey*, held that absent an agreement permitting court-ordered provisional measures, the "unmistakably clear congressional purpose" was to bar such measures.

* * *

In 1981, the U.S. and Iran established the Iran-U.S. Claims Tribunal under treaties known as the Algiers Declarations. The two countries intended the Tribunal to settle claims of U.S. nationals against the government of Iran and between the two governments. The Declarations provide for awards by the Tribunal to U.S. nationals to be satisfied out of an account in the Netherlands Central Bank under the control of the Tribunal and the government of Algeria. The original funds in the account came from Iranian assets frozen by the U.S. when U.S. nationals were taken hostage in the U.S. embassy in 1979–1981.[1] The following excerpt concerns an interim award or order of one of the Tribunal's three chambers.

---

1. Declaration of the Government of the Democratic and Popular Republic of Algeria, Jan. 19, 1981, U.S.-Iran-Alg., 1 IRAN-U.S. CL. TRIB. REP. 3, 20 I.L.M. 224 (1981); Undertakings of the Government of the United States of America and the Government of the Islamic Republic of Iran with Respect to

RCA Globcom Communications, Inc., et al., Claimants v. The Islamic Republic of Iran, et al., Respondents

Case No. 160, Award No. ITM 29-160-1
Iran-United States Claims Tribunal
(Chamber One: Lagergren, Chair; Kashani, Holtzman, members)
31 October 1983

INTERIM AWARD

The Claimants filed a Statement of Claim in this case on 17 December 1981. One of the claims asserted by the Claimants arises out of a contract, dated 16 April 1974, between RCA Globcom Disc and the then Imperial Iranian Supreme Commander's Staff, Military's Switching Project Office, now the Islamic Republic of Iran's Army Joint Staff (the "MSPO Contract") in which the Military's Switching Project Office agreed to purchase certain switching equipment for automatic telegraphic services in Iran together with related installations and services. In the Statement of Claim RCA Globcom Disc and RCA Globcom Systems seek, *inter alia*, damages arising out of an alleged breach by the Switching Project Office of the MSPO Contract and cancellation of certain letters of guarantee and standby letters of credit that were issued. In the Statement of Claim RCA Globcom Disc contends that it invoked force majeure in December 1978 and, in accordance with a provision of the MSPO Contract, which permitted cancellation of the contract in case of force majeure, cancelled the contract in March 1979.

The Army Joint Staff and The Government of the Islamic Republic of Iran filed Statements of Defence on 29 December 1982 and on 12 January 1983, respectively. The Army Joint Staff denies that RCA Globcom Disc was entitled to cancel the MSPO Contract by reason of force majeure and asserts that RCA Globcom Disc breached the contract by failing to perform all of its contractual obligations.

Prior to 17 May 1983 the Army Joint Staff of the Islamic Republic of Iran filed with the Public Court of Tehran, Second Branch, a claim against RCA Globcom Disc in the amount of Rials 672,543,983. In the case before the Public Court of Tehran, the Army Joint Staff seeks to recover damages for RCA Globcom Disc's alleged breaches of the MSPO Contract. The damages sought comprise Rials 615,927,887 for losses due to delays caused by RCA Globcom Disc, compensation in the amount of Rials 53,230,240 for taxes owed to the Ministry of Finance and Economic Affairs and compensation in the amount of Rials 33,856,856 for insurance premiums owed to the Social Security Organization of Iran.

Following the filing of the claim with the Public Court of Tehran, RCA Globcom Disc received from the Iranian Interests Section of the Algerian Embassy in Washington, D.C., a notification that a summons had been issued in the case before the Tehran Court directing RCA Globcom Disc to appear before the Court on 12 November 1983. The summons was accompanied by a copy of the claim and a number of exhibits.

On 12 September 1983 the Claimants in Case No. 160 filed with the Tribunal a Motion in which they requested the Tribunal *inter alia* to direct the Government of the Is-

---

the Declaration of the Government of the Democratic and Popular Government of Algeria, Jan. 19, 1981, U.S.-Iran-Alg., 1 Iran-U.S. Cl. Trib. Rep. 13, 20 I.L.M. 229 (1981); Declaration of the Government of the Democratic and Popular Republic of Algeria. Concerning the Settlement of Claims by the Government of the United States of America and the Government of the Islamic Republic of Iran, Jan. 19, 1981, U.S.-Iran-Alg., 1 Iran-U.S. Cl. Trib. Rep. 9, 20 I.L.M. 230 (1981); and Escrow Agreement, 1 Iran-U.S. Cl. Trib. Rep. 16, 20 I.L.M. 234.

lamic Republic of Iran and the Army Joint Staff to stay further proceedings against RCA Globcom Disc in the case before the Public Court of Tehran until Case No. 160 before the Tribunal has been resolved. In this Motion the Claimants contend that the claims brought before the Court in Tehran all arise out of the same contract, i.e. the MSPO Contract, as the claim previously submitted to the Tribunal by the Claimants.

In an Order dated 20 September 1983 the Tribunal requested the Respondents to file a Reply to the Claimants' Motion by 17 October 1983. On 18 October 1983 the Ministry of Defence of the Islamic Republic of Iran filed a Reply to the Claimants' Motion in which it denied the Tribunal's jurisdiction over the case as well as its competence to order Respondents to stay proceedings in the Iranian Court. The Ministry contends that the MSPO Contract contains a clause which confers exclusive jurisdiction on the competent Courts of Iran and that, consequently, the claim is excluded from the Tribunal's jurisdiction by virtue of Article II, paragraph 1, of the Claims Settlement Declaration, which excludes "claims arising under a binding contract between the parties, specifically providing that any disputes thereunder shall be within the sole discretion of the competent Iranian courts, in response to the Majlis position".

The Ministry further alleges that the interim relief sought by the Claimant falls outside the scope of the discretion to take interim measures conferred upon the Tribunal by Article 26 of the Tribunal Rules.

Lastly, the Ministry contends that this Tribunal with an *ad hoc* jurisdiction, cannot order stay or suspension of proceedings in a municipal forum with inherent and general jurisdiction, and further that the laws of Iran do not permit the Government to comply with the Tribunal's request to move for stay of proceedings before the Public Court of Tehran.

In the light of the determination by the Full Tribunal in its Interlocutory Award No. ITL 6-159-FT in the Case *Ford Aerospace & Communications Corporation et al. and The Air Force of the Islamic Republic of Iran et al.*, Case No. 159, that the Tribunal has jurisdiction over a claim based on a contract containing a forum selection clause similar to the above mentioned clause, it would appear that the Tribunal has jurisdiction over RCA Globcom Disc's claim in the instant case.

Further, it appears from the copy of the Army Joint Staff's Claim which accompanied the summons received by RCA Globcom Disc that the Claim filed before the Public Court of Tehran involves the same legal and factual issues as the claims by RCA Globcom Disc and RCA Globcom Systems before the Tribunal.

As to the contention that the Tribunal does not have power to grant the interim relief sought by the Claimants, the Tribunal notes that the Full Tribunal concluded in its Interim Award No. ITM 13-388-FT in the Case *E-Systems, Inc. and The Government of the Islamic Republic of Iran et al.*, Case No. 388, that the Algiers Declarations leave the Government of Iran free in principle to initiate claims before Iranian Courts even where the claim would have been admissible as a counterclaim before the Tribunal. However, in that Interim Award it is also stated that the Tribunal has an inherent power to issue such orders as may be necessary to conserve the respective rights of the parties and to ensure that its jurisdiction and authority are made fully effective. It is also stated that any award to be rendered in the case by the Tribunal, which was established by inter-governmental agreement, will prevail over any decision inconsistent with it rendered by Iranian or United States Courts.

The consistent practice of the Tribunal indicates, that this inherent power is in no way restricted by the language in Article 26 of the Tribunal Rules. Further, the Government of Iran and the Government of the United States have agreed in the Algiers Declarations to confer upon this Tribunal jurisdiction over certain claims. It follows that both Governments are under an international obligation to comply with any decisions rendered by the Tribunal pursuant to this agreement.

For these reasons,

The Tribunal requests the Government of the Islamic Republic of Iran or the Islamic Republic of Iran's Army Joint Staff to take all appropriate measures to ensure that the present proceedings before the Public Court of Tehran be stayed, pending the Tribunal's final determination in Case No. 160.

[The following note is appended to the signature of Mr. Kashani:]

I dissent from the majority since the claim is based on a contract specifically providing for jurisdiction of Iranian courts, and in accordance with the Single Article Act passed by the Islamic Consultative Assembly of Iran and Article II, paragraph 1, of the Claims Settlement Declaration this arbitral Tribunal is excluded from jurisdiction to proceed with the claim and, a priori, it is without jurisdiction to issue the interim award and make such a request from the Government of the Islamic Republic of Iran in this case.

RCA Global Communications, Inc., et al., Claimants v. The Islamic Republic of Iran, Respondents

Case No. 160
Iran-United States Claims Tribunal
(Chamber One: Lagergren, Chair)
2 June 1983

ORDER

The following is the text as issued by the Tribunal:

In a Motion filed with the Tribunal on 6 May 1983 the Claimants have requested the Tribunal to direct the Government of Iran to stay further proceedings regarding a claim filed with the Public Court of Tehran by Iran Insurance Company against RCA Global Communications, Inc, and RCA Global Communications Disc, Inc.

RCA Global Communications, Inc. has been requested to appear before the Public Court of Tehran on 8 June 1983,

In its Order of 12 May 1983 the Tribunal has requested the Respondents to file a Reply to the Claimant's Motion by 23 May 1983, addressing in particular the question as to whether the litigation before the Public Court of Tehran involves any issue that can lead to decisions by the Tribunal inconsistent with decisions by the Public Court or Tehran.

Following a request for an extension submitted by the Deputy Agent of the Islamic Republic of Iran on 23 May 1983, the Tribunal has granted an extension to file said Reply by 1 August 1983.

However, in view of the Claimants' statement that RCA Global Communications, Inc. has been ordered to appear before the Public Court of Tehran on 8 June 1983 and the Tribunal's inherent power to issue orders to conserve the respective rights of the Parties and to ensure that its jurisdiction and authority are made fully effective, the Tribunal finds it appropriate immediately to request the Government of Iran to move for a stay of the proceedings before the Public Court of Tehran until such time that the Tribunal can make a decision on the Claimants' request based on the views of both Parties.

For these reasons, the Tribunal requests the Government of the Islamic Republic of Iran to take all appropriate measures to ensure that the proceedings before the Public Court of Tehran be stayed until 15 August 1983.

The following excerpt provides background for an important decision on interim measures. Ireland was seeking to resolve its dispute with the United Kingdom through arbitration, but it sought an award of interim measures from the United Nations Law of the Sea Tribunal, a court.

Barbara Kwiatkowska, The *Ireland v. United Kingdom (Mox Plant) Case*: Applying the Doctrine of Treaty Parallelism*

Introduction

The *Ireland v United Kingdom (Mox Plant)* case was the tenth case brought before the International Tribunal for the Law of the Sea (ITLOS) and the third case involving prescription of provisional measures under Article 290 of the 1982 United Nations Convention on the Law of the Sea (LOSC) and Article 25 of the ITLOS Statute, forming the Convention's Annex VI.

* * *

The History of the *Mox Plant* Dispute

In its Request for Provisional Measures and Statement of Case filed with the ITLOS Registry on 9 November 2001, Ireland broadly characterised the instant dispute as "concerning the Mox Plant, international movements of radioactive materials, and the protection of the marine environment of the Irish Sea". The Request was prompted by the British Justification Decision of 3 October 2001 and a subsequent belief that the process of plutonium commissioning at the Mox Plant would commence on 23 November (later changed to 20 December 2001). Ireland's concerns dated, however, back to the 1970s, when routine and accidental discharges of artificial radionuclides from the Sellafield site (occurring since the early 1950s) into the semi-enclosed Irish Sea increased. The Sellafield (originally called Windscale) site is located in Cumbria, in the North-west of England, on the coast of the Irish Sea, a distance of some 112 miles from Ireland's coast at its closest point (at Clogher Head). The British Nuclear Fuels (BNFL) company, which was created out of the UK Atomic Energy Authority in 1971, has been responsible for most of the activities carried out at this site. In 1984 BNFL became a separate company, intended to operate on a commercial basis, although the British Secretary of State for Trade and Industry and the Treasury Solicitor held all the shares in the company. The BNFL's shipping arm, Pacific Nuclear Transport Limited, operates two vessels—*Pacific Pintail* and *Pacific Teal.*

Both Ireland and Britain were in 1976 amongst the first claimants of 200-mile exclusive fisheries zones, which are divided by equidistance for fishery control purposes and which are subject to the EC Common Fisheries Policy (CFP), developed since the late 1970s and to be reviewed in 2002. Within the CFP, Irish fishermen continue to fish within six miles of Sellafield, and the Irish coastline, south-east from Northern Ireland is in-

---

* 18 Int'l J. Marine & Coastal L. 1, 1–13 (2003) (footnotes omitted).

habited by some 1.5 million people (out of a total population of 3.8 million). Ireland ratified the LOSC on 21 June 1996, followed by Britain's accession on 25 July 1997 and formal confirmation by the European Community on 1 April 1998.

According to Ireland's Request and Statement of Claim, a Mox Plant (Mox Demonstration Facility—MDF) began producing small quantities of Mixed Oxide (Mox) Fuel for Light Water Reactors (LWRs) in 1993, followed by commencement in 1994 of the operation of the Thermal Oxide Reprocessing Plant (THORP), separating plutonium and uranium from fission products. BNFL intended to increase significantly Mox fuel production for use in other reactors so as to have a maximum output of 120 tonnes of heavy metal per year (tHM/y). As no British nuclear reactors currently use Mox, all the Mox fuel produced at this facility was to be exported. The unique three-stage process to be used at the new Mox Plant has been considered as constituting "an experiment with unacceptable risks for Ireland" and formed the subject of concerns expressed by Ireland since 1993, when the present dispute originated. The three stages include: transporting, mainly by sea, spent reactor fuel elements, containing plutonium, unused uranium and fission products, from Japan to Sellafield; reprocessing the spent reactor fuel at THORP to separate these elements, followed by the mixing at the Mox Plant of the plutonium oxide with uranium oxide, so as to make Mox pellets which are then placed into new fuel rods; assembling of these rods into fuel assemblies for use in nuclear power reactors and transporting of fuel assemblies, again mainly by sea, from Sellafield to Japan and possibly to other states.

In the view of Ireland, the process of authorisation of the Mox Plant that began in the early 1990s has been badly flawed and inconsistent with the UK's obligations under the LOSC. Britain approved the construction—but not the operation—of the Mox Plant on the basis of in Ireland's opinion, an inadequate 1993 Environmental Statement, which has never been updated, despite regular repeated requests from Ireland. After the completion of the Mox Plant's construction in 1996, BNFL sought to separately obtain three other necessary and closely related authorisations from Britain for uranium and plutonium processing and full operation of the plant, subject to environmental and economic requirements. The shipments of radioactive materials associated with the Mox Plant's operation into and out of Britain have, to Ireland's knowledge—never been subjected to any environmental assessment.

In its Written Response filed with the ITLOS Registry on 15 November 2001, the United Kingdom pointed out that according to the Opinion of the EC Commission of 25 February 1997, which has never been contested by Ireland, even when the Mox Plant is fully operational its discharges will be "negligible from the health point of view", and in the period pending the plant's full operation, any discharges would be "infinitesimally small".

Ireland's Request and Statement of Claim repeatedly stressed that the "economic justification" of the Mox Plant (in terms of its economic benefits exceeding its economic costs) was assessed during five rounds of public consultations held between April 1997 and August 2001 by the UK authorities in accordance with Directives 80/836/EURATOM and 96/29/EURATOM. The resultant reports placed in public circulation were—according to Ireland—heavily censored by Britain on the ground that the excluded information would unreasonably damage the Mox Plant, and Ireland's requests to obtain complete texts of these reports were repeatedly refused. The United Kingdom, while maintaining that the Environment Agency was responsive to public concerns on environmental and other matter, contested Ireland's entitlement to obtain commercially confidential information contained in those reports, followed by review in the High Court of London.

In its Letter of 30 July 1999, Ireland first raised its specific concerns with regard to the LOSC. They were further clarified in its Letter of 23 December 1999, also drawing Britain's attention to the significant change in the circumstances in which the Mox Plant was to be authorised, which change necessitated a review of authorisation. The concerns of Ireland were, in its view, confirmed by the Report of the UK Nuclear Installations Inspectorate (NII Report) of 18 February 2000. In its Letter of 9 March 2000 responding to Ireland, Britain merely stated that when a final decision regarding the full operation of the Mox Plant was taken, it would set out the reasons in full, and that this would be sent to Ireland. Given, in Ireland's view, the inadequate 1993 UK Environment Statement referred to above, Ireland's Letter of 23 December 1999 called upon Britain to carry out a revised environmental impact assessment (EIA), in accordance with the LOSC, the UN/ECE Espoo Convention on EIA in a Transboundary Context of 25 February 1991, the 1992 OSPAR Convention (including the precautionary principle), the EC Council Directive 85/337/EEC as amended by Directive 97/11/EEC, and the 1998 Sintra Ministerial Declaration of the OSPAR Ministers/European Commission that provided for reduction of radioactive discharges by the year 2020 to levels close to zero. The UK Letter of 9 March 2000 did not respond to the EIA related point at all. In its Written Response to Ireland's Request and Statement of Claim, Britain maintained, however, that its Environmental Assessment fully conformed with the EURATOM and the EC Council Directives referred to above, and that:

> "Precautionary dictates cannot be relied upon as a substitute for a basic foundation of evidence supporting the tangible reality of the risk that is alleged. In this case, Ireland has not adduced such a basic foundation of evidence showing a real risk of harm such as to warrant pre-emptive restraint of the rights of the United Kingdom on grounds of precaution."

In support of its argument that as a result of radioactive pollution from Sellafield site, the semi-enclosed Irish Sea is amongst the most radioactively polluted seas in the world, Ireland relied on the Report on Possible Toxic Effects from the Nuclear Reprocessing Plants at Sellafield (UK) and Cap de La Hague (France) (STOA Report) which was commissioned by the European Parliament's Directory General for Research, under the auspices of its Panel on Scientific and Technological Office Assessment (STOA), which was submitted to the European Parliament in August 2001, Britain stressed that the STOA Report has been "slammed" as "unscientific" and was not concerned with the alleged risks arising from the Mox Plant. In Ireland's view, moreover, the horrifying atrocities at the World Trade Centre and the Pentagon on 11 September 2001 notably increased the risk of devastating effects on human health and the environment as a result of nuclear terrorism.

In view of the failure to obtain the reports on the Mox Plant's "economic justification" prepared pursuant to EURATOM Directives referred to above, Ireland instituted on 15 June 2001 arbitral proceedings against Britain under the 1992 OSPAR Convention on the ground of the allegedly repeated violation of Article 9 on Access to Information. The OSPAR *Mox Plant* Arbitral Tribunal, established in pursuance of Article 32, comprised Chairman W. Michael Reisman, Arbitrators Gavan Griffith QC and Lord Mustill PC, while its Registry was placed at the Permanent Court of Arbitration (PCA), Peace Palace, The Hague. Following Ireland's requests of June and August 2001 for confirmation that the United Kingdom would not authorise the Mox Plant's operation pending the conclusion of the OSPAR arbitral proceedings, Britain declined on 13 September 2001 to provide such a confirmation.

On 3 October 2001, the British authorities decided that the Mox Plant was "economically justified" in accordance with Directives 80/836/EURATOM and 96/29/EURATOM (referred to above) and that over the course of its life it would make a net operating profit between UK£199M and £216M. In the view of Britain, this decision "was in fact the culmination of a process lasting eight years that reveals how, at every step, the United Kingdom has insisted that the environmental and other requirements for the construction and operation of the Mox Plant have been satisfied." Ireland noted that BNFL was reported to have closed its two Sellafield reprocessing plants due to its inability to reduce the production of high-level liquid radioactive waste (HLW) sufficiently to meet the regulators' requirements. At the meeting of the UK and Irish Agents in the OSPAR *Mox Plant* arbitration held in London on 5 October, Ireland notified Britain that—as Ireland's Letter of 16 October reiterated—the UK decision on economic justification of the Mox Plant violated various LOSC provisions, and that there existed a dispute between them in relation *inter alia* to the interpretation and application of these provisions. By Letter of 18 October 2001 Britain responded that: "[T]he UK is anxious to exchange views on the points you raise in your letter as soon as possible. In order to do so meaningfully we need to understand why the Irish Government considers the UK to be in breach of the provisions and principles identified in your letter."

According to Ireland's Request and Statement of Claim, the UK Letter did not respond to Ireland's request that the authorisation of the Mox Plant be suspended with immediate effect, nor did it address the question of plutonium movements or the increased threat of terrorist attacks. In its written response, Britain maintained that although Ireland's letter of 16 October 1002 referred to above, which raised the issue of the risk of terrorist attacks for the first time, did not contain an offer to treat any information received on a confidential basis, the UK responded two days later offering and exchange of views, which offer Ireland did not accept. Britain also stated that there were to be no maritime transports, in the Irish Sea or elsewhere, arising from the commissioning of the Mox Plant, prior to the establishment of the Annex VII Arbitral Tribunal. Thereafter, exports from the Mox Plant will not be of separated plutonium (in the form of plutonium dioxide powder) but of Mox fuel (in the form of ceramic pellets), which reduces any security threat because Mox fuel is less attractive to potential terrorists and has safety advantages during transport which can be carried out in full compliance with international regulations on the transport of nuclear materials by sea, including the 1999 IAEA/IMO INF Code.

By Letter of 23 October, Ireland stated that no useful purpose could be served by any exchange of views unless Britain indicated a willingness to suspend authorisation or operation of the Mox Plant. Since by Letter of 24 October the United Kingdom declined to indicate such willingness, it became clear to Ireland that the dispute could not be settled by negotiations. Accordingly, by Letter of 25 October 2001 Ireland notified Britain that a situation of urgency now existed, that views had been exchanged between the parties, and that it reserved its right to initiate LOSC proceedings without further notice.

The Mox Plant Case
(*Ireland v. United Kingdom*)

International Tribunal for the Law of the Sea
Case No. 10 (Request for Interim Measures)
Dec. 3, 2001

ORDER

Present: President Chandrasekhara Rao; Vice-President Nelson; Judges Caminos, Marotta Rangel, Yankov, Yamamoto, Kolodkin, Park, Bamela, Engo, Mensah, Akl, Anderson,

Vukas, Wolfrum, Treves, Marsit, Eiriksson, Ndiaye, Jesus, Xu; Judge *ad hoc* Székely; Registrar Gautier.

The Tribunal,

composed as above,

after deliberation,

Having regard to article 290 of the United Nations Convention on the Law of the Sea (hereinafter "the Convention") and articles 21, 25 and 27 of the Statute of the Tribunal (hereinafter "the Statute"),

Having regard to articles 89 and 90 of the Rules of the Tribunal (hereinafter "the Rules"),

Having regard to the fact that Ireland and the United Kingdom of Great Britain and Northern Ireland (hereinafter "the United Kingdom") have not accepted the same procedure for the settlement of disputes in accordance with article 287 of the Convention and are therefore deemed to have accepted arbitration in accordance with Annex VII to the Convention,

Having regard to the Notification and Statement of Claim submitted by Ireland to the United Kingdom on 25 October 2001 instituting arbitral proceedings as provided for in Annex VII to the Convention "in the dispute concerning the MOX plant, international movements of radioactive materials, and the protection of the marine environment of the Irish Sea",

Having regard to the Request for provisional measures submitted by Ireland to the United Kingdom on 25 October 2001 pending the constitution of an arbitral tribunal under Annex VII to the Convention,

Having regard to the Request submitted by Ireland to the Tribunal on 9 November 2001 for the prescription of provisional measures by the Tribunal in accordance with article 290, paragraph 5, of the Convention,

* * *

26. *Whereas*, in the Notification and Statement of Claim of 25 October 2001, Ireland requested the arbitral tribunal to be constituted under Annex VII (hereinafter "the Annex VII arbitral tribunal") to adjudge and declare:

1) that the United Kingdom has breached its obligations under Articles 192 and 193 and/or Article 194 and/or Article 207 and/or Articles 211 and 213 of UNCLOS in relation to the authorisation of the MOX plant, including by failing to take the necessary measures to prevent, reduce and control pollution of the marine environment of the Irish Sea from (1) intended discharges of radioactive materials and/or wastes from the MOX plant, and/or (2) accidental releases of radioactive materials and/or wastes from the MOX plant and/or international movements associated the MOX plant, and/or (3) releases of radioactive materials and/or wastes from the MOX plant and/or international movements associated the MOX plant with the of resulting from terrorist act;
2) that the United Kingdom has breached its obligations under Articles 192 and 193 and/or Article 194 and/or Article 207 and/or Articles 211 and 213 of UNCLOS in relation to the authorisation of the MOX plant by failing (1) properly or at all to assess the risk of terrorist attack on the MOX plant and international movements of radioactive material associated with the plant, and/or (2) properly or at all to prepare a comprehensive response strategy or plan to prevent,

contain and respond to terrorist attack on the MOX plant and international movements of radioactive waste associated with the plant;

3) That the United Kingdom has breached its obligations under Articles 123 and 197 of UNCLOS in relation to the authorisation of the MOX plant, and has failed to cooperate with Ireland in the protection of the marine environment of the Irish Sea *inter alia* by refusing to share information with Ireland and/or refusing to carry out a proper environmental assessment of the impacts on the marine environment of the MOX plant and associated activities and/or proceeding to authorise the operation of the MOX plant whilst proceedings relating to the settlement of a dispute on access to information were still pending;

4) That the United Kingdom has breached its obligations under Article 206 of UNCLOS in relation to the authorisation of the MOX plant, including by

   (a) failing, by its 1993 Environmental Statement, properly and fully to assess the potential effects of the operation of the MOX plant on the marine environment of the Irish Sea; and/or

   (b) failing, since the publication of its 1993 Environmental Statement, to assess the potential effects of the operation of the MOX plant on the marine environment by reference to the factual and legal developments which have arisen since 1993, and in particular since 1998; and/or

   (c) failing to assess the potential effects on the marine environment of the Irish Sea of international movements of radioactive materials to be transported to and from the MOX plant; and/or

   (d) failing to assess the risk of potential effects on the marine environment of the Irish Sea arising from terrorist act or acts on the MOX plant and/or on international movements of radioactive material to and from the MOX plant.

5) That the United Kingdom shall refrain from authorizing or failing to prevent (a) the operation of the MOX plant and/or (b) international movements of radioactive materials into and out of the United Kingdom related to the operation of the MOX plant or any preparatory or other activities associated with the operation of the MOX until such time as (1) there has been carried out a proper assessment of the environmental impact of the operation of the MOX plant as well as related international movements of radioactive materials, and (2) it is demonstrated that the operation of the MOX plant and related international movements of radioactive materials will result in the deliberate discharge of no radioactive materials, including wastes, directly or indirectly into the marine environment of the Irish Sea, and (3) there has been agreed and adopted jointly with Ireland a comprehensive strategy or plan to prevent, contain and respond to terrorist attack on the MOX plant and international movements of radioactive waste associated with the plant;

* * *

29. *Whereas* Ireland, in its final submissions at the public sitting held on 20 November 2001, requested the prescription by the Tribunal of the following provisional measures:

(1) that the United Kingdom immediately suspend the authorisation of the MOX plant dated 3 October, 2001, alternatively take such other measures as are necessary to prevent with immediate effect the operation of the MOX plant;

(2) that the United Kingdom immediately ensure that there are no movements into or out of the waters over which it has sovereignty or exercises sovereign

rights of any radioactive substances or materials or wastes which are associated with the operation of, or activities preparatory to the operation of, the MOX plant;

(3) that the United Kingdom ensure that no action of any kind is taken which might aggravate, extend or render more difficult of solution the dispute submitted to the Annex VII tribunal (Ireland hereby agreeing itself to act so as not to aggravate, extend or render more difficult of solution that dispute); and

(4) that the United Kingdom ensure that no action is taken which might prejudice the rights of Ireland in respect of the carrying out of any decision on the merits that the Annex VII tribunal may render (Ireland likewise will take no action of that kind in relation to the United Kingdom);

30. *Whereas*, at the public sitting held on 20 November 2001, the United Kingdom presented its final submissions as follows:

The United Kingdom requests the International Tribunal for the Law of the Sea to:

(1) reject Ireland's request for provisional measures;

(2) order Ireland to bear the United Kingdom's costs in these proceedings;

31. *Considering* that, in accordance with article 287 of the Convention, Ireland has, on 25 October 2001, instituted proceedings before the Annex VII arbitral tribunal against the United Kingdom "in the dispute concerning the MOX plant, international movements of radioactive materials, and the protection of the marine environment of the Irish Sea";

32. *Considering* that Ireland on 25 October 2001 notified the United Kingdom of the submission of the dispute to the Annex VII arbitral tribunal and of the Request for provisional measures;

33. *Considering* that, on 9 November 2001, after the expiry of the time-limit of two weeks provided for in article 290, paragraph 5, of the Convention, and pending the constitution of the Annex VII arbitral tribunal, Ireland submitted to the Tribunal a Request for provisional measures;

34. *Considering* that article 290, paragraph 5, of the Convention provides in the relevant part that:

> Pending the constitution of an arbitral tribunal to which a dispute is being submitted under this section, any court or tribunal agreed upon by the parties or, failing such agreement within two weeks from the date of the request for provisional measures, the International Tribunal for the Law of the Sea ... may prescribe, modify or revoke provisional measures in accordance with this article if it considers that *prima facie* the tribunal which is to be constituted would have jurisdiction and that the urgency of the situation so requires;

35. *Considering* that, before prescribing provisional measures under article 290, paragraph 5, of the Convention, the Tribunal must satisfy itself that *prima facie* the Annex VII arbitral tribunal would have jurisdiction;

36. *Considering* that Ireland maintains that the dispute with the United Kingdom concerns the interpretation and application of certain provisions of the Convention, including, in particular, articles 123, 192 to 194, 197, 206, 207, 211, 212 and 213 thereof;

37. *Considering* that Ireland has invoked as the basis of jurisdiction of the Annex VII arbitral tribunal article 288, paragraph 1, of the Convention which reads as follows:

> A court or tribunal referred to in article 287 shall have jurisdiction over any dispute concerning the interpretation or application of this Convention which is submitted to it in accordance with this Part;

38. *Considering* that the United Kingdom maintains that Ireland is precluded from having recourse to the Annex VII arbitral tribunal in view of article 282 of the Convention which reads as follows:

> If the States Parties which are parties to a dispute concerning the interpretation or application of this Convention have agreed, through a general, regional or bilateral agreement or otherwise, that such dispute shall, at the request of any party to the dispute, be submitted to a procedure that entails a binding decision, that procedure shall apply in lieu of the procedures provided for in this Part, unless the parties to the dispute otherwise agree;

39. *Considering* that the United Kingdom maintains that the matters of which Ireland complains are governed by regional agreements providing for alternative and binding means of resolving disputes and have actually been submitted to such alternative tribunals, or are about to be submitted;

40. *Considering* that the United Kingdom referred to the fact that Ireland has under article 32 of the 1992 Convention for the Protection of the Marine Environment of the North-East Atlantic (hereinafter "the OSPAR Convention") submitted a dispute between Ireland and the United Kingdom "concerning access to information under article 9 of the OSPAR Convention in relation to the economic 'justification' of the proposed MOX plant" to an arbitral tribunal (hereinafter "the OSPAR arbitral tribunal");

41. *Considering* that the United Kingdom has further stated that certain aspects of the complaints of Ireland are governed by the Treaty establishing the European Community (hereinafter "the EC Treaty") or the Treaty establishing the European Atomic Energy Community (hereinafter "the Euratom Treaty") and the Directives issued thereunder and that States Parties to those Treaties have agreed to invest the Court of Justice of the European Communities with exclusive jurisdiction to resolve disputes between them concerning alleged failures to comply with such Treaties and Directives;

42. *Considering* that the United Kingdom has also stated that Ireland has made public its intention of initiating separate proceedings in respect of the United Kingdom's alleged breach of obligations arising under the EC Treaty and the Euratom Treaty;

43. *Considering* that the United Kingdom maintains that the main elements of the dispute submitted to the Annex VII arbitral tribunal are governed by the compulsory dispute settlement procedures of the OSPAR Convention or the EC Treaty or the Euratom Treaty;

44. *Considering* that, for the above reasons, the United Kingdom maintains that the Annex VII arbitral tribunal would not have jurisdiction and that, consequently, the Tribunal is not competent to prescribe provisional measures under article 290, paragraph 5, of the Convention;

45. *Considering* that Ireland contends that the dispute concerns the interpretation or application of the Convention and does not concern the interpretation or application of either the OSPAR Convention or the EC Treaty or the Euratom Treaty;

46. *Considering* that Ireland further states that neither the OSPAR arbitral tribunal nor the Court of Justice of the European Communities would have jurisdiction that extends to all of the matters in the dispute before the Annex VII arbitral tribunal;

47. *Considering* that Ireland further maintains that the rights and duties under the Convention, the OSPAR Convention, the EC Treaty and the Euratom Treaty are cumulative, and, as a State Party to all of them, it may rely on any or all of them as it chooses;

48. *Considering* that, in the view of the Tribunal, article 282 of the Convention is concerned with general, regional or bilateral agreements which provide for the settlement of disputes concerning what the Convention refers to as "the interpretation or application of this Convention";

49. *Considering* that the dispute settlement procedures under the OSPAR Convention, the EC Treaty and the Euratom Treaty deal with disputes concerning the interpretation or application of those agreements, and not with disputes arising under the Convention;

50. *Considering* that, even if the OSPAR Convention, the EC Treaty and the Euratom Treaty contain rights or obligations similar to or identical with the rights or obligations set out in the Convention, the rights and obligations under those agreements have a separate existence from those under the Convention;

51. *Considering* also that the application of international law rules on interpretation of treaties to identical or similar provisions of different treaties may not yield the same results, having regard to, *inter alia*, differences in the respective contexts, objects and purposes, subsequent practice of parties and *travaux préparatoires*;

52. *Considering* that the Tribunal is of the opinion that, since the dispute before the Annex VII arbitral tribunal concerns the interpretation or application of the Convention and no other agreement, only the dispute settlement procedures under the Convention are relevant to that dispute;

53. *Considering* that, for the reasons given above, the Tribunal considers that, for the purpose of determining whether the Annex VII arbitral tribunal would have *prima facie* jurisdiction, article 282 of the Convention is not applicable to the dispute submitted to the Annex VII arbitral tribunal;

54. *Considering* that the United Kingdom contends that the requirements of article 283 of the Convention have not been satisfied since, in its view, there has been no exchange of views regarding the settlement of the dispute by negotiation or other peaceful means;

55. *Considering* that article 283 of the Convention reads as follows:

> 1. When a dispute arises between States Parties concerning the interpretation or application of this Convention, the parties to the dispute shall proceed expeditiously to an exchange of views regarding its settlement by negotiation or other peaceful means.
>
> 2. The parties shall also proceed expeditiously to an exchange of views where a procedure for the settlement of such a dispute has been terminated without a settlement or where a settlement has been reached and the circumstances require consultation regarding the manner of implementing the settlement;

56. *Considering* that the United Kingdom maintains that the correspondence between Ireland and the United Kingdom did not amount to an exchange of views on the dispute said to arise under the Convention;

57. *Considering* that the United Kingdom contends further that its request for an exchange of views under article 283 of the Convention was not accepted by Ireland;

58. *Considering* that Ireland contends that, in its letter written as early as 30 July 1999, it had drawn the attention of the United Kingdom to the dispute under the Convention and that further exchange of correspondence on the matter took place up to the submission of the dispute to the Annex VII arbitral tribunal;

59. *Considering* that Ireland contends further that it has submitted the dispute to the Annex VII arbitral tribunal only after the United Kingdom failed to indicate its willingness to consider the immediate suspension of the authorization of the MOX plant and a halt to related international transports;

60. *Considering* that, in the view of the Tribunal, a State Party is not obliged to continue with an exchange of views when it concludes that the possibilities of reaching agreement have been exhausted;

61. *Considering* that, in the view of the Tribunal, the provisions of the Convention invoked by Ireland appear to afford a basis on which the jurisdiction of the Annex VII arbitral tribunal might be founded;

62. *Considering* that, for the above reasons, the Tribunal finds that the Annex VII arbitral tribunal would *prima facie* have jurisdiction over the dispute;

63. *Considering* that, in accordance with article 290, paragraph 1, of the Convention, the Tribunal may prescribe provisional measures to preserve the respective rights of the parties to the dispute or to prevent serious harm to the marine environment;

64. *Considering* that, according to article 290, paragraph 5, of the Convention, provisional measures may be prescribed pending the constitution of the Annex VII arbitral tribunal if the Tribunal considers that the urgency of the situation so requires in the sense that action prejudicial to the rights of either party or causing serious harm to the marine environment is likely to be taken before the constitution of the Annex VII arbitral tribunal;

65. *Considering* that the Tribunal must, therefore, decide whether provisional measures are required pending the constitution of the Annex VII arbitral tribunal;

66. *Considering* that, in accordance with article 290, paragraph 5, of the Convention, the Annex VII arbitral tribunal, once constituted, may modify, revoke or affirm any provisional measures prescribed by the Tribunal;

67. *Considering* that Ireland contends that its rights under certain provisions of the Convention, in particular articles 123, 192 to 194, 197, 206, 207, 211, 212 and 213 thereof, will be irrevocably violated if the MOX plant commences its operations before the United Kingdom fulfils its duties under the Convention;

68. *Considering* that Ireland contends further that once plutonium is introduced into the MOX plant and it commences operations some discharges into the marine environment will occur with irreversible consequences;

69. *Considering* that Ireland contends further that, if the plant becomes operational, the danger of radioactive leaks and emissions, whether arising from the operation of the plant, or resulting from industrial accidents, terrorist attacks, or other causes, would be greatly magnified;

70. *Considering* that Ireland argues that the commissioning of the plant is, in practical terms, itself a near-irreversible step and it is not possible to return to the position that existed before the commissioning of the MOX plant simply by ceasing to feed plutonium into the system;

71. *Considering* that Ireland argues that the precautionary principle places the burden on the United Kingdom to demonstrate that no harm would arise from discharges and

other consequences of the operation of the MOX plant, should it proceed, and that this principle might usefully inform the assessment by the Tribunal of the urgency of the measures it is required to take in respect of the operation of the MOX plant;

72. *Considering* that the United Kingdom contends that it has adduced evidence to establish that the risk of pollution, if any, from the operation of the MOX plant would be infinitesimally small;

73. *Considering* that the United Kingdom maintains that the commissioning of the MOX plant on or around 20 December 2001 will not, even arguably, cause serious harm to the marine environment or irreparable prejudice to the rights of Ireland, in the period prior to the constitution of the Annex VII arbitral tribunal or at all;

74. *Considering* that the United Kingdom contends that neither the commissioning of the MOX plant nor the introduction of plutonium into the system is irreversible, although decommissioning would present the operator of the plant with technical and financial difficulties, if Ireland were to be successful in its claim before the Annex VII arbitral tribunal;

75. *Considering* that the United Kingdom argues that Ireland has failed to supply proof that there will be either irreparable damage to the rights of Ireland or serious harm to the marine environment resulting from the operation of the MOX plant and that, on the facts of this case, the precautionary principle has no application;

76. *Considering* that the United Kingdom states that the manufacture of MOX fuel presents negligible security risks and it has in place very extensive security precautions in terms of the protection of the Sellafield site;

77. *Considering* that the United Kingdom states that it hopes to reach agreement with Ireland on the constitution of the Annex VII arbitral tribunal within a short space of time;

78. *Considering* that, at the public sitting held on 20 November 2001, the United Kingdom has stated that "there will be no additional marine transports of radioactive material either to or from Sellafield as a result of the commissioning of the MOX plant";

79. *Considering* that at the same sitting the United Kingdom stated further that "there will be no export of MOX fuel from the plant until summer 2002" and that "there is to be no import to the THORP plant of spent nuclear fuel pursuant to contracts for conversion to the MOX plant within that period either" and clarified that the word "summer" should be read as "October";

80. *Considering* that the Tribunal places on record the assurances given by the United Kingdom as specified in paragraphs 78 and 79;

81. *Considering* that, in the circumstances of this case, the Tribunal does not find that the urgency of the situation requires the prescription of the provisional measures requested by Ireland, in the short period before the constitution of the Annex VII arbitral tribunal;

82. *Considering*, however, that the duty to cooperate is a fundamental principle in the prevention of pollution of the marine environment under Part XII of the Convention and general international law and that rights arise therefrom which the Tribunal may consider appropriate to preserve under article 290 of the Convention;

83. *Considering* that, in accordance with article 89, paragraph 5, of the Rules, the Tribunal may prescribe measures different in whole or in part from those requested;

84. *Considering* that, in the view of the Tribunal, prudence and caution require that Ireland and the United Kingdom cooperate in exchanging information concerning risks

or effects of the operation of the MOX plant and in devising ways to deal with them, as appropriate;

85. *Considering* that Ireland and the United Kingdom should each ensure that no action is taken which might aggravate or extend the dispute submitted to the Annex VII arbitral tribunal;

86. *Considering* that, pursuant to article 95, paragraph 1, of the Rules, each party is required to submit to the Tribunal a report and information on compliance with any provisional measures prescribed;

87. *Considering* that it may be necessary for the Tribunal to request further information from the parties on the implementation of provisional measures and that it is appropriate that the President be authorized to request such information in accordance with article 95, paragraph 2, of the Rules;

88. *Considering* that, in the present case, the Tribunal sees no need to depart from the general rule, as set out in article 34 of its Statute, that each party shall bear its own costs;

89. *For these reasons,*

The Tribunal,

1. Unanimously,

Prescribes, pending a decision by the Annex VII arbitral tribunal, the following provisional measure under article 290, paragraph 5, of the Convention:

Ireland and the United Kingdom shall cooperate and shall, for this purpose, enter into consultations forthwith in order to:

(a) exchange further information with regard to possible consequences for the Irish Sea arising out of the commissioning of the MOX plant;

(b) monitor risks or the effects of the operation of the MOX plant for the Irish Sea;

(c) devise, as appropriate, measures to prevent pollution of the marine environment which might result from the operation of the MOX plant.

2. Unanimously,

Decides that Ireland and the United Kingdom shall each submit the initial report referred to in article 95, paragraph 1, of the Rules not later than 17 December 2001, and *authorizes* the President of the Tribunal to request such further reports and information as he may consider appropriate after that date.

3. Unanimously,

Decides that each party shall bear its own costs.

Notes and Questions on Interim Orders in Arbitration

1. In *RCA*, did the Tribunal issue an order? What is an "order"? (Note other terms for decisions prior to a final decision include: interim measures, provisional measures, injunctive relief, interlocutory decisions, and interim award. Some of these terms are synonymous; some have somewhat different meanings. Check the relevant rules to be certain.)

2. Consider Iran's three arguments against RCA's request for an order. Does the Tribunal answer them all adequately?

3. In *Mox*, why does Ireland request provisional measures from ITLOS and not the arbitral tribunal that is actually deciding the case? Note the same steps were followed in *SBT*.

4. Who won the provisional measures phase of the *Mox Plant Case?*

5. Based on the materials in this chapter, create arguments for and against the proposition that arbitral tribunals have the authority to issue interim orders even when such authority is not specified in the agreement establishing the tribunal. Should an *ad hoc* arbitral tribunal have such authority? Would you argue differently with respect to institutional tribunals or semi-permanent tribunals like the Iran-U.S. Claims Tribunal?

6. After Ireland requested provisional measures in the *Mox Plant Case*, the Commission of the European Communities instituted proceedings against Ireland for doing so:

Action Brought on 30 October 2003 by the Commission of the European Communities against Ireland

(Case C-459/03)
(2004/C 7/39)

An action against Ireland was brought before the Court of Justice of the European Communities on 30 October 2003 by the Commission of the European Communities, represented by P.J. Kuijper and B. Martenczuk, acting as agents, with an address for service in Luxembourg.

The Applicant claims that the Court should:

—declare that, by instituting dispute settlement proceedings against the United Kingdom under the UN Convention for the Law of the Sea concerning the MOX Plant located at Sellafield, Ireland has failed to fulfil its obligations under Article 10 and 292 EC and Article 192 and 193 Euratom;

—order Ireland to pay the costs.

Pleas in law and main arguments

The Commission submits that Ireland has instituted the proceedings against the United Kingdom without taking due account of the fact that the European Community is a party to the UN Convention for the Law of the Sea (UNCLOS). It has further failed to appreciate that the provisions of UNCLOS invoked by it, as well as a number of other Community acts invoked by Ireland, are provisions of Community law. By submitting the dispute to a Tribunal outside the Community legal order, Ireland has violated the exclusive jurisdiction of the Court of Justice enshrined in Articles 292 EC and 193 Euratom. Furthermore, Ireland has also violated the duty of cooperation incumbent on it under Articles 10 EC and 192 Euraton.

7. For further reading on interim orders, see, Dana Renée Bucy, *How to Best Protect Party Rights: The Future of Interim Relief in International Commercial Arbitration Under the Awarded UNCITRAL Model Law,* 25 AM. U. INT'L L. REV. 579 (2010).

Chapter Seven

Issues Arising in the Course of Arbitration

Introduction

Law relevant to conducting an arbitration at the inter-state level comes from the agreement of the parties and from international law (the *lex arbitri*). Within international law we find core principles that must be observed, such as the equal treatment of the parties. See the International Law Commission Draft Model Arbitration Procedure in the Annex.[1] Significant failure to abide by the law found in either source can result in the invalidation of the arbitral award. Some arbitral tribunals, such as the Iran-U.S. Claims Tribunal, use a standard set of rules to supplement the basic agreement to arbitrate. The ILC's Model Rules on Arbitration contain provisions for both establishing an *ad hoc* tribunal and for conducting an arbitration. In addition to such rules, arbitration has certain characteristic features. Some of these are described in the excerpt below for international commercial arbitration, but they are basically true of all international arbitrations.

Andreas Lowenfeld,
The Conduct of an International Arbitration[*]

1. None of the sets of rules ... in common use[] actually prescribe the conduct of an arbitration. Once the tribunal has been constituted, ... and both parties have appeared, how the arbitration goes forward depends largely on the background and disposition of the arbitrators and counsel—as well as, of course, on the nature of the controversy....

2. If arbitration in many ways resembles litigation, arbitration does offer many opportunities for more flexibility.... [Arbitrators may not, however, ignore] the basic principle common to all the rules (and to *ad hoc* arbitration as well) that the parties shall be treated equally and fairly.

3. It is often said that one of the advantages of arbitration (or disadvantages, depending on one's point of view) is that it proceeds without discovery. In fact, parties in significant cases do exchange documents, and submit requests for documents to one another for documents not in their own possession....

---

1. *See also* United Nations Commission on International Trade Law (UNCITRAL) Arbitration Rules (1976) (amended 2010), *available at* http://www.uncitral.org/pdf/english/texts/arbitration/arb-rules-revised/arb-rules-revised-2010-e.pdf (a widely used set of rules for disputes involving both private and state parties).

* International Litigation and Arbitration 339–43 (2d ed. 2002) (footnotes omitted).

4. Outsiders often think that arbitrators—whether sitting alone or in a panel of three—tend to compromise, to "cut up the baby," in the common reference to the judgment of Solomon, who of course did not do that but used the suggestion merely as a discovery device. Most persons who have served as arbitrators in international controversies, including the present author, disagree with this perception. They point out that arbitrators not only view themselves as carrying out a judicial (or quasi-judicial) function, but as being required by rule and tradition to write reasoned, and often very detailed, opinions. Of course as in any collegial decision, whether by an appellate court, a jury, a committee, or a board of trustees, exchange of views is likely to lead to some accommodation of views. It is also true that most presiding arbitrators aim for a unanimous verdict, and in a great many cases achieve it. But the suggestion that if there are two issues the tribunal will award one to each side is not borne out in international commercial arbitration.

* * *

Judicial Review

Appeal from arbitral awards is generally not available. In most countries there is some possibility of setting aside awards for "gross miscarriage of justice," misconduct (including undisclosed conflict of interests) by the arbitrators, or "manifest disregard" of law. Courts are generally sensitive to attempts by losing parties to use such allegations as a substitute for appeal. In principle, if all parties were heard and represented by counsel, a finding of fact different from what a court might have made, or misapplication of legal standards, is not a ground for setting aside an award. The idea is that if the parties chose to submit their disputes to arbitration, they should be bound by the results, unless wholly unforeseeable corruption of the process has occurred.

The two cases that follow concern arbitrations reviewed before the ICJ that used both the agreements and general principles of international law for the conduct of the arbitration. The ICJ is reviewing the awards in both cases for failures to comply with either the agreement to arbitrate or the general principles.

Case Concerning the Arbitral Award made by the King of Spain on 23 December 1906 (*Honduras v. Nicaragua*)

1960 ICJ 192 (Nov. 18)

* * *

Present: President Klaestad; Vice-President Zafrulla Khan; Judges Hackworth, Winiarski, Badawi, Armand-Ugon, Kojevnikov, Moreno Quintana, Cordova, Wellington Koo, Spiropoulos, Sir Percy Spender, Alfaro; Judges Ad Hoc Ago and Urrutia Holguin; Registrar Garnier-Coignet.

* * *

The Court,
composed as above,
delivers the following Judgment:

* * *

On 7 October 1894 Honduras and Nicaragua concluded a Treaty—hereinafter referred to as the Gámez-Bonilla Treaty—Articles I to XI of which are as follows:

[*Translation from the Spanish revised by the Registry*]

Article I

The Governments of Honduras and Nicaragua shall appoint representatives who duly authorized, shall organize a Mixed Boundary Commission, whose duty it shall be to settle in a friendly manner all pending doubts and differences, and to demarcate on the spot the dividing line which is to constitute the boundary between the two Republics.

Article II

The Mixed Commission, composed of an equal number of members appointed by both parties, shall meet at one of the border towns which offers the greater conveniences for study, and shall there begin its work, adhering to the following rules:

1. Boundaries between Honduras and Nicaragua shall be those lines on which both Republics may be agreed or which neither of them may dispute.

2. Those lines drawn in public documents not contradicted by equally public documents of greater force shall also constitute the boundary between Honduras and Nicaragua.

3. It is to be understood that each Republic is owner of the territory which at the date of independence constituted, respectively, the provinces of Honduras and Nicaragua.

4. In determining the boundaries, the Mixed Commission shall consider fully proven ownership of territory and shall not recognize juridical value to de facto possession alleged by one party or the other.

5. In case of lack of proof of ownership the maps of both Republics and public or private documents, geographical or of any other nature, which may shed light upon the matter, shall be consulted; and the boundary line between the two Republics shall be that which the Mixed Commission shall equitably determine as a result of such study.

6. The same Mixed Commission, if it deems it appropriate, may grant compensations and even fix indemnities in order to establish, in so far as possible, a well-defined, natural boundary line.

7. In studying the plans, maps and other similar documents which the two Governments may submit, the Mixed Commission shall prefer those which it deems more rational and just.

8. In case the Mixed Commission should fail to reach a friendly agreement on any point, it shall record this fact separately in two special books, signing the double detailed record, with a statement of the allegations of both parties, and it shall continue its study in regard to the other points of the line of demarcation, disregarding the above referred point until the limit at the extreme end of the dividing line is fixed.

9. The books referred to in the preceding clause shall be sent by the Mixed Commission, one to each of the interested Governments, for its custody in the national archives.

Article III

The point or points of the boundary line which may not have been settled by the Mixed Commission referred to in this Treaty, shall be submitted, no later than one month after the final session of the said Commission, to the decision, without appeal, of an arbitral tribunal which shall be composed of one representative for Honduras and another for Nicaragua, and of one Member of the foreign Diplomatic Corps accredited to Guatemala, the latter to be elected by the first two, or chosen by lot from two lists each containing three names, and proposed one by each party.

Article IV

The arbitral Tribunal shall be organized in the city of Guatemala within twenty days following dissolution of the Mixed Commission, and within the next ten days shall begin its work, which is to be recorded in a Minutes Book, kept in duplicate, the majority vote constituting law.

Article V

In case the foreign Diplomatic Representative should decline the appointment, another election shall take place within the following ten days, and so on. When the membership of the foreign Diplomatic Corps is exhausted, any other foreign or Central American public figure may be elected, by agreement of the Commissions of Honduras and Nicaragua, and should this agreement not be possible, the point or points in controversy shall be submitted to the decision of the Government of Spain, and, failing this, to that of any South American Government upon which the Foreign Offices of both countries may agree.

Article VI

The procedure and time-limit to which the arbitration shall be subject, are as follows:

1. Within twenty days following the date on which the acceptance of the third arbitrator shall have been notified to the parties, the latter shall present to him, through their counsel, their pleadings, plans, maps and documents.

2. Should there be pleadings, he shall submit these, within eight days following their presentation, to the respective opposing counsel, who shall have a period of ten days within which to rebut them and to present any other documents they may deem appropriate.

3. The arbitral award shall be rendered within twenty days following the date on which the period for rebutting pleadings shall have expired, whether these have been presented or not.

Article VII

The arbitral decision, whatever it be, rendered by a majority vote, shall be held as a perfect, binding and perpetual treaty between the High Contracting Parties, and shall not be subject to appeal.

Article VIII

This Convention shall be submitted in Honduras and in Nicaragua to constitutional ratifications, the exchange of which shall take place in Tegucigalpa or in Managua, within sixty days following the date on which both Governments shall have complied with the stipulations of this article.

Article IX

The provision in the preceding article shall in no way hinder the immediate organization of the Mixed Commission, which shall begin its studies no later than two months after the last ratification, in conformity with the provisions of the present Convention, without prejudice to so doing prior to the ratifications, should these be delayed, in order to take advantage of the dry or summer season.

Article X

Immediately following exchange of ratifications of this Convention, whether the work of the Mixed Commission has begun or not, the Governments of Honduras and Nicaragua shall appoint their representatives, who, in conformity with Article IV, shall constitute the arbitral Tribunal, in order that, by organizing themselves in a preliminary meeting, they may name the third arbitrator and so communicate it to the respective Ministers of Foreign Affairs, in order to obtain the acceptance of the appointee. If the latter should decline to serve they shall forth with proceed to the appointment of another third arbitrator in the manner stip ulated, and so on until the arbitral Tribunal shall have been organized.

Article XI

The periods stipulated in this Treaty for the appointment of arbitrators, the initiation of studies, the ratifications and the exchange thereof, as well as any other periods herein fixed, shall not be fatal nor shall they in any way produce nullity.

The object of these periods has been to speed up the work; but if for any reason they cannot be complied with, it is the will of the High Contracting Parties that the negotiation be carried on to its conclusion in the manner herein stipulated, which is the one they deem most appropriate. To this end they agree that this Treaty shall be in force for a period of ten years, in case its execution should be interrupted, within which period it may be neither revised nor amended in any manner whatever, nor the matter of boundaries be settled by any other means.

The Mixed Boundary Commission provided for in Article I of the Treaty met from 24 February 1900 onwards and succeeded in fixing the boundary from the Pacific Coast to the *Portillo de Teotecacinte*; it was however unable to agree on the boundary from that point to the Atlantic Coast and recorded its disagreement at its meeting of 4 July 1901. With regard to the latter section of the boundary, the King of Spain handed down, on 23 December 1906, an arbitral award—hereinafter referred to as the Award.

* * *

Following upon a series of exchanges between the two Governments, some of which will be referred to later, the Foreign Minister of Honduras in a Note dated 25 April 1911 brought to the notice of the Foreign Minister of Nicaragua certain steps taken by Honduras in execution of the Award and made a proposal relating to the demarcation of a certain part of the boundary line in accordance with the concluding portion of the operative clause. In reply to this Note, the Foreign Minister of Nicaragua, in a Note dated 19 March 1912, challenged the validity and binding character of the Award. This gave rise to a dispute between the Parties.

Subsequently, the two Governments made several attempts at settlement by direct negotiation or through the good offices or mediation of other States, but these were all unfruitful. The good offices of the United States of America in 1918–1920 did not succeed. The Irias-Ulloa protocol of 21 January 1931, negotiated directly between the two Governments, failed of ratification. Nor was the joint mediation of Costa Rica, the United States of America and Venezuela in 1937 productive of positive result. Certain incidents between the two Parties having taken place in 1957, the Organization of American States, acting as a consultative body, was led to deal with the dispute with the result that on 21 July 1957, Honduras and Nicaragua reached an agreement at Washington by virtue of which they undertook to submit:

> "to the International Court of Justice, in accordance with its Statute and Rules of Court, the disagreement existing between them with respect to the Arbitral Award handed down by His Majesty the King of Spain on 23 December 1906, with the understanding that each, in the exercise of its sovereignty and in accordance with the procedures outlined in this instrument, shall present such facets of the matter in disagreement as it deems pertinent."

* * *

By the Application instituting proceedings in the present case, Honduras asks the Court *inter alia* to declare that Nicaragua is under an obligation to give effect to the Award. This request was maintained in the final Submissions presented by Honduras at the hearing.

In its final Submissions presented at the hearing, Nicaragua asks the Court to reject the Submissions of Honduras and to adjudge and declare *inter alia* that the decision given by King Alfonso XIII on 23 December 1906, invoked by Honduras, does not possess the character of a binding arbitral award and that the so-called "arbitral" decision is in any case incapable of execution by reason of its omissions, contradictions and obscurities.

Honduras alleges that there is a presumption in favour of the binding character of the Award as it presents all the outward appearances of regularity and was made after the Parties had every opportunity to put their respective cases before the Arbitrator. It contends that the burden lay upon Nicaragua to rebut this presumption by furnishing proof that the Award was invalid.

Nicaragua contends that, as Honduras relies upon the Award, it is under an obligation to prove that the person giving the decision described as an award was invested with the powers of an arbitrator, and it argues that the King of Spain was not so invested inasmuch as:

> (a) he was not designated arbitrator in conformity with the provisions of the Gámez-Bonilla Treaty, and
>
> (b) the Treaty had lapsed before he agreed to act as arbitrator.

* * *

Some support for Nicaragua's contention was sought to be drawn from the suggestion made by the Spanish Minister to Central America to the President of Honduras on 21 October 1904 and to the President of Nicaragua on 24 October 1904 that the period of the Treaty might be extended. In the opinion of the Court, the time at which this initiative was taken shows that it did not carry with it any implication that the Treaty had expired on 7 October 1904. In actual fact, no action was taken to extend the duration of the Treaty. This furnishes confirmation of the view which the Court takes that the Treaty was not due to expire till ten years after the date of the exchange of ratifications, that is to say, on 24 December 1906. Had this not been so, the two Governments, when confronted with the suggestion made by the Spanish Minister to Central America, would either have taken immediate appropriate measures for the renewal or extension of the Treaty or would have terminated all further proceedings in respect of the arbitration on the ground that the Treaty providing for arbitration had already lapsed. On the contrary, the two Governments proceeded with the arbitration and submitted their respective cases to the arbitrator. This shows that the intention of the Parties had been that the Treaty should come into force on the date of the exchange of ratifications.

Again, it may be noted that no objection was taken before the King of Spain to his proceeding with the arbitration on the ground that the Gámez-Bonilla Treaty had already expired. Indeed, the very first allegation that the Treaty had expired on 7 October 1904 was made as late as 1920 during a mediation procedure undertaken by the Government of the United States of America in an effort to resolve the boundary dispute between Honduras and Nicaragua.

The Court, therefore, concludes that the Gámez-Bonilla Treaty was in force till 24 December 1906, and that the King's acceptance on 17 October 1904 of his designation as arbitrator was well within the currency of the Treaty.

Finally, the Court considers that, having regard to the fact that the designation of the King of Spain as arbitrator was freely agreed to by Nicaragua, that no objection was taken by Nicaragua to the jurisdiction of the King of Spain as arbitrator either on the ground of irregularity in his designation as arbitrator or on the ground that the Gámez-Bonilla Treaty had lapsed even before the King of Spain had signified his acceptance of the office of arbitrator, and that Nicaragua fully participated in the arbitral proceedings before the King, it is no longer open to Nicaragua to rely on either of these contentions as furnishing a ground for the nullity of the Award.

Honduras is thus seeking execution of the Award made on 23 December 1906 by the King of Spain who, in the opinion of the Court, was validly designated arbitrator by the Parties during the currency of the Gámez-Bonilla Treaty. Nicaragua urges that even under those conditions the Award is a nullity and seeks to establish the nullity of the Award on the grounds that it was vitiated by

(a) excess of jurisdiction;

(b) essential error;

(c) lack or inadequacy of reasons in support of the conclusions arrived at by the Arbitrator.

Nicaragua also contends that the Award is in any case incapable of execution by reason of its omissions, contradictions and obscurities.

Honduras contends that the conduct and attitudes of Nicaragua show that it accepted the Award as binding and that in consequence of that acceptance and of its failure to raise any objection to the validity of the Award for a number of years, it is no longer open to Nicaragua to question the validity of the Award on the grounds alleged or indeed on any ground at all. Honduras further contends that the Award is clear and definite and is not incapable of execution.

As already stated, the Award was handed down on 23 December 1906. On 24 December 1906 the President of Nicaragua received a telegram from the Nicaraguan Minister in Madrid, which summarized the operative clause of the Award as follows:

> "Boundary begins mouth principal arm River Segovia leaving to Nicaragua Island San Pío, with the bay and the town of Gracias and arm called Gracias; line follows Segovia upstream until encounters Guineo; thereafter boundary takes direction corresponding Sitio Teotecacinte, according to marking established

> 1720, finishing at Portillo de Teotecacinte, said Sitio remaining entirely to Nicaragua."

On the next day, the President of Nicaragua sent the following telegram to the President of Honduras:

> "Through a cable of today's date I have taken cognizance of the arbitral award made by the King of Spain in the matter of the delimitation of the frontier. Having regard to this decision, it appears that you have won the day, upon which I congratulate you. A strip of land more or less is of no importance when it is a question of good relations between two sister nations. The irksome question of the delimitation of the frontier has been resolved in such a satisfactory manner thanks to friendly arbitration. I hope that in the future no obstacle will disturb the good relations between our respective countries."

In a Note dated 9 January 1907, addressed to the Spanish Charge d'affaires in Central America, the Foreign Minister of Nicaragua expressed the appreciation of his Government "for the graciousness of the King of Spain who, by his arbitral award, has terminated our frontier dispute with the neighbouring state of Honduras."

On 28 January 1907, the full text of the Award was published in the Official Gazette of Nicaragua.

On 1 December 1907, the President of Nicaragua, in his message to the National Legislative Assembly of Nicaragua, stated as follows:

> "On 23 December 1906, His Majesty the King of Spain made the Arbitral Award in the matter of the delimitation of the frontier between this Republic and that of Honduras. My Government has noted with satisfaction that this important dispute has been terminated by the highly civilized method of arbitration and, although it accepts this decision with pleasure, it has given instructions to Minister Crisanto Medina with a view to requesting a relevant clarification since this decision contains some points that are obscure and even contradictory."

In the course of his report (*Memoria*) to the National Legislative Assembly of Nicaragua, dated 26 December 1907, covering the period between 1 December 1905 and 30 November 1907, the Foreign Minister of Nicaragua, José Dolores Gámez, referring to Honduras, stated: "Our long-standing question of boundaries with this sister Republic, which, as you will remember, we had submitted to arbitration by the King of Spain, was finally settled by the latter on 23 December 1906, on which date he made his Award." He went on to explain that, despite every effort that had been made by the Government of Nicaragua to obtain a more favourable decision, the decision was somewhat disappointing. The report continued: "The Award in question also contains contradictory concepts which make it difficult to put it into effect, for which reason our Minister in Spain has been instructed to ask for a clarification to avoid possible difficulties in the interpretation of these concepts by the parties interested in the case." The report then stated that, if satisfactory light was not thrown by the King upon the points submitted to him, a friendly approach would be made to the Government of Honduras so that "these final details" might be settled in all harmony and to the satisfaction of both countries. The report affirmed "that the irksome question of frontiers which has preoccupied us for so many years and which might at any moment have impaired the good relations which have always attached us to our Honduran brothers, has been settled. Boundary questions are normally of a very serious and dangerous character, and as a rule they leave in their wake feelings of deep resentment which are difficult to overcome. For that reason we must rejoice at the friendly solution we have been able to find in the settlement of so delicate a question, whatever lines of demarcation have today been laid down for our frontiers with Honduras." In conclusion the report sounded a note of caution for the future with regard to the seeking of settlements by arbitration without appeal.

The section of the report dealing with Spain set out the Award in full.

The National Legislative Assembly of Nicaragua took note of the report and by decree of 14 January 1908 approved 'the acts of the executive power in the field of foreign affairs between 1 December 1905 and 26 December 1907'.

On 25 April 1911, the Foreign Minister of Honduras addressed a Note to the foreign Minister of Nicaragua pointing out that

> "it would be desirable to demarcate the small portion of the line which, in conformity with the last paragraph of the Arbitral Award, extends from the junction of the River Poteca or Bodega with the River Guineo or Namasli as far as the *Portillo de Teotecacinte*, since the Arbitral Award fixed the rest of the line along natural boundaries; for this purpose, as soon as the time is thought opportune, my Government will approach Your Excellency's Government with a view to carrying out this demarcation by agreement."

Early in September 1911, certain Nicaraguan papers carried a report attributed to the Ministry of Foreign Affairs of Nicaragua that one of its representatives, who was then in Europe, had been instructed to request the King of Spain for a clarification of the Award. The Honduran Charge d'affaires in Nicaragua thereupon approached the Foreign Minister of Nicaragua and enquired whether the newspaper report was accurate. According to the Note of the Honduran Charge d'affaires dated 8 September 1911, addressed to his own Foreign Minister, a document presented to the Court by Nicaragua, the Foreign Minister of Nicaragua replied that the press reports were not true and

> "that all that he had intimated to the journalists was that, together with the Charge d'affaires, he was engaged in examining whatever had any reference to fixing, in accordance with the Award, the line of demarcation running from the junction of the Poteca or Bodega River as far as the *Portillo de Teotecacinte*; and that everything would be done in a satisfactory manner in view of the sincere and cordial relations existing between the Governments of Honduras and Nicaragua."

It follows from the facts referred to above that Nicaragua took cognizance of the Award and on several occasions between the date of the Award and 19 March 1912 expressed its satisfaction to Honduras that the dispute concerning the delimitation of frontiers between the two countries had been finally settled through the method of arbitration.

Nicaragua urges that, when the President of Nicaragua dispatched his telegram of 25 December 1906 to the President of Honduras, he was not aware of the actual terms of the Award. From the telegram of the Minister of Nicaragua in Madrid of 24 December 1906, the President of Nicaragua had however learned where the boundary line was to begin under the Award, and the course it was to follow in order to join up with the point reached by the Mixed Boundary Commission. The President's own telegram to the President of Honduras shows that he considered that the Award was on the whole in favour of Honduras, and he gave expression to his feeling that the loss of a certain area of territory was not too serious a sacrifice as against the strengthening of friendly relations between the two countries. In any event, the full terms of the Award must have become available to the Nicaraguan Government fairly soon since the Award was published in the Official Gazette of Nicaragua on 28 January 1907. Even thereafter, the attitude of Nicaragua towards the Award continued to be one of acceptance, subject to a desire to seek clarification of certain points which would facilitate the carrying into effect of the Award. This desire was, however, not carried beyond the giving of certain instructions to the Nicaraguan Minister in Madrid and no request for clarification was in fact submitted to the King of Spain. Changes of Government in Nicaragua and Honduras did not bring about any change in this attitude till March of 1912 when the Foreign Minister of Nicaragua, in his reply dated 19 March 1912 to the Note of the Foreign Minister of Honduras, dated 25 April 1911, for the first time raised the question of the validity of the Award on the grounds that the King of Spain had not been validly designated arbitrator, that the Award did not comply with the conditions laid down by the Gámez-Bonilla Treaty and that it was not "a clear, really valid, effective and compulsory Award."

* * *

In the judgment of the Court, Nicaragua, by express declaration and by conduct, recognized the Award as valid and it is no longer open to Nicaragua to go back upon that recognition and to challenge the validity of the Award. Nicaragua's failure to raise any question with regard to the validity of the Award for several years after the full terms of the Award had become known to it further confirms the conclusion at which the Court has arrived. The attitude of the Nicaraguan authorities during that period was in conformity with Article VII of the Gámez-Bonilla Treaty which provided that the arbitral decision whatever it might be—and this, in the view of the Court, includes the decision of the King of Spain as arbitrator—"shall be held as a perfect, binding and perpetual Treaty between the High Contracting Parties, and shall not be subject to appeal."

* * *

... [T]he Court will observe that the Award is not subject to appeal and that the Court cannot approach the consideration of the objections raised by Nicaragua to the validity of the Award as a Court of Appeal. The Court is not called upon to pronounce on whether the arbitrator's decision was right or wrong. These and cognate considerations have no relevance to the function that the Court is called upon to discharge in these proceedings, which is to decide whether the Award is proved to be a nullity having no effect.

Nicaragua's first complaint is that the King of Spain exceeded his jurisdiction by reason of non-observance of the rules laid down in Article II of the Gámez-Bonilla Treaty. It is contended in the first place that the arbitrator failed to observe the rules laid down in paragraphs 3 and 4 of that Article. The first of these two rules states that "each Republic is owner of the territory which at the date of Independence constituted respectively the provinces of Honduras and Nicaragua." The rule in paragraph 4 calls upon the arbitrator to consider "fully proven ownership of territory" and precludes recognition of "juridical value to de facto possession alleged by one party or the other." Nicaragua contends that the arbitrator fixed what he regarded as a natural boundary line without taking into account the Laws and Royal Warrants of the Spanish State which established the Spanish administrative divisions before the date of Independence. In the judgment of the Court this complaint is without foundation inasmuch as the decision of the arbitrator is based on historical and legal considerations (*derecho historico*) in accordance with paragraphs 3 and 4 of Article II.

With regard to the same complaint, Nicaragua, in the second place, stresses that the arbitrator purported to exercise his discretion in granting compensations in order to establish, in so far as possible, a well-defined natural boundary line as provided for in paragraph 6 of Article II of the Treaty. Nicaragua contends that this discretion was, under the said paragraph, vested in the Mixed Boundary Commission and could not be exercised by the arbitrator. In exercising this discretion, the arbitrator, it is urged, exercised a power which he did not possess, or which, if conferred upon him, he exercised far beyond its legitimate limit. The Court is unable to share this view. An examination of the Treaty shows that the rules laid down in Article II were intended not only for the guidance of the Mixed Commission to which they expressly referred, but were also intended to furnish guidance for the arbitration. No convincing reason has been adduced by Nicaragua in support of the view that, while the remaining paragraphs of Article II were applicable to the arbitrator, paragraph 6 was excluded and that, if it was not excluded, the arbitrator, in applying it, exceeded his powers. In the view of the Court, the arbitrator was under obligation to take into account the whole of Article II, including paragraph 6, to assist him in arriving at his conclusions with regard to the delimitation of the frontier between the two States and, in applying the rule in that paragraph, he did not go beyond its legitimate scope.

The Court, having carefully considered the allegations of Nicaragua, is unable to arrive at the conclusion that the King of Spain went beyond the authority conferred upon him.

Nicaragua next contends that the Award is a nullity by reason of "essential error." The Court has not been able to discover in the arguments of Nicaragua any precise indication of "essential error" which would have the effect, as alleged by Nicaragua, of rendering the Award a nullity. Under paragraph 7 of Article II of the Gámez-Bonilla Treaty, "in studying the plans, maps and other similar documents which the two Governments may submit," the arbitrator was to prefer those which he "deems more rational and just." The instances of "essential error" that Nicaragua has brought to the notice of the Court amount to no more than evaluation of documents and of other evidence submitted to the arbitrator. The appraisal of the probative value of documents and evidence appertained to the discretionary power of the arbitrator and is not open to question.

The last ground of nullity raised by Nicaragua is the alleged lack or inadequacy of reasons in support of the conclusions arrived at by the arbitrator. However, an examination of the Award shows that it deals in logical order and in some detail with all relevant considerations and that it contains ample reasoning and explanations in support of the conclusions arrived at by the arbitrator. In the opinion of the Court, this ground is without foundation.

* * *

It was further argued by Nicaragua that the Award is not capable of execution by reason of its omissions, contradictions and obscurities, and that therefore on this ground the Court must reject the submission of Honduras praying that the Court should adjudge and declare that Nicaragua is under an obligation to give effect to the Award.

The operative clause of the Award fixes the common boundary point on the coast of the Atlantic as the mouth of the river Segovia or Coco where it flows out into the sea, taking as the mouth of the river that of its principal arm between Hara and the Island of San Pío where Cape Gracias a Dios is situated, and directs that, from that point, the frontier line will follow the thalweg of the river Segovia or Coco upstream without interruption until it reaches the place of its confluence with the Poteca or Bodega and that thence the frontier line will depart from the river Segovia or Coco continuing along the thalweg of the Poteca or Bodega upstream until it joins the river Guineo or Namasli. From this junction, the line will follow the direction which corresponds to the demarcation of the *Sitio* of Teotecacinte in accordance with the demarcation made in 1720 to terminate at the *Portillo de Teotecacinte* in such manner that the said *Sitio* remains wholly within the jurisdiction of Nicaragua.

Nicaragua has argued that the mouth of a river is not a fixed point and cannot serve as a common boundary between two States, and that vital questions of navigation rights would be involved in accepting the mouth of the river as the boundary between Honduras and Nicaragua. The operative clause of the Award, as already indicated, directs that "starting from the mouth of the Segovia or Coco the frontier line will follow the vaguada or thalweg of this river upstream." It is obvious that in this context the thalweg was contemplated in the Award as constituting the boundary between the two States even at the "mouth of the river." In the opinion of the Court, the determination of the boundary in this section should give rise to no difficulty.

Nicaragua argues further that the delimitation in the operative clause leaves a gap of a few kilometres between the point of departure of the frontier line from the junction of the Poteca or Bodega with the Guineo or Namasli up to the *Portillo de Teotecacinte*, which was the point to which the Mixed Commission had brought the frontier line from its western boundary point. An examination of the Award fails to reveal that there is in fact any gap with regard to the drawing of the frontier line between the junction of the Poteca or Bodega with the Guineo or Namasli and the *Portillo de Teotecacinte.*

In view of the clear directive in the operative clause and the explanations in support of it in the Award, the Court does not consider that the Award is incapable of execution by reason of any omissions, contradictions or obscurities.

For these reasons,

THE COURT,

by fourteen votes to one,

finds that the Award made by the King of Spain on 23 December 1906 is valid and binding and that Nicaragua is under an obligation to give effect to it.

* * *

Note on the Case Concerning the Arbitral Award of 31 July 1989

The case that follows is an ICJ review of an arbitral award on the maritime boundary of Guinea-Bissau and Senegal. As you will see from the map, these two states are adjacent, sharing a land and maritime boundary. The land boundary was delineated by the former colonial powers in the area, France and Portugal. That agreement also divided the existing maritime zones of the time: the territorial sea, contiguous zone, and continental shelf. In 1982, with the adoption of UNCLOS, these zones were modified and new zones were added: the territorial sea became twelve miles, the zone contiguous to the territorial sea was extended another twelve miles, and a new zone, the exclusive economic zone, was created, extending 200 miles. Fisheries zones are not specifically provided for in UNCLOS. These zones often intersect with those of neighboring states and must be delineated. France and Portugal provided that the land boundary should extend as the maritime boundary into the sea at 240° from a designated lighthouse. The case refers to the demarcation line as a "loxodromic line," meaning it follows the curve of the earth.[2]

---

2. For more on the law of the sea, *see* ROBIN CHURCHILL & ALAN VAUGHAN LOWE, THE LAW OF THE SEA (new rev'd. 1988).

Case Concerning the Arbitral Award of 31 July 1989 (*Guinea-Bissau v. Senegal*)

1991 ICJ Rep. 53 (Nov. 12, 1991)

* * *

Present: President Sir Robert Jennings; Vice-President Oda; Judges Lachs, Ago, Schwebel, Ni, Evensen, Tarassov, Guillaume, Shahabuddeen, Aguilar Mawdsley, Weeramantry, Ranjeva; Judges ad hoc Thierry, Mbaye; Registrar Valencia-Ospina.

* * *

THE COURT,
composed as above,
after deliberation,
delivers the following Judgment:

* * *

12. The events leading up to the present proceedings are as follows. On 26 April 1960 an Agreement by exchange of letters was concluded between France, on its own behalf and that of the *Communauté*, and Portugal for the purpose of defining the maritime boundary between the Republic of Senegal (at that time an autonomous State within the *Communauté*) and the Portuguese Province of Guinea. The letter of France proposed (*inter alia*) as follows:

> "As far as the outer limit of the territorial sea, the boundary shall consist of a straight line drawn at 240 degrees from the intersection of the prolongation of the land frontier and the low-water mark, represented for that purpose by the Cape Roxo lighthouse.
>
> As regards the contiguous zones and the continental shelf, the delimitation shall be constituted by the prolongation in a straight line, in the same direction, of the boundary of the territorial seas."

The letter of Portugal expressed its agreement to this proposal.

13. After the accession to independence of Senegal and Guinea-Bissau a dispute arose between them concerning the delimitation of their maritime areas. This dispute was the subject of negotiations between them from 1977 onward, in the course of which Senegal asserted, *inter alia*, that the line defined in the 1960 Agreement had been validly established, while Guinea-Bissau disputed the validity of that Agreement and its opposability to Guinea-Bissau, and insisted that the maritime areas in question be delimited without reference to the Agreement.

14. On 12 March 1985 the Parties concluded an Arbitration Agreement for submission of that dispute to an arbitration tribunal; the terms of the Agreement, so far as relevant to the questions now before the Court, were as follows:

"The Government of the Republic of Senegal and the Government of the Republic of Guinea-Bissau,

Recognizing that they have been unable to settle by means of diplomatic negotiation the dispute relating to the determination of their maritime boundary,

Desirous, in view of their friendly relations, to reach a settlement of that dispute as soon as possible and, to that end, having decided to resort to arbitration,

Have agreed as follows:

Article 1

1. The Arbitration Tribunal (hereinafter called "the Tribunal") shall consist of three members designated in the following manner:

Each Party shall appoint one arbitrator of its choice;

The third arbitrator, who shall function as President of the Tribunal, shall be appointed by mutual agreement of the two Parties or, in the absence of such agreement, by agreement of the two arbitrators after consultation with the two Parties.

* * *

Article 2

The Tribunal is requested to decide in accordance with the norms of international law on the following questions:

1. Does the Agreement concluded by an exchange of letters on 26 April 1960, and which relates to the maritime boundary, have the force of law in the relations between the Republic of Guinea-Bissau and the Republic of Senegal?

2. In the event of a negative answer to the first question, what is the course of the line delimiting the maritime territories appertaining to the Republic of Guinea-Bissau and the Republic of Senegal respectively?

* * *

Article 4

1. The Tribunal shall take its decisions only in its full composition.

2. The decisions of the Tribunal relating to all questions of substance or procedure, including all questions relating to the jurisdiction of the Tribunal and the interpretation of the Agreement, shall be taken by a majority of its members.

* * *

Article 9

1. Upon completion of the proceedings before it, the Tribunal shall inform the two Governments of its decision regarding the questions set forth in Article 2 of the present Agreement.

2. That decision shall include the drawing of the boundary line on a map. To that end, the Tribunal shall be empowered to appoint one or more technical experts to assist it in the preparation of such map.

3. The Award shall state in full the reasons on which it is based.

* * *

Article 10

1. The Arbitral Award shall be signed by the President of the Tribunal and by the Registrar. The latter shall hand to the Agents of the two Parties a certified copy in the two languages.

2. The Award shall be final and binding upon the two States which shall be under a duty to take all necessary steps for its implementation.

* * *

Article 11

1. No activity of the Parties during the course of the proceedings may be deemed to prejudge their sovereignty over the areas the subject of the Arbitration Agreement.

* * *

Done in duplicate in Dakar, on 12 March 1985, in the French and Portuguese languages, both texts being equally authentic."

15. An Arbitration Tribunal was duly constituted under the Agreement, by the appointment first of Mr. Mohammed Bedjaoui and then of Mr. Andre Gros, arbitrators, and of Mr. Julio A. Barberis, President. On 31 July 1989 the Tribunal pronounced the Award the existence and validity of which have been challenged in the present proceedings. According to this Award it was adopted by the votes of the President of the Tribunal and Mr. Gros, over the negative vote of Mr. Bedjaoui.

16. The findings of the Tribunal may for the purposes of the present judgment be summarized as follows. The Tribunal concluded that the 1960 Agreement was valid and could be opposed to Senegal and to Guinea-Bissau (Award, para. 80); that it had to be interpreted in the light of the law in force at the date of its conclusion (*ibid.*, para. 85); that

> "the 1960 Agreement does not delimit those maritime spaces which did not exist at that date, whether they be termed exclusive economic zone, fishery zone or whatever ...",

but that

> "the territorial sea, the contiguous zone and the continental shelf ... are expressly mentioned in the 1960 Agreement and they existed at the time of its conclusion" (*ibid.*).

The Tribunal went on to say that:

> "As regards the continental shelf, the question of determining how far the boundary line extends can arise today, in view of the evolution of the definition of the concept of 'continental shelf'. In 1960, two criteria served to determine the extent of the continental shelf: that of the 200-metre bathymetric line and that of exploitability. The latter criterion involved a dynamic conception of the continental shelf, since the outer limit would depend on technological developments and could consequently move further and further to seaward. In view of the fact that the 'continental shelf' existed in the international law in force in 1960, and that the definition of the concept of that maritime space then included the dynamic criterion indicated, it may be concluded that the Franco-Portuguese Agreement delimits the continental shelf between the Parties over the whole extent of that maritime space as defined at present." (Award, para. 85.)

17. The Tribunal then explained that

> "Bearing in mind the above conclusions reached by the Tribunal and the wording of Article 2 of the Arbitration Agreement, in the opinion of the Tribunal it is not called upon to reply to the second question.

Furthermore, in view of its decision, the Tribunal considered that there was no need to append a map showing the course of the boundary line." (*Ibid.*, para. 87.)

18. The operative clause of the Award was as follows:

"For the reasons stated above, the Tribunal decides by two votes to one:

> To reply as follows to the first question formulated in Article 2 of the Arbitration Agreement: The Agreement concluded by an exchange of letters of 26 April 1960, and relating to the maritime boundary, has the force of law in the relations between the Republic of Guinea-Bissau and the Republic of Senegal with regard solely to the areas mentioned in that Agreement, namely the territorial sea, the contiguous zone and the continental shelf. The 'straight line drawn at 240 degrees' is a loxodromic line." (Para. 88.)

19. Mr. Barberis, President of the Arbitration Tribunal, appended a declaration to the Award, and Mr. Bedjaoui, who had voted against the Award, appended a dissenting opinion. The declaration of President Barberis read as follows:

> "I feel that the reply given by the Tribunal to the first question put by the Arbitration Agreement could have been more precise. I would have replied to that question as follows:
>
> 'The Agreement concluded by an exchange of letters of 26 April 1960, and relating to the maritime boundary, has the force of law in the relations between the Republic of Guinea-Bissau and the Republic of Senegal with respect to the territorial sea, the contiguous zone and the continental shelf, but does not have the force of law with respect to the waters of the exclusive economic zone or the fishery zone. The "straight line drawn at 240 degrees" mentioned in the Agreement of 26 April 1960 is a loxodromic line.'
>
> This partially affirmative and partially negative reply is, in my view, the exact description of the legal position existing between the Parties. As suggested by Guinea-Bissau in the course of the present arbitration (Reply, p. 248), this reply would have enabled the Tribunal to deal in its Award with the second question put by the Arbitration Agreement. The partially negative reply to the first question would have conferred on the Tribunal a partial competence to reply to the second, i.e., to do so to the extent that the reply to the first question would have been negative.

In that case, the Tribunal would have been competent to delimit the waters of the exclusive economic zone* or the fishery zone between the two countries. The Tribunal thus could have settled the whole of the dispute, because, by virtue of the reply to the first question of the Arbitration Agreement, it would have determined the boundaries for the territorial sea, the contiguous zone and the continental shelf, as the Award has just done and, by its answer to the second question, the Tribunal could have determined the boundary for the waters of the exclusive economic zone or the fishery zone, a boundary which might or might not have coincided with the line drawn by the 1960 Agreement.

20. In his dissenting opinion, Mr. Bedjaoui referred to the declaration by President Barberis, which, he said,

> "shows to what an extent the Award is incomplete and inconsistent with the letter and spirit of the Arbitration Agreement with regard to the single line desired by the Parties. Since it emanates from the President of the Tribunal himself, that Declaration, by its very existence as well as by its contents, justifies more fundamental doubts as to the existence of a majority and the reality of the Award." (Para. 161.)

---

* "I refer to the 'waters' of the exclusive economic zone. I think it necessary to be as specific as to this, because it sometimes occurs that the notion of this zone covers also the continental shelf as, for example, in Article 56 of the 1982 Montego Bay Convention."

21. A public sitting of the Tribunal was held on 31 July 1989 for delivery of the Award, at which President Barberis and Mr. Bedjaoui were present, but not Mr. Gros. At that sitting, after the Award had been delivered, the representative of Guinea-Bissau indicated that, pending full reading of the documents and consultation with his Government, he reserved the position of Guinea-Bissau regarding the applicability and validity of the Award, as he alleged that it did not satisfy the requirements laid down by agreement between the two Parties. After contacts between the Governments of the two Parties, in which Guinea-Bissau indicated its reasons for not accepting the Award, the present proceedings were brought before the Court by Guinea-Bissau ...

... As the Court had occasion to observe with respect to the contention of nullity advanced in the case of the *Arbitral Award Made by the King of Spain on 23 December 1906:*

> "the Award is not subject to appeal and ... the Court cannot approach the consideration of the objections raised by Nicaragua to the validity of the Award as a Court of Appeal. The Court is not called upon to pronounce on whether the arbitrator's decision was right or wrong. These and cognate considerations have no relevance to the function that the Court is called upon to discharge in these proceedings, which is to decide whether the Award is proved to be a nullity having no effect." (*I.C.J. Reports 1960*, p. 214.)

* * *

26. The Court will now consider a contention by Senegal that Guinea-Bissau's Application is inadmissible, insofar as it seeks to use the declaration of President Barberis for the purpose of casting doubt on the validity of the Award (see paragraph 30 below). Senegal argues that that declaration is not part of the Award, and therefore that any attempt by Guinea-Bissau to make use of it for that purpose "must be regarded as an abuse of process aimed at depriving Senegal of the rights belonging to it under the Award." Senegal also contends that the remedies sought are disproportionate to the grounds invoked and that the proceedings have been brought for the purpose of delaying the final solution of the dispute.

27. The Court considers that Guinea-Bissau's Application has been properly presented in the framework of its right to have recourse to the Court in the circumstances of the case. Accordingly, it does not accept Senegal's contention that Guinea-Bissau's Application, or the arguments used in support of it, amount to an abuse of process.

28. Guinea-Bissau contends that the absence of Mr. Gros from the meeting of the Arbitration Tribunal at which the Award was pronounced amounted to a recognition that the Tribunal had failed to resolve the dispute. Guinea-Bissau accepts that at this meeting

> "it was not intended that a 'decision' should be taken, and by a formal and strict interpretation it would be possible to avoid applying to it Article 4, paragraph 1 [of the Arbitration Agreement], requiring that the Tribunal be in its full composition ...".

Guinea-Bissau however takes the view that this was a particularly important meeting of the Tribunal and that the absence of Mr. Gros lessened the Tribunal's authority.

29. The Court notes that it is not disputed that Mr. Gros participated in the voting when the Award was adopted. Thereafter the Award had to be delivered to the Parties. In this respect Article 10, paragraph 1, of the Arbitration Agreement provided that the Award having been signed by the President and the Registrar, the Registrar was to "hand to the Agents of the two Parties a certified copy in the two languages". This was done. A meeting was held at which the Award was read. The absence of Mr. Gros from that meeting could not affect the validity of the Award which had already been adopted.

30. The Court will now examine the submissions of Guinea-Bissau that the Arbitral Award is inexistent, or subsidiarily that it is absolutely null and void. In support of its principal contention, that the Award is inexistent, the Applicant claims that the Award was not supported by a real majority. Guinea-Bissau does not dispute the fact that the Award was expressed to have been adopted by the votes of President Barberis and Mr. Gros; it contends however that President Barberis's declaration contradicted and invalidated his vote, thus leaving the Award unsupported by a real majority. The Tribunal, having concluded, in reply to the first question in the Arbitration Agreement, that the 1960 Agreement "has the force of law in the relations between" the Parties, held that that was so "with regard solely to the areas mentioned in that Agreement, namely, the territorial sea, the contiguous zone and the continental shelf ..." (Award, para. 88). However, Guinea-Bissau drew attention to the fact that, in his declaration, President Barberis stated that he would have replied to the effect that the Agreement had the force of law in the relations between the Parties "with respect to the territorial sea, the contiguous zone and the continental shelf, but does not have the force of law with respect to the waters of the exclusive economic zone or the fishery zone ..." (paragraph 19 above).

31. The Court considers that, in putting forward this formulation, what President Barberis had in mind was that the Tribunal's answer to the first question "could have been more precise"—to use his own words—, not that it had to be more precise in the sense indicated in his formulation, which was, in his view, a preferable one, not a necessary one. In the opinion of the Court, the formulation discloses no contradiction with that of the Award.

32. Guinea-Bissau also drew attention to the fact that President Barberis expressed the view that his own formulation "would have enabled the Tribunal to deal in its Award with the second question put by the Arbitration Agreement" and that the Tribunal would in consequence "have been competent to delimit the waters of the exclusive economic zone or the fishery zone between the two countries," in addition to the other areas. The Court considers that the view expressed by President Barberis, that the reply which he would have given to the first question would have enabled the Tribunal to deal with the second question, represented, not a position taken by him as to what the Tribunal was required to do, but only an indication of what he considered would have been a better course. His position therefore could not be regarded as standing in contradiction with the position adopted by the Award.

33. Furthermore, even if there had been any contradiction, for either of the two reasons relied on by Guinea-Bissau, between the view expressed by President Barberis and that stated in the Award, such contradiction could not prevail over the position which President Barberis had taken when voting for the Award. In agreeing to the Award, he definitively agreed to the decisions, which it incorporated, as to the extent of the maritime areas governed by the 1960 Agreement, and as to the Tribunal not being required to answer the second question in view of its answer to the first. As the practice of international tribunals shows, it sometimes happens that a member of a tribunal votes in favour of a decision of the tribunal even though he might individually have been inclined to prefer another solution. The validity of his vote remains unaffected by the expression of any such differences in a declaration or separate opinion of the member concerned, which are therefore without consequence for the decision of the tribunal.

34. Accordingly, in the opinion of the Court, the contention of Guinea-Bissau that the Award was inexistent for lack of a real majority cannot be accepted ...

* * *

36. The Court will examine Guinea-Bissau's contentions, whether presented as of *exces de pouvoir* or as lack of reasoning, which are based on the absence of a reply to the sec-

ond question put by the Arbitration Agreement, before dealing with those relating to the absence of a map....

* * *

39. Guinea-Bissau's complaint on the ground that the Tribunal did not give an answer to the second question in Article 2 of the Arbitration Agreement involves three arguments. It questions whether the Tribunal really took a decision not to give an answer; it contends that, even if there was such a decision, there was insufficient reasoning in support of it; and, finally, it contests the validity of any such decision.

40. As to the first of these three arguments, Guinea-Bissau suggests that what the Tribunal did was not to decide not to answer the second question put to it; it simply omitted, for lack of a real majority, to reach any decision at all on the issue. In this respect Guinea-Bissau stresses that what is referred to in the first sentence of paragraph 87 of the Award as an "opinion of the Tribunal" on the point appears in the statement of reasoning, not in the operative clause of the Award; that the Award does not specify the majority by which that paragraph would have been adopted; and that only Mr. Gros could have voted in favour of this paragraph. In the light of the declaration made by President Barberis, Guinea-Bissau questions whether any vote was taken on paragraph 87.

41. The Court recognizes that the structure of the Award is, in that respect, open to criticism. Article 2 of the Arbitration Agreement put two questions to the Tribunal; and the Tribunal was, according to Article 9, to "inform the two Governments of its decision regarding the questions set forth in Article 2." Consequently, it would have been normal to include in the operative part of the Award, i.e., in a final paragraph, both the answer given to the first question and the decision not to answer the second. It is to be regretted that this course was not followed. However, when the Tribunal adopted the Award by two votes to one, it was not only approving the content of paragraph 88, but was also doing so for the reasons already stated in the Award and, in particular, in paragraph 87. It is clear from that paragraph, taken in its context, and also from the declaration of President Barberis, that the Tribunal decided by two votes to one that, as it had given an affirmative answer to the first question, it did not have to answer the second. By so doing, the Tribunal did make a decision: namely, not to answer the second question put to it. The Award is not flawed by any failure to decide.

42. Guinea-Bissau argues, secondly, that any arbitral award must, in accordance with general international law, be a reasoned one. Moreover, according to Article 9, paragraph 3, of the Arbitration Agreement, the Parties had specifically agreed that "the Award shall state in full the reasons on which it is based." Yet, according to Guinea-Bissau, the Tribunal in this case did not give any reasoning in support of its refusal to reply to the second question put by the Parties or, at the very least, gave "wholly insufficient" reasoning, which did not even make it possible to "determine the line of argument followed" and did not "reply on any point to the questions raised and discussed during the arbitral proceedings." On this ground also, it is claimed that the Award is null and void.

43. In paragraph 87 of the Award, referred to above, the Tribunal, "bearing in mind the ... conclusions" that it had reached, together with "the wording of Article 2 of the Arbitration Agreement," took the view that it was not called upon to reply to the second question put to it. This reasoning is brief, and could doubtless have been developed further. But the references in paragraph 87 to the Tribunal's conclusions and to the wording of Article 2 of the Arbitration Agreement make it possible to determine, without difficulty, the reasons why the Tribunal decided not to answer the second question. By referring to the wording of Article 2 of the Arbitration Agreement, the Tribunal was tak-

ing note that, according to that Article, it was asked, first, whether the 1960 Agreement had "the force of law in the relations" between Guinea-Bissau and Senegal, and then, "in the event of a negative answer to the first question, what is the course of the line delimiting the maritime territories" of the two countries. By referring to the conclusions that it had already reached, the Tribunal was noting that it had, in paragraphs 80 et seq. of the Award, found that the 1960 Agreement, in respect of which it had already determined the scope of its substantive validity, was "valid and can be opposed to Senegal and to Guinea-Bissau." Having given an affirmative answer to the first question, and basing itself on the actual text of the Arbitration Agreement, the Tribunal found as a consequence that it did not have to reply to the second question. That statement of reasoning, while succinct, is clear and precise. The second contention of Guinea-Bissau must also be dismissed.

44. Thirdly, Guinea-Bissau challenges the validity of the reasoning thus adopted by the Tribunal on the issue whether it was required to answer the second question. In this respect Guinea-Bissau presents two arguments: first that the Arbitration Agreement, on its true construction, required an answer to the second question whatever might have been its reply to the first; secondly, that in any event an answer to the second question was required because the answer to the first question was in fact partially negative.

45. Guinea-Bissau's first argument is that the Arbitration Agreement was concluded on the basis of an agreement

> "that a two-fold question should be posed to the Tribunal, in order to ensure that whatever [the Tribunal's] reply concerning the value of the Franco-Portuguese exchange of letters, the Tribunal would be called upon to proceed to a comprehensive delimitation of the maritime territories."

In the view of Guinea-Bissau, even if the Tribunal upheld the validity and opposability of the 1960 Agreement, the effect would not be to produce a complete delimitation, and a complete delimitation by a single line was the object and purpose of the Arbitration Agreement. Accordingly, Guinea-Bissau is in effect contending that that Agreement required the Tribunal to answer the second question whatever was its answer to the first.

46. In this connection the Court would first recall

> "a rule consistently accepted by general international law in the matter of international arbitration. Since the Alabama case, it has been generally recognized, following the earlier precedents, that, in the absence of any agreement to the contrary, an international tribunal has the right to decide as to its own jurisdiction and has the power to interpret for this purpose the instruments which govern that jurisdiction." (*Nottebohm, Preliminary Objection, Judgment, I.C.J. Reports* 1953, p. 119.)

In the present case, Article 4, paragraph 2, of the Arbitration Agreement confirmed that the Tribunal had the power to determine its own jurisdiction and to interpret the Agreement for that purpose.

47. By its argument set out above, Guinea-Bissau is in fact criticizing the interpretation in the Award of the provisions of the Arbitration Agreement which determine the Tribunal's jurisdiction, and proposing another interpretation. However, the Court does not have to enquire whether or not the Arbitration Agreement could, with regard to the Tribunal's competence, be interpreted in a number of ways, and if so to consider which would have been preferable. By proceeding in that way the Court would be treating the request as an appeal and not as a *recours en nullite*. The Court could not act in that way

in the present case. It has simply to ascertain whether by rendering the disputed Award the Tribunal acted in manifest breach of the competence conferred on it by the Arbitration Agreement, either by deciding in excess of, or by failing to exercise, its jurisdiction.

48. Such manifest breach might result from, for example, the failure of the Tribunal properly to apply the relevant rules of interpretation to the provisions of the Arbitration Agreement which govern its competence. An arbitration agreement (*compromis d'arbitrage*) is an agreement between States which must be interpreted in accordance with the general rules of international law governing the interpretation of treaties....

These principles are reflected in Articles 31 and 32 of the Vienna Convention on the Law of Treaties, which may in many respects be considered as a codification of existing customary international law on the point.

49. Furthermore, when States sign an arbitration agreement, they are concluding an agreement with a very specific object and purpose: to entrust an arbitration tribunal with the task of settling a dispute in accordance with the terms agreed by the parties, who define in the agreement the jurisdiction of the tribunal and determine its limits. In the performance of the task entrusted to it, the tribunal "must conform to the terms by which the Parties have defined this task" (*Delimitation of the Maritime Boundary in the Gulf of Maine Area, Judgment, I.C.J. Reports* 1984, p. 266, para. 23).

50. In the present case, Article 2 of the Arbitration Agreement presented a first question concerning the 1960 Agreement, and then a second question relating to delimitation. A reply had to be given to the second question "in the event of a negative answer to the first question." The Court notes that those last words, which were originally proposed by Guinea-Bissau itself, are categorical. The situation in the present case differs from that faced by the Court or by arbitral tribunals when they had to reply to successive questions which were not made conditional on each other, and to each of which some meaning had in any event to be attributed in order for a reply to be given thereto, as for example in the case of the *Free Zones of Upper Savoy and the District of Gex (Order of 19 August 1929, P.C.I.J., Series A, No.* 22, p. 13), or *Corfu Channel, Merits (Judgment, I.C.J. Reports* 1949, p. 24). Where, however, successive questions were put to the Court which were made conditional on each other, the Court replied, or found no room to reply, according to whether or not the governing condition had been fulfilled, as, for example, in *Interpretation of the Greco-Bulgarian Agreement of 9 December 1927 (Advisory Opinion, 1932, P.C.I.J., Series A/B, No.* 45, pp. 70, 86–87); and *Interpretation of Peace Treaties with Bulgaria, Hungary and Romania (First Phase, Advisory Opinion, I.C.J. Reports 1950, pp. 65, 67–68, 75, 76, 77; Second Phase, Advisory Opinion, ibid.*, pp. 225, 226, 230).

51. In fact in the present case the Parties could have used some such expression as that the Tribunal should answer the second question "taking into account" the reply given to the first, but they did not; they directed that the second question should be answered only "in the event of a negative answer" to that first question. In that respect, the wording was very different from that to be found in another Arbitration Agreement to which Guinea-Bissau is a party, that concluded on 18 February 1983 with the Republic of Guinea. By that Agreement, those two States asked another tribunal to decide on the legal value and scope of another Franco-Portuguese delimitation convention and annexed documents, and then, "according to the answers given" to those initial questions, to determine the "course of the boundary between the maritime territories" of the two countries.

52. Faced with the problem presented by the prefatory words of the second question, the Applicant stresses that, according to the Preamble of the Arbitration Agreement, its object was to settle the dispute that had arisen between the two countries relating to the

determination of their maritime boundary. The first sentence of Article 2 requested the Tribunal to decide on the two questions put to it. The Tribunal was, according to Article 9, to "inform the two Governments of its decision regarding the questions set forth in Article 2." That decision was to "include the drawing of the boundary line on a map." According to Guinea-Bissau, the Tribunal was therefore required to delimit by a single line the whole of the maritime areas appertaining to each State. As, for the reasons given by the Tribunal, its answer to the first question put in the Arbitration Agreement could not lead to a comprehensive delimitation, it followed, in Guinea-Bissau's view, that, notwithstanding the prefatory words to the second question the Tribunal was required to answer that question and to effect the overall delimitation desired by both Parties.

53. It is useful to recall, in order to assess the weight of that line of argument, the circumstances in which the Arbitration Agreement was drawn up. Following various incidents, Senegal and Guinea-Bissau engaged in negotiations, from 1977 to 1985, with regard to their maritime boundary. Two opposing views were asserted. Senegal maintained that the Agreement concluded in 1960 between France, on its own behalf and that of the *Communauté*, and Portugal had the force of law in the relations between the two States, by virtue of the rules relating to State succession, and that the line defined by that Agreement defined the boundary. Guinea-Bissau however considered that that Agreement was inexistent, null and void, and in any case not opposable to it. From this it inferred that it would be appropriate to proceed *ex novo* to a maritime delimitation between the two States. When the time came to draft the Arbitration Agreement, Senegal proposed that the Tribunal should decide solely whether the 1960 Agreement had the force of law in the relations between the Parties. Guinea-Bissau asked that the Tribunal should be entrusted only with the task of drawing the line delimiting the maritime territories in dispute. After lengthy discussions, it was agreed that there should first be put to the Tribunal the question proposed by Senegal. Guinea-Bissau suggested in addition that, "in the event of a negative answer to the first question," the Tribunal should be asked to define the course of the delimitation line. That form of words was ultimately adopted.

54. It will be apparent that the two questions had a completely different subject matter. The first concerned the issue whether an international agreement had the force of law in the relations between the Parties, while the second was directed to a maritime delimitation in the event that that agreement did not have such force. Senegal was counting on an affirmative reply to the first question, and concluded that the straight line on a bearing of 240 degrees, adopted by the 1960 Agreement, would constitute the single line separating the whole of the maritime areas of the two countries. Guinea-Bissau was counting on a negative answer to the first question, and concluded that a single dividing line for the whole of the maritime areas of the two countries would be fixed *ex novo* by the Tribunal in reply to the second question. The two States intended to obtain a delimitation of the whole of their maritime areas by a single line. But Senegal was counting on achieving this result through an affirmative answer to the first question, and Guinea-Bissau through a negative answer to that question. No agreement had been reached between the Parties as to what should happen in the event of an affirmative answer leading only to a partial delimitation, and as to what might be the task of the Tribunal in such case. The *travaux preparatoires* accordingly confirm the ordinary meaning of Article 2.

55. The Court considers that this conclusion is not at variance with the circumstance that the Tribunal adopted as its title "Arbitration Tribunal for the Determination of the Maritime Boundary: Guinea-Bissau/Senegal," or with its definition, in paragraph 27 of the Award, of the "sole object of the dispute" as being one relating to "the determination of the maritime boundary between the Republic of Senegal and the Republic of Guinea-

Bissau, a question which they have not been able to settle by means of negotiation...." In the opinion of the Court, that title and that definition are to be read in the light of the Tribunal's conclusion, which the Court shares, that, while its mandate did include the making of a delimitation of all the maritime areas of the Parties, this fell to be done only under the second question and "in the event of a negative answer to the first question."

56. In short, although the two States had expressed in general terms in the Preamble of the Arbitration Agreement their desire to reach a settlement of their dispute, their consent thereto had only been given in the terms laid down by Article 2. Consequently the Tribunal did not act in manifest breach of its competence to determine its own jurisdiction by deciding that it was not required to answer the second question except in the event of a negative answer to the first. The first argument must be rejected.

57. The Court now turns to Guinea-Bissau's second argument. Apart from its contention that, on a true construction, the Arbitration Agreement required recourse to the second question whatever was the answer to the first, Guinea-Bissau argues that the answer in fact given by the Tribunal to the first question was a partially negative answer and that this sufficed to satisfy the prescribed condition for entering into the second question. Accordingly, and as was to be shown by the declaration of President Barberis, the Tribunal was, it is said, both entitled and bound to answer the second question.

58. It is true that the Arbitration Tribunal, when answering the first question, in paragraph 88 of the Award, explained that the 1960 Agreement had the force of law in the relations between the Parties "with regard solely to the areas mentioned in that Agreement, namely the territorial sea, the contiguous zone and the continental shelf." Consequently "the 1960 Agreement does not delimit those maritime spaces which did not exist at that date, whether they be termed exclusive economic zone, fishery zone or whatever" (Award, para. 85).

59. In his declaration appended to the Award reproduced in paragraph 19 above, President Barberis added that he would have preferred that, in paragraph 88 of the Award, an affirmative answer be given with respect to the areas delimited by the 1960 Agreement, and a negative answer with respect to the areas not delimited by that Agreement. In his opinion, such a partially negative wording would have conferred on the Tribunal a partial competence to reply to the second question, and to determine the boundary of the waters of the exclusive economic zones or fishery zones between the two countries.

60. The Court would first observe that the Tribunal did not, in paragraph 88 of its Award, adopt the form of words that President Barberis would have preferred. Guinea-Bissau thus cannot base its arguments upon a form of words that was not in fact adopted by the Tribunal. The Tribunal found, in reply to the first question, that the 1960 Agreement had the force of law in the relations between the Parties, and at the same time it defined the substantive scope of that Agreement. Such an answer did not permit a delimitation of the whole of the maritime areas of the two States, and a complete settlement of the dispute between them. It achieved a partial delimitation. But that answer was nonetheless both a complete and an affirmative answer to the first question; it recognized that the Agreement of 1960 had the force of law in the relations between Senegal and Guinea-Bissau. The Tribunal could thus find, without manifest breach of its competence, that its answer to the first question was not a negative one, and that it was therefore not competent to answer the second question. In this respect also, the contention of Guinea-Bissau that the entire Award is a nullity must be rejected.

61. Finally, Guinea-Bissau recalls that, according to Article 9, paragraph 2, of the Arbitration Agreement, the decision of the Tribunal was to "include the drawing of the

boundary line on a map," and that no such map was produced by the Arbitration Tribunal. Guinea-Bissau contends that the Tribunal also did not give sufficient reasons for its decision on that point. It is contended that the Award should, for these reasons, be considered wholly null and void.

62. The Court observes that the Award states that the 1960 Agreement "clearly determines the maritime boundary as regards the territorial sea, the contiguous zone and the continental shelf" by adopting "a straight line drawn at 240 degrees" (paras. 80 and 85). The Award states that this terminology "makes it possible to rule out any geodesic line," so that the line would have to be a loxodromic line, which, moreover is in accordance with the "sketch included in the preparatory work of the 1960 Agreement" (paras. 86 and 88). Then, after deciding not to answer the second question, the Tribunal adds that: "Furthermore, in view of its decision, the Tribunal considered that there was no need to append a map showing the course of the boundary line."

63. The Court is unable to uphold the contention that the reasoning of the Tribunal was insufficient on this point. The reasoning mentioned above is, once again, brief but sufficient to enlighten the Parties and the Court as to the reasons that guided the Tribunal.

* * *

69. For these reasons,

THE COURT,

(1) Unanimously,

Rejects the submission of the Republic of Guinea-Bissau that the Arbitral Award given on 31 July 1989 by the Arbitration Tribunal established pursuant to the Agreement of 12 March 1985 between the Republic of Guinea-Bissau and the Republic of Senegal, is inexistent;

(2) By eleven votes to four,

Rejects the submission of the Republic of Guinea-Bissau that the Arbitral Award of 31 July 1989 is absolutely null and void;

IN FAVOUR: *President* Sir Robert Jennings; *Vice-President* Oda; *Judges* Lachs, Ago, Schwebel, Ni, Evensen, Tarassov, Guillaume, Shahabuddeen; *Judge* ad hoc Mbaye.

AGAINST: *Judges* Aguilar Mawdsley, Weeramantry, Ranjeva; *Judge* ad hoc Thierry.

(3) By twelve votes to three.

Rejects the submission of the Republic of Guinea-Bissau that the Government of Senegal is not justified in seeking to require the Government of Guinea-Bissau to apply the Arbitral Award of 31 July 1989; and, on the submission to that effect of the Republic of Senegal, finds that the Arbitral Award of 31 July 1989; and, on the submission to that effect of the Republic of Senegal, *finds* that the Arbitral Award of 31 July 1989 is valid and binding for the Republic of Senegal and the Republic of Guinea-Bissau, which have the obligation to apply it.

IN FAVOUR: *President* Sir Robert Jennings; *Vice-President* Oda; *Judges* Lachs, Ago, Schwebel, Ni, Evensen, Tarassov, Guillaume, Shahabuddeen, Ranjeva; *Judge* ad hoc Mbaye.

AGAINST: *Judges* Aguilar Mawdsley, Weeramantry; *Judge* ad hoc Thierry.

The Government of Sudan and The Sudan People's Liberation Movement/Army (Abyei Arbitration) Final Award, Permanent Court of Arbitration July 22 2009

CHAPTER I—PROCEDURAL HISTORY

A. The Arbitration Agreement

1. On July 7, 2008, the Government of Sudan ("GoS") and the Sudan People's Liberation Movement/Army ("SPLM/A," and together with the GoS, the "Parties") signed the "Arbitration Agreement between The Government of Sudan and The Sudan People's Liberation Movement/Army on Delimiting Abyei Area" ("Arbitration Agreement").
2. As stated in the Arbitration Agreement, a dispute has arisen between the Parties regarding whether or not the experts ("ABC Experts" or "Experts") of the Abyei Boundaries Commission ("ABC"), established pursuant to the Comprehensive Peace Agreement signed by the Parties on January 9, 2005 ("CPA"), exceeded their mandate as per the provisions of the CPA, the Protocol signed by the Parties on May 26, 2004 on the Resolution of Abyei Conflict ("Abyei Protocol"), the appendix to the Abyei Protocol ("Abyei Appendiz" or "Abyei Annex"),[1] and the ABC's terms of reference ("Terms of Reference") and rules of procedure ("Rules of Procedure").
3. Under Article 1.1 of the Arbitration Agreement, the Parties agreed to refer their dispute to final and binding arbitration under the Arbitration Agreement and the PCA Optional Rules for Arbitrating Disputes between Two Parties of Which Only One is a State ("PCA Rules"), subject to such modifications as the Parties agreed in the Arbitration Agreement or may agree in writing. Under Article 1.2, the Parties agreed to form an arbitration tribunal ("Tribunal") to arbitrate their dispute.
4. In accordance with Article 12.1 of the Arbitration Agreement, on July 11, 2008, the Parties deposited the Arbitration Agreement with the Secretary-General of the Permanent Court of Arbitration ("PCA").
5. Under Article 1.3 of the Arbitration Agreement, the Parties agreed that the International Bureau of the PCA is to act as registry and provide administrative support in accordance with the Arbitration Agreement and the PCA Rules. Pursuant to Article 1.4, the Parties designated the Secretary-General of the PCA as the appointing authority for the proceedings.

* * *

CHAPTER II—INTRODUCTION

95. The GoS and the SPLM/A agreed in 2004 to define the "Abyei Area" in the following terms: "The territory [of the Abyei Area] is defined as the area of the nine Ngok Dinka chiefdoms transferred to Kordofan in 1905."[13] (In appropriate instances, this phrase is also referred to in this Award as the "Formula") However, the Parties do not agree on the boundaries of the Abyei Area that the application of that Formula should produce. It is

1. The Parties use the terms interchangeably to refer to the same instrument.
13. Abyei Protocol, section 1.1.2.

this disagreement that constitutes the essence of the dispute submitted for arbitration to the Tribunal.

* * *

133. Upon the delivery of the ABC Experts' Report, disagreements arose between the Parties as to whether the ABC Experts exceeded their mandate.

134. On June 8, 2008, the Parties signed "The Road Map for Return of IDPs and Implementation of Abyei Protocol" (the "Abyei Road Map") in Khartoum. Through the Abyei Road Map, the Parties committed, among other matters, to refer this dispute to arbitration, and to "abide by and implement the award of the arbitration tribunal."[92] They also agreed, without prejudice the outcome of the arbitration, on interim boundaries for the Abyei Area for administrative purposes.[93]

* * *

401. ... [B]oth Parties drew upon these general principles [of international law] in analogizing and comparing the Tribunal's function with that of a court or tribunal reviewing a prior decision of a different and independent institution for *excés de pouvoir* (or excess of jurisdiction). Given the paucity of authority on what "excess of mandate" concretely represents in law, the Tribunal agrees that principles of review applicable in public international law and national legal systems, insofar as the latter's practices are commonly shared, may be relevant as "general principles of law and practices" to its Article 2(a) inquiry.[805]

402. National courts' process of judicial review in relation to administrative bodies (specifically, regulatory bodies imbued with quasi-judicial and rule-making powers) commonly involves an assessment of whether the original decision-maker exceeded its powers. In situations involving review of the findings of expert groups and specialized bodies, many jurisdictions permit courts to defer to the expertise of those groups and bodies. In the United States of America, for example, the review of agency decision-making and rule-making is marked by a high degree of deference:[806] the judiciary defers to the agency's presumed expertise, instead of conducting a *de novo* review.[807] Such judicial restraint is also practiced in the United Kingdom, provided that an issue is within the particular expertise of the prior decision-maker.[808] Certain continental European legal systems, including Germany, accord a more limited degree of deference to the original decision-maker, extending only to the decision-maker's appreciation of the facts and its choice among

92. Abyei Road Map, Section 4.

93. *See* Abyei Road Map, Section 3 and SPLM/A Map Atlas vol. 1, Map 58 (Abyei Area: Area Calculations).

805. Arbitration Agreement, Article 3(1).

806. *Chevron U.S.A. Inc. v. Natural Resources Defense Council*, 467 U.S. 837 (1984), 843–44 (if Congress has expressly given the agency authority to elucidate a statutory provision through regulations, then such legislative regulations are given controlling weight "unless ... arbitrary, capricious, or manifestly contrary to the statute." If Congress' statute is silent or ambiguous with respect to the issue in question, then the court must simply ask whether the agency's interpretation is based on a "permissible construction of the statute.")

807. *Skidmore v. Swift & Co.*, 323 U.S. 134, 139 (1944), noting that agencies formulate policy "based upon more specialized experience and broader investigation and information than is likely to come to a judge."

808. *R v. Social Fund Inspector, ex p Ali* (1994) 6 ADMIN LR 205, 210E (Brooke, J). The English courts have been reluctant to interfere when Parliament has entrusted an expert body, whether the expert body be tribunals or civil servants, or a combination of civil servants and independent inspectors, with the task of fulfilling the intentions of Parliament in a specialist sphere.

various permissible decision options.[809] However, this more limited deference presumably results from the fact that in these jurisdictions, the review is conducted by specialized administrative courts which themselves have both substantive expertise and superior knowledge of the legal rules applicable to pertinent areas of activity. The Tribunal notes this national practice only to indicate the extent to which patterns of deference to the decisions of expert bodies are widespread and general.

403. In public international law, it is an established principle of arbitral and, more generally, institutional review that the original decision-maker's findings will be subject to limited review only. The relevant case law draws a clear distinction between an appeal on the merits—to determine whether the original decision was legally and factually "right or wrong"—and a review of whether the decision-maker that rendered a decision exceeded its powers. A reviewing body that is seized of the issue of putative excess of powers will not "pronounce on whether the [original] decision was right or wrong," as this question is legally irrelevant within an excess of powers inquiry.[810]

404. Legal authorities on arbitral review do not directly apply to the present proceedings, because (as will be discussed further *infra*) the ABC was not an adjudicatory body *strictu sensu*, such that it would be inapposite to transpose, without appropriate qualification, the legal principles governing excesses of jurisdiction of powers to the ABC. That said, the established case law regarding *excès de pouvoir* of arbitral tribunals, which was relied on by both Parties in their submissions, may *mutatis mutandis* inform the interpretation of "excess of mandate" pursuant to the Arbitration Agreement.

405. There is no dearth of international case law confirming that the remedy of annulment of arbitral awards is granted only under exceptional circumstances. Reviewing bodies have noted that only "weighty" or "exceptional circumstances" will justify a finding of invalidity and that the party seeking to impugn an arbitral award bears a "very great" burden of proof.[811] In addition, reviewing bodies have limited their review to *"clear"* cases[812] and have noted that the reviewing body must "not intrude into the legal and factual decision-making of the [original decision-making body]."[813] This body of case law suggests that the scope of review in international proceedings leading to the annulment of a prior decision is generally very limited.

406. It is clear that a reviewing body's task cannot take the form of an appeal with respect to the *correctness* of the findings of the original decision-maker when the reviewing body's methodology differs from that of the original decision-maker. Otherwise, the reviewing body would be prone to strike down the findings of the original decision-maker. The fact that the original decision-making body (the ABC Experts) and the reviewing body (this Tribunal) are each programmed to assess the facts using quite different methodologies (i.e. the methodology of science vis-à-vis the methodology of law) distinguishes these proceedings from proceedings in which the annulment of arbitral awards is sought—

---

809. *See Judgment of the Federal Supreme Court in Administrative Matters of May 28, 1965*, BVerwGE 21, 184.

810. *Case Concerning the Arbitral Award Made by the King of Spain on 23 December 1906*, Judgment, ICJ Reports 1960, p. 192, 214. Cited with approval in *Case concerning the Arbitral Award of July 31, 1989 (Guinea-Bissau v. Senegal)*, ICJ Reports 1991, p. 62, para. 25.

811. *See* the compilation of case law in the SPLM/A Counter-Memorial, paras. 613–621.

812. *See Vivendi v. Argentina*, Decision on Annulment, July 3, 2002, Case No. ARB/97/3, paras. 64–65.

813. *CDC Group plc v Republic of the Seychelles, Decision on the Application by the Republic of the Seychelles for Annulment of the Award dated December 17, 2003*, June 29, 2005, Case No. ARB/02/14, para. 70.

the classic field of application of the doctrine of *excès de pouvoir.* This unusual feature further underscores the inappropriateness of applying a standard of correctness in these proceedings....

B. Initial Matters: Alleged Procedural Violations; Waiver, Estoppel, Res Judicata Issues

1. Alleged Procedural Violations by the ABC Experts

436. Before proceeding to the key aspects of the Tribunal's analysis, a number of issues raised by the Parties may be dealt with in short order. The first of these relates to the alleged procedural violations which one of the Parties claims the ABC Experts committed.

437. The GoS argues that certain acts and omissions of the ABC Experts violated the procedures specified by the Parties in the Abyei Appendix, Terms of Reference, and Rules of Procedure, to wit: (1) they allegedly took evidence from Ngok Dinka informants without procedural safeguards and without informing the GoS; (2) they allegedly unilaterally sought and relied on an e-mail from an official of the United States Government to establish their interpretation of the mandate; and (3) they allegedly failed to act through the ABC (*i.e.* the Commission as a whole) in reaching their decision and failed to seek a consensus before rendering their Report (collectively, the "alleged acts and omissions").[840] Emphasizing that the Parties specifically defined the issues to be addressed by the Tribunal with reference to the Abyei Appendix, Terms of Reference, and Rules of Procedure,[841] the GoS asserts that the Tribunal should interpret a violation of procedures specified in these instruments as an excess of mandate.

438. The SPLM/A rejects this view, contending that a dispute regarding an excess of mandate does not extend to procedural complaints and that, alternatively, a party seeking to invalidate an arbitral award on procedural grounds must demonstrate serious prejudice.

439. Having considered the Parties' arguments, the Tribunal finds, as explained below, that the alleged acts and omissions do not individually or collectively fall within the scope of "excess of mandate" review under Article 2(a) of the Arbitration Agreement, which does not permit the review of alleged procedural violations.

440. Article 2(a) restates the ABC Experts' mandate in clear terms: "to define (i.e., delimit) and demarcate the area of the nine Ngok Dinka chiefdoms transferred to Kordofan in 1905." To aid in the "Functioning"[842] of their mandate, the ABC Experts were guided by procedural rules expressed in the Abyei Appendix, Terms of Reference, and Rules of Procedure. These rules are not intrinsic components of the mandate itself; rather, they

---

840. *See* discussion on "Procedural Excess of Mandate" in the summary of the Parties' arguments, *supra* paras. 141 to 163.

841. *See* Article 2(a) of the Arbitration Agreement at para. 395 *supra.*

842. Notably, a clear distinction between "Mandate" and "Functioning" exists within the text of the Terms of Reference (an instrument drawn up and agreed upon by both Parties). The ABC's "Mandate" as provided in the Terms of Reference is:

> *1.1 The Abyei area is defined in the Abyei Protocol in article 1.1.2 as "The area of the Nine Ngok Dinka chiefdoms transferred to Kordofan in 1905." The ABC shall confirm this definition.*
> 1.2 The ABC shall demarcate the area, specified above and on land.
> *A subsequent section in the Terms of Reference, captioned "Functioning of the ABC," defines the principal procedures to be followed by the ABC Experts. See* Section 3 of the Terms of Reference, with the caption "Functioning of the ABC." Among others, the listed procedures pertain to public hearings, consulting third-party sources, and the preparation of the final report.

provided for a flexible[843] process to aid in the implementation of the ABC's mandate. By its plain terms, Article 2(a)'s inquiry as to whether the ABC Experts had "exceeded their mandate, *which is* to define (i.e., and delimit) and demarcate" the Abyei Area, concentrates the Tribunal's scope of review to decisions made by the ABC Experts *ultra petita*, i.e., purporting to decide matters outside the scope of the dispute submitted by the Parties. That is evident from the Parties' use of the words "*exceeded* their mandate," which referred to situations where the ABC Experts might have gone beyond the scope of the *substantive* issues submitted to them.

441. Thus, Article 2(a) does not recognize putative violations of procedural rights within the concept of "excess of mandate." Nor does Article 2(a) refer more generally to concepts of nullity or invalidity of arbitral awards, or incorporate the well-known grounds for invalidity or nullity based on procedural or due process violations included in instruments such as the 1958 New York Convention, the ICSID Convention, or the International Law Commission's ("ILC") Draft Convention on Arbitral Procedure/ILC Model Rules on Arbitral Procedure 1958. Any of these approaches could have been adopted, but none of these were. There is no basis for expanding this single ground for invalidity to include other grounds that were not specified.

442. As the alleged acts and omissions fall outside the category of permissible review under Article 2(a) of the Arbitration Agreement, the Tribunal need not proceed further on this line of inquiry.

443. The Tribunal further emphasizes that for a majority of its members, even assuming *arguendo* that the alleged acts and omissions occurred and were departures from rigidly-enforceable procedural rules, such improprieties did not amount to an excess of mandate, not having individually or collectively resulted in a violation of the fundamental rights of either Party. A procedural irregularity alone cannot invalidate a decision; a *significant injustice* must have also have occurred as a result of the irregularity.[844] For the majority, this "prejudice" requirement has not been met, as the GoS has not demonstrated that any of the alleged procedural violations would have affected the decision outcome. Thus, the GoS's submissions on this point cannot be sustained, not having met the "significant injustice" standard.

1. Waiver, Estoppel, and Res Judicata Arguments

444. The Tribunal also considers it convenient to discuss, at this early stage, two specific objections which the SPLM/A raised in connection with the Tribunal's ability to review the ABC Experts' Report.

---

843. *See* Terms of Reference, Sections 3.3 and 3.4; Rules of Procedure, Sections 2, 4, 7, 8, 10, and 11. *See further infra* at paras. 468.

844. *See* SPLM/A Counter Memorial, p. 76, para. 298, citing J. Lew, L. Mistelis & S. Kröll, Comparative International Commercial Arbitration ¶ 25–37 (2003) ("The prevailing view is that a procedural irregularity or defect alone will not invalidate an award. The test is that of a significant injustice so that the tribunal would have decided otherwise had the tribunal not made a mistake."); C. Schreuer, The ICSID Convention: A Commentary Art. 52 ¶ 230 (2001) ("In order to be serious, the departure must be more than minimal. It must be substantial. In addition, this departure must have had a material effect on the affected party. It must have deprived that party of the benefit of the rule in question.... if it is clear from the circumstances that the party had not intended to exercise the right [said to be breached], there would be no material effect and the departure would not be "serious" under this analysis."); D. Sutton, J. Gill & M. Gearing (Eds.), Russell on Arbitration ¶ 8.106 (2007) ("If ... correcting or avoiding the serious irregularity would make no difference to the outcome, substantial injustice will not be shown."); R. Merkin, Arbitration Law ¶ 20.8 (update 2008) ("there is substantial injustice if it can be shown that the irregularity in the procedure caused the arbitrators to reach a conclusion which, but for the irregularity, they might not have reached ...").

(a) *Waiver/Estoppel*

445. The SPLM/A argues that the GoS effectively waived its objections to the ABC Experts' Report because it agreed, as provided in the ABC's constitutive instruments, that the Report would be "final and binding."[845] The GoS counters that the entire point of these proceedings is to allow the Tribunal to determine whether or not the ABC Experts committed an excess of mandate; hence, in the GoS's view, the Arbitration Agreement precludes the SPLM/A from raising this waiver argument.

446. The claim of a waiver of the GoS's right to seek a review of the ABC Experts' Report is hardly consonant with the GoS's subsequent recourse to this arbitration, to which the SPLM/A has also consented. Moreover, from the initial presentation of the ABC Experts' Report, the GoS has been clear in expressing its disagreement with the ABC Experts, and no evidence of waiver can be found or implied by the course of its conduct.

447. Insofar as there is any ground for a claim of estoppel (which is doubtful), the Tribunal would agree with the GoS that the SPLM/A, as a party to the Arbitration Agreement and, in particular, its Article 2, is estopped from objecting to the Tribunal's review of the ABC Experts' Report. As provided in the Arbitration Agreement, the scope of the dispute submitted to arbitration is covered by Article 2.[846]

448. The language of Article 2 makes clear that both the GoS and the SPLM/A have submitted to the Tribunal the question of whether or not the ABC Experts had exceeded their mandate. To the extent that the Tribunal finds that this is not the case, the Tribunal will make a declaration that no excess of mandate was committed. To the extent that the Tribunal does find that an excess of mandate occurred, it will proceed to the delimitation of the Abyei Area. The mandate of the Tribunal, as agreed by both Parties in the Arbitration Agreement, necessarily requires a review and (if necessary) an annulment and revision of parts of the ABC Experts' decision. This thus estops the SPLM/A from arguing that the ABC Experts' Report was final and binding. Indeed, by agreeing to Article 2 of the Arbitration Agreement, the SPLM/A has specifically accepted the authority of the Tribunal to review the Report, and if necessary, to declare an excess of mandate and proceed with a revision of the findings of the ABC Experts.

(b) *Res Judicata*

449. The SPLM/A further contends that the ABC Experts' Report enjoys *res judicata* status and hence, cannot be impugned by the GoS. It asserts that inasmuch as the ABC conducted itself in the manner of an adjudicative body and rendered an adjudicative decision, the Report's findings are *res judicata* for both Parties. The GoS disagrees, arguing that by agreeing to the Arbitration Agreement, the Parties understood that there was still the possibility that the border was not definitely settled, and that issue is to be finally determined by the Tribunal.

450. The Tribunal sees no need to enter into an extended discourse on whether, as a matter of legal theory, the ABC Experts' Report is of such a juridical nature that *res judicata* can attach to it. The critical question is whether the fact that the Parties agreed to the finality of the Report in 2005 precluded them from consenting to submit questions about it to another Tribunal. Whatever the status of the ABC Experts' Report, the Arbitration Agreement concluded by the Parties in 2008 had the effect of reopening questions

845. Section 5 of the Abyei Appendix, text at *supra* note 107.
846. *See* text at para. 395 *supra.*

that had been accepted as "final and binding," thus novating the issues for decision in accordance with the contingencies in Article 2.

451. When both Parties consented to this arbitration, that consent extended to all the matters provided under Article 2 of the Arbitration Agreement, and had the effect of reopening the ABC Experts' Report to "excess of mandate" review under Article 2(a) and a potential new delimitation exercise under Article 2(c).

C. Characterization of the ABC

452. Through the Arbitration Agreement, the Parties have asked that the Tribunal determine whether another body (the ABC Experts) exceeded its mandate. As the ABC is quite singular in character, there is no neatly established standard against which to assess the ABC Experts' conduct. Instead, the ABC's nature must be ascertained from its constitutive instruments, its composition, the conduct of the Parties, and the function to be performed by the ABC in the larger peace process. These factors will form the basis for ascertaining the normative framework and proper conduct of the ABC Experts in fulfillment of their mandate.

453. In international law, the spectrum of entities designed to engage in dispute settlement varies widely in terms of institutional permanence, composition, and the procedural regimes according to which these entities operate. Some, such as the ICJ, are composed of legal professionals and have a highly articulated procedural regime. At the other end of the spectrum, entities (often established on an *ad hoc* basis) include non-lawyers and follow very informal procedures, which may not be fully articulated in writing. What is procedurally permissible in some of the decision entities is prohibited in others. Thus, for example, mediators are expected to meet each of the disputing parties separately and to respect, in full confidence, what one party may say, while an arbitral or judicial body would be prohibited from entertaining such *ex parte* communications. International law is creative and innovative in these matters and may sometimes graft some of these procedures onto others in combinations that may appear anomalous to those unfamiliar with international law. For example, in the *Taba* arbitration (discussed in further detail below), three of the five arbitrators were also to function as mediators and to seek a compromise settlement while serving as arbitrators.

454. It is clear from its constitutive instruments that the ABC was designed by the GoS and the SPLM/A, along with others who participated in the process of conceiving and establishing it, to make a specified decision according to criteria specified in the texts. Although the Parties committed themselves to accept the Report as "final and binding," a formulation often found in arbitration agreements, the ABC was plainly not an "arbitration tribunal" and certainly not an international arbitration tribunal. None of the constitutive texts referred to it in those terms. Yet, along with the criteria for making a final and binding decision, the ABC also had a quasi-mediatory role, for its expert members were authorized to try to seek a consensus between the disputing parties in parallel; mediators, as noted above, operate according to procedures very different from those of arbitrators.

455. Taking account of the ABC's constitutive instruments as well as contextual factors, a majority of the members of the Tribunal has no difficulty to conclude that the ABC Experts' essential function was to reach a final decision with regard to the boundaries of the Abyei Area, even in the face of scarce factual evidence. In ascertaining the nature of the ABC, one of the Tribunal's members, Professor Hafner, did not share the view of the other members, preferring to see the ABC as a fact-finding body with a more limited na-

ture (his views are explained in some detail *infra*). Nevertheless, these different views on this matter do not affect the substance of the Tribunal's conclusions.

1. The Non-uniform Nature of Boundary Commissions

456. The mere fact that the ABC was termed a "boundary commission" does not by itself clarify the scope and nature of the ABC's mandate. Historically, many bodies, with many different titles, have been endowed with the specific task of delineating and/or demarcating boundaries. The role and mandate of such bodies differ as a function of the parties' agreement on what each particular "boundary commission," "boundary committee," "mixed commission," *etc.* was designed to do.

457. Thus, the *Ethiopia-Eritrea Boundary Commission*, though charged with delimitation and demarcation, was clearly in the nature of an international arbitral tribunal; it was composed of international lawyers and jurists and its mandate, functions, and procedures meticulously followed those of a formal arbitral proceeding.[847]

458. By contrast, a chamber of the ICJ in the *Frontier Dispute, Burkina Faso v. Mali*[848] constituted a commission of three experts for the specific purpose of demarcating the boundary delimited by the ICJ chamber itself; the commission did not undertake any adjudicatory or arbitral functions.

459. Uniquely, in the *Taba Arbitration*[849] (referred to above), before the tribunal constituted to determine the boundary dispute rendered a decision, some of the arbitrators were required to "explore the possibilities of a settlement of a dispute," and the "boundary commission" thus undertook a parallel conciliation function.

460. The Cameroon-Nigeria Mixed Commission, constituted to implement the ICJ ruling in *Land and Maritime Boundary between Cameroon and Nigeria (Equatorial Guinea intervening)*[850] had as part of its mandate (in addition to demarcating the land boundary) the development of projects to promote joint economic ventures, troop withdrawal from relevant areas along the land boundary, and the reactivation of the Lake Chad Basin Commission.[851]

461. Finally, despite its name, the Iraq-Kuwait Boundary Demarcation Commission arguably performed delimitation functions as well.[852]

462. These examples demonstrate that the term "boundary commission" has encompassed bodies with a wide spectrum of functions, their mandates, with varying degrees of formality, ranging from pure fact-finding to full adjudication (and many with facets of both). Like other boundary commissions, the ABC is best considered a singular entity whose nature is to be derived from its own, specific features....

---

847. *See Decision Regarding Delimitation of the Border between The State of Eritrea and The Federal Democratic Republic of Ethiopia*; 41 ILM 1057 (2002).

848. *See Frontier Dispute, Burkina Faso v. Mali*, Nomination of Experts, Order of April 9, 1987 ICJ Reports 1985, p. 7.

849. *See* Egypt-Israel Arbitration Tribunal*: Award in Boundary Dispute Concerning the Taba Area*, 27 ILM 1421 (1988).

850. *Case Concerning the Land and Maritime Boundary Between Cameroon and Nigeria (Cameroon v. Nigeria: Equatorial Guinea intervening)*, Judgment ICJ Reports (2002), p. 203.

851. *See* Meeting between the Secretary-General and President Biya and President Obasanjo on the October 10, 2002 ruling of the ICJ, Geneva, November 15, 2002, available at http://www.un.org/unowa/cnmc/preleas/sgstmts.htm#3.

852. *See* Letter From the Secretary-General Transmitting to the Security Council the Final Report on the Demarcation of the International Boundary Between Iraq and Kuwait, 32 ILM 1425 (1993).

D. Reasonableness is the Applicable Standard for Reviewing the Interpretation and Implementation of the ABC Experts' Mandate

486. Recalling the limited scope of the Tribunal's review authority over the ABC Experts' Report under Article 2(a) of the Arbitration Agreement, a consideration of what such a limited review entails in relation to the GoS's alleged grounds for finding an "excess of mandate" is in order. This section will therefore discuss the standard of review that the Tribunal must apply with respect to the ABC Experts' *interpretation* and *implementation* of their mandate. These two aspects—interpretation and implementation—raise slightly different issues, and will be discussed in turn.

1. Standard of Review Regarding the ABC's Interpretation of Its Mandate

487. The Tribunal has no doubt that a fundamental misinterpretation by the ABC Experts of the instruments establishing the ABC's competence could in principle qualify as an excess of mandate. This view is consistent with the position taken in international arbitral awards such as the *Orinoco Steamship Company* arbitration, where the tribunal found that an excessive exercise of powers could arise from "misinterpreting the express provisions of the relevant agreement in respect of the way in which [the arbitrators] are to reach their decisions."[888]

* * *

496. The proper reading of Article 2(a) in, and consistent with the context of Article 2 as a whole, is that, at that phase, the Tribunal must confine itself to determining whether the ABC Experts' interpretation of their mandate was reasonable. However, the Tribunal must stop short of deciding whether one or the other interpretation proffered by the Parties is more correct; the question of which interpretation the Tribunal deems correct is not a question of "excess of mandate" but rather a component of the Tribunal's contingent delimitation inquiry under Article 2(c).

(ii) The ABC Experts Had the Authority to Interpret Their Mandate

497. Contextual as well as teleological analyses support the conclusion of the confined inquiry required by Article 2(a). The ABC Experts possessed the authority to interpret their mandate and, thus, the limits of their "jurisdiction," and the Tribunal is required to defer to that interpretation within the context of its Article 2(a) analysis.

498. In an arbitral context, a tribunal's power to interpret the instrument on which its jurisdiction is founded is typically discussed under the heading of *Kompetenz-Kompetenz*. Pursuant to this doctrine, which is accepted with certain variations in most national arbitration laws and is a postulate in international arbitration, an arbitral tribunal must be deemed competent to determine the limits of its own jurisdiction. Allocating decision-making authority to the party-selected arbitrator rather than the courts is more respectful of the parties' intention to have specially-appointed arbitrators (often possessing specific expertise in a particular area) decide disputes over their relationships.

499. In international arbitral proceedings, *Kompetenz-Kompetenz* is even a necessity, as no higher court of law with compulsory jurisdiction exists to adjudge the limits of a tribunal's competence when one of the parties disputes it. Without a principle of *Kompetenz-Kompetenz,* any form of third party decision in international law could be paralyzed by a party which challenged jurisdiction.

500. The authority of international tribunals to declare their own competence and, to that end, interpret the *compromis* and other relevant documents was already enshrined

888. *The Orinoco Steamship Company Case (United States/Venezuela)* XI UNRIAA 227, 239 (1910).

in the 1899 and 1907 Hague Conventions.[895] In its first judgment in the *Nottebohm* case dealing with Guatemala's jurisdictional objections, the ICJ affirmed the *Kompetenz-Kompetenz* principle as accepted in international law:

> Since the *Alabama* case, it has been generally recognized, following the earlier precedents, that, in the absence of any agreement to the contrary, an international tribunal has the right to decide as to its own jurisdiction and has the power to interpret for this purpose the instruments which govern that jurisdiction.[896]

501. Other notable expressions of the *Kompetenz-Kompetenz* principle subsequent to the ICJ's pronouncement can be found in the 1953 Draft Convention on Arbitral Procedure of the International Law Commission (ILC),[897] the 1958 ILC Model Rules on Arbitral Procedure,[898] the PCA Optional Rules for Arbitrating Disputes between Two States,[899] the PCA Optional Rules for Arbitrating Disputes between Two Parties of Which Only One Is a State,[900] the 1965 ICSID Convention,[901] the UNCITRAL Arbitration Rules[902] and the UNCITRAL Model Law.[903]

502. As noted, because international law lacks a hierarchy of courts endowed with compulsory jurisdiction, the operation of any of the range of decision institutions could be paralyzed by an objection to its competence, if it, too, did not have some form of *Kompetenz-Kompetenz.* Thus, the fact that the ABC was not an adjudicatory body *strictu sensu* does not mean that it lacked *Kompetenz-Kompetenz*....

505. The practice of courts and tribunals in public international law is broadly supportive of the proposition that an instance of review must defer, and give special weight, to the interpretation of a jurisdictional instrument by the decision-making body designated under that instrument. The ICJ's judgment in the *Case concerning the Arbitral Award of 31 July 1989* is particularly instructive.[904] In that case, the Republic of Guinea-Bissau requested the Court to declare an arbitral award null and void because the original arbitral tribunal allegedly "did not comply with the provisions of the Arbitration Agreement."[905] The Court reaffirmed its previous distinction between appellate review—that the Court is "called upon to pronounce on whether the arbitrator's decision was right or wrong"[906]—and the requested review of the validity of the award. On this basis, the Court noted that, in the context of a *recours en nullité*, it

895. Article 48 of the Hague Convention for the Pacific Settlement of International Disputes of 1899, 1 BEVANS 230; 1 AJIL (1907) 103; Article 73 of the Hague Convention for the Pacific Settlement of International Disputes of 1907, 1 *Bevans* 577; 2 AJIL SUPP. (1908) 43.

896. *Nottebohm Case* (Preliminary Objection), Judgment, ICJ Reports 1953, p. 111, 119.

897. Article 11, Report of the International Law Commission Covering the Work of its Fifth Session, 1 June–14 August 1953, Official Records of the General Assembly, Eighth Session, Supplement No. 9 (A/2456), A/CN.4/76.

898. Article 9, Yearbook of the International Law Commission, 1958, vol. II.

899. *See* Article 21. These rules are available at http://www.pca-cpa.org.

900. *See* Article 21. These rules are available at http://www.pca-cpa.org; *see also* the 1962 Optional Rules, reprinted in J.G. Wetter, THE INTERNATIONAL ARBITRAL PROCESS, PUBLIC AND PRIVATE, Vol. V, p. 54 (1979).

901. Article 41, Convention on the Settlement of Investment Disputes Between States and Nationals of Other States, 575 *UNTS* 159.

902. Article 21, UN Doc. A/RES/31/98; 15 ILM 701 (1976).

903. Article 16, 24 ILM 1302 (1985).

904. The Tribunal notes that both Parties repeatedly relied on this judgment in their submissions, thus making the judgment an appropriate consensual reference point.

905. *Arbitral Award of July 31, 1989*, ICJ Reports 1991, p. 56, para. 10.

906. *Arbitral Award Made by the King of Spain*, ICJ Reports (1960), p. 214.

has simply to ascertain whether by rendering the disputed Award the Tribunal acted in *manifest breach* of the competence conferred on it by the Arbitration Agreement, either by deciding in excess of, or by failing to exercise, its jurisdiction.[907] (emphasis added)

506. In addition to confirming the applicability of the "manifest breach" standard to decisions on jurisdiction, the Court specifically noted that the reviewing body must accord deference to the original decision maker in its interpretation of its own competence. The Court noted that "[b]y its argument set out above, Guinea-Bissau is in fact criticizing the interpretation in the Award of the provisions of the Arbitration Agreement which determine the Tribunal's jurisdiction, and proposing another interpretation." The Court rejected Guinea-Bissau's argument and ruled that it was not competent to determine which of several plausible interpretations of the original arbitration agreement was the correct one, explaining that "the Court does not have to enquire whether or not the Arbitration Agreement could, with regard to the Tribunal's competence, be interpreted in a number of ways, and if so to consider which would have been preferable."[908]

507. In the Tribunal's view, the ICJ's analysis in the *Case concerning the Arbitral Award of 31 July 1989,* which is based on explicitly reasoned legal principles that apply by analogy to these proceedings, provides the best method for establishing the appropriate standard of review. The review of arbitral awards on grounds of excess of powers serves to protect the parties from the rendering of binding third-party decisions to which they have not consented. Consistent with this fundamental principle of consent, third-party jurisdictional determinations against the will of the parties cannot stand. But as long as a decision can still be reconciled with the parties' consent, the arbitrators who were appointed by the parties constitute the preferred forum for settling the substantive disagreement between the parties, as it is they who were specifically entrusted with this task on the basis of their specific expertise....

(a) *Review for "Substantive Errors" is Outside the Tribunal's Competence*

512. With regard to substantive error as a potential ground for annulment, the "general principles of law and practices" applied by international tribunals undertaking a review function do not appear to be entirely consistent. On the one hand, relevant international treaties (including the 1958 New York Convention and the 1965 ICSID Convention) and the UNCITRAL Model Law on International Commercial Arbitration do not recognize "manifest error" as a ground for setting aside an award. Recent arbitral decisions within the context of ICSID annulment proceedings confirm the irrelevance of substantive errors at the review stage.[910] On the other hand, the relevance of "essential errors" or "manifest error[s]" of law or fact was acknowledged in several, especially older, decisions, including the *Trail Smelter* case[911] and the *Drier* case.[912]

513. For purposes of the present proceedings, however, the question of whether substantive errors are altogether outside the scope of its review or subject to review in "man-

---

907. *Arbitral Award of July 31, 1989,* ICJ Reports 1991, p. 69, para. 47.

908. *Arbitral Award of July 31, 1989,* ICJ Reports 1991, p. 56, para. 47.

910. *Maritime International Nominees Establishment (MINE) v. Government of Guinea (Guinea),* ICSID Case ARB/84/4, Decision on the Application by Guinea for Partial Annulment of the Arbitral Award dated January 6, 1988, *see* especially para. 4.04 and para. 5.08; *AMCO Asia Corp. v. The Republic of Indonesia,* ICSID Case ARB/81/1, Decision on the Application by Indonesia for Annulment of the Arbitral Award dated November 20, 1984, May 16, 1986, para. 23.

911. *Canada v. U.S.,* Final Award of March 11, 1941, III UNRIAA 1905, 1957.

912. *Katharine M. Drier (United States) v. Germany,* Award of July 29, 1935, VIII UNRIAA 127, 157.

ifest" cases is academic and without relevance for the Tribunal's decision. The Tribunal notes that while the GoS believes the ABC Experts' findings to be substantively incorrect, these perceived errors are not as such the basis for GoS's excess of mandate claim. The GoS does not ground its claim on "essential error" or "manifest error" but on the proposition that the ABC's findings—whether substantively right or wrong—went beyond or failed to accomplish what the Parties agreed to.[913]

514. This characterization of the GoS's claims was again confirmed during the oral hearings, when the GoS explained that:

> while an essential error of law or fact of an arbitral tribunal is a ground for nullity of the award, this Tribunal has probably no jurisdiction to that effect ... In other words, the [ABC Experts] have made an essential error of interpretation, but this error ... bears upon the mandate itself, not on its implementation, not on the answer to the question.[914]

515. Thus, leaving aside other, distinct grounds for excess of mandate (such as alleged procedural violations and failure to state reasons) and criticism of its substance, the GoS's disagreement with the ABC Experts' Report is in essence a disagreement concerning the ABC Experts' *interpretation* of the mandate, not with its *implementation*. Similarly, the SPLM/A has consistently argued during these proceedings that substantive errors are beyond the Tribunal's jurisdiction of review.[915]

516. The Tribunal sees no reason for departing from this understanding of its mandate, which is consensual between the Parties. As noted above, the Parties have defined the Tribunal's mandate as comprising two distinct juridical and intellectual tasks, and the first of these tasks, pursuant to Article 2(a), does not authorize the Tribunal to ascertain the correctness of the ABC Experts' findings. The interpretation of the scope of a decision-making body's competence is analytically distinct from the use of that competence, and the Parties authorized the Tribunal, for purposes of the present proceedings, to review only the former but not the latter.

517. The Tribunal's review of the ABC Experts' findings, under Article 2(a), will thus extend neither to the appreciation of evidence by the ABC Experts nor to the ABC Experts' substantive conclusions (except for the determination of an excess of mandate). Consistent with its mandate, the Tribunal will not engage in an academic excursus into the ABC Experts' reading of the evidence or their conclusions.

(b) *Failure to State Reasons for a Decision May Lead to an "Excess of Mandate"*

518. A final consideration relates to the GoS's contention that the ABC Experts' committed an excess of mandate by allegedly failing to state reasons for some of their findings. As with the other alleged grounds for excess of mandate, the Tribunal will discuss, as a preliminary matter, to what extent it is authorized to review the cogency of the reasons advanced by the ABC Experts under Article 2(a). To that end, the Tribunal must address two questions: first, were the ABC Experts under a duty to state the reasons for their decisions in the first place? If so, then what is the threshold that determines when deficient reasoning amounts to an excess of mandate?

---

913. In its Rejoinder, the GoS groups these allegations under the headings of "Decisions *Ultra Petita*" and "*Infra Petita.*"

914. GoS Oral Pleadings, April 18, 2009, Transcr. 165/20-23 and 166/16-20.

915. SPLM/A Counter-Memorial, para. 44.

(i) The ABC's Mandate Included the Duty to State Reasons

519. Both Parties, relying on arbitral precedent as, presumably, an expression of "general principles of law and practices," disagree as to whether the ABC Experts were under an obligation to state reasons. The GoS averred a requirement incumbent upon arbitrators to explain the basis for their decision. The SPLM/A adduced evidence of legal systems that stipulate no reasoning requirement.

520. In the Tribunal's view, the primary and secondary authorities adduced by the Parties are not dispositive of the question of whether reasons were required, nor do they establish a presumption that, absent an express agreement by the Parties to the contrary, the ABC Experts were under such an obligation. Whether reasons had to be presented is not conclusively resolved by "general principles of law and practices" but by evidence of the Parties' expectations, which may be inferred from the context in which the ABC was intended to operate and from the function it had been assigned within the peace process. The ABC was created as part of an extraordinarily complex political process, which is not comparable to ordinary commercial or investment arbitrations. Whether reasons are required is therefore a question of proper interpretation of the ABC's constitutive instruments in light of their ordinary meaning and object and purpose.

521. An initial, textual argument (reiterated by the GoS throughout the proceedings) relates to the instructions by the Parties that the decision taken in the ABC Experts' Report be "based on scientific analysis and research."[916] The preference for a scientific methodology suggests that the Parties expected the ABC Experts to disclose the fruits of their research in some manner appropriate to their respective fields of scientific research. While there is nothing in the relevant instruments requiring a comprehensive analytic discussion of all the evidence found, an exposition of the key evidence in support of the ABC Experts' "final and binding decision" was clearly imported in the words "based on scientific analysis and research."

522. The clear purport of the text is confirmed by the object and purpose of the ABC's constitutive instruments. The principal consideration in these instruments is the important role played by the ABC in the context of the Sudan peace process; after years of uncertainty as to the location and boundaries of the Abyei Area, which in turn contributed to the untold hardship of millions of victims in the Civil War, the ABC was to definitively determine the boundaries of the Abyei Area. It was obvious that the ABC Experts' Report, whatever its conclusions, would have a major political impact on the country and especially on the life of Misseriya and Ngok Dinka in and around the Abyei Area. Stakeholders were entitled to know on what grounds the ABC Experts' decision was made. Indeed, such knowledge could be critical to the legitimacy and acceptability of the decision.

523. An additional indication of the expectation of a reasoned decision is found in the contradictory nature of the ABC proceedings.[917] It would be unusual to invite the Parties to make extensive presentations to the ABC and then take a decision that in no way assesses the Parties' respective presentations.

524. Finally, in the absence of a standing and compulsory body in which an appeal may be lodged (which is the normal situation in international law), the requirement to state the reasons on which a decision is based also functions as an informal control mechanism.

---

916. Section 4 of the Abyei Appendix.
917. *See* Section 3.1 of the Terms of Reference.

Since the ABC Experts' findings were not subject to appeal, an explanation of the rationale for the decision would dispel any hint of arbitrariness and ensure the presence of fairness which is indisputably necessary for the acceptability and successful conclusion of the peace process.

525. It follows that a failure to state reasons on the part of the ABC Experts would amount to the contravention of an obligation that was integral to their mandate and, as explained immediately below, could constitute an excess of mandate.

(ii) Lack of Any Reasons or Obviously Contradictory or Frivolous Reasons Would Amount to an Excess of Mandate

526. This does not yet answer the question as to the appropriate minimum standard that applies to the ABC Experts' reasoning. In their submissions, the Parties were in agreement that, assuming that the ABC Experts were required to provide reasons, the Tribunal's review of the "quality" of the ABC Experts' reasons would be constrained. Both Parties quoted (with approval) the standard of review endorsed by the *Vivendi v. Argentina* annulment committee,[918] and the GoS explained:

> [T]he GoS maintains the absolute relevance of the *Vivendi v. Argentina* annulment decision according to which the failure to state reasons will only constitute grounds for the annulment of a decision if—but only if—it leaves "the decision on a particular point essentially lacking in any expressed rationale" and if that point itself is necessary to the decision.[919]

527. Under general international law, the number of relevant precedents dealing with the minimum standard of "motivation" of arbitral awards is limited. The most authoritative decision in this respect is the ICJ's judgment in the *Case concerning the Arbitral Award made by the King of Spain on 23 December 1906.* In that case, Nicaragua challenged the award handed down by the King of Spain, *inter alia,* for the alleged lack or inadequacy of reasons. The Court flatly rejected Nicaragua's argument, noting that

> an examination of the Award shows that it deals in logical order and in some detail with all relevant considerations and that it contains ample reasoning and explanation in support of the conclusions arrived at by the arbitrator. In the opinion of the Court, this ground is without foundation.[920]

* * *

531. As the standards endorsed by the ICJ and the more recent ICSID annulment committees significantly converge, it is possible to draw a tentative conclusion regarding the "general principles of law and practices" applicable to the setting aside of arbitral awards on the ground of failure to state reasons. To meet the minimum requirement, an award should contain sufficient ratiocination to allow the reader to understand how the tribunal reached its binding conclusions (regardless of whether the ratiocination might persuade a disengaged third party that the award is substantively correct). As to the substantive issue, awards may be set aside for failure to state reasons where conclusions are not supported by any reasons at all, where the reasoning is incoherent or where the reasons provided are obviously contradictory or frivolous.

532. Given the very specific context of these proceedings, which do not easily analogize to annulment proceedings in the area of investment arbitration, the Tribunal con-

---

918. GoS Memorial, para. 164; GoS Rejoinder, para. 156; SPLM/A Counter-Memorial, para. 740.

919. GoS Rejoinder, para. 156.

920. *Arbitral Award made by the King of Spain*, Judgment of November 18, 1960, ICJ Reports 1960, p. 216.

siders it appropriate to examine the standard it has derived from practice in light of the object and purpose of the ABC's constitutive instruments.

533. The Parties subjected the ABC Experts to significant time constraints. Both Parties clearly expected the ABC Experts to be able to complete their Report within the allotted short time frame of three months (from the beginning of their fact-finding procedure until the rendering of the Report).[929] This suggests that the Parties could only have expected a short and concise Report that would be limited to elucidating the key reasons on which the conclusions were based. Even under time constraints, however, the Parties were entitled to expect that the Experts' reasons would be clear, coherent, and free from contradiction.[930]

534. Whatever the constraints the ABC Experts may have experienced in terms of methodology or timing, the Parties reasonably expected and were entitled, as a matter of fairness, that each of the Report's essential rulings be supported by sufficient reasons. The degree of reasoning provided in the Report for each of its conclusions had to be commensurate with the importance of those conclusions, as the articulation of reasons is the principal way by which reviewing bodies such as this Tribunal may ascertain reasonableness. A standard that liberally permits derogation from the obligation to state reasons due to external constraints could not have been expected in the absence of truly unforeseen and compelling reasons (or the Parties' explicit consent that the decision not be reasoned, which is not the case here). The Tribunal realizes, of course, that much of the evidence in this case is marked, in varying degrees, by some imprecision and is often circumstantial, and to that extent, the subjective assessment necessary when evaluating such evidence can be taken into account. This does not dilute the necessity of articulating reasons in itself, however.

535. For these reasons, the Tribunal considers that the foregoing standard, quite similar to the one endorsed by both Parties, is appropriate for the present proceedings. The Tribunal must verify whether the ABC Experts' Report contains sufficient explication to allow the reader to understand how the ABC Experts reached each conclusion of their "final and binding decision" (regardless of whether these explanations are persuasive or the decision was right). The ABC Experts will have exceeded their mandate if some or all of their conclusions are unsupported by any reasons at all, if the reasoning is incoherent, or if the reasons provided are obviously contradictory or frivolous....

E. Assessing the Reasonableness of the ABC Experts' Interpretation of the Formula

537. Having established that *reasonableness* is the proper standard by which the Tribunal should review the ABC Experts' Report, the Tribunal must now determine whether the ABC Experts' interpretation of their mandate can be considered a reasonable one. The Tribunal stresses that its assessment of the ABC Experts' construction of the Formula must remain within the confines of the reasonableness standard, and cannot amount to a *de novo* decision on the correct meaning of the Formula....

---

929. The Abyei Protocol initially provided that the ABC should complete its work "within the first two years of the Interim Period." (Abyei Protocol, Section 5.2). This schedule was subsequently revised by the Parties, who required that the ABC instead present its final report to the Sudanese Presidency "before the end of the Pre-Interim Period." (Abyei Appendix, Section 5) The Parties gave their preliminary presentations on April 12, 2005, and the report was presented to the Sudanese Presidency approximately three months later, on July 14, 2005. The Terms of Reference, drawn up by the Parties, also prescribe this three month schedule, though the actual schedule followed was delayed by approximately fifteen days. (See "Program of Work" in the Terms of Reference).

930. Indeed, despite similar time constraints, the Parties have obliged this Tribunal to "comprehensively state the reasons upon which the [A]ward is based." Arbitration Agreement, Article 9(2).

540. Secondly, the Tribunal will consider what the ABC Experts themselves understood the mandate to mean. The ABC Experts did not spell out in a separate section of their Report what they considered to be the meaning of the mandate, but they made specific comments on what they conceived the mandate to be and, of course, drew conclusions from the analysis of the Parties' various propositions and the evidence they submitted. These elements reveal quite clearly what their interpretation of the mandate was.

541. The Tribunal will then move on to assess the reasonableness of the Expert's construction of the mandate, having regard not only to the text, context, object and purpose of the ABC's mandate as it was set out in the 2004 Abyei Protocol, but also to other means of interpretation such as the historical context of the transfer (abundantly discussed by the Parties), the travaux préparatoires (also relied upon by the GoS and the SPLM/A), and the further agreements between the Parties that led to the Arbitration Agreement. The reasonableness of a predominantly territorial interpretation will also be examined in a subsequent section.

* * *

647. The Tribunal further observes that the very notion of "Indirect Rule," a British governmental policy which "relied on local and traditional tribal and other mechanisms for most aspects of administration"[1132] and which started with *The Power of Nomad Sheikhs Ordinance 1922,*[1133] is additional evidence that the British officials considered it more expedient to exercise their administration through tribal mediation. This policy was in line with the approach that had been previously adopted by the government by which, for example, "tribal *shaykhs* were left in place but held responsible for collecting taxes levied by the government."[1134]

648. [It]can reasonably be interpreted [that] … the British administration's intention [was] to place the *totality* of a semi-nomadic tribe, who moved between two provinces according to the seasons, under a single jurisdiction, in order to protect the whole of the Ngok Dinka people at *all* times, regardless of where they might have been located in each season of the year.

649. The foregoing suggests that it was entirely plausible for the ABC Experts to choose the tribal view [over a territorial view] as a reasonable and, indeed, the more probable interpretation of what the officials intended when they engaged in the 1905 transfer.…

PCA PRESS RELEASE
ABYEI ARBITRATION:
FINAL AWARD RENDERED

THE HAGUE, July 22, 2009*

* * *

The Tribunal adds that, since the interpretation made by the ABC Experts is subject to a reasonableness test (rather than a correctness test), its conclusion should not be taken to suggest that the opposite, predominantly territorial, interpretation was less reasonable. Rather, the Tribunal is not required or authorized to decide which out of the two possible interpretations is more "correct."

1132. SPLM/A Memorial, para. 358.
1133. Daly Expert Report, p. 45, Appendix to SPLM/A Memorial.
1134. Daly Expert Report, p. 13, Appendix to SPLM/A Memorial.
* http://www.pca-cpa.org/upload/files/Abyei%20Press%20Release%2022-07-09%20EN.pdf.

The Tribunal therefore finds that the ABC Experts did not exceed their mandate in interpreting their mandate in the manner that Experts did.

Implementation of the ABC Experts' Mandate

However, the Tribunal decides that the ABC Experts exceeded their mandate in certain areas of its implementation. Specifically, the ABC Experts failed to state sufficient reasons concerning some aspects of their decisions and thus exceeded their mandate with respect to some of their conclusions.

Notes and Questions on Issues Arising during Arbitration

1. What is the source of the law the ICJ looked to evaluate the King of Spain and Guinea Bissau-Senegal arbitrations? What international law rules can you derive from the two cases as generally applicable to the conduct of arbitration?

2. Compare the international arbitration rules you found for Question 1 with Article 36 of the ILC's Model Procedure (Annex) and Article V of the New York Convention on Recognition and Enforcement of Foreign Arbitral Awards:

1. Recognition and enforcement of the award may be refused, at the request of the party against whom it is invoked, only if that party furnishes to the competent authority where the recognition and enforcement is sought, proof that:
   (a) The parties to the agreement referred to in article II were, under the law applicable to them, under some incapacity or the said agreement is not valid under the law to which the parties have subjected it or, failing any indication thereon, under the law of the country where the award was made;
   (b) The party against whom the award is invoked was not given proper notice of the appointment of the arbitrator or of the arbitration proceedings or was otherwise unable to present his case;
   (c) The award deals with a difference not contemplated by not falling within the terms of the submission to arbitration, or it contains decisions on matters beyond the scope of the submission to arbitration, provided that, if the decisions on matters submitted to arbitration can be separated from those not so submitted, that part of the award which contain decisions on matters submitted to arbitration may be recognized and enforced;
   (d) The composition of the arbitral authority or the arbitral procedure was not in accordance with the agreement of the parties, or, failing such agreement, was not in accordance with the law of the country where the arbitration took place; or
   (e) The award has not yet become binding on the parties, or has been set aside or suspended by a competent authority of the country in which, or under the law of which, that award was made.
2. Recognition and enforcement of an arbitral award may also be refused if the competent authority in the country where recognition and enforcement is sought finds that:
   (a) The subject matter of the dispute is not capable of settlement by arbitration under law of that country; or

(b) The recognition or enforcement of the award would be contrary to the public policy of that country.

June 10, 1958, 21 U.S.T. 2517, 330 U.N.T.S. 38.

3. Note the ground for nullifying part of the Abyei Boundary Commission decision—that it exceeded its mandate by failing to give reasons. Did the ABC really "exceed" its mandate in your view?

4. Where did the Abyei Tribunal find the law to apply in the case?

5. The Abyei Tribunal made its decision in July 2009. In July 2011, South Sudan voted for independence. In the weeks prior to the referendum and continuing after, Sudan launched attacks in Abyei and other border regions:

> Almost 113,000 people have fled Sudan's disputed border region of Abyei since fighting started last month between troops from the north and south, the United Nations said today....
>
> Abyei is contested between the region's Ngok Dinka people, who are settled in the area and consider themselves southerners, and Misseriya nomads who herd their cattle south in the dry season and are supported by the government in Khartoum.
>
> The Permanent Court of Arbitration in The Hague, in a 2009 ruling, set Abyei's borders to the area around Ngok Dinka settlements. That largely excluded the Misseriya....
>
> The court also set key oilfields run by the Greater Nile Petroleum Operating Co., which is 40 percent owned by Beijing-based China National Petroleum Corp., outside of the Abyei region. Abyei produces less than 2,500 barrels a day, according to Sudan's Oil Ministry.

Maram Mazen, *Sudan's Abyei Clashes Displace 113,000 People, UN Reports*, BLOOMBERG.COM, June 17, 2011, http://www.bloomberg.com/news/2011-06-17/sudan-fighting-causes-almost-113-000-to-flee-abyei-border-region-un-says.html.

6. States involved in arbitration can go to the ICJ for review of their arbitral awards. International organizations may not bring such requests for review to the ICJ. Where might international organizations bring an award for review? On the role of the ICJ as a court of review, see W. Michael Reisman, *The Supervisory Jurisdiction of the International Court of the Justice*, 258 RECUEIL DES COURS (1996).

7. Arbitral awards made by domestic arbitral tribunals are generally reviewable to some extent in national courts. Should international arbitrations also be reviewable as a matter of law? If so, where and for what purposes?

Chapter Eight

Compliance and Enforcement

Introduction

We return to the problem of enforcement that we first encountered with interim orders. Now the problem is not whether the outcome is binding and enforceable, but how to ensure enforcement when the arbitral tribunal itself does not have control over persons or assets. The excerpts below describe two different approaches by arbitral tribunals. The first is from the *Rainbow Warrior Case* where the parties organized a formal arbitration to consider the question of whether France was in compliance with a decision of the UN Secretary General. The second, a decision of the Iran-U.S. Claims Tribunal, takes a very different approach to enforcement from that of the *Rainbow Warrior* tribunal.

Rainbow Warrior
(*New Zealand v. France*)

France-New Zealand Arbitration Tribunal, April 30, 1990
(Jiménez de Aréchaga, *Chairman*; Sir Kenneth Keith and
Professor Bredin, *Members*)*

SUMMARY [82 I.L.R. 500 (1990)]: *The facts:*—In July 1985 a team of French agents sabotaged and sank the *Rainbow Warrior*, a vessel belonging to Greenpeace International, while it lay in harbor in New Zealand. One member of the crew was killed. Two of the agents, Major Mafart and Captain Prieur, were subsequently arrested in New Zealand and, having pleaded guilty to charges of manslaughter and criminal damage, were sentenced by a New Zealand court to ten years imprisonment.[1] A dispute arose between France, which demanded the release of the two agents, and New Zealand, which claimed compensation for the incident. New Zealand also complained that France was threatening to disrupt New Zealand trade with the European Communities unless the two agents were released.

The two countries requested the Secretary-General of the United Nations to mediate and to propose a solution in the form of a ruling, which both Parties agreed in advance to accept. The Secretary-General's ruling, which was given in 1986, required France to pay US $7 million to New Zealand and to undertake not to take certain defined measures injurious to New Zealand trade with the European Communities.[2] The ruling also provided that Major Mafart and Captain Prieur were to be released into French custody but were

---

* Some footnotes omitted.
1. *R v. Mafart and Prieur* 74 *ILR* 241 at 243.
2. *Rainbow Warrior*, 74 *ILR* 241 at 256.

to spend the next three years on an isolated French military base in the Pacific. The two States concluded an agreement in the form of an exchange of letters on 9 July 1986 ("the First Agreement"),[3] which provided for the implementation of the ruling. Under the terms of the First Agreement, Major Mafart and Captain Prieur were to be

> ... transferred to a French military facility on the island of Hao for a period of not less than three years. They will be prohibited from leaving the island for any reason, except with the mutual consent of the two governments.

The actual transfer took place on 23 July 1986.

Following concern about Major Mafart's health, a French medical team advised that he be evacuated to France for treatment on 10 December 1987. On 11 December France sought New Zealand's consent to this "urgent, health-related transfer" but New Zealand's request that its own medical team should also examine Mafart before he was repatriated was denied when France refused to allow a New Zealand military aircraft carrying a doctor to land at Hao. On 14 December 1987 Mafart left Hao without the consent of New Zealand. Following medical treatment in Paris, Mafart was permitted to remain in France. New Zealand doctors who examined Mafart after his return to Paris agreed that he could not have been satisfactorily examined in Hao but denied that the evacuation was an emergency measure and concluded that Mafart's health was not such as to preclude his being returned to Hao after the treatment had been concluded.

Captain Prieur was repatriated in May 1988. On 3 May 1988 the French authorities notified New Zealand that she was expecting her first child and asked consent to her repatriation. New Zealand again requested that an independent medical examination be made. France acceded to this request and a New Zealand doctor was due to arrive in Hao on 6 May. On 5 May, however, the French authorities notified New Zealand that Captain Prieur's father was dying of cancer and that her immediate evacuation had thus become necessary. She was repatriated on 5 May 1988 without the consent of New Zealand and never returned to Hao.

The 1986 Agreement contained provision for arbitration of any dispute arising out of the agreement. After New Zealand invoked this provision, France and New Zealand concluded a further agreement on 14 February 1989 ("the Supplementary Agreement"), designating the three arbitrators and dealing with the procedure for the arbitration.

* * *

The Applicable Law

72. The first question that the Tribunal must determine is the law applicable to the conduct of the Parties.

According to Article 2 of the Supplementary Agreement of 14 February 1989:

> "The decisions of the Tribunal shall be taken on the basis of the Agreements concluded between the Government of New Zealand and the Government of the French Republic by Exchange of Letters of 9 July 1986, this Agreement and the applicable rules and principles of international law."

This provision refers to two sources of international law: the conventional source, represented by certain bilateral agreements concluded between the Parties, and the customary source, constituted by the "applicable rules and principles of international law."

The customary source, in turn, compromises two important branches of general international law: the Law of Treaties, codified in the 1969 Vienna Convention, and the

3. *Ibid.* at 274.

Law of State Responsibility, in process of codification by the International Law Commission.

The Parties disagree on the question of which of these two branches should be given primacy or emphasis in the determination of the primary obligations to France.

While New Zealand emphasizes the terms of the 1986 Agreement and related aspects of the Law of Treaties, France relies much more on the Law of State Responsibility. So far as remedies are concerned both are in broad agreement that the main law applicable is the Law of State Responsibility.

73. In this respect New Zealand contests three French legal propositions which it describes as bad law. The first one is that the Treaty of 9 July 1986 must be read subject to the customary Law of State Responsibility; thus France is trying to shift the question at issue out of the Law of Treaties, as codified in the Vienna Convention of 1969.

New Zealand contends that the question at issue must be decided in accordance with the Law of Treaties, because the treaty governs and the reference to customary international law may be made only if there were a need (1) to clarify some ambiguity in the treaty, (2) to fill an evident gap, or (3) to invalidate a treaty provision by reference to a rule of *jus cogens* in customary international law. But, it adds, there is otherwise no basis upon which a clear treaty obligation can be altered by reference to customary international law.

A second French proposition contested by New Zealand is that Article 2 of the Supplementary Agreement of 14 February 1989 refers to the rules and principles of international law and thus, France argues, requires the Tribunal to refer to Law of International Responsibility. New Zealand contends that Article 2 makes clear that the Tribunal is to decide in accordance with the Agreements, so the Treaty of 9 July 1986 governs and, consequently, customary international law applies only to the extent it is applicable as a source supplementary to the Treaty; not to change the treaty obligation but only to resolve an ambiguity in the treaty language or to fill some gap, which does not exist since the text is crystal clear. Thus, New Zealand takes the position that the Law of Treaties is the law relevant to this case.

Finally, New Zealand contests a third French proposition by which France relies upon the general concept of circumstances excluding illegality, as derived from the work of the International Law Commission on State Responsibility, contending that those circumstances arise in this case because there were determining factors beyond France's control, such as humanitarian reasons of extreme urgency making the action necessary. New Zealand asserts that a State Party to a treaty, and seeking to excuse its own non-performance, is not entitled to set aside the specific grounds for termination or suspension of a treaty, enumerated in the 1969 Vienna Convention, and rely instead on grounds relevant to general State responsibility. New Zealand adduces that it is not a credible proposition to admit that the Vienna Convention identifies and defines a number of lawful excuses for non-performance—such as supervening impossibility of performance; a fundamental change of circumstances; the emergence of a new rule of *jus cogens*—and yet contend that there may be other excuses, such as *force majeure* or distress, derived from the customary Law of State Responsibility. Consequently, New Zealand asserts that the excuse of *force majeure*, invoked by France, does not conform to the grounds for termination or suspension recognized by the Law of Treaties in Article 61 of the Vienna Convention, which requires absolute impossibility of performing the treaty as the grounds for terminating or withdrawing from it.

74. France, for its part, points out that New Zealand's request calls into question France's international responsibility towards New Zealand and that everything in this

request is characteristic of a suit for responsibility; therefore, it is entirely natural to apply the Law of Responsibility. The French Republic maintains that the Law of Treaties does not govern the breach of treaty obligations and that the rules concerning the consequences of a "breach of treaty" should be sought not in the Law of Treaties, but exclusively in the Law of Responsibility. France further states that within the Law of International Responsibility, "breach of treaty" does not enjoy any special status and that the breach of a treaty obligation falls under exactly the same legal regime as the violation of any other international obligation. In this connection, France points out that the Vienna Convention of the Law of Treaties is constantly at pains to exclude or reserve questions of responsibility, and that the sole provision concerning the consequences of the breach of a treaty is that of Article 60, entitled "Termination of a treaty or suspension of its application as a result of breach," but the provisions of this Article are not applicable in this instance. But even in this case, the French Republic adds, the State that is the victim of the breach is not deprived of its right to claim reparation under the general Law of Responsibility. France points out, furthermore, that the origin of an obligation in breach has no impact either on the international wrongfulness of an act nor on the regime of international responsibility applicable to such an act; this approach is explained in Article 17 of the draft of the International Law Commission on State Responsibility.

In particular, the French Republic adds, citing the report of the International Law Commission, the reasons which may be invoked to justify the non-execution of a treaty are a part of the general subject matter of the international responsibility of States.

The French Republic does admit, in this connection, that it is the Law of Treaties that makes it possible to determine the content and scope of the obligations assumed by France, but, even supposing that France had breached certain of these obligations, this breach would not entail any repercussion stemming from the Law of Treaties. On the contrary, it is exclusively within the framework of the Law on International Responsibility that the effects of a possible breach by France of its treaty obligations must be determined and it is within the context of the Law of Responsibility that the reasons and justificatory facts adduced by France must be assessed. Consequently, the French Republic further states, it is up to the Tribunal to decide whether the circumstances under which France was led to take the contested decisions are of such a nature as to exonerate it of responsibility, and this assessment must be made within the context of the Law of Responsibility and not solely in the light of Article 61 of the 1969 Vienna Convention.

75. The answer to the issue discussed in the two preceding paragraphs is that, for the decision of the present case, both the customary Law of Treaties and the customary Law of State Responsibility are relevant and applicable. The customary Law of Treaties, as codified in the Vienna Convention, proclaimed in Article 26, under the title "*Pacta sunt servanda*" that

> "Every treaty in force is binding upon the parties to it and must be performed by them in good faith."

This fundamental provision is applicable to the determination whether there have been violations of that principle, and in particular, whether material breaches of treaty obligations have been committed.

Moreover, certain specific provisions of customary law in the Vienna Convention are relevant in this case, such as Article 60, which gives a precise definition of the concept of a material breach of a treaty, and Article 70, which deals with the legal consequences of the expiry of a treaty.

On the other hand, the legal consequences of a breach of a treaty, including the determination of the circumstances that may exclude wrongfulness (and render the breach only apparent) and the appropriate remedies for breach are subjects that belong to the customary Law of State Responsibility.

The reason is that the general principles of International Law concerning State responsibility are equally applicable in the case of breach of treaty obligation, since in the international law field there is no distinction between contractual and tortuous responsibility, so that any violation by a State of any obligation, of whatever origin, gives rise to State responsibility and consequently, to the duty of reparation. The particular treaty itself might of course limit or extend the general Law of State Responsibility, for instance by establishing a system of remedies for it.

The Permanent Court proclaimed this fundamental principle in the Chorzów Factory (Jurisdiction) case, stating:

> "It is a principle of international law that the breach of an engagement involves an obligation to make reparation in an adequate form. Reparation, therefore, is the indispensable complement of a failure to apply a convention. (P.C.I.J., Series A, Nos. 9, 21 (1927)).

And the present Court has said:

> "It is clear that refusal to fulfill a treaty obligation involves international responsibility."

(Peace Treaties (second phase) 1950, ICJ Reports 221, 228).[[9] 17 *ILR* 318 at 321.]

The conclusion to be reaches on this issue is that, without prejudice to the terms of the agreement which the Parties signed and the applicability of certain important provisions of the Vienna Convention on the Law of Treaties, the existence in this case of circumstances excluding wrongfulness as well as the questions of appropriate remedies, should be answered in the context and in the light of the customary Law of State Responsibility.

Circumstances Precluding Wrongfulness

76. Under the title "Circumstances Precluding Wrongfulness" the International Law Commission proposed in Articles 29 to 35 a set of rules which include three provisions, on *force majeure* and fortuitous event (Article 31), distress (Article 32), and state of necessity (Article 33), which may be relevant to the decision on this case.

As to *force majeure*, it was invoked in the French note of 14 December 1987, where, referring to the removal of Major Mafart, the French authorities stated that "*in this case of force majeure*" (emphasis added), they "are compelled to proceed without further delay with the repatriation of the French officer for health reasons."

In the oral proceedings, counsel for France declared that France "did not invoke *force majeure* as far as the Law of Responsibility is concerned." However, the Agent for France was not so categorical in excluding *force majeure*, because he stated: "It is substantively incorrect to claim that France has invoked *force majeure* exclusively. Our written submissions indisputably show that we have referred to the whole theory of special circumstances that exclude or 'attenuate' illegality."

Consequently, the invocation of "*force majeure*" has not been totally excluded. It is therefore necessary to consider whether it is applicable to the present case.

77. Article 31 (1) of the ILC draft reads:

> "The wrongfulness of an act of a State not in conformity with an international obligation of that State is precluded if the act was due to an irresistible force or to an unforeseen external event beyond its control which made it materially impossible for the State to act in conformity with that obligation or to know that its conduct was not in conformity with that obligation."

In the light of this provision, there are several reasons for excluding the applicability of the excuse of *force majeure* in this case. As pointed out in the report of the International Law Commission, Article 31 refers to "a situation facing the subject taking the action, which leads it, as it were, *despite itself*, to act in a manner not in conformity with the requirements of an international obligation incumbent on it" (Ybk. ILC, 1979, vol. II, para. 2, p. 122, emphasis in the original). *Force majeure* is "generally invoked to justify *involuntary*, or at least unintentional conduct," it refers "to an irresistible force or an unforeseen external event against which it has no remedy and which makes it 'materially impossible' for it to act in conformity with the obligation," since "no person is required to do the impossible" (Ibid., p. 123, para. 4).

The report of the International Law Commission insists on the strict meaning of Article 31, in the following terms:

> "the wording of paragraph 1 emphasizes, by the use of the adjective 'irresistible' qualifying the word 'force,' that there must, in the case in point, be a constraint which the State was unable to avoid or to oppose by its own means ... The event must be an act which occurs and produces its effect without the State being able to do anything which might rectify the event or might avert its consequences. The adverb 'materially' preceding the word 'impossible' is intended to show that, for the purposes of the article, it would not suffice for the 'irresistible force' or the 'unforeseen external event' to have made it *very difficult* for the State to act in conformity with the obligation ... the Commission has sought to emphasize that the State must not have had any option in that regard" (Ybk. cit., p. 133, para. 40, emphasis in the original).

In conclusion, New Zealand is right in asserting that the excuse of *force majeure* is not of relevance in this case because the test of its applicability is of absolute and material impossibility, and because a circumstance rendering performance more difficult or burdensome does not constitute a case of *force majeure*. Consequently, this excuse is of no relevance in the present case.

78. Article 32 of the Articles drafted by the International Law Commission deals with another circumstance which may preclude wrongfulness in international law, namely, that of the "distress" of the author of the conduct which constitutes the act of State whose wrongfulness is in question.

Article 32 (1) reads as follows:

> "The wrongfulness of an act of a State not in conformity with an international obligation of that State is precluded if the author of the conduct which constitutes the act of that State had no other means, in a situation of extreme distress, of saving his life or that of persons entrusted to his care."

The commentary of the International Law Commission explains that " 'distress' means a situation of extreme peril in which the organ of the State which adopts that conduct has, at that particular moment, no means of saving himself or persons entrusted to his care other than to act in a manner not in conformity with the requirements of the obligation in question" (Ybk. cit. 1979, p. 133, para. 1).

The Report adds that in international practice distress, as a circumstance capable of precluding the wrongfulness of an otherwise wrongful act of the State, "has been invoked and recognized primarily in cases involving the violation of a frontier of another State, particularly its airspace and its sea—for example, when the captain of a State vessel in distress seeks refuge from storm in a foreign port without authorization, or when the pilot of a State aircraft lands without authorization on foreign soil to avoid an otherwise inevitable disaster" (Ibid., p. 134, para. 4)....

Both parties recognized that the return of Major Mafart to Hao depended mainly on his state of health. Thus, the French Ministry of Foreign Affairs in its note of 30 December 1987 to the New Zealand Embassy referring to France's respect for the 1986 Agreement had said that Major Mafart will return to Hao when his state of health allowed.

Consequently, there was no valid ground for Major Mafart continuing to remain in metropolitan France and the conclusion is unavoidable that this omission constitutes a material breach by the French Government of the First Agreement.

For the foregoing reasons the Tribunal:

> by a majority declares that the French Republic did not breach its obligations to New Zealand by removing Major Mafart from the island of Hao on 13 December 1987;
>
> declares that the French Republic committed a material and continuing breach of its obligations to New Zealand by failing to order the return of Major Mafart to the island of Hao as from 12 February 1988.

* * *

94. On the other hand, it appears that during the day of 5 May the French Government suddenly decided to present the New Zealand Government with the *fait accompli* of Captain Prieur's hasty return for a new reason, the health of Mrs. Prieur's father, who was seriously ill, hospitalized for cancer. Indisputably the health of Mrs. Prieur's father, who unfortunately would die on 16 May, and the concern for allowing Mrs. Prieur to visit her dying father constitute humanitarian reasons worthy of consideration by both Governments under the 1986 Agreement. But the events of 5 May (French date) prove that the French Republic did not make efforts in good faith to obtain New Zealand's consent. First of all, it must be remembered that France and New Zealand agreed that Captain Prieur would be examined in Hao on 6 May, which would allow her to return to France immediately. For France, in this case, it was only a question of gaining 24 or 36 hours. Of course, the health of Mrs. Prieur's father, who had been hospitalized for several months, could serve as grounds for such acute and sudden urgency; but, in this case, New Zealand would have had to be informed very precisely and completely, and not be presented with a decision that had already been made.

However, when the French Republic notified the Ambassador of New Zealand on 5 May at 11:00 a.m. (French time), the latter was merely told that Mrs. Dominique Prieur's father, hospitalized for cancer treatment, was dying. Of course, it was explained that the New Zealand Government could verify "the validity of this information" using a physician of its choice, but the telegram the French Minister of Foreign Affairs sent to the Embassy of France in Wellington on 5 May 1988 clearly stated that the decision to repatriate was final. And this singular announcement was addressed to New Zealand: "After all, New Zealand should understand that it would be incomprehensible for both French and New Zealand opinion for the New Zealand Government to stand in the way of allowing Mrs. Prieur to see her father on his death bead ..." Thus, New Zealand was really not asked for its approval, as compliance with France's obligations required, even under extremely urgent circumstances; it was indeed demanded so firmly that it was bound to provoke a strong reaction from New Zealand.

* * *

96. Pondering the reasons for the haste of France, New Zealand contended that Captain Prieur's "removal took place against the backdrop of French presidential elections in which the Prime Minister was a candidate" and New Zealand pointed out that Captain Prieur's departure and arrival in Paris had been widely publicized in France. During the oral proceedings, New Zealand produced the text of an interview given on 27 September 1989 by the Prime Minister at the relevant time, explaining the following on the subject of the "Turenge couple": "I take responsibility for the decision that was made, and could not imagine how these two officers could be abandoned after having obeyed the highest authorities of the State. Because it was the last days of my Government, I decided to bring Mrs. Prieur, who was pregnant, back from the Pacific atoll where she was stationed. Had I failed to do so, she would surely still be there today." New Zealand alleges that the French Government acted in this way for reasons quite different from the motive or pretext invoked. The Tribunal need not search for the French Government's motives, nor examine the hypotheses alleged by New Zealand. It only observes that, during the day of 5 May 1988, France did not seek New Zealand's approval in good faith for Captain Prieur's sudden departure; and accordingly, that the return of Captain Prieur, who left Hao on Thursday, 5 May at 11:30 p.m. (French time) and arrived in Paris on Friday, 6 May, thus constituted a violation of the obligations under the 1986 Agreement.

This violation seems even more regrettable because, as of 12 February 1988, France had been in a state of continuing violation of its obligations concerning Major Mafart, as stated above, which normally should have resulted in special care concerning compliance with the Agreement in Captain Prieur's case.

97. Moreover, France continued to fall short of its obligations by keeping Captain Prieur in Paris after the unfortunate death of her father on 16 May 1988. No medical report supports or demonstrates the original claim by French authorities to the effect that Captain Prieur's pregnancy required "particular care" and demonstrating that "the medical facilities on Hao are not equipped to carry out the necessary medical examinations and to give Mrs. Prieur the care required by her condition." There is no evidence either which demonstrates that the facilities in Papeete, originally suggested by the New Zealand Ambassador in Paris, were also inadequate; on the contrary, positive evidence has been presented by New Zealand as to their adequacy and sophistication.

The Only medical report in the files concerning Captain Prieur's health is one from Dr. Croxson, dated 21 July 1988, which appears to discard the necessity of "particular care" for a pregnancy which is "proceeding uneventfully." This medical report adds that "no special arrangements for later pregnancy or delivery are planned, and I formed the opinion that management would be conducted on usual clinical criteria for a 39-year-old, fit, healthy woman in her first pregnancy."

So, the record provides no justification for the failure to return Captain Prieur to Hao some time after the death of her father.

98. The fact that "pregnancy in itself normally constitutes a contra-indication for overseas appointment" is not a valid explanation, because the return to Hao was not an assignment to service, or "an assignment" or military posting, for the reasons already indicated in the case of Major Mafart.

Likewise, the fact that Captain Prieur benefited, under French regulations, from "military leave which she had not taken previously," as well as "the maternity and nursing leaves established by French law," may be measures provided by French military laws or regulations.

But in this case, as in that of Major Mafart, French military laws or regulations do not constitute the limit of the obligations of France or of the consequential rights deriving for New Zealand from those obligations. The French rules "governing military discipline" are referred to in the fourth paragraph of the First Agreement not as the limit of New Zealand rights, but as the means of enforcing the stipulated conditions and ensuring that they "will be strictly complied with." Moreover, French military laws or regulations can never be invoked to justify the breach of a treaty. As the French Counter-Memorial properly stated: "the principle according to which the existence of a domestic regulation can never be an excuse for not complying with an international obligation is well established, and France subscribes to it completely."

99. In summary, the circumstances of distress, of extreme urgency and the humanitarian considerations invoked by France may have been circumstances excluding responsibility for the unilateral removal of Major Mafart without obtaining New Zealand's consent, but clearly these circumstances entirely fail to justify France's responsibility for the removal of Captain Prieur and from the breach of its obligations resulting from the failure to return the two officers to Hao (in the case of Major Mafart once the reasons for their removal had disappeared). There was here a clear breach of its obligations and a breach of a material character.

100. According to Article 60 (3)(b) of the Vienna Convention on the Law of Treaties, a material breach of a treaty consists in "the violation of a provision essential to the accomplishment of the object or purpose of the treaty."

The main object or purpose of the obligations assumed by France in the Clauses 3 to 7 of the First Agreement was to ensure that the two agents, Major Mafart and Captain Prieur, were transferred to the island of Hao and remained there for a period of not less than three years, being subject to the special regime stipulated in the Exchange of Letters.

To achieve this object or purpose, the third and fourth paragraphs of the First Agreement provide that New Zealand will transfer the two agents to the French military authorities and these authorities will immediately transfer them to a French military facility in Hao. The prohibition "from leaving the island for any reason without the mutual consent of the two Governments" was the means to guarantee the fulfillment of the fundamental obligation assumed by France; to keep the agents in Hao and submit them to the special regime of isolation and restriction of contact described in the fourth paragraph of the Exchange of Letters.

The facts show that the essential object or purpose of the First Agreement was not fulfilled, since the two agents left the island before the expiry of the three-year period.

This leads the Tribunal to conclude that there have been material breaches by France of its international obligations.

101. In its codification of the Law of State Responsibility, the International Law Commission has made another classification of the different types of breaches, taking into account the time factor as an ingredient of the obligation. It is based on the determination of what is described as *tempus commissi delictu*, that is to say, the duration or continuation in time of the breach. Thus the Commission distinguishes the breach which does not extend in time, or instantaneous breach, defined in Article 24 of the draft, from the breach having

a continuing character or extending in time. In the latter case, according to paragraph 1 of Article 25, "the time of commission of the breach extends over the entire period during which the act continues and remains not in conformity with the international obligation."

Applying this classification to the present case, it is clear that the breach consisting in the failure of returning to Hao the two agents has been not only a material but also a continuous breach.

And this classification is not purely theoretical, but, on the contrary, it has practical consequences, since the seriousness of the breach and its prolongation in time cannot fail to have considerable bearing on the establishment of the reparation which is adequate for a violation presenting these two features.

For the foregoing reasons the Tribunal:

- declares that the French Republic committed a material breach of its obligations to New Zealand by not endeavouring in good faith to obtain on 5 May 1988 New Zealand's consent to Captain Prieur's leaving the island of Hao;
- declares that as a consequence the French Republic committed a material breach of its obligations by removing Captain Prieur from the island of Hao on 5 and 6 may 1988;
- declares that the French Republic committed a material and continuing breach of its obligations to New Zealand by failing to order the return of Captain Prieur to the island of Hao.

Duration of the Obligations

102. The Parties in this case are in complete disagreement with respect to the duration of the obligations assumed by France in paragraphs 3 to 7 of the First Agreement.

New Zealand contends that the obligation in the Exchange of Letters envisaged that in the normal course of events both agents would remain on Hao for a continuous period of three years. It point out that the First Agreement does not set an expiry date for the three year term but rather describes the term as being for "a period of not less than three years." According to the New Zealand Government, this is clearly not a fixed period ending on a predetermined date. "The three-year period, in its context, clearly means the period of time to be spent by Major Mafart and Captain Prieur on Hao rather than a continuous or fixed time span. In the event of an interruption to the three year period, the obligation assumed by France to ensure that either or both agents serve the balance of the three years would remain." Consequently, concludes the Government of New Zealand, "France is under an ongoing obligation to return Major Mafart and Captain Prieur to Hao to serve out the balance of their three-year confinement."

103. For its part, the French Government answers: "it is true that the 1986 Agreement does not fix the exact date of expiry of the specific regime that it sets up for the two agents. But neither does it fix the exact date that this regime will take effect." The reason, adds the French Government, is that in paragraph 7 of the First Agreement, it is provided that the undertakings relating to "the transfer of Major Mafart and Captain Prieur will be implemented not later than 25 July 1986." Consequently, adduces the French Government, "it is quite obviously the effective date of transfer to Hao which should constitute the *dies a quo* and thus determine the *dies ad quem* ... The obligation assumed by France to post the two officers to Hao and to subject them there to a regime that restricts some of their freedoms was planned by the parties to last for three years beginning on the day the transfer to Hao became effective; this transfer having taken place on 22 July 1986, the three year

period allotted for the obligatory stay on Hao and its attendant obligations" expired three years after, that is to say, on 22 July 1989.

The French Government adds in the Reply that "a period is quite precisely a continuous and fixed interval of time" and "even if no exact expiry date was expressly stated in advance, this date necessarily follows from the determination of both a time period and the *dies a quo*." The French Government remarks, moreover, that there is no rule of international law extending the length of an obligation by reason of its breach.

104. It results from paragraph 7 of the Agreement of 9 July 1986 that both parties agreed that "the undertakings relating to an apology, the payment of compensation and the transfer of Major Mafart and Captain Prieur" should be implemented as soon as possible. For that purpose, they fixed a completion date of not later than 25 July 1986. In respect of the two agents, the date of their delivery to French military authorities was 22 July 1986, thus bringing to an end their prison term in New Zealand. In order to avoid any gap or interval, paragraph 3 of the Agreement required that the two agents should be transferred to a French military base "immediately thereafter" their delivery. There is no question therefore that the special regimen stipulated and the undertakings assumed by the French Government began to operate uninterruptedly on 22 July 1986. It follows that such a special regime, intended to last for a minimum period of three years, expired on 22 July 1989. It would be contrary to the principles concerning treaty interpretation to reach a more extensive construction of the provisions which thus established a limited duration to the special undertakings assumed by France.

105. The characterization of the breach as one extending or continuing in time, in accordance with Article 25 of the draft on State Responsibility (see para. 101), confirms the previous conclusion concerning the duration of the relevant obligations by France under the First Agreement.

According to Article 25, "the time of commission of the breach" extends over the entire period during which the unlawful act continues to take place. France committed a continuous breach of its obligations, without any interruption or suspension, during the whole period when the two agents remained in Paris in breach of the Agreement.

If the breach was a continuous one, as established in paragraph 101 above, that means that the violated obligation also had to be running continuously and without interruption. The "time of commission of the breach" constituted an uninterrupted period, which was not and could not be intermittent, divided into fractions or subject to intervals. Since it had begun on 22 July 1986, it had to end on 22 July 1989, at the expiry of the three years stipulated.

Thus, while France continues to be liable for the breaches which occurred before 22 July 1989, it cannot be said today that France is *now* in breach of its international obligations.

106. This does not mean that the French Government is exempt from responsibility on account of the previous breaches of its obligations, committed while these obligations were in force.

Article 70(1) of the Vienna Convention on the Law of Treaties provides that:

> "the termination of a treaty under its provisions ...
>
> b) does not affect any right, obligation or legal situation of the parties created through the execution of the treaty prior to its termination."

Referring to claims based on the previous infringement of a treaty which had since expired, Lord McNair stated:

> "such claims acquire an existence independent of the treaty whose breach gave rise to them" (ICJ Reports, 1952, p. 63).

In this case it is undisputed that the breaches of obligation incurred by the French Government discussed in paragraphs 88 and 101 of the award—the failure to return Major Mafart and the removal of and failure to return Captain Prieur—were committed at a time when the obligations assumed in the First Agreement were still in force.

Consequently, the claims advanced by New Zealand have an existence independent of the expiration of the First Agreement and entitle New Zealand to obtain adequate relief for these breaches.

For the foregoing reason the Tribunal:

> by a majority declares that the obligations of the French Republic requiring the stay of Major Mafart and Captain Prieur on the island of Hao ended on 22 July 1989.

Existence of Damage

107. Before examining the question of adequate relief for the aggrieved State, it is necessary to deal with a fundamental objection which has been raised by the French Government. The French Government opposes the New Zealand claim for relief on the ground that such a claim "completely ignores a central element, the damage," since it does not indicate that "the slightest damage has been suffered, even moral damage."

And, the French Republic adds, in the theory of international responsibility, damage is necessary to provide a basis for liability to make reparation.

108. New Zealand gives a two-fold answer to the French objection: first, it contends that it has been confirmed by the International Law Commission draft on State Responsibility that damage is not a precondition of liability or responsibility and second, that in any event, New Zealand has suffered in this case legal and moral damage. New Zealand asserts that it is not claiming material damage in the sense of physical or direct injury to persons or property resulting in an identifiable economic loss, but it is claiming legal damage by reason of having been victim of a violation of its treaty rights, even if there is no question of a material or pecuniary loss. Moreover, New Zealand claims moral damage since in this case there is not a purely technical breach of a treaty, but a breach causing deep offence to the honour, dignity and prestige of the State New Zealand points out that the affront it suffered by the premature release of the two agents in breach of the treaty revived all the feelings of outrage which had resulted from the Rainbow Warrior incident.

109. In the oral proceedings, France made it clear that it had never said, as New Zealand had once maintained, that only material or economic damage is taken into consideration by international law. It added that there exist other damages, including moral and even legal damage. In light of this statement, New Zealand remarked in the hearings that France recognized in principle that there can be legal or moral damage, and that material loss is not the only form of damage in this case. Consequently, the doctrinal controversy between the parties over whether damage is or is not a precondition to responsibility became moot, so long as there was legal or moral damage in this case. Accordingly, both parties agree that

> "in inter-State relations, the concept of damage does not possess an exclusive material or patrimonial character. Unlawful action against non-material interests, such as acts affecting the honor, dignity or prestige of a State, entitle the victim State to receive adequate reparation, even if those acts have not resulted in a pecuniary or material loss for the claimant State" (Cf. Soerensen, Manual cit., p. 534).

110. In the present case the Tribunal must find that the infringement of the special regime designed by the Secretary-General to reconcile the conflicting views of the Parties has provoked indignation and public outrage in New Zealand and caused a new, additional non-material damage. This damage is of a moral, political and legal nature, resulting from the affront to the dignity and prestige not only of New Zealand as such, but of its highest judicial and executive authorities as well.

* * *

For the forgoing reasons the Tribunal:

- declares that it cannot accept the request of New Zealand for a declaration and an order that Major Mafart and Captain Prieur return to the island of Hao.

115. On the other hand, the French contention that satisfaction is the only appropriate remedy for non-material damage is also not justified in the circumstances of the present.

The granting of a form or reparation other than satisfaction has been recognized and admitted in the relations between the parties by the Ruling of the Secretary general of 9 July 1986, which has been accepted and implemented by both Parties to this case.

In the Memorandum presented to the Secretary-General, the New Zealand Government requested compensation for non-material damage, stating that it was "entitled to compensation for the violation of sovereignty and the affront and insult that that involved."

The French Government opposed this claim, contending that the compensation "could concern only the material damage suffered by New Zealand, the moral damage being compensated by the offer of apologies."

But the Secretary-General did not make any distinction, ruling instead that the French Government "should pay the sum of US dollars 7 million to the Government of New Zealand as *compensation for all the damage it has suffered*" (*Ibid*., p. 32, emphasis added.)

In the Rejoinder in this case, the French Government has admitted that "the Secretary-General granted New Zealand double reparation for moral wrong, i.e., both satisfaction, in the form of an official apology from France, and reparations in the form of damages and interest in the amount of 7 million dollars."

In compliance with the Ruling, both parties agreed in the second paragraph of the First Agreement that "the French Government will pay the sum of US 7 million to the Government of New Zealand as *compensation for all the damage which it has suffered*" (emphasis added).

It clearly results from these terms, as well as from the amount allowed, that the compensation constituted a reparation not just for material damage—such as the cost of the police investigation—but for non-material damage as well, regardless of material injury and independent therefrom. Both parties thus accepted the legitimacy of monetary compensation for non-material damages.

On Monetary Compensation

116. The Tribunal has found that France has committed serious breaches of its obligations to New Zealand. But it has also concluded that no order can be made to give effect to these obligations requiring the agents to return to the island of Hao, because these obligations have already expired. The Tribunal has accordingly considered whether it should add to the declarations it will be making an order for the payment by France of damages.

117. The Tribunal considers that it has power to make an award of monetary compensation for breach of the 1986 Agreement under its jurisdiction to decide "any dispute con-

cerning the interpretation or the application" of the provisions of that Agreement (*Chorzów Factory Case (Jurisdiction)* PCIJ Pubs. Ser A. No. 9, p. 21).

118. The Tribunal next considers that an order for the payment of monetary compensation can be made in respect of the breach of international obligations involving, as here, serious moral and legal damage, even though there is no material damage. As already indicated, the breaches are serious ones, involving major departures from solemn treaty obligations entered into in accordance with a binding ruling of the United Nations Secretary-General. It is true that such orders are unusual but one explanation of that is that these requests are relatively rare, for instance by France in the *Carthage* and *Manouba* cases (1913) (11 UNRIAA 449, 463), and by New Zealand in the 1986 process before the Secretary-General, accepted by France in the First Agreement. Moreover, such orders have been made, for instance in the last case.

119. New Zealand has not however requested the award of monetary compensation—even as a last resort should the Tribunal not make the declarations and orders for the return of the agents. The Tribunal can understand that position in terms of an assessment made by a State of its dignity and its sovereign rights. The fact that New Zealand has not sought an order for compensation also means that France has not addressed this quite distinct remedy in its written pleadings and oral arguments, or even had the opportunity to do so. Further, the Tribunal itself has not had the advantage of the argument of the two Parties on the issues mentioned in paragraphs 117 and 118, or on other relevant matters, such as the amount of damages.

120. For these reasons, and because of the issue mentioned in paragraphs 124 to 126 following, the Tribunal has decided not to make an order for monetary compensation.

On Declaration of Unlawfulness as Satisfaction

121. The Tribunal considers in turn satisfaction by way of declarations of breach. Furthermore, in light of the foregoing considerations, it will make a recommendation to the two Governments.

122. There is a long established practice of States and international Courts and Tribunals of using satisfaction as a remedy or form of reparation (in the wide sense) for the breach of an international obligation. This practice relates particularly to the case of moral or legal damage done directly to the State, especially as opposed to the case of damage to persons involving international responsibilities. The whole matter is valuably and extensively discussed by Professor Arangio-Ruiz in his second report (1989) for the International Law Commission on State Responsibility (A/CN.4/425 paras. 7–19 and Ch. 3 paras. 106–145; see also Ch. 4 paras. 146–161 "Guarantees of Non-Repetition in the Wrongful Act"). He demonstrates wide support in the writing as well as in judicial and State practice of satisfaction as "the special remedy for injury to the State's dignity, honour and prestige" (para. 106).

Satisfaction in this sense can take and has taken various forms. Arangio-Ruiz mentions regrets, punishment of the responsible individuals, safeguards against repetition, the payment of symbolic or nominal damages or of compensation on a broader basis, and a decision of an international tribunal declaring the unlawfulness of the State's conduct (para. 107; see also his draft article 10, A/CN.4/425/add. 1, p. 25).

123. It is to the last of these forms of satisfaction for an international wrong that the Tribunal now turns. The Parties in the present case are agreed that in principle such a declaration of breach could be made—although France denied that it was in breach of its obligations and New Zealand sought as well a declaration and order of return. There is

no doubt both that this power exists and that it is seen as a significant sanction. In two related cases brought by France against Italy for unlawful interference with French ships, the Permanent Court of Arbitration, having made an order for the payment of compensation for material loss, stated that:

> in the case in which a Power has failed to meet its obligations ... to another Power, the statement of that fact, especially in an arbitral award, constitutes in itself a serious sanction (*Carthage* and *Manouba* cases (1913) 11 UNRIAA 449–463).

Most notable is the judgment of the International Court of Justice in the *Corfu Channel (Merits) Case* (1949 ICJ Reports 4). The Court, having found that the British Navy had acted unlawfully, in the operative part of its decision:

> "gives judgment that ... the United Kingdom Government violated the sovereignty of the People's Republic of Albania, and that this declaration of the Court constitutes in itself appropriate satisfaction."

The Tribunal accordingly decides to make four declarations of material breach of its obligations by France and further decides in compliance with Article 8 of the Agreement of 14 February 1989 to make public the text of its Award.

For the foregoing reasons the Tribunal:

- declares that the condemnation of the French Republic for its breaches of its treaty obligations to New Zealand, made public by the decision of the Tribunal, constitutes in the circumstances appropriate satisfaction for the legal and moral damage caused to New Zealand.

* * *

For the foregoing reasons the Tribunal:

- in light of the above decisions, recommends that the Governments of the French Republic and of New Zealand set up a fund to promote close and friendly relations between the citizens of the two countries, and that the Government of the French Republic make an initial contribution equivalent to US Dollars 2 million to that fund.

The Islamic Republic of Iran v. The United States of America

Case No. A21, Full Tribunal, Decision No. Dec. 62-A21-FT
Iran-United States Claims Tribunal
May 4, 1987

DECISION

Request for interpretation by the Full Tribunal of the Algiers Declarations with respect to whether the United States is obligated to satisfy promptly any award of this Tribunal rendered in favor of Iran against nationals of the United States.

* * *

I. THE PROCEEDINGS

1. On 19 July 1985, the Islamic Republic of Iran filed a request for interpretation by the Full Tribunal of the provisions of the Algiers Declarations "concerning the commitment of the United States to promptly satisfy any award of this Tribunal rendered in

favour of 'Iran' against the nationals of the United States." The request invoked the provisions of Paragraph 17 of the General Declaration, as well as Article II, paragraph 3, and Article VI, paragraph 4, of the Claims Settlement Declaration, as the basis of the Full Tribunal's jurisdiction to interpret the Declarations.

2. In its request, Iran contended that the United States was obligated to satisfy awards rendered by the Tribunal in favor of Iran against nationals of the United States. It cited an exchange of letters between the Agents of the respective Governments to demonstrate how the dispute had arisen on this issue. In a letter to the Agent of the United States dated 28 January 1985, the Agent of the Islamic Republic of Iran had listed, inter alia, five monetary awards or orders rendered by the Tribunal in favor of Iran against United States nationals, either granting counterclaims or awarding costs of arbitration, which remained unpaid. Iran requested the "prompt compliance" of the United States with respect to such awards. In his reply dated 30 January 1985, the Agent of the United States denied that the United States was obligated either by the Algiers Declarations or by any principle of customary international law to satisfy awards rendered against its nationals.

3. On 18 October 1985, the United States filed its Reply to Iran's request. On 15 May 1986, Iran filed a further Memorial. The United States filed its Response on 4 September 1986. A hearing took place on 3 December 1986 at which both Governments presented oral argument. Mr. Carl F. Salans participated in the deliberations in this Case as a substitute arbitrator in the place of Mr. Charles N. Brower. See Presidential Order No. 51 of 2 February 1987.

4. In its written pleadings, Iran argues that the "final and binding" nature of the Tribunal's awards, as this term is used in Article IV, paragraph 1, of the Claims Settlement Declaration[5] and Article 32, paragraph 2, of the Tribunal Rules,[6] imposes an obligation on the United States to satisfy such awards. Iran seeks to sustain this proposition by reference both to the Algiers Declarations themselves and to the principles of customary international law in the light of which the Declarations must be interpreted. It asserts that the Algiers Declarations establish a "reciprocal system of commitments" that obligates the United States to pay awards if its nationals fail to do so. Relying on the "international" character of the Tribunal, Iran contends that the United States has espoused the claims of its nationals, and that this carries with it the obligation to satisfy Tribunal awards against such nationals. It further asserts that the principles of customary international law require the commitment of a government to satisfy awards rendered by an international tribunal established by a treaty to which it was party.

5. At the hearing, Iran advanced further arguments. It contends that the obligation on the United States is, by nature, one of result—the result being the assured enforcement of Tribunal awards rendered against its nationals, without the need for Iran to take any action to secure enforcement. It suggests that a number of alternative means are open to the United States to satisfy this obligation. In Iran's view, the United States might elect to pay such awards directly, and thereby assume the right to enforce them against the nationals concerned; or it could enact special legislation enabling the enforcement of Tribunal awards on a "full faith and credit" basis as it has done in the

5. Art. IV, para. 1, of the Claims Settlement Declaration provides that "[a]ll decisions and awards of the Tribunal shall be final and binding."

6. Art. 32, para. 2, of the Tribunal Rules provides that "[t]he award shall be made in writing and shall be final and binding on the parties." Iran acknowledges that in this context the term "parties" refers to "arbitrating parties," i.e., the particular claimant and respondent in any case. *See* Tribunal Rules, Introduction and Definitions, paragraph 3(c).

case of awards rendered pursuant to the ICSID Convention.[7] Iran argues that the failure of the United States to take any such steps has exposed Iran to the risk that the Tribunal's awards would not be found to be enforceable in the United States, even by means of proceedings under the New York Convention.[8] Such uncertainty is, Iran contends, inconsistent with the "reciprocal system of commitments" embodied in the Algiers Declarations.

6. The United States denies that it is obligated to satisfy awards rendered against its nationals. First, the United States argues that Iran has not presented an interpretative dispute over which the Tribunal has jurisdiction under Article II, paragraph 3, or Article VI, paragraph 4, of the Claims Settlement Declaration because the Algiers Declarations contain no express or implied provision requiring the United States to enforce such awards. Second, the United States argues that even if Iran has presented an interpretative issue, the Tribunal lacks jurisdiction because no outstanding dispute exists on this issue since the Tribunal has in all relevant cases rendered awards against a named United States national, not against the United States. Third, the United States argues that, even if the Tribunal has jurisdiction, Iran's request fails on the merits. In particular, the United States argues that the very fact that an award against a United States national is "final and binding" does not endow the Tribunal or the United States with responsibility for paying such an award. Finally, the United States argues that the Algiers Declarations do not relieve Iran of the necessity to seek enforcement in the United States or other national courts in the event that a United States national fails voluntarily to satisfy such an award, and notes that Iran has failed to do so to date.

II. REASONS FOR DECISION

A. Jurisdiction

7. The question raised by Iran involves an examination not only of the express terms of the respective Algiers Declarations, but of the totality of those instruments in the context of general principles of international law. The obligation Iran is seeking to establish is not to be found in the express words of the Declarations. However, this fact alone does not remove the present dispute from the ambit of Article VI, paragraph 4, of the Claims Settlement Declaration: it remains a "question concerning the interpretation or application" of that agreement, and as such it is properly brought before the Tribunal.

B. The Merits

8. The task of the Tribunal is to ascertain the nature and content of the obligations undertaken by the respective States Parties to the Algiers Declarations. The means to be employed in the process of interpretation of an international agreement of this nature are set out in the Vienna Convention on the Law of Treaties.[9] Article 31, paragraph 1, of the Convention provides:

---

7. Convention on the Settlement of Investment Disputes Between States and Nationals of Other States, Mar. 18, 1965, 17 U.S.T. 1270, T.I.A.S. No. 6090, 575 U.N.T.S. 159 (1966). Pursuant to the legislation implementing the ICSID Convention in the United States, pecuniary obligations imposed by an award rendered pursuant to the Convention "shall be enforced and shall be given the same full faith and credit as if the award were a final judgment of a court of general jurisdiction of one of the several States" 22 U.S.C. § 1650a.

8. United Nations Convention on the Recognition and Enforcement of Foreign Arbitral Awards, June 10, 1958, 21 U.S.T. 2517, T.I.A.S. No. 6997, 330 U.N.T.S. 3, (effective Dec. 29, 1970).

9. Vienna Convention on the Law of Treaties, May 23, 1969, U.N. Doc. A/CONF.39/27, 8 I.L.M. 679 (1969).

"A treaty shall be interpreted in good faith in accordance with the ordinary meaning to be given to the terms of the treaty in their context and in the light of its object and purpose."

9. In its written pleadings and oral argument, Iran has focused principally on the interpretation of the words "final and binding" as they appear in Article IV, paragraph 1, of the Claims Settlement Declaration, which provides that "[a]ll decisions and awards of the Tribunal shall be final and binding." Iran invests these words with particular significance because, it argues, they reflect the statement in General Principle B of the General Declaration that:

"It is the purpose of both parties, within the framework of and pursuant to the provisions of the two Declarations ... to terminate all litigation as between the government of each party and the nationals of the other, and to bring about the settlement and termination of all such claims through binding arbitration."

Iran contends that the effect of these provisions is to commit the United States to ensure the satisfaction of Tribunal awards in Iran's favor against United States nationals. The term "final and binding", Iran argues, means that no further proceedings are required in order to obtain satisfaction of such Tribunal awards, and the consequence of this is that the United States bears a direct responsibility to pay awards when its nationals fail to do so.

10. The Tribunal notes at the outset that the Algiers Declarations contain no express provision obligating the United States to pay a Tribunal award made against one of its nationals. Indeed, in all the awards at issue, the dispositif obligates named United States nationals—not their Government—to make payments. Moreover, no obligation of the United States can be implied, as Iran contends, from the inclusion in the Declarations of the words "final" and "binding". The terms "final" and "binding," when used in instruments relating to international arbitration, do not ordinarily mean that an award is self-enforcing. Rather, as is generally recognized, a "final" and "binding" award is one with which the parties must comply and which is ripe for enforcement. Thus, when a party fails to comply voluntarily with a final and binding arbitral award, the other party is free to seek enforcement of the award through municipal court procedures. The Tribunal considers that these terms as used in the Algiers Declarations should be given this ordinary and generally recognized meaning.

11. Nor can the Tribunal agree with Iran's argument that the Algiers Declarations establish a "reciprocal system of commitments" that automatically obligates the United States to step in and pay awards against its nationals in the event that those nationals do not do so voluntarily. The principle of reciprocity applies to the agreement taken as a whole; furthermore, it cannot override the specific terms of a treaty freely entered into. Iran's construction would ignore the express provisions of the Declarations which, in establishing a Security Account as the source for payments of awards against the Government of Iran and its controlled entities and in not imposing an identical obligation of payment upon the United States, clearly contemplated something other than parity of treatment of the two States Parties as regards enforcement mechanisms. Further, the Tribunal notes that the Algiers Declarations contain express provisions that carefully define the circumstances in which the two Governments are responsible for paying Tribunal awards. Thus, Article IV, paragraph 3, of the Claims Settlement Declaration provides that awards rendered "against either government shall be enforceable against such government in the courts of any nation in accordance with its laws." On its face, this provision excludes any reference to awards against nationals of either State. In addition, Paragraphs

16 and 17 of the General Declaration relate only to the responsibility of the two Governments concerning fulfillment of their respective obligations under the Declaration; they do not impose a duty to pay the obligations of nationals. The inclusion of specific provisions in both the Claims Settlement Declaration and the General Declaration describing the limited instances in which the two Governments are obligated to satisfy Tribunal Awards is a strong indication that no such obligation exists in other circumstances that are not mentioned, except in the event that a breach of a treaty obligation were to be found, giving rise to liability in damages.

12. Iran also contends that the United States has espoused the claims of its nationals and that this carries with it the obligation for it to pay Tribunal awards against those nationals. However, as the Full Tribunal has previously stated:

> "[T]his Tribunal is clearly an international tribunal.... [I]t is the rights of the claimant, not of his nation, that are to be determined by the Tribunal. *This should be contrasted with the situation of espousal of claims in international law....* Moreover, the object and purpose of the Algiers Declarations was to resolve a crisis in relations between Iran and the United States, *not to extend diplomatic protection in the normal sense.* (Emphasis added.) (Decision No. DEC. 32-A18-FT, pp. 18–19 (6 April 1984))"

Tribunal awards uniformly recognize that no espousal of claims by the United States is involved in the cases before it. Thus, all Tribunal awards requiring payment by nationals of the United States are directed against specifically named nationals, not against their Government. Indeed, all of the counterclaims and requests for costs by Iranian parties are similarly directed against particular nationals of the United States.

13. In view of the conclusions set forth above, the Tribunal cannot find that any obligation of the United States to satisfy Tribunal awards against its nationals flows from the "international" character of the Tribunal, or from any principle of customary international law based on the United States having been a party to the treaty that established the Tribunal.

14. On the other hand, the act of entering into a treaty in good faith carries with it the obligation to fulfill the object and purpose of that treaty—in other words, to take steps to ensure its effectiveness. In this respect, the Algiers Declarations impose upon the United States a duty to implement the Algiers Declarations in good faith so as to ensure that the jurisdiction and authority of the Tribunal are respected. The Parties to the Algiers Declarations are obligated to implement them in such a way that the awards of the Tribunal will be treated as valid and enforceable in their respective national jurisdictions. Such a conclusion is inescapable if one examines the totality of the reciprocal obligations embodied in the Declarations in the light of their stated "object and purpose," as the Vienna Convention requires. General Principle B of the General Declaration expressly states that the purpose of the Tribunal is "to bring about the settlement and termination" of claims between the nationals of one State and the government of the other through "binding arbitration." That purpose is fulfilled and implemented by specific provisions in both Declarations governing the manner in which such arbitration is to be carried out, including the characterisation of the Tribunal's awards as "final and binding".

15. This good faith obligation leaves a considerable latitude to the States Parties as to the nature of the procedures and mechanisms by which Tribunal awards rendered against their nationals may be enforced. The Tribunal has no authority under the Algiers Declarations to prescribe the means by which each of the States provides for such enforcement. Certainly, if no enforcement procedure were available in a State Party, or if recourse to

such procedure were eventually to result in a refusal to implement Tribunal awards, or unduly delay their enforcement, this would violate the State's obligations under the Algiers Declarations. It is therefore incumbent on each State Party to provide some procedure or mechanism whereby enforcement may be obtained within its national jurisdiction, and to ensure that the successful Party has access thereto. If procedures did not already exist as part of the State's legal system they would have to be established, by means of legislation or other appropriate measures. Such procedures must be available on a basis at least as favorable as that allowed to parties who seek recognition or enforcement of foreign arbitral awards.

16. The Tribunal finds no grounds on which to conclude that the United States has failed in its obligation in this respect. To date, Iran has made no attempt to avail itself of the procedures which exist for the enforcement of arbitral awards in United States courts. It is thus premature to make any pronouncement as to whether the mechanisms currently existing in municipal law are adequate. Only if it were to be established that recourse by Iran to the mechanisms or systems existing in the United States had not resulted in the enforcement of awards of this Tribunal against United States nationals would the question arise as to what further measures, if any, the United States might be required to take in order to ensure the "effectiveness" of the Algiers Declarations. A request to the Tribunal as to the "application" of the Algiers Declarations pursuant to Article VI, paragraph 4, of the Claims Settlement Declaration would be appropriate at that stage. However, that is not the question before the Tribunal at the present time.

17. Accordingly, Iran's request that the Tribunal find that "the United States is responsible for the satisfaction of awards rendered by this Tribunal in favour of Iran and against nationals of the United States" cannot be granted and is therefore denied.

Separate Opinion of Hamid Bahrami-Ahmadi and Mohsen Mostafavi with Respect to Case No. A21

* * *

In view of the above, we believe that paragraph 17 of the Decision should read as follows:

> "Accordingly, Iran's request that the Tribunal find that 'the United States is responsible for the satisfaction of awards rendered by this Tribunal in favor of Iran and against nationals of the United States' may be entertained by this Tribunal if and when the United States courts refuse to enforce the said awards, or where there is an undue delay in the enforcement thereof."

Separate Opinion of Judge Parviz Ansari

* * *

5. While in my opinion the United States Government has the responsibility to enforce awards and decisions rendered in favor of Iran directly, the Decision by the Tribunal in the instant Case does, at any rate, constitute a step in the direction of expediting and ensuring enforcement of awards and decisions rendered in favor of Iran. Moreover, in terms of ensuring both the validity and binding nature of Tribunal awards and decisions, and the right of the prevailing party to have the award or decision enforced within the jurisdiction of the United States, the present Decision also merits careful scrutiny and consideration.

Iran Aircraft Industries and Iran Helicopter Support and Renewal Company, Petitioners-Appellants v. Avco Corporation, Respondent-Appellee

980 F.2d 141 (2d Cir. 1992)*

Before: Meskill, Chief Judge, Lumbard, and Cardamone, Circuit Judges.

Lumbard, Circuit Judge:

Iran Aircraft Industries and Iran Helicopter Support and Renewal Company (collectively the "Iranian parties"), both agencies and instrumentalities of the Islamic Republic of Iran, appeal from the December 10, 1991 order of the District Court for the District of Connecticut, Daly, J., granting defendant Avco Corporation's motion for summary judgment.

In granting Avco's motion, which was not timely opposed by the Iranian parties, the district court declined to enforce an award of the Iran-United States Claims Tribunal which resulted in a net balance of $3,513,086[1] due from Avco to the Iranian parties (the "Award"). The Iranian parties argue that the district court erred in declining to enforce the Award because, as claimed by the Iranian parties, the Tribunal's awards are "directly" enforceable in United States courts. In the alternative, the Iranian parties contend that the Award is enforceable under the United Nations Convention on the Recognition and Enforcement of Foreign Arbitral Awards, June 10, 1958, 21 U.S.T. 2517 (the "New York Convention"). Because we find that the district court properly denied enforcement of the Award, we affirm.

Beginning in 1976, Avco entered into a series of contracts whereby it agreed to repair and replace helicopter engines and related parts for the Iranian parties. After the Iranian Revolution of 1978–79, disputes arose as to Avco's performance of, and the Iranian parties' payments under, those contracts. On January 14, 1982, the parties' disputes were submitted to the Tribunal for binding arbitration.

The Tribunal was created by the Algiers Accords (the "Accords"), an agreement between the United States and Iran, through the mediation of Algeria, which provided for the release of the 52 hostages seized at the American Embassy in Tehran on November 4, 1979. In addition to providing conditions for the release of the hostages[3] the Accords established the Tribunal to serve as a forum for the binding arbitration of all existing disputes between the governments of each country and the nationals of the other. Accordingly, the Tribunal was vested with exclusive jurisdiction over claims by nationals of the United States against Iran, claims by nationals of Iran against the United States, and counterclaims arising from the same transactions.[4] *See* Claims Settlement Declaration, Art. II(1).

On May 17, 1985, the Tribunal held a pre-hearing conference to consider, *inter alia*, "whether voluminous and complicated data should be presented through summaries,

* Some footnotes omitted.

1. This figure includes pre-award, but not post-award interest.

3. The Accords provided that upon the release of the American hostages, the U.S. would permit the return to Iran of some twelve billion dollars in Iranian assets frozen in the U.S. and abroad by President Jimmy Carter's Executive Order.... *See* Exec. Order No. 12,170, 3 C.F.R. 457 (1980).

4. The Tribunal was also vested with jurisdiction to hear "official claims of the United States and Iran against each other arising out of contractual arrangements between them for the purchase and sale of goods and services," and "dispute[s] as to the interpretation or performance of any provision" of the General Declaration.... Claims Settlement Declaration, Art. II(2)-(3).

tabulations, charts, graphs or extracts in order to save time and costs." *See Avco Corp. v. Iran Aircraft Indus.*, Case No. 261, 19 Iran-U.S.Cl.Trib.Rep. 200, 235 (1988) (Brower, *J.*, concurring and dissenting). At the conference, Avco's counsel, Dean Cordiano, requested guidance from the Tribunal as to the appropriate method for proving certain of its claims which were based on voluminous invoices, stating:

> In the interest of keeping down some of the documentation for the Tribunal we have not placed in evidence as of yet the actual supporting invoices. But we have those invoices and they are available and if the Tribunal would be interested in seeing them we can obviously place them in evidence or we can use a procedure whereby an outside auditing agency, uh, certifies to the amounts of the, uh, summaries vis-a-vis the underlying invoices. Both of those approaches can be taken. But I want to assure the Tribunal that all of the invoices reflected in our exhibits to the memorial ... exist and are available.

Id. at 235–36. After noting that the Iranian parties "obviously have had those invoices all along," Cordiano stated that he would:

> like the Tribunal's guidance as to whether, uh, you would like this outside certifying agency to go through the underlying invoices and certify as to the summary amounts or that the Tribunal feels at this point that the, uh—that you would rather have the, uh, raw data, so to speak—the underlying invoices. Uh, we're prepared to do it either way.

Id. at 236.

The Chairman of Chamber Three. Judge Nils Mangard of Sweden, then engaged in the following colloquy with Cordiano:

> Mangard: I don't think we will be very, very much enthusiastic getting kilos and kilos of invoices.
>
> Cordiano: That, that's what I thought so ...
>
> Mangard: So I think it will help us ...
>
> Cordiano: We'll use ...
>
> Mangard: To use the alternative rather.
>
> Cordiano: Alright ...
>
> Mangard: On the other hand, I don't know if, if any, if there are any objections to any specific invoices so far made by the Respondents. But anyhow as a precaution maybe you could ...
>
> Cordiano: Yes sir.
>
> Mangard: Get an account made.

Id. at 236. Neither counsel for the Iranian parties nor the Iranian Judge attended the prehearing conference.

On July 22, 1985, Avco submitted to the Tribunal a Supplemental Memorial, which stated in part:

> In response to the Tribunal's suggestion at the Prehearing Conference, Avco's counsel has retained Arthur Young & Co., an internationally recognized public accounting firm, to verify that the accounts receivable ledgers submitted to the Tribunal accurately reflect the actual invoices in Avco's records.

Attached to the Supplemental Memorial was an affidavit of a partner at Arthur Young & Co. which verified that the accounts receivable ledgers submitted by Avco tallied with Avco's original invoices, with the exception of one invoice for $240.14. *Id.* at 237.

The Tribunal held its hearing on the merits on September 16–17, 1986. By that time, Judge Mangard had resigned as Chairman of Chamber Three and had been replaced by Judge Michel Virally of France. At the hearing, Judge Parviz Ansari of Iran engaged in the following colloquy with Cordiano

> Ansari: May I ask a question? It is about the evidence. It was one of the first or one of the few cases that I have seen that the invoices have not been submitted. So what is your position on this point about the substantiation of the claim?
>
> Cordiano: Your Honor, this point was raised at the pre-hearing conference in May of last year.
>
> Ansari: I was not there.
>
> Cordiano: I remember that you weren't there. I think we were kind of lonely that day. We were on one side of the table, the other side was not there ... We could have produced at some point the thousands of pages of invoices, but we chose to substantiate our invoices through ... the Arthur Young audit performed specifically for this tribunal proceeding.

Id. at 237.

The Tribunal issued the Award on July 18, 1988. Of particular relevance here, the Tribunal disallowed Avco's claims which were documented by its audited accounts receivable ledgers, stating, "[T]he Tribunal cannot grant Avco's claim solely on the basis of an affidavit and a list of invoices, even if the existence of the invoices was certified by an independent audit." *Id.* at 211 (majority opinion).

Judge Brower, the American judge and the only judge of the panel who was present at the pre-hearing conference, filed a separate Concurring and Dissenting Opinion in which he stated:

> I believe the Tribunal has misled the Claimant, however, unwittingly, regarding the evidence it was required to submit, thereby depriving Claimant, to that extent, of the ability to present its case ...

Since Claimant did exactly what it previously was told to do by the Tribunal the denial in the present Award of any of those invoice claims on the ground that more evidence should have been submitted constitutes a denial to Claimant of the ability to present its case to the Tribunal.

Id. at 231, 238.

A. *"Direct" Enforceability of the Award*

[1][2] The Iranian parties contend that the district court erred in refusing to enforce the Award because the Tribunal's awards are "directly" enforceable in United States courts, irrespective of the defenses to the enforcement of foreign arbitral awards provided for in the New York Convention. The Iranian parties do not, and cannot, point to any mechanism in the Accords for direct enforcement of Tribunal awards issued against United States nationals.[6] Nevertheless, the Iranian parties argue that Tribunal awards must be "directly"

6. In contrast, the Accords provided that approximately one billion dollars of the previously frozen Iranian assets would be placed in a "security account" from which the U.S. or its nationals who prevailed on claims against Iran would be able to satisfy their awards ... Iran agreed to maintain a

enforced because the Accords state that "All decisions and awards of the Tribunal shall be final and binding." *See* Claims Settlement Declaration, Art. IV(1).

The Tribunal's own interpretation of the Accords reveals the lack of merit in the Iranian parties' position. In *Islamic Republic of Iran v. United States,* Case No. A/21, 14 Iran-U.S.Cl.Trib.Rep. 324 (1987), the Tribunal considered whether the Accords obligated the United States to satisfy awards issued in favor of Iran or its nationals upon the default of United States nationals. The Tribunal ruled that while the United States had no such obligation under the Accords, it had assumed a treaty obligation to provide an enforcement mechanism for the Tribunal's awards, stating:

> It is therefore incumbent on each State Party to provide some procedure or mechanism whereby enforcement may be obtained within its national jurisdiction, and to ensure that the successful Party has access thereto. If procedures did not already exist as part of the State's legal system they would have to be established, by means of legislation or other appropriate measures. Such procedures must be available on a basis *at least as favorable* as that allowed to parties who seek recognition or enforcement of foreign arbitral awards.

Id. at 331 (emphasis added). Accordingly, the Accords require only that we grant the Award "at least as favorable" treatment as we grant other "final and binding" foreign arbitral awards.

The Iranian parties argue that where parties agree to "final" or "binding" arbitration, the resulting arbitral award must be treated as a final, res judicata judgment against the non-prevailing party. We disagree. The terms "final" and "binding" merely reflect a contractual intent that the issues joined and resolved in the arbitration may not be tried de novo in any court. *See I/S Stavborg v. National Metal Converters, Inc.,* 500 F.2d 424, 427 (2d Cir.1974). Furthermore, we have held that even a "final" and "binding" arbitral award is subject to the defenses to enforcement provided for in the New York Convention. *See Fotochrome, Inc. v. Copal Co., Ltd.,* 517 F.2d 512, 519 (2d Cir.1975). Accordingly, the "final and binding" language in the Accords does not bar consideration of the defenses to enforcement provided for in the New York Convention.

B. *The New York Convention*

[3] Avco argues that the district court properly denied enforcement of the Award pursuant to Article V(1)(b) of the New York Convention because it was unable to present its case to the Tribunal. The New York Convention provides for nonenforcement where:

> The party against whom the award is invoked was not given proper notice of the appointment of the arbitrator or of the arbitration proceedings or was *otherwise unable to present his case …*

New York Convention, Art. V(1)(b) (emphasis added).

We have recognized that the defense provided for in Article V(1)(b) "essentially sanctions the application of the forum state's standards of due process," and that due process rights are "entitled to full force under the Convention as defenses to enforcement." *Parsons & Whittemore Overseas Co., Inc. v. Societe Generale de L'Industrie du Papier (RAKTA),* 508 F.2d 969, 975–76 (2d Cir.1974). Under our law, "[t]he fundamental requirement of due process is the opportunity to be heard 'at a meaningful time and in a meaningful manner.'" *Mathews v. Eldridge,* 424 U.S. 319, 333, 96 S.Ct. 893, 902, 47 L.Ed.2d 18 (1976)

---

minimum balance of $500 million in the security account until all awards of the Tribunal are paid … General Declaration, Sec. 7.

(quoting *Armstrong v. Manzo,* 380 U.S. 545, 552, 85 S.Ct. 1187, 1191, 14 L.Ed.2d 62 (1965)). Accordingly, if Avco was denied the opportunity to be heard in a meaningful time or in a meaningful manner, enforcement of the Award should be refused pursuant to Article V(1)(b).

At the pre-hearing conference, Judge Mangard specifically advised Avco not to burden the Tribunal by submitting "kilos and kilos of invoices." Instead, Judge Mangard approved the method of proof proposed by Avco, namely the submission of Avco's audited accounts receivable ledgers. Later, when Judge Ansari questioned Avco's method of proof, he never responded to Avco's explanation that it was proceeding according to an earlier understanding. Thus, Avco was not made aware that the Tribunal now required the actual invoices to substantiate Avco's claim. Having thus led Avco to believe it had used a proper method to substantiate its claim, the Tribunal then rejected Avco's claim for lack of proof.

We believe that by so misleading Avco, however unwittingly, the Tribunal denied Avco the opportunity to present its claim in a meaningful manner. Accordingly, Avco was "unable to present [its] case" within the meaning of Article V(1)(b), and enforcement of the Award was properly denied.

Affirmed.

Cardamone, Circuit Judge, dissenting:

The issue before us is whether Avco was denied an opportunity to present its case before the Iran-United States Claims Tribunal at the Hague. To rule, as the majority does, that it was denied such an opportunity renders the Tribunal's award unenforceable under article V(1)(b) of the United Nations Convention on the Recognition and Enforcement of Foreign Arbitral Awards, June 10, 1958, 21 U.S.T. 2517 (the New York Convention). I respectfully dissent because it seems to me that a fair reading of this record reveals that Avco was not denied such an opportunity. Thus, in my view the arbitral award is enforceable under the New York Convention.

* * *

One of the reasons for this dissent is because until today no federal or foreign case appears to have used article V(1)(b)'s narrow exception as a reason to refuse to enforce an arbitral award due to the arbitration panel's failure to consider certain evidence. Moreover, some decisions have rejected the article V(1)(b) defense under other, somewhat analogous circumstances. For example, in *Parsons & Whittemore Overseas Co.,* 508 F.2d at 975–76, we refused to use the defense to bar enforcement based on an arbitral Tribunal's refusal to accommodate a key witness' schedule, stating that the inability to present one's witness was "a risk inherent in an agreement to submit to arbitration." Similarly, another court has held that a party was not denied the opportunity to present its defenses under article V(1)(b) when it had notice of an arbitration, but chose not to respond. *See Goetech Lizenz AG v. Evergreen Systems,* 697 F.Supp. 1248, 1253 (E.D.N.Y.1988). The court in *Evergreen Systems* ruled that the defendant's "failure to participate was a decision that was reached only after the Company had full knowledge of the peril at which it acted." *Id.* In the face of Judge Ansari's repeated questioning of Avco's counsel, Avco was plainly placed on similar notice of the possible risk that the panel would choose not to rely on invoice summaries in determining whether to grant it an award.

* * *

The present picture is vastly different. Avco had a full opportunity to present its claims, and was on notice that there might be a problem with its proof, especially given

Judge Ansari's concerns voiced at trial. The earlier panel surely had never said that the invoices themselves would not be accepted or considered as evidence at trial. Nor did the pre-trial colloquy clearly indicate that the earlier panel had issued a definitive ruling that account summaries would be sufficient substitute proof for the invoices. Avco did not declare, after hearing Judge Ansari's comments, that it had been precluded by the pre-trial colloquy from producing the invoices, nor did it then attempt to introduce them before the panel. Rather than address Judge Ansari's concerns through producing the invoices themselves, Avco reiterated its "choice" to produce only a summary of the invoices. In so doing it took a calculated risk. Under these circumstances, Avco can scarcely credibly maintain that it was prevented from presenting its case before the Tribunal.

III

When reviewing the grant of summary judgment which dismissed the action to enforce the award, we must view the facts in the light most favorable to the Iranian parties. When so viewed those facts fail to demonstrate that Avco was denied the opportunity to present its claims to the Tribunal. For the reasons stated I think the district court erred in reaching the opposite conclusion. Accordingly, I dissent and vote to enforce the award.

The Islamic Republic of Iran, Claimant v. The United States of America, Respondent

Case No. A27, Full Tribunal, Award No. 586-A27-FT
Iran-United States Claims Tribunal
June 5, 1998

AWARD

* * *

I. INTRODUCTION

1. At issue in this Case are the United States obligations under the Algiers Declarations[1] concerning the enforcement in the United States of Tribunal awards rendered against United States nationals in favor of Iran. Relevant to this Case are the Tribunal's findings in Islamic Republic of Iran and United States of America, Decision No. DEC 62-A21-FT (4 May 1987), reprinted in 14 Iran-U.S. C.T.R. 324 (hereinafter "Case A21").

2. In Case A21, Iran had requested that the Tribunal hold that the Algiers Declarations obliged the United States to satisfy any award rendered by the Tribunal against United States nationals in favor of Iran. The Tribunal concluded that the Algiers Declarations did not impose on the United States any obligation, either express or implicit, to satisfy any such awards, and it denied Iran's request. In reaching this conclusion, the Tribunal pointed out, however, that "[t]he Parties to the Algiers Declarations are obligated to implement them in such a way that the awards of the Tribunal will be treated as

---

1. Declaration of the Government of the Democratic and Popular Republic of Algeria ("General Declaration") and Declaration of the Government of the Democratic and Popular Republic of Algeria Concerning the Settlement of Claims by the Government of the United States of America and the Government of the Islamic Republic of Iran ("Claims Settlement Declaration"), both dated 19 January 1981.

valid and enforceable in their national jurisdictions." *Id.* at para. 14, 14 Iran-U.S.C.T.R. at 330.

3. In this Case, Iran contends that the United States has breached its obligations under the Algiers Declarations concerning the enforcement of Tribunal awards, which obligations, Iran asserts, were delineated by the Tribunal in its Decision in Case A21. As a basis for its claim, Iran invokes the refusal by the United States courts to enforce the Tribunal's Partial Award in Avco Corporation and Iran Aircraft Industries, et al., Partial Award No. 377-261-3 (18 Jul. 1988), reprinted in 19 Iran-U.S.C.T.R. 200 (hereinafter "Avco"). Iran also adduces an alleged undue delay by the United States courts in enforcing the Tribunal's Award in Gould Marketing, Inc. and Ministry of Defence of the Islamic Republic of Iran, Award No. 136-49/50-2 (29 Jun. 1984), reprinted in 6 Iran-U.S.C.T.R. 272 (hereinafter "Gould"). The United States denies liability.

4. According to its final pleadings, Iran seeks U.S.$3,513,086.03, the amount that the Tribunal awarded the Iranian parties in Avco, and U.S.$48,914, the legal expenses that Iran allegedly incurred in connection with the Avco enforcement proceedings in the United States. In addition, Iran seeks U.S.$344,767.80, the total amount of arbitration costs that the Tribunal awarded Iran in twenty-four other awards. Iran concedes that it has not attempted to seek enforcement of those cost awards in the courts of the United States. In Iran's view, in light of the unsatisfactory outcome of the Avco and Gould enforcement proceedings, it would have been futile to do so. Iran seeks interest on all claimed amounts.

5. A Hearing in this Case was held on 27 and 28 February 1996 in the Peace Palace, The Hague.

* * *

IV. MERITS

A. THE CLAIM RELATED TO THE NONENFORCEMENT OF THE AWARD IN AVCO AND THE ALLEGED UNDUE DELAY

56. In its Decision in Case A21, the Tribunal held that "[t]he Parties to the Algiers Declarations are obligated to implement them in such a way that the awards of the Tribunal will be treated as valid and enforceable in their respective national jurisdictions." Case A21, *supra*, at para. 14, 14 Iran-U.S.C.T.R. at 330. The task before the Tribunal is to determine whether the United States, by virtue of the refusal by its courts to enforce the Avco award, has breached that obligation.

57. Before turning to this task the Tribunal will deal with the question of its own legal nature, as that nature has been discussed by the parties and forms a backdrop against which the Tribunal may view the actions of the United States. Article II, paragraph 1, of the Claims Settlement Declaration in relevant part provides:

> An international arbitral tribunal (the Iran-United States Claims Tribunal) is hereby established for the purpose of deciding claims of nationals of the United States against Iran and claims of nationals of Iran against the United States, and any counterclaim which arises out of the same contract, transaction or occurrence that constitutes the subject matter of that national's claim....

Pursuant to paragraph 2 of that Article, the Tribunal shall also have jurisdiction to decide official claims of the High Contracting Parties against each other arising out of contractual arrangements between them for the purchase and sale of goods and services. Pursuant to Paragraph 17 of the General Declaration and Article VI, paragraph 4, of the Claims Settlement Declaration, moreover, the Tribunal shall have jurisdiction over any dispute as to the interpretation or performance of the Algiers Declarations.

58. The Tribunal was established by an international agreement concluded between Iran and the United States. The States Parties empowered it to decide intergovernmental claims as well as claims by nationals of one State Party against the government of the other State Party. Under contemporary international law, the fact that an individual or a private entity is party to proceedings before a forum created by an international agreement does not deprive that forum and its proceedings of their international legal nature. The Tribunal is "clearly an international tribunal," Islamic Republic of Iran and United States of America, Decision No. DEC 32-A18-FT, at 18 (6 Apr. 1984), reprinted in 5 Iran-U.S.C.T.R. 251, 261, and "it is subject to international law," Anaconda Iran, Inc. and Islamic Republic of Iran, et al., Interlocutory Award No. ITL 65-167-3, para. 97 (10 Dec. 1986), reprinted in 13 Iran-U.S.C.T.R. 199, 223. By definition, international arbitral awards, if final, are binding. Recourse to this Tribunal implies the undertaking to respect its awards.

59. In Case A21, the Tribunal stated that it was "incumbent on each State Party [to the Algiers Declarations] to provide some procedure or mechanism whereby enforcement [of Tribunal awards] may be obtained within its national jurisdiction, and to ensure that the successful Party has access thereto." Decision in Case A21, para. 15, 14 Iran-U.S.C.T.R. at 331. In this connection, it should be noted that "[t]he Tribunal has no authority under the Algiers Declarations to prescribe the means by which each of the States provides for such enforcement." Id. The States Parties enjoy "considerable latitude ... as to the nature of the procedures and mechanisms by which Tribunal awards rendered against their nationals may be enforced." Id. However, that latitude, though "considerable," has its limits. In its Decision in Case A21, the Tribunal held that those procedures "must be available on a basis at least as favorable as that allowed to parties who seek recognition or enforcement of foreign arbitral awards." Id. The procedures and mechanisms among which a State Party to the Algiers Declarations may choose must also be adequate to achieve the objective envisaged by the Declarations, i.e., the enforceability of Tribunal decisions and awards as final and binding. That limitation on the Parties' latitude in choosing those procedures and mechanisms clearly follows from the Tribunal's Decision in Case A21. See *infra*, para. 61.

60. In paragraph 15 of its Decision in Case A21, the Tribunal also stated that

> if recourse to [a municipal enforcement] procedure were eventually to result in a refusal to implement Tribunal awards, or unduly delay their enforcement, this would violate the State's obligations under the Algiers Declarations.

This interpretation of the Algiers Declarations by the Decision in Case A21 conforms to international law. *See supra*, para. 58. As paragraph 14 of that Decision points out, it is important to ensure the "effectiveness" of the Algiers Declarations and ensure that the

> jurisdiction and authority of the Tribunal are respected. The Parties to the Algiers Declarations are obligated to implement them in such a way that the awards of the Tribunal will be treated as valid and enforceable in their respective national jurisdictions.

61. The mechanism available in the United States for the enforcement of Tribunal awards is the 1958 New York Convention on the Recognition and Enforcement of Foreign Arbitral Awards. *See supra*, footnote 2. As noted, in the Gould and Avco enforcement proceedings, the United States courts held that Tribunal awards were enforceable pursuant to that Convention. *See supra*, paras. 14 and 22.

62. In its decision denying enforcement of the Avco award, the Second Circuit held that the Algiers Declarations did not bar consideration of the defenses to enforcement

provided for in Article V of the New York Convention.[5] *See supra*, para. 22. In the statement of interest it filed in the Gould enforcement proceedings before the District Court of the Central District of California, *see supra*, para. 12, the United States, for its part, while arguing that in principle Article V of the New York Convention applied to Tribunal awards, recognized that subparagraphs (1)(a) and (2)(b) thereof did not apply to such awards. With respect to the balance of the Article V exceptions to enforcement (subparagraphs (1)(b) through (1)(e) and subparagraph 2(a)), at the Hearing, the Legal Adviser to the United States Department of State conceded that there appeared to be, on the surface, "some infelicities."

63. The Tribunal agrees that those provisions are problematic in the context of Tribunal awards, particularly when viewed in the light of the States Parties' obligations under the Algiers Declarations relating to the enforcement of those awards. Indeed, Article IV, paragraph 1, of the Claims Settlement Declaration, which provides that "[a]ll decisions and awards of the Tribunal shall be final and binding," rules out the possibility of readjudication of the merits of Tribunal awards by a municipal court, either under the guise of Article V of the New York Convention or by any other means. See infra, para. 70.

64. Indeed, it is difficult for the Tribunal to believe that any of its awards could fall within the scope of Article V of the New York Convention. In any event, the fact that the mechanism chosen by the United States to enforce this Tribunal's awards is the New York Convention does not exempt the United States from liability if its courts err by denying enforcement of an award that should, by virtue of the Algiers Declarations, have been enforced.[6] See also Decision in Case A21, para. 15, 14 Iran-U.S.C.T.R. at 331.

65. In denying enforcement of the Avco award, the Second Circuit held that Avco had been "unable to present [its] case" before the Tribunal within the meaning of Article V(1)(b) of the New York Convention. *See supra*, para. 23. In reaching the conclusion that the Tribunal had "denied Avco the opportunity to present its claim in a meaningful manner," the Second Circuit found (1) that at a Pre-Hearing Conference held in 1985, the then-Chairman of Chamber Three approved the method of proof proposed by Avco to substantiate its invoice claim, namely the "submission of Avco's audited accounts receivable ledgers" and (2) that the Tribunal never made Avco aware that "the Tribunal now required the actual invoices to substantiate Avco's claim." In the Second Circuit's view, "[h]aving thus led Avco to believe it had used a proper method to substantiate its claim, the Tribunal then rejected Avco's claim for lack of proof." *See supra*, para. 23.

66. This decision by the Second Circuit was erroneous. A careful reading of the Tribunal's award in Avco shows that it was based not on the absence of the invoices underlying Avco's claims, but on a lack of proof that those invoices were payable. *See supra*, para. 17. Indeed, the Tribunal stated at paragraph 32 of its Award that it did not question the existence of the invoices, but rather, whether Iran Aircraft Industries owed Avco on the basis of them, a defect in proof the invoices themselves could not have cured. Consequently, this erroneous decision by the Second Circuit places the United States in violation of its obligation to make the Avco award enforceable in the United States.

---

5. Article V of the New York Convention.

6. The Tribunal recognizes that no tribunal can declare itself immune from procedural error or the possibility of fraud, forgery, or perjury that it may not detect. In such hypothetical cases, however, revision of the award could be done only by the Tribunal (if it concluded that it had the authority to do so), not by any other court. See Harold Birnbaum and Islamic Republic of Iran, Decision No. DEC 124-967-2, paras. 14–19 (14 Dec. 1995); Ram International Industries Inc., et al. and Air Force of the Islamic Republic of Iran, Decision No. DEC 118-148-1, para. 20 (28 Dec. 1993).

67. The United States elected not to file a statement of interest before the Second Circuit in Avco. The Tribunal believes that a statement should have pointed out why the Avco award deserved enforcement and, if filed, might have improved the chances that the majority of the court would have paid due attention to the text of the Tribunal's award, rather than apparently relying on the Dissenting and Concurring Opinion of one of the Members of the Tribunal, *see supra*, para. 18.

68. Indeed, the fact that the Second Circuit effectively adopted the dissenting view of the Tribunal Member in the minority illustrates an additional problem with its decision. That Member argued that Avco had been unable to prove its claim solely because the Tribunal supposedly misled it into not submitting its invoices. A majority of Chamber Three of the Tribunal considered this argument and, by not adopting the minority's view, rejected it. The Second Circuit thus reconsidered a specific question raised and conclusively decided by the Tribunal; in effect, the Second Circuit repudiated the merits of the Tribunal's award in Avco.

69. By reconsidering an issue that had been already aired and decided by the Tribunal, the Second Circuit, in violation of Article IV, paragraph 1, of the Claims Settlement Declaration, failed to treat the Tribunal's decision as "final and binding." Once an issue has been raised and decided by the Tribunal, no enforcing court may reexamine that same issue—whether under the guise of the New York Convention or by any other means—without violating that Article's proviso that "[a]ll decisions and awards of the Tribunal shall be final and binding." In this connection, see also Case Concerning the Factory at Chorzów (Interpretation) (*Germany vs. Poland*), 1927 P.C.I.J. (ser. A) No. 13, at 19 (16 Dec.); Case Concerning the Factory at Chorzów (Claim for Indemnity) (Merits) (*Germany vs. Poland*), 1928 P.C.I.J. (ser. A) No. 17, at 33–34 (13 Sep.).

70. In other words, a party to a case before the Tribunal cannot evade findings made by the Tribunal by relitigating them in an enforcing court. The Claims Settlement Declaration requires the States Parties to stand behind the Tribunal's findings and makes them liable if their courts second-guess decisions the Tribunal has made. In this Case, the significance of the invoices underlying Avco's claims and of the colloquy between the Chairman of Chamber Three and Avco's Counsel at the 1985 Pre-Hearing Conference were considered and decided by the Tribunal. It was not open to the enforcing courts of one of the sovereign parties to decide that the dissenting arbitrator was right after all.

71. Based on the foregoing, the Tribunal holds that, through the refusal by the United States Court of Appeals for the Second Circuit to enforce the Avco award, the United States has violated its obligation under the Algiers Declarations to ensure that a valid award of the Tribunal be treated as final and binding, valid, and enforceable in the jurisdiction of the United States. It is a well-settled principle of international law that every international wrongful act of the judiciary of a state is attributable to that state.[7] Consequently, the United States is liable for damages pursuant to paragraph 17 of the General Declaration and Article VI, paragraph 4, of the Claims Settlement Declaration. It is appropriate to recall here that the Parties to the Algiers Declarations undertook to respect the jurisdiction and the authority of the Tribunal.

---

7. Lord McNair writes: "[I]f ... the courts ... decline to give effect to the treaty..., their judgments involve the State in a breach of treaty." Lord McNair, The Law of Treaties 346 (1961). The Draft Articles on State Responsibility adopted by the International Law Commission of the UN provide that if an act of a judicial organ of the state constitutes a breach of an international obligation of that state, such an act produces an internationally wrongful act of the state, entailing its international responsibility. See Articles 1–6, International Law Commission, 48th Sess., at 125–126, U.N. Doc. A/51/10 (1996).

72. To be sure, there were imperfections in the way Iran pursued enforcement of the Avco award before the United States courts. For example, Iran failed to respond to Avco's motion for summary judgment before the District Court, it did not seek a rehearing en banc by the Second Circuit, and it did not petition the Supreme Court of the United States for a writ of certiorari. *See supra*, paras. 19–20 and 25. Nevertheless, while an enforcing party must carry the burden of enforcement, the Tribunal does not believe that, taken as a whole, the evidence compels it to refuse relief to Iran because of those shortcomings. It should be noted, in particular, that, despite Iran's failure to respond to Avco's motion before the District Court, the Second Circuit heard arguments upon and reviewed the question of the enforceability of the Avco award.

73. With respect to the alleged delay of enforcement, the Tribunal finds that the record, as it stands, does not support Iran's contentions that the procedures available in the United States unduly delay enforcement of Tribunal awards and that it is not cost-effective to attempt to enforce Tribunal awards in the United States. *See supra*, para. 34.

74. In view of its decision in this Case, the Tribunal need not address Iran's request for an order requiring the United States to establish a suitable procedure for the enforcement of all future Tribunal awards rendered in favor of Iran against United States nationals.

75. Where it finds that one of the State Parties has not fulfilled its obligations under the Algiers Declarations, the Tribunal has, according to paragraph 17 of the General Declaration, authority to award the other State Party damages to compensate for losses resulting from such a breach. In the circumstances, the Tribunal holds that the United States is liable to compensate Iran in the amount of the award in Avco, namely U.S.$3,513,086.03.

76. The Tribunal further holds that Iran is entitled to pre-judgment interest on that amount, as the Second Circuit would likely have awarded such interest if its decision had been to grant enforcement of the Avco award.[8] The Tribunal therefore awards Iran simple pre-judgment interest at the annual rate of 10 percent[9] (365-day basis) from 18 July 1988, the date the Avco award was issued, until 24 November 1992, the date the Second Circuit rendered its decision denying enforcement of that award.

77. Iran also seeks reimbursement of the legal expenses it incurred in pursuing the enforcement of the award in Avco after the United States District Court for the District of Connecticut denied enforcement of that award on 10 December 1991. These expenses, however, would have been incurred even if the decision of the Second Circuit had been to grant enforcement. Consequently, they are not recoverable as damages.

78. Consequently, the Tribunal awards Iran a total of U.S.$5,042,481.65 on its claim related to the nonenforcement of the Tribunal's award in Avco. This amount includes the amount awarded by the Tribunal in Avco, U.S.$3,513,086.03, plus U.S.$1,529,395.62, the aggregate pre-judgment interest awarded *supra*, at para. 76. The Tribunal further

8. See Born, International Commercial Arbitration in the United States: Commentary & Materials (Deventer-Boston 1994) 623–24.

9. In Avco, the Tribunal awarded U.S.$886,127 to the Respondent Iran Aircraft Industries ("IACI") and U.S.$2,626,959.03 to the Respondent Iran Helicopter Support and Renewal Company ("IHSRC"), for a total of U.S.$3,513,086.03. It further awarded simple interest at the rate of ten percent per annum on the amount awarded IACI, U.S.$886,127, from the date of the award up to and including the date of payment. The Tribunal did not grant post-award interest on the amount owing to IHSRC because IHSRC had limited its interest request to the pre-award period. *See* Avco, *supra*, para. 139, 19 Iran-U.S.C.T.R. at 229. Given the inequity of the fact that IHSRC was not paid promptly after the Avco award, however, the Tribunal believes an enforcing U.S. court would likely have exercised its discretion to award post-award interest on the amount owed to IHSRC as well.

awards simple post-judgment interest on U.S.$5,042,481.65 at the annual rate of 5 percent (365-day basis) from 25 November 1992 up to and including the date of payment of this Award.

B. THE CLAIM RELATED TO THE 24 COST AWARDS

79. Iran seeks U.S.$344,767.80—the total amount of arbitration costs that the Tribunal awarded it in twenty-four awards. Iran argues that, having demonstrated that there is no realistic prospect of enforcing Tribunal awards in the United States, it is entitled to seek payment of the cost awards in question directly from the United States. *See supra*, para. 36. The issue is whether the United States is obliged to satisfy such awards, though Iran has never made any attempt to enforce them in United States courts.

80. In its Decision in Case A21, the Tribunal held that the Algiers Declarations did not contain any express or implied obligation of the United States to step in and satisfy Tribunal awards rendered against its nationals in favor of Iran. *See Case* A21, *supra*, paras. 10–13, 14 Iran-U.S.C.T.R. at 328–30. On the evidence before it, the Tribunal is not prepared to assume that, because United States courts denied enforcement of a single award, they will also deny or unduly delay enforcement of the cost awards that are the subject of this claim.

81. Only after Iran has made timely attempts to enforce those cost awards in United States courts, and only if Iran establishes that those courts have wrongfully refused to implement the awards or have unduly delayed their enforcement, "would the question arise as to what … measures, if any, the United States might be required to take in order to ensure the 'effectiveness' of the Algiers Declarations." Id. para. 16, 14 Iran-U.S.C.T.R. at 331. A request by Iran to the Tribunal as to the performance of the Algiers Declarations pursuant to Article 17 of the General Declaration and Article VI, paragraph 4, of the Claims Settlement Declaration "would be appropriate at that stage." Id.

82. Consequently, Iran's claim relating to the twenty-four cost awards must be dismissed.

V. AWARD

83. In view of the foregoing.

THE TRIBUNAL DETERMINES AS FOLLOWS:

a. By virtue of the refusal by the United States Court of Appeals for the Second Circuit to enforce the Avco award, the United States has violated its obligation under the Algiers Declarations to ensure that a valid award of the Tribunal be treated as final and binding, valid, and enforceable in the jurisdiction of the United States.

b. Consequently, the United States is obligated to pay Iran the sum of Five Million Forty-Two Thousand Four Hundred Eighty-One United States Dollars and Sixty-Five Cents (U.S.$5,042,481.65), plus simple interest at the annual rate of 5 percent (365-day basis) from 24 November 1992 up to and including the date of payment of this award.

c. Iran's claim related to the reimbursement of the legal expenses it incurred in pursuing the enforcement of the award in Avco before the Second Circuit and Iran's claim related to the total amount of arbitration costs awarded to Iran by the Tribunal in twenty-four awards are both dismissed.

Request for Revision

Decision No. DEC 134-A3/A8/A9/A14/B61-FT
Iran-United States Claims Tribunal
July 1, 2011

* * *

44. Iran invokes an alleged "inherent power" of the Tribunal to reopen and reconsider its awards as a basis for its present Request for Revision of Section VI.C of Partial Award No. 601. The Tribunal considers below whether it possesses any such power to do so.

45. The trend for quite some years has been for international courts and tribunals to be expressly empowered in their respective constitutive instruments, in their rules of procedure, or in both to revise otherwise final and binding awards and judgments. This is not surprising given that revision is an extraordinary remedy that can be admissible only in exceptional and stringent circumstances.[52] "The concept of revision adversely affects and undermines the fundamental principle of *res judicata*," so "if applied incorrectly or without the requisite stringency the concept of revision is capable of impairing the stability of juridical relations and legal security."[53]

46. Thus, as early as 1899, a provision was included in the Hague Convention for the Pacific Settlement of International Disputes to the effect that arbitral tribunals would be empowered to revise their awards so long as the parties to the dispute reserved such power to the tribunal in their *compromis*.[54] The same provision was included in the 1907 Hague Convention for the Pacific Settlement of International Disputes.[55] Further, the Statute of the Permanent Court of International Justice ("P.C.I.J.") expressly conferred on the P.C.I.J. the power to revise its judgments,[56] as does the Statute of the International Court of Justice ("I.C.J.") with respect to the I.C.J.[57] The Convention on the Settlement of Investment Disputes Between States and Nationals of Other States ("ICSID Convention"), too, explicitly

---

52. *See, e.g.*, Kaiyan Homi Kaikobad, Interpretation and Revision of International Boundary Decisions 257 (stating that revision is a judicial remedy that must be exercised restrictively, in exceptional circumstances, and as such cannot lightly be provided).

53. 53 Richard Kreindler, *Applications for "Revision" in Investment Arbitration: Selected Current Issues, in* Liber Amicurom Bernardo Cremades 679, 681–82 (M.Á. Fernández-Ballesteros & D. Arias eds., 2010). *See a/so* 3 Shabtai Rosenne, The Law and Practice of the International Court 1920–2005, 1613 (4th ed. 2006) (emphasizing the exceptional nature of the remedy of revision "as possibly impairing the stability of the jural relations established by the *res judicata")*; W. Michael Reisman, Nullity and Revision—The Review and Enforcement of International Judgments and Awards 219–20 (1971) ("While interpretation attempts to sustain a myth of finality, revision incontrovertibly destroys it."); Derek W. Bowett, *Res Judicata and the Limits of Rectification of Decisions by International Tribunals,* 8 AFR. J. Int'l and Comp. L. 577, 577 (1996) (stating that the respect which States show for awards would be undermined if the awards lacked finality and binding force).

54. Convention for the Pacific Settlement of International Disputes art. 55, 29 July 1899 ("1899 Hague Convention") (English translation *reprinted in* Permanent Court of Arbitration Basic Documents 3 (2005)). Article 55, paragraph 1, of the 1899 Hague Convention provides that "[t]he parties can reserve in the 'Compromis' the right to demand the revision of the Award."

55. Convention for the Pacific Settlement of International Disputes art. 83, 18 Oct. 1907 (English translation *reprinted in* Permanent Court of Arbitration Basic Documents 19 (2005)).

56. Statute of the Permanent Court of International Justice art. 61,16 Dec. 1920 (amended 14 Sept. 1929), P.C.U. Publications (ser. D) No.1, at 26.

57. Statute of the International Court of Justice art. 61.

empowers ICSID arbitral tribunals to revise their awards.[58] Other courts and tribunals that have been specifically authorized by their constitutive instruments to revise their judgments include the European Court of Justice,[59] the United Nations Dispute Tribunal,[60] and the United Nations Appeals Tribunal.[61]

47. The rules of procedure of several mixed arbitral tribunals established after the two World Wars expressly empowered the respective tribunals to revise their decisions.[62] Further, the European Court of Human Rights, in establishing the Rules of Court, and the International Tribunal for the Law of the Sea, in establishing the Rules of the Tribunal, have also conferred upon themselves the power to revise their judgments.[63]

48. The practice of international courts and tribunals with respect to the existence of a power of revision in the absence of any textual basis is inconsistent.[64]

49. With respect to this Tribunal, neither the Claims Settlement Declaration nor the Tribunal Rules provide for the reopening and reconsideration of a case on the merits after an award has been rendered.

50. Article IV, paragraph 1, of the Claims Settlement Declaration commands that "[a]ll decisions and awards of the Tribunal shall be final and binding."[65] this command is confirmed by Article 32, paragraph 2, of the Tribunal Rules, which states that an award rendered by the Tribunal "shall be final and binding on the parties." The Tribunal Rules

58. Convention on the Settlement of Investment Disputes Between States and Nationals of Other States art. 51, *opened/or signature* 18 Mar. 1965,575 U.N.T.S. 159 (entered into force 14 Oct. 1966).

59. Protocol on the Statute of the Court of Justice of the European Union art. 44, C 83 OFFICIAL JOURNAL OF THE EUROPEAN UNION 210, 220 (30 Mar. 2010).

60. Statute of the United Nations Dispute Tribunal art. 12, para. 1, G.A. Res. *63/253,* U.N. Doc. *AlRES/63/253,* at 13 (17 Mar. 2009).

61. Statute of the United Nations Appeals Tribunal art. 11, para. I, G.A. Res. *63/253,* U.N. Doc. *A/RES/63/253,* at 19 (17 Mar. 2009).

62. *See, e.g.,* Rules of Procedure of the Belgo-German Mixed Arbitral Tribunal art. 76, *reprinted in* 1 RECUEIL DES DECISIONS DES TRIBUNAUX ARBITRAUX MIXTES INSTITUÉS PAR LES TRAITES DÉ PAIX 33, 43 (1922); Rules of Procedure of the Franco-German Mixed Arbitral Tribunal art. 79, *id.* at 44,55; Rules of Procedure of the AngloAustrian Mixed Arbitral Tribunal art. 91, *id.* at 622, 635. *See also* Rules of Procedure of the Arbitral Tribunal and Mixed Commission for the London Agreement on German External Debts art. 48 (a), *reprinted in* KARIN OELLERS-FRAHM & NORBERT WOHLER, DISPUTE SETTLEMENT IN PUBLIC INTERNATIONAL Law 772, 779–80 (1984); Rules of Procedure of the Arbitral Commission on Property, Rights and Interests in Germany rule 68, [1957] 2 BUNDESGESETZBLATT 230, 249–50.

63. European Court of Human Rights, Rules of Court rule 80, *available at* http://www.echr.coe.int; International Tribunal for the Law of the Sea, Rules of the Tribunal art. 127, *available at* http://www.itlos.org.

64. International decisions recognizing the existence of an international court's or tribunal's inherent power to revise final and binding awards include: George Moore v. Mexico (U.S.-Mex. Mixed Claims Comm. 26 Jul. 1871), 2 J.B. MOORE, HISTORY AND DIGEST OF THE INTERNATIONAL ARBITRATIONS TO WHICH THE UNITED STATES HAS BEEN A PARTY 1357 (1898); Lehigh Valley Railroad ("The Sabotage Cases"), 8 R.I.A.A. 160, 18790 (U.S.-Ger. Mixed Claims Comm. 15 Dec. 1933); Trail Smelter Arbitration (U.S. v. Can.), 3 R.I.A.A. 1938, 1953–54 (U.S.-Can. Arb. Trib. 1941); Effect of Awards of Compensation Made by the United Nations Administrative Tribunal, Advisory Opinion, 1954 I.C.J. 47, 55 (13 July); Antoine Biloune (Syria), et al. v. Ghana Investments Centre, et al., Award on Damages and Costs, paras. 32–35 *(Ad Hoc* UNCITRAL Arb. Trib. 30 June 1990), XIX Y.B. COMMERCIAL ARBITRATION II, 22–23 (1994). International decisions declining to recognize the existence of a power of revision in the absence of an express authorization include: Benjamin Weil and the La Abra Silver Mining Co. (U.S.-Mex. Mixed Claims Comm. 20 Oct. 1876), 2 J.B. MOORE, *supra,* 1324, 1329; A.H. Lazare (U.S.-Haiti 1886), 2 J.B. MOORE] 749, 1801; Question of Jaworzina (Polish-Czechoslovakian Frontier), Advisory Opinion, 1923 P.C.I.J. (ser. B) No.8, at 38.

65. Claims Settlement Declaration art. IV (I), 1 IRAN-U.S. C.T.R. at 10.

provide a narrow exception to the basic rule of finality of awards in Articles 35, 36, and 37. Following the issuance of an award, the Tribunal may, in accordance with those provisions, give an interpretation of the award (Article 35), correct "any errors in computation, any clerical or typographical errors, or any errors of similar nature" (Article 36), or "make an additional award as to claims presented in the arbitral proceedings but omitted from the award" (Article 37).

51. In its practice thus far in Tribunal Chambers, the Tribunal has raised but left open the question whether, given the absence of an express grant of authority to the Tribunal to reopen and reconsider cases on the merits after the issuance of an award, it possesses the inherent power to do so "under exceptional circumstances." The Tribunal examined that question at some length in the following two cases.

52. In *Ram International Industries, Inc.,* the Air Force of the Islamic Republic of Iran requested that Chamber One of the Tribunal reopen the original award in that case[68] on grounds of forgery and perjury. In addressing the question whether it had the inherent power to do so, Chamber One, after considering a number of international decisions and scholarly writings, concluded as follows:

> On the basis of the foregoing review, it might possibly be concluded that a tribunal, like the present one, which is to adjudicate a large group of cases and for a protracted period of time would by implication, until the adjournment and dissolution of the tribunal, have the authority to revise decisions induced by fraud.[69]

Chamber One did not deem it necessary to fully pursue and decide that question for the purpose of that case given that the "required preconditions" for any possible revision had not been met.

53. In *Harold Birnbaum,* Iran requested that Chamber Two of the Tribunal reconsider its original award. In support of its request, Iran cited Chamber One's Decision in *Ram International Industries, Inc.* Chamber Two, however, took a skeptical approach to the question whether the Tribunal possesses an inherent power to revise its awards. While stating that, "in the absence of exceptional circumstances, for example, allegations of fraud or perjury, it need not decide whether it has an inherent or implied power to revise its final and binding awards,"[73] Chamber Two noted:

> There is not much room for reading implied powers into a contemporary bilateral arrangement; for its authors are aware of past experience. It is to be expected that today, two States that intended to allow the revision of awards rendered by a tribunal established pursuant to a treaty between them would do so by an unequivocal expression of their common will. Clearly Iran and the United States did not so provide in the Algiers Declarations.[74]

Quoting *International Schools Services, Inc.,* in which Chamber One of the Tribunal had observed that "it is questionable whether, even in exceptional circumstances, the Tribunal

---

68. *Ram International Industries, Inc., et al.* and *Air Force of the Islamic Republic of Iran,* Award No. 67-148-1 (19 Aug. 1983), *reprinted in* 3 IRAN-U.S. C.T.R. 203.

69. *Ram International Industries, Inc., et al.* and *Air Force of the Islamic Republic of Iran,* Decision No. DEC 118-148-1, para. 20 (28 Dec. 1993), *reprinted in* 29 IRAN-U.S. C.T.R. 383, 390.

73. *Harold Birnbaum* and *Islamic Republic of Iran,* Decision No. DEC 124-967-2, para. 20 (14 Dec. 1995), *reprinted in* 31 IRAN-U.S. C.T.R. 286, 291.

74. *Id.* para. 15,31 IRAN-U.S. C.T.R. at 289–90.

would have authority to act outside [the Tribunal Rules] to revise or correct an award,"[75] in *Harold Birnbaum*, Chamber Two went on to state:

> [T]he final and binding force of an award does not necessarily exclude the possibility of a revision thereof. But the existence of express rules providing that the award is "final and binding," coupled with the silence of the contracting Parties concerning the possibility of revision, makes it difficult to conclude that any inherent power to revise a final award exists.[76]

54. Indeed, in Article IV, paragraph 1, of the Claims Settlement Declaration, which commands that "[a]ll decisions and awards of the Tribunal shall be final and binding,"[77] the State Parties gave expression to the principle of finality of international arbitral awards. This fundamental principle "serves the purpose of efficiency in terms of an expeditious and economical settlement of disputes."[78] The desire for finality is a significant factor in international arbitration.

55. Article III, paragraph 2, of the Claims Settlement Declaration directs that "the Tribunal shall conduct its business in accordance with the arbitration rules of the United Nations Commission on International Trade Law (UNCITRAL) except to the extent modified by the Parties or by the Tribunal to ensure that this Agreement can be carried out." Hence, the Arbitration Rules of the United Nations Commission on International Trade Law ("UNCITRAL Arbitration Rules"), as in force on 19 January 1981, shall govern all Tribunal proceedings except to the extent that those Rules are modified either by the two State Parties to the Claims Settlement Declaration or by the Tribunal itself.

56. In accordance with its mandate, the Tribunal carefully reviewed and modified the UNCITRAL Arbitration Rules after giving the two State Parties full opportunity to express their views. The Tribunal finally adopted the Tribunal Rules in May 1983.

57. Article 1, paragraph 1, of the Tribunal Rules provides that, "[w]ithin the framework of the Algiers Declarations, the initiation and conduct of proceedings before the arbitral tribunal shall be subject to the following Tribunal Rules which may be modified by the Full Tribunal or the two Governments." This provision accords with Article III, paragraph 2, of the Claims Settlement Declaration.

58. During the process of modification of the UNCITRAL Arbitration Rules neither the Tribunal nor the State Parties concluded that, in order for the Tribunal to carry out its functions under the Claims Settlement Declaration—"to ensure that [the Claims Settlement Declaration] can be carried out"—any exceptions to the fundamental rule of finality of awards were required other than the narrow exceptions provided in Articles 35, 36, and 37 of the Tribunal Rules (respectively, interpretation of the award, correction of the award, and making of an additional award). In particular, neither the Tribunal nor the State Parties deemed it necessary to include a provision permitting the revision of an otherwise final and binding award, even though they were "aware of past experience." In connection with the latter, it should be noted that contemporary dispute-settlement in-

---

75. *International Schools Services, Inc.* and *Islamic Republic of Iran, et al.,* Award No. 290-123-1, para. 17 (29 Jan. 1987), *reprinted in* 14 IRAN-U.S. C.T.R. 65,70–71.

76. *Harold Birnbaum,* Decision No. DEC 124-967-2, para. 17, 31 IRAN-U.S. C.T.R. at 290.

77. Claims Settlement Declaration art. IV (1), 1 IRAN-U.S. C.T.R. at 10.

78. Rudolph Dolzer & Christoph Schreuer, Principles of International Investment Law 277 (2008).

struments that were in force on the date of the Algiers Declarations, such as the Statute of the International Court of Justice and the ICSID Convention, expressly provide for the revision of final and binding judgments and awards. Notably, further, the 1899 Hague Convention for the Pacific Settlement of International Disputes, to which both Iran and the United States have been parties since 4 September 1900, provides that "[t]he parties can reserve in the 'Compromis' the right to demand the revision of the Award." As Chamber Two stated in *Harold Birnbaum*, "[i]t is to be expected that today, two States that intended to allow the revision of awards rendered by a tribunal established pursuant to a treaty between them would do so by an unequivocal expression of their common will."

59. The Tribunal now turns to the question of inherent powers of international courts and tribunals. As a general matter, the Tribunal accepts that an international arbitral tribunal, such as the present one, possesses certain inherent powers. Inherent powers "are those powers that are not explicitly granted to the tribunal but must be seen as a necessary consequence of the parties' fundamental intent to create an institution with a judicial nature."[88] It has been suggested that "the source of the inherent powers of international courts is their need to ensure the fulfillment of their functions."[89] Thus, for example, the Tribunal has held that it has "an inherent power to issue such orders as may be necessary to conserve the respective rights of the Parties and to ensure that this Tribunal's jurisdiction and authority are made fully effective."[90]

60. With respect to the existence of an international tribunal's inherent power to revise a final and binding award, opinions of legal scholars diverge,[91] and the practice of international courts and tribunals is inconsistent. The Tribunal is aware that the International Court of Justice, in its 13 July 1954 Advisory Opinion in *Effect of Awards of Compensation Made by the United Nations Administrative Tribunal*,[93] recognized that the power to

88. David D. Caron, et. al., The UNCITRAL Arbitration Rules—A Commentary 915 (2006). *See also* Chester Brown, A Common Law of International Adjudication 56 (2007); Friedl Weiss, *Inherent Powers of National and International Courts: The Practice of the Iran-U.S. Claims Tribunal, in* International Investment Law for the 21st Century-Essays [in Honour of Christoph Schreuer 185, 186 (C. Binder, U. Kriebaum, A. Reinisch, S. Wittich eds., 2009).

89. Chester Brown, *The Inherent Powers of International Courts and Tribunals,* 76 Brit. Y.B. Int'l L. 195,228 *(2005). See also* Paola Gaeta, *Inherent Powers of International Courts and Tribunals, in* Man's Inhumanity to Man—Essays on International Law [in Honour of Antonio Cassese 353, 364–68 (L.C. Vohrah, F. Pocar, Y. Featherstone, O. Fourmy, C. Graham, J. Hocking & N. Robson eds., 2003).

90. *E-Systems, Inc.* and *Islamic Republic of Iran, et al.,* Interim Award No. ITM 13-388-FT, at 10 (4 Feb. 1983), *reprinted in* 2 Iran-U.S. C.T.R. 51, 57.

91. *See, e.g.,* Brown, A Common Law of International Adjudication, *supra* note 88, at 171 (stating that the arguments for the existence of the power of revision as an inherent power "are quite compelling;" and that the proper administration of international justice militates in favor of the admission of a procedure to take account of new evidence, subject to certain conditions, so long as the exercise of the power is not inconsistent with the terms of the constitutive instrument of the international court); Bowett, *supra* note 53, at 590 (stating that it is "doubtful" whether an international tribunal possesses "any inherent power of revision"); Kaikobad, *supra* note 52, at 252 (revision is "a remedy based on consent," and "the power of a tribunal to revise its decisions upon the discovery of a decisive fact is not an inherent power.").

93. Effect of Awards of Compensation Made by the United Nations Administrative Tribunal, Advisory Opinion, 1954 I.C.J. 47 (13 July). As a result of the decision of the United Nations General Assembly to establish a new system of administration of justice, including a two-tier formal system comprising a first instance, the United Nations Dispute Tribunal, and an appellate instance, the United Nations Appeals Tribunal, the United Nations Administrative Tribunal was abolished in 2009. *See* G.A. Res. 63/253, U.N. Doc. A/RES/63/253 (17 Mar. 2009). *See supra* notes 60 and 61.

revise, in special circumstances, a final and binding award is an inherent power.[94] It should be noted, however that the Court's Advisory Opinion was followed by United Nations General Assembly Resolution 888 (IX) of 17 December 1954, in which the General Assembly, after taking note of that Opinion, (i) accepted in principle judicial review of judgments of the United Nations Administrative Tribunal ("U.N.A.T.") and (ii) established a Special Committee to study the question of establishing a review procedure for judgments of the U.N.A.T.[95] by Resolution 957 (X) of 8 November 1955, the General Assembly subsequently amended the Statute of the U.N.A.T. by including, *inter alia*, a new Article 12 on revision, which expressly empowered the U.N.A.T. to revise its judgments on the basis of new, decisive facts.[96] Article 12 of the Statute of the U.N.A.T. mirrored to a large extent Article 61, paragraph 1, of the Statute of the International Court of Justice.

61. In the Tribunal's view, in order to determine which powers international courts and tribunals may exercise as inherent powers one must take into account the particular features of each specific court or tribunal, including the circumstances surrounding its establishment, the object and purpose of its constitutive instrument, and the consent of the parties as expressed in that and related instruments.[98] This principle will guide the Tribunal in determining whether it possesses the inherent power to revise its awards.

62. On 19 January 1981, after protracted and difficult negotiations conducted through the Government of Algeria acting as the official intermediary, Iran and the United States entered into the Algiers Declarations, which consist of a General Declaration and a Claims Settlement Declaration. The Algiers Declarations ended a long and acute political crisis between two Governments that had essentially severed all diplomatic relations and that regarded each other with extreme distrust. This Tribunal, which was one of the measures intended to defuse that crisis, was established through the Claims Settlement Declaration for the purpose of deciding certain claims by nationals of one State against the Government of the other and certain claims between the two Governments.[100] The final settlement of such claims was one of the crucial features of the bargain struck by the two Governments to end the crisis; this aspect is also reflected in Article I of the Claims Settlement Declaration, which provides that "Iran and the United States will promote the settlement of the claims described in Article II by the parties directly concerned."[101] Against this backdrop, the State Parties' agreement, in Article IV, paragraph 1, of the Claims Settlement Declaration, that "[a]ll decisions and awards of the Tribunal shall be final and binding"[102] acquires particular significance.

63. In the Tribunal's view, to avoid upsetting the strict and careful construction and application of the politically sensitive Algiers Declarations, the Tribunal must be especially cautious in finding that it possesses inherent powers.

---

94. In its Advisory Opinion, the International Court of Justice found that a rule that a judgment is final and without appeal "cannot ... be considered as excluding the [United Nations Administrative] Tribunal from itself revising a judgment in special circumstances when new facts of decisive importance have been discovered...." Effect of Awards of Compensation Made by the United Nations Administrative Tribunal, Advisory Opinion, 1954 I.e.J. at 55.

95. G.A. Res. 888 (IX) (17 Dec. 1954), *available at* http://www.un.org/documents/ga/res/9?ares9.htm.

96. G.A. Res. 957 (X) (8 Nov. 1955), *available at* http://www.un.org/documents/ga/res/10/ares10.htm.

98. *See also* Gaeta, *supra* note 89, at 370 ("[I]n assessing the inherent nature of an 'unexpressed' power, the unique features of each particular court or tribunal should be taken into account.").

100. Claims Settlement Declaration art. II & art. VI (4), 1 IRAN-U.S. C.T.R. at 9–11.

101. *Id.* art. 1, 1 IRAN-U.S. C.T.R. at 10.

102. *Id.* art. IV (1), 1 IRAN-U.S. C.T.R. at 10.

64. In light of the above and considering (i) that, when the Tribunal, in consultation with the two State Parties to the Claims Settlement Declaration, modified the UNCITRAL Arbitration Rules, neither the Tribunal nor the two State Parties considered the remedy of revision of a final and binding award necessary "to ensure that [the Claims Settlement Declaration] can be carried out"[103] and (ii) that a mechanism is available under the Claims Settlement Declaration and Article 1, paragraph 1, of the Tribunal Rules to modify those Rules should the Tribunal or the two State Parties to the Claims Settlement Declaration at any point in time deem it necessary and appropriate to provide the remedy of revision,[104] the Tribunal is not prepared to hold that it has an inherent power to revise a final and binding award.[105] Equally crucial, the Tribunal believes that it is, not in the context of a Tribunal decision in a particular case, but rather in the context of a formal modification of the Tribunal rules that essential features and modalities relating to a remedy of revision—such as its scope, the time limits within which an application for revision may be submitted, and the structure of the revision proceeding[106]—can be established with the proper degree of rigor.

65. Additionally, the Tribunal notes that, to its knowledge, the statutes and rules of procedure of modern international courts and tribunals expressly providing the remedy of revision do not provide for "manifest errors of law" or "fundamental errors of procedure" as grounds for revising a final and binding decision. Rather, they typically provide that an application for revision of such a decision may be made only if it is based upon the discovery of some new and decisive fact; they also specify the time limits within which any such application may be submitted.

---

103. *Id.* art. III (2), 1 IRAN-U.S. C.T.R. at 10. *See supra* paras. 55–58. After their adoption, the Tribunal Rules have been amended only once. This amendment, which consisted of the addition of a new paragraph—paragraph 5—to Article 13 (providing that a Tribunal Member who resigned would continue as a member with respect to all cases in which he had participated in a hearing on the merits) was adopted finally on 7 March 1984. *See* Amendment to Tribunal Rules, Article 13, *reprinted in* 7 IRAN-U.S. C.T.R. 317 (1984).

104. Of course, by agreement of the two State Parties, the Claims Settlement Declaration may be amended to empower the Tribunal to revise final and binding awards.

105. It has been suggested that, because a decision proven to have been induced by fraud or perjury does not constitute a "decision in law, ... the right and indeed the duty to render a valid judgment or award must be seen to continue;" and that the "argument that, in such circumstances, the reopening of the case can hardly be described as revision in the normal understanding of the notion is clearly a strong one." KAIKOBAD, *supra* note 52, at 257; *see also* BIN CHENG, GENERAL PRINCIPLES OF LAW AS APPLIED BY INTERNATIONAL COURTS AND TRIBUNALS 159 (Grotius Publications Ltd., 1987) ("A judgment, which in principle calls for the greatest respect, will not be upheld if it is the result of fraud."); KENNETH S. CARLSTON, THE PROCESS OF INTERNATIONAL ARBITRATION 58 (1946) ("The principle that an award procured through false evidence or other fraud is void has been sustained by a number of writers.... It is clear that authority and practice sustain the conclusion that an award fraudulently procured is without obligatory force."); L. OPPENHEIM, 2 INTERNATIONAL LAW-A TREATISE 28 (4th ed., 1926) ("[S]hould one of the parties have intentionally and maliciously led the arbitrators into an essential material error, the award would have no binding force whatever."). Neither fraud nor perjury are alleged in the present case. Consequently, the Tribunal need not address the matter for present purposes.

106. For example, Article 61 of the Statute of the International Court of Justice *(supra* note 57) provides for a two-stage revision proceeding: the first stage consists of a preliminary hearing on the question whether the petition for revision is admissible; the second stage consists of the hearing on the merits of the question whether and to what extent a particular judgment should be revised (if the petition for revision has been found to be admissible).

Notes and Questions to Compliance and Enforcement in Arbitration

1. Did New Zealand get the original decision in its favor enforced in *Rainbow Warrior II?* Did it have a right to have the decision enforced?

2. Why did New Zealand not simply invoke the New York Convention and go to a French national court to get an order against the French government requiring Prieur and Mafart to serve out their terms on Hao?

3. What effect might *Rainbow Warrior II* have on the attractiveness of arbitration for dispute resolution among states? What about the impact of the Iran-U.S. Claims Tribunal's decisions on enforcement?

4. Compare the *Southern Blue Fin Tuna* decision on jurisdiction with the Iran-U.S. Claims Tribunal's decisions on enforcement. In one case, the Tribunal seeks the most explicit possible consent from the parties. In the other, the Tribunal finds that it can act on implied authority. Discuss these two decisions. Is implied consent a more acceptable basis for obligation at the enforcement phase versus the outset of an arbitration? Which is more supportive of international dispute settlement?

5. The U.S. eventually paid Iran the awards at issue in Case A27, though not before U.S. civil plaintiffs with judgments against Iran tried to attach the funds the U.S. intended to pay to Iran. This case is discussed in Chapter Fourteen as an example of dispute resolution in national courts.

6. Consider carefully the evidence in the *Request for Revision* case. Are you persuaded that arbitral tribunals do not have inherent power to revise their own decisions? Are the arguments particular to the Iran-U.S. Claims Tribunal that you can make for or against such inherent power?

7. According to the Global Arbitration Review, by July 2011, the Iran-U.S. Claims Tribunal was hearing only interstate claims. It has rendered over 600 awards valued at $2.5 billion.

The Weapons Manufacturer Problem

Johnson's Advanced Weapons Systems (JAWS), a U.S. national, manages manufacturing plants globally. The plants produce high technology weapons, operating through joint ventures between governments and JAWS. JAWS has just entered into a joint venture agreement with the government of Boleru, South America. JAWS has a seventy-percent interest in the Boleru plant, the government has thirty percent. The agreement also contains the following clause:

> The Government and JAWS hereby consent to submit to the jurisdiction of the International Centre for the Settlement of Investment Disputes all disputes arising out of this Agreement, or relating to any investment made hereunder, for settlement by arbitration, pursuant to the Convention on the Settlement of Investment Disputes (SID). The government further waives any right of sovereign immunity as to it and its property in respect of this agreement both during any arbitration and in respect of the enforcement and execution of any award resulting therefrom.

JAWS pours a sizable investment into the plant, but never makes much money. After some years, JAWS tells the government it needs to downsize the workforce. The government refuses to agree, but JAWS has majority control and goes ahead. The government takes over the plant, throws out the JAWS directors, and refuses to pay JAWS anything for its investment, pointing to the corporate accounting scandals involving the Enron and Worldcom corporations in the United States and opining that JAWS has been well compensated despite what the accounts say.

JAWS invokes the arbitration clause and asks the U.S. government to freeze certain of Boleru's commercial assets. Can the U.S. lawfully freeze Boleru's assets?

An arbitration panel with five arbitrators is formed, and the case begins. After the hearings conclude and the deliberations begin, one of the arbitrators fails to show up. The other four continue, and reach a decision—three to one in JAWS' favor. In their confidential decision, the four do not mention that one arbitrator was absent. JAWS goes to a U.S. court to get the award enforced out of the frozen assets. Can a U.S. court lawfully enforce the award? If Boleru fails to point to the absence of the fifth vote, must JAWS refer to it?

What if JAWS discovers that Boleruan agents detained the fifth arbitrator?

II. Binding Methods

B. Judicial Settlement

1. International Courts

Chapter Nine

International Courts

Introduction

International dispute resolution scholars have long worked toward the goal of creating an international court as the premier means of resolving international disputes. Chapter One's brief history of IDR describes the first significant unofficial discussions concerning an international court that began in the United States in the 1890s and the first official discussions that occurred at the First Hague Peace Conference of 1899. From those years until today, international law theorists have continued to view the existence of a court with compulsory jurisdiction over all important international law disputes as the step that would finally resolve the question, is international law law? And the inevitable follow-up question, should anyone care about law that is left to the governed to judge and enforce through self-help?

Despite more than a century of efforts, the world still has no court analogous to the highest courts of national legal systems. The International Court of Justice comes closest to the ideal.[1] The next four chapters are generally devoted to the ICJ, how it functions, and why. We will focus on the Court's jurisdiction to hear disputes between states. The ICJ also has authority to give advisory opinions to organs of the UN. Advisory opinions are technically non-binding and serve to clarify questions of international law. The law that is being clarified is generally binding, however, so that advisory opinions often have as much or more weight in the international system as decisions in contentious cases between states. As we saw in the discussion of inquiry, resolving questions of law can help resolve international disputes.

Before reaching the ICJ and its procedures, this chapter will consider more generally the development of international courts in the international system. The Project on International Courts and Tribunals (PICT) has identified about 125 dispute settlement mechanisms that have existed over time or are planned. Some 20 meet PICT's narrower definition of "international court." These are impressive numbers that lead some to question whether the growth in courts and tribunals may pose challenges to the international legal system. There may be negative as well as positive aspects of this growth. For example, while the ICJ has had a healthy number of important cases since the 1980s, the work toward expanding its jurisdiction and its caseload seems to have been set aside in favor of a variety of subject-matter specific courts rather than one global court. One of the most active international courts in the world today that hears inter-state disputes is the WTO's Dispute Settlement Body.[2]

1. For more on the ICJ, see its website: www.icj-cij.org.

2. For a history of the development of a court for international trade disputes at the WTO, see, Ernst-Ulrich Petersmann, *From Trade Diplomacy to Judging in International Trade Law*, *in* The Role of International Courts 23 (Carl Baudenbacher and Erhard Busek eds., 2010).

(The European Court of Human Rights and the European Court of Justice also have heavy dockets, but these are regional rather than international courts. Most of their cases concern individuals bringing complaints against states.) The WTO has a good website with a complete record of its cases at www.wto.org. The UN Law of the Sea Tribunal is also receiving regular submissions (www.itlos.org). The most dramatic development on the international courts front, however, is the creation of the International Criminal Court (ICC). The ICC was designed as a forum to bring to account individuals accused of international crimes. Some argue that the ICC plays a role in IDR, although admittedly an indirect role compared to the ICJ, WTO DSU, or ITLOS.

International courts have much in common with arbitral tribunals as a method of dispute resolution. Both render binding decisions, usually on the basis of law. Both methods are bound by basic procedural rules seen in the previous chapters—parties must be treated as equal before the law and must be given an opportunity to be heard. Courts, in contrast to arbitral tribunals, however, are usually permanent institutions. They are established under multilateral treaties and have rules of procedure specially designed for the court. The judges themselves update and adapt their own rules. Unlike arbitrators, judges are not selected by the parties to a dispute, but through a neutral process. Judges are expected to be neutral and impartial in a case. "Party" judges do not exist, unlike "party arbitrators."[3] These distinguishing features may account for the greater prestige attached to an ICJ decision, say, than to an arbitral tribunal decision.

The ICJ is the chief judicial organ of the UN. It hears contentious cases between sovereign states and provides advisory opinions to organs and agencies of the UN. We have already seen several decisions of the ICJ in prior chapters. We have also seen decisions of the International Tribunal of the Law of the Sea, another international court. The WTO Dispute Settlement Understanding (DSU) does not use the term "court" or "tribunal" for any of its bodies. States first take disputes to a "panel" and may appeal the resulting reports to the "Appellate Body." Panelists are chosen by the secretariat out of a pool, something more typical of arbitration than judicial settlement, but the Appellate Body has judges selected for a term of office and not by the parties. In the view of Petersmann, the WTO DSU is the result of evolution from trade diplomacy to "judicialization."[4]

The regional human rights courts of Europe, Africa, and the Americas have broader jurisdiction than does the ICJ. In addition to inter-state disputes, individuals may petition these courts when their governments have violated the human rights treaties with which the courts are associated. These courts do not, however, hold individuals accountable. In the early 1990s, states could finally agree to establish a court that would hold individuals responsible for serious violations of human rights law. The International Criminal Tribunal for the former Yugoslavia (ICTY) moved beyond the human rights courts, returning the legacy of the Nuremberg and Tokyo war crimes tribunals. The ICTY was expanded after the 1994 massacres in Rwanda, and from these two courts, the next natural step was the establishment of a court of general criminal jurisdiction, the International Criminal Court.[5] But are criminal courts usually considered places where disputes are resolved? Professors Luigi Condorelli and Santiago Villaplando state that the

3. Helmut Steinberger, *Judicial Settlement of Disputes*, *in* I Encyclopedia of Public International Law 120, 120–132 (1981).

4. Petersmann, *supra* note 2, at 26.

5. Leila N. Sadat & S. Richard Carden, *The International Criminal Court: An Uneasy Revolution*, 88 Geo. L. J. 381 (2000).

Security Council began forming criminal tribunals to help maintain peace and security in the world:

> Through the establishment of the ICTY and the ICTR, the Security Council gave a new dimension to the exercise of its powers for the maintenance of international peace and security, by becoming active in the field of the prosecution of international crimes. In this perspective, the Rome Statute takes over from the Security Council's pioneering action and consolidates the progress accomplished in the field of international criminal law. But it also provides for a new instrument at the Security Council's disposal for the fulfillment of its primary responsibility under the UN Charter. By establishing a permanent international criminal court, providing for the basic rules that govern its functioning and defining its jurisdiction, and then by allowing the Security Council to 'trigger' the proceedings before the Court, the Rome Statute encourages and considerably simplifies this UN organ's action. In the future, the prosecution of international crimes could be initiated immediately, without the need to establish new tribunals and to define their constitutive elements. In other words, in 1998, the States participating in the Rome Conference seemed to make a 'gift' to the Security Council for the accomplishment of its duties under the Charter.[6]

Regardless of whether the ICC will ever help to prevent inter-communal violence, it is an important example of the proliferation of international courts. Even before the ICC Statute was drafted a prescient judge of the ICJ, Judge Sir Robert Jennings, predicted that the rise of a number of new international courts would result in certain challenges for the international legal system. His early, informal comments constitute the first excerpt below, followed by an updated set of thoughts on the same topic by Ruth MacKenzie.

Statute of the International Court of Justice

June 26, 1945, 59 Stat. 1055, T.S. No. 993, 3 Bevans 1179

See Annex

World Trade Organization, Understanding on Rules and Procedures Governing the Settlement of Dispute

Apr. 15, 1994, WTO Agreement, Annex 2, 33 I.L.M. 1224, 1228

See Annex

---

6. Luigi Condorelli & Santiago Villalpando, *Can the Security Council Extend the ICC's Jurisdiction?*, *in* I The Rome Statute of the International Criminal Court: A Commentary 571, 571–72 (Antonio Cassese et al. eds., 2002).

United Nations Convention on the Law of the Sea

Annex VI. Statute of the International Tribunal for the Law of the Sea

Dec. 10, 1982, UN Doc. A/CONF.62/ 122 (1982)

See Annex

Rome Statute on the International Criminal Court

July 17, 1998, U.N. Doc. A/CONF.183/9*

See Annex

Sir Robert Y. Jennings, *The Proliferation of Adjudicatory Bodies: Dangers and Possible Answers**

I take it that my task, this morning, on this question of proliferation of international tribunals, is to throw out problems rather than to offer solutions. I can say at once that I have no simple solutions for this problem. I will try to be a little provocative from time to time, and you must not mind too much if I say something that politically is not quite correct.

The Quiet Revolution in International Law

The first thing I wanted to say is to point out something which is very often not noticed so much today, that is the quiet revolution that has been going on in international law as a whole in the last couple of decades or so, and with accelerating vigor. I mean of course the way in which international law has recently, in the perspective of the history of international law, radically changed in character. What I am thinking of is especially evident in the field of treaty law.

Most governments make a lot of treaties every year, and an increasing number of them are not the old political kind of treaties one used to read about in history books; they are treaties that affect the life of every one of us daily in our ordinary occupations. These are interpreted and applied by municipal courts and there, I think, is a very big change, certainly in my time as an international lawyer. More and more, international law is a little doubtfully international law as it were; the boundary between municipal law and international law has been breaking down. To take an example, the great body of air law: one can still give a lecture on the international law of the air, but if you wanted to advise an air company, for example, on what is happening in the real world, just to be an international lawyer would not be very much use. You would have to know at least some municipal law and about its enforcement by municipal courts. You would have to be something of a comparativist. And you would certainly have to be something of a private international lawyer, as well as a public international lawyer.

So that is the first thing I wanted to do; to put the problem in the perspective of the very considerable change in the nature of international law and the breaking down of those old barriers. The idea I was taught as an undergraduate that public international

---

* ASIL Bulletin, No. 9, Nov. 1995, 2–7.

law was something on a special plane of its own and quite different from municipal law and the work of municipal court, is no longer even approximately true. So it is not surprising perhaps that, in this crucial and new context, there has been a proliferation of adjudicating tribunals of various kinds.

Reasons Requiring the Establishment of New Tribunals

There are a number of reasons for having more tribunals. There is of course the regional idea; that is people sometimes prefer a local tribunal. One recently established tribunal of that kind is the Badinter Commission, established under the auspices of the Peace Conference on Yugoslavia, where there was the feeling that security within Europe was a European problem. It was perhaps unfortunate that the first big problem that occurred before it turned out not to be European at all, but universal. The efforts were about as successful as all the other efforts—whether on a regional or a universal scale—in dealing with the problem of the former Yugoslavia which is still with us.

But there is this idea, and I think it is reasonable, that local tribunals sometimes can understand the local requirements better than more general tribunals. One may think, for example, of the criticisms that used to be leveled against the ICJ about the *Asylum* case by South American states, which felt that the local tradition of asylum in an embassy was not really properly understood by what was then, a predominantly European court. On the other hand, it is also true that it is possible for a universal court to understand local variations. I think the chamber of the ICJ in the *Honduras/El Salvador* case coped pretty well with the problem of *uti possidetis juris*; indeed, it was difficult not to understand it after all the explanations we heard from counsel in the course of that case.

This regional prejudice, however, is very capricious. I am thinking of disputes in which I was somewhat involved, between Argentina and Chile. In the most recent arbitration concerning a part of the long frontier between them—with which arbitration I had nothing to do, because I was a judge on the ICJ by then—I gathered that the parties agreed that it was better to have a Latin American tribunal, because that seemed reasonable in the circumstances, since it was a Latin American matter. But in the earlier one, the *Beagle Channel* case, when it came to the choosing of the court which was a sort of a compromise between arbitration and the International Court, I remember very well at a meeting in London, the counsel from both sides have agreed upon one basic principle: that was "no Latin Americans," because the feeling then was that, any Latin American would be *parti pris* in this very well-known and debated for eighty or ninety years dispute between Chile and Argentina. So, the regional idea for new tribunals is a capricious one. You can never be quite sure how it will work, except that one way or another, it will produce more and more tribunals. I am sure of that.

Perhaps this is the place to mention one disturbing development, at least very disturbing to my mind. That is the idea, that comes, I suppose, from Muslim fundamentalism and that has been embodied recently in a *fatwa* issued in Saudi Arabia, that Muslim countries are not to go to any tribunal other than one which applies Mahometan law. Now this, of course, is a challenge to the universality principle of our system of international law. Obviously, one cannot go into this, but I just wanted to mention it. I find it a very disturbing challenge and one which demands a lot of serious thought.

Then there are courts and tribunals established for special subjects, such as the courts of human rights. The European Court of Human Rights, for example, was established on a European basis because of the European Convention and because it was possible to provide machinery with teeth to enforce human rights in this regional group, which was not possible on a larger basis. That is obviously a very good reason for having a special, regional tribunal.

There are many other new tribunals of course, but I cannot go through a whole list of the examples because there are so many. I do not know if anybody has a complete list. That should be almost the first thing we ought to do, to get a comprehensive list of these international tribunals. One of a different kind is the World Trade Organization tribunals recently invented, but I confess I do not know a great deal about them. But there seems to be a rather different idea, that is members of the tribunals should be experts in this particular subject and it includes, which seems more unusual if I got it right, the possibility of making policy decisions and not merely the application of a system of law. If I am right, we have here what could be a very important new development.

There are also the international criminal courts, the proposed general one, the one for former Yugoslavia and the one for Rwanda; the last two, peculiar tribunals because they were established by the Security Council under the machinery for the keeping of the peace. Thus, they are purely *ad hoc* and should come to an end when their purpose is accomplished. But how far the tribunals will assist in establishing peace in those regions remains to be seen. There is one problem that I would like to mention, at least to me it seems to be a problem, and this would apply also, I think, to the proposal in the International Law commission for a permanent tribunal. I understand that a policy decision was made to go ahead with the tribunal before the work on the code of law it is to apply was accomplished. There was suppose to be a code of international humanitarian criminal law and this is not forthcoming and so we will have a tribunal without it. That, I think, is going to raise very considerable problems in certain cases, especially in the offenses like murder which are common to the municipal law systems. I suppose in international criminal law, they are thinking of murder with the added factor of a sort of illegitimate policy behind it.

Another point on these new tribunals I would like to mention is that I think we have to be careful—if I may put it that way, I said I might be a bit provocative—of the arrogance of public International lawyers. What I mean is: Is it right that most of these tribunals, except the trade ones, seem to be jobs for public international lawyers? There is little sign, even in the Law of the Sea tribunals for example, of the use of other disciplines and other kinds of experts. If I could just illustrate it in a sort of personal way, the first time I appeared as a counsel in an international arbitration was in the *Encuentro* or *Palena* case between Argentina and Chile. The tribunal had a retired professor of international law and indeed former President of the ICJ, Lord McNair as its president, but the other two members: one of them was the Secretary of the Royal Geographical Society, not a lawyer at all, and the other one was a soldier and an engineer. That, I am bound to say was one of the best tribunals I ever had anything to do with. I discovered the hard way that it is very important not to underestimate the military. The soldier arbitrator had rather played the ignorant soldier in all the preparations up to the actual hearings, but when addressing the tribunal one realized that he was producing all the documents just at the right moment to the president from the pile in front of him, and the frightening thing was that he not only produced the one you mentioned but also had ready all the others you were going to mention. As for the Secretary of the Royal Geographical Society, he was able to exclude one legal argument. The Argentineans were very concerned that the Chileans were bringing a lot of evidence of the allegiance and nationality of people who lived in this rather remote area of the Andes. We—I was for Argentina—were concerned about it because Chileans of course had always gone to Argentina for work, and there was indeed a place on the Atlantic coast with a larger population of Chileans than Argentineans, so we were naturally bothered by this evidence and objected. McNair was impressed as a lawyer with the objections, not so the geographer. He said he did not understand the legal objection, but as a geographer he wanted to know about "land-use." It was a good point, and all that evidence was thus admitted before the tribunal. That is one of the illustrations of the use of other disciplines. One can think that in the law of the sea surely, one ought to use more experts, such as maritime surveyors and hydrographers, not merely as advisers but as members of the court; but that is not very popular with international lawyers, I fear.

The Dangers of Proliferation

There are thus various good reasons for producing more tribunals of different kinds, but the problem really is the possible dangers that could arise from this proliferation. I think the main point can be put this way: looking at it as a whole, you see that this proliferation has been flourishing, but without system. It is simply that tribunals have been thought of and produced from time to time for local and other reasons, but the result as a whole is a mess. And to put it in better words, there is a recent article written by my colleague Judge Shahabuddeen, whom I quote:

> The adjudicating machinery on the international plane consists of a number of tribunals, some instituted on a bilateral basis, others on a multilateral basis, but with nothing to hold them together in a coherent system. They all make decisions which can influence the development of international law. If that influence can amount to law-making in the case of all of them, the absence of hierarchical authority to impose order is a prescription for conflicting precepts.

Now, that is probably the main danger of proliferation, the fragmentation of international law; and by fragmentation I do not mean the very proper local variations for particular purposes. It so happens that the Strasbourg Court of Human Rights has produced for me the ideal case to illustrate this danger. In the last few weeks, in the case of *Loizidou v. Turkey*, a complaint against Turkey was brought by Cyprus before the European Court about the alleged difficulty of a Cypriot national of the Greek community who wanted to visit the family property in the Turkish part of Cyprus. The question first before the Court was a question of competence or jurisdiction. The Convention has a clause providing for declaration by governments accepting the jurisdiction of the Strasbourg Court and that clause is, word for word, based on Article 36(2) of the Statute of the ICJ, the optional clause. So the same machinery was provided and governments that wish to accept the jurisdiction of the Court did so by making a declaration. Most of them, and apparently practically all of them, if they wished to accept the jurisdiction, did so unconditionally by simply filing a declaration. Turkey acted differently. It agreed to the application of the Convention and the competence of the Court in respect of "matters coming within Article 1 of the Convention and performed within the boundary of the national territory of the Republic of Turkey," a reservation obviously intended to exclude the northern part of Cyprus from the jurisdiction of the tribunal.

The decision of the Court on this matter—the merits have not yet come before the Court—was that it did have jurisdiction and the reasoning was as follows. First, other governments in accepting the Court's jurisdiction had accepted it without reservation. Therefore, in the light of this consistent practice, the making of reservations was not permissible. The Court went on to say that the decisions of the ICJ to this matter, which of course had been pleaded before them, were irrelevant because of the special character of the Strasbourg Court. The surprising thing to me is that it is not unlike the famous separate opinion of Judge Lauterpacht, where he felt that the "automatic" reservation of France to its optional declaration was invalid and void because contrary to the Statute. He agreed, however, with the majority of the Court that the reservation was unseverable and that therefore the French attempt to create jurisdiction was itself invalid. To the contrary, the Strasboug Court decided that the Turkish "invalid" reservation was severable and therefore Turkey must be taken to have accepted the competence of the Court without any reservation at all. The passage of the Court's decision that I want to mention is:

> The fundamental difference in the role and purpose of the respective tribunals [that is Strasbourg and the Hague], coupled with the existence of a practice of unconditional acceptance, provided a compelling basis for distinguishing Convention practice from that of the International Court.

Now, of course, one can say this is merely a question of jurisdiction, and not of substance, but there are red lights there. It indicates that tendency of particular tribunals to regard themselves as different, as separate little empires which must as far as possible be augmented. Of course, one can appreciate that the Strasbourg Court, applying and interpreting the European Convention, is in a different position from the ICJ applying a universal system of international law. It might be acceptable to rely on the regional differences for a question of jurisdiction; but obviously, there is a possibility that the technique might also be extended to matters of substance. This could lead to a law of human rights increasingly different from the universal system, which is part of general international law, and under the custody of the ICJ. I merely point out the danger. I have no solution, all I can say is that I am sure this tendency will increase rather than decrease. We ought to be thinking about it.

Possible Answers

Coming back to this question of the control raised by Judge Shahabuddeen, what can we do about this glut of tribunals with no hierarchical pattern? We do not even have a list of these different tribunals anywhere easily available, much less an analysis. Well, one thinks immediately of the ICJ, the principal judicial organ of the United Nations, as possibly providing the head of some sort of hierarchy, a court of last resort, of appeal, review or cassation. But there are difficulties about that and the principal one is Article 34(1) of the Statute of the Court, which says that only states may be parties before the Court. It means that for the contentious jurisdiction at any rate, it is not easy to think of any machinery for tribunals dealing with other entities than states having recourse to the Court. It may happen incidentally sometimes in a contentious case. It did happen in the Guinea-Bissau case. The Court did pass upon an arbitral award which was, according to the agreement establishing the arbitration, to have been final. The Court confirmed the validity of the award, but it did hear the case. So there is a sort of precedent there. The other difficulty with the International Court's attempt to control these other tribunals would be that, according to Article 34(1), it does not have contentious jurisdiction over any of the international organizations which exist in the international sphere. This is a most extraordinary position. It is extraordinary that you have this UN system of law, a universal system of international law, you have a principal judicial organ of the United Nations and no state or government can cite an international organization before the ICJ; for example, in regard of allegedly *ultra vires* activities. Maybe the International Court itself is not the proper instrument, but there ought to be some way of getting international organizations, as well as other entities, before the tribunals.

I had the privilege in the UN Congress in New York, a few weeks ago, to hear the very remarkable speech by Ambassador Owada about the tension in international relations between the requirements of stability and the requirements of justice. I think it was one of the most important things that has been said about international law by anybody for quite a long time. I cite only one paragraph just to show the problem:

> The single most important fact behind this change is that the world today suffers from the dichotomy that has come to exist between the fast-growing socio-economic reality that entrepreneurs as individuals engage in activities on a global basis and the equally stark reality that the competence to regulate these activities are still compartmentalized by nations states, within the system based on the Westphalian legal order.

Article 34(1) of the Statute of the International Court is the embodiment of the Westphalian legal order. I suppose something can be done. Another colleague of the Court, Judge Guillaume has suggested that there might be a possibility of reference by other tribunals to the Court, corresponding to Article 177 of the Rome Treaty. They might be encouraged to ask the Court for advice on questions of international law. The advisory jurisdiction of the ICJ is much more flexible, and it could accommodate a procedure of reference. Whether tribunals would in fact refer is perhaps doubtful; but at any rate, even if there were the possibility, it might serve as a beginning for some sort of order and system.

We have a proliferation of adjudicating bodies of various kinds, but we still do not have that political machinery, that Ambassador Owada was calling for, to control activities on the international plane. In the domestic sphere, we have tribunals or courts which have compulsory jurisdiction. That works for the simple reason that you also have political bodies within their own sphere controlled by constitutional and administrative law; political bodies that make decisions for political and administrative reasons and not for legal reasons; for reasons of statesmanship, for reasons of policy, for reasons of expediency and convenience, for reasons of general wisdom and need to change things. We do not have that in the international sphere, except to an inadequate extent. There is the Security Council, but even the Security Council has only been able to begin activities of that kind recently, has relatively little experience and, in any case, it is practically all we have got. I do think that the call of international lawyers for more and more tribunals, for more and more activity by international lawyers needs to be balanced by a call for more and more thinking about the need for political decisions, wise political decisions on the international plane. There are summits and so on, but we need something better and seems to me that we ought to be thinking not only of the sort of tribunal that we might need, but we ought as well to be thinking about the other kind of decisions that are needed in a healthy international society.

Ruth MacKenzie, *Introduction, in the Role of International Courts**

* * *

For a long time the Permanent Court of International Justice stood alone, but the situation clearly has moved on significantly in the period since 1945. My colleague in the Project on International Courts and Tribunals, Cesare Romano, produced a chart a number of years ago (with subsequent updates), which some of you may have seen. The chart

* pp. 10–13 (Carl Baudenbacher and Erhard Busek eds., 2010).

is available on the Project on International Courts and Tribunals website.[4] It identifies some 125 international dispute settlement mechanisms that have existed in the past or currently exist, that are in the process of establishment or that are under serious consideration, or that have been proposed. Not all of these, of course, are what we would understand as international courts proper. Nonetheless, Romano identifies around 20 existing bodies that fulfill certain criteria that might enable them to be classified as 'international courts' or 'international judicial bodies'. The criteria that he uses, and there can be some debate about the criteria perhaps, are that: they are standing or permanent institutions; they are composed of independent judges who are not appointed specifically for the case which they are about to hear, but who are available on a standing basis; they deal with disputes in which at least one party of a state or international organization (although they may be open to other entities, such as non-state actors, corporations or individuals); they work on the basis of pre-determined rules and procedures; and they render binding decisions.[5] Many of these international judicial bodies are established, of course, within the context of or under the auspices of existing international organisations which can have implications for their functioning.

The remaining bodies on the chart are extremely diverse, ranging from the administrative tribunals established within international organisations to deal with staff cases, to the committees established under human rights treaties, to which individuals can bring complaints in certain circumstances, to bodies established to deal with issues of non-compliance under multilateral environmental agreements, and to some of the new 'hybrid' or 'mixed' criminal tribunals which exhibit characteristics or combine elements of international and domestic courts. Professor Baudenbacher has touched some of the factors that might explain this multiplication, proliferation or even 'explosion', as it has been described, of international courts and tribunals, including the opportunities for new forms of international cooperation afforded by the end of the Cold War, the growth in the number of transnational actors, the growth of new or enhanced forms of regional cooperation, particularly in the field of trade, and the widening or deepening of international law itself with the development of new more detailed sectoral rules in different areas. Whatever the reasons for the proliferation, it raises numerous questions that some of the panelists might explore in more detail.

First of all I think that, notwithstanding the growth in the number of tribunals, one can legitimately ask: has there really been a move from diplomacy to judging? Is it a very clear cut move or are we still looking at a situation in which a rather broad continuum of dispute settlement options are available? Not all of the new courts deal with the cases that lend themselves to diplomatic resolution, and numerous disputes are still dealt with through diplomatic means.

Secondly, with the growth in the number of courts and tribunals, issues and concerns about fragmentation and coherence among international courts have attracted much attention. So, is it a problem that for the most part formal relations have not been put in place between the different components of the international judicial system, if one can

4. C. Romano, PICT Synoptic Chart: The International Judiciary in Context, version 3.0, November 2004, available at: http://www.pict-pcti.org/publications/synoptic_chart/Synop_C4.pdf.

5. […] C. Romano, "The Proliferation of International Judicial Bodies: the Pieces of the Puzzle," 31 New York University Journal of International Law and Politics (1999) 709, at 713–714, citing C. Tomuschat, "International Courts and Tribunals with Regionally Restricted and/or Specialized Jurisdiction" in Judicial Settlement of International Disputes: International Court of Justice, Other Courts and Tribunals, Arbitration and Conciliation: an international symposium (Max Planck Institut for Ausländisches Őffentliches Recht and Vőlkerrecht, 1987).

even say that there is an international judicial system?[6] Moreover, where courts operate primarily through chambers or through panels, whether because their caseload makes that the only feasible way to operate or because that is the way states parties to a particular dispute might prefer them to operate, might there even be questions of internal coherence or fragmentation that need to be addressed or additional measures that need to be taken to ensure collegiality or coherence?

Thirdly, what is it that we and the states that create international judicial bodies, expect them to do? Questions have been raised about the proper scope, and indeed the proper limits of the judicial function in international law. There has been much attention paid to constitutional or constitutionalizing roles of international courts in certain contexts, aspects of which some of the panelists will discuss. A related aspect of this question perhaps is, as the number of specialized fields of international law expands, courts and tribunals are often called upon to do much more than to apply existing rules to particular factual scenarios. As numerous commentators have observed, they may be asked to consolidate, even almost to complete, treaty negotiations to 'take up the legislative slack',[7] addressing the consequences of constructive ambiguities in international agreements, or even of gaps in relevant treaty regimes. These two aspects raise a number of issues related to the law-making role of international courts.

And fourthly, as international judicial bodies play an increasing role in international affairs, more focus is placed on the judiciary itself and particularly on modes of judicial appointment and on issues of independence and impartiality. I should declare some interest here, in that our Centre at UCL is in the process of conducting a research project on processes for the nomination and appointment of international judges. So, it would certainly be interesting in the course of these discussions and in the conference to hear any views on this aspect. There are questions about the extent to which states can or do exercise a degree of control over international courts and tribunals through judicial appointment processes or, indeed, through other mechanisms such as budgetary controls and other means. As compared to elections to other international judicial bodies, the first election of judges to the International Criminal Court attracted massive attention among non-governmental organizations around the world: emails were being circulated saying who was standing for election and how the different rounds of elections had turned out. In another international court, the Caribbean Court of Justice, the judicial appointments process has been taken away from states entirely, at least in principle, by the establishment of a Regional Legal and Judicial Services Commission.[8] So the judges of that Court are appointed not by states or an intergovernmental political body, but by a standing commission of individuals drawn from various branches of the legal profession and the civil society. Furthermore, of course, the process of judicial appointments to the European Court of Human Rights has also undergone some changes and evolution in recent years. We might ask whether similar such developments are useful, necessary or desirable in other international courts and tribunals.

And there is perhaps a further question I would raise which is to what extent it is possible to talk about international courts and tribunals as a distinct category of international organization, as if they were a homogenous group of institutions.

---

6. See generally, New York University Journal of International Law and Politics, Volume 31, Number 4 (1999) "The Proliferation of International Courts and Tribunals: Piecing Together the Puzzle."

7. See J. Alvarez, International Organizations as Law-Makers, 533 (Oxford University Press 2005); L. Boisson de Chazournes and S. Heathcote, "The Role of the New International Adjudicator," 95 ASIL Proc. (2001) 129, at 132–134.

8. Agreement establishing the Caribbean Court of Justice, Articles IV and V.

Notes and Questions for the Introduction to International Courts

1. Why did states make the leap from arbitral tribunals to permanent courts? In addition to the materials in this chapter, refer again to the historical introduction in Chapter One.

2. Do you agree with Sir Robert that the proliferation of courts could be a challenge for the unity of international law? The ICJ was viewed as a higher court by the parties to the Guinea Bissau-Senegal and King of Spain arbitrations. But the International Criminal Tribunal for the former Yugoslavia in its decision in the *Tadić Case* did not strictly follow the ICJ's lead in the important question of state responsibility for non-state actors.

In the *Nicaragua Case*, the ICJ found that acts of the *Contra* rebels were not attributable to the U.S. because the U.S. did not exercise "effective control" over the *Contras. Military and Paramilitary Activities in and against Nicaragua* (Nicar. v. U.S.) 1986 ICJ 64–65 (June 14). In the *Hostages Case*, the ICJ found that Iran was responsible for the hostage-taking at the U.S. Embassy because of the "failure on the part of the Iranian authorities to oppose the armed attack by militants" and "the almost immediate endorsement by those authorities of the situation thus created." *United States Diplomatic and Consular Staff in Tehran* (U.S. v. Iran), 1980 ICJ 3, 42.

In *Tadić*, the ICTY found: "The control required by international law may be deemed to exist when a State (or, in the context of an armed conflict, the party to the conflict) *has a role in organizing, coordinating or planning the military actions* of the military actions of the military group, in addition to financing, training and equipping or providing operational support to that group." *Prosecutor v. Tadić*, Judgment, No. IT-94-1-A, para. 137 (July 15, 1999) (emphasis in the original). But then in the *Genocide* case, the ICJ held:

> [T]he ICTY presented the "overall control" test as equally applicable under the law of State responsibility for the purpose of determining—as the Court is required to do in the present case—when a State is responsible for acts committed by paramilitary units, armed forces which are not among its official organs. In this context, the argument in favour of that test is unpersuasive.
>
> * * *
>
> 406. It must next be noted that the "overall control" test has the major drawback of broadening the scope of State responsibility well beyond the fundamental principle governing the law of international responsibility: a State is responsible only for its own conduct, that is to say the conduct of persons acting, on whatever basis, on its behalf. That is true of acts carried out by its official organs, and also by persons or entities which are not formally recognized as official organs under internal law but which must nevertheless be equated with State organs because they are in a relationship of complete dependence on the State. Apart from these cases, a State's responsibility can be incurred for acts committed by persons or groups of persons—neither State organs nor to be equated with such organs—only if, assuming those acts to be internationally wrongful, they are attributable to it under the rule of customary international law reflected in Article 8 cited above (paragraph 398). This is so where an organ of the State gave the instructions or provided the direction pursuant to which the perpetrators of the wrongful act acted or where it exercised effective control over the action during

> which the wrong was committed. In this regard the "overall control" test is unsuitable, for it stretches too far, almost to breaking point, the connection which must exist between the conduct of a State's organs and its international responsibility.
>
> 407. Thus it is on the basis of its settled jurisprudence that the Court will determine whether the Respondent has incurred responsibility under the rule of customary international law set out in Article 8 of the ILC Articles on State Responsibility.

Application of the Convention on the Prevention and Punishment of the Crime of Genocide (Bosnia v. Serbia) 2007 I.C.J. 43 (Feb. 26).

This divergence of opinion on a fundamental aspect of international law might seem to be a problem. Perhaps it simply reveals that the ICJ is moving to the position of superior court for questions of general international law? In the view of most commentators "fragmentation" of this type does not seem to be a serious problem. Courts and tribunals cite each other in a constructive way, perhaps even recognizing which court is superior on certain questions. *See* Gilbert Guillaume, *The Use of Precedent by International Judges and Arbitrators*, 2(1) J. DISP. SETTLEMENT 5 (2011); Chester Brown, *The Cross-Fertilization of Principles Relating to Procedure and Remedies in the Jurisprudence of International Courts and Tribunals*, 30 LOY. L.A. INT'L & COMP. L. REV. 219 (2008); Fragmentation of International Law: Difficulties Arising from the Diversification and Expansion of International Law (Chair of the Study Group, Martti Koskenniemmi) Report of the International Law Commission, 58th Session, A/61/10 (1 May–9 June and 3 July–11 August 2006).

Not all observers are unconcerned, however. What might be the concerns?

4. The International Criminal Court has certainly captured the imagination of many devoted to the advancement of human rights and international humanitarian law. What does its founding say about the evolution of international law that before working out problems regarding enforcement of ICJ decisions, a court for individual accountability has been formed?

5. And how do you answer Professor MacKenzie's questions? What should the international community expect from courts? Is there any danger in expecting too much?

6. How do criminal courts help maintain peace and security? Do international criminal courts belong in a course on international dispute resolution? In its first few years of existence the ICC is associated with the breakdown of peace talks in two armed conflicts (Sudan and Dafuri rebels; Uganda and the Lord's Resistance Army) and the increase in intensity in a third armed conflict (Libya). No one seems to report on the ICC as playing any role in the end or decline of any armed conflict. Nevertheless, there is a widely held view that without "justice" there can be no peace. What are your views respecting the ICC and the promotion of peace?

7. The literature on international courts is as vast as international legal scholars' interest in the subject. Some noteworthy titles include:

THE INTERNATIONAL COURT OF JUSTICE AT A CROSSROADS (Lori F. Damrosch ed., 1987).

INTERNATIONAL COURTS FOR THE TWENTY-FIRST CENTURY (Mark W. Janis ed., 1992).

SHABTAI ROSENNE, THE WORLD COURT: WHAT IT IS AND HOW IT WORKS (1995).

FIFTY YEARS OF THE INTERNATIONAL COURT OF JUSTICE: ESSAYS IN HONOUR OF SIR ROBERT JENNINGS (Vaughan Lowe & Malgosia Fitzmaurice eds., 1996).

MOHAMED SHAHABUDDEEN, PRECEDENT IN THE WORLD COURT (1996).

ARTHUR EYFFINGER, THE INTERNATIONAL COURT OF JUSTICE, 1946–1996 (1996).

THE INTERNATIONAL CRIMINAL COURT: THE MAKING OF THE ROME STATUTE—ISSUES, NEGOTIATIONS, RESULTS (Roy S. Lee ed., in cooperation with the Project on International Courts and Tribunals, 1999).

THE INTERNATIONAL TRIBUNAL FOR THE LAW OF THE SEA: LAW AND PRACTICE (P. Chandrasekhara Rao & Rahmatullah Khan eds., 2001).

LEILA NADYA SADAT, THE INTERNATIONAL CRIMINAL COURT AND THE TRANSFORMATION OF INTERNATIONAL LAW: JUSTICE FOR THE NEW MILLENNIUM (2002).

BRUCE BROOMHALL, INTERNATIONAL JUSTICE AND THE INTERNATIONAL CRIMINAL COURT; BETWEEN SOVEREIGNTY AND THE RULE OF LAW (2003).

THE STATUTE OF THE INTERNATIONAL COURT OF JUSTICE, A COMMENTARY (Andreas Zimmermann et al. eds., 2006).

CHITTHARANJAN F. AMERASINGHE, JURISDICTION OF SPECIFIC INTERNATIONAL TRIBUNALS (2009).

RUTH MACKENZIE, ET AL., MANUAL ON INTERNATIONAL COURTS AND TRIBUNALS (2d ed. 2010).

RUTH MACKENZIE, ET AL., SELECTING INTERNATIONAL JUDGES: PRINCIPLE, PROCESS, AND POLITICS (2010).

Chapter Ten

Jurisdiction and Admissibility

Introduction

In international relations there is no compulsory system of courts where an injured state, organization or individual has the right to bring a claim in the absence of a state or organization's consent. Once a state or organization gives consent, however, an international court will have jurisdiction and keep it, even if the consent is later withdrawn. Consent is key to a court's authority, and courts are, therefore, careful to make certain that consent has been given in any particular case. The treaty establishing a court will set out the scope of the court's authority to adjudicate and the process of giving consent to the court's authority. The Statute of the ICJ provides for the court's jurisdiction in Article 36:*

Article 36

1. The jurisdiction of the Court comprises all cases which the parties refer to it and all matters specially provided for in the Charter of the United Nations or in treaties and conventions in force.

2. The states parties to the present Statute may at any time declare that they recognize as compulsory ipso facto and without special agreement, in relation to any other state accepting the same obligation, the jurisdiction of the Court in all legal disputes concerning:

a. the interpretation of a treaty;

b. any question of international law;

c. the existence of any fact which, if established, would constitute a breach of an international obligation;

d. the nature or extent of the reparation to be made for the breach of an international obligation.

3. The declarations referred to above may be made unconditionally or on condition of reciprocity on the part of several or certain states, or for a certain time.

4. Such declarations shall be deposited with the Secretary-General of the United Nations, who shall transmit copies thereof to the parties to the Statute and to the Registrar of the Court.

5. Declarations made under Article 36 of the Statute of the Permanent Court of International Justice and which are still in force shall be deemed, as between

* ICJ Statute, see Annex.

> the parties to the present Statute, to be acceptances of the compulsory jurisdiction of the International Court of Justice for the period which they still have to run and in accordance with their terms.
>
> 6. In the event of a dispute as to whether the Court has jurisdiction, the matter shall be settled by the decision of the Court.

In addition to Article 36, which outlines the ICJ's primary jurisdiction in inter-state cases, the ICJ also has jurisdiction to give advisory opinions:

Article 65

> 1. The Court may give an advisory opinion on any legal question at the request of whatever body may be authorized by or in accordance with the Charter of the United Nations to make such a request.

The UN Charter provides for advisory opinions under Article 96:

Article 96

> 1. The General Assembly or the Security Council may request the International Court of Justice to give an advisory opinion on any legal question.
>
> 2. Other organs of the United Nations and specialized agencies, which may at any time be so authorized by the General Assembly, may also request advisory opinions of the Court on legal questions arising within the scope of their activities.

In addition to these primary bases for exercising jurisdiction, the ICJ also has secondary bases provided for in Article 60 (request for construal of a judgment), Article 61 (request for revision), Article 62 (discretionary intervention) and Article 63 (intervention as of right). The UN Headquarters case, excerpted in Chapter Two, is an example of an advisory opinion. Articles 62 and 63 are discussed below in Chapter Twelve. Articles 60 and 61 are discussed in Chapter Thirteen.

In inter-state cases, one or more states will be unhappy about being brought before the ICJ and will typically argue that the court has no jurisdiction. Jurisdictional arguments are found in both cases excerpted below.

In the first, the *Hostages Case* brought by the U.S. against Iran, the U.S. founded jurisdiction on dispute resolution provisions in the multilateral Vienna Conventions on Diplomatic and Consular Relations, committing the parties to go to the ICJ. It also founded jurisdiction on a bilateral convention of friendship, commerce, and navigation. That agreement, too, committed the parties to resolve disputes before the ICJ. The U.S. was able, therefore, to found the ICJ's jurisdiction under Article 36(1) on the basis of two treaties.

In the second excerpt, it is Nicaragua bringing a case against the U.S. Nicaragua founds jurisdiction mostly on an optional clause acceptance, so Article 36(2). Some lawyers in the U.S. still dispute that the ICJ had jurisdiction in the *Nicaragua Case*. It is also worth emphasizing, however, that the U.S. had a treaty of commerce, friendship, and navigation with Nicaragua, just as it had with Iran. Certain issues were going to the ICJ under Article 36(1) regardless of the 36(2) jurisdiction. The ICJ decided a case in 2003 brought by Iran against the U.S. In that case, as in the *Nicaragua Case*, the issues concerned the unlawful use of armed force. Iran founded jurisdiction on the friendship treaty alone. *See Oil Platforms* (*Iran v. U.S.*) 2003 I.C.J. 161 (Nov. 6), *available at* www.icj-cij.org.

In addition to arguing against jurisdiction, states resisting litigation before the ICJ will also argue that the case is inadmissible. The ICJ Statute contains nothing explicit on the subject of admissibility, but principles governing admissibility are necessary in litigation and are found in the general principles of international law. Even where the ICJ has jurisdiction, it may decline to take a case for any of a variety of reasons well known to students of civil procedure. Courts will decline to take cases, for example, where the case is moot, where the parties bringing the case are not sufficiently interested, or where the Court will be unable to render a decision. Both excerpts also include arguments by Iran and the U.S. against the admissibility of the respective cases before the Court.

Case Concerning United States Diplomatic and Consular Staff in Tehran (*United States of America v. Iran*)

1980 ICJ Rep. (Judgment of May 24)

Present: *President* Sir Humphrey Waldock; *Vice-President* ELIAS; *Judges* Forster, Gros, Lachs, Morozov, Nagendra Singh, Ruda, Mosler, Tarazi, Oda, Ago, El-Erian, Sette-Camara, Baxter; *Registrar* Aquarone.

* * *

12. The essential facts of the present case are, for the most part, matters of public knowledge which have received extensive coverage in the world press and in radio and television broadcasts from Iran and other countries....

13. The result is that the Court has available to it a massive body of information from various sources concerning the facts and circumstances of the present case, including numerous official statements of both Iranian and United States authorities. So far as newspaper, radio and television reports emanating from Iran are concerned, the Court has necessarily in some cases relied on translations into English supplied by the Applicant. The information available, however, is wholly consistent and concordant as to the main facts and circumstances of the case. This information, as well as the United States Memorial and the records of the oral proceedings, has all been communicated by the Court to the Iranian Government without having evoked from that Government any denial or questioning of the facts alleged before the Court by the United States. Accordingly, the Court is satisfied that, within the meaning of Article 53 of the Statute, the allegations of fact on which the United States bases its claims in the present case are well founded.

* * *

16. On 1 November 1979, while a very large demonstration was being held elsewhere in Tehran, large numbers of demonstrators marched to and fro in front of the United States Embassy. Under the then existing security arrangements the Iranian authorities normally maintained 10 to 15 uniformed policemen outside the Embassy compound and a contingent of Revolutionary Guards nearby; on this occasion the normal complement of police was stationed outside the compound and the Embassy reported to the State Department that it felt confident that it could get more protection if needed. The Chief of Police came to the Embassy personally and met the Charge d'affaires, who informed Washington that the Chief was 'taking his job of protecting the Embassy very seriously'. It was announced on the radio, and by the prayer leader at the main demonstration in another location in the city, that people should not go to the Embassy. During the day, the number of demonstrators at the Embassy was around 5,000, but protection was maintained by Iranian security forces. That evening, as the crowd dispersed, both the Iranian Chief of Protocol and the Chief of Police expressed relief to the Charge d'affaires that everything had gone well.

17. At approximately 10.30 a.m. on 4 November 1979, during the course of a demonstration of approximately 3,000 persons, the United States Embassy compound in Tehran was overrun by a strong armed group of several hundred people. The Iranian security personnel are reported to have simply disappeared from the scene; at all events it is established that they made no apparent effort to deter or prevent the demonstrators from seizing the Embassy's premises. The invading group (who subsequently described themselves as 'Muslim Student Followers of the Imam's Policy', and who will hereafter be referred to as 'the militants') gained access by force to the compound and to the ground floor of the Chancery building. Over two hours after the beginning of the attack, and after the militants had attempted to set fire to the Chancery building and to cut through the upstairs steel doors with a torch, they gained entry to the upper floor; one hour later they gained control of the main vault. The militants also seized the other buildings, including the various residences, on the Embassy compound. In the course of the attack, all the diplomatic and consular personnel and other persons present in the premises were seized as hostages, and detained in the Embassy compound; subsequently other United States personnel and one United States private citizen seized elsewhere in Tehran were brought to the compound and added to the number of hostages.

18. During the three hours or more of the assault, repeated calls for help were made from the Embassy to the Iranian Foreign Ministry, and repeated efforts to secure help from the Iranian authorities were also made through direct discussions by the United States Charge d'affaires, who was at the Foreign Ministry at the time, together with two other members of the mission. From there he made contact with the Prime Minister's Office and with Foreign Ministry officials. A request was also made to the Iranian Charge d'affaires in Washington for assistance in putting an end to the seizure of the Embassy. Despite these repeated requests, no Iranian security forces were sent in time to provide relief and protection to the Embassy. In fact when Revolutionary Guards ultimately arrived on the scene, despatched by the Government 'to prevent clashes', they considered that their task was merely to 'protect the safety of both the hostages and the students', according to statements subsequently made by the Iranian Government's spokesman, and by the operations commander of the Guards. No attempt was made by the Iranian Government to clear the Embassy premises, to rescue the persons held hostage, or to persuade the militants to terminate their action against the Embassy.

19. During the morning of 5 November, only hours after the seizure of the Embassy, the United States Consulates in Tabriz and Shiraz were also seized; again the Iranian Government took no protective action. The operation of these Consulates had been suspended since the attack in February 1979 (paragraph 14 above), and therefore no United States personnel were seized on these premises.

20. The United States diplomatic mission and consular posts in Iran were not the only ones whose premises were subjected to demonstrations during the revolutionary period in Iran. On 5 November 1979, a group invaded the British Embassy in Tehran but was ejected after a brief occupation. On 6 November 1979 a brief occupation of the Consulate of Iraq at Kermanshah occurred but was brought to an end on instructions of the Ayatollah Khomeini; no damage was done to the Consulate or its contents. On 1 January 1980 an attack was made on the Embassy in Tehran of the USSR by a large mob, but as a result of the protection given by the Iranian authorities to the Embassy, no serious damage was done.

21. The premises of the United States Embassy in Tehran have remained in the hands of militants; and the same appears to be the case with the Consulates at Tabriz and Shiraz. Of the total number of United States citizens seized and held as hostages, 13 were re-

leased on 18–20 November 1979, but the remainder have continued to be held up to the present time. The release of the 13 hostages was effected pursuant to a decree by the Ayatollah Khomeini addressed to the militants, dated 17 November 1979, in which he called upon the militants to "hand over the blacks and the women, if it is proven they did not spy, to the Ministry of Foreign Affairs so that they may be immediately expelled from Iran."

22. The persons still held hostage in Iran include, according to the information furnished to the Court by the United States, at least 28 persons having the status, duly recognized by the Government of Iran, of 'member of the diplomatic staff' within the meaning of the Vienna Convention on Diplomatic Relations of 1961; at least 20 persons having the status, similarly recognized, of 'member of the administrative and technical staff' within the meaning of that Convention; and two other persons of United States nationality not possessing either diplomatic or consular status. Of the persons with the status of member of the diplomatic staff, four are members of the Consular Section of the Mission.

23. Allegations have been made by the Government of the United States of inhumane treatment of hostages; the militants and Iranian authorities have asserted that the hostages have been well treated, and have allowed special visits to the hostages by religious personalities and by representatives of the International Committee of the Red Cross. The specific allegations of ill-treatment have not however been refuted. Examples of such allegations, which are mentioned in some of the sworn declarations of hostages released in November 1979, are as follows: at the outset of the occupation of the Embassy some were paraded bound and blindfolded before hostile and chanting crowds; at least during the initial period of their captivity, hostages were kept bound, and frequently blindfolded, denied mail or any communication with their government or with each other, subjected to interrogation, threatened with weapons.

24. Those archives and documents of the United States Embassy which were not destroyed by the staff during the attack on 4 November have been ransacked by the militants. Documents purporting to come from this source have been disseminated by the militants and by the Government-controlled media.

25. The United States Charge d'affaires in Tehran and the two other members of the diplomatic staff of the Embassy who were in the premises of the Iranian Ministry of Foreign Affairs at the time of the attack have not left the Ministry since; their exact situation there has been the subject of conflicting statements. On 7 November 1979, it was stated in an announcement by the Iranian Foreign Ministry that 'as the protection of foreign nationals is the duty of the Iranian Government', the Charge d'affaires was 'staying in' the Ministry. On 1 December 1979, Mr. Sadegh Ghotbzadeh, who had become Foreign Minister, stated that

> "it has been announced that, if the U.S. Embassy's charge d'affaires and his two companions, who have sought asylum in the Iranian Ministry of Foreign Affairs, should leave this ministry, the ministry would not accept any responsibility for them."

According to a press report of 4 December, the Foreign Minister amplified this statement by saying that as long as they remained in the ministry he was personally responsible for ensuring that nothing happened to them, but that "as soon as they leave the ministry precincts they will fall back into the hands of justice, and then I will be the first to demand that they be arrested and tried." The militants made it clear that they regarded the Charge and his two colleagues as hostages also. When in March 1980 the Public Prosecutor of the Islamic Revolution of Iran called for one of the three diplomats to be handed over to him, it was announced by the Foreign Minister that

> "Regarding the fate of the three Americans in the Ministry of Foreign Affairs, the decision rests first with the imam of the nation [i.e., the Ayatollah Khomeini]; in case there is no clear decision by the imam of the nation, the Revolution Council will make a decision on this matter."

26. From the outset of the attack upon its Embassy in Tehran, the United States protested to the Government of Iran both at the attack and at the seizure and detention of the hostages. On 7 November a former Attorney-General of the United States, Mr. Ramsey Clark, was instructed to go with an assistant to Iran to deliver a message from the President of the United States to the Ayatollah Khomeini. The text of that message has not been made available to the Court by the Applicant, but the United States Government has informed the Court that it thereby protested at the conduct of the Government of Iran and called for release of the hostages, and that Mr. Clark was also authorized to discuss all avenues for resolution of the crisis. While he was en route, Tehran radio broadcast a message from the Ayatollah Khomeini dated 7 November, solemnly forbidding members of the Revolutionary Council and all the responsible officials to meet the United States representatives. In that message it was asserted that "the U.S. Embassy in Iran is our enemies' centre of espionage against our sacred Islamic movement," and the message continued:

> "Should the United States hand over to Iran the deposed shah ... and give up espionage against our movement, the way to talks would be opened on the issue of certain relations which are in the interest of the nation."

Subsequently, despite the efforts of the United Sates Government to open negotiations, it became clear that the Iranian authorities would have no direct contact with representatives of the United States Government concerning the holding of the hostages.

27. During the period which has elapsed since the seizure of the Embassy a number of statements have been made by various governmental authorities in Iran which are relevant to the Court's examination of the responsibility attributed to the Government of Iran in the submissions of the United States. These statements will be examined by the Court in considering these submissions (paragraphs 59 and 70–74 below).

28. On 9 November 1979, the Permanent Representative of the United States to the United Nations addressed a letter to the President of the Security Council, requesting urgent consideration of what might be done to secure the release of the hostages and to restore the 'sanctity of diplomatic personnel and establishments'. The same day, the President of the Security Council made a public statement urging the release of the hostages, and the President of the General Assembly announced that he was sending a personal message to the Ayatollah Khomeini appealing for their release. On 25 November 1979, the Secretary-General of the United Nations addressed a letter to the President of the Security Council referring to the seizure of the United States Embassy in Tehran and the detention of its diplomatic personnel, and requesting an urgent meeting of the Security Council "in an effort to seek a peaceful solution to the problem." The Security Council met on 27 November and 4 December 1979; on the latter occasion, no representative of Iran was present, but the Council took note of a letter of 13 November 1979 from the Supervisor of the Iranian Foreign Ministry to the Secretary-General. The Security Council then adopted resolution 457 (1979), calling on Iran to release the personnel of the Embassy immediately, to provide them with protection and to allow them to leave the country. The resolution also called on the two Governments to take steps to resolve peacefully the re-

maining issues between them, and requested the Secretary-General to lend his good offices for the immediate implementation of the resolution, and to take all appropriate measures to that end. It further stated that the Council would "remain actively seized of the matter" and requested the Secretary-General to report to it urgently on any developments with regard to his efforts.

29. On 31 December 1979, the Security Council met again and adopted resolution 461 (1979), in which it reiterated both its calls to the Iranian Government and its request to the Secretary-General to lend his good offices for achieving the object of the Council's resolution. The Secretary-General visited Tehran on 1–3 January 1980, and reported to the Security Council on 6 January. On 20 February 1980, the Secretary-General announced the setting up of a commission to undertake a "fact-finding mission" to Iran. The Court will revert to the terms of reference of this commission and the progress of its work in connection with a question of admissibility of the proceedings (paragraphs 39–40 below).

* * *

32. During the night of 24–25 April 1980 the President of the United States set in motion, and subsequently terminated for technical reasons, an operation within Iranian territory designed to effect the rescue of the hostages by United States military units. In an announcement made on 25 April, President Carter explained that the operation had been planned over a long period as a humanitarian mission to rescue the hostages, and had finally been set in motion by him in the belief that the situation in Iran posed mounting dangers to the safety of the hostages and that their early release was highly unlikely. He stated that the operation had been under way in Iran when equipment failure compelled its termination; and that in the course of the withdrawal of the rescue forces two United States aircraft had collided in a remote desert location in Iran. He further stated that preparations for the rescue operations had been ordered for humanitarian reasons, to protect the national interests of the United States, and to alleviate international tensions. At the same time, he emphasized that the operation had not been motivated by hostility towards Iran or the Iranian people....

33. It is to be regretted that the Iranian Government has not appeared before the Court in order to put forward its arguments on the questions of law and of fact which arise in the present case; and that, in consequence, the Court has not had the assistance it might have derived from such arguments or from any evidence adduced in support of them. Nevertheless, in accordance with its settled jurisprudence, the Court, in applying Article 53 of its Statute, must first take up, *proprio motu*, any preliminary question, whether of admissibility or of jurisdiction, that appears from the information before it to arise in the case and the decision of which might constitute a bar to any further examination of the merits of the Applicant's case. The Court will, therefore, first address itself to the considerations put forward by the Iranian Government in its letters of 9 December 1979 and 16 March 1980, on the basis of which it maintains that the Court ought not to take cognizance of the present case.

34. The Iranian Government in its letter of 9 December 1979 drew attention to what it referred to as the "deep rootedness and the essential character of the Islamic Revolution of Iran, a revolution of a whole oppressed nation against its oppressors and their masters." The examination of the "numerous repercussions" of the revolution, it added, is "a matter essentially and directly within the national sovereignty of Iran." However, as the Court pointed out in its Order of 15 December 1979,

> "a dispute which concerns diplomatic and consular premises and the detention of internationally protected persons, and involves the interpretation or applica-

> tion of multilateral conventions codifying the international law governing diplomatic and consular relations, is one which by its very nature falls within international jurisdiction" (*I.C.J. Reports 1979*, p. 16, para. 25).

In its later letter of 16 March 1980 the Government of Iran confined itself to repeating the observations on this point which it had made in its letter of 9 December 1979, without putting forward any additional arguments or explanations. In these circumstances, the Court finds it sufficient here to recall and confirm its previous statement on the matter in its Order of 15 December 1979.

35. In its letter of 9 December 1979 the Government of Iran maintained that the Court could not and should not take cognizance of the present case for another reason, namely that the case submitted to the Court by the United States, is "confined to what is called the question of the 'hostages of the American Embassy in Tehran.'" It then went on to explain why it considered this to preclude the Court from taking cognizance of the case:

> "For this question only represents a marginal and secondary aspect of an overall problem, one such that it cannot be studied separately, and which involves, *inter alia*, more than 25 years of continual interference by the United States in the internal affairs of Iran, the shameless exploitation of our country, and numerous crimes perpetrated against the Iranian people, contrary to and in conflict with all international and humanitarian norms.
>
> The problem involved in the conflict between Iran and the United States is thus not one of the interpretation and the application of the treaties upon which the American Application is based, but results from an overall situation containing much more fundamental and more complex elements. Consequently, the Court cannot examine the American Application divorced from its proper context, namely the whole political dossier of the relations between Iran and the United States over the last 25 years. This dossier includes, *inter alia*, all the crimes perpetrated in Iran by the American Government, in particular the coup d'etat of 1953 stirred up and carried out by the CIA, the overthrow of the lawful national government of Dr. Mossadegh, the restoration of the Shah and of his regime which was under the control of American interests, and all the social, economic, cultural and political consequences of the direct interventions in our internal affairs, as well as grave, flagrant and continuous violations of all international norms, committed by the United States in Iran."

36. The Court, however, in its Order of 15 December 1979, made it clear that the seizure of the United States Embassy and Consulates and the detention of internationally protected persons as hostages cannot be considered as something "secondary" or "marginal," having regard to the importance of the legal principles involved. It also referred to a statement of the Secretary-General of the United Nations, and to Security Council resolution 457 (1979), as evidencing the importance attached by the international community as a whole to the observance of those principles in the present case as well as its concern at the dangerous level of tension between Iran and the United States. The Court, at the same time, pointed out that no provision of the Statute or Rules contemplates that the Court should decline to take cognizance of one aspect of a dispute merely because that dispute has other aspects, however important. It further underlined that, if the Iranian Government considered the alleged activities of the United States in Iran legally to have a close connection with the subject-matter of the United States' Application, it was open to that Government to present its own arguments regarding those activities to the Court either by way of defence in a Counter-Memorial or by way of a counter-claim.

37. The Iranian Government, notwithstanding the terms of the Court's Order, did not file any pleadings and did not appear before the Court. By its own choice, therefore, it has forgone the opportunities offered to it under the Statute and Rules of Court to submit evidence and arguments in support of its contention in regard to the "overall problem." Even in its later letter of 16 March 1980, the Government of Iran confined itself to repeating what it had said in its letter of 9 December 1979, without offering any explanations in regard to the points to which the Court had drawn attention in its Order of 15 December 1979. It has provided no explanation of the reasons why it considers that the violations of diplomatic and consular law alleged in the United States' Application cannot be examined by the Court separately from what it describes as the "overall problem" involving "more than 25 years of continual interference by the United States in the internal affairs of Iran." Nor has it made any attempt to explain, still less define, what connection, legal or factual, there may be between the "overall problem" of its general grievances against the United States and the particular events that gave rise to the United States' claims in the present case which, in its view, precludes the separate examination of those claims by the Court. This was the more necessary because legal disputes between sovereign States by their very nature are likely to occur in political contexts, and often form only one element in a wider and longstanding political dispute between the States concerned. Yet never has the view been put forward before that, because a legal dispute submitted to the Court is only one aspect of a political dispute, the Court should decline to resolve for the parties the legal questions at issue between them. Nor can any basis for such a view of the Court's functions or jurisdiction be found in the Charter or the Statute of the Court; if the Court were, contrary to its settled jurisprudence, to adopt such a view, it would impose a far-reaching and unwarranted restriction upon the role of the Court in the peaceful solution of international disputes.

38. It follows that the considerations and arguments put forward in the Iranian Government's letters of 9 December 1979 and 16 March 1980 do not, in the opinion of the Court, disclose any ground on which it should conclude that it cannot or ought not to take cognizance of the present case.

39. The Court, however, has also thought it right to examine, *ex officio*, whether its competence to decide the present case, or the admissibility of the present proceedings, might possibly have been affected by the setting up of the Commission announced by the Secretary-General of the United Nations on 20 February 1980. As already indicated, the occupation of the Embassy and detention of its diplomatic and consular staff as hostages was referred to the United Nations Security Council by the United States on 9 November 1979 and by the Secretary-General on 25 November. Four days later, while the matter was still before the Security Council, the United States submitted the present Application to the Court together with a request for the indication of provisional measures. On 4 December, the Security Council adopted resolution 457 (1979) (the terms of which have already been indicated in paragraph 28 above), whereby the Council would "remain actively seized of the matter" and the Secretary-General was requested to report to it urgently on developments regarding the efforts he was to make pursuant to the resolution. In announcing the setting up of the Commission on 20 February 1980, the Secretary-General stated its terms of reference to be "to undertake a fact-finding mission to Iran to hear Iran's grievances and to allow for an early solution of the crisis between Iran and the United States;" …

40. … It is for the Court, the principal judicial organ of the United Nations, to resolve any legal questions that may be in issue between parties to a dispute; and the resolution of such legal questions by the Court may be an important, and sometimes decisive,

factor in promoting the peaceful settlement of the dispute. This is indeed recognized by Article 36 of the Charter, paragraph 3 of which specifically provides that:

> "In making recommendations under this Article the Security Council should also take into consideration that legal disputes should as a general rule be referred by the parties to the International Court of Justice in accordance with the provisions of the Statute of the Court."

* * *

44. It follows that neither the mandate given by the Security Council to the Secretary-General in resolutions 457 and 461 of 1979, nor the setting up of the Commission by the Secretary-General, can be considered as constituting any obstacle to the exercise of the Court's jurisdiction in the present case. It further follows that the Court must now proceed, in accordance with Article 53, paragraph 2, of the Statute, to determine whether it has jurisdiction to decide the present case and whether the United States' claims are well founded in fact and in law.

45. Article 53 of the Statute requires the Court, before deciding in favour of an Applicant's claim, to satisfy itself that it has jurisdiction, in accordance with Articles 36 and 37, empowering it to do so. In the present case the principal claims of the United States relate essentially to alleged violations by Iran of its obligations to the United States under the Vienna Conventions of 1961 on Diplomatic Relations and of 1963 on Consular Relations. With regard to these claims the United States has invoked as the basis for the Court's jurisdiction Article I of the Optional Protocols concerning the Compulsory Settlement of Disputes which accompany these Conventions....

46. The terms of Article I, which are the same in the two Protocols, provide:

> "Disputes arising out of the interpretation or application of the Convention shall lie within the compulsory jurisdiction of the International Court of Justice and may accordingly be brought before the Court by an application made by any party to the dispute being a Party to the present Protocol."

The United States' claims here in question concern alleged violations by Iran of its obligations under several articles of the Vienna Conventions of 1961 and 1963 with respect to the privileges and immunities of the personnel, the inviolability of the premises and archives, and the provision of facilities for the performance of the functions of the United States Embassy and Consulates in Iran. In so far as its claims relate to two private individuals held hostage in the Embassy, the situation of these individuals falls under the provisions of the Vienna Convention of 1961 guaranteeing the inviolability of the premises of embassies, and of Article 5 of the 1963 Convention concerning the consular functions of assisting nationals and protecting and safeguarding their interests. By their very nature all these claims concern the interpretation or application of one or other of the two Vienna Conventions.

* * *

48. Articles II and III of the Protocols, it is true, provide that within a period of two months after one party has notified its opinion to the other that a dispute exists, the parties may agree either: (a) "to resort not to the International Court of Justice but to an arbitral tribunal," or (b) "to adopt a conciliation procedure before resorting to the International Court of Justice." The terms of Articles II and III however, when read in conjunction with those of Article I and with the Preamble to the Protocols, make it crystal clear that they are not to be understood as laying down a precondition of the applicability of the precise and categorical provision contained in Article I establishing the compulsory juris-

diction of the Court in respect of disputes arising out of the interpretation or application of the Vienna Convention in question. Articles II and III provide only that, as a substitute for recourse to the Court, the parties may agree upon resort either to arbitration or to conciliation. It follows, first, that Articles II and III have no application unless recourse to arbitration or conciliation has been proposed by one of the parties to the dispute and the other has expressed its readiness to consider the proposal. Secondly, it follows that only then may the provisions in those articles regarding a two months' period come into play, and function as a time-limit upon the conclusion of the agreement as to the organization of the alternative procedure.

49. In the present instance, neither of the parties to the dispute proposed recourse to either of the two alternatives, before the filing of the Application or at any time afterwards. On the contrary, the Iranian authorities refused to enter into any discussion of the matter with the United States, and this could only be understood by the United States as ruling out, *in limine*, any question of arriving at an agreement to resort to arbitration or conciliation under Article II or Article III of the Protocols, instead of recourse to the Court. Accordingly, when the United States filed its Application on 29 November 1979, it was unquestionably free to have recourse to Article I of the Protocols, and to invoke it as a basis for establishing the Court's jurisdiction with respect to its claims under the Vienna Conventions of 1961 and 1963.

50. However, the United States also presents claims in respect of alleged violations by Iran of Articles II, paragraph 4, XIII, XVIII and XIX of the Treaty of Amity, Economic Relations, and Consular Rights of 1955 between the United States and Iran, which entered into force on 16 June 1957. With regard to these claims the United States has invoked paragraph 2 of Article XXI of the Treaty as the basis for the Court's jurisdiction. The claims of the United States under this Treaty overlap in considerable measure with its claims under the two Vienna Conventions and more especially the Convention of 1963. In this respect, therefore, the dispute between the United States and Iran regarding those claims is at the same time a dispute arising out of the interpretation or application of the Vienna Conventions which falls within Article I of their Protocols. It was for this reason that in its Order of 15 December 1979 indicating provisional measures the Court did not find it necessary to enter into the question whether Article XXI, paragraph 2, of the 1955 Treaty might also have provided a basis for the exercise of its jurisdiction in the present case. But taking into account that Article II, paragraph 4, of the 1955 Treaty provides that "nationals of either High Contracting Party shall receive the most constant protection and security within the territories of the other High Contracting Party...," the Court considers that at the present stage of the proceedings that Treaty has importance in regard to the claims of the United States in respect of the two private individuals said to be held hostage in Iran. Accordingly, the Court will now consider whether a basis for the exercise of its jurisdiction with respect to the alleged violations of the 1955 Treaty may be found in Article XXI, paragraph 2, of the Treaty.

51. Paragraph 2 of that Article reads:

> "Any dispute between the High Contracting Parties as to the interpretation or application of the present Treaty, not satisfactorily adjusted by diplomacy, shall be submitted to the International Court of Justice, unless the High Contracting Parties agree to settlement by some other pacific means."

As previously pointed out, when the United States filed its Application on 29 November 1979, its attempts to negotiate with Iran in regard to the overrunning of its Embassy and detention of its nationals as hostages had reached a deadlock, owing to the refusal of the

Iranian Government to enter into any discussion of the matter. In consequence, there existed at that date not only a dispute but, beyond any doubt, a "dispute ... not satisfactorily adjusted by diplomacy" within the meaning of Article XXI, paragraph 2, of the 1955 Treaty; and this dispute comprised, *inter alia*, the matters that are the subject of the United States' claims under that Treaty.

52. The provision made in the 1955 Treaty for disputes as to its interpretation or application to be referred to the Court is similar to the system adopted in the Optional Protocols to the Vienna Conventions which the Court has already explained. Article XXI, paragraph 2, of the Treaty establishes the jurisdiction of the Court as compulsory for such disputes, unless the parties agree to settlement by some other means. In the present instance, as in the case of the Optional Protocols, the immediate and total refusal of the Iranian authorities to enter into any negotiations with the United States excluded *in limine* any question of an agreement to have recourse to "some other pacific means" for the settlement of the dispute. Consequently, under the terms of Article XXI, paragraph 2, the United States was free on 29 November 1979 to invoke its provisions for the purpose of referring its claims against Iran under the 1955 Treaty to the Court. While that Article does not provide in express terms that either party may bring a case to the Court by unilateral application, it is evident, as the United States contended in its Memorial, that this is what the parties intended. Provisions drawn in similar terms are very common in bilateral treaties of amity or of establishment, and the intention of the parties in accepting such clauses is clearly to provide for such a right of unilateral recourse to the Court, in the absence of agreement to employ some other pacific means of settlement.

53. The point has also been raised whether, having regard to certain counter-measures taken by the United States vis-à-vis Iran, it is open to the United States to rely on the Treaty of Amity, Economic Relations, and Consular Rights in the present proceedings. However, all the measures in question were taken by the United States after the seizure of its Embassy by an armed group and subsequent detention of its diplomatic and consular staff as hostages. They were measures taken in response to what the United States believed to be grave and manifest violations of international law by Iran, including violations of the 1955 Treaty itself. In any event, any alleged violation of the Treaty by either party could not have the effect of precluding that party from invoking the provisions of the Treaty concerning pacific settlement of disputes.

* * *

56. The principal facts material for the Court's decision on the merits of the present case have been set out earlier in this Judgment. [The remainder of the Judgment turned to the merits of the U.S. allegations against Iran.]

* * *

95. For these reasons,

THE COURT,

1. By thirteen votes to two,

> *Decides* that the Islamic Republic of Iran, by the conduct which the Court has set out in this Judgment, has violated in several respects, and is still violating, obligations owed by it to the United States of America under international conventions in force between the two countries, as well as under long-established rules of general international law;

IN FAVOUR: *President* Sir Humphrey Waldock; *Vice-President* Elias; *Judges* Forster, Gros, Lachs, Nagendra Singh, Ruda, Mosler, Oda, Ago, El-Erian, Sette-Camara and Baxter.

AGAINST: *Judges* Morozov and Tarazi.

2. By thirteen votes to two,

Decides that the violations of these obligations engage the responsibility of the Islamic Republic of Iran towards the United States of America under international law;

IN FAVOUR: *President* Sir Humphrey Waldock; *Vice-President* Elias; *Judges* Forster, Gros, Lachs, Nagendra Singh, Ruda, Mosler, Oda, Ago, El-Erian, Sette-Camara and Baxter.

AGAINST: *Judges* Morozov and Tarazi.

3. Unanimously,

Decides that the Government of the Islamic Republic of Iran must immediately take all steps to redress the situation resulting from the events of 4 November 1979 and what followed from these events, and to that end:

(*a*) must immediately terminate the unlawful detention of the United States Charge d'affaires and other diplomatic and consular staff and other United States nationals now held hostage in Iran, and must immediately release each and every one and entrust them to the protecting Power (Article 45 of the 1961 Vienna Convention on Diplomatic Relations);

(*b*) must ensure that all the said persons have the necessary means of leaving Iranian territory, including means of transport;

(*c*) must immediately place in the hands of the protecting Power the premises, property, archives and documents of the United States Embassy in Tehran and of its Consulates in Iran;

4. Unanimously,

Decides that no member of the United States diplomatic or consular staff may be kept in Iran to be subjected to any form of judicial proceedings or to participate in them as a witness;

5. By twelve votes to three,

Decides that the Government of the Islamic Republic of Iran is under an obligation to make reparation to the Government of the United States of America for the injury caused to the latter by the events of 4 November 1979 and what followed from these events;

IN FAVOUR: *President* Sir Humphrey Waldock; *Vice-President* Elias; *Judges* Forster, Gros, Nagendra Singh, Ruda, Mosler, Oda, Ago, El-Erian, Sette-Camara and Baxter.

AGAINST: *Judges* Lachs, Morozov and Tarazi.

6. By fourteen votes to one,

Decides that the form and amount of such reparation, failing agreement between the Parties, shall be settled by the Court, and reserves for this purpose the subsequent procedure in the case.

IN FAVOUR: *President* Sir Humphrey Waldock; *Vice-President* Elias; *Judges* Forster, Gros, Lachs, Nagendra Singh, Ruda, Mosler, Tarazi, Oda, Ago, El-Erian, Sette-Camara and Baxter.

AGAINST: *Judge* Morozov.

Done in English and in French, the English text being authoritative, at the Peace Palace, The Hague, this twenty-fourth day of May, one thousand nine hundred and eighty, in three copies, one of which will be placed in the archives of the Court, and the others transmitted to the Government of the United States of America and the Government of the Islamic Republic of Iran, respectively.

(Signed) Humphrey WALDOCK,
President.

(Signed) S. AQUARONE,
Registrar.

Judge LACHS appends a separate opinion to the Judgment of the Court.

Judges MOROZOV and TARAZI append dissenting opinions to the Judgment of the Court.

(*Initialled*) H.W.

(*Initialled*) S.A.

Case Concerning Military and Paramilitary Activities in and against Nicaragua (*Nicaragua v. United States of America*)

1984 ICJ Rep. (Judgment of Nov. 26, 1984)

Present: *President* Elias; *Vice-President* Sette-Camara; *Judges* Lachs, Morozov, Nagendra Singh, Ruda, Mosler, Oda, Ago, Elkhani, Schwebel, Sir Robert Jennings, De Lacharriere, Mbaye, Bedjaoui; *Judge* ad hoc Colliard; *Registrar* Torres Bernardez.

* * *

11. The present case concerns a dispute between the Government of the Republic of Nicaragua and the Government of the United States of America occasioned, Nicaragua contends, by certain military and paramilitary activities conducted in Nicaragua and in the waters off its coasts, responsibility for which is attributed by Nicaragua to the United States. In the present phase the case concerns the jurisdiction of the Court to entertain and pronounce upon this dispute, and the admissibility of the Application by which it was brought before the Court. The issue being thus limited, the Court will avoid not only all expressions of opinion on matters of substance, but also any pronouncement which might prejudge or appear to prejudge any eventual decision on the merits.

12. To found the jurisdiction of the Court in the present proceedings, Nicaragua in its Application relied on Article 36 of the Statute of the Court and the declarations, described below, made by the Parties accepting compulsory jurisdiction pursuant to that Article. In its Memorial, Nicaragua, relying on a reservation contained in its Application (para. 26) of the right to "supplement or to amend this Application," also contended that the Court has jurisdiction under Article XXIV, paragraph 2, of a Treaty of Friendship, Commerce and Navigation between the Parties signed at Managua on 21 January 1956.

13. ... On 6 April 1984 the Government of the United States of America deposited with the Secretary-General of the United Nations a notification, signed by the United States Secretary of State. Mr. George Shultz, referring to the Declaration deposited on 26 August 1946, and stating that:

> "the aforesaid declaration shall not apply to disputes with any Central American State or arising out of or related to events in Central America, any of which disputes shall be settled in such manner as the parties to them may agree.

Notwithstanding the terms of the aforesaid declaration, this proviso shall take effect immediately and shall remain in force for two years, so as to foster the continuing regional dispute settlement process which seeks a negotiated solution to the interrelated political, economic and security problems of Central America."

This notification will be referred to, for convenience, as the "1984 notification."

14. In order to be able to rely upon the United States Declaration of 1946 to found jurisdiction in the present case, Nicaragua has to show that it is a "State accepting the same obligation" within the meaning of Article 36, paragraph 2, of the Statute. For this purpose, Nicaragua relies on a Declaration made by it on 24 September 1929 pursuant to Article 36, paragraph 2, of the Statute of the Permanent Court of International Justice. That Article provided that:

"The Members of the League of Nations and the States mentioned in the Annex to the Covenant may, either when signing or ratifying the Protocol to which the present Statute is adjoined, or at a later moment, declare that they recognize as compulsory *ipso facto* and without special agreement, in relation to any other Member or State accepting the same obligation, the jurisdiction of the Court"

in any of the same categories of dispute as listed in paragraph 2 of Article 36 of the Statute of the postwar Court, set out above. Nicaragua relies further on paragraph 5 of Article 36 of the Statute of the present Court, which provides that:

"Declarations made under Article 36 of the Statute of the Permanent Court of International Justice and which are still in force shall be deemed, as between the parties to the present Statute, to be acceptances of the compulsory jurisdiction of the International Court of Justice for the period which they still have to run and in accordance with their terms."

15. The circumstances of Nicaragua's Declaration of 1929 were as follows. The Members of the League of Nations (and the States mentioned in the Annex to the League of Nations Covenant) were entitled to sign the Protocol of Signature of the Statute of the Permanent Court of International Justice, which was drawn up at Geneva on 16 December 1920. That Protocol provided that it was subject to ratification, and that instruments of ratification were to be sent to the Secretary-General of the League of Nations. On 24 September 1929, Nicaragua, as a Member of the League, signed this Protocol and made a declaration under Article 36, paragraph 2, of the Statute of the Permanent Court which read:

[*Translation from the French*]

"On behalf of the Republic of Nicaragua I recognize as compulsory unconditionally the jurisdiction of the Permanent Court of International Justice.

Geneva, 24 September 1929.

(Signed) T. F. MEDINA."

16. According to the documents produced by both Parties before the Court, on 4 December 1934, a proposal for the ratification of (*inter alia*) the Statute of the Permanent Court of International Justice and of the Protocol of Signature of 16 December 1920 was approved by the "Ejecutivo" (executive power) of Nicaragua. On 14 February 1935, the Senate of Nicaragua decided to ratify these instruments, its decision being published in *La Gaceta*, the Nicaraguan official journal, on 12 June 1935, and on 11 July 1935 the Chamber of Deputies of Nicaragua adopted a similar decision, similarly published on 18 September 1935. On 29 November 1939, the Ministry of External Relations of Nicaragua sent the following telegram to the Secretary-General of the League of Nations: ...

[*Translation*]

> (Statute and Protocol Permanent Court International Justice The Hague have already been ratified. Will send you in due course Instrument Ratification-Relations.)

The files of the League of Nations however contain no record of an instrument of ratification ever having been received. No evidence has been adduced before the Court to show that such an instrument of ratification was ever despatched to Geneva. On 16 December 1942, the Acting Legal Adviser of the Secretariat of the League of Nations wrote to the Foreign Minister of Nicaragua to point out that he had not received the instrument of ratification "dont le depot est necessaire pour faire naitre effectivement l'obligation" (the deposit of which is necessary to cause the obligation to come into effective existence). In the Nicaraguan Memorial, it was stated that "Nicaragua never completed ratification of the old Protocol of Signature;" at the hearings, the Agent of Nicaragua explained that the records are very scanty, and he was therefore unable to certify the facts one way or the other. He added however that if instruments of ratification were sent, they would most likely have been sent by sea, and, the Second World War being then in progress, the attacks on commercial shipping may explain why the instruments appear never to have arrived. After the war, Nicaragua took part in the United Nations Conference on International Organization at San Francisco and became an original Member of the United Nations, having ratified the Charter on 6 September 1945; on 24 October 1945 the Statute of the International Court of Justice, which is an integral part of the Charter, came into force.

17. On the basis of these facts, the United States contends, first, that Nicaragua never became a party to the Statute of the Permanent Court of International Justice, and that accordingly it could not and did not make an effective acceptance of the compulsory jurisdiction of the Permanent Court; the 1929 acceptance was therefore not 'still in force' within the meaning of the English version of Article 36, paragraph 5, of the Statute of the present Court. In the contention of the United States, the expression in the French version of the Statute corresponding to "still in force" in the English text, namely "pour une duree qui n'est pas encore expiree," also requires that a declaration be binding under the Statute of the Permanent Court in order to be deemed an acceptance of the jurisdiction of the present Court under Article 36, paragraph 5, of its Statute.

18. Nicaragua does not contend that its 1929 Declaration was in itself sufficient to establish a binding acceptance of the compulsory jurisdiction of the Permanent Court of International Justice, for which it would have been necessary that Nicaragua complete the ratification of the Protocol of Signature of the Statute of that Court. It rejects however the interpretation of Article 36, paragraph 5, of the Statute of the present Court advanced by the United States: Nicaragua argues that the phrase "which are still in force" or "pour une duree qui n'est pas encore expiree" was designed to exclude from the operation of the Article only declarations that had already expired, and has no bearing whatever on a declaration, like Nicaragua's, that had not expired, but which, for some reason or another, had not been perfected. Consistently with the intention of the provision, which in Nicaragua's view was to continue the pre-existing situation as regards declarations of acceptance of compulsory jurisdiction, Nicaragua was in exactly the same situation under the new Statute as it was under the old. In either case, ratification of the Statute of the Court would perfect its Declaration of 1929. Nicaragua contends that the fact that this is the correct interpretation of the Statute is borne out by the way in which the Nicaraguan declaration was handled in the publications of the Court and of the United Nations Secretariat; by the conduct of the Parties to the present case, and of the Government of Honduras, in relation to the dispute in 1957–1960 between Honduras and

Nicaragua in connection with the arbitral award made by the King of Spain in 1906, which dispute was eventually determined by the Court; by the opinions of publicists; and by the practice of the United States itself.

19. With regard to Nicaragua's reliance on the publications of the Court, it may first be noted that in the Sixteenth Report (the last) of the Permanent Court of International Justice, covering the period 15 June 1939 to 31 December 1945, Nicaragua was included in the "List of States having signed the Optional Clause" (p. 358), but it was recorded on another page (p. 50) that Nicaragua had not ratified the Protocol of Signature of the Statute, and Nicaragua was not included in the list of "States bound by the Clause" (i.e., the Optional Clause) on the same page. The first Yearbook, that for 1946–1947, of the present Court contained (p. 110) a list entitled "Members of the United Nations, other States parties to the Statute and States to which the Court is open. (An asterisk denotes a State bound by the compulsory jurisdiction clause)," and Nicaragua was included in that list, with an asterisk against it, and with a footnote (common to several States listed) reading "Declaration made under Article 36 of the Statute of the Permanent Court and deemed to be still in force (Article 36, 5, of Statute of the present Court)." On another page (p. 210), the text of Nicaragua's 1929 Declaration was reproduced, with the following footnote:

> "According to a telegram dated November 29th, 1939, addressed to the League of Nations, Nicaragua had ratified the Protocol of Signature of the Statute of the Permanent Court of International Justice (December 16th, 1920), and the instrument of ratification was to follow. Notification concerning the deposit of the said instrument has not, however, been received in the Registry."

The *Yearbook 1946–1947* also includes a list (p. 221) entitled "List of States which have recognized the compulsory jurisdiction of the International Court of Justice or which are still bound by their acceptance of the Optional Clause of the Statute of the Permanent Court of International Justice (Article 36 of the Statute of the International Court of Justice)" and this list includes Nicaragua (with a footnote cross-reference to the page where its 1929 Declaration is reproduced).

20. Subsequent *Yearbooks* of the Court, up to and including *I.C.J. Yearbook 1954–1955*, list Nicaragua among the States with regard to which there were "in force" declarations of acceptance of the compulsory jurisdiction of the Court, made in accordance with the terms either of the Permanent Court of International Justice Statute or of the Statute of the present Court (see, e.g., *Yearbook 1954–1955*, p. 39); however, a reference was also given to the page of the *Yearbook 1946–1947* at which the text of Nicaragua's 1929 Declaration was printed (ibid., p. 187). Nicaragua also continued to be included in the list of States recognizing compulsory jurisdiction (*ibid.*, p. 195). In the *Yearbook 1955–1956*, the reference to Nicaragua in this list (p. 195) had a footnote appended to it reading as follows:

> "According to a telegram dated November 29th, 1939, addressed to the League of Nations, Nicaragua had ratified the Protocol of Signature of the Statute of the Permanent Court of International Justice (December 16th, 1920), and the instrument of ratification was to follow. It does not appear, however, that the instrument of ratification was ever received by the League of Nations."

A note to the same effect has been included in subsequent *Yearbooks* up to the present time.

21. In 1968 the Court began the practice, which has continued up to the present time, of transmitting a Report to the General Assembly of the United Nations for the past year. Each of these Reports has included a paragraph recording the number of States which

recognize the jurisdiction of the Court as compulsory, and Nicaragua has been mentioned among these. For a number of years the paragraph referred to such States as having so recognized the Court's jurisdiction "in accordance with declarations filed under Article 36, paragraph 2, of the Statute." No reference has been made in these Reports to the issue of ratification of the Protocol of Signature of the Statute of the Permanent Court.

22. Nicaragua also places reliance on the references made to it in a number of publications issued by the Secretariat of the United Nations, all of which include it as a State whose declaration of acceptance of the jurisdiction of the Permanent Court has attracted the operation of Article 36, paragraph 5, of the Statute of the present Court. These publications are the Second *Annual Report* of the Secretary-General to the General Assembly; the annual volume entitled *Signatures, Ratifications, Acceptances, Accessions, etc., concerning the Multilateral Conventions and Agreements in respect of which the Secretary-General acts as Depositary*; the *Yearbook* of the United Nations; and certain ancillary official publications.

23. The United States contention as to these publications is, as to those issued by the Registry of the Court, that the Registry took great care not to represent any of its listings as authoritative; the United States draws attention to the caveat in the Preface to the *I.C.J. Yearbook* that it 'in no way involves the responsibility of the Court', to the footnotes quoted in paragraphs 19 and 20 above, and to a disclaimer appearing for the first time in the *Yearbook 1956–1957* (p. 207) reading as follows:

> "The texts of declarations set out in this Chapter are reproduced for convenience of reference only. The inclusion of a declaration made by any State should not be regarded as an indication of the view entertained by the Registry or, a fortiori, by the Court, regarding the nature, scope or validity of the instrument in question."

It concludes that it is clear that successive Registrars and the *Yearbooks* of the Court never adopted, and indeed expressly rejected, Nicaragua's contention as to the effect of Article 36, paragraph 5, of the Statute. So far as the United Nations publications are concerned, the United States points out that where they cite their source of information, they invariably refer to the *I.C.J. Yearbook*, and none of them purport to convey any authority.

* * *

24. In order to determine whether the provisions of Article 36, paragraph 5, can have applied to Nicaragua's Declaration of 1929, the Court must first establish the legal characteristics of that declaration and then compare them with the conditions laid down by the text of that paragraph.

* * *

27. … [W]hile the declaration had not acquired binding force, it is not disputed that it could have done so, for example at the beginning of 1945, if Nicaragua had ratified the Protocol of Signature of the Statute of the Permanent Court. The correspondence brought to the Court's attention by the Parties, between the Secretariat of the League of Nations and various Governments including the Government of Nicaragua, leaves no doubt as to the fact that, at any time between the making of Nicaragua's declaration and the day on which the new Court came into existence, if not later, ratification of the Protocol of Signature would have sufficed to transform the content of the 1929 Declaration into a binding commitment; no one would have asked Nicaragua to make a new declaration. It follows that such a declaration as that made by Nicaragua had a certain potential effect which could be maintained indefinitely. This durability of potential effect flowed from a

certain characteristic of Nicaragua's declaration; being made "unconditionally," it was valid for an unlimited period. Had it provided, for example, that it would apply for only five years to disputes arising after its signature, its potential effect would admittedly have disappeared as from 24 September 1934. In sum, Nicaragua's 1929 Declaration was valid at the moment when Nicaragua became a party to the Statute of the new Court; it had retained its potential effect because Nicaragua, which could have limited the duration of that effect, had expressly refrained from doing so.

* * *

34. ... [I]t is undeniable that a declaration by which a State recognizes the compulsory jurisdiction of the Court is "in existence," in the sense given above, and that each such declaration does constitute a certain progress towards extending to the world in general the system of compulsory judicial settlement of international disputes. Admittedly, this progress has not yet taken the concrete form of a commitment having binding force, but nonetheless, it is by no means negligible. There are no grounds for maintaining that those who drafted the Statute meant to go back on this progress and place it in a category in opposition to the progress achieved by declarations having binding force. No doubt their main aim was to safeguard these latter declarations, but the intention to wipe out the progress evidenced by a declaration such as that of Nicaragua would certainly not square well with their general concern. As the Court said in the very similar matter of the already existing field of conventional compulsory jurisdiction, it was "a natural element of this compromise" (then accepted by comparison with the ideal of universal compulsory jurisdiction) "that the maximum, and not some merely quasi optimum preservation of this field should be aimed at" (*Barcelona Traction, Light and Power Company, Limited, I.C.J. Reports 1964*, p. 32). Furthermore, if the highly experienced drafters of the Statute had had a restrictive intention on this point, in contrast to their overall concern, they would certainly have translated it into a very different formula from the one which they in fact adopted.

35. On the other hand, the logic of a system substituting a new Court for the former one without the cause of compulsory jurisdiction in any way suffering in the process resulted in the ratification of the new Statute having exactly the same effects as the ratification of the Protocol of Signature of the former one would have had, that is to say, in the case of Nicaragua, the step from potential commitment to effective commitment. The general system of devolution from the old Court to the new thus lends support to the interpretation whereby Article 36, paragraph 5, even covers declarations that had not previously acquired binding force. In this connection, it should not be overlooked that Nicaragua was represented at the San Francisco Conference, and duly signed and ratified the Charter of the United Nations. At that time, the consent which it had given in 1929 to the jurisdiction of the Permanent Court had not become fully effective in the absence of ratification of the Protocol of Signature; but taking into account the interpretation given above, the Court may apply to Nicaragua what it stated in the case of the *Aerial Incident* of 27 July 1955:

> "Consent to the transfer to the International Court of Justice of a declaration accepting the jurisdiction of the Permanent Court may be regarded as effectively given by a State which, having been represented at the San Francisco Conference, signed and ratified the Charter and thereby accepted the Statute in which Article 36, paragraph 5, appears." (*I.C.J. Reports 1959*, p. 142.)

36. This finding as regards the interpretation of Article 36, paragraph 5, must, finally, be compared to the conduct of States and international organizations in regard to this

interpretation. In that respect, particular weight must be ascribed to certain official publications, namely the *I.C.J. Yearbook* (since 1946–1947), the Reports of the Court to the General Assembly of the United Nations (since 1968) and the annually published collection of *Signatures, Ratifications, Acceptances, Accessions, etc., concerning the Multilateral Conventions and Agreements in respect of which the Secretary-General acts as Depositary*. The Court notes that, ever since they first appeared, all these publications have regularly placed Nicaragua on the list of those States that have recognized the compulsory jurisdiction of the Court by virtue of Article 36, paragraph 5, of the Statute. Even if the *I.C.J. Yearbook* has, in the issue for 1946–1947 and as from the issue for 1955–1956 onwards, contained a note recalling certain facts concerning Nicaragua's ratification of the Protocol of Signature of the Statute of the Permanent Court of International Justice, this publication has never modified the classification of Nicaragua or the binding character attributed to its 1929 Declaration—indeed the Yearbooks list Nicaragua among the States "still bound by" their declarations under Article 36 of the Statute of the Permanent Court (see paragraph 19, above). The same observation is valid for the Secretariat publication Signatures, Ratifications, Acceptances, Accessions, etc., which derived its data, including footnotes, from the *I.C.J. Yearbook*. As for the reports of the Court, they are quite categorical in stating that Nicaragua had accepted compulsory jurisdiction, even if the distinction between acceptances made under Article 36, paragraph 2, and those "deemed" to be such acceptances, is not spelled out.

* * *

39. Admittedly, Nicaragua itself, according to the information furnished to the Court, did not at any moment explicitly recognize that it was bound by its recognition of the Court's compulsory jurisdiction, but neither did it deny the existence of this undertaking. The Court notes that Nicaragua, even if its conduct in the case concerning the *Arbitral Award Made by the King of Spain on 23 December 1906* was not unambiguous, did not at any time declare that it was not bound by its 1929 Declaration. Having regard to the public and unchanging nature of the official statements concerning Nicaragua's commitment under the Optional-Clause system, the silence of its Government can only be interpreted as an acceptance of the classification thus assigned to it. It cannot be supposed that that Government could have believed that its silence could be tantamount to anything other than acquiescence. Besides, the Court would remark that if proceedings had been instituted against Nicaragua at any time in these recent years, and it had sought to deny that, by the operation of Article 36, paragraph 5, it had recognized the compulsory jurisdiction of the Court, the Court would probably have rejected that argument. But the Court's jurisdiction in regard to a particular State does not depend on whether that State is in the position of an Applicant or a Respondent in the proceedings. If the Court considers that it would have decided that Nicaragua would have been bound in a case in which it was the Respondent, it must conclude that its jurisdiction is identically established in a case where Nicaragua is the Applicant.

40. As for States other than Nicaragua, including those which could be supposed to have the closest interest in that State's legal situation in regard to the Court's jurisdiction, they have never challenged the interpretation to which the publications of the United Nations bear witness and whereby the case of Nicaragua is covered by Article 36, paragraph 5. Such States as themselves publish lists of States bound by the compulsory jurisdiction of the Court have placed Nicaragua on their lists. Of course, the Court is well aware that such national publications simply reproduce those of the United Nations where that particular point is concerned. Nevertheless, it would be difficult to interpret the fact of such reproduction as signifying an objection to the interpretation thus given; on the contrary,

this reproduction contributes to the generality of the opinion which appears to have been cherished by States parties to the Statute as regards the applicability to Nicaragua of Article 36, paragraph 5.

41. Finally, what States believe regarding the legal situation of Nicaragua so far as the compulsory jurisdiction of the Court is concerned may emerge from the conclusions drawn by certain governments as regards the possibility of obliging Nicaragua to appear before the Court or of escaping any proceedings it may institute. The Court would therefore recall that in the case concerning the *Arbitral Award Made by the King of Spain on 23 December 1906* Honduras founded its application both on a special agreement, the Washington Agreement, and on Nicaragua's Optional-Clause declaration. It is also difficult for the Court not to consider that the United States letter of 6 April 1984 implies that at that date the United States, like other States, believed that Nicaragua was bound by the Court's jurisdiction in accordance with the terms of its 1929 Declaration.

* * *

44. The United States however objects that this contention of Nicaragua is flatly inconsistent with the Statute of the Court, which provides only for consent to jurisdiction to be manifested in specified ways; an "independent title of jurisdiction, as Nicaragua calls it, is an impossibility." The Statute provides the sole bases on which the Court can exercise jurisdiction, under Articles 36 and 37. In the particular case of Article 36, paragraph 5, the Statutes of the two Courts provide a means for States to express their consent, and Nicaragua did not use them. The United States urges what it describes as policy considerations of fundamental importance: that compulsory jurisdiction, being a major obligation, must be based on the clearest manifestation of the State's intent to accept it; that Nicaragua's thesis introduces intolerable uncertainty into the system; and that that thesis entails the risk of consenting to compulsory jurisdiction through silence, with all the harmful consequences that would ensue. The United States also disputes the significance of the publications and conduct on which Nicaragua bases this contention.

45. The Court would first observe that, as regards the requirement of consent as a basis of its jurisdiction, and more particularly as regards the formalities required for that consent to be expressed in accordance with the provisions of Article 36, paragraph 2, of the Statute, the Court has already made known its view in, *inter alia*, the case concerning the *Temple of Preah Vihear*. On that occasion it stated: "The only formality required is the deposit of the acceptance with the Secretary-General of the United Nations under paragraph 4 of Article 36 of the Statute." (*I.C.J. Reports 1961*, p. 31.)

46. The Court must enquire whether Nicaragua's particular circumstances afford any reason for it to modify the conclusion it then reached. After all, the reality of Nicaragua's consent to be bound by its 1929 Declaration is, as pointed out above, attested by the absence of any protest against the legal situation ascribed to it by the publications of the Court, the Secretary-General of the United Nations and major States. The question is therefore whether, even if the consent of Nicaragua is real, the Court can decide that it has been given valid expression even on the hypothesis that the 1929 Declaration was without validity, and given that no other declaration has been deposited by Nicaragua since it became a party to the Statute of the International Court of Justice. In this connection the Court notes that Nicaragua's situation has been wholly unique, in that it was the publications of the Court itself (since 1947, the *I.C.J. Yearbook*; since 1968, the Reports to the General Assembly of the United Nations), and those of the Secretary-General (as depositary of the declarations under the Statute of the present Court) which affirmed (and still affirm today, for that matter) that Nicaragua had accomplished the

formality in question. Hence, if the Court were to object that Nicaragua ought to have made a declaration under Article 36, paragraph 2, it would be penalizing Nicaragua for having attached undue weight to the information given on that point by the Court and the Secretary-General of the United Nations and, in sum, having (on account of the authority of their sponsors) regarded them as more reliable than they really were.

47. The Court therefore recognizes that, so far as the accomplishment of the formality of depositing an optional declaration is concerned, Nicaragua was placed in an exceptional position, since the international organs empowered to handle such declarations declared that the formality in question had been accomplished by Nicaragua. The Court finds that this exceptional situation cannot be without effect on the requirements obtaining as regards the formalities that are indispensable for the consent of a State to its compulsory jurisdiction to have been validly given. It considers therefore that, having regard to the origin and generality of the statements to the effect that Nicaragua was bound by its 1929 Declaration, it is right to conclude that the constant acquiescence of that State in those affirmations constitutes a valid mode of manifestation of its intent to recognize the compulsory jurisdiction of the Court under Article 36, paragraph 2, of the Statute, and that accordingly Nicaragua is, vis-à-vis the United States, a State accepting "the same obligation" under that Article.

48. The United States, however, further contends that even if Nicaragua is otherwise entitled to invoke against the United States the jurisdiction of the Court under Article 36, paragraphs 2 and 5, of the Statute, Nicaragua's conduct in relation to the United States over the course of many years estops Nicaragua from doing so. Having, it is argued, represented to the United States that it was not itself bound under the system of the Optional Clause, Nicaragua is estopped from invoking compulsory jurisdiction under that clause against the United States. The United States asserts that since 1943 Nicaragua has consistently represented to the United States of America that Nicaragua was not bound by the Optional Clause, and when the occasion arose that this was material to the United States diplomatic activities, the United States relied upon those Nicaraguan representations.

* * *

51. For the same reason, the Court does not need to deal at length with the contention based on estoppel. The Court has found that the conduct of Nicaragua, having regard to the very particular circumstances in which it was placed, was such as to evince its consent to be bound in such a way as to constitute a valid mode of acceptance of jurisdiction (paragraph 47, above). It is thus evident that the Court cannot regard the information obtained by the United States in 1943, or the doubts expressed in diplomatic contacts in 1955, as sufficient to overturn that conclusion, let alone to support an estoppel. Nicaragua's contention that since 1946 it has consistently maintained that it is subject to the jurisdiction of the Court, is supported by substantial evidence. Furthermore, as the Court pointed out in the North Sea Continental Shelf cases (*I.C.J. Reports 1969*, p. 26), estoppel may be inferred from the conduct, declarations and the like made by a State which not only clearly and consistently evinced acceptance by that State of a particular regime, but also had caused another State or States, in reliance on such conduct, detrimentally to change position or suffer some prejudice. The Court cannot regard Nicaragua's reliance on the optional clause as in any way contrary to good faith or equity: nor can Nicaragua be taken to come within the criterion of the North Sea Continental Shelf case, and the invocation of estoppel by the United States of America cannot be said to apply to it.

52. The acceptance of jurisdiction by the United States which is relied on by Nicaragua is, as noted above, that dated 14 August 1946. The United States contends however that

effect must also be given to the "1984 notification"—the declaration deposited with the Secretary-General of the United Nations on 6 April 1984. It is conceded by Nicaragua that if this declaration is effective as a modification or termination of the Declaration of 14 August 1946, and valid as against Nicaragua at the date of its filing of the Application instituting the present proceedings (9 April 1984), then the Court is without jurisdiction to entertain those proceedings, at least under Article 36, paragraphs 2 and 5, of the Statute. It is however contended by Nicaragua that the 1984 notification is ineffective because international law provides no basis for unilateral modification of declarations made under Article 36 of the Statute of the Court, unless a right to do so has been expressly reserved.

* * *

59. Declarations of acceptance of the compulsory jurisdiction of the Court are facultative, unilateral engagements, that States are absolutely free to make or not to make. In making the declaration a State is equally free either to do so unconditionally and without limit of time for its duration, or to qualify it with conditions or reservations. In particular, it may limit its effect to disputes arising after a certain date; or it may specify how long the declaration itself shall remain in force, or what notice (if any) will be required to terminate it. However, the unilateral nature of declarations does not signify that the State making the declaration is free to amend the scope and the contents of its solemn commitments as it pleases. In the *Nuclear Tests* cases the Court expressed its position on this point very clearly:

> "It is well recognized that declarations made by way of unilateral acts, concerning legal or factual situations, may have the effect of creating legal obligations. Declarations of this kind may be, and often are, very specific. When it is the intention of the State making the declaration that it should become bound according to its terms, that intention confers on the declaration the character of a legal undertaking, the State being thenceforth legally required to follow a course of conduct consistent with the declaration." (*I.C.J. Reports 1974*, p. 267, para. 43; p. 472, para. 46.)

60. In fact, the declarations, even though they are unilateral acts, establish a series of bilateral engagements with other States accepting the same obligation of compulsory jurisdiction, in which the conditions, reservations and time-limit clauses are taken into consideration. In the establishment of this network of engagements, which constitutes the Optional-Clause system, the principle of good faith plays an important role; the Court has emphasized the need in international relations for respect for good faith and confidence in particularly unambiguous terms, also in the *Nuclear Tests* cases:

> "One of the basic principles governing the creation and performance of legal obligations, whatever their source, is the principle of good faith. Trust and confidence are inherent in international co-operation, in particular in an age when this co-operation in many fields is becoming increasingly essential. Just as the very rule of *pacta sunt servanda* in the law of treaties is based on good faith, so also is the binding character of an international obligation assumed by unilateral declaration. Thus interested States may take cognizance of unilateral declarations and place confidence in them, and are entitled to require that the obligation thus created be respected." (*Ibid.*, p. 268, para. 46; p. 473, para. 49.)

61. The most important question relating to the effect of the 1984 notification is whether the United States was free to disregard the clause of six months' notice which, freely and by its own choice, it had appended to its 1946 Declaration. In so doing the United States entered into an obligation which is binding upon it vis-à-vis other States parties to

the Optional-Clause system. Although the United States retained the right to modify the contents of the 1946 Declaration or to terminate it, a power which is inherent in any unilateral act of a State, it has, nevertheless assumed an inescapable obligation towards other States accepting the Optional Clause, by stating formally and solemnly that any such change should take effect only after six months have elapsed as from the date of notice.

62. The United States has argued that the Nicaraguan 1929 Declaration, being of undefined duration, is liable to immediate termination, without previous notice, and that therefore Nicaragua has not accepted "the same obligation" as itself for the purposes of Article 36, paragraph 2, and consequently may not rely on the six months' notice proviso against the United States. The Court does not however consider that this argument entitles the United States validly to act in non-application of the time-limit proviso included in the 1946 Declaration. The notion of reciprocity is concerned with the scope and substance of the commitments entered into, including reservations, and not with the formal conditions of their creation, duration or extinction. It appears clearly that reciprocity cannot be invoked in order to excuse departure from the terms of a State's own declaration, whatever its scope, limitations or conditions. As the Court observed in the *Interhandel* case:

> "Reciprocity enables the State which has made the wider acceptance of the jurisdiction of the Court to rely upon the reservations to the acceptance laid down by the other party. There the effect of reciprocity ends. It cannot justify a State, in this instance, the United States, in relying upon a restriction which the other party, Switzerland, has not included in its own Declaration." (*I.C.J. Reports 1959*, p. 23.)

The maintenance in force of the United States Declaration for six months after notice of termination is a positive undertaking, flowing from the time-limit clause, but the Nicaraguan Declaration contains no express restriction at all. It is therefore clear that the United States is not in a position to invoke reciprocity as a basis for its action in making the 1984 notification which purported to modify the content of the 1946 Declaration. On the contrary it is Nicaragua that can invoke the six months' notice against the United States—not of course on the basis of reciprocity, but because it is an undertaking which is an integral part of the instrument that contains it.

63. Moreover, since the United States purported to act on 6 April 1984 in such a way as to modify its 1946 Declaration with sufficiently immediate effect to bar an Application filed on 9 April 1984, it would be necessary, if reciprocity is to be relied on, for the Nicaraguan Declaration to be terminable with immediate effect. But the right of immediate termination of declarations with indefinite duration is far from established. It appears from the requirements of good faith that they should be treated, by analogy, according to the law of treaties, which requires a reasonable time for withdrawal from or termination of treaties that contain no provision regarding the duration of their validity. Since Nicaragua has in fact not manifested any intention to withdraw its own declaration, the question of what reasonable period of notice would legally be required does not need to be further examined: it need only be observed that from 6 to 9 April would not amount to a "reasonable time."

64. The Court would also recall that in previous cases in which it has had to examine the reciprocal effect of declarations made under the Optional Clause, it has determined whether or not the "same obligation" was in existence at the moment of seising of the Court, by comparing the effect of the provisions, in particular the reservations, of the two declarations at that moment. The Court is not convinced that it would be appropri-

ate, or possible, to try to determine whether a State against which proceedings had not yet been instituted could rely on a provision in another State's declaration to terminate or modify its obligations before the Court was seised. The United States argument attributes to the concept of reciprocity, as embodied in Article 36 of the Statute, especially in paragraphs 2 and 3, a meaning that goes beyond the way in which it has been interpreted by the Court, according to its consistent jurisprudence. That jurisprudence supports the view that a determination of the existence of the "same obligation" requires the presence of two parties to a case, and a defined issue between them, which conditions can only be satisfied when proceedings have been instituted. In the case of Right of Passage over Indian Territory, the Court observed that

> "when a case is submitted to the Court, it is always possible to ascertain what are, at that moment, the reciprocal obligations of the Parties in accordance with their respective Declarations" (*I.C.J. Reports 1957*, p. 143).
>
> "It is not necessary that the 'same obligation' should be irrevocably defined at the time of the deposit of the Declaration of Acceptance for the entire period of its duration. That expression means no more than that, as between States adhering to the Optional Clause, each and all of them are bound by such identical obligations as may exist at any time during which the Acceptance is mutually binding." (*Ibid.*, p. 144.)

The coincidence or interrelation of those obligations thus remain in a state of flux until the moment of the filing of an application instituting proceedings. The Court has then to ascertain whether, at that moment, the two States accepted "the same obligation" in relation to the subject-matter of the proceedings; the possibility that, prior to that moment, the one enjoyed a wider right to modify its obligation than did the other, is without incidence on the question.

65. In sum, the six months' notice clause forms an important integral part of the United States Declaration and it is a condition that must be complied with in case of either termination or modification. Consequently, the 1984 notification, in the present case, cannot override the obligation of the United States to submit to the compulsory jurisdiction of the Court vis-à-vis Nicaragua, a State accepting the same obligation.

* * *

67. The question remains to be resolved whether the United States Declaration of 1946, though not suspended in its effects vis-à-vis Nicaragua by the 1984 notification, constitutes the necessary consent of the United States to the jurisdiction of the Court in the present case, taking into account the reservations which were attached to the declaration. Specifically, the United States has invoked proviso (c) to that declaration, which provides that the United States acceptance of the Court's compulsory jurisdiction shall not extend to

> "disputes arising under a multilateral treaty, unless (1) all parties to the treaty affected by the decision are also parties to the case before the Court, or (2) the United States of America specially agrees to jurisdiction."

* * *

73. It may first be noted that the multilateral treaty reservation could not bar adjudication by the Court of all Nicaragua's claims, because Nicaragua, in its Application, does not confine those claims only to violations of the four multilateral conventions referred to above (paragraph 68). On the contrary, Nicaragua invokes a number of principles of customary and general international law that, according to the Application, have been

violated by the United States. The Court cannot dismiss the claims of Nicaragua under principles of customary and general international law, simply because such principles have been enshrined in the texts of the conventions relied upon by Nicaragua. The fact that the abovementioned principles, recognized as such, have been codified or embodied in multilateral conventions does not mean that they cease to exist and to apply as principles of customary law, even as regards countries that are parties to such conventions. Principles such as those of the non-use of force, non-intervention, respect for the independence and territorial integrity of States, and the freedom of navigation, continue to be binding as part of customary international law, despite the operation of provisions of conventional law in which they have been incorporated. Therefore, since the claim before the Court in this case is not confined to violation of the multilateral conventional provisions invoked, it would not in any event be barred by the multilateral treaty reservation in the United States 1946 Declaration.

74. The Court would observe, further, that all three States have made declarations of acceptance of the compulsory jurisdiction of the Court, and are free, at any time, to come before the Court, on the basis of Article 36, paragraph 2, with an application instituting proceedings against Nicaragua—a State which is also bound by the compulsory jurisdiction of the Court by an unconditional declaration without limit of duration—,if they should find that they might be affected by the future decision of the Court. Moreover, these States are also free to resort to the incidental procedures of intervention under Articles 62 and 63 of the Statute, to the second of which El Salvador has already unsuccessfully resorted in the jurisdictional phase of the proceedings, but to which it may revert in the merits phase of the case. There is therefore no question of these States being defenceless against any consequences that may arise out of adjudication by the Court, or of their needing the protection of the multilateral treaty reservation of the United States.

75. The United States Declaration uses the word "affected," without making it clear who is to determine whether the States refered to are, or are not, affected. The States themselves would have the choice of either instituting proceedings or intervening for the protection of their interests, in so far as these are not already protected by Article 59 of the Statute. As for the Court, it is only when the general lines of the judgment to be given become clear that the States "affected" could be identified. By way of example we may take the hypothesis that if the Court were to decide to reject the Application of Nicaragua on the facts, there would be no third State's claim to be affected. Certainly the determination of the States "affected" could not be left to the parties but must be made by the Court.

76. At any rate, this is a question concerning matters of substance relating to the merits of the case: obviously the question of what States may be "affected" by the decision on the merits is not in itself a jurisdictional problem. The present phase of examination of jurisdictional questions was opened by the Court itself by its Order of 10 May 1984, not by a formal preliminary objection submitted by the United States; but it is appropriate to consider the grounds put forward by the United States for alleged lack of jurisdiction in the light of the procedural provisions for such objections. That being so, and since the procedural technique formerly available of joinder of preliminary objections to the merits has been done away with since the 1972 revision of the Rules of Court, the Court has no choice but to avail itself of Article 79, paragraph 7, of the present Rules of Court, and declare that the objection based on the multilateral treaty reservation of the United States Declaration of Acceptance does not possess, in the circumstances of the case, an exclusively preliminary character, and that consequently it does not constitute an obstacle for the Court to entertain the proceedings instituted by Nicaragua under the Application of 9 April 1984.

77. It is in view of this finding on the United States multilateral treaty reservation that the Court has to turn to the other ground of jurisdiction relied on by Nicaragua, even though it is *prima facie* narrower in scope than the jurisdiction deriving from the declarations of the two Parties under the Optional Clause. As noted in paragraphs 1 and 12 above, Nicaragua in its Application relies on the declarations of the Parties accepting the compulsory jurisdiction of the Court in order to found jurisdiction, but in its Memorial it invokes also a 1956 Treaty of Friendship, Commerce and Navigation between Nicaragua and the United States as a complementary foundation for the Court's jurisdiction. Since the multilateral treaty reservation obviously does not affect the jurisdiction of the Court under the 1956 Treaty, it is appropriate to ascertain the existence of such jurisdiction, limited as it is.

* * *

83. ... Accordingly, the Court finds that, to the extent that the claims in Nicaragua's Application constitute a dispute as to the interpretation or the application of the Articles of the Treaty of 1956 described in paragraph 82 above, the Court has jurisdiction under that Treaty to entertain such claims.

84. The Court now turns to the question of the admissibility of the Application of Nicaragua. The United States of America contended in its Counter-Memorial that Nicaragua's Application is inadmissible on five separate grounds, each of which, it is said, is sufficient to establish such inadmissibility, whether considered as a legal bar to adjudication or as "a matter requiring the exercise of prudential discretion in the interest of the integrity of the judicial function." Some of these grounds have in fact been presented in terms suggesting that they are matters of competence or jurisdiction rather than admissibility, but it does not appear to be of critical importance how they are classified in this respect. These grounds will now be examined; but for the sake of clarity it will first be convenient to recall briefly what are the allegations of Nicaragua upon which it bases its claims against the United States.

85. In its Application instituting proceedings, Nicaragua asserts that:

> "The United States of America is using military force against Nicaragua and intervening in Nicaragua's internal affairs, in violation of Nicaragua's sovereignty, territorial integrity and political independence and of the most fundamental and universally accepted principles of international law. The United States has created an 'army' of more than 10,000 mercenaries ... installed them in more than ten base camps in Honduras along the border with Nicaragua, trained them, paid them, supplied them with arms, ammunition, food and medical supplies, and directed their attacks against human and economic targets inside Nicaragua,"

and that Nicaragua has already suffered and is now suffering grievous consequences as a result of these activities. The purpose of these activities is claimed to be

> "to harass and destabilize the Government of Nicaragua so that ultimately it will be overthrown, or, at a minimum, compelled to change those of its domestic and foreign policies that displease the United States."

86. The first ground of inadmissibility relied on by the United States is that Nicaragua has failed to bring before the Court parties whose presence and participation is necessary for the rights of those parties to be protected and for the adjudication of the issues raised in the Application....

* * *

88. There is no doubt that in appropriate circumstances the Court will decline, as it did in the case concerning Monetary Gold Removed from Rome in 1943, to exercise the jurisdiction conferred upon it where the legal interests of a State not party to the proceedings "would not only be affected by a decision, but would form the very subject-matter of the decision" (*I.C.J. Reports 1954*, p. 32). Where however claims of a legal nature are made by an Applicant against a Respondent in proceedings before the Court, and made the subject of submissions, the Court has in principle merely to decide upon those submissions, with binding force for the parties only, and no other State, in accordance with Article 59 of the Statute. As the Court has already indicated (paragraph 74, above) other States which consider that they may be affected are free to institute separate proceedings, or to employ the procedure of intervention....

89. Secondly, the United States regards the Application as inadmissible because each of Nicaragua's allegations constitutes no more than a reformulation and restatement of a single fundamental claim, that the United States is engaged in an unlawful use of armed force, or breach of the peace, or acts of aggression against Nicaragua, a matter which is committed by the Charter and by practice to the competence of other organs, in particular the United Nations Security Council. All allegations of this kind are confided to the political organs of the Organization for consideration and determination; the United States quotes Article 24 of the Charter, which confers upon the Security Council "primary responsibility for the maintenance of international peace and security." The provisions of the Charter dealing with the ongoing use of armed force contain no recognition of the possibility of settlement by judicial, as opposed to political, means. Under Article 52 of the Charter there is also a commitment of responsibility for the maintenance of international peace and security to regional agencies and arrangements, and in the view of the United States the Contadora process is precisely the sort of regional arrangement or agency that Article 52 contemplates.

* * *

91. It will be convenient to deal with this alleged ground of inadmissibility together with the third ground advanced by the United States namely that the Court should hold the Application of Nicaragua to be inadmissible in view of the subject-matter of the Application and the position of the Court within the United Nations system, including the impact of proceedings before the Court on the ongoing exercise of the "inherent right of individual or collective self-defence" under Article 51 of the Charter. This is, it is argued, a reason why the Court may not properly exercise "subject-matter jurisdiction" over Nicaragua's claims. Under this head, the United States repeats its contention that the Nicaraguan Application requires the Court to determine that the activities complained of constitute a threat to the peace, a breach of the peace, or an act of aggression, and proceeds to demonstrate that the political organs of the United Nations, to which such matters are entrusted by the Charter, have acted, and are acting, in respect of virtually identical claims placed before them by Nicaragua. The United States points to the approach made by Nicaragua to the Security Council on 4 April 1984, a few days before the institution of the present proceedings: the draft resolution then presented, corresponding to the claims submitted by Nicaragua to the Court, failed to achieve the requisite majority under Article 27, paragraph 3, of the Charter. However, this fact, it is argued, and the perceived likelihood that similar claims in future would fail to secure the required majority, does not vest the Court with subject-matter jurisdiction over the Application. Since Nicaragua's Application in effect asks the Court for a judgment in all material respects identical to the decision which the Security Council did not take, it amounts to an appeal to the Court from an adverse consideration in the Security Council. Furthermore, in order to reach a

determination on what amounts to a claim of aggression the Court would have to decide whether the actions of the United States, and the other States not before the Court, are or are not unlawful: more specifically, it would have to decide on the application of Article 51 of the Charter, concerning the right of self-defence. Any such action by the Court cannot be reconciled with the terms of Article 51, which provides a role in such matters only for the Security Council. Nor would it be only in case of a decision by the Court that the inherent right of self-defence would be impaired: the fact that such claims are being subjected to judicial examination in the midst of the conflict that gives rise to them may alone be sufficient to constitute such impairment.

* * *

93. The United States is thus arguing that the matter was essentially one for the Security Council since it concerned a complaint by Nicaragua involving the use of force. However, having regard to the *United States Diplomatic and Consular Staff in Tehran* case, the Court is of the view that the fact that a matter is before the Security Council should not prevent it being dealt with by the Court and that both proceedings could be pursued *pari passu.*

* * *

96. It must also be remembered that, as the *Corfu Channel* case (*I.C.J. Reports 1949*, p. 4) shows, the Court has never shied away from a case brought before it merely because it had political implications or because it involved serious elements of the use of force. The Court was concerned with a question of a "demonstration of force" (cf. loc. cit., p. 31) or "violation of a country's sovereignty" (*ibid.*); the Court, indeed, found that

> "Intervention is perhaps still less admissible in the particular form it would take here; for, from the nature of things, it would be reserved for the most powerful States, and might easily lead to perverting the administration of international justice itself." (*Ibid.*, p. 35.)

What is also significant is that the Security Council itself in that case had "undoubtedly intended that the whole dispute should be decided by the Court" (p. 26).

97. It is relevant also to observe that while the United States is arguing today that because of the alleged ongoing armed conflict between the two States the matter could not be brought to the International Court of Justice but should be referred to the Security Council, in the 1950s the United States brought seven cases to the Court involving armed attacks by military aircraft of other States against United States military aircraft; the only reason the cases were not dealt with by the Court was that each of the Respondent States indicated that it had not accepted the jurisdiction of the Court, and was not willing to do so for the purposes of the case. The United States did not contradict Nicaragua's argument that the United States indeed brought these suits against the Respondents in this Court, rather than in the Security Council. It has argued further that in both the Corfu Channel case and the *Aerial Incident* cases, the Court was asked to adjudicate the rights and duties of the parties with respect to a matter that was fully in the past. To a considerable extent this is a question relevant to the fourth ground of inadmissibility advanced by the United States, to be examined below. However the United States also contends that the *Corfu Channel* case, at least, shows that it was the fact that the incident in question was not part of an ongoing use of armed force that led the Security Council to conclude that its competence was not engaged. In the view of the Court, this argument is not relevant.

98. Nor can the Court accept that the present proceedings are objectionable as being in effect an appeal to the Court from an adverse decision of the Security Council. The Court

is not asked to say that the Security Council was wrong in its decision, nor that there was anything inconsistent with law in the way in which the members of the Council employed their right to vote. The Court is asked to pass judgment on certain legal aspects of a situation which has also been considered by the Security Council, a procedure which is entirely consonant with its position as the principal judicial organ of the United Nations. As to the inherent right of self-defence, the fact that it is referred to in the Charter as a "right" is indicative of a legal dimension; if in the present proceedings it becomes necessary for the Court to judge in this respect between the Parties—for the rights of no other State may be adjudicated in these proceedings—it cannot be debarred from doing so by the existence of a procedure for the States concerned to report to the Security Council in this connection.

99. The fourth ground of inadmissibility put forward by the United States is that the Application should be held inadmissible in consideration of the inability of the judicial function to deal with situations involving ongoing conflict. The allegation, attributed by the United States to Nicaragua, of an ongoing conflict involving the use of armed force contrary to the Charter is said to be central to, and inseparable from, the Application as a whole, and is one with which a court cannot deal effectively without overstepping proper judicial bounds. The resort to force during ongoing armed conflict lacks the attributes necessary for the application of the judicial process, namely a pattern of legally relevant facts discernible by the means available to the adjudicating tribunal, establishable in conformity with applicable norms of evidence and proof, and not subject to further material evolution during the course of, or subsequent to, the judicial proceedings.... The United States does not argue that the Application must be dismissed because it presents a "political" question rather than a "legal" question, but rather that an allegation of an ongoing use of unlawful armed force was never intended by the drafters of the Charter to be encompassed by Article 36, paragraph 2, of the Statute. It is also recalled that the circumstances alleged in the Application involve the activities of 'groups indigenous to Nicaragua' that have their own motivations and are beyond the control of any State. The United States emphasizes, however, that to conclude that the Court cannot adjudicate the merits of the complaints alleged does not require the conclusion that international law is neither directly relevant nor of fundamental importance in the settlement of international disputes, but merely that in this respect the application of international legal principles is the responsibility of other organs set up under the Charter.

* * *

101. The Court is bound to observe that any judgment on the merits in the present case will be limited to upholding such submissions of the Parties as have been supported by sufficient proof of relevant facts, and are regarded by the Court as sound in law. A situation of armed conflict is not the only one in which evidence of fact may be difficult to come by, and the Court has in the past recognized and made allowance for this (*Corfu Channel, I.C.J. Reports 1949*, p. 18; *United States Diplomatic and Consular Staff in Tehran, I.C.J. Reports 1980*, p. 10, para. 13). Ultimately, however, it is the litigant seeking to establish a fact who bears the burden of proving it; and in cases where evidence may not be forthcoming, a submission may in the judgment be rejected as unproved, but is not to be ruled out as inadmissible *in limine* on the basis of an anticipated lack of proof. As to the possibility of implementation of the judgment, the Court will have to assess this question also on the basis of each specific submission, and in the light of the facts as then established; it cannot at this stage rule out a priori any judicial contribution to the settlement of the dispute by declaring the Application inadmissible. It should be observed however that the Court "neither can nor should contemplate the contingency of the judgment not

being complied with" (*Factory at Chorzów, P.C.I.J., Series A, No. 17*, p. 63). Both the Parties have undertaken to comply with the decisions of the Court, under Article 94 of the Charter; and

> "Once the Court has found that a State has entered into a commitment concerning its future conduct it is not the Court's function to contemplate that it will not comply with it." (*Nuclear Tests, I.C.J. Reports 1974*, p. 272, para. 60; p. 477, para. 63.)

102. The fifth and final contention of the United States under this head is that the Application should be held inadmissible because Nicaragua has failed to exhaust the established processes for the resolution of the conflicts occurring in Central America. In the contention of the United States, the Contadora process, to which Nicaragua is party, is recognized both by the political organs of the United Nations and by the Organization of American States, as the appropriate method for the resolution of the issues of Central America....

* * *

105. On this latter point, the Court would recall that in the United States Diplomatic and Consular Staff in Tehran case it stated:

> "The Court, at the same time, pointed out that no provision of the Statute or Rules contemplates that the Court should decline to take cognizance of one aspect of a dispute merely because that dispute has other aspects, however important." (*I.C.J. Reports 1980*, p. 19, para. 36.)

And, a little later, added:

> "Yet never has the view been put forward before that, because a legal dispute submitted to the Court is only one aspect of a political dispute, the Court should decline to resolve for the parties the legal questions at issue between them. Nor can any basis for such a view of the Court's functions or jurisdiction be found in the Charter or the Statute of the Court; if the Court were, contrary to its settled jurisprudence, to adopt such a view, it would impose a far-reaching and unwarranted restriction upon the role of the Court in the peaceful solution of international disputes." (*I.C.J. Reports 1980*, p. 20, para. 37.)

106. With regard to the contention of the United States of America that the matter raised in the Nicaraguan Application was part of the Contadora Process, the Court considers that even the existence of active negotiations in which both parties might be involved should not prevent both the Security Council and the Court from exercising their separate functions under the Charter and the Statute of the Court....

107. The Court does not consider that the Contadora process, whatever its merits, can properly be regarded as a "regional arrangement" for the purposes of Chapter VIII of the Charter of the United Nations. Furthermore, it is also important always to bear in mind that all regional, bilateral, and even multilateral, arrangements that the Parties to this case may have made, touching on the issue of settlement of disputes or the jurisdiction of the International Court of Justice, must be made always subject to the provisions of Article 103 of the Charter which reads as follows:

> "In the event of a conflict between the obligations of the Members of the United Nations under the present Charter and their obligations under any other international agreement, their obligations under the present Charter shall prevail."

108. In the light of the foregoing, the Court is unable to accept either that there is any requirement of prior exhaustion of regional negotiating processes as a precondition to seising the Court; or that the existence of the Contadora process constitutes in this case

an obstacle to the examination by the Court of the Nicaraguan Application and judicial determination in due course of the submissions of the Parties in the case. The Court is therefore unable to declare the Application inadmissible, as requested by the United States, on any of the grounds it has advanced as requiring such a finding.

* * *

113. For these reasons,

THE COURT,

(1)

(a) *finds*, by eleven votes to five, that it has jurisdiction to entertain the Application filed by the Republic of Nicaragua on 9 April 1984, on the basis of Article 36, paragraphs 2 and 5, of the Statute of the Court;

IN FAVOUR: *President* Elias; *Vice-President* Sette-Camara; *Judges* Lachs, Morozov, Nagendra Singh, Ruda, El-Khani, de Lacharriere, Mbaye, Bedjaoui; *Judge* ad hoc Colliard;

(AGAINST): *Judges* Mosler, Oda, Ago, Schwebel and Sir Robert Jennings.

(b) *finds*, by fourteen votes to two, that it has jurisdiction to entertain the Application filed by the Republic of Nicaragua on 9 April 1984, in so far as that Application relates to a dispute concerning the interpretation or application of the Treaty of Friendship, Commerce and Navigation between the United States of America and the Republic of Nicaragua signed at Managua on 21 January 1956, on the basis of Article XXIV of that Treaty;

IN FAVOUR; *President* Elias; *Vice-President* Sette-Camara; *Judges* Lachs, Morozov, Nagendra Singh, Mosler, Oda, Ago, El-Khani, Sir Robert Jennings, de Lacharriere, Mbaye, Bedjaoui; *Judge* ad hoc Colliard;

AGAINST: *Judges* Ruda and Schwebel.

(c) *finds*, by fifteen votes to one, that it has jurisdiction to entertain the case;

IN FAVOUR: *President* Elias; *Vice-President* Sette-Camara; *Judges* Lachs, Morozov, Nagendra Singh, Ruda, Mosler, Oda, Ago, El-Khani, Sir Robert Jennings, de Lacharriere, Mbaye, Bedjaoui; *Judge* ad hoc Colliard;

AGAINST: *Judge* Schwebel.

(2) *finds*, unanimously, that the said Application is admissible.

Done in English and in French, the English text being authoritative, at the Peace Palace, The Hague, this twenty-sixth day of November, one thousand nine hundred and eighty-four, in three copies, one of which will be placed in the archives of the Court and the others will be transmitted to the Government of Nicaragua and to the Government of the United States of America, respectively.

(*Signed*) Taslim O. ELIAS,
President.

(*Signed*) Santiago TORRES BERNÁRDEZ,
Registrar.

Judges NAGENDRA SINGH, RUDA, MOSLER, ODA, AGO and Sir Robert JENNINGS append separate opinions to the Judgment of the Court.

Judge SCHWEBEL appends a dissenting opinion to the Judgment of the Court.

(*Initialled*) T.O.E.

(*Initialled*) S.T.B.

Notes and Questions on Jurisdiction and Admissibility

1. Describe the difference between jurisdiction and admissibility.

2. Having argued in favor of jurisdiction in the *Iran Hostages Case*, do you believe it was inappropriate for the U.S. to argue against jurisdiction in the *Nicaragua Case*? Or at least with regard to some of the arguments? Or is it always appropriate for any litigant to make all colorable arguments? The U.S. withdrew from the ICJ's compulsory jurisdiction as a result of the *Nicaragua Case*. Would it have been wiser for the ICJ to avoid finding jurisdiction to keep the U.S. committed to compulsory jurisdiction? See a discussion of this and other issues surrounding the *Nicaragua Case* and U.S. relations to the ICJ in The International Court of Justice at a Crossroads (Lori F. Damrosch ed. 1987). Ironically, the U.S. has participated in far more cases at the ICJ in the fifteen years after withdrawing from compulsory jurisdiction than in the fifteen years before.

3. In 2005, U.S. Secretary of State Condoleeza Rice withdrew the U.S. acceptance of the Protocol to the Vienna Convention on Consular Relations providing for ICJ jurisdiction over disputes under the Convention. A number of years after the *Hostage Case*, the U.S. was brought to the ICJ by Paraguay, Germany, and Mexico in disputes under the Convention. These cases are discussed further in Chapter 15.

In October 2009, the chairs of the Human Rights Committee of the American Branch of the International Law Association sent a letter to Harold Koh, Legal Adviser to the State Department to urge action in several international law issue areas including that the U.S.:

> *Recommit to the Optional Protocol to the Vienna Convention on Consular Relations.*
>
> The United States, as you know, deployed the Optional Protocol to great effect in 1979, bringing a claim against the Government of Iran following its detention of Americans at the U.S. Embassy. The claim helped mobilize international opinion against the outrageous behavior of the Iranian Government. Yet in the wake of several cases brought under the Protocol against the United States, the previous administration withdrew from the Optional Protocol, stating the following:
>
>> ... we will continue to live up to our obligations under the Vienna Convention. We will continue to believe in the importance of consular notification. But this particular optional protocol was in our federal system being interpreted in ways that we thought were inappropriate for a system in which there is a jurisdictional issue between the federal government and the states. And that's really what this is about.
>
> *See Briefing En Route to Mexico*, Secretary Condoleezza Rice, Mexico City, Mexico, Mar. 10, 2005.
>
> The federalism excuse should be seen as a hurdle to overcome rather than a solid barrier that precludes U.S. participation. And it is solvable through concerted federal action to educate local law enforcement officials, as the previous administration wisely did. Fair or not, the withdrawal has been seen as part of a broader rejection by the United States of international treatymaking. At the same time, the withdrawal reduces the levers for the United States when dealing with future hostile entities that wish to detain and possibly abuse American citizens. Re-

> turning to the Protocol would be a mark of American leadership, likely encouraging others to join and thus expanding the U.S. ability to defend Americans abroad.

Letter from American Branch of International Law Association to Harold Koh (Oct. 19, 2009) *available at* http://ila-americanbranch.org/reports/2009-10-19_ABILA_Ltr_to_Koh.pdf. As of July 2011, no steps had been taken to rejoin the protocol.

4. Think of issues on which courts cannot or should not make decisions. Were any of these issues present in the two cases summarized in this chapter?

5. Refer to the jurisdiction and admissibility provisions of the Rome Statute of the International Criminal Court found in the Annex. Do those provisions represent progressive development of international adjudication compared with the comparable provisions of the ICJ or ITLOS? (Also included in the Annex.) Before developing a court for individual criminal responsibility, should international lawyers and pro-law NGOs have used their energies to press for broader ICJ jurisdiction, especially wider compulsory jurisdiction?

6. In the 1960s, Liberia and Ethiopia brought a case against South Africa to the ICJ, arguing that South Africa was in breach of its obligations as the Mandatory or Trustee of South West Africa, today Namibia. In 1962, the ICJ held that the Mandate was still in effect and that Liberia's and Ethiopia's claims were justiciable. During the merits phase, however, the ICJ reversed itself, finding that Ethiopia and Liberia lacked a legal interest in the case, which the Court then dismissed. This case generated great criticism against the Court. It was seen as a decision made more on political than legal grounds, favoring a more powerful state. This view of the Court was not finally put aside until the *Nicaragua Case* where the Court viewed Nicaragua's arguments for jurisdiction generously and ultimately handed a small state a major victory against a powerful one.

Following the *Nicaragua Case*, the ICJ enjoyed new popularity. Indeed, the Court has had record numbers of cases on its dockets since that time. In late 2004 and early 2005, however, the Court ruled against jurisdiction on questionable grounds, both cases brought by much smaller states against far more powerful ones. In 2004, in a case brought by Serbia against eight members of NATO, the ICJ found that Serbia was not a state party to the ICJ Statute at the time the case was brought. This was a startling outcome given that the Court had another case on its docket brought by Bosnia against Serbia, alleging genocide and the ICJ had found Serbia was a party to the Statute. *Application of the Convention on the Prevention and Punishment of the Crime of Genocide* (Bosnia v. Serbia) 1996 I.C.J. 595 (July 11).

Just two months later, the ICJ dismissed a case brought by Liechtenstein against Germany on a narrow reading of its jurisdiction. Liechtenstein argued that Prince Hans Adam II had been denied justice before the German courts in 1991 when the courts refused to hear his claim to ownership of a painting held by the Czech Republic that was on loan to an art gallery in Cologne, Germany. Liechtenstein founded ICJ jurisdiction on the European Convention for the Peaceful Settlement of disputes, which allowed it to bring cases arising after 1980 to the ICJ. The ICJ, however, found the facts of the dispute arose in the 1940s and refused to grant jurisdiction on the basis *ratione temporis*. *Certain Property* (Liecht. v. F.R.G.) 2001 I.C.J. 565 (June 28). (This case, too, is discussed further below.)

It remains to be seen how states will react to these decisions, but it appears fair to say that they do not comport with the goal of expanding the jurisdiction of the ICJ mentioned by Judge Elias in the *Nicaragua Case*.

Chapter Eleven

Provisional Measures

Introduction

After jurisdiction and admissibility, the procedural issues that most commonly confront the ICJ relate to provisional measures orders and intervention. We have seen provisional measures before in our consideration of arbitration. The ICJ Statute explicitly grants the Court the authority to order provisional measures:

Article 41

1. The Court shall have the power to indicate, if it considers that circumstances so require, any provisional measures which ought to be taken to preserve the respective rights of either party.

2. Pending the final decision, notice of the measures suggested shall forthwith be given to the parties and to the Security Council.

Until the *LaGrand* case, scholars debated whether provisional measures orders were binding. After *LaGrand* we know that they are, but, ensuring respect for such orders has proven far more challenging than in the case of final orders and judgments as seen in the *Request for Interpretation* case brought by Mexico against the United States. The first excerpt is from a case brought by the United States against Iran. It demonstrates the importance of provisional measures.

United States Diplomatic and Consular Staff in Tehran (*United States of America v. Iran*)

1979 ICJ 7 (Order of Dec. 15)

Request for the Indication of Provisional Measures

Having regard to the Application by the United States of America filed in the Registry of the Court on 29 November 1979, instituting proceedings against the Islamic Republic of Iran in respect of a dispute concerning the situation in the United States Embassy in Tehran and the seizure and holding as hostages of members of the United States diplomatic and consular staff in Iran;

1. Whereas in the above-mentioned Application the United States Government invokes jurisdictional provisions in certain treaties as bases for the Court's jurisdiction in the present case; whereas it further recounts a sequence of events, beginning on 4 November 1979 in and around the United States Embassy in Tehran and involving the invasion of the Embassy premises, the seizure of United States diplomatic and consular staff and their

continued detention; and whereas, on the basis of the facts there alleged, it requests the Court to adjudge and declare:

(a) That the Government of Iran, in tolerating, encouraging, and failing to prevent and punish the conduct described in the preceding Statement of Facts [in the Application], violated its international legal obligations to the United States as provided by

—Articles 22, 24, 25, 27, 29, 31, 37 and 47 of the Vienna Convention on Diplomatic Relations,

—Articles 28, 31, 33, 34, 36 and 40 of the Vienna Convention on Consular Relations,

—Articles 4 and 7 of the Convention on the Prevention and Punishment of Crimes against Internationally Protected Persons, including Diplomatic Agents, and

—Articles II (4), XIII, XVIII and XIX of the Treaty of Amity, Economic Relations, and Consular Rights between the United States and Iran, and

—Articles 2 (3), 2 (4) and 33 of the Charter of the United Nations;

(b) That pursuant to the foregoing international legal obligations, the Government of Iran is under a particular obligation immediately to secure the release of all United States nationals currently being detained within the premises of the United States Embassy in Tehran and to assure that all such persons and all other United States nationals in Tehran are allowed to leave Iran safely;

(c) That the Government of Iran shall pay to the United States, in its own right and in the exercise of its right of diplomatic protection of its nationals, reparation for the foregoing violations of Iran's international legal obligations to the United States, in a sum to be determined by the Court; and

(d) That the Government of Iran submit to its competent authorities for the purpose of prosecution those persons responsible for the crimes committed against the premises and staff of the United States Embassy and against the premises of its Consulates';

2. Having regard to the request dated 29 November 1979 and filed in the Registry the same day, whereby the Government of the United States of America, relying on Article 41 of the Statute and Articles 73, 74 and 75 of the Rules of Court, asks the Court urgently to indicate, pending the final decision in the case brought before it by the above-mentioned Application of the same date, the following provisional measures:

(a) That the Government of Iran immediately release all hostages of United States nationality and facilitate the prompt and safe departure from Iran of these persons and all other United States officials in dignified and humane circumstances.

(b) That the Government of Iran immediately clear the premises of the United States Embassy, Chancery and Consulate of all persons whose presence is not authorized by the United States Charge d'Affaires in Iran, and restore the premises to United States control.

(c) That the Government of Iran ensure that all persons attached to the United States Embassy and Consulate should be accorded, and protected in, full freedom within the Embassy and Chancery premises, and the freedom of movement within Iran necessary to carry out their diplomatic and consular functions.

(d) That the Government of Iran not place on trial any person attached to the Embassy and Consulate of the United States and refrain from any action to implement any such trial.

(e) That the Government of Iran ensure that no action is taken which might prejudice the rights of the United States in respect of the carrying out of any decision which the Court may render on the merits, and in particular neither take nor permit action that would threaten the lives, safety, or well-being of the hostages;

* * *

8. Whereas on 9 December 1979 a letter, dated the same day and transmitted by telegram, was received from the Minister for Foreign Affairs of Iran, which reads as follows:

[Translation from French]

I have the honour to acknowledge receipt of the telegrams concerning the meeting of the International Court of Justice on 10 December 1979, at the request of the Government of the United States of America, and to submit to you below the position of the Government of the Islamic Republic of Iran in this respect.

1. First of all, the Government of the Islamic Republic of Iran wishes to express its respect for the International Court of Justice, and for its distinguished members, for what they have achieved in the quest for just and equitable solutions to legal conflicts between States. However, the Government of the Islamic Republic of Iran considers that the Court cannot and should not take cognizance of the case which the Government of the United States of America has submitted to it, and in a most significant fashion, a case confined to what is called the question of the "hostages of the American Embassy in Tehran."

2. For this question only represents a marginal and secondary aspect of an overall problem, one such that it cannot be studied separately, and which involves, *inter alia*, more than 25 years of continual interference by the United States in the internal affairs of Iran, the shameless exploitation of our country, and numerous crimes perpetrated against the Iranian people, contrary to and in conflict with all international and humanitarian norms.

3. The problem involved in the conflict between Iran and the United States is thus not one of the interpretation and the application of the treaties upon which the American Application is based, but results from an overall situation containing much more fundamental and more complex elements. Consequently, the Court cannot examine the American Application divorced from its proper context, namely the whole political dossier of the relations between Iran and the United States over the last 25 years. This dossier includes, *inter alia*, all the crimes perpetrated in Iran by the American Government, in particular the *coup d'état* of 1953 stirred up and carried out by the CIA, the overthrow of the lawful national government of Dr. Mossadegh, the restoration of the Shah and of his regime which was under the control of American interests, and all the social, economic, cultural, and political consequences of the direct interventions in our internal affairs, as well as grave, flagrant and continuous violations of all international norms, committed by the United States in Iran.

4. With regard to the request for provisional measures, as formulated by the United States, it in fact implies that the Court should have passed judgment on the actual substance of the case submitted to it, which the Court cannot do without breach of the norms governing its jurisdiction. Furthermore, since provisional mea-

sures are by definition intended to protect the interests of the parties, they cannot be unilateral, as they are in the request submitted by the American Government.

In conclusion, the Government of the Islamic Republic of Iran respectfully draws the attention of the Court to the deep-rootedness and the essential character of the Islamic revolution of Iran, a revolution of a whole oppressed nation against its oppressors and their masters; any examination of the numerous repercussions thereof is a matter essentially and directly within the national sovereignty of Iran;

* * *

13. Noting that the Government of Iran was not represented at the hearing; and whereas the non-appearance of one of the States concerned cannot by itself constitute an obstacle to the indication of provisional measures;

14. Whereas the treaty provisions on which, in its Application and oral observations, the United States Government claims to found the jurisdiction of the Court to entertain the present case are the following:

(i) the Vienna Convention on Diplomatic Relations of 1961, and Article I of its accompanying Optional Protocol concerning the Compulsory Settlement of Disputes;

(ii) the Vienna Convention on Consular Relations of 1963, and Article I of its accompanying Optional Protocol concerning the Compulsory Settlement of Disputes;

(iii) Article XXI, paragraph 2, of the Treaty of Amity, Economic Relations, and Consular Rights of 1955 between the United States of America and Iran; and

(iv) Article 13, paragraph 1, of the Convention of 1973 on the Prevention and Punishment of Crimes against Internationally Protected Persons, including Diplomatic Agents;

* * *

18. Whereas, accordingly, it is manifest from the information before the Court and from the terms of Article I of each of the two Protocols that the provisions of these Articles furnish a basis on which the jurisdiction of the Court might be founded with regard to the claims of the United States under the Vienna Conventions of 1961 and 1963;

* * *

21. Whereas, therefore, the Court does not find it necessary for present purposes to enter into the question whether a basis for the exercise of its powers under Article 41 of the Statute might also be found under Article XXI, paragraph 2, of the Treaty of Amity, Economic Relations, and Consular Rights of 1955, and Article 13, paragraph 1, of the Convention on the Prevention and Punishment of Crimes against Internationally Protected Persons, including Diplomatic Agents, of 1973.

22. Whereas, on the other hand, in the above-mentioned letter of 9 December 1979 the Government of Iran maintains that the Court cannot and should not take cognizance of the present case, for the reason that the question of the hostages forms only 'a marginal and secondary aspect of an overall problem' involving the activities of the United States in Iran over a period of more than 25 years; and whereas it further maintains that any examination of the numerous repercussions of the Islamic revolution of Iran is essentially and directly a matter within the national sovereignty of Iran;

23. Whereas, however important, and however connected with the present case, the iniquities attributed to the United States Government by the Government of Iran in that

letter may appear to be to the latter Government, the seizure of the United States Embassy and Consulates and the detention of internationally protected persons as hostages cannot, in the view of the Court, be regarded as something "secondary" or "marginal," having regard to the importance of the legal principles involved; whereas the Court notes in this regard that the Secretary-General of the United Nations has indeed referred to these occurrences as 'a grave situation' posing 'a serious threat to international peace and security' and that the Security Council in resolution 457 (1979) expressed itself as deeply concerned at the dangerous level of tension between the two States, which could have grave consequences for international peace and security;

24. Whereas, moreover, if the Iranian Government considers the alleged activities of the United States in Iran legally to have a close connection with the subject-matter of the United States Application, it remains open to that Government under the Court's Statute and Rules to present its own arguments to the Court regarding those activities either by way of defence in a Counter-Memorial or by way of a counter-claim filed under Article 80 of the Rules of Court; whereas, therefore, by not appearing in the present proceedings, the Government of Iran, by its own choice, deprives itself of the opportunity of developing its own arguments before the Court and of itself filing a request for the indication of provisional measures; and whereas no provision of the Statute or Rules contemplates that the Court should decline to take cognizance of one aspect of a dispute merely because that dispute has other aspects, however important;

25. Whereas it is no doubt true that the Islamic revolution of Iran is a matter "essentially and directly within the national sovereignty of Iran;" whereas however a dispute which concerns diplomatic and consular premises and the detention of internationally protected persons, and involves the interpretation or application of multilateral conventions codifying the international law governing diplomatic and consular relations, is one which by its very nature falls within international jurisdiction;

26. Whereas accordingly the two considerations advanced by the Government of Iran in its letter of 9 December 1979 cannot, in the view of the Court, be accepted as constituting any obstacle to the Court's taking cognizance of the case brought before it by the United States Application of 29 November 1979;

27. Whereas in that same letter of 9 December 1979 the Government of Iran also puts forward two considerations on the basis of which it contends that the Court ought not, in any event, to accede to the United States request for provisional measures in the present case;

28. Whereas, in the first place, it maintains that the request for provisional measures, as formulated by the United States, "in fact implies that the Court should have passed judgment on the actual substance of the case submitted to it;" whereas it is true that in the *Factory at Chorzów* case the Permanent Court of International Justice declined to indicate interim measures of protection on the ground that the request in that case was "designed to obtain an interim judgment in favour of a part of the claim" (*Order of 21 November 1927, P.C.I.J., Series A, No. 12,* at p. 10); whereas, however, the circumstances of that case were entirely different from those of the present one, and the request there sought to obtain from the Court a final judgment on part of a claim for a sum of money; whereas, moreover, a request for provisional measures must by its very nature relate to the substance of the case since, as Article 41 expressly states, their object is to preserve the respective rights of either party; and whereas in the present case the purpose of the United States request appears to be not to obtain a judgment, interim or final, on the merits of its claims but to preserve the substance of the rights which it claims *pendente lite*;

* * *

33. Whereas by the terms of Article 41 of the Statute the Court may indicate such measures only when it considers that circumstances so require in order to preserve the rights of either party;

34. Whereas the circumstances alleged by the United States Government which, in the submission of that Government, require the indication of provisional measures in the present case may be summarized as follows:

(i) On 4 November 1979, in the course of a demonstration outside the United States Embassy compound in Tehran, demonstrators attacked the Embassy premises; no Iranian security forces intervened or were sent to relieve the situation, despite repeated calls for help from the Embassy to the Iranian authorities. Ultimately the whole of the Embassy premises was invaded. The Embassy personnel, including consular and non-American staff, and visitors who were present in the Embassy at the time were seized. Shortly afterwards, according to the United States Government, its consulates in Tabriz and Shiraz, which had been attacked earlier in 1979, were also seized, without any action being taken to prevent it.

(ii) Since that time, the premises of the United States Embassy in Tehran, and of the consulates in Tabriz and Shiraz, have remained in the hands of the persons who seized them. These persons have ransacked the archives and documents both of the diplomatic mission and of its consular section. The Embassy personnel and other persons seized at the time of the attack have been held hostage with the exception of 13 persons released on 18 and 20 November 1979. Those holding the hostages have refused to release them, save on condition of the fulfilment by the United States of various demands regarded by it as unacceptable. The hostages are stated to have frequently been bound, blindfolded, and subjected to severe discomfort, complete isolation and threats that they would be put on trial or even put to death. The United States Government affirms that it has reason to believe that some of them may have been transferred to other places of confinement.

(iii) The Government of the United States considers that not merely has the Iranian Government failed to prevent the events described above, but also that there is clear evidence of its complicity in, and approval of, those events.

(iv) The persons held hostage in the premises of the United States Embassy in Tehran include, according to the information furnished to the Court by the Agent of the United States, at least 28 persons having the status, duly recognized by the Government of Iran, of 'member of the diplomatic staff' within the meaning of the Vienna Convention on Diplomatic Relations of 1961; at least 20 persons having the status, similarly recognized, of "member of the administrative and technical staff" within the meaning of that Convention; and two other persons of United States nationality not possessing either diplomatic or consular status. Of the persons with the status of member of the diplomatic staff, four are members of the Consular Section of the Embassy.

(v) In addition to the persons held hostage in the premises of the Tehran Embassy, the United States Chargé d'Affaires in Iran and two other United States diplomatic agents are detained in the premises of the Iranian Ministry of Foreign Affairs, in circumstances which the Government of the United States has not been able to make entirely clear, but which apparently involve restriction of their freedom of movement, and a threat to their inviolability as diplomats;

38. Whereas there is no more fundamental prerequisite for the conduct of relations between States than the inviolability of diplomatic envoys and embassies, so that throughout history nations of all creeds and cultures have observed reciprocal obligations for that purpose; and whereas the obligations thus assumed, notably those for assuring the personal safety of diplomats and their freedom from prosecution, are essential, unqualified, and inherent in their representative character and their diplomatic function;

39. Whereas the institution of diplomacy, with its concomitant privileges and immunities, has withstood the test of centuries and proved to be an instrument essential for effective co-operation in the international community, and for enabling States, irrespective of their differing constitutional and social systems, to achieve mutual understanding and to resolve their differences by peaceful means;

40. Whereas the unimpeded conduct of consular relations, which have also been established between peoples since ancient times, is no less important in the context of present-day international law, in promoting the development of friendly relations among nations, and ensuring protection and assistance for aliens resident in the territories of other States; and whereas therefore the privileges and immunities of consular officers and consular employees, and the inviolability of consular premises and archives, are similarly principles deep-rooted in international law;

41. Whereas, while no State is under any obligation to maintain diplomatic or consular relations with another, yet it cannot fail to recognize the imperative obligations inherent therein, now codified in the Vienna Conventions of 1961 and 1963, to which both Iran and the United States are parties;

42. Whereas continuance of the situation the subject of the present request exposes the human beings concerned to privation, hardship, anguish and even danger to life and health and thus to a serious possibility of irreparable harm;

* * *

47. Accordingly,

THE COURT,

unanimously,

1. Indicates, pending its final decision in the proceedings instituted on 29 November 1979 by the United States of America against the Islamic Republic of Iran, the following provisional measures:

A. (i) The Government of the Islamic Republic of Iran should immediately ensure that the premises of the United States Embassy, Chancery and Consulates be restored to the possession of the United States authorities under their exclusive control, and should ensure their inviolability and effective protection as provided for by the treaties in force between the two States, and by general international law;

(ii) The Government of the Islamic Republic of Iran should ensure the immediate release, without any exception, of all persons of United States nationality who are or have been held in the Embassy of the United States of America or in the Ministry of Foreign Affairs in Tehran, or have been held as hostages elsewhere, and afford full protection to all such persons, in accordance with the treaties in force between the two States, and with general international law;

(iii) The Government of the Islamic Republic of Iran should, as from that moment, afford to all the diplomatic and consular personnel of the United States the full protection, privileges and immunities to which they are entitled under the treaties in force between the two States, and under general international law, including immunity from any form of criminal jurisdiction and freedom and facilities to leave the territory of Iran;

B. The Government of the United States of America and the Government of the Islamic Republic of Iran should not take any action and should ensure that no action is taken which may aggravate the tension between the two countries or render the existing dispute more difficult of solution;

2. Decides that, until the Court delivers its final judgment in the present case, it will keep the matters covered by this Order continuously under review.

LaGrand
(*Germany v. United States of America*)

2001 ICJ 104 (June 27)

* * *

Present: *President* Guillaume; *Vice-President* Shi; *Judges* Oda, Bedjaoui, Ranjeva, Herczegh, Fleischhauer, Koroma, Vereshchetin, Higgnes, Parra-Aranguren, Kooijmans, Rezek, Al-Khasawneh, Buergenthal; *Registrar* Couvreur.

* * *

13. Walter LaGrand and Karl LaGrand were born in Germany in 1962 and 1963 respectively, and were German nationals. In 1967, when they were still young children, they moved with their mother to take up permanent residence in the United States. They returned to Germany only once, for a period of about six months in 1974. Although they lived in the United States for most of their lives, and became the adoptive children of a United States national, they remained at all times German nationals, and never acquired the nationality of the United States. However, the United States has emphasized that both had the demeanour and speech of Americans rather than Germans, that neither was known to have spoken German, and that they appeared in all respects to be native citizens of the United States.

14. On 7 January 1982, Karl LaGrand and Walter LaGrand were arrested in the United States by law enforcement officers on suspicion of having been involved earlier the same day in an attempted armed bank robbery in Marana, Arizona, in the course of which the bank manager was murdered and another bank employee seriously injured. They were subsequently tried before the Superior Court of Pima County, Arizona, which, on 17 February 1984, convicted them both of murder in the first degree, attempted murder in the first degree, attempted armed robbery and two counts of kidnapping. On 14 December 1984, each was sentenced to death for first degree murder and to concurrent sentences of imprisonment for the other charges.

15. At all material times, Germany as well as the United States were parties to both the Vienna Convention on Consular Relations and the Optional Protocol to that Convention. Article 36, paragraph 1*(b)*, of the Vienna Convention provides that:

> "if he so requests, the competent authorities of the receiving State shall, without delay, inform the consular post of the sending State if, within its consular district, a national of that State is arrested or committed to prison or to custody pending trial or is detained in any other manner. Any communication ad-

> dressed to the consular post by the person arrested, in prison, custody or detention shall be forwarded by the said authorities without delay. The said authorities shall inform the person concerned without delay of his rights under this subparagraph."

It is not disputed that at the time the LaGrands were convicted and sentenced, the competent United States authorities had failed to provide the LaGrands with the information required by this provision of the Vienna Convention, and had not informed the relevant German consular post of the LaGrands' arrest. The United States concedes that the competent authorities failed to do so, even after becoming aware that the LaGrands were German nationals and not United States nationals, and admits that the United States has therefore violated its obligations under this provision of the Vienna Convention.

16. However, there is some dispute between the Parties as to the time at which the competent authorities in the United States became aware of the fact that the LaGrands were German nationals. Germany argues that the authorities of Arizona were aware of this from the very beginning, and in particular that probation officers knew by April 1982. The United States argues that at the time of their arrest, neither of the LaGrands identified himself to the arresting authorities as a German national, and that Walter LaGrand affirmatively stated that he was a United States citizen. The United States position is that its "competent authorities" for the purposes of Article 36, paragraph 1*(b)*, of the Vienna Convention were the arresting and detaining authorities, and that these became aware of the German nationality of the LaGrands by late 1984, and possibly by mid-1983 or earlier, but in any event not at the time of their arrest in 1982. Although other authorities, such as immigration authorities or probation officers, may have known this even earlier, the United States argues that these were not "competent authorities" for the purposes of this provision of the Vienna Convention. The United States has also suggested that at the time of their arrest, the LaGrands may themselves have been unaware that they were not nationals of the United States.

17. At their trial, the LaGrands were represented by counsel assigned by the court, as they were unable to afford legal counsel of their own choice. Their counsel at trial did not raise the issue of non-compliance with the Vienna Convention, and did not themselves contact the German consular authorities.

18. The convictions and sentences pronounced by the Superior Court of Pima County, Arizona, were subsequently challenged by the LaGrands in three principal sets of legal proceedings.

19. The first set of proceedings consisted of appeals against the convictions and sentences to the Supreme Court of Arizona, which were rejected by that court on 30 January 1987. The United States Supreme Court, in the exercise of its discretion, denied applications by the LaGrands for further review of these judgments on 5 October 1987.

20. The second set of proceedings involved petitions by the LaGrands for post-conviction relief, which were denied by an Arizona state court in 1989. Review of this decision was denied by the Supreme Court of Arizona in 1990, and by the United States Supreme Court in 1991.

21. At the time of these two sets of proceedings, the LaGrands had still not been informed by the competent United States authorities of their rights under Article 36, paragraph 1*(b)*, of the Vienna Convention, and the German consular post had still not been informed of their arrest. The issue of the lack of consular notification, which had not been raised at trial, was also not raised in these two sets of proceedings.

22. The relevant German consular post was only made aware of the case in June 1992 by the LaGrands themselves, who had learnt of their rights from other sources, and not from the Arizona authorities. In December 1992, and on a number of subsequent occasions between then and February 1999, an official of the Consulate-General of Germany in Los Angeles visited the LaGrands in prison. Germany claims that it subsequently helped the LaGrands' attorneys to investigate the LaGrands' childhood in Germany, and to raise the issue of the omission of consular advice in further proceedings before the federal courts.

23. The LaGrands commenced a third set of legal proceedings by filing applications for writs of *habeas corpus* in the United States District Court for the District of Arizona, seeking to have their convictions—or at least their death sentences—set aside. In these proceedings they raised a number of different claims, which were rejected by that court in orders dated 24 January 1995 and 16 February 1995. One of these claims was that the United States authorities had failed to notify the German consulate of their arrest, as required by the Vienna Convention. This claim was rejected on the basis of the "procedural default" rule. According to the United States, this rule:

> "is a federal rule that, before a state criminal defendant can obtain relief in federal court, the claim must be presented to a state court. If a state defendant attempts to raise a new issue in a federal *habeas corpus* proceeding, the defendant can only do so by showing cause and prejudice. Cause is an external impediment that prevents a defendant from raising a claim and prejudice must be obvious on its face. One important purpose of this rule is to ensure that the state courts have an opportunity to address issues going to the validity of state convictions before the federal courts intervene."

The United States District Court held that the LaGrands had not shown an objective external factor that prevented them from raising the issue of the lack of consular notification earlier. On 16 January 1998, this judgment was affirmed on appeal by the United States Court of Appeals, Ninth Circuit, which also held that the LaGrands' claim relating to the Vienna Convention was "procedurally defaulted", as it had not been raised in any of the earlier proceedings in state courts. On 2 November 1998, the United States Supreme Court denied further review of this judgment.

24. On 21 December 1998, the LaGrands were formally notified by the United States authorities of their right to consular access.

25. On 15 January 1999, the Supreme Court of Arizona decided that Karl LaGrand was to be executed on 24 February 1999, and that Walter LaGrand was to be executed on 3 March 1999. Germany claims that the German Consulate learned of these dates on 19 January 1999.

26. In January and early February 1999, various interventions were made by Germany seeking to prevent the execution of the LaGrands. In particular, the German Foreign Minister and German Minister of Justice wrote to their respective United States counterparts on 27 January 1999; the German Foreign Minister wrote to the Governor of Arizona on the same day; the German Chancellor wrote to the President of the United States and to the Governor of Arizona on 2 February 1999; and the President of the Federal Republic of Germany wrote to the President of the United States on 5 February 1999. These letters referred to German opposition to capital punishment generally, but did not raise the issue of the absence of consular notification in the case of the LaGrands. The latter issue was, however, raised in a further letter, dated 22 February 1999, two days before the scheduled date of execution of Karl LaGrand, from the German Foreign Minister to the United States Secretary of State.

27. On 23 February 1999, the Arizona Board of Executive Clemency rejected an appeal for clemency by Karl LaGrand. Under the law of Arizona, this meant that the Governor of Arizona was prevented from granting clemency.

28. On the same day, the Arizona Superior Court in Pima County rejected a further petition by Walter LaGrand, based *inter alia* on the absence of consular notification, on the ground that these claims were "procedurally precluded."

29. On 24 February 1999, certain last-minute federal court proceedings brought by Karl LaGrand ultimately proved to be unsuccessful. In the course of these proceedings the United States Court of Appeals, Ninth Circuit, again held the issue of failure of consular notification to be procedurally defaulted. Karl LaGrand was executed later that same day.

30. On 2 March 1999, the day before the scheduled date of execution of Walter LaGrand, at 7.30 p.m. (The Hague time), Germany filed in the Registry of this Court the Application instituting the present proceedings against the United States (see paragraph 1 above), accompanied by a request for the following provisional measures:

> "The United States should take all measures at its disposal to ensure that Walter LaGrand is not executed pending the final decision in these proceedings, and should inform the Court of all the measures which it has taken in implementation of that Order."

By a letter of the same date, the German Foreign Minister requested the Secretary of State of the United States "to urge [the] Governor [of Arizona] for a suspension of Walter LaGrand's execution pending a ruling by the International Court of Justice."

31. On the same day, the Arizona Board of Executive Clemency met to consider the case of Walter LaGrand. It recommended against a commutation of his death sentence, but recommended that the Governor of Arizona grant a 60-day reprieve having regard to the Application filed by Germany in the International Court of Justice. Nevertheless, the Governor of Arizona decided, "in the interest of justice and with the victims in mind," to allow the execution of Walter LaGrand to go forward as scheduled.

32. In an Order of 3 March 1999, this Court found that the circumstances required it to indicate, as a matter of the greatest urgency and without any other proceedings, provisional measures in accordance with Article 41 of its Statute and with Article 75, paragraph 1, of its Rules (*I.C.J. Reports 1999*, p. 9, para. 26); it indicated provisional measures in the following terms:

> "*(a)* The United States of America should take all measures at its disposal to ensure that Walter LaGrand is not executed pending the final decision in these proceedings, and should inform the Court of all the measures which it has taken in implementation of this Order;
>
> *(b)* The Government of the United States of America should transmit this Order to the Governor of the State of Arizona."

33. On the same day, proceedings were brought by Germany in the United States Supreme Court against the United States and the Governor of Arizona, seeking *inter alia* to enforce compliance with this Court's Order indicating provisional measures. In the course of these proceedings, the United States Solicitor-General as counsel of record took the position, *inter alia*, that "an order of the International Court of Justice indicating provisional measures is not binding and does not furnish a basis for judicial relief." On the same date, the United States Supreme Court dismissed the motion by Germany, on the ground of the tardiness of Germany's application and of jurisdictional barriers under United States domestic law.

34. On that same day, proceedings were also instituted in the United States Supreme Court by Walter LaGrand. These proceedings were decided against him. Later that day, Walter LaGrand was executed.

* * *

92. The Court will now consider Germany's third submission, in which it asks the Court to adjudge and declare:

> "that the United States, by failing to take all measures at its disposal to ensure that Walter LaGrand was not executed pending the final decision of the International Court of Justice on the matter, violated its international legal obligation to comply with the Order on Provisional Measures issued by the Court on 3 March 1999, and to refrain from any action which might interfere with the subject matter of a dispute while judicial proceedings are pending."

93. In its Memorial, Germany contended that "[p]rovisional [m]easures indicated by the International Court of Justice [were] binding by virtue of the law of the United Nations Charter and the Statute of the Court." In support of its position, Germany developed a number of arguments in which it referred to the "principle of effectiveness," to the "procedural prerequisites" for the adoption of provisional measures, to the binding nature of provisional measures as a "necessary consequence of the bindingness of the final decision," to "Article 94 (1), of the United Nations Charter," to "Article 41 (1), of the Statute of the Court" and to the "practice of the Court."

Referring to the duty of the "parties to a dispute before the Court ... to preserve its subject-matter", Germany added that:

> "[a]part from having violated its duties under Art. 94 (1) of the United Nations Charter and Art. 41 (1) of the Statute, the United States has also violated the obligation to refrain from any action which might interfere with the subject-matter of a dispute while judicial proceedings are pending."

At the hearings, Germany further stated the following:

> "A judgment by the Court on jurisdiction or merits cannot be treated on exactly the same footing as a provisional measure ... Article 59 and Article 60 [of the Statute] do not apply to provisional measures or, to be more exact, apply to them only by implication; that is to say, to the extent that such measures, being both incidental and provisional, contribute to the exercise of a judicial function whose end-result is, by definition, the delivery of a judicial decision. There is here an inherent logic in the judicial procedure, and to disregard it would be tantamount, as far as the Parties are concerned, to deviating from the principle of good faith and from what the German pleadings call 'the principle of institutional effectiveness'... [P]rovisional measures ... are indeed legal decisions, but they are decisions of procedure ... Since their decisional nature is, however, implied by the logic of urgency and by the need to safeguard the effectiveness of the proceedings, they accordingly create genuine legal obligations on the part of those to whom they are addressed."

94. Germany claims that the United States committed a threefold violation of the Court's Order of 3 March 1999:

> "(1) Immediately after the International Court of Justice had rendered its Order on Provisional Measures, Germany appealed to the U.S. Supreme Court in order to reach a stay of the execution of Walter LaGrand, in accordance with the International Court's Order to the same effect. In the course of these proceed-

> ings—and in full knowledge of the Order of the International Court—the Office of the Solicitor General, a section of the U.S. Department of Justice—in a letter to the Supreme Court argued once again that: 'an order of the International Court of Justice indicating provisional measures is not binding and does not furnish a basis for judicial relief.'

This statement of a high-ranking official of the Federal Government ... had a direct influence on the decision of the Supreme Court....

> (2) In the following, the U.S. Supreme Court—an agency of the United States—refused by a majority vote to order that the execution be stayed. In doing so, it rejected the German arguments based essentially on the Order of the International Court of Justice on Provisional Measures ...
>
> (3) Finally, the Governor of Arizona did not order a stay of the execution of Walter LaGrand although she was vested with the right to do so by the laws of the State of Arizona. Moreover, in the present case, the Arizona Executive Board of Clemency—for the first time in the history of this institution—had issued a recommendation for a temporary stay, not least in light of the international legal issues involved in the case ..."

95. The United States argues that it "did what was called for by the Court's 3 March Order, given the extraordinary and unprecedented circumstances in which it was forced to act." It points out in this connection that the United States Government "immediately transmitt[ed] the Order to the Governor of Arizona," that "the United States placed the Order in the hands of the one official who, at that stage, might have had legal authority to stop the execution" and that by a letter from the Legal Counselor of the United States Embassy in The Hague dated 8 March 1999, it informed the International Court of Justice of all the measures which had been taken in implementation of the Order.

The United States further states that:

> "[t]wo central factors constrained the United States ability to act. The first was the extraordinarily short time between issuance of the Court's Order and the time set for the execution of Walter LaGrand ...

The second constraining factor was the character of the United States of America as a federal republic of divided powers."

96. The United States also alleges that the "terms of the Court's 3 March Order did not create legal obligations binding on [it]." It argues in this respect that "[t]he language used by the Court in the key portions of its Order is not the language used to create binding legal obligations" and that

> "the Court does not need here to decide the difficult and controversial legal question of whether its orders indicating provisional measures would be capable of creating international legal obligations if worded in mandatory ... terms."

It nevertheless maintains that those orders cannot have such effects and, in support of that view, develops arguments concerning "the language and history of Article 41 (1) of the Court's Statute and Article 94 of the Charter of the United Nations," the "Court's and State practice under these provisions," and the "weight of publicists' commentary."

Concerning Germany's argument based on the "principle of effectiveness," the United States contends that

> "[i]n an arena where the concerns and sensitivities of States, and not abstract logic, have informed the drafting of the Court's constitutive documents, it is

perfectly understandable that the Court might have the power to issue binding final judgments, but a more circumscribed authority with respect to provisional measures."

Referring to Germany's argument that the United States "violated the obligation to refrain from any action which might interfere with the subject matter of a dispute while judicial proceedings are pending," the United States further asserts that:

"The implications of the rule as presented by Germany are potentially quite dramatic, however. Germany appears to contend that by merely filing a case with the Court, an Applicant can force a Respondent to refrain from continuing any action that the Applicant deems to affect the subject of the dispute. If the law were as Germany contends, the entirety of the Court's rules and practices relating to provisional measures would be surplussage. This is not the law, and this is not how States or this Court have acted in practice."

97. Lastly, the United States states that in any case, "[b]ecause of the press of time stemming from Germany's last-minute filing of the case, basic principles fundamental to the judicial process were not observed in connection with the Court's 3 March Order" and that

"[t]hus, whatever one might conclude regarding a general rule for provisional measures, it would be anomalous—to say the least—for the Court to construe this Order as a source of binding legal obligations."

98. Neither the Permanent Court of International Justice, nor the present Court to date, has been called upon to determine the legal effects of orders made under Article 41 of the Statute. As Germany's third submission refers expressly to an international legal obligation "to comply with the Order on Provisional Measures issued by the Court on 3 March 1999," and as the United States disputes the existence of such an obligation, the Court is now called upon to rule expressly on this question.

99. The dispute which exists between the Parties with regard to this point essentially concerns the interpretation of Article 41, which is worded in identical terms in the Statute of each Court (apart from the respective references to the Council of the League of Nations and the Security Council). This interpretation has been the subject of extensive controversy in the literature. The Court will therefore now proceed to the interpretation of Article 41 of the Statute. It will do so in accordance with customary international law, reflected in Article 31 of the 1969 Vienna Convention on the Law of Treaties. According to paragraph 1 of Article 31, a treaty must be interpreted in good faith in accordance with the ordinary meaning to be given to its terms in their context and in the light of the treaty's object and purpose.

100. The French text of Article 41 reads as follows:

"1. La Cour a le pouvoir *d'indiquer*, si elle estime que les circonstances l'exigent, quelles mesures conservatoires due droit de chacun *doivent* être prises à titre provisoire.

2. En attendant l'arrêt définitif, *l'indication* de ces mesures est immédiatement notifiée aux parties et au Conseil de sécurité." (Emphasis added.)

In this text, the terms "indiquer" and "l'indication" may be deemed to be neutral as to the mandatory character of the measure concerned; by contrast the words "doivent être prises" have an imperative character.

For its part, the English version of Article 41 reads as follows:

> "1. The Court shall have the power to *indicate*, if it considers that circumstances so require, any provisional measures which *ought* to be taken to preserve the respective rights of either party.
>
> 2. Pending the final decision, notice of the measures *suggested* shall forthwith be given to the parties and to the Security Council." (Emphasis added.)

According to the United States, the use in the English version of "indicate" instead of "order," of "ought" instead of "must" or "shall," and of "suggested" instead of "ordered," is to be understood as implying that decisions under Article 41 lack mandatory effect. It might however be argued, having regard to the fact that in 1920 the French text was the original version, that such terms as "indicate" and "ought" have a meaning equivalent to "order" and "must" or "shall."

101. Finding itself faced with two texts which are not in total harmony, the Court will first of all note that according to Article 92 of the Charter, the Statute "forms an integral part of the present Charter." Under Article 111 of the Charter, the French and English texts of the latter are "equally authentic." The same is equally true of the Statute.

In cases of divergence between the equally authentic versions of the Statute, neither it nor the Charter indicates how to proceed. In the absence of agreement between the parties in this respect, it is appropriate to refer to paragraph 4 of Article 33 of the Vienna Convention on the Law of Treaties, which in the view of the Court again reflects customary international law. This provision reads "when a comparison of the authentic texts discloses a difference of meaning which the application of Articles 31 and 32 does not remove the meaning which best reconciles the texts, having regard to the object and purpose of the treaty, shall be adopted."

The Court will therefore now consider the object and purpose of the Statute together with the context of Article 41.

102. The object and purpose of the Statute is to enable the Court to fulfil the functions provided for therein, and in particular, the basic function of judicial settlement of international disputes by binding decisions in accordance with Article 59 of the Statute. The context in which Article 41 has to be seen within the Statute is to prevent the Court from being hampered in the exercise of its functions because the respective rights of the parties to a dispute before the Court are not preserved. It follows from the object and purpose of the Statute, as well as from the terms of Article 41 when read in their context, that the power to indicate provisional measures entails that such measures should be binding, inasmuch as the power in question is based on the necessity, when the circumstances call for it, to safeguard, and to avoid prejudice to, the rights of the parties as determined by the final judgment of the Court. The contention that provisional measures indicated under Article 41 might not be binding would be contrary to the object and purpose of that Article.

103. A related reason which points to the binding character of orders made under Article 41 and to which the Court attaches importance, is the existence of a principle which has already been recognized by the Permanent Court of International Justice when it spoke of

> "the principle universally accepted by international tribunals and likewise laid down in many conventions ... to the effect that the parties to a case must abstain from any measure capable of exercising a prejudicial effect in regard to the execution of the decision to be given, and, in general, not allow any step of any kind to be taken which might aggravate or extend the dispute" (*Electricity Company of Sofia and Bulgaria, Order of 5 December 1939, P.C.I.J., Series A/B, No. 79*, p. 199).

Furthermore measures designed to avoid aggravating or extending disputes have frequently been indicated by the Court. They were indicated with the purpose of being implemented (see *Nuclear Tests (Australia v. France), Interim Protection, Order of 22 June 1973, I.C.J. Reports 1973*, p. 106; *Nuclear Tests (New Zealand v. France), Interim Protection, Order of 22 June 1973, I.C.J. Reports 1973*, p. 142; *Frontier Dispute, Provisional Measures, Order of 10 January 1986, I.C.J. Reports 1986*, p. 9, para. 18, and p. 11, para. 32, point 1 A; *Application of the Convention on the Prevention and Punishment of the Crime of Genocide, Provisional Measures, Order of 8 April 1993, I.C.J. Reports 1993*, p. 23, para. 48, and p. 24, para. 52 B; *Application of the Convention on the Prevention and Punishment of the Crime of Genocide, Provisional Measures, Order of 13 September 1993, I.C.J. Reports 1993*, p. 349, para. 57, and p. 350, para. 61 (3); *Land and Maritime Boundary between Cameroon and Nigeria, Provisional Measures, Order of 15 March 1996, I.C.J. Reports 1996 (I)*, pp. 22–23, para. 41, and p. 24, para. 49 (1)).

104. Given the conclusions reached by the Court above in interpreting the text of Article 41 of the Statute in the light of its object and purpose, it does not consider it necessary to resort to the preparatory work in order to determine the meaning of that Article. The Court would nevertheless point out that the preparatory work of the Statute does not preclude the conclusion that orders under Article 41 have binding force.

105. The initial preliminary draft of the Statute of the Permanent Court of International Justice, as prepared by the Committee of Jurists established by the Council of the League of Nations, made no mention of provisional measures. A provision to this effect was inserted only at a later stage in the draft prepared by the Committee, following a proposal from the Brazilian jurist Raul Fernandes.

Basing himself on the Bryan Treaty of 13 October 1914 between the United States and Sweden, Raul Fernandes had submitted the following text:

> "Dans le cas où la cause due différend consiste en actes déterminés déjà effectués ou sur le point de l'être, la Cour pourra ordonner, dans le plus bref délai, à titre provisoire, des mesures conservatoires adéquates, en attendant le jugement définitif." (Comité consultatif de juristes, *Procès-verbaux des séances due comité*, 16 juin–24 juillet 1920 (avec annexes), La Haye, 1920, p. 609.)

In its English translation this text read as follows:

> "In case the cause of the dispute should consist of certain acts already committed or about to be committed, the Court may, provisionally and with the least possible delay, order adequate protective measures to be taken, pending the final judgment of the Court." (Advisory Committee of Jurists, *Procès-verbaux of the Proceedings of the Committee*, 16 June–24 July 1920 (with Annexes), The Hague, 1920, p. 609.)

The Drafting Committee prepared a new version of this text, to which two main amendments were made: on the one hand, the words "la Cour pourra ordonner" ("the Court may ... order") were replaced by "la Cour a le pouvoir d'indiquer" ("the Court shall have the power to suggest"), while, on the other, a second paragraph was added providing for notice to be given to the parties and to the Council of the "measures suggested" by the Court. The draft Article 2*bis* as submitted by the Drafting Committee thus read as follows:

> "Dans le cas où la cause due différend consiste en un acte effectué ou sur le point de l'être, la Cour a le pouvoir d'indiquer, si elle estime que les circonstances l'exigent, quelles mesures conservatoires due droit de chacun doivent être prises à titre provisoire.
>
> "En attendant son arrêt, cette suggestion de la Cour est immédiatement transmise aux parties et au Conseil." (Comité consultatif de juristes, *Procès-verbaux*

> *des séances due comité*, 16 juin–24 juillet 1920 (avec annexes), La Haye, 1920, p. 567–568.)

The English version read:

> "If the dispute arises out of an act which has already taken place or which is imminent, the Court shall have the power to suggest, if it considers that circumstances so require, the provisional measures that should be taken to preserve the respective rights of either party.
>
> Pending the final decision, notice of the measures suggested shall forthwith be given to the parties and the Council." (Advisory Committee of Jurists, *Procès-verbaux of the Proceedings of the Committee*, 16 June–24 July 1920 (with Annexes), The Hague, 1920, pp. 567–568.)

The Committee of Jurists eventually adopted a draft Article 39, which amended the former Article 2*bis* only in its French version: in the second paragraph, the words "*cette suggestion*" were replaced in French by the words "*l'indication*."

106. When the draft Article 39 was examined by the Sub-Committee of the Third Committee of the first Assembly of the League of Nations, a number of amendments were considered. Raul Fernandes suggested again to use the word "ordonner" in the French version. The Sub-Committee decided to stay with the word "indiquer," the Chairman of the Sub-Committee observing that the Court lacked the means to execute its decisions. The language of the first paragraph of the English version was then made to conform to the French text: thus the word "suggest" was replaced by "indicate," and "should" by "ought to." However, in the second paragraph of the English version, the phrase "measures suggested" remained unchanged.

The provision thus amended in French and in English by the Sub-Committee was adopted as Article 41 of the Statute of the Permanent Court of International Justice. It passed as such into the Statute of the present Court without any discussion in 1945.

107. The preparatory work of Article 41 shows that the preference given in the French text to "*indiquer*" over "*ordonner*" was motivated by the consideration that the Court did not have the means to assure the execution of its decisions. However, the lack of means of execution and the lack of binding force are two different matters. Hence, the fact that the Court does not itself have the means to ensure the execution of orders made pursuant to Article 41 is not an argument against the binding nature of such orders.

108. The Court finally needs to consider whether Article 94 of the United Nations Charter precludes attributing binding effect to orders indicating provisional measures. That Article reads as follows:

> "1. Each Member of the United Nations undertakes to comply with the decision of the International Court of Justice in any case to which it is a party.
>
> 2. If any party to a case fails to perform the obligations incumbent upon it under a judgment rendered by the Court, the other party may have recourse to the Security Council, which may, if it deems necessary, make recommendations or decide upon measures to be taken to give effect to the judgment."

The question arises as to the meaning to be attributed to the words "the decision of the International Court of Justice" in paragraph 1 of this Article. This wording could be understood as referring not merely to the Court's judgments but to any decision rendered by it, thus including orders indicating provisional measures. It could also be interpreted to mean only judgments rendered by the Court as provided in paragraph 2 of Article 94.

In this regard, the fact that in Articles 56 to 60 of the Court's Statute, both the word "decision" and the word "judgment" are used does little to clarify the matter.

Under the first interpretation of paragraph 1 of Article 94, the text of the paragraph would confirm the binding nature of provisional measures; whereas the second interpretation would in no way preclude their being accorded binding force under Article 41 of the Statute. The Court accordingly concludes that Article 94 of the Charter does not prevent orders made under Article 41 from having a binding character.

109. In short, it is clear that none of the sources of interpretation referred to in the relevant Articles of the Vienna Convention on the Law of Treaties, including the preparatory work, contradict the conclusions drawn from the terms of Article 41 read in their context and in the light of the object and purpose of the Statute. Thus, the Court has reached the conclusion that orders on provisional measures under Article 41 have binding effect.

110. The Court will now consider the Order of 3 March 1999. This Order was not a mere exhortation. It had been adopted pursuant to Article 41 of the Statute. This Order was consequently binding in character and created a legal obligation for the United States.

111. As regards the question whether the United States has complied with the obligation incumbent upon it as a result of the Order of 3 March 1999, the Court observes that the Order indicated two provisional measures, the first of which states that

> "[t]he United States of America should take all measures at its disposal to ensure that Walter LaGrand is not executed pending the final decision in these proceedings, and should inform the Court of all the measures which it has taken in implementation of this Order."

The second measure required the Government of the United States to "transmit this Order to the Governor of the State of Arizona." The information required on the measures taken in implementation of this Order was given to the Court by a letter of 8 March 1999 from the Legal Counsellor of the United States Embassy at The Hague. According to this letter, on 3 March 1999 the State Department had transmitted to the Governor of Arizona a copy of the Court's Order. "In view of the extremely late hour of the receipt of the Court's Order," the letter of 8 March went on to say, "no further steps were feasible."

The United States authorities have thus limited themselves to the mere transmission of the text of the Order to the Governor of Arizona. This certainly met the requirement of the second of the two measures indicated. As to the first measure, the Court notes that it did not create an obligation of result, but that the United States was asked to "take all measures at its disposal to ensure that Walter LaGrand is not executed pending the final decision in these proceedings." The Court agrees that due to the extremely late presentation of the request for provisional measures, there was certainly very little time for the United States authorities to act.

112. The Court observes, nevertheless, that the mere transmission of its Order to the Governor of Arizona without any comment, particularly without even so much as a plea for a temporary stay and an explanation that there is no general agreement on the position of the United States that orders of the International Court of Justice on provisional measures are non-binding, was certainly less than could have been done even in the short time available. The same is true of the United States Solicitor General's categorical statement in his brief letter to the United States Supreme Court that "an order of the Inter-

national Court of Justice indicating provisional measures is not binding and does not furnish a basis for judicial relief" (see paragraph 33 above). This statement went substantially further than the amicus brief referred to in a mere footnote in his letter, which was filed on behalf of the United States in earlier proceedings before the United States Supreme Court in the case of Angel Francisco Breard (see *Breard v. Greene*, United States Supreme Court, 14 April 1998, *International Legal Materials*, Vol. 37 (1988), p. 824; Memorial of Germany, Ann. 34). In that amicus brief, the same Solicitor General had declared less than a year earlier that "there is substantial disagreement among jurists as to whether an ICJ order indicating provisional measures is binding ... The better reasoned position is that such an order is not binding."

113. It is also noteworthy that the Governor of Arizona, to whom the Court's Order had been transmitted, decided not to give effect to it, even though the Arizona Clemency Board had recommended a stay of execution for Walter LaGrand.

114. Finally, the United States Supreme Court rejected a separate application by Germany for a stay of execution, "[g]iven the tardiness of the pleas and the jurisdictional barriers they implicate." Yet it would have been open to the Supreme Court, as one of its members urged, to grant a preliminary stay, which would have given it "time to consider, after briefing from all interested parties, the jurisdictional and international legal issues involved ..." (*Federal Republic of Germany et al. v. United States et al.*, United States Supreme Court, 3 March 1999).

115. The review of the above steps taken by the authorities of the United States with regard to the Order of the International Court of Justice of 3 March 1999 indicates that the various competent United States authorities failed to take all the steps they could have taken to give effect to the Court's Order. The Order did not require the United States to exercise powers it did not have; but it did impose the obligation to "take all measures at its disposal to ensure that Walter LaGrand is not executed pending the final decision in these proceedings...." The Court finds that the United States did not discharge this obligation.

Under these circumstances the Court concludes that the United States has not complied with the Order of 3 March 1999.

116. The Court observes finally that in the third submission Germany requests the Court to adjudge and declare only that the United States violated its international legal obligation to comply with the Order of 3 March 1999; it contains no other request regarding that violation. Moreover, the Court points out that the United States was under great time pressure in this case, due to the circumstances in which Germany had instituted the proceedings. The Court notes moreover that at the time when the United States authorities took their decision the question of the binding character of orders indicating provisional measures had been extensively discussed in the literature, but had not been settled by its jurisprudence. The Court would have taken these factors into consideration had Germany's submission included a claim for indemnification.

In 2004, Mexico brought a case very similar to *LaGrand* against the U.S. *Avena and Other Mexican Nationals* (Mex. v. U.S.) 2004 I.C.J. 12 (Mar. 31). The *Avena* judgment and Mexico's attempt to enforce it through a request for interpretation are discussed in Chapter Thirteen. Pending the ICJ's decision on Mexico's request for interpretation, Mexico asked for an order of provisional measures.

Request for Interpretation of the Judgment of 31 March in *Avena and Other Mexican Nationals (Mexico v. United States)*

Request for Provisional Measures
2008 ICJ (Order of July 16)

* * *

44. Whereas the Court's jurisdiction on the basis of Article 60 of the Statute is not preconditioned by the existence of any other basis of jurisdiction as between the parties to the original case; and whereas it follows that, even if the basis of jurisdiction in the original case lapses, the Court, nevertheless, by virtue of Article 60 of the Statute, may entertain a request for interpretation;

45. Whereas in the case of a request for the indication of provisional measures made in the context of a request for interpretation under Article 60 of the Statute, the Court has to consider whether the conditions laid down by that Article for the Court to entertain a request for interpretation appear to be satisfied; whereas Article 60 provides that: "The judgment is final and without appeal. In the event of dispute as to the meaning or scope of the judgment, the Court shall construe it upon the request of any party"; and whereas this provision is supplemented by Article 98 of the Rules of Court, paragraph 1 of which reads: "In the event of dispute as to the meaning or scope of a judgment any party may make a request for its interpretation ...";

46. Whereas, therefore, by virtue of the second sentence of Article 60, the Court may entertain a request for interpretation of any judgment rendered by it provided that there is a "dispute as to the meaning or scope of [the said] judgment";

47. Whereas Mexico requests the Court to interpret paragraph 153 (9) of the operative part of the Judgment delivered by the Court on 31 March 2004 in the case concerning *Avena and Other Mexican Nationals (Mexico v. United States of America)*; whereas a request for interpretation must relate to a dispute between the parties relating to the meaning or scope of the operative part of the judgment and cannot concern the reasons for the judgment except in so far as these are inseparable from the operative part (*Interpretation of Judgments Nos. 7 and 8 (Factory at Chorzów), Judgment No. 11, 1927, P.C.I.J., Series A, No. 13*, p. 11; *Request for Interpretation of the Judgment of 11 June 1998 in the Case concerning the* Land and Maritime Boundary between Cameroon and Nigeria (Cameroon *v.* Nigeria), Preliminary Objections (*Nigeria v. Cameroon*), *Judgment, I.C.J. Reports 1999 (I)*, p. 35, para. 10);

48. Whereas Mexico asks the Court to confirm its understanding that the language in that provision of the *Avena* Judgment establishes an obligation of result that obliges the United States, including all its component organs at all levels, to provide the requisite review and reconsideration irrespective of any domestic law impediment; whereas Mexico further submits that the obligation imposed by the *Avena* Judgment requires the United States to prevent the execution of any Mexican national named in the Judgment unless and until that review and reconsideration has been completed and it has been determined whether any prejudice resulted from the Vienna Convention violations found by this Court" (see also paragraph 9 above); whereas, in Mexico's view, the fact that

> "[n]either the Texas executive, nor the Texas legislature, nor the federal executive, nor the federal legislature has taken any legal steps at this point that would stop th[e] execution [of Mr. Medellín] from going forward ... reflects a dispute over the meaning and scope of [the] *Avena*" Judgment;

49. Whereas, according to Mexico, "by its actions thus far, the United States understands the Judgment to constitute merely an obligation of means, not an obligation of result" despite the formal statements by the United States before the Court to the contrary; whereas Mexico contends that notwithstanding the Memorandum issued by the President of the United States in 2005, whereby he directed state courts to provide review and reconsideration consistent with the *Avena* Judgment, "petitions by Mexican nationals for the review and reconsideration mandated in their cases have repeatedly been denied by domestic courts"; whereas Mexico claims that the decision by the Supreme Court of the United States in Mr. Medellín's case on 25 March 2008 has rendered the President's Memorandum without force in state courts; and whereas

> "[a]part from having issued the President's 2005 Memorandum, a means that fell short of achieving its intended result, the United States to date has *not* taken the steps necessary to prevent the executions of Mexican nationals until the obligation of review and reconsideration is met" (emphasis in the original);

50. Whereas the United States contends that Mexico's understanding of paragraph 153 (9) of the *Avena* Judgment as an "obligation of result", i.e., that the United States is subject to a binding obligation to provide review and reconsideration of the convictions and sentences of the Mexican nationals named in the Judgment, "is *precisely* the interpretation that the United States holds concerning the paragraph in question" (emphasis in the original); and whereas, while admitting that, because of the structure of its Government and its domestic law, the United States faces substantial obstacles in implementing its obligation under the *Avena* Judgment, the United States confirmed that "it has clearly accepted that the obligation to provide review and reconsideration is an obligation of result and it has sought to achieve that result";

51. Whereas, in the view of the United States, in the absence of a dispute with respect to the meaning and scope of paragraph 153 (9) of the *Avena* Judgment, Mexico's "claim is not capable of falling within the provisions of Article 60" and thus it would be "inappropriate for the Court to grant relief, including provisional measures, in respect to that claim"; whereas the United States contends that the Court lacks "jurisdiction *ratione materiae*" to entertain Mexico's Application and accordingly lacks "the prima facie jurisdiction required for the indication of provisional measures";

52. Whereas the United States submits that, in light of the circumstances, the Court "should give serious consideration to dismissing Mexico's Request for interpretation in its entirety at this stage of the proceedings";

53. Whereas the French and English versions of Article 60 of the Statute are not in total harmony; whereas the French text uses the term "contestation" while the English text refers to a "dispute"; whereas the term "contestation" in the French text has a wider meaning than the term used in the English text; whereas Article 60 of the Statute of the International Court of Justice is identical to Article 60 of the Statute of the Permanent Court of International Justice; whereas the drafters of the Statute of the Permanent Court of International Justice chose to use in the French text of Article 60 a term ("contestation") which is different from the term ("différend") used notably in Article 36, paragraph 2, and in Article 38 of the Statute; whereas, although in their ordinary meaning, both terms in a general sense denote opposing views, the term "contestation" is wider in scope than the term "différend" and does not require the same degree of opposition; whereas, compared to the term"différend," the concept underlying the term "contestation" is more flexible in its application to a particular situation; and whereas a dispute ("contestation" in the French text) under Article 60 of the Statute, understood as a difference of opinion be-

tween the parties as to the meaning and scope of a judgment rendered by the Court, therefore does not need to satisfy the same criteria as would a dispute ("différend" in the French text) as referred to in Article 36, paragraph 2, of the Statute; whereas, in the present circumstances, a meaning shall be given that best reconciles the French and English texts of Article 60 of its Statute, bearing in mind its object; whereas this is so notwithstanding that the English texts of Article 36, paragraph 2, and Articles 38 and 60 of the Statute all employ the same word, "dispute"; and whereas the term "dispute" in English also may have a more flexible meaning than that generally accorded to it in Article 36, paragraph 2, of the Statute;

54. Whereas the question of the meaning of the term "dispute" ("contestation") as employed in Article 60 of the Statute has been addressed in the jurisprudence of the Court's predecessor; whereas "the manifestation of the existence of the dispute in a specific manner, as for instance by diplomatic negotiations, is not required" for the purposes of Article 60, nor is it required that "the dispute should have manifested itself in a formal way"; whereas recourse could be had to the Permanent Court as soon as the interested States had in fact shown themselves as holding opposing views in regard to the meaning or scope of a judgment of the Court (*Interpretation of Judgments Nos. 7 and 8 (Factory at Chorzów), Judgment No. 11, 1927, P.C.I.J., Series A, No. 13*, pp. 10–11); and whereas this reading of Article 60 was confirmed by the present Court in the case concerning *Application for Revision and Interpretation of the Judgment of 24 February 1982 in the Case concerning the* Continental Shelf (Tunisia/Libyan Arab Jamahiriya) *(Tunisia v. Libyan Arab Jamahiriya) (Judgment, I.C.J. Reports 1985*, pp. 217–218, para. 46);

55. Whereas the Court needs now to determine whether there appears to be a dispute between the Parties within the meaning of Article 60 of the Statute; whereas, according to the United States, its executive branch, which is the only authority entitled to represent the United States internationally, understands paragraph 153 (9) of the *Avena* Judgment as an obligation of result; whereas, in Mexico's view, the fact that other federal and state authorities have not taken any steps to prevent the execution of Mexican nationals before they have received review and reconsideration of their convictions and sentences reflects a dispute over the meaning and scope of the *Avena* Judgment; whereas, while it seems both Parties regard paragraph 153 (9) of the *Avena* Judgment as an international obligation of result, the Parties nonetheless apparently hold different views as to the meaning and scope of that obligation of result, namely, whether that understanding is shared by all United States federal and state authorities and whether that obligation falls upon those authorities;

56. Whereas, in light of the positions taken by the Parties, there appears to be a difference of opinion between them as to the meaning and scope of the Court's finding in paragraph 153 (9) of the operative part of the Judgment and thus recourse could be had to the Court under Article 60 of the Statute;

57. Whereas, in view of the foregoing, it appears that the Court may, under Article 60 of the Statute, deal with the Request for interpretation; whereas it follows that the submission of the United States, that the Application of Mexico be dismissed *in limine* "on grounds of manifest lack of jurisdiction", can not be upheld; and whereas it follows also that the Court may address the present request for the indication of provisional measures;

58. Whereas the Court, when considering a request for the indication of provisional measures, "must be concerned to preserve ... the rights which may subsequently be adjudged by the Court to belong either to the Applicant or to the Respondent" (*Land and*

Maritime Boundary between Cameroon and Nigeria (Cameroon v. Nigeria), Provisional Measures, Order of 15 March 1996, I.C.J. Reports 1996 (I), p. 22, para. 35); whereas a link must therefore be established between the alleged rights the protection of which is the subject of the provisional measures being sought, and the subject of the principal request submitted to the Court;

59. Whereas Mexico contends that its request for the indication of provisional measures is intended to preserve the rights that Mexico asserts in its Request for interpretation of paragraph 153 (9) of the *Avena* Judgment; whereas, according to Mexico, the indication of provisional measures would be required to preserve the said rights during the pendency of the proceedings, as "in executing Mr. Medellín or others, the United States *will forever* deprive these nationals of the correct interpretation of the Judgment" (emphasis in the original); whereas, in Mexico's view, paragraph 153 (9) establishes an obligation of result incumbent upon the United States, namely it "must not execute any Mexican national named in the Judgment unless and until review and reconsideration is completed and either no prejudice as a result of the treaty violation is found or any prejudice is remedied";

60. Whereas Mexico argues that, given the dispute between the Parties as to the meaning and scope of paragraph 153 (9) of the *Avena* Judgment, "there can be no doubt that the provisional relief requested arises from the rights that Mexico seeks to protect and preserve until this Court clarifies the obligation imposed by [that] paragraph";

61. Whereas the United States submits that Mexico's request for the indication of provisional measures aims to prohibit the United States from carrying out sentences with regard to Mexican nationals named therein prior to the conclusion of the Court's proceedings on Mexico's Request for interpretation; whereas the United States contends that, in its Application, Mexico asks the Court to interpret the *Avena* Judgment to mean that the United States must not carry out sentences "unless the individual affected has received review and reconsideration and it is determined that no prejudice resulted from the violation of the Vienna Convention", rather than an absolute prohibition on the United States carrying out sentences in regard to each of the individuals mentioned in *Avena*; whereas the United States claims that, by focusing in the request for the indication of provisional measures on the carrying out of the sentence and not on its review and reconsideration, Mexico seeks to protect rights that are not asserted in its Application for interpretation;

62. Whereas the United States asserts that, as is clear from the Court's case law, "any provisional measures indicated must be designed to preserve [the] rights" which are the subject of the principal request submitted to the Court; and whereas it contends that the provisional measures requested by Mexico do not satisfy the Court's test because they go beyond the subject of the proceedings before the Court on the Request for interpretation;

63. Whereas, in proceedings on interpretation, the Court is called upon to clarify the meaning and the scope of what the Court decided with binding force in a judgment (*Request for Interpretation of the Judgment of 20 November 1950 in the Asylum Case (Colombia v. Peru), Judgment, I.C.J. Reports 1950*, p. 402; *Application for Revision and Interpretation of the Judgment of 24 February 1982 in the Case concerning the* Continental Shelf (Tunisia/Libyan Arab Jamahiriya) *(Tunisia v. Libyan Arab Jamahiriya), Judgment, I.C.J. Reports 1985*, p. 223, para. 56); whereas Mexico seeks clarification of the meaning and the scope of paragraph 153 (9) of the operative part of the 2004 Judgment in the *Avena* case, whereby the Court found that the United States is under an obligation to provide, by

means of its own choosing, review and reconsideration of the convictions and sentences of the Mexican nationals, taking into account both the violation of the rights set forth in Article 36 of the Vienna Convention and paragraphs 138 to 141 of the Judgment; whereas it is the interpretation of the meaning and scope of that obligation, and hence of the rights which Mexico and its nationals have on the basis of paragraph 153 (9) that constitutes the subject of the present proceedings before the Court on the Request for interpretation; whereas Mexico filed a request for the indication of provisional measures in order to protect these rights pending the Court's final decision;

64. Whereas, therefore, the rights which Mexico seeks to protect by its request for the indication of provisional measures (see paragraph 40 above) have a sufficient connection with the Request for interpretation;

65. Whereas the power of the Court to indicate provisional measures under Article 41 of its Statute "presupposes that irreparable prejudice shall not be caused to rights which are the subject of a dispute in judicial proceedings" (*LaGrand (Germany v. United States of America), Provisional Measures, Order of 3 March 1999, I.C.J. Reports 1999 (I)*, p.15, para. 22);

66. Whereas the power of the Court to indicate provisional measures will be exercised only if there is urgency in the sense that action prejudicial to the rights of either party is likely to be taken before the Court has given its final decision (see, for example, Passage through the Great Belt (Finland v. Denmark), Provisional Measures, Order of 29 July 1991, I.C.J. Reports 1991, p. 17, para. 23; Certain Criminal Proceedings in France (Republic of the Congo v. France), Provisional Measure, Order of 17 June 2003, I.C.J. Reports 2003, p. 107, para. 22; Pulp Mills on the River Uruguay (Argentina v. Uruguay), Provisional Measures, Order of 23 January 2007, I.C.J. Reports 2007 (I), p. 11, para. 32);

67. Whereas Mexico's principal request is that the Court should order that the United States

> "take all measures necessary to ensure that José Ernesto Medellín, César Roberto Fierro Reyna, Rubén Ramírez Cárdenas, Humberto Leal García, and Roberto Moreno Ramos are not executed pending the conclusion of the proceedings [concerning the Request for the interpretation of paragraph 153 (9) of the *Avena* Judgment,] unless and until [these] five Mexican nationals have received review and reconsideration consistent with paragraphs 138 to 141 of [that] Judgment";

68. Whereas Mexico asserts that it faces a real danger of irreparable prejudice and that the circumstances are sufficiently urgent as to justify the issuance of provisional measures; whereas Mexico, relying on the Court's previous case law, states that irreparable prejudice to the rights of Mexico would be caused by the execution of any persons named in the *Avena* Judgment pending this Court's resolution of the present Request for interpretation; whereas, according to Mexico,

> "[t]he execution of a Mexican national subject to the *Avena* Judgment, and hence entitled to review and reconsideration before the Court has had the opportunity to resolve the present Request for interpretation, would forever deprive Mexico of the opportunity to vindicate its rights and those of its nationals";

69. Whereas Mexico claims that there indisputably is urgency in the present circumstances given that Mr. Medellín's execution is scheduled for 5 August 2008, another Mexican national named in the *Avena* Judgment shortly could receive an execution date on 30 days' notice and three more shortly could receive execution dates on 90 days' notice; and whereas Mexico states that it "asks the Court to indicate provisional measures only

in respect of those of its nationals who have exhausted all available remedies and face an imminent threat of execution" and reserves its right to "return to this Court for protection for additional individuals if changing circumstances make that necessary";

70. Whereas Mexico requests the Court to

> "specify that the obligation to take all steps necessary to ensure that the execution *not* go forward applies to all competent organs of the United States and all its constituent subdivisions, including all branches of government and any official, state or federal, exercizing government authority" (emphasis in the original)

and to order that the United States inform the Court of the measures taken;

71. Whereas the United States argues that, as in the present case there are no rights in dispute, "*none* of the requirements for provisional measures are met" (emphasis in the original);

72. Whereas the execution of a national, the meaning and scope of whose rights are in question, before the Court delivers its judgment on the Request for interpretation "would render it impossible for the Court to order the relief that [his national State] seeks and thus cause irreparable harm to the rights it claims" (*Vienna Convention on Consular Relations (Paraguay v. United States of America), Provisional Measures, Order of 9 April 1998, I.C.J. Reports 1998*, p. 257, para. 37);

73. Whereas it is apparent from the information before the Court in this case that Mr. José Ernesto Medellín Rojas, a Mexican national, will face execution on 5 August 2008 and other Mexican nationals, Messrs. César Roberto Fierro Reyna, Rubén Ramírez Cárdenas, Humberto Leal García, and Roberto Moreno Ramos, are at risk of execution in the coming months; whereas their execution would cause irreparable prejudice to any rights, the interpretation of the meaning and scope of which is in question; and whereas it could be that the said Mexican nationals will be executed before this Court has delivered its judgment on the Request for interpretation and therefore there undoubtedly is urgency;

74. Whereas the Court accordingly concludes that the circumstances require that it indicate provisional measures to preserve the rights of Mexico, as Article 41 of its Statute provides;

75. Whereas the Court is fully aware that the federal Government of the United States has been taking many diverse and insistent measures in order to fulfil the international obligations of the United States under the *Avena* Judgment;

76. Whereas the Court notes that the United States has recognized that, were any of the Mexican nationals named in the request for the indication of provisional measures to be executed without the necessary review and reconsideration required under the *Avena* Judgment, that would constitute a violation of United States obligations under international law; whereas, in particular, the Agent of the United States declared before the Court that "[t]o carry out Mr. Medellín's sentence without affording him the necessary review and reconsideration obviously would be inconsistent with the *Avena* Judgment";

77. Whereas the Court further notes that the United States has recognized that "it is responsible under international law for the actions of its political subdivisions", including "federal, state, and local officials", and that its own international responsibility would be engaged if, as a result of acts or omissions by any of those political subdivisions, the United States was unable to respect its international obligations under the *Avena* Judgment; whereas, in particular, the Agent of the United States acknowledged before the Court that "the United States would be responsible, clearly, under the principle of State responsibility for the internationally wrongful actions of [state] officials";

78. Whereas the Court regards it as in the interest of both Parties that any difference of opinion as to the interpretation of the meaning and scope of their rights and obligations under paragraph 153 (9) of the *Avena* Judgment be resolved as early as possible; whereas it is therefore appropriate that the Court ensure that a judgment on the Request for interpretation be reached with all possible expedition;

79. Whereas the decision given in the present proceedings on the request for the indication of provisional measures in no way prejudges any question that the Court may have to deal with relating to the Request for interpretation;

80. For these reasons,

THE COURT,

I. By seven votes to five,

Finds that the submission by the United States of America seeking the dismissal of the Application filed by the United Mexican States can not be upheld;

IN FAVOUR: *President* Higgins; *Vice-President* Al-Khasawneh; *Judges* Ranjeva, Koroma, Abraham, Sepúlveda-Amor, Bennouna; AGAINST: *Judges* Buergenthal, Owada, Tomka, Keith, Skotnikov;

II. *Indicates* the following provisional measures:

(a) By seven votes to five,

The United States of America shall take all measures necessary to ensure that Messrs. José Ernesto Medellín Rojas, César Roberto Fierro Reyna, Rubén Ramírez Cárdenas, Humberto Leal García, and Roberto Moreno Ramos are not executed pending judgment on the Request for interpretation submitted by the United Mexican States, unless and until these five Mexican nationals receive review and reconsideration consistent with paragraphs 138 to 141 of the Court's Judgment delivered on 31 March 2004 in the case concerning *Avena and Other Mexican Nationals (Mexico v. United States of America)*;

IN FAVOUR: *President* Higgins; *Vice-President* Al-Khasawneh; *Judges* Ranjeva, Koroma, Abraham, Sepúlveda-Amor, Bennouna; AGAINST: *Judges* Buergenthal, Owada, Tomka, Keith, Skotnikov;

(b) By eleven votes to one,

The Government of the United States of America shall inform the Court of the measures taken in implementation of this Order;

IN FAVOUR: *President* Higgins; *Vice-President* Al-Khasawneh; *Judges* Ranjeva, Koroma, Owada, Tomka, Abraham, Keith, Sepúlveda-Amor, Bennouna, Skotnikov;

AGAINST: *Judge* Buergenthal;

Request for Interpretation of the Judgment of 31 March in *Avena and Other Mexican Nationals* (*Mexico v. United States*)

2009 I.C.J. (Judgment of Jan. 19)

52. ... [A]fter having unsuccessfully filed an application for a writ of *habeas corpus* and applications for stay of execution and after having been refused a stay of execution through the clemency process. Mr. Medellín was executed without being afforded the review and reconsideration provided for by paragraphs 138 to 141 of the *Avena* Judgment,

contrary to what was directed by the Court in its Order indicating provisional measures of 16 July 2008.]

53. The Court thus finds that the United States did not discharge its obligation under the Court's Order of 16 July 2008, in the case of Mr. José Ernesto Medellín Rojas.

54. The Court further notes that the Order of 16 July 2008 stipulated that five named persons were to be protected from execution until they received review and reconsideration or until the Court had rendered its Judgment upon Mexico's Request for interpretation. The Court recalls that the obligation upon the United States not to execute Messrs. César Roberto Fierro Reyna, Rubén Ramírez Cárdenas, Humberto Leal García, and Roberto Moreno Ramos pending review and reconsideration being afforded to them is fully intact by virtue of subparagraphs (4), (5), (6), (7) and (9) of paragraph 153 of the Avena Judgment itself. The Court further notes that the other persons named in the Avena Judgment are also to be afforded review and reconsideration in the terms there specified.

55. The Court finally recalls that, as the United States has itself acknowledged, until all of the Mexican nationals referred to in subparagraphs (4), (5), (6) and (7) of paragraph 153 of the Avena Judgment have had their convictions and sentences reviewed and reconsidered, by taking account of Article 36 of the Vienna Convention on Consular Relations and paragraphs 138 to 141 of the Avena Judgment, the United States has not complied with the obligation incumbent upon it.

56. As regards the additional claim by Mexico asking the Court to declare that the United States breached the *Avena* Judgment by executing José Ernesto Medellín Rojas without having provided him review and reconsideration consistent with the terms of that Judgment, the Court notes that the only basis of jurisdiction relied upon for this claim in the present proceedings is Article 60 of the Statute, and that that Article does not allow it to consider possible violations of the Judgment which it is called upon to interpret.

57. In view of the above, the Court finds that the additional claim by Mexico concerning alleged violations of the *Avena* Judgment must be dismissed.

58. Lastly, Mexico requests the Court to order the United States to provide guarantees of non-repetition (point (2) (c) of Mexico's submissions) so that none of the Mexican nationals mentioned in the Avena Judgment is executed without having benefited from the review and reconsideration provided for by the operative part of that Judgment.

59. The United States disputes the jurisdiction of the Court to order it to furnish guarantees of non-repetition, principally inasmuch as the Court lacks jurisdiction under Article 60 of the Statute to entertain Mexico's Request for interpretation or, in the alternative, since the Court cannot, in any event, order the provision of such guarantees within the context of interpretation proceedings.

60. The Court finds it sufficient to reiterate that its Avena Judgment remains binding and that the United States continues to be under an obligation fully to implement it.

61. For these reasons,

THE COURT,

(1) By eleven votes to one,

> *Finds* that the matters claimed by the United Mexican States to be in issue between the Parties, requiring an interpretation under Article 60 of the Statute, are not matters which have been decided by the Court in its Judgment of 31 March 2004 in the case concerning *Avena and Other Mexican Nationals (Mexico v. United*

States of America), including paragraph 153 (9), and thus cannot give rise to the interpretation requested by the United Mexican States;

IN FAVOUR : *President* Higgins; *Vice-President* Al-Khasawneh; *Judges* Ranjeva, Koroma, Buergenthal, Owada, Tomka, Abraham, Keith, Bennouna,

Skotnikov;

AGAINST: *Judge* Sepúlveda-Amor;

(2) Unanimously,

Finds that the United States of America has breached the obligation incumbent upon it under the Order indicating provisional measures of 16 July 2008, in the case of Mr. José Ernesto Medellín Rojas;

(3) By eleven votes to one,

Reaffirms the continuing binding character of the obligations of the United States of America under paragraph 153 (9) of the *Avena* Judgment and *takes note* of the undertakings given by the United States of America in these proceedings;

IN FAVOUR : *President* Higgins; *Vice-President* Al-Khasawneh; *Judges* Ranjeva, Koroma, Buergenthal, Owada, Tomka, Keith, Sepúlveda-Amor, Bennouna, Skotnikov;

AGAINST: *Judge* Sepúlveda-Amor

Mary Ellen O'Connell, *The Failure to Observe Provisional Measures of Protection in the Case of Bosnia v. Yugoslavia**

* * *

Does the Court have the authority to take measures which could be categorized as enforcement measures? Article 94 of the UN Charter states that "If any party to a case fails to perform the obligations incumbent upon it under a judgment rendered by the Court, the other party may have recourse to the Security Council, which may, if it deems necessary, make recommendations or decide upon measures to be taken to give effect the judgment." This suggests to some that the Security Council has the sole authority to enforce.

But Article 94 does not bar the Court from taking responsive action. The purpose of Article 94 is to lend support to the Court by linking it with the Security Council and the Council's greater competence. Article 94 does not appear to be a limitation on the competence the Court does have, which includes enforcement certainly through procedural means. *Rosenne*, agent for Yugoslavia, has written:

> ... the failure of a State to comply with an interlocutory decision can lead to the automatic imposition by the Court itself of a sanction against that State ...[47]

Rosenne goes on to write that the Court cannot sanction non-compliance with provisional measures. He does not, however, provide any explanation why provisional measures

---

* Vortrag gehalten im Rahmen des Walther-Schücking-Kollegs, Institut für Internationales Recht an der Universität Kiel, 12 November, 1993 (some footnotes omitted).

47. *Shabtai Rosenne*, The Law and Practice of the International Court of Justice (1985), pp. 124–25.

should be treated differently from other interlocutory measures and indeed, no distinction seems apparent.[48]

* * *

Admittedly, the Court's options in this case were limited, but some additional, creative measures to respond to the non-compliance would have been available. In particular, procedural sanctions, as *Rosenne* suggests above, were available....

* * *

Among the procedural measures available, the most limited response to non-compliance is remonstration. The Court did use this response. Another possibility was suggested by Judge *Ajibola*. He suggested that all requests for additional orders should be rejected until prior orders are fulfilled....[49]

Judge *Ajibola* then characterized the Court's Order of 13 September as such a sanction, saying that the reiteration of the earlier order was a refusal to issue a new order. The Court, however, does not anywhere indicate this was its intention. Indeed, such intention does not seem even implicit in the court's opinion. Instead, the Court said "... the present perilous situation demands, not an indication of provisional measures additional to those indicated ... but immediate and effective implementation of those measures....[50]

Another procedural sanction is to shift the burden of proof. The Genocide Convention requires proof that the accused intended to commit genocide. Intent is always difficult to prove and it could make Bosnia's case much easier if the Court shifted the burden from Bosnia to Yugoslavia, requiring Yugoslavia to prove it had no intent to commit genocide. Colleagues from the civil law tradition have reacted to this suggestion as unfair because it manipulates the discovery of truth. But, of course, the imposition of the burden is not an organic part of the search for truth. In common law the burden is associated with those who society favors in a particular search for truth. It would seem that the party which cannot show it took measures to prevent genocide should not be favored.[51]

In Nicaragua's case against the United States, Nicaragua requested yet another type of sanction for the U.S.'s failure to observe provisional measures. Nicaragua requested that the Court deny the U.S. the Court's facilities in all cases. The Court's president at the time denied the request without much explanation....

* * *

Professor Schachter has written well before the Bosnia case:

> If the Court has satisfied itself that an order for provisional measures is justified in the circumstances, it should be prepared to impose some sanction on the recalcitrant State, whether applicant or respondent ... Admittedly, the Court is limited in the enforcement it can take but it can always express strong censure of non-complying conduct. To do nothing more than mention the fact of disobedience provides little deterrent to contumacious behavior by a party. The result is to weaken the authority of the judicial process.[53]

48. *Id.*
49. *Ajibola*, I.C.J. Reports 1993, p. 406.
50. Order of 13 September, I.C.J. Reports 1993, p. 349.
51. However, Bosnia's failure to provide evidence on this question raises further problems.
53. *Oscar Schachter*, International Law in Theory and Practice (1991), p. 232.

Notes and Questions on Provisional Measures

1. Does it matter that the *LaGrand* Court held provisional measures are binding if states consistently ignore them? In other words, provisional measures are, in effect, only advisory as a practical matter, are they not?

2. Or are they? Recall how interim orders might be enforced in arbitration. Might similar methods be used regarding judicial orders? As a theoretical matter, would it make sense for provisional measures to be advisory only? Recall why courts and tribunals have the power to issue interim measures.

3. As will be discussed in Chapter Thirteen, the UN Charter provides for the Security Council in Article 94 to act in cases where parties fail to fulfill their obligations regarding the ICJ, but the article says the Council may make recommendations or decide on measures "to give effect to the judgment." Still, the U.K. invoked Article 94 in a provisional measures case. It requested that the Security Council enforce provisional measures ordered by the ICJ in the Anglo-Iranian Oil Co. Case. *Anglo-Iranian Oil Co.* (U.K. v. Iran), 1951 I.C.J. 4 (Order of July 5). Article 94's reference to "judgments" led the Council to debate whether it had the authority to enforce interim measures. The issue became moot before the Council reached a decision.

4. In 1999, while NATO bombed Yugoslavia, Yugoslavia requested that the ICJ issue an order of interim measures requiring NATO to stop the bombing. The emergency request was intended to save lives during an evidently unlawful use of force by NATO. *See* Mary Ellen O'Connell, *The UN, NATO and International Law After Kosovo*, 22 HUM. RTS. Q. 57 (2000). In such a case, even where the basis for ICJ jurisdiction is weak, the Court has in the past ordered interim measures. In this instance, Yugoslavia had a basis for jurisdiction in the Genocide Convention—the same basis used by Bosnia in the *Genocide Case*. To avoid taking action in the case, however, the Court narrowly construed a time limit in Yugoslavia's acceptance of the Court's jurisdiction. See *Case Concerning Legality of Use of Force* (Yugoslavia v. Belgium), Request for the Indication of Provisional Measures, Order, 1999 I.C.J. 124 (June 2). In a dramatic reversal of its earlier decision, the ICJ then found it had jurisdiction over the remaining part of Yugoslavia, Serbia, in *Application of the Convention on the Prevention and Punishment of the Crime of Genocide* (Bosnia v. Serbia) 2007 I.C.J. 43 (Feb. 26). Some argue that the ICJ should avoid highly political cases in order to conserve support in the international community. Would the ICJ have any cases if it took this view? How should the ICJ or any court look upon the political aspects of its case?

5. The attempts by Ernesto Medellin and other Mexican nationals named in the *Avena* case to have the ICJ orders enforced in the United States Supreme Court are discussed in Chapter Fifteen.

6. In March 2011, the ICJ ordered interim measures in a boundary dispute between Costa Rica and Nicaragua. Tensions had been high with Nicaraguan troops refusing to leave an area claimed by Costa Rica. The ICJ ordered all government personnel out of the area but made the unusual and creative exception for Costa Rica:

> civilian personnel charged with the protection of the environment in the disputed territory..., but only in so far as it is necessary to avoid irreparable prejudice being caused to the part of the wetland where that territory is situated; Costa Rica shall consult with the Secretariat of the Ramsar Convention in re-

gard to these actions, give Nicaragua prior notice of them and use its best endeavors to find common solutions with Nicaragua in this respect. *Certain Activities Carried Out by Nicaragua in the Border Area* (Costa Rica v. Nicar.), Order, ¶ 80 (Mar. 8, 2011), *available at* http://www.icj-cij.org/docket/files/150/16324.pdf.

If Nicaragua or Costa Rica failed to honor the requirements of this order, how might the ICJ in its final decision on the merits take such a failure into account? Is the ICJ really in any position to enforce an order like this?

7. In July 2011, the ICJ ordered interim measures in another serious boundary conflict between Cambodia and Thailand in which a number had been killed in the preceding years. *See Request for Interpretation of the Judgment of 15 June 1962 in the Case Concerning the Temple of Preah Vihear* (Thai. v. Cambodia), Order, (July 18, 2011), *available at* http://www.icj-cij.org/docket/files/151/16564.pdf. Among other orders, the court held: "Both Parties shall refrain from any action which might aggravate or extend the dispute before the Court or make it more difficult to resolve." Fifteen judges voted in favor of the Order. Only Judge Donoghue of the United States voted against. This is highly unusual as sole dissenters are almost always a judge of the nationality of a party to the case or is the judge *ad hoc* appointed by a party. What might account for Judge Donoghue's unusual voting record? The *Request for Interpretation in the Temple of Preah Vihear* case is discussed further in Chapter Thirteen.

8. For further reading on provisional measures *see*:

INTERIM MEASURES INDICATED BY INTERNATIONAL COURTS (Rudolph Bernard ed., 1994).

JERZY SZTUCKI, INTERIM MEASURES IN THE HAGUE COURT: AN ATTEMPT AT A SCRUTINY (1983).

Chapter Twelve

Intervention and Indispensable Parties

Introduction

Unlike the topic of provisional measures, we have not yet seen a discussion of either intervention or indispensable parties (also called "necessary" parties). While there are instances of parties trying to intervene in commercial arbitration, apparently we have no prominent examples of states or international organizations attempting to intervene in an arbitration or of an arbitration being dismissed by the arbitrators because of the absence of indispensable parties. These facts provide insights into the nature of courts versus arbitral tribunals. Arbitral tribunals are focused more narrowly on the parties that create the tribunal and ask the questions, while courts have a larger role with respect to the rule of law in society more generally.

A. Intervention

Several states have sought to intervene in cases before the ICJ during the Court's sixty year history. As the excerpted article by Judge Ruda explains, the ICJ has resisted allowing intervention with the exception of one case, despite the fact that the ICJ Statute provides for intervention:

Article 62

1. Should a state consider that it has an interest of a legal nature which may be affected by the decision in the case, it may submit a request to the Court to be permitted to intervene.
2. It shall be for the Court to decide upon this request.

J.M. Ruda, *Intervention before the International Court of Justice**

INTRODUCTION

The jurisdiction of the International Court of Justice to entertain interventions is part of the Court's incidental jurisdiction. This form of the Court's jurisdiction is termed 'in-

* Fifty Years of the International Court of Justice: Essays in Honour of Sir Robert Jennings 487 (Vaughan Lowe and Malgosia Fitzmaurice eds., 1996) (Footnotes omitted. For provisions of the ICJ. Statute and Rules, see Annex.).

cidental' because 'it is a jurisdiction which the Court may be called upon to exercise as an incident of proceedings already before it'.

The Statute of the ICJ envisions two types of intervention: discretionary intervention, which is covered by article 62 of the Statute; and intervention as of right, which is provided for by article 63 of the Statute. In the following, these two types of intervention will be discussed separately.

DISCRETIONARY INTERVENTION

The provisions of the Statute and the Rules of the Court

Discretionary intervention is covered by article 62 of the Statute of the Court, which reads as follows:

> (1) Should a state consider that it has an interest of a legal nature which may be affected by the decision in the case, it may submit a request to the Court to be permitted to intervene.
>
> (2) It shall be for the Court to decide upon this request.

Although under paragraph 2 of article 62 it is 'for the Court to decide upon' a request for permission to intervene, this provision does not supply the Court with unlimited powers to accept or reject a request for permission to intervene. As the Court stated in the *Continental Shelf* case between Tunisia and Libya:

> The Court observes that under paragraph 2 of Article 62 it is for the Court itself to decide upon any request for permission to intervene. The Court, at the same, emphasizes that it does not consider paragraph 2 to confer upon it any general discretion to accept or reject a request for permission to intervene for reasons simply of policy. On the contrary, in the view of the Court the task entrusted to it by that paragraph is to determine the admissibility or otherwise the request by reference to the relevant provisions of the Statute.

The procedure governing intervention under article 62 is regulated by article 81 of the Rules of the Court. This article reads as follows:

> 1. An application for permission to intervene under the terms of Article 62 of the Statute, signed in the manner provided for in Article 38, paragraph 3, of these Rules, shall be filed as soon as possible, and not later than the closure of the written proceedings. In exceptional circumstances, an application submitted at a later stage may however be admitted.
>
> 2. The application shall state the name of an agent. It shall specify the case to which it relates, and shall set out:
>
>   (a) the interest of a legal nature which the State applying to intervene considers may be affected by the decision in that case;
>
>   (b) the precise object of the intervention;
>
>   (c) any basis of jurisdiction which is claimed to exist as between the State applying to intervene and the parties to the case.
>
> 3. The application shall contain a list of the documents in support, which documents shall be attached.

It can be noted that article 81 of the Rules of the Court is more specific than article 62 of the Statute. Of particular interest is paragraph 2 of article 81 of the Rules, which specifies the contents of an application for permission to intervene, and requires that the application must not only specify 'the interest of a legal nature which the State applying to intervene considers may be affected by the decision in th[e] case', which requirement is also embodied in article 62 of the Statute, but also 'the precise object of the intervention', and 'any basis of jurisdiction which is claimed to exist as between the State applying to intervene and the parties to the case'.

The inclusion of the last-mentioned requirement in the Rules of the Court, i.e., that a state seeking intervention shall set out any jurisdictional link that is claimed to exist between that state and the parties in the case, reflects a long-standing controversy within the Court concerning the institution of intervention; namely, whether or not there must exist a jurisdictional link between the state seeking to intervene and the parties to the case. This controversy dates from 1922 when the predecessor of the present Court, the Permanent Court of International Justice, began to consider its rules of procedure for applying article 62 of the Statute. This controversy has been described by the present Court as follows:

> When the Permanent Court began, in 1922, to consider its rules of procedure for applying Article 62 of the Statute, it became apparent that different views were held as to the object and form of the intervention allowed under that Article, and also as to the need for a basis of jurisdiction vis-à-vis the parties to the case. Some Members of the Permanent Court took the view that only an interest of a legal nature in the actual subject of the dispute itself would justify the intervention under Article 62; others considered that it would be enough for the State seeking to intervene to show that its interests might be affected by the position adopted by the Court in the particular case. Similarly, while some Members of the Court regarded the existence of a link of jurisdiction with the parties to the case as a further necessary condition for intervention under Article 62, others thought that it would be enough simply to establish the existence of an interest of a legal nature which might be affected by the Court's decision in the case. The outcome of the discussion was that it was agreed not to try to resolve in the Rules of the Court the various questions which had been raised, but to leave them to be decided as and when they occurred in practice and in the light of the circumstances of each particular case.

Subsequently, when the present Rules of the Court, which date from 1978, were drafted, a new subparagraph (c) was included, requiring an application for permission to intervene.... The Court has explained that this was done in order to ensure that, when the question did arise in a concrete case, [the Court] would be in possession of all the elements which might be necessary for its decision. At the same time the Court left any question with which it might in future be confronted in regard to intervention to be decided on the basis of the Statute and in the light of the particular circumstances of each case.'

The practice of the Court

Article 62 of the Statute has been invoked as a basis of intervention in three relatively recent cases before the Court. In the case concerning the *Continental Shelf between Tunisia and Libya*, Malta sought intervention, and in the case concerning the *Continental Shelf between Libya and Malta*, Italy requested permission to intervene. Most recently, Nicaragua sought intervention in the case concerning the *Land, Island and Maritime Frontier Dispute* between El Salvador and Honduras.

In the *Tunisia/Libya Continental Shelf* case, the Court unanimously denied Malta's application on the grounds that Malta had failed to demonstrate an interest of a legal nature that might be affected by the decision of the Court within the meaning of article 62 of the Statute. Having reached that conclusion, the Court found 'it unnecessary to decide in the present case the question whether the existence of a valid link of jurisdiction with the parties to the case is an essential condition for the granting of permission to intervene under Article 62 of the Statute'.

The *Libya/Malta Continental Shelf* case was more controversial, and Italy's application for permission to intervene was denied only after a vote, by eleven votes to five. In this case, Italy argued that article 62 of the Statute created 'direct jurisdiction' for the Court to entertain Italy's intervention, and that article 81, paragraph 2(c) of the Rules was not intended to impose the existence of a basis of jurisdiction as a condition for intervention, but was included in the Rules merely to ensure that the Court would be provided with all relevant information of the circumstances of the case. Like the *Tunisia/Libya Continental Shelf* case, the Court did not reach this issue. It concluded that Italy's request could not be granted because, in the Court's view, Italy was requesting the Court to decide on the rights Italy had claimed and not merely to ensure that these rights were not affected. Consequently, according to the Court, 'to permit the intervention would involve the introduction of a fresh dispute' to the Court; and in the absence of consent of the parties, the Court could not entertain any such dispute. The Court held that these consequences of the Court's finding '[could] be defined by reference to either of the two approaches to the interpretation of Article 62 of the Statute'. The Court explained:

> The first way of expressing this reality [i.e., 'the basic principle that the jurisdiction of the Court to deal with and judge a dispute depends on the consent of the parties thereto'] would be to find that, having ... reached the conclusion that Italy is requesting it to decide on the rights which it has claimed and not merely to ensure that these rights be not affected, the Court must state whether it is competent to give, by way of intervention procedure, the decision requested by Italy ... The view could be taken that Article 62 does not permit an intervention of the kind referred to except when the third State desiring to intervene can rely on a basis of jurisdiction making it possible for the Court to take a decision on the dispute or disputes submitted to it by the third State ... A second method of expressing the Court's conviction that Article 62 of its Statute is not an exception to the principle of consent to its jurisdiction to deal with a dispute would be to find that, in a case where the State requesting the intervention asked the Court to give a judgment on the rights which it was claiming, this would not be a genuine intervention within the meaning of Article 62. In such a situation, the State requesting the intervention ought to have instituted mainline proceedings in application of Article 36, and possibly to have asked for the two proceedings to be joined ... Thus, according to this second approach, Article 62 would not derogate from the consensualism which underlies the jurisdiction of the Court, since the only cases of intervention afforded by that Article would be those in which the intervener was only seeking the preservation of its rights, without attempting to have them recognized, the latter objective appertaining rather to a direct action. Article 62 of the Statute envisages that the object of the intervening State is to ensure the protection or safeguarding of its 'interest of a legal nature' by preventing it from being 'affected' by the decision. There is nothing in Article 62 to suggest that it was intended as an alternative means of bringing an additional dispute as a case before the Court ... or as a method of asserting the individual rights of a State not party to the case.

The Court concluded that, 'in order to arrive at its decision on the Application of Italy to intervene in the present case, [the Court] does not have to rule on the question whether, in general, any intervention based on Article 62 must, as a condition for its admission, show the existence of a valid jurisdictional link'.

The first case in the history of the present Court and its predecessor in which a state was accorded permission to intervene under article 62 of the Statute was the *Case Concerning the Land, Island and Maritime Frontier Dispute* between El Salvador and Honduras. The Chamber that was formed to deal with the case found that the intervening state, Nicaragua, had shown that it had 'an interest of a legal nature which may be affected by part of the Judgment of the Chamber in the present case, namely its decision on the legal regime of the waters of the Gulf of Fonseca'. Consequently, the Chamber permitted Nicaragua to intervene in the case 'to the extent, in the manner and for the purposes set out in the Judgment'.

Pursuant to article 2 of the Special Agreement concluded between the parties, El Salvador and Honduras, by which Agreement they submitted the dispute to the Chamber, the function of the Chamber was: '1. To delimit the frontier line in the areas or sections not described in Article 16 of the General Peace Treaty of 30 October 1980; [and] 2. To determine the legal situation of the islands and maritime spaces.' Nicaragua's application for permission to intervene was not related to the first aspect of the proceedings, i.e., the delimitation of the land frontier line, but only to the determination by the Chamber of the legal situation of the islands, the waters of the Gulf of Fonseca, and the waters outside the Gulf.

Referring to article 81, paragraph 2 of the Rules of the Court, the Chamber examined in detail Nicaragua's arguments in support of its application. Dismissing El Salvador's objection that Nicaragua's request was out of time, the Court focused on whether Nicaragua had been able to show an interest of a legal nature which might be affected by the Chamber's decision in the case, the criterion stated in article 62 of the Statute and article 81, paragraph 2(a) of the Rules of the Court. Noting that the Chamber was not required, by the Special Agreement, to give a decision on a single circumscribed issue, but several decisions on various aspects of the overall dispute between the parties, the Chamber considered 'the possible effect on legal interests asserted by Nicaragua of its eventual decision on each of the different issues which might fall to be determined, in order to define the scope of any intervention which may be found to be justified under Article 62 of the Statute'.

Regarding the extent of the burden of proof on a state seeking to intervene, the Chamber noted the differences between the parties and the state seeking to intervene, and concluded:

> In the Chamber's opinion, however, it is clear, first, that it is for a State seeking to intervene to demonstrate convincingly what it asserts, and thus to bear the burden of proof; and, second, that it has only to show that its interest 'may' be affected, not that it will or must be affected. What needs to be shown by a State seeking permission to intervene can only be judged *in concreto* and in relation to all the circumstances of a particular case. It is for the State seeking to intervene to identify the interest of a legal nature which it considers may be affected by the decision in the case, and to show in what way that interest may be affected; it is not for the Court itself—or in the present case the Chamber—to substitute itself for the State in that respect.

Having examined the question whether the decision of the Chamber regarding the legal situation of the islands may affect the legal interest of Nicaragua, the Chamber concluded that:

> Insofar as the dispute relates to sovereignty over the islands, [the Chamber] should not grant permission for intervention by Nicaragua, in the absence of

> any Nicaraguan interest liable to be directly affected by a decision on that issue. Any possible effects of the islands as relevant circumstances for delimitation of maritime spaces fall to be considered in the context of the question whether Nicaragua should be permitted to intervene on the basis of a legal interest which may be affected by a decision on the legal situation of the waters of the Gulf.

The Chamber then examined the parties' and Nicaragua's arguments regarding the existence of 'an objective legal régime' of a condominium in the waters of the Gulf of Fonseca. The Chamber noted, in particular, Nicaragua's argument to the effect that 'the condominium, if it is declared to be applicable, would by its very nature involve three riparians, and not only the parties to the Special Agreement'. The Chamber concluded that this was a sufficient demonstration by Nicaragua that it has an interest of a legal nature in the determination whether or not this is the régime governing the waters of the Gulf: the very definition of a condominium points to this conclusion'. The Chamber likewise held that, on the basis of the Honduran theory to the effect that there was a 'community of interest' in the waters of the Gulf, the result was the same: Nicaragua, as one of the three riparian states, was also interested in that question. However, the Chamber was not satisfied that, were it to hold that there was no such condominium or community of interests in the Gulf, Nicaragua had also a legal interest that may be affected by the Chamber's decision in the delimitation within the Gulf. The Chamber reached the same conclusion as to the possible effect on Nicaragua's legal interests of its future decision on the waters outside the Gulf.

As to the two remaining conditions of intervention embodied in article 81, paragraph 2 of the Rules of the Court, the Chamber was satisfied that the two 'objects' of intervention put forward by Nicaragua—to protect its legal rights in the Gulf of Fonseca and the adjacent maritime areas, and to inform the Chamber of the nature of its legal rights in issue in the dispute—were proper ones. The remaining—and controversial—issues was the requirement of article 81, paragraph 2(c) of the Rules, or the question of the existence of a valid jurisdictional link between Nicaragua and the parties to the case. The Chamber noted that in its application Nicaragua had not invoked any jurisdictional basis for its intervention other than the Statute itself. Referring to the Court's past practice, the Chamber stated:

> Although that Judgment [i.e., *Libya/Malta Continental Shelf* case (*Intervention*)] contains a number of valuable observations on the subject, the question remains unresolved. Since in the present case the Chamber has reached the conclusion that Nicaragua has shown the existence of an interest of a legal nature which may be affected by the decision, and that the intervention of Nicaragua has a proper object, the only remaining question is whether a jurisdictional link is required; and since it is conceded that no such link exists, the Chamber is obliged to decide the point.

The Chamber then proceeded to consider 'the general principle of consensual jurisdiction in its relation with the institution of intervention'. Recalling that, as between the parties, consent is the source of the Court's jurisdiction, the Chamber continued:

> Nevertheless, procedures for a 'third' State to intervene in a case are provided in Articles 62 and 63 of the Court's Statute. The competence of the Court in this matter of intervention is not, like its competence to hear and determine the dispute referred to it, derived from the consent of the parties to the case, but from the consent given by them, in becoming parties to the Court's Statute, to the Court's exercise of its powers conferred by the Statute. There is no need to interpret the reference in Article 36, paragraph 1, of the Statute to 'treaties in force'

to include the Statute itself; acceptance of the Statute entails acceptance of the competence conferred on the Court by Article 62. Thus the Court has competence to permit an intervention even though it be opposed by one or both of the parties to the case; as the Court stated in 1984, 'the opposition [to an intervention] of the parties to a case is, though very important, no more than one element to be taken into account by the Court' (*ICJ Reports 1984*, p. 28, para. 46). The nature of the competence thus created by Article 62 of the Statute is definable by reference to the object and purpose of intervention, as this appears from Article 62 of the Statute.

The Chamber added that intervention was 'not intended to enable a third State to tack on a new case, to become a new party, and so have its own claims adjudicated by the Court'. The difference between intervention and the joining of a new party to the case was not, in the Chamber's view, merely a difference in degree, but a difference in kind. Observing that intervention appears in section D of the Rules of the Court, headed 'Incidental Proceedings', the Chamber emphasized that 'incidental proceedings by definition must be those which are incidental to a case which is already before the Court or Chamber'. Accordingly, 'an incidental proceeding cannot be one which transforms a case into a different case with different parties'. In other words, according to the Chamber, intervention could not have been intended to be employed as a substitute for contentious proceedings.

> Acceptance of the Statute by a State does not of itself create jurisdiction to entertain a particular case: the specific consent of the parties is necessary for that. If an intervener were held to become a party to a case merely as a consequence of being permitted to intervene in it, this would be a very considerable departure from this principle of consensual jurisdiction.

Referring to the *Libya/Malta Continental Shelf* case, the Chamber concluded:

> It is therefore clear that a State which is allowed to intervene in a case, does not, by reason only of being an intervener, become also a party to the case. It is true, conversely, that provided that there be the necessary consent by the parties to the case, the intervener is not prevented by reason of that status from itself becoming a party to the case ... It thus follows from the juridical nature and from the purposes of intervention that the existence of a valid link of jurisdiction between the would-be intervener and the parties is not a requirement for the success of the application. On the contrary, the procedure for intervention is to ensure that a State with possibly affected interests may be permitted to intervene even though there is no jurisdictional link and it therefore cannot become a party. Article 81, paragraph 2(c), of the Rules of the Court states that an application under Article 62 of the Statute shall set out 'any basis of jurisdiction which is claimed to exist as between the State applying to intervene and the parties to the case'; the use of the words 'any basis' (and in French the formula 'toute base de competence qui ... existerait') shows that a valid link of jurisdiction is not treated as a *sine qua non* for intervention ... The Chamber therefore concludes that the absence of a jurisdictional link between Nicaragua and the Parties to the case is no bar to permission being given for intervention.

Noting that this was the first case in the history of the two Courts in which a state had been permitted to intervene under article 62 of the Statute, the Chamber found it 'appropriate to give some indication of the extent of the procedural rights acquired by the intervening State as a result of that permission'. The rights were, first, that 'the intervening State does not become party to the proceedings, and does not acquire the rights, or become subject to the obligations, which attach to the status of a party, under the Statute and the Rules of the Court, or the general principles of procedural law'. Second, the intervening state has a right to be heard, which right is regulated by article 85 of the Rules of the Court. Third, the intervening state is permitted to address only such issues with respect to which it has demonstrated an interest of a legal nature in accordance with article 62 of the Statute, i.e., in this case the intervening state, Nicaragua, was permitted to address only such issues as relate to the legal regime of the waters of the Gulf of Fonseca.

The Chamber delivered its judgment on the merits of the *Land, Island and Maritime Frontier Dispute* on 11 September 1992. Recalling that this was the first time in the history of the Court and its predecessor in which a third state had been permitted to intervene under article 62 of the Statute, the Chamber considered it appropriate 'to make some observations on the effect of the present Judgment for the intervening State'.

The Chamber first noted that pursuant to its judgment on the application by Nicaragua for permission to intervene of 13 September 1990, the intervening state, Nicaragua, had not become a party to the proceedings. Based on this, the Chamber held that 'the binding force of the present Judgment for the Parties, as contemplated by Article 59 of the Statute of the Court, does not therefore extend also to Nicaragua as intervener'. The Chamber then took note of the fresh attitude of Nicaragua to the effect that Nicaragua no longer regarded itself as being obligated to treat the judgment as binding upon it, and went on to consider 'the effect, if any, to be given to the statement made in Nicaragua's Application for permission to intervene that it "intends to submit itself to the binding effect of the decision to be given"'. The Chamber opined:

> In the Chamber's Judgment of 13 September 1990, emphasis was laid on the need, if an intervener is to become a party, for the consent of the existing parties to the case, either consent *ad hoc* or in the form of a pre-existing link of jurisdiction. This is essential because the force of *res judicata* does not operate in one direction only if an intervener becomes a party, and is thus bound by the judgment, it becomes entitled equally to assert the binding force of the judgment against the other parties. A non-party to a case before the Court, whether or not admitted to intervene, cannot by its own unilateral act place itself in the position of a party, and claim to be entitled to rely on the judgment against the original parties. In the present case, El Salvador requested the Chamber to deny the permission to intervene sought by Nicaragua; and neither Party has given any indication of consent to Nicaragua's being recognized to have any status which would enable it to rely on the Judgment. The Chamber therefore concludes that in the circumstances of the present case, this Judgment is not *res judicata* for Nicaragua.

INTERVENTION AS OF RIGHT

Another type of intervention, often termed intervention as of right, is provided for in article 63 of the Statute of the Court. This provision states:

> 1. Whenever the construction of a convention to which states other than those concerned in the case are parties is in question, the Registrar shall notify all such states forthwith.
> 2. Every state so notified has the right to intervene in the proceedings; but if it uses this right, the construction given by the judgment will be equally binding upon it.

This provision was applied by the Permanent Court of International Justice only once, in the case concerning the *SS Wimbledon*. There, the Court admitted the intervention sought by Poland under article 63 of the Statute, although the application was initially filed under article 62. Taking note of the change of attitude by Poland in the course of the proceedings, abandoning article 62 as the basis of its intervention and instead relying on article 63, the Court found it unnecessary 'to consider and satisfy itself whether Poland's intervention in the suit before it is justified by an interest of a legal nature, within the meaning of Article 62 of the Statute'. The Court then noted that the interpretation of certain clauses of the Treaty of Versailles was involved in the case and that Poland was one of the states parties to the Treaty. Based on this, the Court merely 'recorded' that 'the Polish Government intend[ed] to avail itself of the right to intervene conferred upon it by Article 63 of the Statutes', and accepted Poland's intervention.

In the *Haya de la Torre* case, Cuba filed a Declaration of Intervention with the Court, invoking article 63 of the Statute, together with a Memorandum stating its views concerning the interpretation of the Havana Convention of 1928. One of the parties to the case, Peru, having objected to Cuba's Declaration of Intervention on grounds, *inter alia*, that the intervention sought by Cuba did not constitute a proper intervention but rather 'an attempt by a third State to appeal against the Judgment delivered by the Court on November 20th, 1950', the Court stated in that regard:

> The Court observes that every intervention is incidental to the proceedings in a case; it follows that a declaration filed as an intervention only acquires that character, in law, if it actually relates to the subject-matter of the pending proceedings. The subject-matter of the present case differs from that of the case which was terminated by the Judgment of November 20th, 1950: it concerns a question—the surrender of Haya de la Torre to the Peruvian authorities—which in the previous case was completely outside the Submissions of the Parties, and which was in consequence in no way decided by the above-mentioned Judgment.

The Court then examined whether the object of Cuba's intervention was in fact the interpretation of the Havana Convention. Observing that Cuba's Memorandum was 'almost entirely [devoted] to a discussion of the questions which the Judgment of November 20th, 1950, had already decided with the authority of *res judicata*', the Court found that, to that extent, Cuba's Declaration of Intervention did not satisfy the conditions of a genuine intervention. The Court also held, however, that the statement of the Agent of Cuba at the hearing to the effect that Cuba's intervention was based on the fact that the Court was required to interpret a new aspect of the Havana Convention not subject to the Court's determination in the *Asylum* case conformed to the conditions of article 63 of the Statute. Consequently, 'reduced in this way, and operating within these limits', the Court admitted Cuba's intervention.

The most recent case in which a Declaration of Intervention was submitted to the Court by invoking article 63 of the Statute was the *Case Concerning Military and Paramilitary Activities in and against Nicaragua* between Nicaragua and the US, in which El Salvador sought intervention. The Court summarily disposed of El Salvador's Declaration of Intervention, deciding not to hold a hearing on it and declaring it inadmissible 'inasmuch as it relate[d] to the current phase of the proceedings'; i.e., a phase of the proceedings in which the proceedings on the merits of the case were suspended pending the Court's determination of whether it had jurisdiction to entertain Nicaragua's application and whether the application was admissible. The Court found that El Salvador's Declaration of Intervention 'addresse[d] itself to matters, including the construction of conventions, which presuppose that the Court has jurisdiction to entertain the dispute ... and that Nicaragua's Application ... [was] admissible'.

CONCLUSION

The two forms of intervention contemplated in the Statute of the Court—discretionary intervention under article 62 and intervention as of right under article 63—are quite distinct and the juridical issues relating to the former appear to be more complicated than those relating to the latter. While the language of article 62 of the Statute is reasonably clear, the differences between the Statute and the Rules of the Court have created some confusion for the Court as well as for the states appearing before it. However, some of the issues have been clarified by the practice of the two Courts, in particular by the recent practice of the present Court. As regards article 62 of the Statute, the following conclusions can be drawn based on that practice:

1. A state seeking intervention may be granted a permission to intervene in a case even in the absence of a jurisdictional link between that state and the parties to the case; however, in the absence of a consent by the parties to the case, the state seeking intervention does not become a party to the case and therefore will not be bound by the judgment on the Merits nor can it oppose the judgment as against the parties; i.e., the judgment is not *res judicata* as regards the state permitted to intervene.
2. If a state seeking intervention is able to establish a jurisdictional link as between itself and the parties to the case, or if the parties do not object to the intervention, the state seeking intervention may be granted permission to intervene and it may become a party to the case; in such circumstances, it will also be bound by the decision and will be able to oppose the decision *vis-à-vis* the original parties.

As regards article 63 of the Statute, there appear to be no 'grand' jurisprudential issues and for the states seeking intervention under this article such intervention appears to be, indeed, one 'as of right'. The following limitations, however, can be drawn from the practice of the two Courts:

1. The state seeking intervention under article 63 must satisfy the Court that its intervention relates to the subject matter of the dispute between the parties, or that the convention it invokes, or the interpretation thereof, is 'in question' in the case.
2. The state seeking intervention is required to submit its declaration at an appropriate stage of the proceedings; i.e., if the proceedings on the merits of the case have been suspended due to a preliminary objection to the jurisdiction of the Court to entertain the application, and the convention relied on as a basis of intervention is at issue in the merits phase of the case but not in the jurisdictional phase, the state seeking intervention may intervene only in the merits phase (assuming, of course, that jurisdiction is found and the eventual merits of the application reached), but not in the jurisdictional phase. If the convention the intervening state is invoking is also, or solely, at issue in the jurisdictional phase, it is unclear, in light of the practice of the Court, whether such intervention would be permissible, or whether any jurisdictional disputes would be considered strictly bilateral in nature and therefore out of bounds for third parties for purposes of intervention.

Case Concerning Military and Paramilitary Activities in and against Nicaragua (*Nicaragua v. United States of America*)

1984 ICJ 215 (Order of 4 October)

* * *

... Having regard to the Declaration of Intervention, under the terms of Article 63 of the Statute, made by the Republic of El Salvador on 15 August 1984 and filed in the Registry the same day, in relation to the proceedings instituted by Nicaragua against the United States of America, as supplemented by a letter dated 10 September 1984,

Having regard to the written observations on that Declaration submitted by the Government of Nicaragua and the Government of the United States of America, respectively,

Makes the following Order:

1. Whereas by its Order of 10 May 1984 the Court decided *inter alia* that the written proceedings in the case should first be addressed to the question of the jurisdiction of the Court to entertain the dispute between Nicaragua and the United States of America and of the admissibility of Nicaragua's Application;

2. Whereas the Declaration of Intervention of the Republic of El Salvador, which relates to the present phase of the proceedings, addresses itself also in effect to matters, including the construction of conventions, which presuppose that the Court has jurisdiction to entertain the dispute between Nicaragua and the United States of America and that Nicaragua's Application against the United States of America in respect of that dispute is admissible;

3. Whereas the Court notes that in its Declaration of Intervention the Republic of El Salvador:

> "reserves the right in a later substantive phase of the case to address the interpretation and application of the conventions to which it is also a party relevant to that phase;"

THE COURT,

(i) By nine votes to six,

> *Decides* not to hold a hearing on the Declaration of Intervention of the Republic of El Salvador,

IN FAVOUR: *President* Elias; *Vice-President* Sette-Camara; *Judges* Lachs, Morozov, Nagendra Singh, Oda, El-Khani, Mbaye, Bedjaoui.

AGAINST: *Judges* Ruda, Mosler, Ago, Schwebel, Sir Robert Jennings, de Lacharriere.

(ii) By fourteen votes to one,

> *Decides* that the declaration of intervention of the Republic of El Salvador is inadmissible inasmuch as it relates to the current phase of the proceedings brought by Nicaragua against the United States of America,

IN FAVOUR: *President* Elias; *Vice-President* Sette-Camara; *Judges* Lachs, Morozov, Nagendra Singh, Ruda, Mosler, Oda, Ago, El-Khani, Sir Robert Jennings, de Lacharriere, Mbaye, Bedjaoui.

AGAINST: Judge Schwebel.

* * *

SEPARATE OPINION OF JUDGES RUDA, MOSLER, AGO, SIR ROBERT JENNINGS AND DE LACHARRIERE

1. Article 63 of the Statute of the Court provides for a right of intervention in proceedings before it, "Whenever the construction of a convention to which States other than those concerned in the case are parties is in question." Where those conditions are fulfilled, a State wishing to intervene has a right to do so, and it is not for the Court to grant or withhold permission. Nevertheless, it is for the Court to decide in each case whether or not the conditions for such intervention, laid down in Article 63, are fulfilled.

2. Accordingly, Article 82 of the Court's Rules provides that a State desiring to avail itself of the right of intervention conferred upon it by Article 63 shall file a declaration; which declaration shall contain *inter alia*:

> "*(b)* identification of the particular provisions of the convention the construction of which it considers to be in question;
>
> *(c)* a statement of the construction of those provisions for which it contends."

3. We have voted with the majority of the Court in deciding that El Salvador's declaration of intervention is inadmissible in the present phase of the proceedings, because we have not been able to find, in El Salvador's written communications to the Court, the necessary identification of such particular provision or provisions which it considers to be in question in the jurisdictional phase of the case between Nicaragua and the United States; nor of the construction of such provision or provisions for which it contends. Furthermore, the brief references made in this regard have not convinced us that El Salvador's request is in accordance with what is contemplated by Article 63 of the Court's Statute.

4. We differ, however, from the Court on the question whether or not El Salvador should have been granted an oral hearing. In our opinion, it would have been more in accordance with judicial propriety if the Court had granted a hearing to the State seeking to intervene, and had not decided only on the basis of the written communications.

(*Signed*) J. M. RUDA.

(*Signed*) Hermann MOSLER.

(*Signed*) Roberto AGO.

(*Signed*) R. Y. JENNINGS.

(*Signed*) Guy DE LACHARRIERE.

* * *

DISSENTING OPINION OF JUDGE SCHWEBEL

I regret that I must dissent from the Court's Order. I dissent because of the decision of the Court not to hold a hearing on the Declaration of Intervention of El Salvador, a decision which departs from the observance of due process of law which the Court has traditionally upheld. Moreover, in the absence of hearing El Salvador, it has not been possible to resolve satisfactorily questions which its Declaration poses. That Declaration raises doubts, but for my part I am unwilling to resolve those doubts against El Salvador without affording it the opportunity of clarifying its position. Accordingly, once the Court declined to hear El Salvador, I felt obliged to vote in favour of admitting its right of intervention under Article 63 of the Statute, even though I recognize that neither the terms of its Declaration nor the law of the matter are altogether clear.

I. THE TERMS AND MEANING OF EL SALVADOR'S DECLARATION OF INTERVENTION

* * *

El Salvador filed a Declaration of Intervention under Article 63 on 15 August 1984. Paragraph XIV of that Declaration sets forth what El Salvador maintains are the grounds of its intervention:

> "... Nicaragua bases its jurisdictional claim on Article 36 of the Statute of the Court ... Nicaragua founds its principal claim against the United States on supposed violations of the Charter of the United Nations, the Charter of the Organization of American States, the Convention on Rights and Duties of States, and the Convention Relative to the Duties and Rights of States in the Event of Civil Strife ...
>
> Assuming *arguendo* the supposed validity of Nicaragua's jurisdictional allegation, El Salvador also is a party to the Statute of the International Court, ... and ... the Charter of the United Nations ... It became a member of the Organization of American States ... It became a member of the Convention Relative to the Duties and Rights of States in the Event of Civil Strife ... It ratified the Convention on Rights and Duties of States ... Therefore, El Salvador is party to all the multilateral conventions on which Nicaragua alleges the jurisdictional basis of its substantive claims.
>
> These treaties give to El Salvador equally the right to demand that Nicaragua cease in its overt intervention in our internal affairs, and El Salvador considers, and this is a reason for intervening in the case of Nicaragua v. the United States, that all these multilateral treaties and conventions constitute the lawful mechanisms for the resolution of conflicts, having priority over the assumption of jurisdiction by the International Court of Justice ...
>
> In the opinion of El Salvador, ... it is not possible for the Court to adjudicate Nicaragua's claims against the United States without determining the legitimacy or the legality of any armed action in which Nicaragua claims the United States has engaged and, hence, without determining the rights of El Salvador and the United States to engage in collective actions of legitimate defence. Nicaragua's claims against the United States are directly interrelated with El Salvador's claims against Nicaragua.
>
> * * *
>
> Any case against the United States based on the aid provided by that nation at El Salvador's express request, in order to exercise the legitimate act of self defence, cannot be carried out without involving some adjudication, acknowledgment, or attribution of the rights which any nation has under Article 51 of the United Nations Charter to act collectively in legitimate defence. This makes inadmissible jurisdictional action by the Court in the absence of the participation of Central America and specifically El Salvador, in whose absence the Court lacks jurisdiction.
>
> Finally, El Salvador points to the fact that it has entered a reservation concerning acceptance of the Court's jurisdiction, with specific reference to disputes relating to facts or situations involving hostilities, armed conflicts, individual or collective acts of legitimate defence, resistance to aggression, fulfilment of obligations imposed by international organizations, and other similar acts, measures, or situations in which El Salvador is, has been, or might be an involved party."

This Declaration did not adequately meet the specifications set forth in Article 82, paragraph 2, of the Rules of Court; in particular, it failed to identify the particular provisions of the conventions whose construction El Salvador considered to be in question, and it did not contain a statement of the construction of those provisions for which El Salvador contends.

However, on 10 September 1984, El Salvador submitted to the Registrar a letter which amplified its Declaration in clearer terms, which conformed to the essential requirements of Article 82, paragraph 2, of the Rules. Paragraphs 1 and 3 of that letter read as follows:

> "1. The construction of international conventions to which El Salvador is a party is centrally involved in the Court's forthcoming consideration of the Jurisdiction of the Court and of the admissibility of Nicaragua's application. El Salvador asserts its automatic right to intervene in this phase or stage of the proceedings in order to address the threshold questions of the construction of Article 36 of the Statute of the Court, and correlatively the construction of the relevant provisions of the Charter of the United Nations, in particular Articles 39, 51 and 52. El Salvador is a party to both these conventions, as set forth in its Declaration. El Salvador will contend that those provisions should be construed to deny the jurisdiction of the Court to consider and apply the conventional principles of international law relied on by Nicaragua to an ongoing armed conflict such as is presently underway in Central America, and will contend that the application of Nicaragua is inadmissible by a process of similar reasoning. El Salvador will particularly contend that this construction is appropriate with respect to Articles 39, 51 and 52 of the Charter, *inter alia*, and to Article 36 of the Statute, ...
>
> * * *
>
> 3. El Salvador thus invokes its right to intervene in a way which strictly conforms to the conditions of Article 63. Its intervention is limited. It seeks to speak only to the construction of the conventions to which it is a party. Thus, it does not propose to address the question whether Nicaragua ratified the Protocol of Signature of the Statute of the Permanent Court of International Justice, referred to in the Court's Order of 10 May 1984 ... El Salvador may address the effectiveness of the declaration of the United States of 6 April 1984, under Article 36, paragraph 2, of the Statute, referred to in ... the Order of 10 May 1984, only to the extent that the Court's determination of the question might affect the reservation of El Salvador to the Court's jurisdiction."

It is accordingly clear that El Salvador sought to intervene in the jurisdictional phase of the proceedings between Nicaragua and the United States to argue that a proper construction of Article 36 of the Statute of the Court, and of Articles 39, 51 and 52 of the Charter, debar the Court from addressing the merits of Nicaragua's claims. Its argument appears to be more addressed to the admissibility of the claims of Nicaragua than to the Court's jurisdiction over them; the principal thrust of El Salvador's contentions is that the resolution of an ongoing armed conflict is remitted to the political organs of the international system (in this case, the United Nations and regional arrangements) rather than to the Court.

However, this does not appear to be the whole of El Salvador's argument, for it also relies on the terms of Article 36 of the Statute and on adherences to the Court's compulsory jurisdiction under the Optional Clause of that article, as well as on provisions of the OAS Charter and two other inter-American conventions. The intendment of El Salvador's argument in these respects requires clarification, clarification which could have been sought by putting questions to El Salvador, either in the course of an oral hearing of otherwise.

* * *

II. THE FAILURE TO ACCORD EL SALVADOR A HEARING

Article 84 of the Rules of Court provides:

> "1. The Court shall decide ... whether an intervention under Article 63 of the Statute is admissible, as a matter of priority unless in view of the circumstances of the case the Court shall otherwise determine.
>
> 2. If, ... an objection is filed ... to the admissibility of a declaration of intervention, the Court shall hear the State seeking to intervene and the parties before deciding."

Pursuant to Article 83 of the Rules, Nicaragua and the United States were invited to furnish their written observations on El Salvador's Declaration. The United States, in a letter of 14 September 1984, extensively examined the right of intervention under Article 63, and concluded that it is....

> .... In sum, the United States respectfully submits its view that El Salvador is entitled to intervene in this case pursuant to Article 63 of the Statute of the Court, as a State party to multilateral conventions whose construction is at issue in this phase of the case. Further, as we understand the object and scope of El Salvador's proposed intervention, it is appropriately related and inherently limited to the current phase of proceedings. Accordingly, the United States sees no ground for objection to the admissibility of this intervention."

Nicaragua's letter of 10 September 1984 was not as straightforward. Since interpretation of the terms of that letter is essential to evaluating the Court's application of Article 84 of its Rules, it will be extensively quoted:

> "1. Nicaragua has no objection in principle to a proper intervention by El Salvador in this case in accordance with Article 63 of the Statute of the Court and Articles 82–85 of the Rules of Court. Nicaragua's Application, in addition to claims under general international law, asserts claims under certain conventions. It is well established that any State may intervene as of right under Article 63 in a case involving the interpretation of a convention to which it is a party if it meets the requirements of the Article and the relevant Rules.
>
> 2. Although Nicaragua has no intention to oppose El Salvador's intervention, it feels bound to call the Court's attention to certain deficiencies, both as to form and substance, in the Declaration of Intervention.

* * *

Thus, while Nicaragua purported in its letter not to have filed "an objection" to the admissibility of El Salvador's Declaration of Intervention, it voiced objections. It characterized these objections as "deficiencies, both as to form and substance, in the Declaration of Intervention." Those of form related to requirements which Nicaragua describes as "necessary to ensure that the intervention falls properly within the provisions of Article 63 of the Statute." Those of substance led Nicaragua to conclude that "Article 63 of the Statute ... does not permit intervention for the purpose of opposing jurisdiction ...," that is, the very purpose for which El Salvador sought to intervene. Now it is plain that if what Nicaragua called deficiencies in form were so serious as to result in El Salvador's having failed to do what was "necessary" to comply with Article 63, and that if what Nicaragua called deficiencies of substance were so serious as not to "permit intervention" under Article 63, then Nicaragua objected to El Salvador's Declaration on these grounds. It objected in fact even if it professed to agree "in principle".

* * *

The Court, however, disregarded not only what El Salvador's letter of 17 September says but what Nicaragua's letter of 10 September says. The Court insisted on taking at full and face value what Nicaragua's letter says it says rather than what it plainly said. The Court thereby found it possible not to apply the mandatory terms of Article 84, paragraph 2, of its Rules, which prescribe that, if an objection is filed to the admissibility of a declaration of intervention, "the Court shall hear the State seeking to intervene and the Parties before deciding." Nicaragua's written observations contained in its letter of 10 September were carefully, indeed artfully, crafted, but this was hardly reason to reward them with such an application of the Court's Rules....

* * *

III. THE RIGHT OF EL SALVADOR TO INTERVENE IN THE JURISDICTIONAL PHASE OF THE CURRENT PROCEEDINGS ON THE GROUNDS STATED BY IT

While under Article 63 of the Statute, a State has "the right" to intervene whenever the construction of a convention to which it is a party is in question in proceedings before the Court, it always has been accepted that the Court must pass upon whether the State seeking to intervene is such a party, and whether the construction of the convention cited is in question in the proceedings. If the Court so finds, the Court does not need to grant permission to intervene; it simply—and, as the distinguished President of the Court has put it, "rather significantly" (Taslim O. Elias, *The International Court of Justice and Some Contemporary Problems*, 1983, p. 86)—"records" that the declarant State intends to avail itself of the right to intervene conferred upon it by Article 63 of the Statute and "accepts" its intervention. (*S.S. 'Wimbledon', Judgments, 1923, P.C.I.J, Series A, No. 1*, p. 13. But in the *Haya de la Torre* case, *supra*, the Court "decided ... to admit" the intervention.)

* * *

[Several questions remain:]

—May intervention under Article 63 take place in the jurisdictional phase of a proceeding?

—If so, is such intervention confined to conventions other than the Statute of the Court and the Charter of the United Nations?

—If such intervention is not so confined, does it embrace the Statute as well as the Charter?

—If so, may intervention embrace not only the Charter and the Statute but declarations submitted under the Optional Clause of the Statute?

It will be convenient to begin with jurisdictional intervention in general.

[Judge Schwebel answered all questions favorably for El Salvador.]

In *Case Concerning the Land and Maritime Boundaries between Cameroon and Nigeria, Application of Costa Rica for Permission to Intervene* (Cameroon v. Nigeria) 1999 ICJ 1059 (Order of Oct. 21) Equatorial Guinea wished to intervene to assert its legal rights to its maritime boundaries. Equatorial Guinea was concerned that a decision by the Court prolonging the maritime boundary between Cameroon and Nigeria could encroach upon its rights and interests. The Court cited *Land, Island and Maritime Frontier Dispute* (discussed in the Ruda article) for the rule that intervention is permissible where a state wishes to inform the Court of its legal rights at issue in the dispute whether or not it has a valid jurisdictional link to the parties (paras. 14–15). The ICJ permitted the intervention by Equatorial Guinea. What must have been different about Equatorial Guinea's reason for intervening in comparison to Costa Rica's in the next case?

Territorial and Maritime Dispute Application of Costa Rica for Permission to Intervene (*Nicaragua v. Colombia*)

2011 ICJ (Judgment of May 4)

1. On 6 December 2001, the Republic of Nicaragua (hereinafter "Nicaragua") filed in the Registry of the Court an Application instituting proceedings against the Republic of Colombia (hereinafter "Colombia") in respect of a dispute consisting of a "group of related legal issues subsisting" between the two States "concerning title to territory and maritime delimitation" in the western Caribbean. As a basis for the jurisdiction of the Court, the Application invoked the provisions of Article XXXI of the American Treaty on Pacific Settlement signed on 30 April 1948, officially designated, according to Article LX thereof, as the "Pact of Bogotá" (hereinafter referred to as such), as well as the declarations made by the Parties under Article 36 of the Statute of the Permanent Court of International Justice, which are deemed, for the period which they still have to run, to be acceptances of the compulsory jurisdiction of the present Court pursuant to Article 36, paragraph 5, of its Statute.

2. Pursuant to Article 40, paragraph 2, of the Statute, the Registrar immediately communicated the Application to the Government of Colombia; and, pursuant to paragraph 3 of that Article, all other States entitled to appear before the Court were notified of the Application.

3. Pursuant to the instructions of the Court under Article 43 of the Rules of Court, the Registrar addressed to all States parties to the Pact of Bogotá the notifications provided for in Article 63, paragraph 1, of the Statute.

* * *

12. On 25 February 2010, Costa Rica filed an Application for permission to intervene in the case pursuant to Article 62 of the Statute. In this Application, it stated in particular that its intervention "would have the limited purpose of informing the Court of the nature of Costa Rica's legal rights and interests and of seeking to ensure that the Court's decision regarding the maritime boundary between Nicaragua and Colombia does not affect those rights and interests".

* * *

53. The Court will now turn to consider whether Costa Rica has sufficiently set out an "interest of a legal nature" which may be affected by the decision of the Court in the main proceedings. The Court will examine both of the elements, namely the existence of an interest of a legal nature on the part of Costa Rica and the effects that the Court's eventual decision on the merits might have on this interest, in order for the request for intervention to succeed (see *Continental Shelf (Tunisia/Libyan Arab Jamahiriya), Application for Permission to Intervene, Judgment, I.C.J. Reports 1981*, p. 19, para. 33).

54. In its Application, Costa Rica states that its:

> "interest of a legal nature which may be affected by the decision of the Court is Costa Rica's interest in the exercise of its sovereign rights and jurisdiction in the maritime area in the Caribbean Sea to which it is entitled under international law by virtue of its coast facing on that sea".

It takes the view that the arguments developed by Nicaragua and Colombia in their delimitation dispute affect its legal interest, which it wishes to assert before the Court. According to Costa Rica, such interest is established in reference to the "hypothetical delimitation scenario between Costa Rica and Nicaragua" and, consequently, if it does not intervene, "the delimitation decision in this case may affect the legal interest of Costa Rica".

55. Costa Rica has indicated that the area in question is bounded in the north by a putative equidistance line with Nicaragua and in the east by a line that is 200 nautical miles from Costa Rica's coast, which was identified as the "minimum area of interest" of Costa Rica.

At the hearings, the geographical scope of Costa Rica's claimed interest was clearly depicted through several illustrations, in many of which the area in dispute in the main proceedings and the "minimum area of interest" of Costa Rica were shown in distinctive colours, used as references in later submissions."

* * *

85. The Court recalls that it has stated in the past that "in the case of maritime delimitations where the maritime areas of several States are involved, the protection afforded by Article 59 of the Statute may not always be sufficient" (*Land and Maritime Boundary between Cameroon and Nigeria (Cameroon v. Nigeria: Equatorial Guinea intervening), Judgment, I.C.J. Reports 2002*, p. 421, para. 238).

At the same time, it is equally true, as the Chamber of the Court noted in its Judgment on the Application by Nicaragua for permission to intervene in the case concerning the Land, Island and Maritime Frontier Dispute (El Salvador/Honduras), that

> "the taking into account of all the coasts and costal relationships ... as a geographical fact for the purpose of effecting on eventual delimitation as between two riparian States ... in no way signifies that by such an operation itself the legal interest of a third ... State ... may be affected" (*Judgment, I.C.J. Reports, 1990*, p. 124, para. 77).

Furthermore, in the case concerning *Maritime Delimitation in the Black Sea (Romania v. Ukraine),* the Court, after noting that "the delimitation [between Romania and Ukraine] will occur within the enclosed Black Sea, with Romania being both adjacent to, and opposite Ukraine, and with Bulgaria and Turkey lying to the south" (*Judgment, I.C.J. Reports 2009*, p. 100, para. 112), stated that "[i]t will stay north of any area where third party interests could become involved" (ibid.).

86. It follows that a third State's interest will, as a matter of principle, be protected by the Court, without it defining with specificity the geographical limits of an area where that interest may come into play (see also paragraph 65 above). The Court wishes to emphasize that this protection is to be accorded to any third State, whether intervening or not. For instance, in its Judgment concerning *the Land and Maritime Boundary between Cameroon and Nigeria (Cameroon v. Nigeria: Equatorial Guinea intervening)*, the Court adopted the same position with regard to Equatorial Guinea, which had intervened as a non-party, and to Sao Tome and Principe, which had not (*I.C.J. Reports 2002*, p. 421, para. 238).

87. The Court, in its above-mentioned Judgment, had occasion to indicate the existence of a certain relationship between Articles 62 and 59 of the Statute. Accordingly, to succeed with its request, Costa Rica must show that its interest of a legal nature in the maritime area bordering the area in dispute between Nicaragua and Colombia needs a protection that is not provided by the relative effect of decisions of the Court under Article 59 of the Statute, i.e., Costa Rica must fulfil the requirement of Article 62, paragraph 1, by showing that an interest of a legal nature which it has in the area "may be affected" by the decision in the case (see paragraph 26 above).

88. The Court recalls in this connection that, in the present case, Colombia has not requested that the Court fix the southern endpoint of the maritime boundary that it has to determine. Indeed, as the Court noted earlier (paragraph 77), Colombia asserts that its claims deliberately leave open the endpoints of the delimitation so as not to affect third State's interests. The Court further recalls that Nicaragua has agreed "that any delimitation line established by the Court should stop well short of the area [in which, according to Costa Rica, it has an interest of a legal nature,] and terminate [with] an arrow pointing in the direction of Costa Rica's area".

89. In the present case, Costa Rica's interest of a legal nature may only be affected if the maritime boundary that the Court has been asked to draw between Nicaragua and Colombia were to be extended beyond a certain latitude southwards. The Court, following its jurisprudence, when drawing a line delimiting the maritime areas between the Parties to the main proceedings, will, if necessary, end the line in question before it reaches an area in which the interests of a legal nature of third States may be involved (see *Maritime Delimitation in the Black Sea (Romania v. Ukraine), Judgment, I.C.J. Reports 2009*, p. 100, para. 112).

90. In view of the above, the Court concludes that Costa Rica has not demonstrated that it has an interest of a legal nature which may be affected by the decision in the main proceedings.

91. For these reasons,

THE COURT,

By nine votes to seven,

> Finds that the Application for permission to intervene in the proceedings filed by the Republic of Costa Rica under Article 62 of the Statute of the Court cannot be granted.

IN FAVOUR: *President* Owada; *Vice-President* Tomka; *Judges* Koroma, Keith, Sepúlveda-Amor, Bennouna, Skotnikov, Xue; *Judge* ad hoc Cot;

AGAINST: *Judges* Al-Khasawneh, Simma, Abraham, Cançado Trindade, Yusuf, Donoghue; *Judge* ad hoc Gaja.

B. Indispensable Parties

The issue of indispensable parties is in a sense the flip side of the intervention issue. The intervention cases involved states that wanted to have a part in a case between two or more other states. The indispensable party cases involve states that want no part of a case between others. As a result of such abstention, however, the ICJ has seen fit to dismiss cases. That is what occurred when Portugal tried to bring a case against Australia:

Case Concerning East Timor
(*Portugal v. Australia*)
1995 ICJ 90 (June 30)

* * *

11. The Territory of East Timor corresponds to the eastern part of the island of Timor; it includes the island of Atauro, 25 kilometres to the north, the islet of Jaco to the east, and the enclave of Oe-Cusse in the western part of the island of Timor. Its capital is Dili, situated on its north coast. The south coast of East Timor lies opposite the north coast of Australia, the distance between them being approximately 430 kilometres.

In the sixteenth century, East Timor became a colony of Portugal; Portugal remained there until 1975. The western part of the island came under Dutch rule and later became part of independent Indonesia.

12. In resolution 1542(XV) of 15 December 1960 the United Nations General Assembly recalled "differences of views ... concerning the status of certain territories under the administrations of Portugal and Spain and described by these two States as 'overseas provinces' of the metropolitan State concerned"; and it also stated that it considered that the territories under the administration of Portugal, which were listed therein (including "Timor and dependencies") were non-self-governing territories within the meaning of Chapter XI of the Charter. Portugal, in the wake of its "Carnation Revolution", accepted this position in 1974.

13. Following internal disturbances in East Timor, on 27 August 1975 the Portuguese civil and military authorities withdrew from the mainland of East Timor to the island of Atauro. On 7 December 1975 the armed forces of Indonesia intervened in East Timor. On 8 December 1975 the Portuguese authorities departed from the island of Atauro, and thus left East Timor altogether. Since their departure, Indonesia has occupied the Territory, and the Parties acknowledge that the Territory has remained under the effective control of that State. Asserting that on 31 May 1976 the people of East Timor had requested Indonesia "to accept East Timor as an integral part of the Republic of Indonesia", on 17 July 1976 Indonesia enacted a law incorporating the Territory as part of its national territory.

14. Following the intervention of the armed forces of Indonesia in the Territory and the withdrawal of the Portuguese authorities, the question of East Timor became the subject of two resolutions of the Security Council and of eight resolutions of the General Assembly, namely, Security Council resolutions 384 (1975) of 22 December 1975 and 389 (1976) of 22 April 1976, and General Assembly resolutions 3485(XXX) of 12 December 1975, 31/53 of 1 December 1976, 32/34 of 28 November 1977, 33/39 of 13 December 1978, 34/40 of 21 November 1979, 35/27 of 11 November 1980, 36/50 of 24 November 1981 and 37/30 of 23 November 1982.

15. Security Council resolution 384 (1975) of 22 December 1975 called upon "all States to respect the territorial integrity of East Timor as well as the inalienable right of its people to self-determination"; called upon "the Government of Indonesia to withdraw without delay all its forces from the Territory"; and further called upon

> "the Government of Portugal as administering Power to co-operate fully with the United Nations so as to enable the people of East Timor to exercise freely their right to self-determination".

Security Council resolution 389 (1976) of 22 April 1976 adopted the same terms with regard to the right of the people of East Timor to self-determination; called upon "the Government of Indonesia to withdraw without further delay all its forces from the Territory"; and further called upon "all States and other parties concerned to co-operate fully with the United Nations to achieve a peaceful solution to the existing situation ...".

General Assembly resolution 3485(XXX) of 12 December 1975 referred to Portugal "as the administering Power"; called upon it "to continue to make every effort to find a solution by peaceful means"; and "strongly deplore[d] the military intervention of the armed forces of Indonesia in Portuguese Timor". In resolution 31/53 of 1 December 1976, and again in resolution 32/34 of 28 November 1977, the General Assembly rejected

> "the claim that East Timor has been incorporated into Indonesia, inasmuch as the people of the Territory have not been able to exercise freely their right to self-determination and independence".

Security Council resolution 389 (1976) of 22 April 1976 and General Assembly resolutions 31/53 of 1 December 1976, 32/34 of 28 November 1977 and 33/39 of 13 December 1978 made no reference to Portugal as the administering Power. Portugal is so described, however, in Security Council resolution 384 (1975) of 22 December 1975 and in the other resolutions of the General Assembly. Also, those resolutions which did not specifically refer to Portugal as the administering Power recalled another resolution or other resolutions which so referred to it.

16. No further resolutions on the question of East Timor have been passed by the Security Council since 1976 or by the General Assembly since 1982. However, the Assembly has maintained the item on its agenda since 1982, while deciding at each session, on the recommendation of its General Committee, to defer consideration of it until the following session. East Timor also continues to be included in the list of non-self-governing territories within the meaning of Chapter XI of the Charter; and the Special Committee on the Situation with Regard to the Implementation of the Declaration on the Granting of Independence to Colonial Countries and Peoples remains seised of the question of East Timor. The Secretary-General of the United Nations is also engaged in a continuing effort, in consultation with all parties directly concerned, to achieve a comprehensive settlement of the problem.

17. The incorporation of East Timor as part of Indonesia was recognized by Australia de facto on 20 January 1978. On that date the Australian Minister for Foreign Affairs stated: "The Government has made clear publicly its opposition to the Indonesian intervention and has made this known to the Indonesian Government." He added: "[Indonesia's] control is effective and covers all major administrative centres of the territory." And further:

> "This is a reality with which we must come to terms. Accordingly, the Government has decided that although it remains critical of the means by which integration was brought about it would be unrealistic to continue to refuse to recognize de facto that East Timor is part of Indonesia."

On 23 February 1978 the Minister said: "we recognize the fact that East Timor is part of Indonesia, but not the means by which this was brought about".

On 15 December 1978 the Australian Minister for Foreign Affairs declared that negotiations which were about to begin between Australia and Indonesia for the delimitation of the continental shelf between Australia and East Timor, "when they start, will signify *de jure* recognition by Australia of the Indonesian incorporation of East Timor"; he added: "The acceptance of this situation does not alter the opposition which the Government has consistently expressed regarding the manner of incorporation." The negotiations in question began in February 1979.

18. Prior to this, Australia and Indonesia had, in 1971–1972, established a delimitation of the continental shelf between their respective coasts; the delimitation so effected stopped short on either side of the continental shelf between the south coast of East Timor and the north coast of Australia. This undelimited part of the continental shelf was called the "Timor Gap".

The delimitation negotiations which began in February 1979 between Australia and Indonesia related to the Timor Gap; they did not come to fruition. Australia and Indonesia then turned to the possibility of establishing a provisional arrangement for the joint exploration and exploitation of the resources of an area of the continental shelf. A Treaty to this effect was eventually concluded between them on 11 December 1989, whereby a "Zone of Cooperation" was created "in an area between the Indonesian Province of East Timor and Northern Australia". Australia enacted legislation in 1990 with a view to implementing the Treaty; this law came into force in 1991.

19. In these proceedings Portugal maintains that Australia, in negotiating and concluding the 1989 Treaty, in initiating performance of the Treaty, in taking internal legislative measures for its application, and in continuing to negotiate with Indonesia, has acted unlawfully, in that it has infringed the rights of the people of East Timor to self-determination and to permanent sovereignty over its natural resources, infringed the rights of Portugal as the administering Power, and contravened Security Council resolutions 384 and 389. Australia raised objections to the jurisdiction of the Court and to the admissibility of the Application. It took the position, however, that these objections were inextricably linked to the merits and should therefore be determined within the framework of the merits. The Court heard the Parties both on the objections and on the merits. While Australia concentrated its main arguments and submissions on the objections, it also submitted that Portugal's case on the merits should be dismissed, maintaining, in particular that its actions did not in any way disregard the rights of Portugal.

20. According to one of the objections put forward by Australia, there exists in reality no dispute between itself and Portugal. In another objection, it argued that Portugal's Application would require the Court to rule on the rights and obligations of a State which is not a party to the proceedings, namely Indonesia. According to further objections of Australia, Portugal lacks standing to bring the case, the argument being that it does not have a sufficient interest of its own to institute the proceedings, notwithstanding the references to it in some of the resolutions of the Security Council and the General Assembly as the administering Power of East Timor, and that it cannot, furthermore, claim any right to represent the people of East Timor; its claims are remote from reality, and the judgment the Court is asked to give would be without useful effect; and finally, its claims concern matters which are essentially not legal in nature which should be resolved by negotiation within the framework of ongoing procedures before the political organs of the United Nations. Portugal requested the Court to dismiss all these objections.

21. The Court will now consider Australia's objection that there is in reality no dispute between itself and Portugal. Australia contends that the case as presented by Portugal is artificially limited to the question of the lawfulness of Australia's conduct, and that the true respondent is Indonesia, not Australia. Australia maintains that it is being sued in place of Indonesia. In this connection, it points out that Portugal and Australia have accepted the compulsory jurisdiction of the Court under Article 36, paragraph 2, of its Statute, but that Indonesia has not.

In support of the objection, Australia contends that it recognizes, and has always recognized, the right of the people of East Timor to self-determination, the status of East Timor as a non-self-governing territory, and the fact that Portugal has been named by the United Nations as the administering Power of East Timor; that the arguments of Portugal, as well as its submissions, demonstrate that Portugal does not challenge the capacity of Australia to conclude the 1989 Treaty and that it does not contest the validity of the Treaty; and that consequently there is in reality no dispute between itself and Portugal.

Portugal, for its part, maintains that its Application defines the real and only dispute submitted to the Court.

22. The Court recalls that, in the sense accepted in its jurisprudence and that of its predecessor, a dispute is a disagreement on a point of law or fact, a conflict of legal views or interests between parties (see *Mavrommatis Palestine Concessions, Judgment No. 2, 1924, P.C.I.J., Series A, No. 2*, p. 11; *Northern Cameroons, Judgment, I.C.J. Reports 1963*, p. 27; and Applicability of the Obligation to Arbitrate under Section 21 of the *United Nations Headquarters Agreement of 26 June 1947, Advisory Opinion, I.C.J. Reports 1988*, p. 27, para. 35). In order to establish the existence of a dispute, "It must be shown that the claim of one party is positively opposed by the other" (*South West Africa, Preliminary Objections, Judgment, I.C.J. Reports 1962*, p. 328); and further, "Whether there exists an international dispute is a matter for objective determination" (*Interpretation of Peace Treaties with Bulgaria, Hungary and Romania, First Phase, Advisory Opinion, I.C.J. Reports 1950*, p. 74).

For the purpose of verifying the existence of a legal dispute in the present case, it is not relevant whether the "real dispute" is between Portugal and Indonesia rather than Portugal and Australia. Portugal has, rightly or wrongly, formulated complaints of fact and law against Australia which the latter has denied. By virtue of this denial, there is a legal dispute.

On the record before the Court, it is clear that the Parties are in disagreement, both on the law and on the facts, on the question whether the conduct of Australia in negotiating, concluding and initiating performance of the 1989 Treaty was in breach of an obligation due by Australia to Portugal under international law.

Indeed, Portugal's Application limits the proceedings to these questions. There nonetheless exists a legal dispute between Portugal and Australia. This objection of Australia must therefore be dismissed.

23. The Court will now consider Australia's principal objection, to the effect that Portugal's Application would require the Court to determine the rights and obligations of Indonesia. The declarations made by the Parties under Article 36, paragraph 2, of the Statute do not include any limitation which would exclude Portugal's claims from the jurisdiction thereby conferred upon the Court. Australia, however, contends that the jurisdiction so conferred would not enable the Court to act if, in order to do so, the Court were required to rule on the lawfulness of Indonesia's entry into and continuing presence in East Timor, on the validity of the 1989 Treaty between Australia and Indonesia, or on the rights and obligations of Indonesia under that Treaty, even if the Court did not have to determine its validity.

Portugal agrees that if its Application required the Court to decide any of these questions, the Court could not entertain it. The Parties disagree, however, as to whether the Court is required to decide any of these questions in order to resolve the dispute referred to it.

24. Australia argues that the decision sought from the Court by Portugal would inevitably require the Court to rule on the lawfulness of the conduct of a third State, namely Indonesia, in the absence of that State's consent. In support of its argument, it cites the

Judgment in the case concerning Monetary Gold Removed from Rome in 1943, in which the Court ruled that, in the absence of Albania's consent, it could not take any decision on the international responsibility of that State since "Albania's legal interests would not only be affected by a decision, but would form the very subject-matter of the decision" (*I.C.J. Reports 1954*, p. 32).

25. In reply, Portugal contends, first, that its Application is concerned exclusively with the objective conduct of Australia, which consists in having negotiated, concluded and initiated performance of the 1989 Treaty with Indonesia, and that this question is perfectly separable from any question relating to the lawfulness of the conduct of Indonesia. According to Portugal, such conduct of Australia in itself constitutes a breach of its obligation to treat East Timor as a non-self-governing territory and Portugal as its administering Power; and that breach could be passed upon by the Court by itself and without passing upon the rights of Indonesia. The objective conduct of Australia, considered as such, constitutes the only violation of international law of which Portugal complains.

26. The Court recalls in this respect that one of the fundamental principles of its Statute is that it cannot decide a dispute between States without the consent of those States to its jurisdiction. This principle was reaffirmed in the Judgment given by the Court in the case concerning Monetary Gold Removed from Rome in 1943 and confirmed in several of its subsequent decisions (see *Continental Shelf (Libyan Arab Jamahiriya/Malta), Application for Permission to Intervene, Judgment, I.C.J. Reports 1984*, p. 25, para. 40; *Military and Paramilitary Activities in and against Nicaragua (Nicaragua v. United States of America), Jurisdiction and Admissibility, Judgment, I.C.J. Reports 1984*, p. 431, para. 88; *Frontier Dispute (Burkina Faso/Republic of Mali), Judgment, I.C.J. Reports 1986*, p. 579, para. 49; *Land, Island and Maritime Frontier Dispute (El Salvador/Honduras), Application to Intervene, Judgment, I.C.J. Reports 1990*, pp. 114–116, paras. 54–56, and p. 112, para. 73; and *Certain Phosphate Lands in Nauru (Nauru v. Australia), Preliminary Objections, Judgment, I.C.J. Reports 1992*, pp. 259–262, paras. 50–55).

27. The Court notes that Portugal's claim that, in entering into the 1989 Treaty with Indonesia, Australia violated the obligation to respect Portugal's status as administering Power and that of East Timor as a non-self-governing territory, is based on the assertion that Portugal alone, in its capacity as administering Power, had the power to enter into the Treaty on behalf of East Timor; that Australia disregarded this exclusive power, and, in so doing, violated its obligations to respect the status of Portugal and that of East Timor.

The Court also observes that Australia, for its part, rejects Portugal's claim to the exclusive power to conclude treaties on behalf of East Timor, and the very fact that it entered into the 1989 Treaty with Indonesia shows that it considered that Indonesia had that power. Australia in substance argues that even if Portugal had retained that power, on whatever basis, after withdrawing from East Timor, the possibility existed that the power could later pass to another State under general international law, and that it did so pass to Indonesia; Australia affirms moreover that, if the power in question did pass to Indonesia, it was acting in conformity with international law in entering into the 1989 Treaty with that State, and could not have violated any of the obligations Portugal attributes to it. Thus, for Australia, the fundamental question in the present case is ultimately whether, in 1989, the power to conclude a treaty on behalf of East Timor in relation to its continental shelf lay with Portugal or with Indonesia.

28. The Court has carefully considered the argument advanced by Portugal which seeks to separate Australia's behaviour from that of Indonesia. However, in the view of the

Court, Australia's behaviour cannot be assessed without first entering into the question why it is that Indonesia could not lawfully have concluded the 1989 Treaty, while Portugal allegedly could have done so; the very subject-matter of the Court's decision would necessarily be a determination whether, having regard to the circumstances in which Indonesia entered and remained in East Timor, it could or could not have acquired the power to enter into treaties on behalf of East Timor relating to the resources of its continental shelf. The Court could not make such a determination in the absence of the consent of Indonesia.

29. However, Portugal puts forward an additional argument aiming to show that the principle formulated by the Court in the case concerning Monetary Gold Removed from Rome in 1943 is not applicable in the present case. It maintains, in effect, that the rights which Australia allegedly breached were rights *erga omnes* and that accordingly Portugal could require it, individually, to respect them regardless of whether or not another State had conducted itself in a similarly unlawful manner.

In the Court's view, Portugal's assertion that the right of peoples to self-determination, as it evolved from the Charter and from United Nations practice, has an *erga omnes* character, is irreproachable. The principle of self-determination of peoples has been recognized by the United Nations Charter and in the jurisprudence of the Court (see *Legal Consequences for States of the Continued Presence of South Africa in Namibia (South West Africa) notwithstanding Security Council Resolution 276 (1970), Advisory Opinion, I.C.J. Reports 1971*, pp. 31–32, paras. 52–53; *Western Sahara, Advisory Opinion, I.C.J. Reports 1975*, pp. 31–33, paras. 54–59); it is one of the essential principles of contemporary international law. However, the Court considers that the *erga omnes* character of a norm and the rule of consent to jurisdiction are two different things. Whatever the nature of the obligations invoked, the Court could not rule on the lawfulness of the conduct of a State when its judgment would imply an evaluation of the lawfulness of the conduct of another State which is not a party to the case. Where this is so, the Court cannot act, even if the right in question is a right *erga omnes*.

30. Portugal presents a final argument to challenge the applicability to the present case of the Court's jurisprudence in the case concerning Monetary Gold Removed from Rome in 1943. It argues that the principal matters on which its claims are based, namely the status of East Timor as a non-self-governing territory and its own capacity as the administering Power of the Territory, have already been decided by the General Assembly and the Security Council, acting within their proper spheres of competence; that in order to decide on Portugal's claims, the Court might well need to interpret those decisions but would not have to decide de novo on their content and must accordingly take them as "givens"; and that consequently the Court is not required in this case to pronounce on the question of the use of force by Indonesia in East Timor or upon the lawfulness of its presence in the Territory.

Australia objects that the United Nations resolutions regarding East Timor do not say what Portugal claims they say; that the last resolution of the Security Council on East Timor goes back to 1976 and the last resolution of the General Assembly to 1982, and that Portugal takes no account of the passage of time and the developments that have taken place since then; and that the Security Council resolutions are not resolutions which are binding under Chapter VII of the Charter or otherwise and, moreover, that they are not framed in mandatory terms.

31. The Court notes that the argument of Portugal under consideration rests on the premise that the United Nations resolutions, and in particular those of the Security Coun-

cil, can be read as imposing an obligation on States not to recognize any authority on the part of Indonesia over the Territory and, where the latter is concerned, to deal only with Portugal. The Court is not persuaded, however, that the relevant resolutions went so far.

For the two Parties, the Territory of East Timor remains a non-self-governing territory and its people has the right to self-determination. Moreover, the General Assembly, which reserves to itself the right to determine the territories which have to be regarded as non-self-governing for the purposes of the application of Chapter XI of the Charter, has treated East Timor as such a territory. The competent subsidiary organs of the General Assembly have continued to treat East Timor as such to this day. Furthermore, the Security Council, in its resolutions 384 (1975) and 389 (1976) has expressly called for respect for "the territorial integrity of East Timor as well as the inalienable right of its people to self-determination in accordance with General Assembly resolution 1514(XV)".

Nor is it at issue between the Parties that the General Assembly has expressly referred to Portugal as the "administering Power" of East Timor in a number of the resolutions it adopted on the subject of East Timor between 1975 and 1982, and that the Security Council has done so in its resolution 384 (1975). The Parties do not agree, however, on the legal implications that flow from the reference to Portugal as the administering Power in those texts.

32. The Court finds that it cannot be inferred from the sole fact that the above-mentioned resolutions of the General Assembly and the Security Council refer to Portugal as the administering Power of East Timor that they intended to establish an obligation on third States to treat exclusively with Portugal as regards the continental shelf of East Timor. The Court notes, furthermore, that several States have concluded with Indonesia treaties capable of application to East Timor but which do not include any reservation in regard to that Territory. Finally, the Court observes that, by a letter of 15 December 1989, the Permanent Representative of Portugal to the United Nations transmitted to the Secretary-General the text of a note of protest addressed by the Portuguese Embassy in Canberra to the Australian Department of Foreign Affairs and Trade on the occasion of the conclusion of the Treaty on 11 December 1989; that the letter of the Permanent Representative was circulated, at his request, as an official document of the forty-fifth session of the General Assembly, under the item entitled "Question of East Timor", and of the Security Council; and that no responsive action was taken either by the General Assembly or the Security Council.

Without prejudice to the question whether the resolutions under discussion could be binding in nature, the Court considers as a result that they cannot be regarded as "givens" which constitute a sufficient basis for determining the dispute between the Parties.

33. It follows from this that the Court would necessarily have to rule upon the lawfulness of Indonesia's conduct as a prerequisite for deciding on Portugal's contention that Australia violated its obligation to respect Portugal's status as administering Power, East Timor's status as a non-self-governing territory and the right of the people of the Territory to self-determination and to permanent sovereignty over its wealth and natural resources.

34. The Court emphasizes that it is not necessarily prevented from adjudicating when the judgment it is asked to give might affect the legal interests of a State which is not a party to the case. Thus, in the case concerning *Certain Phosphate Lands in Nauru (Nauru v. Australia)*, it stated, *inter alia*, as follows:

> "In the present case, the interests of New Zealand and the United Kingdom do not constitute the very subject-matter of the judgment to be rendered on the merits of Nauru's Application ... In the present case, the determination of the responsibility of New Zealand or the United Kingdom is not a prerequisite for the determination of the responsibility of Australia, the only object of Nauru's claim ... In the present case, a finding by the Court regarding the existence or the content of the responsibility attributed to Australia by Nauru might well have implications for the legal situation of the two other States concerned, but no finding in respect of that legal situation will be needed as a basis for the Court's decision on Nauru's claim against Australia. Accordingly, the Court cannot decline to exercise its jurisdiction." (*I.C.J. Reports 1992*, pp. 261–262, para. 55.)

However, in this case, the effects of the judgment requested by Portugal would amount to a determination that Indonesia's entry into and continued presence in East Timor are unlawful and that, as a consequence, it does not have the treaty-making power in matters relating to the continental shelf resources of East Timor. Indonesia's rights and obligations would thus constitute the very subject-matter of such a judgment made in the absence of that State's consent. Such a judgment would run directly counter to the "well-established principle of international law embodied in the Court's Statute, namely, that the Court can only exercise jurisdiction over a State with its consent" (*Monetary Gold Removed from Rome in 1943, Judgment, I.C.J. Reports 1954*, p. 32).

35. The Court concludes that it cannot, in this case, exercise the jurisdiction it has by virtue of the declarations made by the Parties under Article 36, paragraph 2, of its Statute because, in order to decide the claims of Portugal, it would have to rule, as a prerequisite, on the lawfulness of Indonesia's conduct in the absence of that State's consent. This conclusion applies to all the claims of Portugal, for all of them raise a common question: whether the power to make treaties concerning the continental shelf resources of East Timor belongs to Portugal or Indonesia, and, therefore, whether Indonesia's entry into and continued presence in the Territory are lawful. In these circumstances, the Court does not deem it necessary to examine the other arguments derived by Australia from the non-participation of Indonesia in the case, namely the Court's lack of jurisdiction to decide on the validity of the 1989 Treaty and the effects on Indonesia's rights under that treaty which would result from a judgment in favour of Portugal.

36. Having dismissed the first of the two objections of Australia which it has examined, but upheld its second, the Court finds that it is not required to consider Australia's other objections and that it cannot rule on Portugal's claims on the merits, whatever the importance of the questions raised by those claims and of the rules of international law which they bring into play.

37. The Court recalls in any event that it has taken note in the present Judgment (paragraph 31) that, for the two Parties, the Territory of East Timor remains a non-self-governing territory and its people has the right to self-determination.

38. For these reasons,

THE COURT,

By fourteen votes to two,

> Finds that it cannot in the present case exercise the jurisdiction conferred upon it by the declarations made by the Parties under Article 36, paragraph 2, of its Statute to adjudicate upon the dispute referred to it by the Application of the Portuguese Republic.

IN FAVOUR: *President* Bedjaoui; *Vice-President* Schwebel; Judges Oda, Sir Robert Jennings, Guillaume, Shahabuddeen, Aguilar-Mawdsley, Ranjeva, Herczegh, Shi, Fleischhauer, Koroma, Vereshchetin; *Judge* ad hoc Sir Ninian Stephen;

AGAINST: *Judge* Weeramantry; *Judge* ad hoc Skubiszewski.

Notes and Questions on Intervention and Indispensable Parties

1. Why did the ICJ change its pattern and allow an intervention? Is this a good development? Why had the Court been reluctant to allow intervention? Judge Ruda predicts that the ICJ will be more hospitable to intervention requests in the future. In light of the several ICJ cases included in these materials that came down after Ruda's article was published, do you agree?

Two months after the ICJ declined Costa Rica's request to intervene in the maritime delimitation case between Nicaragua and Colombia, the court permitted Greece to intervene in a case between Germany and Italy. See *Jurisdictional Immunities of the State* (Germany v. Italy), Application by the Hellenic Republic for Permission to Intervene, 2011 ICJ (Order of July 4). Go to the ICJ's website (www.icj-cij.org) and review Greece's application to intervene. Why did it succeed but Costa Rica did not?

2. Should the Court have allowed El Salvador to have a hearing even though all but one judge thought it was intervening at the wrong phase of the case? Seven judges thought it should have such a hearing. Does it make a difference to your thinking to know that El Salvador did not seek to intervene during the merits phase of the case?

3. Given that states may intervene, should the ICJ ever dismiss a case because an indispensable party is absent? What is the purpose of the indispensable party rule? Does it unnecessarily restrict the possibility of states resolving their disputes?

4. Did Portugal have other options beside the ICJ to resolve its dispute with Australia over East Timor? If Portugal could have taken Australia to arbitration, would that option have allowed it to avoid the application of the ICJ's indispensable party rule?

5. Did Portugal accomplish its purpose, in some respects, in going to the ICJ even if the Court did not finally decide the case? Why did it go to the Court?

6. The form of "intervention" discussed in the Chapter concerns intervention by a state. Non-state actors have petitioned to submit documents to the WTO, ITLOS, and other international courts. Here is the ICJ's Practice Direction XII (*available at* http://www.icj-cij.org/documents/index.php?p1=4&p2=4&p3=0):

> 1. Where an international non-governmental organization submits a written statement and/or document in an advisory opinion case on its own initiative, such statement and/or document is not to be considered as part of the case file.
>
> 2. Such statements and/or documents shall be treated as publications readily available and may accordingly be referred to by States and intergovernmental organizations presenting written and oral statements in the case in the same manner as publications in the public domain.
>
> 3. Written statements and/or documents submitted by international non-governmental organizations will be placed in a designated location in the Peace Palace. All States as well as intergovernmental organizations presenting written or oral statements under Article 66 of the Statute will be informed as to the lo-

cation where statements and/or documents submitted by international non-governmental organizations may be consulted.

7. For further reading on intervention and indispensable parties, see:

SHABTAI ROSENNE, INTERVENTION IN THE INTERNATIONAL COURT OF JUSTICE (1993).

CHRISTINE CHINKIN, THIRD PARTIES IN INTERNATIONAL LAW (1993)

Chapter Thirteen

Compliance and Enforcement

Introduction

Many have the perception that international law in general and ICJ decisions, in particular, are unenforceable. As the article excerpted in this chapter seeks to demonstrate, however, ICJ decisions are in fact enforceable in several ways. One way is through the Security Council. In the last chapter, we saw how the drafters of the UN Charter provided for enforcement of ICJ judgments by the Security Council in Article 94 of the Charter. As was mentioned in the discussion of provisional measures, the Council has only considered one case of non-compliance, the *Anglo-Iranian Oil Company Case*, which involved Iran's failure to comply with a provisional measures order, not a final judgment. The Security Council, therefore, has not been faced with the task of actually enforcing an ICJ judgment. Nicaragua sought the Council's assistance, but the U.S. vetoed the request. Eventually, the U.S. and Nicaragua reached something that can be characterized as a settlement of the judgment. Indeed, the vast majority of ICJ judgments are honored. Several states have delayed actually implementing boundary decisions, but for many purposes, the ICJ's judgment on respecting the location of an international boundary will be followed by mapmakers, oil companies, and others. Far more problematic is the U.S. failure to comply with the ICJ's decision in the *Avena* case. This decision and its companion, *Request for Interpretation of Avena*, have already been introduced in previous chapters and are introduced again here.

While the ICJ does not have express authority to enforce judgments, the drafters of the UN Charter provided that authority to the Security Council. The ICJ, nevertheless, does have jurisdiction for two post-judgment tasks: requests for interpretation and revisions. These requests would be made prior to any of the more affirmative steps toward enforcement suggested in the article excerpt on general enforcement that follows the discussion of revision and interpretation.

ICJ Statute

Article 59

The decision of the Court has no binding force except between the parties and in respect of that particular case.

Article 60

The judgment is final and without appeal. In the event of dispute as to the meaning or scope of the judgment, the Court shall construe it upon the request of any party.

Article 61

1. An application for revision of a judgment may be made only when it is based upon the discovery of some fact of such a nature as to be a decisive factor, which fact was, when the judgment was given, unknown to the Court and also to the party claiming revision, always provided that such ignorance was not due to negligence.

2. The proceedings for revision shall be opened by a judgment of the Court expressly recording the existence of the new fact, recognizing that it has such a character as to lay the case open to revision, and declaring the application admissible on this ground.

3. The Court may require previous compliance with the terms of the judgment before it admits proceedings in revision.

4. The application for revision must be made at latest within six months of the discovery of the new fact.

5. No application for revision may be made after the lapse of ten years from the date of the judgment.

United Nations Charter

Article 94

1. Each Member of the United Nations undertakes to comply with the decision of the International Court of Justice in any case to which it is a party.

2. If any party to a case fails to perform the obligations incumbent upon it under a judgment rendered by the Court, the other party may have recourse to the Security Council, which may, if it deems necessary, make recommendations or decide upon measures to be taken to give effect to the judgment.

Application for Revision of the Judgment of 11 September 1992 (*El Salvador v. Honduras, Nicaragua Intervening*)

2003 ICJ 127 (Judgment of Dec. 18)

* * *

Present: *Judge* Guillaume, *President of the Chamber*; *Judges* Rezek, Buergenthal; *Judges* ad hoc Torres Bernardez, Paolillo; Registrar Couvreur.

* * *

15. By a Judgment of 11 September 1992, the Chamber of the Court formed to deal with the case concerning the *Land, Island and Maritime Frontier Dispute (El Salvador/Honduras: Nicaragua intervening)* decided the course of the land boundary between El Salvador and Honduras in six disputed sectors of that boundary. By the same Judgment the Chamber settled the dispute between the Parties over the legal status of various islands in the Gulf of Fonseca and the legal status of waters in the Gulf and outside it.

16. El Salvador has submitted an Application to the Court for revision of the 1992 Judgment in respect of the sixth sector of the land boundary, lying between Los Amates

and the Gulf of Fonseca. During the original proceedings, it was the contention of Honduras that in that sector "the boundary ... follows the present stream [of the River Goascorán], flowing into the Gulf north-west of the Islas Ramaditas in the Bay of La Unión". El Salvador however claimed that the boundary was defined by "a previous course followed by the river ... and that this course, since abandoned by the stream, can be traced, and it reaches the Gulf at Estero La Cutú" (Judgment, para. 306). In the Judgment revision of which is now sought, the Chamber unanimously upheld the submissions of Honduras (*ibid.*, paras. 321, 322 and 430).

17. In its Application for revision of the 1992 Judgment, El Salvador relies on Article 61 of the Statute, which provides:

> "1. An application for revision of a judgment may be made only when it is based upon the discovery of some fact of such a nature as to be a decisive factor, which fact was, when the judgment was given, unknown to the Court and also to the party claiming revision, always provided that such ignorance was not due to negligence.
>
> 2. The proceedings for revision shall be opened by a judgment of the Court expressly recording the existence of the new fact, recognizing that it has such a character as to lay the case open to revision, and declaring the application admissible on this ground.
>
> 3. The Court may require previous compliance with the terms of the judgment before it admits proceedings in revision.
>
> 4. The application for revision must be made at latest within six months of the discovery of the new fact.
>
> 5. No application for revision may be made after the lapse of ten years from the date of the judgment."

18. Article 61 provides for revision proceedings to open with a judgment of the Court declaring the application admissible on the grounds contemplated by the Statute; Article 99 of the Rules of Court makes express provision for proceedings on the merits if, in its first judgment, the Court has declared the application admissible.

Thus the Statute and the Rules of Court foresee a "two-stage procedure". The first stage of the procedure for a request for revision of the Court's judgment should be "limited to the question of admissibility of that request" (*Application for Revision and Interpretation of the Judgment of 24 February 1982 in the Case concerning the* Continental Shelf (Tunisia/Libyan Arab Jamahiriya) *(Tunisia v. Libyan Arab Jamahiriya), Judgment, I.C.J. Reports 1985*, p. 197, paras. 8 and 10; *Application for Revision of the Judgment of 11 July 1996 in the Case concerning* Application of the Convention on the Prevention and Punishment of the Crime of Genocide (Bosnia and Herzegovina *v.* Yugoslavia), Preliminary Objections *(Yugoslavia v. Bosnia and Herzegovina), Judgment*, 3 February 2003, para. 15).

19. Therefore, at this stage, the present Chamber's decision is limited to the question whether El Salvador's request satisfies the conditions contemplated by the Statute....

20. The Chamber observes lastly that "an application for revision is admissible only if each of the conditions laid down in Article 61 is satisfied. If any one of them is not met, the application must be dismissed." (*Application for Revision of the Judgment of 11 July 1996 in the Case concerning* Application of the Convention on the Prevention and Punishment of the Crime of Genocide (Bosnia and Herzegovina *v.* Yugoslavia), Preliminary Objections *(Yugoslavia v. Bosnia and Herzegovina), Judgment*, 3 February 2003, para. 17.)

21. However, El Salvador appears to argue *in limine* that there is no need for the Chamber to consider whether the conditions of Article 61 of the Statute have been satisfied. According to the Applicant,

> "Honduras implicitly acknowledged the admissibility of El Salvador' Application when, by letter dated 29 October 2002, it informed the distinguished President of the Court that, pursuant to Article 61, paragraph 3, of the Statute, it would ask that the Court require previous compliance with the 1992 Judgment as a condition precedent to the admissibility of the Application for revision."

In El Salvador's view, "The back step that Honduras took with its letter of 24 July 2003", by which it decided not to ask for prior compliance with the judgment, "does nothing to diminish [the] acknowledgment [of the admissibility of the Application], and instead serves to confirm it". The Chamber is consequently requested to "adjudge and decide accordingly".

22. The Chamber observes first that, in its letter of 29 October 2002, Honduras informed the President of the Court that it would "request that the Court make the admission of the proceedings in revision conditional on previous compliance with the judgment" and that accordingly it would "submit a formal petition" to that effect. However, Honduras never submitted that request and stated in its observations of 24 July 2003 (see paragraph 9 above) that it had "decided, on reflection, not to ask the Chamber to require prior compliance with the terms of the Judgment". Thus, Honduras's conduct cannot be construed as implying a tacit acceptance of the admissibility of El Salvador's Application for revision.

Further, paragraph 3 of Article 61 of the Statute and paragraph 5 of Article 99 of the Rules of Court afford the Court the possibility at any time to require previous compliance with the terms of the judgment whose revision is sought, before it admits proceedings in revision; accordingly, even if Honduras had submitted a request to the Court to require previous compliance without awaiting the Chamber's decision on the admissibility of El Salvador's Application, the request would not have implied recognition of the admissibility of the Application.

Finally, the Chamber notes that, regardless of the parties' views on the admissibility of an application for revision, it is in any event for the Court, when seised of such an application, to ascertain whether the admissibility requirements laid down in Article 61 of the Statute have been met. Revision is not available simply by consent of the parties, but solely when the conditions of Article 61 are met.

23. In order properly to understand El Salvador's present contentions, it is necessary to recapitulate at the outset part of the reasoning in the 1992 Judgment in respect of the sixth sector of the land boundary.

El Salvador admitted before the Chamber hearing the original case that the river Goascorán had been adopted as the provincial boundary during the period of Spanish colonization. It argued, however, that

> "at some date [the Goascorán] abruptly changed its course to its present position. On this basis El Salvador's argument of law [was] that where a boundary is formed by the course of a river, and the stream suddenly leaves its old bed and forms a new one, this process of 'avulsion' does not bring about a change in the boundary, which continues to follow the old channel." (Para. 308.)

That was claimed to be the rule under both Spanish colonial law and international law. Thus, according to El Salvador, the boundary between the two States should be established not along the present stream of the river, flowing into the Bay of La Unión, but along the "previous course ... since abandoned by the stream", probably during the seventeenth century, emptying into the Estero La Cutú (paras. 306 and 311).

24. After setting out this argument by El Salvador, the Chamber stated in its Judgment of 11 September 1992 that "No record of such an abrupt change of course having occurred has been brought to the Chamber's attention" (para. 308). It added: "were the Chamber satisfied that the river's course was earlier so radically different from its present one, then an avulsion might reasonably be inferred" (para. 308). The Chamber observed, however, that: "There is no scientific evidence that the previous course of the Goascorán was such that it debouched in the Estero La Cutú" or in another neighbouring inlet (para. 309). It did not take a position on the consequences that any avulsion, occurring before or after 1821, would have had on provincial boundaries, or boundaries between States, under Spanish colonial law or international law.

The Chamber went on to find that "any claim by El Salvador that the boundary follows an old course of the river abandoned at some time *before* 1821 must be rejected. It is a new claim and inconsistent with the previous history of the dispute." (Para. 312.) In this regard, the Chamber noted *inter alia* that on several occasions, including in particular during the Saco negotiations between the two States in 1880, El Salvador had adopted conduct excluding any "claim ... that the 1821 boundary was not the 1821 course of the river, but an older course, preserved as provincial boundary by a provision of colonial law" (para. 312).

The Chamber then considered "the evidence made available to it concerning the course of the river Goascorán in 1821" (para. 313). It examined in particular a "chart (de scribed as a 'Carta Esférica') of the Gulf of Fonseca prepared by the captain and navigators of the brig or brigantine *El Activo*, who sailed in 1794, on the instructions of the Viceroy of Mexico, to survey the Gulf" (para. 314). It noted that the mouth of the Goascorán on that chart was "quite inconsistent with the old course of the river alleged by El Salvador, or, indeed, any course other than the present-day one" (para. 314). The Chamber concluded that "the report of the 1794 expedition and the 'Carta Esférica' leave little room for doubt that the river Goascorán in 1821 was already flowing in its present-day course" (para. 316).

Finally, after having examined various other arguments by El Salvador which it is not necessary to repeat here, the Chamber "found that the boundary follows the present course of the Goascorán" (para. 319) and defined the boundary line in the mouth of the river (paras. 320–322).

* * *

25. In its Application for revision, El Salvador, acting under Article 61 of the Statute, relies on facts which it considers to be new within the meaning of that Article; those facts relate, on the one hand, to the avulsion of the river Goascorán and, on the other, to the "Carta Esférica" and the report of the 1794 *El Activo* expedition.

26. El Salvador first claims to possess scientific, technical and historical evidence showing, contrary to what it understands the decision of the Chamber to have been, that the Goascorán did in the past change its bed, and that the change was abrupt, probably as a result of a cyclone in 1762.

In support of this contention El Salvador submits to the Chamber a report dated 5 August 2002 entitled Geologic, Hydrologic and Historic Aspects of the Goascorán Delta—A Basis for Boundary Determination. It also produces a study it conducted in 2002 "to check for the presence of vestiges of the Goascorán's original riverbed and additional information about its hydrographic behaviour". Finally, it refers to various publications, including in particular *Geografía de Honduras* by Ulises Meza Cálix, published in 1916, and *Monografía del Departamento de Valle*, prepared under the direction of Bernardo Galindo y Galindo and published in 1934.

27. El Salvador argues that evidence can constitute "new facts" for purposes o f Article 61 of the Statute. In this regard it relies on the *travaux préparatoires* of the provision of the Statute of the Permanent Court of International Justice, on which Article 61 is modelled, which are said to confirm that a document can be considered to be a "new fact". It also invokes an arbitral award handed down on 7 August and 25 September 1922 by the Franco-German Mixed Arbitral Tribunal in the *Heim et Chamant c. Etat allemand* case, which, in El Salvador's view, recognized that evidence can constitute "a fact".

El Salvador further contends that the evidence it is now offering establishes the existence of an old bed of the Goascorán debouching in the Estero La Cutú, and the avulsion of the river in the mid-eighteenth century or that at the very least, it justifies regarding such an avulsion as plausible. These are said to be "new facts" for purposes of Article 61.

28. The facts thus set out are, according to El Salvador, decisive. It maintains that the considerations and conclusions of the 1992 Judgment are founded on the rejection of an avulsion which, in the Chamber's view, had not been proved: that avulsion has ceased to be a matter of conjecture—it is an established fact which actually occurred. On the basis of Spanish colonial law, the provincial boundaries remained unchanged, notwithstanding the avulsion, until 1821. El Salvador concludes that, contrary to what the Chamber held in 1992, the boundary arising from the *uti possidetis juris* should accordingly follow those boundaries and not the new course of the Goascorán.

29. El Salvador finally maintains that, given all the circumstances of the case, in particular the "bitter civil war [which] was raging in El Salvador" "for virtually the whole period between 1980 and the handing down of the Judgment on 11 September 1992", its ignorance of the various new facts which it now advances concerning the course of the Goascorán was not due to negligence.

In particular, it states that the scientific and technical studies it has produced could not have been carried out previously, given both the state of science and technology in 1992, and the political situation prevailing at the time in the sixth sector of the boundary and, generally, in El Salvador and the region. As for the publications mentioned above (see paragraph 26), El Salvador contends that it could not have "access to the documents in Honduras's National Archives and, despite all its efforts, could not locate them in the archives of other States to which it did have access".

30. El Salvador concludes from the foregoing that, as the various conditions laid down by Article 61 of the Statute are satisfied, the Application for revision founded on the avulsion of the river Goascorán is admissible.

31. Honduras, for its part, argues that with regard to the application of Article 61 of the Statute, it is "well-established case law that there is a distinction in kind between the facts alleged and the evidence relied upon to prove them and that only the discovery of the former opens a right to revision". It quotes in this connection the Advisory Opinion rendered on 4 September 1924 by the Permanent Court of International Justice concerning the question of the *Monastery of Saint-Naoum*. According to Honduras, a "fact" cannot "include evidentiary material in support of an argument, or an assertion, or an allegation". Accordingly, the evidence submitted by El Salvador cannot open a right to revision.

Honduras adds that El Salvador has not demonstrated the existence of a new fact discovered by El Salvador since 1992 "which establishes that the Goascorán River previously ran in a former bed which debouched at Estero La Cutú or that a process of 'avulsion' occurred, or that it occurred on a particular date". In reality, El Salvador is seeking "a new interpretation of previously known facts" and asking the Chamber for a "genuine reversal" of the 1992 Judgment.

32. Honduras further maintains that the facts relied on by El Salvador, even if assumed to be new and established, are not of such a nature as to be decisive factors in respect of the 1992 Judgment. According to Honduras, "the material presented by El Salvador on that subject is irrelevant to the operative factual determination" made at that time by the Chamber. That decision is alleged to have been founded solely on the finding of fact that "from 1880, during the Saco negotiations, until 1972 El Salvador had treated the boundary as being based on the 1821 course of the river". The Chamber is said to have acted on that basis alone when in paragraph 312 of its Judgment it rejected El Salvador's claim "that the boundary follows an old course of the river abandoned at some time *before* 1821", considering it to be "a new claim and inconsistent with the previous history of the dispute". Thus, according to Honduras, it does not matter whether or not there was avulsion: avulsion is irrelevant to the *ratio decidendi* of the Chamber.

33. Honduras argues lastly that El Salvador's ignorance in 1992 of the facts on which it is relying in the present proceedings in support of its theory of avulsion was due to negligence. El Salvador has "never proved that it exhausted—or even initiated—means that would have given it diligent knowledge of the facts that it is alleging today". In Honduras's view, El Salvador could have had the scientific and technical studies and historical research which it is now relying on carried out before 1992.

34. Honduras concludes from the foregoing that, as the various conditions laid down by Article 61 of the Statute have not been satisfied, the Application for revision founded on the avulsion of the river Goascorán is not admissible.

35. Finally, the Parties raise the question whether the Application for revision was properly made within the six-month time-limit stipulated in paragraph 4 of Article 61 of the Statute. They do acknowledge, however, that the Application was submitted within the ten-year time-limit provided for in paragraph 5 of that Article, specifically, one day before the expiry of that time-limit. Honduras maintains nevertheless that, by proceeding in this fashion, the Applicant showed procedural bad faith. That is denied by El Salvador.

36. Turning to consideration of El Salvador's submissions concerning the avulsion of the Goascorán, the Chamber recalls that an application for revision is admissible only if each of the conditions laid down in Article 61 is satisfied, and that if any one of them is not met, the application must be dismissed; in the present case, the Chamber will begin by ascertaining whether the alleged facts, supposing them to be new facts, are of such a nature as to be decisive factors in respect of the 1992 Judgment.

37. In this regard, it is appropriate first to recall the considerations of principle on which the Chamber hearing the original case relied for its ruling on the disputes between the two States in six sectors of their land boundary.

According to that Chamber, the boundary was to be determined "by the application of the principle generally accepted in Spanish America of the *uti possidetis juris*, whereby the boundaries were to follow the colonial administrative boundaries" (para. 28). The Chamber did however note that "the *uti possidetis juris* position can be qualified by adjudication and by treaty". It reasoned from this that "the question then arises whether it can be qualified in other ways, for example, by acquiescence or recognition". It concluded that "There seems to be no reason in principle why these factors should not operate, where there is sufficient evidence to show that the parties have in effect clearly accepted a variation, or at least an interpretation, of the *uti possidetis juris* position." (Para. 67.)

Applying these principles to the first sector of the land boundary, the Chamber considered that in this sector "The situation was susceptible of modification by acquiescence in the lengthy intervening period" since the early nineteenth century. It added that, whatever may have been the colonial administrative boundaries, "the conduct of Honduras from 1881 until 1972 may be regarded as amounting to such acquiescence" to a part of the boundary claimed by El Salvador in this sector (para. 80).

38. The Chamber proceeded similarly in paragraphs 306 to 322 of its Judgment in respect of the sixth sector. After having identified the object of the dispute in this sector in paragraph 306, the Chamber first observed "that during the colonial period a river called the Goascorán constituted the boundary between two administrative divisions of the Captaincy-General of Guatemala: the province of San Miguel and the Alcaldía Mayor de Minas of Tegucigalpa" (para. 307). The Parties were in agreement that El Salvador had succeeded in 1821 to the territory of the Province of San Miguel. On the other hand, they disagreed as to whether or not the Alcaldía Mayor of Tegucigalpa had passed to Honduras. The Chamber decided that point in favour of Honduras *(ibid.)*.

The Chamber then considered "The contention of El Salvador that a former bed of the river Goascorán forms the *uti possidetis juris* boundary." In this respect, it observed that:

> "[this contention] depends, as a question of fact, on the assertion that the Goascorán formerly was running in that bed, and that at some date it abruptly changed its course to its present position. On this basis El Salvador's argument of law is that where a boundary is formed by the course of a river, and the stream suddenly leaves its old bed and forms a new one, this process of 'avulsion' does not bring about a change in the boundary, which continues to follow the old channel." (Para. 308.)

The Chamber added that:

> "No record of such an abrupt change of course having occurred has been brought to the Chamber's attention, but were the Chamber satisfied that the river's course was earlier so radically different from its present one, then an avulsion might reasonably be inferred." *(Ibid.)*

Pursuing its consideration of El Salvador's argument, the Chamber did however note: "There is no scientific evidence that the previous course of the Goascorán was such that it debouched in the Estero La Cutú ... rather than in any of the other neighbouring inlets in the coastline, such as the Estero El Coyol." (Para. 309.)

Turning to consideration as a matter of law of El Salvador's proposition concerning the avulsion of the Goascorán, the Chamber observed that El Salvador "suggests ... that the change in fact took place in the 17th century" (para. 311). It concluded that "On this basis, what international law may have to say, on the question of the shifting of rivers which form frontiers, becomes irrelevant: the problem is mainly one of Spanish colonial law." (Para. 311.)

At the conclusion of its consideration of El Salvador's line of argument as to the avulsion of the Goascorán, the Chamber did not take any position on the existence of an earlier course of the Goascorán which might have debouched into the Estero La Cutú, or on any avulsion of the river, nor *a fortiori*, on the date of any such avulsion or its legal consequences. It confined itself to defining the framework in which it could possibly have taken a position on these various points.

39. Beginning in paragraph 312 of the Judgment, the Chamber turned to a consideration of a different ground. At the outset, it tersely stated the conclusions which it had reached and then set out the reasoning supporting them. In the view of the Chamber, "any claim by El Salvador that the boundary follows an old course of the river abandoned at some time *before* 1821 must be rejected. It is a new claim and inconsistent with the previous history of the dispute." (Para. 312.)

The Chamber then noted: "A specific assertion that the boundary should follow an abandoned course of the river Goascorán was first made during the Antigua negotiations in 1972" (para. 312). It also quoted an excerpt from the record of the negotiations between the two States at Saco in 1880, stating that the two delegates had agreed "to recognize" the river Goascorán "as the frontier between the two Republics, from its mouth in the Gulf of Fonseca, Bay of La Unión, upstream in a north-easterly direction ..." *(ibid.)*. The Chamber observed that to interpret "the words 'River Goascorán' [in the text] as meaning a Spanish colonial boundary which in 1821 followed a long-abandoned course of the river, is out of the question" *(ibid.)*. It added that similar considerations applied to the circumstances of further negotiations in 1884 (para. 317).

Having on these grounds arrived at the conclusion that the boundary in 1821 followed the course of the Goascorán at that date, the Chamber turned to consideration of the evidence submitted to it in respect of that course (paras. 313 *et seq.*), evidence which will be examined in due course (see paragraph 50 below).

40. It is apparent from this discussion that, while the Chamber in 1992 rejected El Salvador's claims that the 1821 boundary did not follow the course of the river at that date, it did so on the basis of that State's conduct during the nineteenth century. In other words, applying the general rule which it had enunciated in paragraph 67 of the Judgment, the Chamber proceeded, in paragraph 312, concerning the sixth sector of the land boundary, by employing reasoning analogous to that which it had adopted in paragraph 80 in respect of the first sector. In the sixth sector, this reasoning led the Chamber to uphold the submissions of Honduras, while in the first sector it had proved favourable to El Salvador's position. In short, it does not matter whether or not there was an avulsion of the Goascorán. Even if avulsion were now proved, and even if its legal consequences were those inferred by El Salvador, findings to that effect would provide no basis for calling into question the decision taken by the Chamber in 1992 on wholly different grounds. The facts asserted in this connection by El Salvador are not "decisive factors" in respect of the Judgment which it seeks to have revised. In light of the 1992 Judgment, the Chamber cannot but reach such a conclusion, independently of the positions taken by the Parties on this point in the course of the present proceedings.

41. In support of its Application for revision, El Salvador relies on a second "new fact", that is, the discovery in the Ayer Collection of the Newberry Library in Chicago of a further copy of the "Carta Esférica" and of a further copy of the report of the expedition of the *El Activo*, thereby supplementing the copies from the Madrid Naval Museum to which the Chamber made reference in paragraphs 314 and 316 of its Judgment (see paragraph 24 above).

El Salvador states that in 1992, the Chamber had before it only copies of the documents that had been obtained from Madrid, and been produced by Honduras. It contends that it was on the basis of those copies that the Chamber decided the "point at which the Goascorán emptied into the Gulf" and the course of the boundary.

According to El Salvador, the documents discovered in Chicago differ from those in Madrid on several significant points. It maintains that:

> "The fact that there are several versions of the 'Carta Esférica' and the Report of the Gulf of Fonseca from the *El Activo* expedition, that there are differences among them and the anachronisms they share, compromises the evidentiary value that the Chamber attached to the documents that Honduras presented, essential in the Judgment [of 1992]."

Further, the evidentiary value is claimed to be all the more doubtful in that the Madrid documents enjoyed no official status and have not been certified to be originals. Accordingly, maintains El Salvador, there exists "a second *new fact*, whose implications for the Judgment have to be considered once the application for revision is admitted".

42. El Salvador adds that "[t]he discovery of hitherto unknown documents is a typical example of the type of fact which lays a case open to revision ... either because they themselves constitute the *factum* or because they are the source of knowledge of them". It further states that "[e]vidence which rebuts a fact established by a judgment of which revision is sought undoubtedly constitutes a *fact* for purposes of Article 61 of the Statute".

El Salvador asserts that in the present case the fact in question pre-dated the 1992 Judgment but was not "known at the time the Judgment was given". Thus, it is a "new fact" for purposes of Article 61. It is said to be decisive because its discovery has highlighted "the insubstantiality of the Madrid Naval Museum documents" from which the Chamber inferred "such significant" geographical "consequences".

43. Lastly, El Salvador states that the Ayer Collection is "not an indispensable reference source" and that the *El Activo* expedition was not a well-known expedition. It refers in more general terms to the "bitter civil war [which] was raging in El Salvador" "for virtually the whole period between 1980 and the handing down of the Judgment on 11 September 1992". Accordingly, it argues, "El Salvador's ignorance until 2002 of the existence of copies of the *El Activo* documents in collections situated in out-of-the-way places cannot be characterized as 'negligent'".

44. El Salvador concludes from the foregoing that, as the various conditions laid down by Article 61 of the Statute are satisfied, the Application for revision founded on the discovery of the new chart and new report is admissible.

45. For its part, Honduras denies that the production of the documents found in Chicago can be characterized as a new fact. This is simply "another copy of one and the same document already submitted by Honduras during the written stage of the case decided in 1992, and already evaluated by the Chamber in its Judgment". Honduras adds that it "never sought to argue the point whether the spherical chart was an original document (it always spoke of copies) or an official document". But it contends that there are no discrepancies between the three copies of the chart, merely "insignificant differences". Honduras maintains that those differences in no way contradict the content of the logbook. Finally, it notes that all three charts place the mouth of the river Goascorán in its present-day position, a finding on which the 1992 Judgment was based and which in any event remains valid.

46. Honduras further states that the new documents produced by El Salvador were part of a prestigious public collection and have been included in the Newberry Library catalogue at least since 1927. It concludes from this that El Salvador could easily have learned of those documents, and that it breached its duty of diligence in failing to seek them out or produce them before 1992. According to Honduras, no excuse for this fail-

ure can be found in the internal conflict prevailing in El Salvador at the time, as that conflict in no way prevented the conduct of research outside the national territory.

47. Honduras concludes from the foregoing that, as the various conditions laid down by Article 61 of the Statute are not satisfied, the Application for revision founded on the discovery of the new chart and the new report is not admissible.

48. Finally, as regards the conditions laid down in paragraphs 4 and 5 of Article 61 of the Statute, the Parties put forward arguments similar to those they made in respect of the avulsion of the Goascorán (see paragraph 35 above).

49. The Chamber will proceed, as it did in respect of the avulsion (see paragraph 36 above), to determine first whether the alleged facts concerning the "Carta Esférica" and the report of the *El Activo* expedition are of such a nature as to be decisive factors in respect of the 1992 Judgment.

50. It should be recalled in this regard that the Chamber in 1992, after having held El Salvador's claims concerning the old course of the Goascorán to be inconsistent with the previous history of the dispute, considered "the evidence made available to it concerning the course of the river Goascorán in 1821" (para. 313). It paid particular attention to the chart prepared by the captain and navigators of the vessel *El Activo* around 1796, described as a "Carta Esférica", which Honduras had found in the archives of the Madrid Naval Museum. It noted that the chart

> "appears to correspond with considerable accuracy to the topography as shown on modern maps. It shows the 'Estero Cutú' in the same position as modern maps; and it also shows a river mouth, marked 'Ro Goascoran', at the point where the river Goascorán today flows into the Gulf. Since the chart is one of the Gulf, presumably for navigational purposes, no features inland are shown except the '... best known volcanoes and peaks ...' ('... *volcanes y cerros mas conocidos* ...'), visible to mariners; accordingly, no course of the river upstream of its mouth is indicated. Nevertheless, the position of the mouth is quite inconsistent with the old course of the river alleged by El Salvador, or, indeed, any course other than the present-day one. In two places, the chart indicates the old and new mouths of a river (e.g., 'Barra vieja del Rio Nacaume' and 'Nuevo Rio de Nacaume'); since no ancient mouth is shown for the Goascorán, this suggests that in 1796 it had for some considerable time flowed into the Gulf where indicated on the chart." (Para. 314.)

The Chamber then analysed the report of the expedition and observed that it also places "the mouth of the river Goascorán at its present-day position" *(ibid.)*.

The Chamber concluded from the foregoing "that the report of the 1794 expedition and the 'Carta Esférica' leave little room for doubt that the river Goascorán in 1821 was already flowing in its present-day course" (para. 316).

51. The Judgment rendered by the Chamber in 1992 is thus based upon certain information conveyed by the "Carta Esférica" and the report of the *El Activo* expedition, in the versions held in Madrid. It should therefore be determined whether the Chamber might have reached different conclusions in 1992 had it also had before it the versions of those documents from Chicago.

52. The Chamber observes in this connection, that the two copies of the "Carta Esférica" held in Madrid and the copy from Chicago differ only as to certain details, such as for example, the placing of titles, the legends, and the handwriting. These differences reflect the conditions under which documents of this type were prepared in the late eighteenth cen-

tury; they afford no basis for questioning the reliability of the charts that were produced to the Chamber in 1992.

53. The Chamber notes further that the Estero La Cutú and the mouth of the Río Goascorán are shown on the copy from Chicago, just as on the copies from Madrid, at their present-day location. The new chart produced by El Salvador thus does not overturn the conclusions arrived at by the Chamber in 1992; it bears them out.

54. As for the new version of the report of the *El Activo* expedition found in Chicago, it differs from the Madrid version only in terms of certain details, such as the opening and closing indications, spelling, and placing of accents. The body of the text is the same, in particular in the identification of the mouth of the Goascorán. Here again, the new document produced by El Salvador bears out the conclusions reached by the Chamber in 1992.

55. The Chamber concludes from the foregoing that the new facts alleged by El Salvador in respect of the "Carta Esférica" and the report of the *El Activo* expedition are not "decisive factors" in respect of the Judgment whose revision it seeks.

56. Finally, El Salvador contends that proper contextualization of the alleged new facts "necessitates consideration of other facts that the Chamber weighed and that are now affected by the *new facts*". Moreover, El Salvador claims that

> "other evidences and proofs exist that, while not a *new fact*, were not taken up in the proceedings and are useful, even essential, whether to supplement and confirm the *new facts* or to better understand them".

It cites the great eruption of Cosigüina volcano and the appearance of the Farallones del Cosigüina, the Saco negotiations between 1880 and 1884, and the characteristics of the lower reaches of the river Goascorán.

57. Honduras responds that El Salvador, by submitting for the Chamber's consideration "evidence additional to the alleged new facts", is acting "as though the Court had to ignore its previous reasoning, on the pretext that it is in the light of the context that the existence or non-existence of the alleged new facts falls to be assessed". In the view of Honduras, this approach would be tantamount to expanding "the restrictive list of elements in Article 61, paragraph 1, of the Court's Statute to unheard-of lengths, calculated to turn revision into a habitual method of appeal and to undermine the authority of *res judicata*".

58. The Chamber agrees with El Salvador's view that, in order to determine whether the alleged "new facts" concerning the avulsion of the Goascorán, the "Carta Esférica" and the report of the *El Activo* expedition fall within the provisions of Article 61 of the Statute, they should be placed in context, which the Chamber has done in paragraphs 23 to 55 above. However, the Chamber must recall that, under that Article, revision of a judgment can be opened only by "the discovery of some fact of such a nature as to be a decisive factor, which fact was, when the judgment was given, unknown to the Court and also to the party claiming revision, always provided that such ignorance was not due to negligence". Thus, the Chamber cannot find admissible an Application for revision on the basis of facts which El Salvador itself does not allege to be new facts within the meaning of Article 61.

59. Given the conclusions to which it has come in paragraphs 40, 55 and 58 above, it is not necessary for the Chamber to ascertain whether the other conditions laid down in Article 61 of the Statute are satisfied in the present case.

60. For these reasons,

THE CHAMBER,

By four votes to one,

Finds that the Application submitted by the Republic of El Salvador for revision, under Article 61 of the Statute of the Court, of the Judgment given on 11 September 1992, by the Chamber of the Court formed to deal with the case concerning the *Land, Island and Maritime Frontier Dispute (El Salvador/Honduras: Nicaragua intervening)*, is inadmissible.

IN FAVOUR: Judge Guillaume, *President of the Chamber*; *Judges* Rezek, Buergenthal; *Judge* ad hoc Torres Bernárdez;

AGAINST: *Judge* ad hoc Paolillo.

Avena and other Mexican Nationals (*Mexico v. United States of America*)

2004 ICJ 12 (Judgment of Mar. 31)

49. In its final submissions Mexico asks the Court to adjudge and declare that, "the United States of America, in arresting, detaining, trying, convicting, and sentencing the 52 Mexican nationals on death row described in Mexico's Memorial, violated its international legal obligations to Mexico, in its own right and in the exercise of its right to diplomatic protection of its nationals, by failing to inform, without delay, the 52 Mexican nationals after their arrest of their right to consular notification and access under Article 36(1)(b) of the Vienna Convention on Consular Relations, and by depriving Mexico of its right to provide consular protection and the 52 nationals' right to receive such protection as Mexico would provide under Article 36(1)(a) and (c) of the Convention."

50. The Court has already in its Judgment in the *LaGrand* case described Article 36, paragraph 1, as "an interrelated régime designed to facilitate the implementation of the system of consular protection" (*I.C.J. Reports 2001*, p. 492, para. 74).

* * *

61. The Court thus now turns to the interpretation of Article 36, paragraph 1(b), having found in paragraph 57 above that it is applicable to the 52 persons listed in paragraph 16. It begins by noting that Article 36, paragraph 1(b), contains three separate but interrelated elements: the right of the individual concerned to be informed without delay of his rights under Article 36, paragraph 1(b); the right of the consular post to be notified without delay of the individual's detention, if he so requests; and the obligation of the receiving State to forward without delay any communication addressed to the consular post by the detained person.

* * *

90. The Court accordingly concludes that, with respect to each of the individuals listed in paragraph 16, the United States has violated its obligation under Article 36, paragraph 1(b), of the Vienna Convention to provide information to the arrested person.

* * *

Article 36, Paragraph 2

107. In its third final submission Mexico asks the Court to adjudge and declare that

"the United States violated its obligations under Article 36(2) of the Vienna Convention by failing to provide meaningful and effective review and reconsideration of convictions and sentences impaired by a violation of Article 36(1)."

108. Article 36, paragraph 2, provides:

"The rights referred to in paragraph 1 of this article shall be exercised in conformity with the laws and regulations of the receiving State, subject to the proviso, however, that the said laws and regulations must enable full effect to be given to the purposes for which the rights accorded under this article are intended."

109. In this connection, Mexico has argued that the United States

"By applying provisions of its municipal law to defeat or foreclose remedies for the violation of rights conferred by Article 36—thus failing to provide meaningful review and reconsideration of severe sentences imposed in proceedings that violated Article 36— ... has violated, and continues to violate, the Vienna Convention."

* * *

Legal Consequences of the breach

119. The general principle on the legal consequences of the commission of an internationally wrongful act was stated by the Permanent Court of International Justice in the *Factory at Chorzów* case as follows: "It is a principle of international law that the breach of an engagement involves an obligation to make reparation in an adequate form." (*Factory at Chorzów,* Jurisdiction, 1927, P.C.I.J., Series A, No. 9, p. 21.)

120. In the *LaGrand* case the Court made a general statement on the principle involved as follows:

"The Court considers in this respect that if the United States, notwithstanding its commitment [to ensure implementation of the specific measures adopted in performance of its obligations under Article 36, paragraph 1(b)], should fail in its obligation of consular notification to the detriment of German nationals, an apology would not suffice in cases where the individuals concerned have been subjected to prolonged detention or convicted and sentenced to severe penalties. In the case of such a conviction and sentence, it would be incumbent upon the United States to allow the review and reconsideration of the conviction and sentence by taking account of the violation of the rights set forth in the Convention. This obligation can be carried out in various ways. The choice of means must be left to the United States." (*I.C.J. Reports 2001*, pp. 513–514, para. 125.)

121. Similarly, in the present case the Court's task is to determine what would be adequate reparation for the violations of Article 36. It should be clear from what has been observed above that the internationally wrongful acts committed by the United States were the failure of its competent authorities to inform the Mexican nationals concerned, to notify Mexican consular posts and to enable Mexico to provide consular assistance. It follows that the remedy to make good these violations should consist in an obligation on the United States to permit review and reconsideration of these nationals' cases by the United States courts, as the Court will explain further in paragraphs 128 to 134 below, with a view to ascertaining whether in each case the violation of Article 36 committed by the competent authorities caused actual prejudice to the defendant in the process of administration of criminal justice.

* * *

123. It is not to be presumed, as Mexico asserts, that partial or total annulment of conviction or sentence provides the necessary and sole remedy. In this regard, Mexico cites the recent Judgment of this Court in the case concerning the *Arrest Warrant of 11 April 2000* (Democratic Republic of the Congo v. Belgium), in which the "Court ordered the cancellation of an arrest warrant issued by a Belgian judicial official in violation of the international immunity of the Congo Minister for Foreign Affairs." However, the present case has clearly to be distinguished from the *Arrest Warrant* case. In that case, the question of the legality under international law of the act of issuing the arrest warrant against the Congolese Minister for Foreign Affairs by the Belgian judicial authorities was itself the subject-matter of the dispute. Since the Court found that act to be in violation of international law relating to immunity, the proper legal consequence was for the Court to order the cancellation of the arrest warrant in question (*I.C.J. Reports 2002*, p. 33). By contrast, in the present case it is not the convictions and sentences of the Mexican nationals which are to be regarded as a violation of international law, but solely certain breaches of treaty obligations which preceded them.

* * *

135. Mexico, in the latter part of its seventh submission, has stated that "this obligation [of providing review and reconsideration] cannot be satisfied by means of clemency proceedings." Mexico elaborates this point by arguing first of all that "the United States's reliance on clemency proceedings is wholly inconsistent with its obligation to provide a remedy, as that obligation was found by this Court in *LaGrand*."

* * *

138. The Court would emphasize that the "review and reconsideration" prescribed by it in the *LaGrand* case should be effective. Thus it should "tak[e] account of the violation of the rights set forth in [the] Convention" (*I.C.J. Reports 2001*, p. 516, para. 128(7)) and guarantee that the violation and the possible prejudice caused by that violation will be fully examined and taken into account in the review and reconsideration process. Lastly, review and reconsideration should be both of the sentence and of the conviction.

* * *

140. As has been explained in paragraphs 128 to 134 above, the Court is of the view that, in cases where the breach of the individual rights of Mexican nationals under Article 36, paragraph 1(b), of the Convention has resulted, in the sequence of judicial proceedings that has followed, in the individuals concerned being subjected to prolonged detention or convicted and sentenced to severe penalties, the legal consequences of this breach have to be examined and taken into account in the course of review and reconsideration. The Court considers that it is the judicial process that is suited to this task.

Request for Interpretation of the Judgment of 31 March in *Avena and Other Mexican Nationals* *(Mexico v. United States)*

2009 I.C.J. 3 (Judgment of Jan. 19)

* * *

11. The Court recalls that in paragraph 153 (9) of the *Avena* Judgment the Court had found that:

> "the appropriate reparation in this case consists in the obligation of the United States of America to provide, by means of its own choosing, review and recon-

> sideration of the convictions and sentences of the Mexican nationals referred to in subparagraphs (4), (5), (6) and (7) above, by taking account both of the violation of the rights set forth in Article 36 of the [Vienna] Convention [on Consular Relations] and of paragraphs 138 to 141 of this Judgment".

12. Mexico asked for an interpretation as to whether paragraph 153 (9) expresses an obligation of result and requested that the Court should so state, as well as issue certain orders to the United States "pursuant to the foregoing obligation of result" (see paragraph 9 above).

13. Mexico's Request for interpretation of paragraph 153 (9) of the Court's Judgment of 31 March 2004 was made by reference to Article 60 of the Statute. That Article provides that "[t]he judgment is final and without appeal. In the event of dispute ['contestation' in the French version] as to the meaning or scope of the judgment, the Court shall construe it upon the request of any party."

14. The United States informed the Court that it agreed that the obligation in paragraph 153 (9) was an obligation of result and, there being no dispute between the Parties as to the meaning or scope of the words of which Mexico requested an interpretation, Article 60 of the Statute did not confer jurisdiction on the Court to make the interpretation (see para. 41 of the Order of 16 July 2008). In its written observations of 29 August 2008, the United States also contended that the absence of a dispute about the meaning or scope of paragraph 153 (9) rendered Mexico's Application inadmissible.

15. The Court notes that its Order of 16 July 2008 on provisional measures was not made on the basis of prima facie jurisdiction. Rather, the Court stated that "the Court's jurisdiction on the basis of Article 60 of the Statute is not preconditioned by the existence of any other basis of jurisdiction as between the parties to the original case" (Order, para. 44).

The Court also affirmed that the withdrawal by the United States from the Optional Protocol to the Vienna Convention on Consular Relations Concerning the Compulsory Settlement of Disputes since the rendering of the *Avena* Judgment had no bearing on the Court's jurisdiction under Article 60 of the Statute (*ibid.*, para. 44).

16. In its Order of 16 July 2008, the Court had addressed whether the conditions laid down in Article 60 "for the Court to entertain a request for interpretation appeared to be satisfied" (*ibid.*, para. 45), observing that "the Court may entertain a request for interpretation of any judgment rendered by it provided that there is a 'dispute as to the meaning or scope of [the said] judgment'" (*ibid.*, para. 46).

17. In the same Order, the Court pointed out that "the French and English versions of Article 60 of the Statute are not in total harmony" and that the existence of a dispute/"contestation" under Article 60 was not subject to satisfaction of the same criteria as that of a dispute ("différend" in the French text) as referred to in Article 36, paragraph 2, of the Statute (Order, para. 53). The Court nonetheless observed that "it seems both Parties regard paragraph 153 (9) of the *Avena* Judgment as an international obligation of result" (*ibid.*, para. 55).

18. However, the Court also observed that

> "the Parties nonetheless apparently hold different views as to the meaning and scope of that obligation of result, namely, whether that understanding is shared by all United States federal and state authorities and whether that obligation falls upon those authorities" (*ibid.*, para. 55).

19. The Court stated that the decision rendered on the request for the indication of provisional measures "in no way prejudges any question that the Court may have to deal with relating to the Request for interpretation" (*ibid.*, para. 79).

20. Accordingly, in the present procedure it is appropriate for the Court to review again whether there does exist a dispute over whether the obligation in paragraph 153 (9) of the *Avena* Judgment is an obligation of result. The Court will also at this juncture need to consider whether there is indeed a difference of opinion between the Parties as to whether the obligation in paragraph 153 (9) of the *Avena* Judgment falls upon all United States federal and state authorities.

21. As is clear from the settled jurisprudence of the Court, a dispute must exist for a request for interpretation to be admissible (*Request for Interpretation of the Judgment of 20 November 1950 in the Asylum Case (Colombia v. Peru), Judgment, I.C.J. Reports 1950*, p. 402 *Application for Revision and Interpretation of the Judgment of 24 February 1982 in the Case concerning the* Continental Shelf (Tunisia/Libyan Arab Jamahiriya) *(Tunisia v. Libyan Arab Jamahiriya), Judgment, I.C.J. Reports 1985*, pp. 216–217, para. 44; see also *Request for Interpretation of the Judgment of 11 June 1998 in the Case concerning the* Land and Maritime Boundary between Cameroon and Nigeria (Cameroon *v.* Nigeria), Preliminary Objections *(Nigeria v. Cameroon), Judgment, I.C.J. Reports 1999 (I)*, p. 36, para. 12)....

24. Mexico referred in particular to the actions of the United States federal Executive, claiming that certain actions reflected the United States disagreement with Mexico over the meaning or scope of the *Avena* Judgment. According to Mexico, this difference of views manifested itself in the position taken by the United States Government in the Supreme Court: that the *Avena* Judgment was not directly enforceable under domestic law and was not binding on domestic courts without action by the President of the United States; and further that the obligation under Article 94 of the United Nations Charter to comply with judgments of the Court fell solely upon the political branches of the States parties to the Charter. In Mexico's view, "the operative language [of the *Avena* Judgment] establishes an obligation of result reaching all organs of the United States, including the federal and state judiciaries, that must be discharged irrespective of domestic law impediments". Mexico maintains that the United States Government's narrow reading of the means for implementing the Judgment led to its failure to take all the steps necessary to bring about compliance by all authorities concerned with the obligation borne by the United States. In particular, Mexico noted that the United States Government had not sought to intervene in support of Mr. Medellin's petition for a stay of execution before the United States Supreme Court. This course of conduct is alleged to reflect a fundamental disagreement between the Parties concerning the obligation of the United States to bring about a specific result by any necessary means. Mexico further argues that the existence of a dispute is also shown by the fact that the competent executive, legislative and judicial organs at the federal and Texas state levels have taken positions in conflict with Mexico's as to the meaning or scope of paragraph 153 (9) of the *Avena* Judgment....

28. The United States has insisted that it fully accepts that paragraph 153 (9) of the *Avena* Judgment constitutes an obligation of result. It therefore continues to assert that there is no dispute over whether paragraph 153 (9) expresses an obligation of result, and thus no dispute within the meaning of the condition in Article 60 of the Statute. Mexico contends, making reference to certain omissions of the federal government to act and of certain actions and statements of organs of government or other public authorities, that in reality the United States does not accept that it is under an obligation of result; and that therefore there is indeed a dispute under Article 60.

29. It is for the Court itself to decide whether a dispute within the meaning of Article 60 of the Statute does indeed exist (see *Interpretation of Judgments Nos. 7 and 8 (Factory at Chorzów), Judgment No. 11, 1927, P.C.I.J., Series A, No. 13*, p. 12)....

43. [E]ven if a dispute in the present case were ultimately found to exist within the meaning of Article 60 of the Statute. The Parties' different stated perspectives on the existence of a dispute reveal also different contentions as to whether paragraph 153 (9) of the *Avena* Judgment envisages that a direct effect is to be given to the obligation contained therein.

44. The *Avena* Judgment nowhere lays down or implies that the courts in the United States are required to give direct effect to paragraph 153 (9). The obligation laid down in that paragraph is indeed an obligation of result which clearly must be performed unconditionally; non-performance of it constitutes internationally wrongful conduct. However, the Judgment leaves it to the United States to choose the means of implementation, not excluding the introduction within a reasonable time of appropriate legislation, if deemed necessary under domestic constitutional law. Nor moreover does the *Avena* Judgment prevent direct enforceability of the obligation in question, if such an effect is permitted by domestic law. In short, the question is not decided in the Court's original Judgment and thus cannot be submitted to it for interpretation under Article 60 of the Statute (*Request for Interpretation of the Judgment of 20 November 1950 in the Asylum Case (Colombia v. Peru), Judgment, I.C.J. Reports 1950*, p. 402).

45. Mexico's argument, as described in paragraph 31 above, concerns the general question of the effects of a judgment of the Court in the domestic legal order of the States parties to the case in which the judgment was delivered, not the "meaning or scope" of the *Avena* Judgment, as Article 60 of the Court's Statute requires. By virtue of its general nature, the question underlying Mexico's Request for interpretation is outside the jurisdiction specifically conferred upon the Court by Article 60. Whether or not there is a dispute, it does not bear on the interpretation of the *Avena* Judgment, in particular of paragraph 153 (9).

46. For these reasons, the Court cannot accede to Mexico's Request for interpretation.

47. Before proceeding to the additional requests of Mexico, the Court observes that considerations of domestic law which have so far hindered the implementation of the obligation incumbent upon the United States, cannot relieve it of its obligation. A choice of means was allowed to the United States in the implementation of its obligation and, failing success within a reasonable period of time through the means chosen, it must rapidly turn to alternative and effective means of attaining that result.

48. In the context of the proceedings instituted by the Application requesting interpretation, Mexico has presented three additional claims to the Court. First, Mexico asks the Court to adjudge and declare that the United States breached the Order indicating provisional measures of 16 July 2008 by executing Mr. Medellín on 5 August 2008 without having provided him with the review and reconsideration required under the *Avena* Judgment. Second, Mexico also regards that execution as having constituted a breach of the *Avena* Judgment itself. Third, Mexico requests the Court to order the United States to provide guarantees of non-repetition.

49. The United States argues that the Court lacks jurisdiction to entertain the supplemental requests made by Mexico. As regards Mexico's claim concerning the alleged breach of the Order of 16 July 2008, the United States is of the opinion, first, that the lack of a basis of jurisdiction for the Court to adjudicate Mexico's Request for interpretation extends to this ancillary claim. Second, and in the alternative, the United States suggests that such a claim, in any event, goes beyond the jurisdiction of the Court under Article 60 of the Statute. Similarly, the United States submits that there is no basis of jurisdiction for the Court to entertain Mexico's claim relating to an alleged violation of the *Avena*

Judgment. Finally, the United States disputes the Court's jurisdiction to order guarantees of non-repetition.

50. Concerning Mexico's claim that the United States breached the Court's Order indicating provisional measures of 16 July 2008 by executing Mr. Medellín, the Court observes that in that Order it found that "it appears that the Court may, under Article 60 of the Statute, deal with the Request for interpretation" (Order, para. 57). The Court then indicated in its Order that:

> "The United States of America shall take all measures necessary to ensure that Messrs. José Ernesto Medellín Rojas, César Roberto Fierro Reyna, Rubén Ramírez Cárdenas, Humberto Leal García, and Roberto Moreno Ramos are not executed pending judgment on the Request for interpretation submitted by the United Mexican States, unless and until these five Mexican nationals receive review and reconsideration consistent with paragraphs 138 to 141 of the Court's Judgment delivered on 31 March 2004 in the case concerning *Avena and Other Mexican Nationals (Mexico v. United States of America).*" (*Ibid.*, para. 80 (II) *(a)*.)

51. There is no reason for the Court to seek any further basis of jurisdiction than Article 60 of the Statute to deal with this alleged breach of its Order indicating provisional measures issued in the same proceedings. The Court's competence under Article 60 necessarily entails its incidental jurisdiction to make findings about alleged breaches of the Order indicating provisional measures. That is still so even when the Court decides, upon examination of the Request for interpretation, as it has done in the present case, not to exercise its jurisdiction to proceed under Article 60.

52. Mr. Medellín was executed in the State of Texas on 5 August 2008 after having unsuccessfully filed an application for a writ of *habeas corpus* and applications for stay of execution and after having been refused a stay of execution through the clemency process. Mr. Medellín was executed without being afforded the review and reconsideration provided for by paragraphs 138 to 141 of the *Avena* Judgment, contrary to what was directed by the Court in its Order indicating provisional measures of 16 July 2008.

53. The Court thus finds that the United States did not discharge its obligation under the Court's Order of 16 July 2008, in the case of Mr. José Ernesto Medellín Rojas.

[The ICJ goes on to discuss the breach of its order of provisional measures. This part is included in Chapter Eleven.]

61. For these reasons,

THE COURT,

(1) By eleven votes to one,

> *Finds* that the matters claimed by the United Mexican States to be in issue between the Parties, requiring an interpretation under Article 60 of the Statute, are not matters which have been decided by the Court in its Judgment of 31 March 2004 in the case concerning *Avena and Other*
>
> *Mexican Nationals (Mexico v. United States of America)*, including paragraph 153 (9), and thus cannot give rise to the interpretation requested by the United Mexican States ;

IN FAVOUR: *President* Higgins; *Vice-President* Al-Khasawneh; *Judges* Ranjeva,

Koroma, Buergenthal, Owada, Tomka, Abraham, Keith, Bennouna, Skotnikov;

AGAINST: *Judge* Sepúlveda-Amor;

(2) Unanimously,

Finds that the United States of America has breached the obligation incumbent upon it under the Order indicating provisional measures of 16 July 2008, in the case of Mr. José Ernesto Medellín Rojas;

(3) By eleven votes to one,

Reaffirms the continuing binding character of the obligations of the United States of America under paragraph 153 (9) of the *Avena* Judgment and *takes note* of the undertakings given by the United States of America in these proceedings;

IN FAVOUR: *President* Higgins; *Vice-President* Al-Khasawneh; *Judges* Ranjeva, Koroma, Buergenthal, Owada, Tomka, Keith, Sepúlveda-Amor, Bennouna, Skotnikov;

AGAINST: *Judge* Abraham;

(4) By eleven votes to one,

Declines, in these circumstances, the request of the United Mexican States for the Court to order the United States of America to provide guarantees of non-repetition;

IN FAVOUR: *President* Higgins; *Vice-President* Al-Khasawneh; *Judges* Ranjeva, Koroma, Buergenthal, Owada, Tomka, Abraham, Keith, Bennouna, Skotnikov;

AGAINST: *Judge* Sepúlveda-Amor;

(5) By eleven votes to one,

Rejects all further submissions of the United Mexican States.

IN FAVOUR: *President* Higgins; *Vice-President* Al-Khasawneh; *Judges* Ranjeva, Koroma, Buergenthal, Owada, Tomka, Abraham, Keith, Bennouna, Skotnikov;

AGAINST: *Judge* Sepúlveda-Amor.

Mary Ellen O'Connell, *The Prospects for Enforcing Monetary Judgments of the International Court of Justice: A Study of Nicaragua's Judgment against the United States**

In March 1988, Nicaragua's Sandinista government asked the International Court of Justice ("ICJ") to order the United States to pay $12 billion for violations of international law, as determined by the Court in June 1986. Before the Court could rule, however, the Sandinistas were voted out of office in national elections on February 25, 1990. Nicaragua's new government has recently indicated that it does not intend to give up the claim but will seek a settlement of the judgment with the United States government. But if the parties cannot reach a voluntary settlement, can Nicaragua enforce an ICJ judgment against the United States—or any other state, for that matter?

The efficacy of ICJ judgments is surely important to states which may be contemplating whether to seek monetary damages in current or future cases. States considering such cases must determine whether it is worth expending the significant resources necessary to bring an action before the ICJ if the resulting judgments cannot be enforced.

* 30 Va. J. Int'l L. 891 (1990) (footnotes omitted).

* * *

II. Enforcement Through International Organizations

When a judgment creditor ascertains that the debtor is unwilling to satisfy the ICJ's award, the first likely approach to getting the judgment satisfied would be to return to the ICJ itself for help. The Court has the authority and some means available to assist judgment creditors but has often proved unwilling or unable to aid enforcement. A second international organ through which enforcement might be obtained is the U.N. Security Council. The Security Council has specific authority in the U.N. Charter to aid enforcement of ICJ judgments, and may request the assistance of U.N. members, or such powerful agencies as the International Monetary Fund ("IMF") and the World Bank, in aiding enforcement. In many cases, however, the Security Council is unlikely to get the opportunity to assist, due to the possibility of a veto by one of the participating states. The creditor may then have more success seeking enforcement through a third international body, the U.N. General Assembly; it possesses the authority to lend assistance to states with unenforced judgments, though, to date, it has done little to help.

A. *The ICJ*

The ICJ can point to a good record of compliance with final judgments. This effectiveness in enforcing judgments seems widely recognized, as prospects for the ICJ appear better than in forty years. States are bringing increasing numbers of cases to the Court—in 1984 and 1989, the ICJ had record numbers of cases on its docket. The U.S. and U.S.S.R. have been discussing a mutual commitment to use the Court to settle certain types of disputes.

The primary rules governing the ICJ's decisions are found in the Statute of the Court and the United Nations Charter. The Statute provides that parties are bound to comply with the decisions of the ICJ. It says nothing, however, about the proper steps to take when a state fails to comply. Indeed the only hint that a state might not comply appears in article 61(3): "The Court may require previous compliance with the terms of the judgment before it admits proceedings in revision.

The jurisprudence of the ICJ and its predecessor, the Permanent Court of International Justice ("PCIJ"), has added little or nothing to this brief reference because the need to do so simply has yet to arise. Since 1970, the Court has not actually had to consider noncompliance with a final judgment. Moreover, in only one ICJ decision—*Corfu Channel*—has a state repudiated an ICJ judgment which to date remains only partially enforced. In a handful of other cases, states began by repudiating the ICJ's judgment but events obviated the need for enforcement in each case. In *Fisheries Jurisdiction*, for example, Iceland refused to participate in the proceeding before the ICJ. A year after the ICJ's judgment, Iceland and the United Kingdom negotiated a final settlement of the dispute. The ICJ has faced refusals to comply with provisional measures; although such measures may not have the same status as final decisions, in such cases the Court has taken no action in response, even of a procedural nature. In spite of the seemingly high rate of success of ICJ judgments, however, commentators continue to disparage the ICJ's capacity to function as and enjoy the authority of a "real" court. They point out that several states in the last fifteen years have chosen not to appear before the Court and states consistently ignore orders on interim measures.

The state representatives who drafted the Statute of the Court would not be surprised by the ICJ's inaction in the area of enforcement, which they envisioned to be a non-judicial function best left to the Security Council. When devising this plan they could not know how ineffectual the Security Council would become, nor did they even consider enforcement a potential problem at all. The ICJ's predecessor, the Permanent Court of International Justice, had a good record of compliance with its judgments, and the drafters might have expected the ICJ to enjoy the same fortune based on reputation alone.

Despite such broad respect for the ICJ in the international community, however, the historically high rate of judgment enforcement may be due less to compliance compelled by the prestige and stature of the ICJ than to the decentralized enforcement procedures typical to the enforcement of international law. As international law evolves, such a decentralized system of enforcement may no longer be sufficient. An extremely visible repudiation of a monetary judgment, the type most easily enforced in domestic courts, could easily damage the prestige of the Court, which could deal a setback to the use of international fora for the resolution of disputes.

* * *

B. *The Security Council*

The drafters of the U.N. Charter gave responsibility for enforcement to the Security Council:

> If any party to a case fails to perform the obligations incumbent upon it under a judgment rendered by the Court, the other party may have recourse to the Security Council, which may, if it deems necessary, make recommendations or decide upon measures to be taken to give effect to the judgment.

Until recently, however, it seemed very unlikely that the Council would fulfill this responsibility because of internal ideological divisions reflected in liberal use of the veto. The newfound cooperation between the U.S. and U.S.S.R. may mean, however, that the Security Council will in the future become a more viable means of assistance. Enforcement through he Security Council is thus technically available at law, although in practice obtaining it depends heavily upon the sense of responsibility of those who occupy its positions and the political situation at the time assistance is sought.

The Council's enforcement role was patterned after that of the League of Nations Council, which did play a useful role in enforcement. In 1933, Greece received an award against Bulgaria from the PCIJ in the *Rhodopia Forest* case. When Bulgaria appeared unwilling to pay the judgment, Greece simply said it would go to the League and ask for enforcement pursuant to article 13(4) of the Covenant which required that the Council take steps to enforce any judicial decision. As soon as the League put the matter on its agenda, Bulgaria gave assurances that it would comply with the decision.

The mandatory nature of the enforcement clause turned out to be somewhat onerous because in the next case to be brought to the League, the *Optant's Case*, the Council proved reluctant to enforce the decision for political reasons. The *Optant's Case* raised questions regarding an institution's obligation to enforce its tribunal's decisions that have never been adequately answered, and were certainly not discussed, when the Security Council took over the League Council's responsibility.

The drafters of the U.N. Charter were at least aware of the questions related to institutional enforcement because they made some significant changes in article 94 from the League's article 13(3). The *travaus* relating to article 94, however, are scant, and we do not know whether the changes were based on a new view of institutional enforcement or, indeed, whether they were based on much analysis at all. Several delegates may have worried that the Security Council would be overburdened by assuming a new competence not originally considered a part of its role when article 94 was put forth.

The language of article 94 seems to demonstrate that such concerns did in fact exist. Unlike the League Council, which was required to take steps to enforce a judgment, the

Council is granted discretion to enforce a judgment. The Security Council may only deal with matters presented to it by parties rather than *proprio motu* as could the League Council, and it may only be called on to enforce ICJ judgments rather than awards and decisions of other international tribunals. The language of article 94 gives no specific authority, however, to reexamine ICJ judgments.

The fact that judgments are final means the Council is restricted from reviewing the merits of a decision. There are, however, questions concerning the circumstances under which the Council should enforce judgments as a general rule. First, the United States has in the past argued that the Security Council should only enforce judgments relating to threats to the peace. The Security Council certainly possesses special authority for defusing threats to the peace, but the language of article 94 does not support any such subject matter restriction. Moreover, such a restriction would make article 94 redundant since the Security Council may already consider any dispute threatening the peace under chapters VI and VII, regardless of the source of the dispute.

Second, and more interesting, is whether the Security Council members' rights to veto apply to requests for enforcement under article 94. Some commentators have suggested that, because article 94 is not located in the chapters on peace and security, the veto should not apply. Forty years after the creation of the veto this is a difficult interpretation to support. The United States and the Soviet Union have insisted on the use of the veto in so many different contexts it is difficult to conceive of one in which they would not use it. Article 27(3), for example, appears on its face to prohibit the use of the veto in some cases, by requiring that a party to a dispute brought to the Council under chapter VI must abstain from voting; abstention, however, has not been the norm. Security Council practice has apparently modified the requirements of article 27(3), and today it appears that no permanent member of the Council may be expected to recuse itself.

Yet regardless of its authority, the Security Council has never received a request to enforce a final ICJ judgment. In 1954 it did receive a request from the United Kingdom for enforcement of ICJ interim measures against Iran resulting from that country's nationalization of oil concessions held by U.K. citizens. The Council reached no conclusion regarding its capacity to enforce interim measures, however, as the request became moot.

If not for political difficulties inherent to the body, the Security Council could be quite effective in enforcing judgments, given its ability to call on the member states and specialized U.N. agencies to aid in assisting enforcement. For example, the Council could call on member states to apply sanctions against a state refusing to comply with a decision of the ICJ.

It is less certain, however, whether the Council possesses the authority to instruct a member state to seize the assets of a judgment debtor within the member's jurisdiction and turn them over to the creditor in order to satisfy a judgment. The Council's power to call on member states outlined in chapter VII of the Charter is certainly very broad, suggesting that, where a failure to secure compliance with a judgment threatened peace or security, it would indeed possess such authority; but where peace is not threatened, such authority may not obtain.

Another significant variable related to Security Council enforcement of judgments involves the Council's ability to manipulate or direct the specialized agencies of the U.N. in enforcing a judgment. Most of the specialized agency agreements pledge the agencies to assist the Security Council in maintaining international peace and security, which would imply enforcing ICJ judgments, and the agencies provide a number of mechanisms for obtaining compliance with judgments. For example, the Security Council could order the IMF or the World Bank to turn over the debtor's funds to the creditor, the International Civil Aviation Organization ("ICAO") could require that its members deny a defaulter access to air space and landing rights, or the World Health Organization could withhold its programs and information from the debtor. Each of these organizations could increase pressure on a recalcitrant judgment debtor, either individually or part of a coordinated effort.

Some stumbling blocks might limit the effectiveness of attempts to utilize such specialized agencies, although they do not appear insurmountable. For instance, the IMF's specialized agency agreement with the United Nations is slightly different from the others. Under its agreement, the IMF:

> takes note of the obligation assumed, under paragraph 2 of Article 48 of the United Nations Charter, by such of its members as are also Members of the United Nations, to carry out the decisions of the Security Council through their action in the appropriate specialized agencies of which they are members, and will, in the conduct of its activities, have due regard for decisions of the Security Council under Articles 41 and 42 of the United Nations Charter.

The term "due regard" implies that the IMF may refuse a Security Council order, and some commentators have stated that it would likely refuse such an order rather than endanger its working capital by allowing attachment for satisfaction of judgments. The IMF could not refuse to assist the Council in all cases, however, it could always fashion assistance in a minimally confrontational manner. Thus, it appears that the Security Council could make effective use of specialized agencies, although not perhaps in every case in which it sought to utilize them.

The Security Council promises to be a more effective enforcer of judgments than the ICJ itself. Certain aspects of the Council's enforcement potential are still unexplored: the use of the veto in cases in which the member state has an interest, the finality of awards, the ability to command third-party states to seize assets and the extent to which the Council can employ its statutory authority to compel action by international organizations. Long dismissed as irrelevant, recent events have shown that the Security Council may yet prove to be an effective enforcer of judgments.

C. *The General Assembly*

Unlike the Security Council, the U.N. General Assembly has no explicit power to enforce ICJ decisions. Under the U.N. Charter, however, the Assembly possesses indirect authority to do so; it can discuss and make recommendations regarding any question "relating to the powers and functions of any organs provided for in the present charter." This broad authority probably includes discussing and making recommendations when states fail to comply with ICJ judgments, especially where a judgment is related to peace and security concerns.

Under the Charter scheme, the Security Council has primary authority for peace and security, but the General Assembly, via its Uniting for Peace Resolution, can make recommendations which could include calling on members to use force. The Soviet Union has disputed the right of the Assembly to authorize force. Nevertheless the Assembly's actions during the Suez crisis of 1956 and in the Middle East in 1958 under the Resolution show that in the future, the Assembly could plainly recommend economic sanctions against the judgment debtor, deny benefits and services, order a peacekeeping force to patrol borders or send the Secretary General to discuss compliance; nonetheless this avenue for enforcing judgments remains largely unexplored.

III. Enforcement Between the Parties

Despite the authority to enforce ICJ judgments codified in the charters of international organizations, most international law is enforced not through formal international institutions but informally by the state members of the system. Domestic, not international, courts are generally considered to be the primary enforcers of international law, and they could potentially play an important role in ICJ enforcement.

A. *Courts of the Judgment Creditor*

Although domestic courts are its primary enforcers, international law presumably does not require the judgment creditor to resort to its own courts before seizing any of the debtor's assets which may be within the creditor's jurisdiction. On the other hand, the creditor's domestic law may require judicial process in order to transfer title to property lawfully or to accomplish other types of enforcement measures. This section considers how the average domestic court is likely to respond to the request to enforce an ICJ judgment.

No party to either a PCIJ case or an ICJ case has asked a domestic court to enforce a judgment. Over the years, however, individuals who stood to benefit by the enforcement of a judgment have asked various domestic courts for enforcement and these cases raise many of the questions which would arise regardless of who asked for judicial intervention. One of the most prominent, *Socobelge v. Greece*, involved a beneficiary's request for assistance from the courts of the judgment creditor.

In 1951, a Belgian company, Socobelge, sought enforcement in Belgium of a PCIJ decision against Greece, which had affirmed certain arbitral awards in favor of Socobelge as valid and binding on Greece. Greece nevertheless still refused to pay the awards, leading Socobelge to attach monies derived from Marshall Aid funds located in a Belgian bank and to seek enforcement of the award through the Belgian courts.

Greece asserted a defense of sovereign immunity against the claim. The Belgian court dismissed this claim, however, on the ground that the assets in question "were derived from economic activities," making the defense of sovereign immunity inapplicable. Yet, despite its favorable ruling on sovereign immunity, the Belgian court ultimately did not order Greece to pay. Socobelge did not have an *exequatur*, which would have given the ICJ judgment the same effect as the judgment of a Belgian court. The court held that Socobelge required an *exequatur* because "in the absence of an independent power of execution belonging to [the PCIJ], which would enable litigants before it to execute its decisions de plano, these decisions are not exempt from the servitude imposed on Belgian territory on decisions of other than Belgian tribunals. In effect, the Belgian court treated the PCIJ judgment as the judgment of a foreign country.

Commentators have criticized this decision on the grounds that Belgium, as a party to the ICJ decision, was required to enforce the award through all its governmental divisions, including its courts. Such criticism, however, is misplaced. Certainly the Greek courts had the obligation to enforce the judgment, along with all other organs of the Greek government. Belgian courts, however, as beneficiaries of the judgment, had no obligation or duty to enforce the PCIJ's decision in its favor, any more than they were obligated to accept the benefit of the judgment at all.

What is most interesting about *Socobelge* is its treatment of ICJ judgments for purposes of enforcement as foreign domestic judgments. Such treatment may not necessarily be fatal to achieving the goal of enforcement, as it was in *Socobelge*, but there are reasons for trying to convince domestic courts to take a different view of ICJ judgments. Because ICJ judgments are infrequent, state-specific judgments, they are visible to the world community. When not enforced, the community's perception of international law suffers. Only a few domestic courts, at least in the near future, are likely to be called on to enforce ICJ judgments; thus, if those courts are not persuaded that the better approach is to enforce the judgments, damage may occur.

Clearly a major problem in *Socobelge* was the lack of a domestic statute or guideline explicitly calling on the court to enforce the international judgment....

At bottom, then, *Socobelge* stands for the "continuing confusion" on the part of domestic courts regarding the enforcement of ICJ judgments. In response to such confusion, one possible solution would be to encourage states to implement domestic legislation directing courts to enforce ICJ judgments on the same basis as international arbitral awards. It may be possible, however, to get the desired result without waiting for states to adopt such legislation, if a creditor can persuade a domestic court that ICJ judgments should be enforced as an international arbitral award, or a least like one.

1. *Arbitration Enforcement Under the New York Convention*

The United States Court of Appeals for the Ninth Circuit, in *Ministry of Defense of the Islamic Republic of Iran v. Gould*, made considerable strides toward opening up the categories of international cases which may be enforced under current U.S. Statutory law. The *Gould* court held that a decision of the Iran-U.S. Claims Tribunal in favor of the Government of Iran against a U.S. corporation could be enforced in the U.S. through legislation implementing the Convention on the Recognition and Enforcement of Foreign Arbitral Awards. The court of a signatory state must enforce these awards as though they were decisions of its own jurisdiction.

The advantages to a judgment creditor in analogizing its judgment to an arbitral award are several. Before the advent of the enforcement treaties, arbitral awards were also treated as foreign domestic awards and were subject to all their concomitant difficulties, such as the need for an *exequatur*....

* * *

3. *Appropriate Assets*

Getting enforcement of a judgment within the courts of the creditor's home state will be of little use where the debtor possesses few assets derived from "economic activities" within that jurisdiction. Governmental assets such as an embassy, or the property of a debtor's citizens, would be inappropriate. Under *Socobelge*, however, the scope of what may be considered "commercial" is broad enough that even a state like the United States, which does not undertake many commercial ventures, will likely have "real" assets in some jurisdictions, such as scientific equipment (survey vessels undertaking research with commercial applications, for example), pavilions and exhibits at trade fairs and air shows.

* * *

B. *Courts of the Judgment Debtor*

Because World Bank loans and other commercial assets of the debtor do not exist everywhere, some judgment creditors will need to go beyond their jurisdiction in seeking enforcement. One potential avenue of enforcement would be through the debtor's courts because the debtor generally cannot remove all of its property from beyond the power of its courts. Nevertheless, creditors may face insurmountable difficulties receiving a hearing in which the debtor's government actually agrees to payment.

* * *

United States courts, regardless of a state's ability to meet jurisdictional requirements, however, often refrain from ruling in cases that might in some way interfere with the executive branch's ability to conduct foreign affairs. Similarly, the Supreme Court has declined to apply international law where it has felt that the constitutional principle of separation of powers requires retreat from jurisdiction because of the potential for executive embarrassment.

Given this jurisprudence, U.S. courts would find it difficult to aid a creditor enforcing an ICJ order if such an order required the Executive to change its foreign policy. A district court, for example, has already refused to give effect to the *Nicaragua* decision on behalf of Americans living in Nicaragua on political questions grounds. [Committee of U.S. Citizens v. Reagan, 859 F. 2d 929 (D.C. Cir. 1988)] The Court of Appeals in reviewing the decision also dismissed the case, but did so in part on the ground that the plaintiffs did not have a cause of action to enforce the ICJ judgment. Although the court seemed to grant a state's right to bring such a case, it also questioned the status of an ICJ decision when the United States has challenged the International Court's jurisdiction to render such a decision. Thus it failed to acknowledge that ICJ decisions are final and that the courts of the debtor have the same obligation to enforce the decisions as other organs of the debtor's government. In committing to the jurisdiction of the ICJ for purposes of the case or under the optional clauses, a state agrees to accept the Statute of the Court; such consent binds domestic courts not to review.

C. *Unilateral Self-Help*

International law seems to require that the creditor attempt to enforce its judgment through the friendliest means available, such as judicial enforcement, before attempting self-help, but eventually the creditor is free to try self-help. Under traditional international law, self-help was the primary means of enforcing rights: states could go to war to promote foreign policy and war was used to enforce international law. For enforcing the judgments of international tribunals, states could resort to the *guerre d'execution*.

The most recent Restatement describes permissible self-help as consisting of measures "not involving the use of force, that might otherwise be unlawful, if such measures are (a) necessary to terminate the violation, or to remedy the violation and (b) are not out of proportion to the violation and the injury suffered." Nicaragua, for example, could attempt self-help on its own or it could seek assistance of third-party states. Generally, third-party reprisals are unlawful, and third-party judicial enforcement can be a form of third-party reprisals, but international law may make an exception for third-party judicial enforcement, especially in the case of monetary judgments. In attempting unilateral self-help, the creditor decides on the measures to be taken, although international law still lacks precise rules regarding what those measures should be or when they may be taken. For example, it is unclear whether the judgment creditor should go to the Security Council in seeking enforcement.

The permissibility of "reprisals" in a broad sense, as form of self-help in the context of enforcing a judgment, is similarly uncertain. That has been outlawed, so clearly states are prohibited from using force to get compliance with an ICJ judgment. Beyond this delimitation, however, international law has not clarified that actions remain as appropriate responses. The guidelines governing the "acceptable" use of force were always rather rough; except in prohibiting the most extreme responses, such guidelines regarding reprisals not involving the use of force are rougher still. The potential for exacerbating the situation through ever-escalating reprisals may not, however, be as great as in other contexts, e.g., where a monetary judgment is involved, which provides a fixed amount as a limit.

The type of self-help actions which various commentators do consider lawful include suspension and termination of treaties, freezing or confiscating assets, imposing economic sanctions, suspension of arms sales, technology, and food shipments, limitation on economic assistance, fishing rights, landing rights, docking rights or rights of over flight. In terms of measures aimed at enforcement, the Restatement says "[d]ifferent steps may be taken at different states of a dispute. For instance, limited measures are most appropriate when a state refuses to negotiate (e.g., freezing the offending state's assets); stronger measures become permissible when a state refuses to comply with a judgment of an international tribunal (e.g., seizure and appropriation of assets)." In most important judicial pronouncement on the legality of peaceful, unilateral reprisals—*Air Services*—an arbitral tribunal held that peaceful unilateral countermeasures are lawful as long as they remain proportional to the breach.

Attachment of the judgment debtor's property is another possible self-help act. Under international law, only commercial assets belonging to the state can be legally attached; beyond this, it's uncertain whether a party unable to get judicial enforcement may pursue a wider range of property, such as the property of citizens, or property enjoying diplomatic immunity. With a few limitations, the Restatement seems to concede that the judgment creditor may lawfully take a foreign national's property as reprisal. The taking of diplomatic or military property, however, may fall in the category of actions which could further exacerbate the conflict, thus constituting a non-proportional act in enforcement context.

At the very least, alien property does not appear to deserve privileged treatment, unlike military or diplomatic property. Developing countries, for example, have often nationalized and expropriated this property in retaliation for governmental actions. The issue in such cases is primarily whether compensation must be paid, not whether the property in unreachable. A. U.S. court has ruled that taking an alien's property is a permissible reprisal. Presumably, such alien property would include a commercial debt or arbitral award held by aliens against the state seeking enforcement.

As evidenced by *Air Services* and the writings of many commentators, the concern that unilateral reprisals may escalate a dispute perhaps renders it advisable for states for disfavor reprisals. Nevertheless, the general lack of institutional enforcement mechanisms has encouraged reprisals, and unless domestic courts begin to respond to requests for judicial enforcement, judgment creditors such as Nicaragua may be tempted to use unilateral self-help despite the potential risks.

IV. Enforcement Through Third-Party Assistance

Another possible approach for obtaining enforcement of an ICJ judgment would be with the aid of third-party states. While most states, as a matter of foreign policy, may be predisposed toward giving aid to their allies' requests for enforcement of ICJ judgments, "the issue is ... how far the third State has an obligation or right to cooperate with the aggrieved State in seeking compliance by the recalcitrant State." Some commentators argue that third-party states are prohibited from aiding in enforcement because such assistance would amount to unlawful interference with the property or affairs of the judgment debtor approaching the level of expropriation. The documents relating to the ICJ do not mention an explicit right of assistance, but sufficient evidence of state practice suggests that states clearly have a right to aid in enforcement and may even have a duty to do so, although any assistance must be pursuant to fair procedure.

A. *The Right to Assist*

Generally, states are free to act unless prohibited from doing so by the rules of international law. Third-party states seeking to assist in the enforcement of a judgment are free to do so unless a rule exists prohibiting assistance, such as the rules against reprisals or non-interference in the affairs of another state. In such cases, willing third-party states must find applicable exceptions. Rules such as those listed above would be only minor barriers, as they are not very specific and would only require a modest amount of evidence to reestablish a state's right to act.

The evidence will not be found, however, in either the Court's Statute or the U.N. Charter because neither mention a third-party's right to aid in enforcement. Article 94 of the Charter mentions only the Security Council's right to assist, which some commentators have interpreted to mean that third-party states may not assist. Article 59 of the Statute similarly says that the Court's judgment is binding only on the parties; some commentators read this article expansively in order to conclude that states not party to a case must stay out.

Over the last thirty years, however, incidents of third-party assistance in enforcement have occurred, and although state practice in this regard is not yet overwhelming, such customary action, when taken with the writing of several eminent scholars and reasons of policy, supports the finding of a right to assist. The domestic enforcement analogy equally provides support to the finding that states have a right, or even an obligation, to assist.

The most significant judicial precedent available in support of the third-party assistance is *Monetary Gold*. Although the ICJ did not rule in the case, it reveals the position of three states important to the question of third-party enforcement and in particular, that of the United States. The case arose out of claims asserted by Italy and Albania to monetary gold that had been seized during World War II. The matter was eventually referred to the President of the International Court of Justice, who appointed an arbitrator; the gold was ruled to have belonged to Albania. The Western Allies, however, had agreed that any judgment awarding the gold to Albania would be "enforced" and, ultimately, turned over to the United Kingdom as partial payment of the ICJ's award to the U.S. against Albania in *Corfu Channel*. In that event, the Allies nevertheless also pledged that either Italy or Albania could prevent transfer of the gold to the U.K. by initiating a case in the ICJ following the arbitral decision.

Britain's representative in the case asserted its right to take reasonable steps to ensure the enforcement of ICJ judgments (admittedly an act without precedence in the Court's history), but such arguments failed. Italy instituted a case with the ICJ, but because Albania—a necessary party—failed to appear before the Court, questions relating to Albania's behavior could not be decided and the case was dismissed.

Despite the fact that the ICJ could not rule on the Allies' enforcement program, at least one commentator has concluded that the case suggests the following propositions regarding third-party enforcement:

> 1. That states are entitled under international law (and possibly may be considered under a duty) to assist in the execution of a decision of the International Court, if that decision has not been complied with and the successful party requests such assistance;
>
> 2. That such assistance may include transferring to the judgment creditor assets of the judgment debtor which are located in the territory of the third state without obtaining the consent of the debtor state and without obtaining the sanction of the Security Council or a further decision of the International Court.
>
> 3. That the right of the third state to effect such transfer is subject to a duty on its party to make necessary measures to safeguard any competing claims of other

parties as, for example, by providing for judicial control as to the respective claims of all parties.

Notes and Questions on Compliance and Enforcement in Judicial Settlement

1. The Council of the League of Nations was required to enforce PCIJ decisions. The UN Security Council has discretion to enforce ICJ decisions. Why do you think the change was made?

2. Is the suggestion for enforcing ICJ decisions through national courts strengthened or weakened by the Iran-U.S. Claims Tribunal's approach for enforcement outlined in Case A27 (see Chapter Eight)?

3. Is enforcement of ICJ decisions important? Some might argue that the pronouncements of the Court on questions of law are more important than the actual payment of monetary damages. (But see the *Nuclear Tests Case* (Aus. v. France) (N.Z. v. France) 1974 I.C.J., where the applicants requested only a declaration on the legality of atmospheric nuclear weapons testing. France declared it would cease testing, so the Court found the cases moot. If the applicants had requested monetary damages for past actions, the Court would have decide the question of legality.) Is enforcement generally important in international law? Note that most international law is obeyed most of the time. Louis Henkin, How Nations Behave 41 (1979).

4. In 1988, Nicaragua went back to the ICJ to get enforcement of the award. In 1991, it sent a letter to the Court to withdraw the case. The letter contains the following passage:

> Taking into consideration that the Government of Nicaragua and the Government of the United States of America have reached agreements aimed at enhancing Nicaragua's economic, commercial and technical development to the maximum extent possible, the Government of Nicaragua has decided to renounce all further right of action based on the case in reference and, hence, that it does not wish to go on with the proceedings.

See 31 ILM 103 (1992).

5. Another ICJ decision languished unenforced for nearly fifty years. The ICJ made an award of damages to Britain for the loss of ships and sailors in the Corfu Channel. *Corfu Channel* (U.K. v. Alb.), 1949 I.C.J. 4 (Apr. 9). Albania refused to pay. Britain refused to have diplomatic relations until they did. It also held monetary gold belonging to the Albania Central bank (which the Allies had captured in Rome during the Second World War) in the Bank of England. At the end of the Cold War, Britain and Albania finally negotiated an end to the long-standing dispute, and Albania made a payment toward the damages. The U.K. re-established diplomatic relations, and the gold was returned. Richard Norton-Taylor, *Bank Returns Looted Nazi Gold to Albania,* Guardian, Oct. 30, 1996, 1996 WL 13384395.

6. May a state that benefits from an ICJ advisory opinion "enforce" the opinion? *See* UN Charter Article 96 and ICJ Statute Articles 65–68. Compare Charter Article 94, which provides for Security Council assistance in enforcing judgments binding on states. Consider also:

> United Nations, Handbook on the Pacific Settlement of Disputes Between States, p. 70 (1992)

> (v) *Advisory opinions*
>
> 212. International courts may be empowered to give an advisory opinion on a legal question relating to an existing international dispute between States referred to them by an international entity. The opinion does not bind the requesting entity, or any other body, or any State. Nevertheless, procedure in advisory cases, as in contentious cases, involves elaborate written and oral proceedings in accordance with the predetermined rules of the court in question, and as such advisory opinions could assume the character of judicial pronouncements which, while not binding, might entail practical consequences....

7. In 2011, Cambodia filed a case with the ICJ that would appear to meet the terms of the ICJ Statute's Article 61 more closely than the cases reviewed in this chapter. Here is a very brief summary from an ICJ press release:

> THE HAGUE, 2 May 2011. On 28 April, the Kingdom of Cambodia filed an Application requesting interpretation of the Judgment rendered on 15 June 1962 by the International Court of Justice (ICJ) in the case concerning the Temple of Preah Vihear (Cambodia v. Thailand). The filing of such an application gives rise to the opening of a new case. Together with that Application, Cambodia submitted an urgent request for the indication of provisional measures....
>
> In support of its Request for interpretation, Cambodia invokes Article 60 of the Statute of the Court....
>
> In its Application, Cambodia indicates the "points in dispute as to the meaning or scope of the Judgment", as stipulated by Article 98 of the Rules of Court. It states in particular that:
>
> "(1) according to Cambodia, the Judgment [rendered by the Court in 1962] is based on the prior existence of an international boundary established and recognized by both States;
>
> (2) according to Cambodia, that boundary is defined by the map to which the Court refers on page 21 of its Judgment..., a map which enables the Court to find that Cambodia's sovereignty over the Temple is a direct and automatic consequence of its sovereignty over the territory on which the Temple is situated ...;
>
> (3) according to the Judgment, Thailand is under an obligation to withdraw any military or other personnel from the vicinity of the Temple on Cambodian territory. Cambodia believes that this is a general and continuing obligation deriving from the statements concerning Cambodia's territorial sovereignty recognized by the Court in that region."
>
> * * *
>
> The Applicant explains that, while "Thailand does not dispute Cambodia's sovereignty over the Temple—and only over the Temple itself", on the other hand, it calls into question the 1962 Judgment in its entirety. Cambodia contends that "in 1962, the Court placed the Temple under Cambodian sovereignty, because the territory on which it is situated is on the Cambodian side of the boundary", and that "[t]o refuse Cambodia's sovereignty over the area beyond the Temple as far as its 'vicinity' is to say to the Court that the boundary line which it recognized [in 1962] is wholly erroneous, including in respect of the Temple itself".

> Cambodia emphasizes that the purpose of its Request is to seek an explanation from the Court regarding the "meaning and ... scope of its Judgment, within the limit laid down by Article 60 of the Statute". It adds that such an explanation, "which would be binding on Cambodia and Thailand, ... could then serve as a basis for a final resolution of this dispute through negotiation or any other peaceful means".

8. For further reading on enforcement of ICJ judgments, see, CONSTANZE SCHULTE, COMPLIANCE WITH DECISIONS OF THE INTERNATIONAL COURT OF JUSTICE (2004).

The Cilantro Island Problem

Cilantro Island lies in the beautiful Medea Sea about 200 yards from the coast of the Kingdom of Roccom. About one hundred miles north of Roccom, across the Medea, is the Republic of Hispania. Roccom and Hispania have long contested the title to Cilantro. They have found no way of settling the actual title question, but have agreed to a treaty with the following clause:

> On August 1 each year, Roccom and Hispania will hold consultations in the matter of Cilantro Island.
>
> Any dispute between the Kingdom of Roccom and the Republic of Hispania that might arise owing to the fact that the title to Cilantro Island is contested, and which cannot be settled by negotiation, shall be referred to the International Court of Justice.

On August 1, Roccom and Hispania held their annual consultations in Paris. A full day was spent covering a wide range of issues, but no agreements were reached. Later that week, Roccom nationals were fishing near Cilantro (as they have since time immemorial), when Hispanian fishing control vessels chased them away, cutting nets and firing across the bows. One Roccom trawler refused to leave the area, and was fired on by the Hispanian vessels. The trawler sank. The Hispanians rescued and arrested the trawler crew, and took them to Hispania where they are now jailed for fishing in Hispanian waters without a license. They are scheduled to be tried in two weeks. As soon as the Government of Roccom received the reports of what happened, it demanded that Hispania agree to go to the ICJ without delay to finally resolve, once and for all, the whole question of the title to Cilantro. Hispania responded that it will consider consultations, but only after the trial of the trawler crew.

Must Hispania go to the ICJ immediately? What objections might it raise to going immediately? What advantages might it gain by going immediately? Both states are party to UNCLOS. What impact might this have? What enforcement issues might arise?

II. Binding Methods

B. Judicial Settlement

2. National Courts

Chapter Fourteen

National Courts

Introduction

Previous chapters have already introduced the subject of national courts. In the last chapter, for example, we saw how national courts could be employed to enforce an ICJ judgment, and thus resolve an inter-state dispute over the obligation to pay an award. Chapter Eight included excerpts from cases where Iran sought enforcement of an arbitral award in U.S. courts. This chapter focuses on the use of national courts to aid in the resolution of disputes involving states and/or international organizations.

A great many international disputes are resolved in national courts. The vast majority of these cases, however, involve at least one private party. Fewer international disputes involving only states and/or international organizations reach national courts. Because some of these disputes do reach national courts, however, this chapter is important to acquiring a complete understanding of IDR. Most of the relevant legal principles discussed in this chapter also apply to the larger body of international disputes in which private parties are involved.

National courts are, in theory, widely available as IDR fora owing to the fact that international law never developed a set of binding rules restricting jurisdiction for states in general or their courts in particular. Thus, under international law, national courts may take jurisdiction in a broad range of cases. This chapter concerns the jurisdiction of national courts over international disputes and the primary limitation on jurisdiction—the sovereign immunity of states and the privileges and immunities of international organizations. The chapter that follows reviews some of the many issues that may arise in the course of a national court's attempt to resolve an international dispute.

A. Jurisdiction

The single difference between national judicial settlement and every other means reviewed to this point is that national courts may have compulsory jurisdiction over some disputes. In other words, the state or international organization may find itself subject to a national court's jurisdiction without ever having given explicit consent.

International law scholarship typically lists a number of bases, grounds for asserting jurisdiction by courts, including territoriality, nationality, passive personality, protective, and universal. The number of available bases of jurisdiction might lead one to think that national courts play a major role in IDR. In fact, national courts play a far smaller role than they are permitted to play. States grant each other and international organizations broad immunity from jurisdiction, and employ other strategies to avoid taking cases involving sovereign states and international organizations. Some of these barriers to national court jurisdiction are beginning to fall—especially with respect to civil suits brought by individuals against states. We also have a growing number of examples where states and international organizations have initiated cases in national courts to get resolution of a dispute. Several cases of this type are excerpted in the next chapter. Here, we begin with a brief discussion of national court jurisdiction under international law, and move on to a discussion of the immunity from national courts jurisdiction enjoyed by sovereign states and international inter-governmental organizations (IOs).

As mentioned above, states tend to put extensive limits on the jurisdiction of their courts in international matters. These limits are not generally derived from international law. International law affords states broad authority to adjudicate international disputes. The only clear rule restricting courts is that states must respect the principle of non-intervention—they may not interfere in the internal affairs of other states. According to Judge Sir Gerald Fitzmaurice:

> It is true that, under present conditions, international law does not impose hard and fast rules on States delimiting spheres of national jurisdiction ... —but leaves to States a wide discretion in the matter. It does, however, (a) postulate the existence of limits—though in any given case it may be for the tribunal to indicate what these are for the purposes of that case; and (b) involve for every State an obligation to exercise moderation and restraint as to the extent of the jurisdiction assumed by its courts in cases having a foreign element, and to avoid undue encroachment on a jurisdiction more properly appertaining to, or more appropriately exercisable by, another State.[1]

Judge Fitzmaurice's view tracks the 1927 decision of the PCIJ in the *Lotus Case*:

The Case of the S.S. "Lotus" (*France v. Turkey*)

1927 PCIJ Rep. Ser. A. No. 10 (Sept. 7)

The Court,

* * *

has to decide the following questions:

(1) Has Turkey, contrary to Article 15 of the Convention of Lausanne of July 24th, 1923, respecting conditions of residence and business and jurisdiction, acted in conflict with the principles of international law—and if so, what principles—by instituting, following the collision which occurred on August 2nd, 1926, on the high seas between the French steamer *Lotus* and the Turkish steamer *Boz-Kourt* and upon the arrival of the French steamer at Constantinople—as well as against the captain of the Turkish steamship—joint criminal proceedings in pursuance of Turkish law against M. Demons, officer of the watch on board the *Lotus* at the time of the collision, in consequence of the loss of the *Boz-Kourt* having involved the death of eight Turkish sailors and passengers?

---

1. Case Concerning Barcelona Traction, Light and Power Col., Ltd., (Canada v. Spain) 1970 I.C.J. 105 (Opinion of Judge Sir Gerald Fitzmaurice), *cited in* F.A. Mann, *The Doctrine of International Jurisdiction Revisited After Twenty Years, in 186, III* Recuil des Cours 26–27 (1984).

(2) Should the reply be in the affirmative, what pecuniary reparation is due to M. Demons, provided, according to the principles of international law, reparation should be made in similar cases?

* * *

THE FACTS.

According to the statements submitted to the Court by the Parties' Agents in their Cases and in their oral pleadings, the facts in which the affair originated are agreed to be as follows:

On August 2nd, 1926, just before midnight, a collision occurred between the French mail steamer *Lotus*, proceeding to Constantinople, and the Turkish collier *Boz-Kourt*, between five and six nautical miles to the north of Cape Sigri (Mitylene). The *Boz-Kourt*, which was cut in two, sank, and eight Turkish nationals who were on board perished. After having done everything possible to succour the shipwrecked persons, of whom ten were able to be saved, the *Lotus* continued on its course to Constantinople, where it arrived on August 3rd.

At the time of the collision, the officer of the watch on board the *Lotus* was Monsieur Demons, a French citizen, lieutenant in the merchant service and first officer of the ship, whilst the movements of the *Boz-Kourt* were directed by its captain, Hassan Bey, who was one of those saved from the wreck.

As early as august 3rd the Turkish police proceeded to hold an enquiry into the collision on board the *Lotus*; and on the following day, August 4th, the captain of the *Lotus* handed in his master's report at the French Consulate-General, transmitting a copy to the harbour master.

On August 5th, Lieutenant Demons was requested by the Turkish authorities to go ashore to give evidence. The examination, the length of which incidentally resulted in delaying the departure of the *Lotus*, led to the placing under arrest of Lieutenant Demons—without previous notice being given to the French Consul-General—and Hassan Bey, amongst others. This arrest, which has been characterized by the Turkish Agent as arrest pending trial (*arrestation preventive*), was effected in order to ensure that the criminal prosecution instituted against the two officers, on a charge of manslaughter, by the Public Prosecutor of Stamboul, on the complaint of the families of the victims of the collision, should follow its normal course.

The case was first heard by the Criminal Court of Stamboul on August 28th. On that occasion, Lieutenant Demons submitted that the Turkish Courts had no jurisdiction; the Court, however, overruled his objection. When the proceedings were resumed on September 11th, Lieutenant Demons demanded his release on bail; this request was complied with on September 13th, the bail being fixed at 6,000 Turkish pounds.

On September 15th, the Criminal Court delivered its judgment, the terms of which have not been communicated to the Court by the Parties. It is, however, common ground, that it sentenced Lieutenant Demons to eighty days' imprisonment and a fine of twenty-two pounds, Hassan Bey being sentenced to a slightly more severe penalty.

It is also common ground between the Parties that the Public Prosecutor of the Turkish Republic entered an appeal against this decision, which had the effect of suspending its execution until a decision upon the appeal had been given; that such decision has not yet been given; but that the special agreement of October 12th, 1926, did not have the effect of suspending "the criminal proceedings.... now in progress in Turkey."

The action of the Turkish judicial authorities with regard to Lieutenant Demons at once gave rise to many diplomatic representations and other steps on the part of the French Government or its representatives in Turkey, either protesting against the arrest of Lieutenant Demons or demanding his release, or with a view to obtaining the transfer of the case from the Turkish Courts to the French Courts.

As a result of these representations, the Government of the Turkish Republic declared on September 2nd, 1926, that "it would have no objection to the reference of the conflict of jurisdiction to the Court at The Hague."

The French Government having, on the 6th of the same month, given "its full consent to the proposed solution," the two Governments appointed their plenipotentiaries with a view of the drawing up of the special agreement to be submitted to the Court; this special agreement was signed at Geneva on October 12th, 1926, as stated above, and the ratifications were deposited on December 27th, 1926.

THE LAW.

I.

* * *

1.—The collision which occurred on August 2nd, 1926, between the S.S. *Lotus*, flying the French flag, and the S.S. *Boz-Kourt*, flying the Turkish flag, took place on the high seas: the territorial jurisdiction of any State other than France and Turkey therefore does not enter into account.

2.—The violation, if any, of the principles of international law would have consisted in the taking of criminal proceedings against Lieutenant Demons. It is not therefore a question relating to any particular step in these proceedings—such as his being put to trial, his arrest, his detention pending trial or the judgment given by the Criminal Court of Stamboul—but of the very fact of the Turkish Courts exercising criminal jurisdiction. That is why the arguments put forward by the Parties in both phases of the proceedings relate exclusively to the question whether Turkey has or has not, according to the principles of international law, jurisdiction to prosecute in this case.

* * *

II.

* * *

It is Article 15 of the Convention of Lausanne of July 24th, 1923, respecting conditions of residence and business and jurisdiction, which refers the contracting Parties to the principles of international law as regards the delimitation of their respective jurisdiction.

This clause is as follows:

> "Subject to the provisions of Article 16, all questions of jurisdiction shall, as between Turkey and the other contracting Powers, be decided in accordance with the principles of international law."

* * *

III.

The Court, having to consider whether there are any rules of international law which may have been violated by the prosecution in pursuance of Turkish law of Lieutenant Demons, is confronted in the first place by a question of principle which, in the written and oral arguments of the two Parties, has proved to be a fundamental one. The French Government contends that the Turkish Courts, in order to have jurisdiction, should be able to point to some title to jurisdiction recognized by international law in favour of Turkey. On the other hand, the Turkish Government takes the view that Article 15 allows Turkey jurisdiction whenever such jurisdiction does not come into conflict with a principle of international law.

The latter view seems to be in conformity with the special agreement itself, No. 1 of which asks the Court to say whether Turkey has acted contrary to the principles of international law and, if so, what principles. According to the special agreement, therefore, it is not a question of stating principles which would permit Turkey to take criminal proceedings, but of formulating the principles, if any, which might have been violated by such proceedings.

This way of stating the question is also dictated by the very nature and existing conditions of international law.

International law governs relations between independent States. The rules of law binding upon States therefore emanate from their own free will as expressed in conventions or by usages generally accepted as expressing principles of law and established in order to regulate the relations between these co-existing independent communities or with a view to the achievement of common aims. Restrictions upon the independence of States cannot therefore be presumed.

Now the first and foremost restriction imposed by international law upon a State is that—failing the existence of permissive rule to the contrary—it may not exercise its power in any form in the territory of another State. In this sense jurisdiction is certainly territorial; it cannot be exercised by a State outside its territory except by virtue of a permissive rule derived from international custom or from a convention.

It does not, however, follow that international law prohibits a State from exercising jurisdiction in its own territory, in respect of any case which relates to acts which have taken place abroad, and in which it cannot rely on some permissive rule of international law. Such a view would only be tenable if international law contained a general prohibition to States to extend the application of their laws and the jurisdiction of their courts to persons, property and acts outside their territory, and if, as an exception to this general prohibition, it allowed States to do so in certain specific cases. But this is certainly not the case under international law as it stands at present. Far from laying down a general prohibition to the effect that States may not extend the application of their laws and the jurisdiction of their courts to persons, property and acts outside their territory, it leaves them in this respect a wide measure of discretion which is only limited in certain cases by prohibitive rules; as regards other cases, every State remains free to adopt the principles which it regards as best and most suitable.

This discretion left to States by international law explains the great variety of rules which they have been able to adopt without objections or complaints on the part of other States; it is in order to remedy the difficulties resulting from such variety that efforts have been made for many years past, both in Europe and America, to prepare conventions the effect of which would be precisely to limit the discretion at present left to States in this respect by international law, thus making good the existing lacunae in respect of jurisdiction or removing the conflicting jurisdictions arising from the diversity of the principles adopted by the various States.

In these circumstances, all that can be required of a State is that it should not overstep the limits which international law places upon its jurisdiction; within these limits, its title to exercise jurisdiction rests in its sovereignty.

It follows from the foregoing that the contention of the French Government to the effect that Turkey must in each case be able to cite a rule of international law authorizing her to exercise jurisdiction, is opposed to the generally accepted international law to which Article 15 of the Convention of Lausanne refers. Having regard to the terms of Article 15 and to the construction which the Court has just placed upon it, this contention would apply in regard to civil as well as to criminal cases, and would be applicable on conditions of absolute reciprocity as between Turkey and the other contracting Parties; in practice, it would therefore in many cases result in paralyzing the action of the courts, owing to the impossibility of citing a universally accepted rule on which to support the exercise of their jurisdiction.

Nevertheless, it has to be seen whether the foregoing considerations really apply as regards criminal jurisdiction, or whether this jurisdiction is governed by a different principle: this might be the outcome of the close connection which for a long time existed between the conception of supreme criminal jurisdiction and that of a State, and also by the especial importance of criminal jurisdiction from the point of view of the individual.

Though it is true that in all systems of law the principle of the territorial character of criminal law is fundamental, it is equally true that all or nearly all these systems of law extend their action to offences committed outside the territory of the State which adopts them, and they do so in ways which vary from State to State. The territoriality of criminal law, therefore, is not an absolute principle of international law and by no means coincides with territorial sovereignty.

This situation may be considered from two different standpoints corresponding to the points of view respectively taken up by the Parties. According to one of these standpoints, the principle of freedom, in virtue of which each State may regulate its legislation at its discretion, provided that in so doing it does not come in conflict with a restriction imposed by international law, would also apply as regards law governing the scope of jurisdiction in criminal cases. According to the other standpoint, the exclusively territorial character of law relating to this domain constitutes a principle which, except as otherwise expressly provided, would, *ipso facto*, prevent States from extending the criminal jurisdiction of their courts beyond their frontiers; the exceptions in question, which include for instance extraterritorial jurisdiction over nationals and over crimes directed against public safety, would therefore rest on special permissive rules forming part of international law.

* * *

IV.

* * *

The arguments advanced by the French Government, other than those considered above, are, in substance, the three following:

(1) International law does not allow a State to take proceedings with regard to offences committed by foreigners abroad, simply by reason of the nationality of the victim; and such is the situation in the present case because the offence must be regarded as having been committed on board the French vessel.

(2) International law recognizes the exclusive jurisdiction of the State whose flag is flown as regards everything which occurs on board a ship on the high seas.

(3) Lastly, this principle is especially applicable in a collision case.

* * *

No argument has come to the knowledge of the Court from which it could be deduced that States recognize themselves to be under an obligation towards each other only to have regard to the place where the author of the offence happens to be at the time of the offence. On the contrary, it is certain that the courts of many countries, even of countries which have given their criminal legislation a strictly territorial character, interpret criminal law in the sense that offences, the authors of which at the moment of commission are in the territory of another State, are nevertheless to be regarded as having been committed in the national territory, if one of the constituent elements of the offence, and more especially its effects, have taken place there. French courts have, in regard to a variety of situations, given decisions sanctioning this way of interpreting the territorial principle. Again, the Court does not know of any cases in which governments have protested against the fact that the criminal law of some country contained a rule to this effect or that the courts of a country construed their criminal law in this sense. Consequently, once it is admitted that the effects of the offence were produced on the Turkish vessel, it becomes impossible to hold that there is a rule of international law which prohibits Turkey from prosecuting Lieutenant Demons because of the fact that the author of the offence was on board the French ship. Since, as has already been observed, the special agreement does not deal with the provision of Turkish law under which the prosecution was instituted, but only with the question whether the prosecution should be regarded as contrary to the principles of international law, there is no reason preventing the Court from confining itself to observing that, in this case, a prosecution may also be justified from the point of view of the so-called territorial principle.

* * *

The second argument put forward by the French Government is the principle that the State whose flag is flown has exclusive jurisdiction over everything which occurs on board a merchant ship on the high seas.

It is certainly true that—apart from certain special cases which are defined by international law—vessels on the high seas are subject to no authority except that of the State whose flag they fly. In virtue of the principle of the freedom of the seas, that is to say the absence of any territorial sovereignty upon the high seas, no State may exercise any kind of jurisdiction over foreign vessels upon them. Thus, if a war vessel, happening to be at the spot where a collision occurs between a vessel flying its flag and a foreign vessel, were to send on board the latter an officer to make investigations or to take evidence, such an act would undoubtedly be contrary to international law.

But it by no means follows that a State can never in its own territory exercise jurisdiction over acts which have occurred on board a foreign ship on the high seas. A corollary of the principle of the freedom of the seas is that a ship on the high seas is assimilated to the territory of the State the flag of which it flies, for, just as in its own territory, that State exercises its authority upon it, and no other State may do so. All that can be said is that by virtue of the principle of the freedom of the seas, a ship is placed in the same position as national territory; but there is nothing to support the claim according to which the rights of the State under whose flag the vessel sails may go farther than the rights which it exercises within its territory properly so called. It follows that what occurs on board a vessel on the high seas must be regarded as if it occurred on the territory of the State whose flag the ship flies. If, therefore, a guilty act committed on the high seas produces its effects on a vessel flying another flag or in foreign territory, the same principles must be applied as if the territories of two different States were concerned, and the conclusion must therefore be drawn that there is no rule of international law prohibiting the State to which the ship on which the effects of the offence have taken place belongs, from regarding the offence as having been committed in its territory and prosecuting, accordingly, the delinquent.

This conclusion could only be overcome if it were shown that there was a rule of customary international law which, going further than the principle stated above, established the exclusive jurisdiction of the State whose flag was flown. The French Government has endeavoured to prove the existence of such a rule, having recourse for this purpose to the teachings of publicists, to decisions of municipal and international tribunals, and especially to conventions which, whilst creating exceptions to the principle of the freedom of the seas by permitting the war and police vessels of a State to exercise a more or less extensive control over the merchant vessels of another State, reserve jurisdiction to the courts of the country whose flag is flown by the vessel proceeded against.

In the Court's opinion, the existence of such a rule has not been conclusively proved.

In the first place, as regards teachings of publicists, and apart from the question as to what their value may be from the point of view of establishing the existence of a rule of customary law, it is no doubt true that all or nearly all writers teach that ships on the high seas are subject exclusively to the jurisdiction of the State whose flag they fly. But the important point is the significance attached by them to this principle; now it does not appear that in general, writers bestow upon this principle a scope differing from or wider than that explained above and which is equivalent to saying that the jurisdiction of a State over vessels on the high seas is the same in extent as its jurisdiction in its own territory. On the other hand, there is no lack of writers who, upon a close study of the special question whether a State can prosecute for offences committed on board a foreign ship on the high seas, definitely come to the conclusion that such offences must be regarded as if they have been committed in the territory of the State whose flag the ship flies, and that consequently the general rules of each legal system in regard to offences committed abroad are applicable.

In regard to precedents, it should first be observed that, leaving aside the collision cases which will be alluded to later, none of them relates to offences affecting two ships flying the flags of two different countries, and that consequently they are not of much importance in the case before the Court. The case of the *Costa Rica Packet* is no exception, for the prauw on which the alleged depredations took place was adrift without flag or crew, and this circumstance certainly influenced, perhaps decisively, the conclusion arrived at by the arbitrator.

On the other hand, there is no lack of cases in which a State has claimed a right to prosecute for an offense, committed on board a foreign ship, which it regarded as punishable under its legislation....

It only remains to examine the third argument advanced by the French Government and to ascertain whether a rule specially applying to collision cases has grown up, according to which criminal proceedings regarding such cases come exclusively within the jurisdiction of the State whose flag is flown.

* * *

Even if the rarity of the judicial decisions to be found among the reported cases were sufficient to prove in point of fact the circumstances alleged by the Agent for the French Government, it would merely show that States had often, in practice, abstained from instituting criminal proceedings, and not that they recognized themselves as being obligated to do so; for only if such abstention were based on their being conscious of having a duty to abstain would it be possible to speak of an international custom. The alleged fact does not allow one to infer that States have been conscious of having such a duty; on the other hand, as will presently be seen, there are other circumstances calculated to show that the contrary is true.

So far as the Court is aware there are no decisions of international tribunals in this matter; but some decisions of municipal courts have been cited. Without pausing to consider the value to be attributed to the judgments of municipal courts in connection with the establishment of the existence of a rule of international law, it will suffice to observe that the decisions quoted sometimes support one view and sometimes the other. Whilst the French Government have been able to cite the *Ortigia—Oncle-Joseph* case before the Court of Aix and the *Franconia—Stratchclyde* case before the British Court for Crown Cases Reserved, as being in favor of the exclusive jurisdiction of the State whose flag is flown, on the other hand the *Ortigia—Oncle-Joseph* case before the Italian Courts and the *Ekbatana—West-Hinder* case before the Belgian Courts have been cited in support of the opposing contention.

Lengthy discussions have taken place between the Parties as to the importance of each of these decisions as regards the details of which the Court confines itself to a reference to the Cases and Counter-Cases of the Parties. The Court does not think it necessary to stop to consider them. It will suffice to observe that, as municipal jurisprudence is thus divided, it is hardly possible to see in it an indication of the existence of the restrictive rule of international law which alone could serve as a basis for the contention of the French Government.

On the other hand, the Court feels called upon to lay stress upon the fact that it does not appear that the States concerned have objected to criminal proceedings in respect of collision cases before the courts of a country other than that the flag of which was flown, or that they have made protests: their conduct does not appear to have differed appreciably from that observed by them in all cases of concurrent jurisdiction. This fact is directly opposed to the existence of a tacit consent on the part of States to the exclusive jurisdiction of the State whose flag is flown, such as the Agent for the French Government has thought is possible to deduce from the infrequency of questions of jurisdiction before criminal courts. It seems hardly probable, and it would not be in accordance with international practice, that the French Government in the *Ortigia—Oncle-Joseph* case and the German Government in the *Ekbatana—West-Hinder* case would have omitted to protest against the exercise of criminal jurisdiction by the Italian and Belgian Courts, if they had really thought that this was a violation of international law.

* * *

V.

Having thus answered the first question submitted by the special agreement in the negative, the Court need not consider the second question, regarding the pecuniary reparation which might have been due to Lieutenant Demons.

For these reasons,

THE COURT,

having heard both Parties,

gives, by the President's casting vote—the votes being equally divided—, judgment to the effect.

(1) that, following the collision which occurred on August 2nd, 1926, on the high seas between the French steamship *Lotus* and the Turkish steamship *Boz-*

Kourt, and upon the arrival of the French ship at Stamboul, and in consequence of the loss of the *Bos-Kourt* having involved the death of eight Turkish nationals, Turkey, by instituting criminal proceedings in pursuance of Turkish law against Lieutenant Demons, officer of the watch on board the *Lotus* at the time of the collision, has not acted in conflict with the principles of international law, contrary to Article 15 of the Convention of Lausanne of July 24th, 1923, respecting conditions of residence and business and jurisdiction;

(2) that, consequently, there is no occasion to give judgment on the question of the pecuniary reparation which might have been due to Lieutenant Demons if Turkey, by prosecuting him as above stated, had acted in a manner contrary to the principles of international law.

* * *

MM. Loder, former President, Weiss, Vice-President, and Lord Finlay, MM. Nyholm and Altamira, Judges, declaring that they are unable to concur in the judgment delivered by the Court and availing themselves of the right conferred to them by Article 57 of the Statute, have delivered the separate opinions which follow hereafter.

Mr. Moore, dissenting from the judgment of the Court only on the ground of the connection of the criminal proceedings in the case with Article 6 of the Turkish Penal Code, also delivered a separate opinion.

Thus, regarding judicial jurisdiction, it is "hard to resist the conclusion that (apart from the well-known rules of immunity for foreign States, diplomats, international organizations, etc.) customary international law imposes *no* limits on the jurisdiction of municipal courts in civil trials."[1] As to criminal trials, while scholars have agreed that courts required some link to a crime in order to exercise criminal jurisdiction, this no longer appears to be the case, certainly for crimes prohibited under international law. In 1994, Denmark prosecuted a Croatian for abuse of Bosnian detainees during the conflicts in the former Yugoslavia.[2] The only link to Denmark was the defendant's presence there under a temporary grant of asylum. Germany can prosecute international criminal cases against anyone—even persons not present in Germany—under its Code of Crimes Against International Law.

Exercising jurisdiction in some cases, however, may be seen as violating the non-intervention principle. According to the Friendly Relations Declaration: "No State ... has the right to intervene, directly or indirectly, for any reason whatever, in the internal or external affairs of any other State."[3] States try to avoid complaints of interference or encroachment by basing exercises of jurisdiction on one of the bases mentioned above. Again, however, international law does not require that a court have such a basis. On the other hand, most national courts recognize that states and international organizations enjoy at least some immunity from national court jurisdiction. The material below explores whether granting this immunity is required by international law where it is not expressly extended under a treaty.

---

1. Michael Akehurst, *Jurisdiction in International Law*, 46 Brit. Y.B. 171–77 (1972–1973).

2. *The Director of Public Prosecutions v. T.* (Sentence passed by the Eastern High Court (3rd Div.) Denmark, Nov. 22, 1994) (Danish Ministry of Foreign Affairs, Legal Service, Unofficial Translation) (on file with the author).

3. Declaration on Principles of International Law Concerning Friendly Relations and Cooperation Among States in Accordance with the Charter of the United Nations, G.A. Res. 2625 (XXV), U.N. GAOR, 25th Sess., Supp. No. 28, at 121, U.N. Doc. A/8082 (1970).

B. Immunity from Jurisdiction

Immunity from jurisdiction comes in three main categories: (1) diplomatic immunity, (2) official immunity, and (3) state sovereign immunity/international organization immunity. Diplomatic immunity flows from the need of states to communicate with one another, a need that can be hindered if diplomats are subject to the judicial process in potentially hostile foreign states. Official and state immunity flows from the concept of states as coequal on the international plane. States would appear to lose if the state itself or its officials could be subjected to judicial control in another state's courts. Diplomatic immunity is one of the oldest jurisdictional principles of international law. Diplomats and personnel of international organizations are generally immune from the national courts of states in which they are properly accredited. Certain government officials also generally have immunity from process in foreign courts. States, too, enjoy a certain amount of sovereign immunity under customary international law, and international organizations also enjoy a certain amount of immunity—as agreed by treaty. Despite several attempts by the International Law Commission, the international community does not have a comprehensive treaty on immunity. Nevertheless, several treaties on subtopics exist and important aspects of the law of state immunity will be decided in a case pending before the International Court of Justice at time of writing, *Jurisdictional Immunities of the State* (Germany v. Italy), Application Instituting Proceedings (Dec. 28, 2008), *available at* http://www.icj-cij.org/docket/files/143/14923.pdf.

1. Sovereign Immunity

In the famous case of the *Schooner Exchange*, U.S. Supreme Court Chief Justice John Marshall demonstrated how the doctrine of sovereign immunity can be a barrier to judicial jurisdiction over cases involving states. In that case, Americans attached a ship in the Port of Philadelphia in 1812. They claimed the ship had been taken from them illegally by the French navy. Marshall reasoned:

> ... [A public armed ship] constitutes a part of the military force of her nation; acts under the immediate and direct command of the sovereign; is employed by him in national objects. He has many and powerful motives for preventing those objects from being defeated by the interference of a foreign State. Such interference cannot take place without affecting his power and his dignity. The implied license therefore under which such vessel enters a friendly port, may reasonably be construed, and it seems to the Court, ought to be construed, as containing an exemption from the jurisdiction of the sovereign, within whose territory she claims the rights of hospitality.[4]

The ship-owners were not completely without recourse. The U.S. government could complain to the French on their behalf, but the difficulty of that option compared with having the court hand over the attached vessel is clear.

The injustices caused by the doctrine of sovereign immunity have led to its steady curtailment from the absolute immunity of Marshall's time to the more restricted immunity of today. As explained by Lord Wilberforce:

> ... the so called "restrictive theory" arises from the willingness of states to enter into commercial, or other private law, transactions with individuals. It appears

4. The Schooner Exchange v. McFaddon, 11 U.S. (7 Cranch) 116, 144 (1812).

> to have two main foundations: (a) It is necessary in the interest of justice to the individuals having such transactions with states to allow them to bring such transactions before the courts; (b) to require a state to answer a claim based upon such transactions does not involve a challenge to or inquiry into any act of sovereignty or governmental act of that state. It is, in accepted phrases, neither a threat to the dignity of that state, nor any interference with its sovereign functions.[5]

Today most states limit the immunity of foreign states or foreign officials for commercial actions or torts. The mostly civil law members of the Council of Europe drafted the European Convention on State Immunity in 1972 to harmonize their varying laws restricting sovereign immunity. The U.S. first restricted sovereign immunity by statute in the Foreign Sovereign Immunity Act of 1976 (FSIA).[6] The British followed suit with the State Immunity Act 1978.[7] The International Law Commission subsequently drafted a set of Articles on Jurisdictional Immunities of States and Their Properties, which are viewed as restating the current customary international law on sovereign immunity.

Each of these versions of the law allows plaintiffs to bring actions against foreign sovereign states for torts and commercial actions. The cases are inconsistent, however, regarding immunity in cases alleging violations of international law. In such cases, the European Court of Human Rights has refused to order national courts to exercise jurisdiction, but did not prohibit it. The Greek courts limited Germany's immunity in *Perfecture of Voiotia v. Federal Republic of Germany*.[8] The prefecture brought a case against Germany for violations of international law during the Second World War. Greece's highest court found that Article 11 of the European Convention on State Immunity[9] had entered customary international law, and that Article 11 limits sovereign immunity for any torts—regardless of whether they are common torts (acts *jure gestionis*) or acts only a sovereign may perform (acts *jure imperii*).[10] Thus, actions in violation of international law were torts for which a state enjoyed no immunity.[11]

The U.S. position is rather more *ad hoc*. The U.S. has amended the FSIA to lift the sovereign immunity of states for the international law crimes of torture and terrorism,[12] but the U.S. Supreme Court held in *Amerada Hess* that states enjoy immunity in U.S. courts for violations of international law unless Congress has explicitly modified the

---

5. Owners of the Cargo Lately Laden on Board the Marble Islands v. Owners of the I Congresso del Partido [1983] 1 A.C. 244, 262D; [1981] 3 W.L.R. 328; [1981] 2 All E.R. 1064 HL.

6. The Foreign Sovereign Immunity Act of 1976, 28 U.S.C. §§ 1330, 1332(a)(2)-(4), 1391(f), 1441(d), 1602-1611-1336 (1994 and Supp. II 1996).

7. State Immunity Act 1978, ch. 33 (Eng.).

8. Case No. 11/2000.... Aerios Pagos (Hellenic Supreme Court), May 4, 2000.... *See also* Bernard H. Oxman, Maria Gavouneli & Ilias Bantekas, Case Report: *Perfecture of Voitia v. Federal Republic of Germany*, 95 Am. J. Int'l L. 198 (2001).

9. European Convention on State Immunity, May 16, 1972, *entered into force* June 11, 1976, ETS No. 74, 111 ILM 470 (1972) [hereinafter European Convention]. The text of, and other information about, the Convention is available online through the Council of Europe Website, http://www.coe.int/.

10. Prefecture of Voitia, *supra* note 9, at 4.

11. *But see* Andreas Zimmerman, *Sovereign Immunity and Violations of International Jus Cogens—Some Critical Remarks*, 16 Mich. J. Int'l L. 433 (1995); responding to Mathias Reimann, *A Human Rights Exception to Sovereign Immunity: Some Thoughts on Prinz v. Federal Republic of Germany*, 16 Mich. J. Int'l L. 403 (1995).

12. *See* Torture Victim Protection Act of 1991, 106 Stat. 73; Antiterrorism and Effective Death Penalty Act of 1996, 110 Stat. 1214.

FSIA.[13] Nevertheless, in *Altmann v. Austria*, decided in 2004, the Supreme Court greatly expanded the possibility of bringing suit against foreign sovereign states in U.S. courts by holding that the restrictions on immunity in the FSIA could apply to events pre-dating the 1976 adoption of the Act.[14] The decision cleared the way for Maria Altmann to bring a suit arguing that Austria unlawfully expropriated several paintings by Gustav Klimt just after the Second World War.

The U.S. continues to enjoy near absolute immunity in its own courts in suits by foreign states and IOs. Sovereign immunity was one reason the Supreme Court refused to stay the execution of Walter LaGrand following the ICJ's order of provisional measures, discussed below.

The Federal Republic of Germany et al. v. United States et al.

526 U.S. 111, 119 S.Ct. 1016 (1999)

* * *

Per Curiam

The motion of the Federal Republic of Germany, et al. (plaintiffs) for leave to file a bill of complaint and the motion for preliminary injunction against the United States of America and Jane Dee Hull, Governor of the State of Arizona, both raised under this Court's original jurisdiction, are denied. Plaintiffs' motion to dispense with printing requirements is granted. Plaintiffs seek, among other relief, enforcement of an order issued this afternoon by the International Court of Justice, on its own motion and with no opportunity for the United States to respond, directing the United States to prevent Arizona's scheduled execution of Walter LaGrand. Plaintiffs assert that LaGrand holds German citizenship. With regard to the action against the United States, which relies on the *ex parte* order of the International Court of Justice, there are imposing threshold barriers. First, it appears that the United States has not waived its sovereign immunity. Second, it is doubtful that Art. III, § 2, cl. 2, provides an anchor for an action to prevent execution of a German citizen who is not an ambassador or consul. With respect to the action against the State of Arizona, as in *Breard v. Greene*, 523 U.S. 371, 377, 118 S.Ct. 1352, 140 L.Ed.2d 529 (1998) (*per curiam*), a foreign government's ability here to assert a claim against a State is without evident support in the Vienna Convention and in probable contravention of Eleventh Amendment principles. This action was filed within only two hours of a scheduled execution that was ordered on January 15, 1999, based upon a sentence imposed by Arizona in 1984, about which the Federal Republic of Germany learned in 1992. Given the tardiness of the pleas and the jurisdictional barriers they implicate, we decline to exercise our original jurisdiction.

Justice SOUTER, with whom Justice GINSBURG joins, concurring.

I join in the foregoing order, subject to the qualification that I do not rest my decision to deny leave to file the bill of complaint on any Eleventh Amendment principle. In exercising my discretion, I have taken into consideration the position of the Solicitor General on behalf of the United States.

---

13. *Argentine Republic v. Amerada Hess Shipping Corp.*, 488 U.S. 428 (1989).
14. *Republic of Austria v. Maria V. Altmann*, 541 U.S. 677 (2004).

Justice BREYER, with whom Justice STEVENS joins, dissenting.

The Federal Republic of Germany et al. (Germany) has filed a motion for leave to file a complaint, seeking as relief an injunction prohibiting the execution of Walter LaGrand pending final resolution of Germany's case against the United States in the International Court of Justice (ICJ)—a case in which Germany claims that Arizona's execution of LaGrand violates the Vienna Convention. Germany also seeks a stay of that execution "pending the Court's disposition of the motion for leave to file an original bill of complaint after a normal course of briefing and deliberation on that motion." Motion for Leave to File a Bill of Complaint and for a Temporary Restraining Order or Preliminary Injunction 2 (Motion). The ICJ has issued an order "indicat[ing]" that the "United States should take all measures at its disposal to ensure that Walter LaGrand is not executed pending the final decision in these [ICJ] proceedings." ¶ 9, *id.*, at 6–7.

The Solicitor General has filed a letter in which he opposes any stay. In his view, the "Vienna Convention does not furnish a basis for this Court to grant a stay of execution," and "an order of the International Court of Justice indicating provisional measures is not binding and does not furnish a basis for judicial relief." The Solicitor General adds, however, that he has "not had time to read the materials thoroughly or to digest the contents." Letter from Solicitor General Waxman filed Mar. 3, 1999, with Clerk of this Court.

Germany's filings come at what is literally the eleventh hour. Nonetheless, Germany explains that it did not file its case in the ICJ until it learned that the State of Arizona had admitted that it was aware, when LaGrand was arrested, that he was a German national. That admission came only eight days ago, and the ICJ issued its preliminary ruling only today. Regardless, in light of the fact that both the ICJ and a sovereign nation have asked that we stay this case, or "indicate[d]" that we should do so, Motion 6, I would grant the preliminary stay that Germany requests. That stay would give us time to consider, after briefing from all interested parties, the jurisdictional and international legal issues involved, including further views of the Solicitor General, after time for study and appropriate consultation.

The Court has made Germany's motion for a preliminary stay moot by denying its motion to file its complaint and "declin[ing] to exercise" its original jurisdiction in light of the "tardiness of the pleas and the jurisdictional barriers they implicate." *Ante,* at 1017. It is at least arguable that Germany's reasons for filing so late are valid, and the jurisdictional matters are arguable. Indeed, the Court says that it is merely "*doubtful* that Art. III, § 2, cl. 2, provides an anchor" for the suit and that a foreign government's ability to assert a claim against a State is "without *evident* support in the Vienna Convention and in *probable* contravention of Eleventh Amendment principles." *Ante,* at 1017 (emphasis added). The words "doubtful" and "probable," in my view, suggest a need for fuller briefing.

For these reasons I would grant a preliminary stay.

The U.S. also enjoys immunity from attachment of assets absent an express waiver. It was this form of immunity that allowed a U.S. District Court to protect the funds out of which the U.S. was to pay Iran in satisfaction of the decision in Iran-U.S. Claims Tribunal Case A27, discussed in Chapter Eight.

M. Flatow v. The Islamic Republic of Iran

74 F.Supp.2d 18 (S.D.N.Y. 1999)

* * *

Memorandum Opinion

Lamberth, District Judge.

The United States moves to quash the writ of attachment entered by the Clerk of this Court on November 18, 1998, which purports to attach "all credits held by the United States to the benefit of the Islamic Republic of Iran," including U.S. Treasury funds owed to Iran in accordance with an award of the Iran-United States Claims Tribunal, Seeking these funds to satisfy part of his prior judgment against Iran, Plaintiff Stephen Flatow maintains that certain amendments to the Foreign Sovereign Immunities Act waive the United States' sovereign immunity with respect to U.S. funds owed to judgment debtors. 28 U.S.C. § 1610(f)(1)(A) & § 1610(a)(7) (Supp.1999). Because this Court finds that Congress has not clearly and unequivocally waived the United States' sovereign immunity, the Court GRANTS the United States's Motion to Quash the Writ of Attachment. This order, however, is stayed, for ten days, to provide plaintiff the opportunity to seek a further stay from the Court of Appeals.

I. Factual and Procedural Background

In April 1995, Alisa Flatow, Plaintiff Stephen Flatow's 20-year-old daughter, was killed in a terrorist bombing of a tourist bus in Israel. The terrorist group responsible for the suicide bombing mission, the Shaqaqi faction of the Palestine Islamic Jihad, is funded exclusively by the Islamic Republic of Iran ("Iran"). *See Flatow v. The Islamic Republic of Iran,* 999 F.Supp. 1, 6–9 (D.D.C.1998).

A year after Alisa Flatow's murder, Congress amended the Foreign Sovereign Immunities Act, 28 U.S.C. §§ 1602–1611 (1994 & Supp.1999) ("FSIA"), by enacting the Antiterrorism and Effective Death Penalty Act of 1996, which lifts the sovereign immunity of foreign states that commit acts of terrorism or provide material support for terrorism. Pub.I., No. 104-132, Title II, § 221(a), (April 24, 1996), 110 Stat. 1241, *codified at* 28 U.S.C. § 1605 (1996 & Supp.1999). In addition, Congress created a federal cause of action for personal injury or death and provided, *inter alia,* that punitive damages would be available in actions brought under the state-sponsored terrorism exception. 28 U.S.C. § 1605(a)(7) (1996 & Supp.1999). This particular amendment became known as the "Flatow Amendment." *Flatow,* 999 F.Supp. at 12.

Pursuant to these newly enacted provisions, Flatow filed a wrongful death action against Iran, its Ministry of Information & Security, and various government officials. *See Flatow,* 999 F.Supp. at 8–10. Iran failed to appear. Accordingly, after an evidentiary hearing in which the plaintiff "establishe[d] his claim or right to relief by evidence ... satisfactory to the Court," 28 U.S.C. § 1608(e), this Court entered a default judgment against Iran, finding Iran and its codefendants jointly and severally liable for loss of accretions, compensatory damages, solatium and $225,000,000.00 in punitive damages. *See Flatow,* 999 F.Supp. at 5.

Attempting to execute this judgment, plaintiff filed a writ of attachment on November 18, 1998 against certain U.S. Treasury funds owed to Iran. Specifically, plaintiff sought attachment of $5,042,481.65 plus interest in the Treasury Judgment Fund, which was awarded to Iran by the Iran-U.S. Claims Tribunal ("Tribunal"). *See Islamic Republic of Iran v. United States,* Case No. A/27, AWD No. 586-A27-FT, (Iran-United States Claims Tribunal June 5, 1998).

In opposing the United States' motion to quash the writ of attachment, plaintiff contends that these U.S. Treasury funds, which are earmarked for payment of the Tribunal award, represent the property of Iran. *See* Iranian Assets Control Regulations, 31 C.F.R. § 535.311(1999) (recognizing, *inter alia.* debt, indebtedness and judgments as property). As such, plaintiff maintains that these funds are subject to attachment pursuant to the Foreign Sovereign Immunities Act. 28 U.S.C. § 1610(f)(1)(A) & (a)(1)(7) (1998). More specifically, he claims that because he is a judgment-creditor of Iran, he is entitled to these funds as partial satisfaction of his March 11, 1998 judgment.

Needless to say, the United States does not share plaintiff's characterization of these U.S. Treasury funds as "Iranian property." Rather, the United States maintains that attachment of the funds constitutes a suit against the United States, which is barred by the doctrine of sovereign immunity. *Buchanan v. Alexander,* 45 U.S. (4 How.) 20, 21, 11 L.Ed. 857 (1846).

As a preliminary matter, then, this Court must determine whether the funds at issue constitute property of the United States or Iran. As explained below, controlling authority dictates the finding that the Treasury funds are U.S. property. As such, sovereign immunity bars their attachment here, as neither the Iranian Assets Control Regulations nor the Foreign Sovereign Immunities Act contain a clear and unequivocal waiver of the United States' immunity.

II. Sovereign Immunity

Suits against the United States are barred by sovereign immunity, absent an effective waiver. *Department of Army v. Blue Fox, Inc.,* 525 U.S. 255, 119 S.Ct. 687, 690, 142 L.Ed.2d 718 (1999) (holding that sovereign immunity barred subcontractor's equitable lien against United States); *FDIC v. Meyer,* 510 U.S. 471, 475, 114 S.Ct. 996, 127 L.Ed.2d 308 (1994) (finding that "sue-and-be-sued" clause waived government agency's sovereign immunity); *see also United States v. Mitchell,* 463 U.S. 206, 212, 103 S.Ct. 2961, 77 L.Ed.2d 580 (1983) ("It is axiomatic that the United States may not be sued without its consent and that the existence of consent is a prerequisite for jurisdiction."). Waiver of the federal government's sovereign immunity must be "expressed in unequivocal statutory text and cannot be implied." *Blue Fox,* 119 S.Ct. at 690; *Lane v. Pena,* 518 U.S. 187, 192, 116 S.Ct. 2092, 135 L.Ed.2d 486 (1996) ("A waiver of the Federal Government's sovereign immunity must be unequivocally expressed in statutory text."); *United States v. Nordic Village, Inc.,* 503 U.S. 30, 33, 112 S.Ct. 1011, 117 L.Ed.2d 181 (1992) ("Waivers of the Government's sovereign immunity, to be effective, must be 'unequivocally expressed.'") (quoting *Mitchell,* 463 U.S. at 206, 103 S.Ct. 2961). Moreover, courts must construe the scope of such waivers "strictly in favor of the sovereign." *Blue Fox,* 119 S.Ct. at 691; *Lane,* 518 U.S. at 192, 116 S.Ct. 2092; *Nordic Village,* 503 U.S. at 33, 112 S.Ct. 1011. Accordingly, any ambiguities in the statutory text must be resolved in favor of immunity. *United States v. Williams,* 514 U.S. 527, 531, 115 S.Ct. 1611, 131 L.Ed.2d 608 (1995). In sum, these rules of construction derive from the fact that sovereign immunity operates as a jurisdictional bar. As such, "the 'terms of [the United States'] consent to be sued in any court define [a] court's jurisdiction to entertain the suit.'" *Meyer,* 510 U.S. at 475, 114 S.Ct. 996 (quoting *United States v. Sherwood,* 312 U.S. 584, 586, 61 S.Ct. 767, 85 L.Ed. 1058 (1941)).

Principles of sovereign immunity apply with equal force to attachments and garnishments. *See Buchanan v. Alexander,* 45 U.S. (4 How.) 20, 21, 11 L.Ed. 857 (1846); *FHA v. Burr,* 309 U.S. 242, 243, 60 S.Ct. 488, 84 L.Ed. 724 (1940); *see also Neukirchen v. Wood County Head Start, Inc.,* 53 F.3d 809, 811 (7th Cir.1995); *Automatic Sprinkler Corp. v. Darla Envtl. Specialists,* 53 F.3d 181, 182 (7th Cir.1995); *State of Arizona v. Bowsher,* 935

F.2d 332, 334 (D.C.Cir.1991); *Haskins Bros. & Co. v. Morgenthau,* 85 F.2d 677, 681 (App.D.C.1936). Indeed, early Supreme Court precedent established that creditors may not attach funds held by the U.S. Treasury or its agents. *Buchanan,* 45 U.S. at 21, 45 U.S. 20. As the Supreme Court explained, "[s]o long as money remains in the hands of a disbursing officer, it is as much the money of the United States, as if it had not been drawn from the treasury." *Id.* In other words, funds held in the U.S. Treasury—even though set aside or "earmarked" for a specific purpose—remain the property of the United States until the government elects to pay them to whom they are owed. *Id.* ("Until paid over by the agent of the government to the person entitled to it, the fund cannot, in any legal sense, be considered a part of his effects."). Notably, the Supreme Court has recently reaffirmed the continued vitality of this precedent. *See Department of the Army v. Blue Fox, Inc.,* 525 U.S. 255, 119 S.Ct. 687, 692, 142 L.Ed.2d 718 (1999) (Rehnquist, C.J.) (citing *Buchanan*). In holding that a subcontractor's lien against government funds owed to an insolvent prime contractor was barred by sovereign immunity, the Supreme Court stated that such a result "is in accord with our precedent establishing that sovereign immunity bars creditors from attaching or garnishing funds in the Treasury." *Id.*

* * *

Here, it is undisputed that the funds plaintiff seeks to attach are held in the U.S. Treasury. Moreover, plaintiff has pointed to no contrary authority that undermines the continued strength of *Buchanan* and its progeny. Thus, controlling authority requires this Court to find that the Treasury funds at issue here are U.S. property and that the writ of attachment constitutes a suit against the United States, which is barred by sovereign immunity. *Blue Fox,* 119 S.Ct. at 690. Accordingly, the Court must grant the United States' motion to quash, unless plaintiff can identify an explicit, unequivocal waiver of the United States' sovereign immunity with respect to these funds. As explained below, however, plaintiff's endeavors in this regard will prove to be unsuccessful.

III. The Foreign Sovereign Immunities Act

Notwithstanding the authority supporting the United States' contention that sovereign immunity bars attachment of funds held in the U.S. Treasury, plaintiff maintains that this doctrine is inapplicable because these funds are not U.S. property. To the contrary, plaintiff asserts that the Tribunal judgment constitutes Iranian property, as defined by the Iranian Assets Control Regulations. 31 C.F.R. § 535.311 (1999). Thus, according to plaintiff, as Iranian property, these funds are subject to attachment pursuant to two amendments to the Foreign Sovereign Immunities Act. *See* 28 U.S.C.A. § 1610(a)(7) (providing that property in the United States of a foreign state used for a commercial activity is subject to attachment to satisfy Section 1605(a)(7) judgments); 28 U.S.C.A. § 1610(f)(1)(A) (providing that judgments obtained pursuant to 28 U.S.C. § 1605(a)(7) may be satisfied by attachment of property subject to the Iranian Assets Control Regulations). But, as explained below, plaintiff's argument must fail, as he cannot identify a waiver of sovereign immunity that unequivocally and expressly authorizes the attachment and payment of U.S. Treasury funds owed to Iran to third-party judgment-creditors. [FN1]

Plaintiff's argument that the Foreign Sovereign Immunities Act authorizes attachment of these Treasury funds proceeds from the legally untenable assertion that such funds constitute Iranian property under the Iranian Assets Control Regulations. These regulations define property to

> "include, *but not by way of limitation,* money, checks, drafts, bullion, bank deposits, savings accounts, *debts, indebtedness,* ... any other evidences of title, ownership or indebtedness, ... *judgments,* ... and any other property, real, personal,

or mixed, tangible or intangible, or interest or interests therein, present, future or contingent."

Id. (emphasis added). Admittedly, by its plain terms, this definition appears to cover any debt or judgment held by Iran, irrespective of the identity of the debtor. Nevertheless, this Court need not decide whether this seemingly expansive definition of property covers a judgment against the United States held in the U.S. Treasury, for two reasons. First, to obtain money from the U.S. treasury, there must be a *statute* authorizing payment. *See Automatic Sprinkler,* 53 F.3d at 182 (citing, *inter alia, Nordic Village,* 503 U.S. at 33–34, 112 S.Ct. 1011). Here, plaintiff points to a definition contained in a Treasury *regulation.* Second, and more important, plaintiff's characterization of the Treasury funds as Iranian property is refuted by the weight of authority, *see supra,* which is binding on this Court. Moreover, even assuming *arguendo* that the regulation's definition of property does cover debts or judgments against the United States, plaintiff still could not prevail with his claim, as neither the Iranian Assets Control Regulations nor the Foreign Sovereign Immunities Act contain the sort of express and unequivocal waiver required to abrogate the United States' sovereign immunity. *See Blue Fox,* 119 S.Ct. at 690 (instructing that "[w]aiver of the federal government's sovereign immunity must be expressed in unequivocal statutory text and cannot be implied").

* * *

IV. Conclusion

The Court concludes by acknowledging the apparent unfairness that attends its grant of the United States' motion to quash. Indeed, the Court regrets that its ruling today forestalls plaintiff's efforts to execute a judgment that was issued by this Court. *Flatow,* 999 F.Supp. at 5. Moreover, the Court appreciates plaintiff's frustration with the White House's present efforts to block his recovery, *see* Stephen M. Flatow, *In This Case, I Can't Be Diplomatic,* The Washington Post, November 7, 1999, at B2, particularly in light its previous pledges of support. Nonetheless, this Court must remain faithful to its proper role within our constitutional system, which requires courts to follow the rule of law, not their own individual conceptions of what is fair or just. Accordingly, for the foregoing reasons, the United States' Motion to Quash the Writ of Attachment is GRANTED.

A separate order shall issue this date.

ORDER

Upon consideration of the United States' Motion to Quash the November 18, 1998, Writ of Attachment for the funds held in the U.S. Treasury, the responses thereto, and for the reasons set forth in the accompanying memorandum opinion issued this date, it is hereby

ORDERED that the United States' Motion to Quash is GRANTED and the Writ of Attachment is hereby Quashed; and

it is further

ORDERED that this order is STAYED for Ten (10) Days to provide plaintiff the opportunity to seek a further stay from the Court of Appeals.

SO ORDERED.

National and international courts have increasingly taken jurisdiction over persons for international criminal law violations, which are serious violations of human rights law and international humanitarian law. Defendants typically raise a defense of immunity from the jurisdiction of these courts for actions undertaken as a government official or diplomat. As a result, the immunity of government officials and diplomats has been the subject of a number of ICJ decisions and national court decisions in recent years. A 2010 case in the United States Supreme Court, *Samantar v. Yousouf*, 130 S.Ct. 2278 (June 1, 2010) is discussed in relation to international law by David Stewart:

David P. Stewart, *Samantar v. Yousuf: Foreign Official Immunity under Common Law**

* * *

As presented to the Supreme Court, the central issue was whether the Foreign Sovereign Immunities Act ("FSIA") provides individual officials of foreign governments with immunity from suit for actions taken in their official capacity. The petitioner, a former Prime Minister and Defense Minister of Somalia, sought to claim the benefit of the statute in moving to dismiss a suit brought by several plaintiffs alleging that he had sanctioned widespread acts of torture and extrajudicial killing. Without admitting the allegations, Samantar argued that the actions alleged were official in nature and thus fell within the scope of the statute.

* * *

[T]he decision did not finally resolve the question of Samantar's own amenability to suit, much less the broader issue of foreign officials' immunity in other circumstances. On the contrary, the Court said that "[a]lthough Congress clearly intended to supersede the common-law regime for claims against foreign states, we find nothing in the statute's origin or aims to indicate that Congress similarly wanted to codify the law of foreign official immunity." The case was therefore remanded to the federal district court for a determination "whether petitioner may be entitled to immunity under the common law, and whether he may have other valid defenses to the grave charges against him."

The decision thus endorsed the government's longstanding view, which it has advocated since the FSIA was enacted, that the statute neither conferred nor abrogated immunity for foreign officials. However, the precise basis for such immunity decisions going forward is less clear. Did the Court simply endorse the government's position that immunity determinations for officials should be made, as they were prior to the enactment of the FSIA, by the Executive Branch? Or by referring to the "common law" basis of foreign official immunity, did the Court intend to suggest either that relevant principles of customary international law apply directly in such cases or that judges should not take into account the law and practices of other nations?

International immunities can no longer be considered merely a question of grace, comity, or convenience but must be grounded in a clear relationship to customary international law. Given the national interest in U.S. participation in the progressive development of cogent international norms, the need for national uniformity in the resolution of such cases, and the sensitive foreign relations context in which the issues necessarily arise, there may be little debate that this area is presumptively one of *federal* common law. However, individual immunity decisions clearly implicate the President's constitutional authority to "send and receive" ambassadors and to conduct foreign relations.

The Solicitor General's brief contended that the determination of individual official immunity "is properly founded on non-statutory principles articulated by the Executive

---

* ASIL Insights, June 14, 2010, http://www.asil.org (footnotes omitted).

Branch," informed by customary international law and practice, and formally conveyed to the courts. The government's immunity determinations, it said, reflect "sensitive diplomatic and foreign policy judgments" which are "ordinarily committed to the Executive as an aspect of the Executive Branch's prerogative to conduct foreign affairs on behalf of the United States." The Court appeared to agree, noting that "[w]e have been given no reason to believe that Congress saw as a problem, or wanted to eliminate, the State Department's role in determinations regarding individual official immunity."

That traditional method has been followed in most cases involving head of state and head of government immunity, and more recently in the case of special diplomatic mission immunity, where the applicable principles are similarly derived from customary international law. Arguably, such cases differ from "official capacity" situations involving diplomatic and consular officials or public international organizations, their officers, employees and representatives of their member states, where the governing law is provided by relevant self-executing treaties or statutes. Whether the Court's apparent endorsement of the traditional procedure means that the government's views should be treated as determinative will be a matter of debate.

These questions promise to take on particular significance in light of the evolving contours of international law and practice regarding the scope of foreign official immunity. In a given case, the first issue will necessarily be to determine whether the individual in question was in fact a governmental official acting within an official capacity. That determination will often require an assessment of foreign law as well as the weight to be accorded to the views (if any) of the foreign government in question. An even more difficult task will be determining whether an individual should be held accountable, for instance, for egregious violations of international law such as torture, genocide, war crimes, or crimes against humanity when his or her responsibility is based only on actions taken in an official governmental capacity. Making this decision at the outset of the litigation, with respect to jurisdiction and on the basis of allegations that could prove unsubstantiated, will be problematic. The Supreme Court expressly left this issue open, noting only that the district court had rejected the argument that Samantar had necessarily acted beyond the scope of his official authority by allegedly violating international law.

Neither is there a consensus about whether immunity is or should be available to shield former officials like Samantar. Even when it might be justified to accord immunity to a currently serving foreign official, the question remains whether she is amenable to suit after leaving office. Here again, the Court noted but did not express a view on the issue.

Finally, the Court was careful to emphasize that in some cases where individual foreign officials are sued, the "sovereign immunity" of the state itself might still be relevant. It said, for example, that "we do not doubt that in some circumstances the immunity of the foreign state extends to an individual for acts taken in his official capacity." Just what those circumstances or the proper test for making the distinction might be is not clarified, but the Court indicated several potentially relevant factors. The question might turn, for instance, on whether "the effect of exercising jurisdiction would be to enforce a rule of law against the state," or whether the state is the "real party in interest" or an indispensable party. In short, "[e]ven if a suit is not governed by the Act, it may still be barred by foreign sovereign immunity under the common law. And not every suit can successfully be pleaded against an individual official alone."

Pakistani courts confronted a case involving diplomatic and consular immunity in early 2011. It was a case with all of the potential to lead to a serious inter-state dispute.

In January 2011, Raymond Davis, a CIA contractor was arrested by Pakistani officials after allegedly shooting and killing two men in Lahore, Pakistan. While accounts of his actual role in Pakistan differ and the details of his job there with the CIA are unclear, the Obama administration demanded his release on the grounds of diplomatic immunity under the Vienna Convention on Diplomatic Relations, arguing it had notified Pakistan in 2010 of Davis' role as "administrative and technical staff" assigned to the U.S. embassy, and the fact that he was traveling with a diplomatic passport.

Following intense negotiations between Pakistan and the U.S., Davis was freed from detention on March 17, 2011 after $2.4 million was paid to the families of the two men that were killed. Under Pakistani law, a killer can be acquitted by paying compensation, known as *diyat* or "blood money", to the heirs of a victim. While the State Department formally denied paying the families to secure Davis' release, it is unclear where the compensation came from. For details of the incident and the role of the Vienna Convention, see, Scott Horton, *Spy Games*, HARPER'S MAGAZINE, Mar. 14, 2011, http://harper's.org/archive/2011/03/hbc-90008019.

2. International Organization Immunity

Like individual states, organizations of states usually enjoy immunity from the national courts wherever their headquarters exist or are active.[16] In recent years, scholars have called for restrictions on IOs so that they too may be answerable in court for law violations.[17]

Jan Klabbers, *Privileges and Immunities**

Privileges and immunities of international organizations generally are usually explained on one of three possible bases. Traditionally, it was thought that privileges and immunities flowed from the idea that a legation abroad would continue to be the territory of the sending state: the notion, hence, of exterritoriality. Clearly, whatever its merits when it comes to explaining the position of agents of states (and those merits appear to be fairly limited), the theory cannot apply to entities such as international organizations, which have no territory to begin with, yet are by definition located on someone else's territory.

The second theory, according to which privileges and immunities somehow derive from the sovereign dignity of the entities concerned, again must remain without application, for the obvious reason that international organizations, whatever else they may possibly be, are not generally considered to be sovereign in their own right. While on occasion courts have referred to the 'sovereignty' of an organization, or its exercise of 'sovereign powers', such instances are best regarded as examples of courts struggling to come to terms with the nature of international organizations rather than as clear-cut affirmations of sovereignty.

---

16. *See* AUGUST REINISCH, INTERNATIONAL ORGANIZATIONS BEFORE NATIONAL COURTS (2000).

17. *But see* Charles H. Brower, II, *International Immunities' Some Dissident Views on the Role of Municipal Courts* 41 VA. J. INT'L L. 1 (2000).

* AN INTRODUCTION TO INTERNATIONAL INSTITUTIONAL LAW 147–9 (2002) (some footnotes omitted) (A second edition was published in 2009.).

This implies that resort is usually had to the third contending theory on privileges and immunities, that of 'functional necessity'. The idea, then, is that organizations enjoy such immunities as are necessary for their effective functioning: international organizations enjoy what is necessary for the exercise of their functions in the fulfillment of their purposes. Moreover, this is often deemed to be normative proposition: not only do organizations in fact enjoy privileges and immunities on the basis of functional necessity, they actually are entitled to such privileges and immunities, so the argument goes.

There is some obvious, if perhaps somewhat superficial, support for the 'functional necessity' thesis when it comes to international organizations. For instance, Article 105, para. 1 of the United Nations Charter provides that the UN shall enjoy in its member-states 'such privileges and immunities as are necessary for the fulfillment of its purposes', with para. 2 adding a similar provision with respect to representatives of member-states and UN officials. Article 105 Charter is referred to in the preamble to the 1946 Convention on the UN's Privileges and Immunities, and the same thought recurs in s. 27 of the UN-US Headquarters Agreement.

Indeed, several decisions of courts and tribunals, both national and international, can be cited in support of the functional necessity thesis, although their number is surprisingly limited. Moreover, the functional necessity thesis has an intuitive appeal, in that it would seem to be self-evident that the organization must be protected against outside interference; and it is of course in particular the host state that could interfere if the organization were devoid of privileges and immunities.

Still, the functional necessity thesis has some considerable weaknesses as well. For one thing, it may well adopt too instrumentalist a view of international life and ignore that the granting of privileges and immunities is usually, quite simply, the result of negotiations between the organization and its host state rather than the application of any blueprint. To be sure, while the needs of the organization will usually be considered during such negotiations, so too will be other factors: past practice of the host state concerned or of the organization concerned if the establishment of a regional or branch office is at issue; the interests of possible third parties, et cetera.

Participating in such negotiations are also often representatives of the various relevant ministries in the host states, which may hold widely different views on the desirability of certain provisions. Tax authorities might be reluctant to grant broad tax exemptions; social security authorities might not wish to see exceptions for international civil servants from domestic security schemes in the host states; the labour ministry; might have its own views on the need for work permits for spouses of international civil servants, et cetera.

Moreover, there is always the role of negotiating power and the quality of negotiators, as well as the chemistry (or absence thereof) between negotiators. In addition, negotiators may hold widely divergent views as to what the functional needs of their proposed creation amount to.

Indeed, another drawback of the functional necessity thesis (but probably also the main source of its attraction) is precisely its open texture. As Reinisch succinctly puts it: 'The fundamental problem is clearly that functional immunity means different, and indeed contradictory, things to different people or rather different judges and states ...'

* * *

It turns out that concrete decisions relating to the scope of an organization's privileges and immunities are almost unpredictable. At the one extreme, one can find such a case such as *Broadbent v. Organization of American States*,[17] coming close to granting absolute immunity to the organization, whereas at the other end of the continuum there are decisions in which the scope of immunities is considered to be much more narrow. Indeed, even a single dispute gives rise to various conceptions, and a perfectly useful illustration thereof is the case of *Iran-United States Claims Tribunal v. A. S.* In this dispute involving the labour relationship between Mr. and the Tribunal, the Local Court of The Hague initially found that translation activities performed for the Tribunal could not be captured by the notion of *acta jure imperii*. The District Court of the Hague, though, affirmed by the Dutch Supreme Court, found that Mr.'s activities were 'so clearly connected with *acta jure imperii*' that the decision of the lower court was well-nigh incomprehensible.[18]

Yet another problem with anything like the functional necessity thesis has recently been observed to reside in the possibility that the organization can commit violations of public order, or even of human rights, under the shield of its functional necessity. Thus, while it may happen that functional necessity requires that an organization's labour policies are not subject to local jurisdiction, where those labour policies condone discrimination or sexual harassment, the balance between organization and the individual may tilt too strongly in favour of the organization.

Note on the "Oil for Food" Dispute

The U.S. became embroiled in a dispute with the UN over aspects of a UN program called "Oil-for-Food." The program aimed at mitigating the suffering inflicted on the population of Iraq as a result of economic sanctions imposed on Iraq following Iraq's 1990 invasion of Kuwait. The sanctions remained in place until the U.S.-led invasion of Iraq in 2003. Not long after the sanctions were lifted, U.S. officials began accusing UN officials of irregularities in the administration of the program. In April 2004, UN Secretary General Kofi Annan formed the Independent Investigating Committee (IIC) to look into the accusations, but some members of Congress lacked confidence in the Secretary General and began their own investigations through various congressional committees. This parallel effort led to a serious dispute between the UN and these U.S. congressional committees over access to documents. The UN went to U.S. courts to try to resolve the dispute. What follows is the UN's complaint against a former member of the IIC who delivered documents to the U.S. House International Relations Committee, chaired by Congressman Henry Hyde. It is followed by an amendment to the Complaint and two orders by U.S. courts on behalf of the UN.

17. Decision of 28 March, 1978 by the U.S. District Court for the District of Columbia, 63 ILR 162–63. Compare also *Weidner v. International Telecommunications Satellite Organization*, decision of 21 September, 1978 by the U.S. Court of Appeals for the District of Columbia, in 63 ILR 191–94.

18. The three decisions can be found in 94 ILR, 321–30. The European Commission of Human Rights would later hold in respect of the same case, in its 1988 decision in *Spaans v. Netherlands*, that it did not consider that a grant of immunity 'gives rise to an issue' under the European Convention on Human Rights. See 107 ILR 1, at 5.

IN THE UNITED STATES DISTRICT COURT FOR THE DISTRICT OF COLUMBIA

UNITED NATIONS on behalf of the INDEPENDENT INQUIRY COMMITTEE INTO THE UNITED NATIONS OIL-FOR-FOOD PROGRAMME... 825 Third Avenue, 15th Floor New York, NY 10022 Plaintiff, v. ROBERT H. PARTON Defendant.	Civil Action No. 1:05CV00917

COMPLAINT FOR DECLARATORY AND INJUNCTIVE RELIEF

Plaintiff, the United Nations on behalf of the Independent Inquiry Committee Into the United Nations Oil-For-Food Programme, brings this action for declaratory and injunctive relief against Defendant Robert H. Parton, alleging as follows:

* * *

BACKGROUND

United Nations IIC into the Oil-for-Food Programme

14. The Oil-for-Food Programme arose as part of an effort to address humanitarian concerns about the impact on the people of Iraq of the comprehensive economic sanctions that were imposed against Iraq following its invasion of Kuwait in 1990. From approximately 1996 to 2003, the Programme permitted Iraq to sell oil, to have the proceeds of oil sales deposited into a UN-controlled escrow account, and to use funds deposited to the escrow account to purchase food and other civilian goods. The Programme terminated in 2003 in light of the onset of military activities in Iraq that led to the fall of the regime of Saddam Hussein.

15. By early 2004, numerous media reports have surfaced concerning corruption and other irregularities in the inception and administration of the Programme. Among the issues raised in media reports concerned the conduct of Secretary-General Kofi Annan. Questions were raised about the propriety of the United Nations' award of a large contract under the Programme to a goods inspection company (Cotecna Inspection SA) that employed Kojo Annan, the son of the Secretary-General.

16. By April 2004, the Secretary-General decided to designate a three-member committee of persons not employed by the United Nations to conduct an independent investigation of the management and administration of the Oil-for-Food Programme. The Secretary-General appointed Paul A. Volcker (formerly chairman of the Federal Reserve Board) as the Committee's chair. In addition, the Secretary-General appointed as members Richard Goldstone (former justice of the Constitutional Court of South Africa and

presently a visiting professor of law at Harvard Law School) and Mark Pieth (a professor of law at the University of Basel in Switzerland).

17. On April 22, 2004, the members of the United Nations Security Council unanimously passed Resolution 1538 endorsing the Secretary-General's appointment of an "independent high-level inquiry" and calling upon all Member States of the United Nations "to cooperate fully by all appropriate means with the inquiry." The United States voted in favor of Resolution 1538.

18. To date, IIC investigators have conducted more than 400 witness interviews in more than twenty countries, and the IIC has reviewed hundreds of thousands of documents in paper and electronic form.

19. Several committees of the United States Congress have also initiated investigations concerning the Oil-for-Food Programme: (a) the House Committee on International Relations (chaired by Rep. Henry Hyde), (b) the House Subcommittee on national Security, Emerging Threats and International Relations of the Committee on Government Reform (chaired by Rep. Christopher Shays), and (c) the Senate Permanent Subcommittee on Investigations (chaired by Sen. Norm Coleman) of the Senate Committee on Homeland Security & Government Affairs.

Legal Protections from Subpoena or Seizure of the Documents and Communications of the United Nations IIC.

20. In the absence of an express waiver by the United Nations, the archives of the United Nations are "inviolable" and the property and assets of the United Nations "*wherever located and by whomever held,* shall be immune from search ... and from confiscation." 22 U.S.C. 288a(b) and (c) (emphasis added). Similarly, the Convention on the Privileges and Immunities of the United Nations, 21 U.S.T. 1418, T.I.A.S. No. 6900, art. 2, sec. 4 (signed Feb. 13, 1946 and ratified by the United States on April 29, 1970) provides that "[t]he archives of the United Nations, and in general all documents belonging to it or held by it, shall be inviolable wherever located."

21. The Convention further provides that "[t]he property and assets of the United Nations, *wherever located and by whomsoever held*, shall be immune from search, requisition, confiscation, expropriation and any other form of interference, whether by executive, administrative, judicial or legislative action." *Id.*, sec. 3 (emphasis added).

22. Under the terms of Article VI of the Convention on Privileges and Immunities, "experts on mission" "shall be accorded ... inviolability for all papers and documents." *See* Convention, art. VI, sec. 22(c). Staff members of the Independent Inquiry Committee have been designated by the United nations as "experts on mission" within the meaning of Article VI of the Convention.

Defendant Parton's Confidentiality Obligations

23. On July 6, 2004, Defendant Parton entered into a letter agreement of employment with the Independent Inquiry Committee as "Senior Investigative Counsel" and began service on August 9, 2004. Defendant Parton previously served as a law enforcement agent with the Federal Bureau of Investigation and has a law degree from Cornell University.

[The Complaint goes on to detail Parton's contract-based confidentiality Agreement obligation.]

* * *

Defendant Parton's Disclosure of Privileged Documents and Communications without Prior Notice to the Independent Inquiry Committee and in Contravention of Federal and International Law

35. After Mr. Parton left the Committee, media reports soon surfaced that he had done so because of his disagreement with aspects of the Committee's second interim report.

36. Defendant Parton informed the Committee that he had obtained legal counsel, Lanny Davis of the law firm of Orrick, Herrington & Sutcliffe, LLP, in Washington, DC.

37. Mr. Davis informed the Committee on April 26, 2004, that he had received requests from Congressional committees for Robert Parton to appear voluntarily to discuss his work for the Committee and inquiries about whether Defendant Parton would accept service of subpoena. The Committee advised Mr. Davis of the protection accorded to such information under the Convention and of Defendant Parton's confidentiality agreement with the Independent Inquiry Committee. The Committee also told Mr. Davis that the United Nations would have to affirmatively waive any privileges and immunities before Defendant Parton could share information with Congress. Mr. Davis gave no indication that Defendant Parton possessed confidential documents of the Independent Inquiry Committee.

38. On the morning of May 2, 2005, Mr. Davis wrote to the Committee seeking "[d]oes the IIC instruct Mr. Parton to defy any subpoena that the United States Congress issues to him in connection with his work for the IIC?" The letter did not state that Defendant Parton had actually been served with any subpoena from Congress. Mr. Davis sent a similar letter to Bruce Rashkow of the United Nations Office of Legal Affairs.

39. Mr. Rashkow replied on May 2, 2005 by letter to Mr. Davis advising in relevant part that "[a]ll activities of the [Independent Inquiry] Committee and its staff in the performance of their duties for the Committee are immune from legal process," that "[i]t is for the Organization [the United Nations] to waive such privileges and immunities," and that "if Mr. Parton were to receive legal process from a United States Congressional Committee, or any other governmental entity, such process should be immediately forwarded to the United Nations." Mr. Rashkow's letter added that "[t]he Organization would respond accordingly after consulting with the Independent Inquiry Committee."

40. The next day, the Committee's Counsel (Ms. Ringler) wrote to Mr. Davis referring to the letter of Mr. Rashkow and reminding him of "Mr. Parton's confidentiality agreement with the IIC and the protections afforded to the IIC Committee members and staff in the performance of the investigation." The Committee's Counsel also inquired what response, if any, he had made to any requests from Congress.

41. On the following day, May 4, Mr. Davis faxed a letter to Ms. Ringler and Mr. Rashkow disclosing that Defendant Parton had previously been served with a subpoena on Friday, April 29, 2005, by the Committee on International Relations of the United States House of Representatives. Mr. Davis's letter included a copy of the subpoena reflecting that Mr. Davis had received service of the subpoena at his office in Washington, D.C., and that the subpoena commanded production of "[a]ll records produced by Mr. Parton or in his possession relating to the Independent Inquiry Committee into the United Nations Oil-for-Food Programme...." Mr. Davis's letter stated that Defendant Parton had complied with the subpoena.

42. Mr. Davis's letter did not describe what was produced by Defendant Parton in response to the subpoena, and he has yet to respond to the IIC's request for a list of documents produced. According to media reports, however, the subpoena production includes "more than a half-dozen boxes of documents." *See* "Volcker Asks Congress to Back Off," Washington Times (May 6, 2005); *see also* "Volcker Lawyer Asks U.N. to Block U.S. Subpoenas," www.foxnews.com (May 7, 2005) (noting that "boxes" of documents were produced in response to subpoena).

43. As noted above, Robert Parton was obliged by the terms of his Confidentiality Agreement "immediately" to notify the Committee if he were served with legal process seeking confidential information of the Committee. The subpoena was served on April 29, but the Committee was not advised of the subpoena until *after* Robert Parton disclosed documents in response to the subpoena.

44. Mr. Davis's letter of May 4 states that he did not earlier disclose the subpoena to the Independent Inquiry Committee because Robert Parton was "[u]nder threat of being held in contempt of Congress" if he did so. Neither the subpoena nor the attached instructions contain any directive prohibiting Defendant Parton from disclosing the fact of the subpoena to the United Nations or the IIC. The federal "contempt of Congress" statute does not proscribe a witness from disclosing the fact or contents of a subpoena to a third party. *See* 2 U.S.C. 192. Similarly, the subpoena-related provisions of the Standing Rules of the House of Representatives (Rule XI, clause 2) and the Rules of the House Committee on International Relations (Rule 22) do not prohibit a witness from disclosing to a third party that he has been served with a subpoena.

45. Late in the evening of May 4, 2005, Congressman Henry Hyde—the Chairman of the House International Relations Committee—spoke by telephone with Paul Volcker. According to Mr. Volcker, Congressman Hyde denied that his committee had issued any such threat.

<u>The Pending Subpoenas</u>

46. There are presently pending two additional congressional subpoena seeking information from Defendant Parton. The first is a subpoena from the Subcommittee on National Security, Emerging Threats and International Relations of the Committee of the Committee on Government Reform. This subpoena was apparently served by fax on Defendant's counsel, Lanny Davis, on May 5, 2005, and it commands the production of "[a]ll records referring or relating to the Independent Inquiry Committee into the United Nations Oil-for-Food Program" at noon on May 9, 2005.

47. The second subpoena has issued from the Permanent Subcommittee on Investigations of the Senate Committee on Homeland Security & Government Affairs. This subpoena commands production by Defendant Parton by 10:00 a.m. on May 12, 2005, of documents relating to his employment and "relating to the subject matter that you were investigating during the course of your employment at the IIC." The subpoena further commands Defendant Parton's appearance as a witness to testify before the Senate Subcommittee at 10:00 a.m. on May 12.

48. On May 6, 2005, Paul Volcker issued a statement to the press proposing to release Defendant Parton from his obligation of confidentiality to make a public statement concerning his disagreement with the Independent Inquiry Committee's report, on the condition that the congressional committees withdraw their subpoenas and return documents that have been subpoenaed. Mr. Volcker stated his "overriding concern ... is to safeguard the security of witnesses whose lives quite literally would be at risk if information about their cooperation became known."

The Need For Injunctive Relief

49. Irreparable harm will occur if Defendant Parton is not prohibited from further disclosing the documents wrongly taken from the Independent Inquiry Committee. First, unauthorized disclosure of its investigative files will destroy the "inviolability" of the United Nation's archives, which are protected by both treaty and statute from exactly this type of disclosures. Second, it will impair the ability of the Committee to complete its investigation by discouraging witnesses (and governments) from cooperating with the Committee in the future. Third, it will harm the reputation of the United Nations with respect to its ability to assure informants about the use that will be made of sensitive information provided in confidential investigations. Fourth, it will place at risk the lives and safety of Iraqi citizens who have provided information to the Committee under promises of confidentiality.

50. Plaintiff has no adequate remedy at law; the sole remedy available is to protect the confidentiality of the Independent Inquiry Committee's documents and communications in accordance with federal and international law by barring Defendant Parton from wrongfully disclosing any misappropriated documents or confidential communications to others.

51. The fact that Defendant Parton has already supplied the documents to the Hyde Committee does not eliminate the threat of irreparable harm from future dissemination; the more broadly this information is made available, the more complete the breach of confidentiality and the more likely the potential for the harms described above to accrue. The Committee continues to seek to work with the Hyde Committee to obtain the return of these unlawfully produced documents.

* * *

PRAYER FOR RELIEF

WHEREFORE, Plaintiff, United Nations on behalf of the International Inquiry Committee into the United Nations Oil-for-Food Programme, pray for preliminary and permanent relief and a judgment against Defendant Parton as follows:

(1) declaring that Defendant and his agents and assigns are prohibited from disclosing the communications, documents or other confidential information of the Independent Inquiry Committee;

(2) declaring that Defendant has violated the contractual terms of his employment and other contracts by retaining these documents and communications after his resignation and by providing these communications and documents to the Hyde Committee;

(3) ordering Defendant to return the documents and communications, and any copies, to the Independent Inquiry Committee;

(4) enjoining Defendant from engaging in any further violations of his obligations to Plaintiff;

(5) ordering Defendant to specifically perform his duties under his contracts with the Committee;

(6) awarding Plaintiff, as appropriate, their costs, attorneys' fees, and other disbursements for this action; and

(7) granting Plaintiff such other and further relief as this Court deems just and proper.

* * *

UNITED STATES DISTRICT COURT FOR THE DISTRICT OF COLUMBIA

UNITED NATIONS on behalf of the INDEPENDENT INQUIRY COMMITTEE INTO THE UNITED NATIONS OIL-FOR-FOOD PROGRAM,	:	
Plaintiff,	:	Civil Action No.: 05-0917 (RMU)
v.	:	Document No.: 13
ROBERT H. PARTON,	:	
Defendant.	:	

GRANTING THE PLAINTIFF'S EMERGENCY MOTION*

On May 9, 2005, the United Nations ("UN"), acting on behalf of the Independent Inquiry Committee into the United Nations Oil-for-Food Program ("IIC"), requested emergency injunctive relief to prevent former IIC investigator, Robert H. Parton, from responding to congressional subpoenas requiring testimony and the production of documents that Parton allegedly took from the UN. The parties reached a compromise that day and consented to the court entering an order enjoining the defendant from disclosing information that he obtained in the course of his work for the IIC.[1]

Hovering over this case is a political storm the court would rather not enter, a precarious competition by various committees, congressional and otherwise, to figure out exactly what happened at the UN's controversial Oil-for-Food Program. *See generally* Pl.'s Mot. for T.R.O., Decl. of Susan M. Ringler ¶¶ 4–16 (discussing efforts to investigate allegations of impropriety at the Oil-for-Food Program).

The politics of the moment notwithstanding, the court must now address the plaintiff's emergency motion to modify the temporary restraining order to allow the plaintiff access to and inspection of the materials that the defendant allegedly took from the UN and provided to the House International Relations Committee ("HIRC").[2] Pl.'s Emergency Mot. ("Pl.'s Mot.") at 1. Such a request would typically resolve itself through dis-

* Some footnotes omitted.

1. The order, which makes no finding one way or the other as to any of the elements for injunctive relief, remains in effect until the close of business on May 19, 2005. Order (May 9, 2005). Although the order does not apply to "members of Congress and their staffs in their own official capacity," *Id.*, representatives from the House General Counsel's Office and the Senate Permanent Subcommittee on Investigations stated on the record at the hearing that, at least until May 19, the congressional committees that issued the subpoenas in this case would agree to continue to negotiate a resolution short of enforcing the subpoenas, Tr. (May 9, 205) at 12–13.

2. The defendant maintains that he has only provided materials to the HIRC and to his lawyer. Def.'s Opp'n at 4. The court takes this to mean, at the very least, that a copy of the documents exists at the office of defense counsel and at the Ford House Office Building. *See Id.*, Ex. A (Agreement Between the HIRC and Robert Parton) (noting that Mr. Parton and his counsel will provide the HIRC with redacted and unredacted versions of the materials and elaborating procedures for insuring the protection of sensitive information). As the plaintiff points out, however, it has no way of knowing that "*all* material in Mr. Parton's possession relating in any way to the IIC's work is currently in the possession of the HIRC and that the HIRC has unredacted copies of all such material." Pl.'s Reply at 4 (emphasis in original).

covery,[3] but the plaintiff wants this relief immediately so that it can see exactly what the defendant has taken from the plaintiff and, more importantly, whether the plaintiff needs to notify confidential informants, "including residents of a highly volatile part of the world," that their identities may be revealed. *Id.*

As authority for its request, the plaintiff cites to the court's equitable powers "to do what is necessary and appropriate to achieve justice in the individual case." *Id.* at 3 (quoting *Friends for All Children, Inc. v. Lockheed Aircraft Corp.*, 746 F.2d 816, 830 (D.C. Cir. 1984)). The defendant responds that the materials at issue do not contain information that jeopardizes the safety of any sources (and thus, that the plaintiff will suffer no harm if the court denies the relief the plaintiff requests), that the HIRC (to whom the plaintiff provided a copy of the materials) has agreed to protect all sensitive information, and that the plaintiff is attempting "to gather discovery without following the rules or any order of this court." Def.'s Opp'n at 4–5, 7.

As to the defendant's first two arguments, the court finds instructive the plaintiff's comment that

> [i]t is simply not enough to say, "don't worry, the investigator who falsely told the IIC that he was not removing confidential material, who breached his confidentiality agreement, who took no steps to inform the IIC of the HIRC's subpoenas, and who negotiated an agreement with the HIRC that fully protects his interests (but not the IIC's), has assured us that we need not be concerned."

Pl.'s Reply at 3. Without taking a position on those assertions, the court believes that the UN is indeed the party best suited to provide assurances to the international community and to the sources in its investigations. Whatever the defendant and his counsel may be able to declare in an affidavit or state in an agreement with a third party, such gestures are inadequate substitutes for the thorough review of the materials that the plaintiff needs to conduct to determine how best to proceed. The court takes very seriously the plaintiff's claim that the lives and safety of certain IIC witnesses may be at risk, *e.g.*, Pl.'s Mot. for T.R.O. at 3, and there is no time left for the parties to work out an arrangement with the HIRC for viewing the HIRC's copies of the documents,[4] assuming that such a review would even suffice, *see* Pl.'s Reply at 4.

Finally, with regard to the defendant's argument that the plaintiff is sidestepping discovery, the court acknowledges that the plaintiff's request is unusual. But the facts of this rapidly evolving case are quite unusual, and the court has yet to see any reason to delay providing the relief the plaintiff seeks. The court continues to hope that the parties informally and efficiently resolve this case without further judicial intervention.[5] As to the instant motion, however, it is this 16th day of May, 2005,

---

3. Or, perhaps, through a motion for expedited discovery. *See, e.g., In re Fannie Mae Derivative Litigation,* 2005 WL 433271,* 1 (D.D.C. Feb. 23, 2005) (discussing two standards for resolving requests for expedited discovery).

4. *See generally* Def.'s Opp'n at 5 (noting that the HIRC "has advised the IIC that it will permit the IIC to inspect the materials turned over by Mr. Parton in response to the Subpoena"); *id.*, Ex. B (Josua Galper Decl.) (stating that "[m]y understanding is that the [HIRC] has advised the IIC that it intends to make arrangements to provide the IIC access to the materials provided to it by Mr. Parton"); see also Pl.'s Reply at 8–9 (pointing to the tentative nature of such assurances).

5. In the interest of fairness, to the extent that expedited discovery burdens the defendant, the Court is willing to entertain a motion from the defendant seeking an equally burdensome effort from the plaintiff, provided that request has the same legitimate sense of urgency as the request now before the court. The plaintiff has suggested that it "would not object to including a provision in the Court's order specifying that the IIC may not introduce into evidence any documents it obtains through this

ORDERED that, by no later than 12:00 p.m. on Tuesday, May 16, 2005, the defendant shall provide the plaintiff the opportunity to inspect and copy all materials that the defendant allegedly copied, removed or otherwise (directly or indirectly) obtained from the IIC; and it is

FURTHER ORDERED that the temporary restraining order in this case is modified to allow for the above inspection and copying.

SO ORDERED.

RICARDO M. URBINA
United States District Judge

Notes and Questions on National Courts

1. What is the purpose of sovereign immunity and IO immunity? Is either type of immunity required by international law?

2. Following the Supreme Court decision in *Altmann v. Austria*, the parties agreed to arbitrate the question of title to the paintings. *See* Howard Reich, *Austrian Panel to Resolve Klimt Art Dispute*, CHICAGO TRIB. May 19, 2005, 2005 WLNR 7940504.

3. Should a sovereign state be able to plead immunity from suit by other sovereign states in its own courts as the Supreme Court implied the U.S. might be able to do in *LaGrand*? Can you see a difference between the need for immunity from suits brought by a state's own citizens, as in *Flatow v. Iran*, versus the need for immunity from co-equal sovereigns if the forum is the defendant state's own courts? Consider the purpose of immunity in Question 1. Is that purpose served by immunity from suit in a defendant state's own courts?

4. Does the U.S. Congress have the right to investigate the UN without the UN's consent? If the U.S. has an issue with the UN, what is the appropriate way to resolve the issue? Why do you think the IIC sued Parton and not the congressional representatives who received the documents in violation of international law?

5. "Hybrid Courts" is a term coined by international law scholars for national courts that involve international observers or other aspects that create an institutional not wholly national in nature. Such courts have been formed in Sierra Leone, Cambodia, Lebanon, and Iraq. All are criminal courts. Do you think such courts could play a role in international public dispute resolution? *See* Laura Dickinson, *The Promise of Hybrid Courts*, 97 AM. J. INT'L L. 295 (2003); Etelle R. Higonnet, *Restructuring Hybrid Courts: Local Empowerment and National Criminal Justice Reform*, 23 ARIZ. J. INT'L & COMP. L. 347 (2006).

6. For further reading on national courts in the system of international dispute settlement, see

ANDRÉ NOLLKAEMPER, NATIONAL COURTS AND THE INTERNATIONAL RULE OF LAW (2011).

DAVID A. KAYE, JUSTICE BEYOND THE HAGUE, SUPPORTING THE PROSECUTION OF INTERNATIONAL CRIMES IN NATIONAL COURTS (Council on Foreign Relations Special Report No. 61, June 2011).

---

process without independently obtaining the material through discovery or otherwise." Pl.'s Reply at 3. If the defendant wishes the Court to include such a provision in today's order, the Court will do so retroactively on the defendant's motion.

ENFORCING INTERNATIONAL HUMAN RIGHTS IN DOMESTIC COURTS (Benedetto Conforti & Francesco Francioni eds., 1999).

INTERNATIONAL LAW DECISIONS IN NATIONAL COURTS (Thomas M. Franck & Gregory H. Fox eds., 1996).

BENEDETTO CONFORTI, INTERNATIONAL LAW AND THE ROLE OF DOMESTIC LEGAL SYSTEM (1993).

CHRISTOPH SCHEUER, DECISIONS OF INTERNATIONAL INSTITUTIONS BEFORE DOMESTIC COURTS (1981).

Chapter Fifteen

Issues Arising in the Course of National Court Dispute Resolution

Introduction

When a national court takes jurisdiction of a public international law dispute, several issues will commonly arise. Perhaps the most common is the question of what law to apply. This is sometimes referred to as "conflicts of law," or the application of the "proper law" of the case. The first part below concerns this issue, choice of the proper law. The second part reviews several doctrines developed by national courts to avoid deciding cases involving international disputes despite the fact the national court has jurisdiction. These doctrines include: the political question doctrine, the act of state doctrine, and the doctrine of *forum non conveniens*. All are part of national law, not international law, and they result in national courts playing a smaller role in resolving international disputes than they potentially could. Nevertheless, national courts play a significant role as the first experts below demonstrate. If the barriers to national court involvement in dispute resolution could be overcome, the potential for this mechanism of dispute resolution is potentially very large.

A. Proper Law

The first case below shows how a U.S. District Court was able to resolve a dispute between the U.S. and the UN by careful analysis of the proper law. Choice of law rules steer us toward the proper law for any particular matter, whether local, national, regional, or international law. If the matter implicates an international boundary, international choice of law rules will guide the choice. Take a typical issue that arises frequently—the choice of law governing a contract between a farmer in Indiana, U.S. selling soybeans and a buyer in Provence, France. What law governs this contract? The answer lies in international law, and, in this case, the international law on choice of law sends us to neither the contract law of Indiana nor the contract law of France. Choice of law sends us to the United Nations Convention on Contracts for the International Sale of Goods because both France and the United States are parties to this treaty. International law regulates the choice of law and in this example it is international law that governs.

Generally, disputes involving states and inter-governmental organizations will be governed by public international law. National courts may, however, find barriers to applying international law. For example, the next excerpt returns to the PLO Observer Mission dispute introduced in Chapter Two. You will recall that the U.S. Congress passed a statute inconsistent with the UN Headquarters Agreement. Before the dispute went to arbitration between the U.S. and the UN, the U.S. sought to enforce the statute against the PLO, and the matter went to court. The U.S. argued that the statute superseded the Headquarters Agreement because it was later in time. This is the general rule guiding U.S. courts on the choice of the proper law. Such an outcome is not possible in other jurisdictions. Courts in the Netherlands, for example, will not apply a domestic statute that puts the state into violation with treaty obligations. If the U.S. position had been adopted, the dispute would have continued to arbitration. The Court, however, was able to reconcile the statute with the Headquarters Agreement and resolve the dispute.

The series of cases that follow the PLO case concern U.S. courts implementing or refusing to implement decisions of international courts and tribunals. National courts have the potential to be significant enforcers of international judicial decisions, as national courts already are respecting arbitral decisions. In one prominent case, however, the U.S. Supreme Court refused to ensure the implementation of the ICJ's judgment in the *Avena* case. Can you see a reasoned basis for the Supreme Court to refuse to enforce the *Avena* decision in contrast to the enforcement of the decision of the Spanish-U.S. claims tribunal in the *Comegys v. Vasse* case below or President Reagan's agreement to remove cases from U.S. courts in order to send them to the Iran-U.S. Claims Tribunal, the issue in *Dames and Moore v. Regan*, also below?

United States v. The Palestine Liberation Organization

695 F.Supp. 1456 (1988)*

* * *

The Anti-terrorism Act of 1987 (the "ATA"), is the focal point of this lawsuit. At the center of controversy is the right of the Palestine Liberation Organization (the "PLO") to maintain its office in conjunction with its work as a Permanent Observer to the United Nations. The case comes before the court on the government's motion for an injunction closing this office and on the defendants' motions to dismiss.

I. *Background*

The United Nations' Headquarters in New York were established as an international enclave by the Agreement Between the United States and the United Nations Regarding the Headquarters of the United Nations (the "Headquarters Agreement"). This agreement followed an invitation extended to the United Nations by the United States, one of its principal founders, to establish its seat within the United States.

As a meeting place and forum for all nations, the United Nations, according to its charter, was formed to:

> maintain international peace and security ...; to develop friendly relations among nations, based on the principle of equal rights and self-determination of peoples ...; to achieve international cooperation in solving international problems of an economic, social, cultural or humanitarian character ...; and be a centre for harmonizing the actions of nations in the attainment of these common ends.

---

* Some footnotes omitted.

U.N. Charter art. 1. Today, 159 of the United Nations' members maintain missions to the U.N. in New York. U.N. Protocol and Liaison Service, Permanent Missions to the United Nations No. 262 3–4 (1988) (hereinafter "Permanent Missions No. 262"). In addition, the United Nations has, from its incipiency, welcomed various non-member observers to participate in its proceedings. See Permanent Missions to the United Nations: Report of the Secretary-General, 4 U.N. GAOR C.6 Annex (Agenda Item 50) 16, 17 ¶ 14, U.N. Doc. A/939/Rev.1 (1949) (hereinafter Permanent Missions: Report of the Secretary-General). Of these, several non-member nations, intergovernmental organizations, and other organizations currently maintain "Permanent Observer Missions" in New York.

The PLO falls into the last of these categories and is present at the United Nations as its invitee. See Headquarters Agreement, § 11, 61 Stat. at 761 (22 U.S.C. § 287 note). The PLO has none of the usual attributes of sovereignty. It is not accredited to the United States and does not have the benefits of diplomatic immunity. There is no recognized state it claims to govern. It purports to serve as the sole political representative of the Palestinian people. See generally Kassim, The Palestine Liberation Organization Claim to Status: A Juridical Analysis Under International Law, 9 Den. J. International L. & Policy 1 (1980). The PLO nevertheless considers itself to be the representative of a state, entitled to recognition in its relations with other governments, and is said to have diplomatic relations with approximately one hundred countries throughout the world. *Id.* at 19.

* * *

It is important to note for the purposes of this case that a primary goal of the United Nations is to provide a forum where peaceful discussions may displace violence as a means of resolving disputed issues. At times our responsibility to the United Nations may require us to issue visas to persons who are objectionable to certain segments of our society. *Id.*, transcript at 37, partially excerpted in Department of State, 1974 Digest of United States Practice in International Law, 27, 28.

Since 1974, the PLO has continued to function without interruption as a permanent observer and has maintained its Mission to the United Nations without trammel, largely because of the Headquarters Agreement, which we discuss below.

II. *The Anti-Terrorism Act*

In October 1986, members of Congress requested the United States Department of State to close the PLO offices located in the United States. That request proved unsuccessful, and proponents of the request introduced legislation with the explicit purpose of doing so.

The result was the ATA, 22 U.S.C. §§ 5201–5203. It is of a unique nature. We have been unable to find any comparable statute in the long history of Congressional enactments. The PLO is stated to be "a terrorist organization and a threat to the interests of the United States, its allies, and to international law and should not benefit from operating in the United States." 22 U.S.C. § 5201(b). The ATA was added, without committee hearings, as a rider to the Foreign Relations Authorization Act for Fiscal Years 1988–89, which provided funds for the operation of the State Department, including the operation of the United States Mission to the United Nations. Pub. L. 100-204 § 101, 101 Stat. 1331, 1335. The bill also authorized payments to the United Nations for maintenance and operation. *Id.* § 102(a)(1), 101 Stat. at 1336; see also *id.* § 143, 101 Stat. at 1386.

The ATA, which became effective on March 21, 1988, forbids the establishment or maintenance of "an office, headquarters, premises, or other facilities or establishments within the jurisdiction of the United States at the behest or direction of, or with funds provided by" the PLO, if the purpose is to further the PLO's interests. 22 U.S.C. § 5202(3). The ATA also forbids spending the PLO's funds or receiving anything of value except informational material from the PLO, with the same *mens rea* requirement. *Id.* §§ 5202(1) and (2).

Ten days before the effective date, the Attorney General wrote the Chief of the PLO Observer Mission to the United Nations that "maintaining a PLO Observer Mission to the United Nations will be unlawful," and advised him that upon failure of compliance, the Department of Justice would take action in federal court. This letter is reproduced in the record as item 28 of the Compendium prepared at the outset of this litigation pursuant to the court's April 21, 1988 request to counsel (attached as Appendix B). It is entitled "Compendium of the Legislative History of the Anti-Terrorism Act of 1987, Related Legislation, and Official Statements of the Department of Justice and the Department of State Regarding This Legislation." The documents in the compendium are of great interest.

The United States commenced this lawsuit the day the ATA took effect, seeking injunctive relief to accomplish the closure of the Mission. The United States Attorney for this District has personally represented that no action would be taken to enforce the ATA pending resolution of the litigation in this court.

* * *

IV. *The Duty to Arbitrate*

Counsel for the PLO and for the United Nations and the Association of the Bar of the City of New York, as *amici curiae*, have suggested that the court defer to an advisory opinion of the International Court of Justice. *Applicability of the Obligation to Arbitrate Under Section 21 of the United Nations Headquarters Agreement of 26 June 1947*, 1988 I.C.J. 12 (April 26, 1988) (*U.N. v. U.S.*). That decision holds that the United States is bound by Section 21 of the Headquarters Agreement to submit to binding arbitration of a dispute precipitated by the passage of the ATA. Indeed, it is the PLO's position that this alleged duty to arbitrate deprives the court of subject matter jurisdiction over this litigation.

In June 1947, the United States subscribed to the Headquarters Agreement, defining the privileges and immunities of the United Nations' Headquarters in New York City, thereby becoming the "Host Country"—a descriptive title that has followed it through many United Nations proceedings. The Headquarters Agreement was brought into effect under United States law, with an annex, by a Joint Resolution of Congress approved by the President on August 4, 1947. The PLO rests its argument, as do the amici, on Section 21(a) of the Headquarters Agreement, which provides for arbitration in the case of any dispute between the United Nations and the United States concerning the interpretation or application of the Headquarters Agreement. Because interpretation of the ATA requires an interpretation of the Headquarters Agreement, they argue, this court must await the decision of an arbitral tribunal yet to be appointed before making its decision.

Section 21(a) of the Headquarters Agreement provides, in part:

> "Any dispute *between the United Nations and the United States* concerning the interpretation or application of this agreement or of any supplemental agreement, which is not settled by negotiation or other agreed mode of settlement, shall be referred for final decision to a tribunal of three arbitrators...." 61 Stat. at 764 (22 U.S.C. § 287 note) (emphasis supplied).

Because these proceedings are not in any way directed to settling any dispute, ripe or not, between the United Nations and the United States, Section 21, is, by its terms, inapplicable.[18] The fact that the Headquarters Agreement was adopted by a majority of both Houses of Congress and approved by the President, see 61 Stat. at 768, might lead to the conclusion that it provides a rule of decision requiring arbitration any time the interpretation of the Headquarters Agreement is at issue in the United States Courts. That conclusion would be wrong for two reasons.

First, this court cannot direct the United States to submit to arbitration without exceeding the scope of its Article III powers. What sets this case apart from the usual situation in which two parties have agreed to binding arbitration for the settlement of any future disputes, requiring the court to stay its proceedings, cf. 9 U.S.C. § 3 (1982), is that we are here involved with matters of international policy. This is an area in which the courts are generally unable to participate. These questions do not lend themselves to resolution by adjudication under our jurisprudence. *See generally Baker v. Carr*, 369 U.S. 186, 211–13, 82 S.Ct. 691, 707–08, 7 L.Ed.2d 663 (1962). The restrictions imposed upon the courts forbidding them to resolve such questions (often termed "political questions") derive not only from the limitations which inhere in the judicial process but also from those imposed by Article III of the Constitution. *Marbury v. Madison*, 5 U.S. (1 Cranch) 137, 170, 2 L.Ed. 60 (1803) (Marshall, C.J.) ("The province of the court is, solely, to decide on the right of individuals, not to inquire how the executive, or executive officers, perform duties in which they have a discretion. Questions in their nature political, or which are, by the constitution and laws, submitted to the executive can never be made in this Court."). The decision in Marbury has never been disturbed.

The conduct of the foreign relations of our Government is committed by the Constitution to the executive and legislative—the "political"—departments of the government. As the Supreme Court noted in *Baker v. Carr*, supra, 369 U.S. at 211, 82 S. Ct. at 707, not all questions touching upon international relations are automatically political questions. Nonetheless, were the court to order the United States to submit to arbitration, it would violate several of the tenets to which the Supreme Court gave voice in *Baker v. Carr, supra*, 369 U.S. at 217, 82 S. Ct. at 710. Resolution of the question whether the United States will arbitrate requires "an initial policy determination of a kind clearly for nonjudicial discretion;" deciding whether the United States will or ought to submit to arbitration, in the face of a determination not to do so by the executive, would be impossible without the court "expressing lack of the respect due coordinate branches of government;" and such a decision would raise not only the "potentiality" but the reality of "embarrassment from multifarious pronouncements by various departments on one question." It is for these reasons that the ultimate decision as to how the United States should honor its treaty obligations with the international community is one which has, for at least one hundred years, been left to the executive to decide. *Goldwater v. Carter*, 444 U.S. 996, 996–97, 100 S. Ct. 533, 533, 62 L.Ed.2d 428 (1979) (vacating, with instructions to dismiss, an attack on the President's action in terminating a treaty with Taiwan)....

The task of the court in this case is to interpret the ATA in resolving this dispute between numerous parties and the United States. Interpretation of the ATA, as a matter of domestic law, falls to the United States courts. In interpreting the ATA, the effect of the United States' international obligations—the United Nations Charter and the Head-

18. The United Nations has explicitly refrained from becoming a party to this litigation. The International Court of Justice makes a persuasive statement that the proceedings before this court "cannot be an 'agreed mode of settlement' within the meaning of section 21 of the Headquarters Agreement. The purpose of these proceedings is to enforce the Anti-Terrorism Act of 1987; it is not directed to settling the [alleged] dispute, concerning the application of the Headquarters Agreement." U.N. v. U.S., *supra*, 1988 I.C.J. 12, ¶ 14, at 34.

quarters Agreement in particular—must be considered. As a matter of domestic law, the interpretation of these international obligations and their reconciliation, if possible, with the ATA is for the courts....

V. *The Anti-Terrorism Act and the Headquarters Agreement*

If the ATA were construed as the government suggests, it would be tantamount to a direction to the PLO Observer Mission at the United Nations that it close its doors and cease its operations *instanter*. Such an interpretation would fly in the face of the Headquarters Agreement, a prior treaty between the United Nations and the United States, and would abruptly terminate the functions the Mission has performed for many years. This conflict requires the court to seek out a reconciliation between the two.

Under our constitutional system, statutes and treaties are both the supreme law of the land, and the Constitution sets forth no order of precedence to differentiate between them. U.S. Const. art. VI, cl. 2. Wherever possible, both are to be given effect. *E.g. Trans World Airlines, Inc. v. Franklin Mint Corp.*, 466 U.S. 243, 252, 104 S. Ct. 1776, 1783, 80 L.Ed.2d 273 (1984)....

* * *

B. *Reconciliation of the ATA and the Headquarters Agreement*

The lengths to which our courts have sometimes gone in construing domestic statutes so as to avoid conflict with international agreements are suggested by a passage from Justice Field's dissent in *Chew Heong, supra,* 112 U.S. at 560, 560–61, 67 S. Ct. at 267, 267 (1884):

> I am unable to agree with my associates in their construction of the act ... restricting the immigration into this country of Chinese laborers. That construction appears to me to be in conflict with the language of that act, and to require the elimination of entire clauses and the interpolation of new ones. It renders nugatory whole provisions which were inserted with sedulous care. The change thus produced in the operation of the act is justified on the theory that to give it any other construction would bring it into conflict with the treaty; and that we are not at liberty to suppose that Congress intended by its legislation to disregard any treaty stipulations.

Chew Heong concerned the interplay of legislation regarding Chinese laborers with treaties on the same subject. During the passage of the statute at issue in *Chew Heong,* "it was objected to the legislation sought that the treaty of 1868 stood in the way, and that while it remained unmodified, such legislation would be a breach of faith to China...." *Id.* at 569, 67 S. Ct. at 272. In spite of that, and over Justice Field's dissent, the Court, in Justice Field's words, "narrow[ed] the meaning of the act so as measurably to frustrate its intended operation." Four years after the decision in *Chew Heong,* Congress amended the act in question to nullify that decision. Ch. 1064, 25 Stat. 504. With the amended statute, there could be no question as to Congress' intent to supersede the treaties, and it was the later enacted statute which took precedence. *The Chinese Exclusion Case, supra,* 130 U.S. at 598–99, 9 S. Ct. at 627 (1889).

* * *

Congress' failure to speak with one clear voice on this subject requires us to interpret the ATA as inapplicable to the Headquarters Agreement. This is so, in short, for the reasons which follow.

First, neither the Mission nor the Headquarters Agreement is mentioned in the ATA itself. Such an inclusion would have left no doubt as to Congress' intent on a matter which had been raised repeatedly with respect to this act, and its absence here reflects equivocation and avoidance, leaving the court without clear interpretive guidance in the language of the act. Second, while the section of the ATA prohibiting the maintenance of an office applies "notwithstanding any provision of law to the contrary," 22 U.S.C. § 5202(3), it does not purport to apply notwithstanding any *treaty*. The absence of that interpretive instruction is especially relevant because elsewhere in the same legislation Congress expressly referred to "United States law (including any treaty)." 101 Stat. at 1343. Thus Congress failed, in the text of the ATA, to provide guidance for the interpretation of the act, where it became repeatedly apparent before its passage that the prospect of an interpretive problem was inevitable. Third, no member of Congress expressed a clear and unequivocal intent to supersede the Headquarters Agreement by passage of the ATA. In contrast, most who addressed the subject of conflict denied that there would be a conflict: in their view, the Headquarters Agreement did not provide the PLO with any right to maintain an office. Here again, Congress provided no guidance for the interpretation of the ATA in the event of a conflict which was clearly foreseeable. And Senator Claiborne Pell, Chairman of the Senate Foreign Relations Committee, who voted for the bill, raised the possibility that the Headquarters Agreement would take precedence over the ATA in the event of a conflict between the two. His suggestion was neither opposed nor debated, even though it came in the final minutes before passage of the ATA.

A more complete explanation begins, of course, with the statute's language. The ATA reads, in part:

> It shall be unlawful, if the purpose be to further the interests of the PLO
>
> * * *
>
> (3) notwithstanding any provision of law to the contrary, to establish or maintain an office, headquarters, premises, or other facilities or establishments within the jurisdiction of the United States at the behest or direction of, or with funds provided by the PLO....
>
> 22 U.S.C. § 5202(3).

The Permanent Observer Mission to the United Nations is nowhere mentioned *in haec verba* in this act, as we have already observed. It is nevertheless contended by the United States that the foregoing provision requires the closing of the Mission, and this in spite of possibly inconsistent international obligations. According to the government, the act is so clear that this possibility is nonexistent. The government argues that its position is supported by the provision that the ATA would take effect "notwithstanding any provision of law to the contrary," 22 U.S.C. § 5202(3), suggesting that Congress thereby swept away any inconsistent international obligations of the United States. In effect, the government urges literal application of the maxim that in the event of conflict between two laws, the one of later date will prevail: *leges posteriores priores contrarias abrogant.*

We cannot agree. The proponents of the ATA were, at an early stage and throughout its consideration, forewarned that the ATA would present a potential conflict with the Headquarters Agreement. It was especially important in those circumstances for Congress to give clear, indeed unequivocal guidance, as to how an interpreter of the ATA was to resolve the conflict. Yet there was no reference to the Mission in the text of the ATA, despite extensive discussion of the Mission in the floor debates. Nor was there reference to the Headquarters Agreement, or to any treaty, in the ATA or in its "notwithstanding" clause, despite the textual expression of intent to supersede treaty obligations in other sections of the Foreign Relations Authorization Act, of which the ATA formed a part. Thus Congress failed to provide unequivocal interpretive guidance in the text of the ATA, leaving open the possibility that the ATA could be viewed as a law of general application and enforced as such, without encroaching on the position of the Mission at the United Nations.

The interpretation would present no inconsistency with what little legislative history exists. There were conflicting voices both in Congress and in the executive branch before the enactment of the ATA. Indeed, there is only one matter with respect to which there was unanimity—the condemnation of terrorism. This, however, is extraneous to the legal issues involved here. At oral argument, the United States Attorney conceded that there was no evidence before the court that the Mission had misused its position at the United Nations or engaged in any covert actions in furtherance of terrorism. If the PLO is benefiting from operating in the United States, as the ATA implies, the enforcement of its provisions outside the context of the United Nations can effectively curtail that benefit.

The record contains voices of congressmen and senators forceful in their condemnation of terrorism and of the PLO and supporting the notion that the legislation would close the mission. There are other voices, less certain of the validity of the proposed congressional action and preoccupied by problems of constitutional dimension. And there are voices of Congressmen uncertain of the legal issues presented but desirous nonetheless of making a "political statement." During the discussions which preceded and followed the passage of the ATA, the Secretary of State and the Legal Adviser to the Department of State a former member of this Court, voiced their opinions to the effect that the ATA presented a conflict with the Headquarters Agreement.

Yet no member of Congress, at any point, explicitly stated that the ATA was intended to override any international obligation of the United States.

The only debate on this issue focused not on whether the ATA would do so, but on whether the United States in fact had an obligation to provide access to the PLO. Indeed, every proponent of the ATA who spoke to the matter argued that the United States did not have such an obligation. For instance, Senator Grassley, after arguing that the United States had no obligation relating to the PLO Mission under the Headquarters Agreement, noted in passing that Congress had the *power* to modify treaty obligations. But even there, Senator Grassley did not argue that the ATA would supersede the Headquarters Agreement in the event of a conflict. 133 Cong. Rec. S 15,621–22 (daily ed. November 3, 1987). This disinclination to face the prospect of an actual conflict was again manifest two weeks later, when Senator Grassley explained, "as I detailed earlier..., the United States has *no international legal obligation* that would preclude it from closing the PLO Observer Mission." 133 Cong. Rec. S 16,505 (daily ed. November 20, 1987) (emphasis supplied). As the Congressional Record reveals, at the time of the ATA's passage (on December 15 in the House and December 16 in the Senate), its proponents were operating under a misapprehension of what the United States' treaty obligation entailed. 133 Cong. Rec. S 18,190 (daily ed. December 16, 1987) (statement of Sen. Helms) (closing the Mission would be "entirely within our Nation's obligations under international law"); 133 Cong. Rec. H 11,425 (daily ed. December 15, 1988) (statement of Rep. Burton) (observer missions have "no—zero—rights in the Headquarters Agreement.")

In sum, the language of the Headquarters Agreement, the longstanding practice under it, and the interpretation given it by the parties to it leave no doubt that it places an obligation upon the United States to refrain from impairing the function of the PLO Observer Mission to the United Nations. The ATA and its legislative history do not manifest Congress' intent to abrogate this obligation. We are therefore constrained to interpret the ATA as failing to supersede the Headquarters Agreement and inapplicable to the Mission.

* * *

Comegys & Pettit v. Vasse*

26 U.S. (1 Pet.) 193 (1828)

MR. JUSTICE STORY delivered the opinion of the Court.

This was an action ... brought by Ambrose Vasse in the Circuit Court for the District of Pennsylvania to recover from the plaintiffs in error (who were defendants in the court below) a certain sum of money received by them under the following circumstances:

Previous to the year 1802, Vasse was an underwriter on various vessels and cargoes, the property of citizens of the United States, which were captured and carried into the ports of Spain and her dependencies, and abandonments were made thereof to Vasse by the owners, and he paid the losses arising therefrom prior to the year 1802. Vasse became embarrassed in his affairs, and his creditors proceeded against him as a bankrupt under the Act of Congress of 4 April, 1800, ch. 19. An assignment was made accordingly to Jacob Shoemaker (who is deceased), and the defendants, Comegys and Pettit, who proceeded to take upon themselves the duties of assignees and have ever since continued to perform the same. Vasse was discharged [from his debts] under the commission, and his certificate of discharge bears date 28 May, 1802. In the year 1824, the sum of $8,846.14 was received by the defendants from the Treasury of the United States, being the sum awarded by the commissioners sitting at Washington under the treaty with Spain which ceded Florida to the United States, dated 22 February, 1819, on account of the captures and losses aforesaid. On 9 December, 1823, Vasse filed a bill in equity in the Circuit Court of the District of Columbia; ...

Upon these facts, a general verdict was found for the plaintiff Vasse for the sum of $8,846.14..., and the circuit court gave judgment upon the facts in favor of the original defendant. The present is a writ of error brought for the purpose of ascertaining the correctness of that judgment.

Three questions have been argued at the bar [; only one of which is considered here:]

1. Whether the award of the commissioners under the treaty with Spain directing the money to be paid to the defendants as assignees of Vasse (which is assumed to be the true state of the fact) is conclusive upon the rights of Vasse, so as to prevent his recovery in the present action.

* * *

1. As to the first point:

> 1. The treaty with Spain of 22 February, 1819, was ratified on 13 February, 1821, by the government of the United States. In the 9th article it provides that the high contracting parties
>
> > "reciprocally renounce all claims for damages or injuries, which they themselves, as well as their respective citizens and subjects may have suffered, until the time of signing this treaty,"

* Some minor changes have been made to punctuation and format.

and then proceeds to enumerate in separate clauses the injuries to which the renunciation extends.

The 11th article provides that the United States, exonerating Spain from all demands in future on account of the claims of their citizens to which the renunciations herein contained extend, and considering them entirely cancelled, undertakes to make satisfaction for the same to an amount not exceeding $5,000,000. To ascertain the full amount and validity of these claims, a commission, to consist of three commissioners, &c., shall be appointed, &c., and within the space of three years from the time of their first meeting, shall "*receive, examine, and decide upon the amount and validity of all claims* included within the descriptions above mentioned." The remaining part of the article is not material to be mentioned.

It has been justly remarked in the opinion of the learned judge who decided this cause in the circuit court that it does not appear from the statement of facts who were the persons who presented or litigated the claim before the Board of commissioners, nor whether Vasse himself was before the board, nor who were the parties to whom or for whose benefit the award was made. We do not think that the fact is material upon the view which we take of the authority and duties of the commissioners. The object of the treaty was to invest the commissioners with full power and authority to receive, examine, and decide upon the amount and validity of the asserted claims upon Spain for damages and injuries. Their decision, within the scope of this authority, is conclusive and final. If they pronounce the claim valid or invalid, if they ascertain the amount, their award in the premises is not reexaminable. The parties must abide by it as the decree of a competent tribunal of exclusive jurisdiction. A rejected claim cannot be brought again under review in any judicial tribunal; an amount once fixed is a final ascertainment of the damages or injury.

This is the obvious purport of the language of the treaty. But it does not necessarily or naturally follow that this authority, so delegated, includes the authority to adjust all conflicting rights of different citizens to the fund so awarded. The commissioners are to look to the original claim for damages and injuries against Spain itself, and it is wholly immaterial for this purpose upon whom it may in the intermediate time have devolved or who was the original legal, as contradistinguished from the equitable owner, provided he was an American citizen. If the claim was to be allowed as against Spain, the present ownership of it, whether in assignees or personal representatives or bona fide purchasers, was not necessary to be ascertained in order to exercise their functions in the fullest manner. Nor could they be presumed to possess the means of exercising such a broader jurisdiction, with due justice and effect. They had no authority to compel parties asserting conflicting interests to appear and litigate before them, nor to summon witnesses to establish or repel such interests, and under such circumstances it cannot be presumed that it was the intention of either government to clothe them with an authority so summary and conclusive, with means so little adapted to the attainment of the ends of a substantial justice. The validity and amount of the claim being once ascertained by their award, the fund might well be permitted to pass into the hands of any claimant; and his own rights, as well as those of all others, who asserted a title to the fund, be left to the ordinary course of judicial proceedings in the established courts, where redress could be administered according to the nature and extent of the rights or equities of all the parties. We are therefore of opinion that the award of the commissioners, in whatever form made, presents no bar to the action if the plaintiff is entitled to the money awarded by the commissioners.

[The Court then considers the ownership of the claim under the law of bankruptcy. It finds in favor of Vasse's assignees.]

The cause must be remanded with directions to enter a judgment for the original defendants.

Dames & Moore v. Regan

453 U.S. 654 (1981)

We are confined to a resolution of the dispute presented to us. That dispute involves various Executive Orders and regulations by which the President nullified attachments and liens on Iranian assets in the United States, directed that these assets be transferred to Iran, and suspended claims against Iran that may be presented to an International Claims Tribunal. This action was taken in an effort to comply with an Executive Agreement between the United States and Iran. We granted certiorari before judgment in this case, and set an expedited briefing and argument schedule, because lower courts had reached conflicting conclusions on the validity of the President's actions and, as the Solicitor General informed us, unless the Government acted by July 19, 1981, Iran could consider the United States to be in breach of the Executive Agreement ...

IV.

Although we have concluded that the IEEPA [the International Economic Emergency Act] constitutes specific congressional authorization to the President to nullify the attachments and order the transfer of Iranian assets, there remains the question of the President's authority to suspend claims pending in American courts. Such claims have, of course, an existence apart from the attachments which accompanied them. In terminating these claims through Executive Order No. 12294, the President purported to act under authority of both the IEEPA and 22 U.S.C. § 1732, the so-called "Hostage Act." 1 46 Fed. Reg. 14111 (1981).

We conclude that although the IEEPA authorized the nullification of the attachments, it cannot be read to authorize the suspension of the claims. The claims of American citizens against Iran are not in themselves transactions involving Iranian property or efforts to exercise any rights with respect to such property. An *in personam* lawsuit, although it might eventually be reduced to judgment and that judgment might be executed upon, is an effort to establish liability and fix damages and does not focus on any particular property within the jurisdiction. The terms of the IEEPA therefore do not authorize the President to suspend claims in American courts.

[Similarly, the Hostage Act does not authorize the President to suspend the claims.]

Although we have declined to conclude that the IEEPA or the Hostage Act directly authorizes the President's suspension of claims for the reasons noted, we cannot ignore the general tenor of Congress' legislation in this area in trying to determine whether the President is acting alone or at least with the acceptance of Congress. As we have noted, Congress cannot anticipate and legislate with regard to every possible action the President may find it necessary to take or every possible situation in which he might act....

Not infrequently in affairs between nations, outstanding claims by nationals of one country against the government of another country are "sources of friction" between the two sovereigns. *United States v. Pink,* 315 U.S. 203, 225 (1942). To resolve these difficulties, nations have often entered into agreements settling the claims of their respective nationals. As one treatise writer puts it, international agreements settling claims by nationals of one state against the government of another "are established international practice reflecting traditional international theory." L. Henkin, Foreign Affairs and the Constitution 262 (1972). Consistent with that principle, the United States has repeatedly exercised its sovereign authority to settle the claims of its nationals against foreign countries. Though those settlements have sometimes been made by treaty, there has also been a longstanding practice of settling such claims by executive agreement without the advice and consent of the Senate. Under such agreements, the President has agreed to renounce or extinguish claims of United States nationals against foreign governments in return for lump-sum payments or the establishment of arbitration procedures.... It is clear that the practice of settling claims continues today. Since 1952, the President has entered into at least 10 binding settlements with foreign nations, including an $80 million settlement with the People's Republic of China.

Crucial to our decision today is the conclusion that Congress has implicitly approved the practice of claim settlement by executive agreement. This is best demonstrated by Congress' enactment of the International Claims Settlement Act of 1949, 64 Stat. 13, as amended, 22 U.S.C. § 1621 *et seq.* (1976 ed. and Supp. IV).... By creating a procedure to implement future settlement agreements, Congress placed its stamp of approval on such agreements....

In addition to congressional acquiescence in the President's power to settle claims, prior cases of this Court have also recognized that the President does have some measure of power to enter into executive agreements without obtaining the advice and consent of the Senate. In *United States v. Pink,* 315 U.S. 203 (1942), for example, the Court upheld the validity of the Litvinov Assignment, which was part of an Executive Agreement whereby the Soviet Union assigned to the United States amounts owed to it by American nationals so that outstanding claims of other American nationals could be paid. The Court explained that the resolution of such claims was integrally connected with normalizing United States' relations with a foreign state....

[The] inferences to be drawn from the character of the legislation Congress has enacted in the area, such as the IEEPA and the Hostage Act, and from the history of acquiescence in executive claims settlement—we conclude that the President was authorized to suspend pending claims pursuant to Executive Order No. 12294.

Committee of U.S. Citizens Living in Nicaragua v. Reagan

859 F.2d 929 (D.C. Cir. 1988)

MIKVA, Circuit Judge:

Appellants, comprising organizations and individuals who oppose United States policy in Central America, claim to have suffered physical, economic and other injuries from the war in Nicaragua. These facts form the backdrop to this lawsuit.

The suit finds its genesis, however, in a 1986 decision by the International Court of Justice (ICJ), which held that America's support of military actions by the so-called "Contras" against the government of Nicaragua violated both customary international law and a treaty between the United States and Nicaragua. The ICJ concluded that the United States "is under a duty immediately to cease and to refrain from all such acts as may constitute breaches of the foregoing legal obligations." 1986 I.C.J. 14, 149. Included among those acts were the "training, arming, equipping, financing and supplying [of] the *contra* forces." *Id.* at 146.

Prior to the ICJ's decision, the United States withdrew from the merits phase of the court's proceedings, contending that the court lacked jurisdiction over Nicaragua's application. Since the decision, the President has requested and Congress has approved continued funding for the Contras of the sort that the ICJ found illegal. In addition, the U.S. used its veto power in the United Nations (U.N.) Security Council to block consideration of a resolution enforcing the ICJ decision.

Unhappy with their government's failure to abide by the ICJ decision and believing that continued funding of the Contras injures their own interests, appellants filed suit in the United States District Court for the District of Columbia. The suit sought injunctive and declaratory relief against the funding of the Contras on grounds that such funding violates the Administrative Procedure Act, the first and fifth amendments of the United States Constitution, Article 94 of the U.N. Charter, and customary international law.

* * *

B. Appellants Have No Basis in Domestic Law for Enforcing the ICJ Judgment

1. *The status of international law in the United States' domestic legal order*

Appellants argue that the United States' decision to disregard the ICJ judgment and to continue funding the Contras violates three types of international law. First, contravention of the ICJ judgment is said to violate part of a United States treaty, namely Article 94 of the U.N. Charter. That article provides that "[e]ach Member of the United Nations undertakes to comply with the decision of the International Court of Justice in any case to which it is a party." U.N. Charter art. 94. Second, disregard of the ICJ judgment allegedly violates principles of customary international law. One such principle holds that treaties in force shall be observed. Appellants contend that another such principle requires parties to ICJ decisions to adhere to those decisions. Third, the United States may have violated peremptory norms of international law. Such norms, often referred to as *jus cogens* (or "compelling law"), enjoy the highest status in international law and prevail over both customary international law and treaties. Appellants' contention that the United States has violated *jus cogens* forms their primary argument before this court. They contend that the obligation of parties to an ICJ judgment to obey that judgment is not merely a customary rule but actually a peremptory norm of international law.

For purposes of the present lawsuit, the key question is not simply whether the United States has violated any of these three legal norms but whether such violations can be remedied by an American court or whether they can only be redressed on an international level. In short, do violations of international law have domestic legal consequences? The answer largely depends on what form the "violation" takes. Here, the alleged violation is the law that Congress enacted and that the President signed, appropriating funds for the Contras. When our government's two political branches, acting together, contravene an international legal norm, does this court have any authority to remedy the violation? The answer is "no" if the type of international obligation that Congress and the President violate is either a treaty or a rule of customary international law. If, on the other hand, Congress and the President violate a peremptory norm (or *jus cogens*), the domestic legal consequences are unclear. We need not resolve this uncertainty, however, for we find that the principles appellants characterize as peremptory norms of international law are not recognized as such by the community of nations.

* * *

Our conclusion is strengthened when we consider those few norms that arguably do meet the stringent criteria for jus cogens. The recently revised Restatement acknowledges two categories of such norms: "the principles of the United Nations Charter prohibiting the use of force," Restatement s 102 comment k, and fundamental human rights law that prohibits genocide, slavery, murder, torture, prolonged arbitrary detention, and racial discrimination. Id. § 702 & comment n; see also Randall, Universal Jurisdiction Under International Law, 66 Tex.L.Rev. 785, 830 (1988); Whiteman, Jus Cogens In International Law, With a Projected List, 7 Ga. J. Int'l & Comp.L. 609, 625–26 (1977). But see Restatement § 331 comment e (doctrine of jus cogens is of such "uncertain scope" that a "domestic court should not on its own authority refuse to give effect to an agreement on the ground that it violates a peremptory norm").

Such basic norms of international law as the proscription against murder and slavery may well have the domestic legal effect that appellants suggest. That is, they may well restrain our government in the same way that the Constitution restrains it. If Congress adopted a foreign policy that resulted in the enslavement of our citizens or of other individuals, that policy might well be subject to challenge in domestic court under international law. Such a conclusion was indeed implicit in the landmark decision in *Filartiga v. Pena-Irala*, 630 F.2d 876 (2d Cir.1980), which upheld jurisdiction over a suit by a Paraguayan citizen against a Paraguayan police chief for the death by torture of the plaintiff's brother. The court concluded that "official torture is now prohibited by the law of nations." Id. at 884 (footnote omitted). The same point has been echoed in our own court. Judge Edwards observed in *Tel-Oren v. Libyan Arab Republic*, 726 F.2d 774 (D.C.Cir.1984), cert. denied, 470 U.S. 1003, 105 S.Ct. 1354, 84 L.Ed.2d 377 (1985), that "commentators have begun to identify a handful of heinous actions—each of which violates definable, universal and obligatory norms," id. at 781 (Edwards, J., concurring), and that these include, at a minimum, bans on governmental "torture, summary execution, genocide, and slavery." Id. at 791 ... ; see also *Letelier v. Republic of Chile*, 488 F.Supp. 665 (D.D.C.1980) (upholding jurisdiction over claim that foreign government brought about assassination of its own citizen living in the United States, in violation of international law and the U.S. Constitution).

We think it clear, however, that the harm that results when a government disregards or contravenes an ICJ judgment does not generate the level of universal disapprobation aroused by torture, slavery, summary execution, or genocide. Appellants try to bootstrap the ICJ's judgment against the United States into a form of jus cogens by pointing out that the judgment relies on a peremptory norm of international law—that is, that the ICJ invoked the norm proscribing aggressive use of force between nations when it rendered its decision in the Nicaragua case. This argument, however, confuses the judgment itself with the ICJ's rationale for that judgment. The gravamen of appellants' complaint is that compliance with an ICJ judgment is a nonderogable norm of international law, not that a particular judgment constitutes collateral estoppel against the United States as to its violation of a nonderogable norm. Were appellants to advance the latter contention, they would be applying nonmutual, offensive collateral estoppel against the federal government, which generally is not permitted even in domestic law cases, see *United States v. Mendoza*, 464 U.S. 154, 104 S.Ct. 568, 78 L.Ed.2d 379 (1984), much less in international law cases where our government disputes the prior court's jurisdiction. In sum, appellants' attempt to enjoin funding of the Contras on the ground that it violates a peremptory norm of international law by contravening an ICJ judgment is unavailing. The ICJ judgment does not represent such a peremptory norm....

Medellín v. Texas*

552 U.S. 491 (2008)

CHIEF JUSTICE ROBERTS delivered the opinion of the Court.

* * *

II. Medellín first contends that the ICJ's judgment in *Avena* constitutes a "binding" obligation on the state and federal courts of the United States. He argues that "by virtue of the Supremacy Clause, the treaties requiring compliance with the *Avena* judgment are *already* the 'Law of the Land' by which all state and federal courts in this country are 'bound.'" Reply Brief for Petitioner 1. Accordingly, Medellín argues, *Avena* is a binding federal rule of decision that pre-empts contrary state limitations on successive habeas petitions.

No one disputes that the *Avena* decision—a decision that flows from the treaties through which the United States submitted to ICJ jurisdiction with respect to Vienna Convention disputes—constitutes an *international* law obligation on the part of the United States. But not all international law obligations automatically constitute binding federal law enforceable in United States courts. The question we confront here is whether the *Avena* judgment has automatic *domestic* legal effect such that the judgment of its own force applies in state and federal courts.

This Court has long recognized the distinction between treaties that automatically have effect as domestic law, and those that—while they constitute international law commitments—do not by themselves function as binding federal law. The distinction was well explained by Chief Justice Marshall's opinion in *Foster v. Neilson*, 2 Pet. 253, 315 (1829), overruled on other grounds, *United States v. Percheman*, 7 Pet. 51 (1833), which held that a treaty is "equivalent to an act of the legislature," and hence self-executing, when it "operates of itself without the aid of any legislative provision." *Foster, supra,* at 314. When, in contrast, "[treaty] stipulations are not self-executing they can only be enforced pursuant to legislation to carry them into effect." *Whitney v. Robertson*, 124 U.S. 190, 194 (1888). In sum, while treaties "may comprise international commitments ... they are not domestic law unless Congress has either enacted implementing statutes or the treaty itself conveys an intention that it be 'self-executing' and is ratified on these terms."

* * *

A. The interpretation of a treaty, like the interpretation of a statute, begins with its text. *Air France v. Saks*, 470 U.S. 392, 396–397 (1985). Because a treaty ratified by the United States is "an agreement among sovereign powers," we have also considered as "aids to its interpretation" the negotiation and drafting history of the treaty as well as "the post ratification understanding" of signatory nations. *Zicherman v. Korean Air Lines Co.*, 516 U.S. 217, 226 (1996); see also *United States v. Stuart*, 489 U.S. 353, 365–366 (1989); *Choctaw Nation v. United States*, 318 U.S. 423, 431–432 (1943).

As a signatory to the Optional Protocol, the United States agreed to submit disputes arising out of the Vienna Convention to the ICJ. The Protocol provides: "Disputes arising out of the interpretation or application of the [Vienna] Convention shall lie within the compulsory jurisdiction of the International Court of Justice." Art. I, 21 U.S.T., at

* Footnotes omitted.

326. Of course, submitting to jurisdiction and agreeing to be bound are two different things. A party could, for example, agree to compulsory nonbinding arbitration. Such an agreement would require the party to appear before the arbitral tribunal without obligating the party to treat the tribunal's decision as binding. See, *e.g.*, North American Free Trade Agreement, U.S.-Can.-Mex., Art. 2018(1), Dec. 17, 1992, 32 I. L. M. 605, 697 (1993) ("On receipt of the final report of [the arbitral panel requested by a Party to the agreement], the disputing Parties shall agree on the resolution of the dispute, which normally shall conform with the determinations and recommendations of the panel").

The most natural reading of the Optional Protocol is as a bare grant of jurisdiction. It provides only that "[d]isputes arising out of the interpretation or application of the [Vienna] Convention shall lie within the compulsory jurisdiction of the International Court of Justice" and "may accordingly be brought before the [ICJ] ... by any party to the dispute being a Party to the present Protocol." Art. I, 21 U.S.T., at 326. The Protocol says nothing about the effect of an ICJ decision and does not itself commit signatories to comply with an ICJ judgment. The Protocol is similarly silent as to any enforcement mechanism.

The obligation on the part of signatory nations to comply with ICJ judgments derives not from the Optional Protocol, but rather from Article 94 of the United Nations Charter—the provision that specifically addresses the effect of ICJ decisions. Article 94(1) provides that "[e]ach Member of the United Nations *undertakes to comply* with the decision of the [ICJ] in any case to which it is a party." 59 Stat. 1051 (emphasis added). The Executive Branch contends that the phrase "undertakes to comply" is not "an acknowledgement that an ICJ decision will have immediate legal effect in the courts of U.N. members," but rather "a *commitment* on the part of U.N. Members to take *future* action through their political branches to comply with an ICJ decision." Brief for United States as *Amicus Curiae* in *Medellín I*, O. T. 2004, No. 04-5928, p. 34.

We agree with this construction of Article 94. The Article is not a directive to domestic courts. It does not provide that the United States "shall" or "must" comply with an ICJ decision, nor indicate that the Senate that ratified the U.N. Charter intended to vest ICJ decisions with immediate legal effect in domestic courts. Instead, "[t]he words of Article 94 ... call upon governments to take certain action." *Committee of United States Citizens Living in Nicaragua v. Reagan*, 859 F. 2d 929, 938 (CADC 1988) (quoting *Diggs v. Richardson*, 555 F. 2d 848, 851 (CADC 1976); internal quotation marks omitted)....

The remainder of Article 94 confirms that the U.N. Charter does not contemplate the automatic enforceability of ICJ decisions in domestic courts.6 Article 94(2)—the enforcement provision—provides the sole remedy for noncompliance: referral to the United Nations Security Council by an aggrieved state....

("[I]f a state fails to perform its obligations under a judgment of the [ICJ], the other party may have recourse to the Security Council") ... (statement of Leo Paslovsky, Special Assistant to the Secretary of State for International Organizations and Security Affairs) ("[W]hen the Court has rendered a judgment and one of the parties refuses to accept it, then the dispute becomes political rather than legal. It is as a political dispute that the matter is referred to the Security Council") ...

If ICJ judgments were instead regarded as automatically enforceable domestic law, they would be immediately and directly binding on state and federal courts pursuant to the Supremacy Clause. Mexico or the ICJ would have no need to proceed to the Security Council to enforce the judgment in this case. Noncompliance with an ICJ judgment through exercise of the Security Council veto—always regarded as an option by the Executive and ratifying Senate during and after consideration of the U.N. Charter, Optional Protocol, and ICJ Statute—would no longer be a viable alternative. There would be nothing to veto. In light of the U.N. Charter's remedial scheme, there is no reason to believe that the President and Senate signed up for such a result.

In sum, Medellín's view that ICJ decisions are automatically enforceable as domestic law is fatally undermined by the enforcement structure established by Article 94. His construction would eliminate the option of noncompliance contemplated by Article 94(2), undermining the ability of the political branches to determine whether and how to comply with an ICJ judgment....

Neither Medellín nor his *amici* have identified a single nation that treats ICJ judgments as binding in domestic courts....

Medellín and the dissent cite *Comegys v. Vasse,* 1 Pet. 193 (1828), for the proposition that the judgments of international tribunals are automatically binding on domestic courts. See *post,* at 9; Reply Brief for Petitioner 2; Brief for Petitioner 19–20. That case, of course, involved a different treaty than the ones at issue here; it stands only for the modest principle that the terms of a treaty control the outcome of a case. We do not suggest that treaties can never afford binding domestic effect to international tribunal judgments—only that the U.N. Charter, the Optional Protocol, and the ICJ Statute do not do so. And whether the treaties underlying a judgment are self-executing so that the judgment is directly enforceable as domestic law in our courts is, of course, a matter for this Court to decide....

Our holding does not call into question the ordinary enforcement of foreign judgments or international arbitral agreements. Indeed, we agree with Medellín that, as a general matter, "an agreement to abide by the result" of an international adjudication—or what he really means, an agreement to give the result of such adjudication domestic legal effect—can be a treaty obligation like any other, so long as the agreement is consistent with the Constitution. See Brief for Petitioner 20. The point is that the particular treaty obligations on which Medellín relies do not of their own force create domestic law....

[Justice Stevens concurred in the result.]

JUSTICE BREYER, with whom JUSTICE SOUTER and JUSTICE GINSBURG join, dissenting.

The Constitution's Supremacy Clause provides that "all Treaties ... which shall be made ... under the Authority of the United States, shall be the supreme Law of the Land; and the Judges in every State shall be bound thereby." Art. VI, cl. 2. The Clause means that the "courts" must regard "a treaty ... as equivalent to an act of the legislature, whenever it operates of itself without the aid of any legislative provision." *Foster v. Neilson*, 2 Pet. 253, 314 (1829) (majority opinion of Marshall, C. J.).

In the *Avena* case the International Court of Justice (ICJ) (interpreting and applying the Vienna Convention on Consular Relations) issued a judgment that requires the United States to reexamine certain criminal proceedings in the cases of 51 Mexican nationals. *Case Concerning Avena and Other Mexican Nationals (Mex. v. U.S.)*, 2004 I. C. J. 12 (Judgment of Mar. 31) *(Avena)*. The question here is whether the ICJ's *Avena* judgment is enforceable now as a matter of domestic law, *i.e.*, whether it "operates of itself without the aid" of any further legislation.

The United States has signed and ratified a series of treaties obliging it to comply with ICJ judgments in cases in which it has given its consent to the exercise of the ICJ's adjudicatory authority. Specifically, the United States has agreed to submit, in this kind of case, to the ICJ's "compulsory jurisdiction" for purposes of "compulsory settlement." Optional Protocol Concerning the Compulsory Settlement of Disputes (Optional Protocol or Protocol), Art. I, Apr. 24, 1963, [1970] 21 U.S.T. 325, 326 T.I.A.S. No. 6820 (capitalization altered). And it agreed that the ICJ's judgments would have "binding force ... between the parties and in respect of [a] particular case." United Nations Charter, Art. 59, 59 Stat. 1062, T. S. No. 993 (1945). President Bush has determined that domestic courts should enforce this particular ICJ judgment. Memorandum to the Attorney General (Feb. 28, 2005), App. to Pet. for Cert. 187a (hereinafter President's Memorandum). And Congress has done nothing to suggest the contrary. Under these circumstances, I believe the treaty obligations, and hence the judgment, resting as it does upon the consent of the United States to the ICJ's jurisdiction, bind the courts no less than would "an act of the [federal] legislature." ...

Of particular relevance to the present case, the Court has held that the United States may be obligated by treaty to comply with the judgment of an international tribunal interpreting that treaty, despite the absence of any congressional enactment specifically requiring such compliance. See *Comegys v. Vasse,* 1 Pet. 193, 211–212, 7 L.Ed. 108 (1828) (holding that decision of tribunal rendered pursuant to a United States-Spain treaty, which obliged the parties to "undertake to make satisfaction" of treaty-based rights, was "conclusive and final" and "not re-examinable" in American courts); see also *Meade v. United States,* 9 Wall. 691, 725, 19 L.Ed. 687 (1870) (holding that decision of tribunal adjudicating claims arising under United States-Spain treaty "was final and conclusive, and bar[red] a recovery upon the merits" in American court).

All of these cases make clear that self-executing treaty provisions are not uncommon or peculiar creatures of our domestic law; that they cover a wide range of subjects; that the Supremacy Clause itself answers the self-execution question by applying many, but not all, treaty provisions directly to the States; and that the Clause answers the self-execution question differently than does the law in many other nations. See *supra,* at 1354–1357. The cases also provide criteria that help determine *which* provisions automatically so apply....

Mexico claimed that state authorities within the United States had failed to notify the arrested persons of their Vienna Convention rights and, by applying state procedural law in a manner which did not give full effect to the Vienna Convention rights, had deprived them of an appropriate remedy. *Ibid.* The ICJ judgment in *Avena* requires that the United States reexamine "by means of its own choosing" certain aspects of the relevant state criminal proceedings of 51 of these individual Mexican nationals....

[I]n accepting Article 94(1) of the Charter,"[e]ach Member ... undertakes to comply with the decision" of the ICJ "in any case to which it is a party." 59 Stat. 1051. And the ICJ Statute (part of the U.N. Charter) makes clear that, a decision of the ICJ between parties that have consented to the ICJ's compulsory jurisdiction has "*binding force* ... between the parties and in respect of that particular case." Art. 59, *id.,* at 1062 (emphasis added). Enforcement of a court's judgment that has "binding force" involves quintessential judicial activity....

[I]nsofar as today's holdings make it more difficult to enforce the judgments of international tribunals, including technical non-politically-controversial judgments, those holdings weaken that rule of law for which our Constitution stands. Compare Hughes Defends Foreign Policies in Plea for Lodge, N. Y. Times, Oct. 31, 1922, p. 1, col. 1, p. 4, col. 1 (then-Secretary of State Charles Evans Hughes stating that "we favor, and always have favored, an international court of justice for the determination according to judicial standards of justiciable international disputes"); Mr. Root Discusses International Problems, N. Y. Times, July 9, 1916, section 6, book review p. 276 (former Secretary of State and U.S. Senator Elihu Root stating that "'a court of international justice with a general obligation to submit all justiciable questions to its jurisdiction and to abide by its judgment is a primary requisite to any real restraint of law'"); Mills, The Obligation of the United States Toward the World Court, 114 Annals of the American Academy of Political and Social Science 128 (1924) (Congressman Ogden Mills describing the efforts of then-Secretary of State John Hay, and others, to establish a World Court, and the support therefor).

These institutional considerations make it difficult to reconcile the majority's holdings with the workable Constitution that the Founders envisaged. They reinforce the importance, in practice and in principle, of asking Chief Justice Marshall's question: Does a treaty provision address the "Judicial" Branch rather than the "Political Branches" of Government. See *Foster*, 2 Pet., at 314. And they show the wisdom of the well-established precedent that indicates that the answer to the question here is "yes."

* * *

V. In sum, a strong line of precedent, likely reflecting the views of the Founders, indicates that the treaty provisions before us and the judgment of the International Court of Justice address themselves to the Judicial Branch and consequently are self-executing. In reaching a contrary conclusion, the Court has failed to take proper account of that precedent and, as a result, the Nation may well break its word even though the President seeks to live up to that word and Congress has done nothing to suggest the contrary. For the reasons set forth, I respectfully dissent.

B. Other Issues

In addition to confronting the problem of the proper law in international public disputes, national courts will also face such issues as infringement on the foreign policy of the court's executive branch and difficulty in adjudicating cases where the evidence and witnesses may be far away. When courts fear impinging on the state's foreign policy, they may dismiss a case, citing the political question or act of state doctrines. When difficulties relative to adjudication are encountered, the court may dismiss the case on *forum non conveniens* grounds. Few prominent cases involving only states or IOs illustrate these points. Therefore, some of the examples below involve private parties in international disputes. A note at the end of the section discusses these issues specifically regarding IOs before national courts.

1. Political Question

The Political Question Doctrine is frequently used by courts to declare that actions of the state executive in breach of international law are non-justiciable.[1] The doctrine was frequently used by U.S. courts during the Viet Nam War to avoid deciding whether the war violated international law.[2] French courts invoked the political question doctrine to

---

1. Benedetto Conforti, International Law and the Role of Domestic Legal Systems 14 (Rene Provost trans., 1993).

2. There were more than 70 decisions related to the Viet Nam War. *Id.* at 25.

prevent a decision on the legality under international law of a sixty-mile exclusion zone established during nuclear testing on Mururoa.[3]

Liechtenstein brought a case against Germany in the ICJ when German courts refused to hear a claim by Prince Hans Adam II to title to a painting on display in a public gallery in Cologne, Germany, loaned by the Czech Republic.[4] Liechtenstein argued that in an earlier case brought in the German courts to claim title to a painting on loan to a German museum by the Czech Republic, the German courts had denied it justice by refusing to hear the case. The ICJ described the decision of the German courts. The ICJ's description is of a national court avoiding a political question.

Case Concerning Certain Property (*Liechtenstein v. Germany*)

Preliminary Objections
2005 I.C.J. 6 (Feb. 10)

13. During the Second World War Czechoslovakia was an allied country and a belligerent in the war against Germany. In 1945, it adopted a series of decrees (the "Beneš Decrees"), among them Decree No. 12 of 21 June 1945, under which "agricultural property" of "all persons belonging to the German and Hungarian people, regardless of their nationality" was confiscated. Under the terms of this Decree, "agricultural property" included, *inter alia*, buildings, installations and movable property pertaining thereto. The properties confiscated under Decree No. 12 comprised some owned by Liechtenstein nationals, including Prince Franz Josef II of Liechtenstein. These measures were contested by Prince Franz Josef II in his personal capacity before the Administrative Court in Bratislava. On 21 November 1951, it held that the confiscations of the property of the Prince of Liechtenstein were lawful under the law of Czechoslovakia.

14. Following earlier Allied enactments concerning a reparations régime in general and German external assets and other property seized in connection with the Second World War in particular, a special régime dealing with the latter subject was created by Chapter Six of the Convention on the Settlement of Matters Arising out of the War and the Occupation, signed by the United States of America, the United Kingdom, France and the Federal Republic of Germany, at Bonn on 26 May 1952 (as amended by Schedule IV to the Protocol on the Termination of the Occupation Regime in the Federal Republic of Germany, signed at Paris on 23 October 1954) (hereinafter referred to as the "Settlement Convention"). This Convention entered into force on 5 May 1955.

Article 3 of Chapter Six of the Settlement Convention read as follows:

> "1. The Federal Republic shall in the future raise no objections against the measures which have been, or will be, carried out with regard to German external assets or other property, seized for the purpose of reparation or restitution, or as a result of the state of war, or on the basis of agreements concluded, or to be concluded, by the Three Powers with other Allied countries, neutral countries or former allies of Germany.

---

3. *Id.* at 16.
4. *See* Case Concerning Certain Property (Liech. v. Ger.), 2005 I.C.J. 6 (Feb. 10).

* * *

> 3. No claim or action shall be admissible against persons who shall have acquired or transferred title to property on the basis of the measures referred to in paragraph 1 and 2 of this Article, or against international organizations, foreign governments or persons who have acted upon instructions of such organizations or governments."

Article 5 of Chapter Six of the Settlement Convention provided that:

> "The Federal Republic shall ensure that the former owners of property seized pursuant to the measures referred to in Articles 2 and 3 of this Chapter shall be compensated."

15. The régime of the Settlement Convention was intended to be temporary until the problem of reparation was finally settled "by the peace treaty between Germany and its former enemies or by earlier agreements concerning this matter" (Article 1 of Chapter Six). A final settlement was brought about through the conclusion in 1990 of the Treaty on the Final Settlement with respect to Germany (signed at Moscow on 12 September 1990 and entered into force on 15 March 1991). The parties to this Treaty were the four former Occupying Powers, the Federal Republic of Germany and the German Democratic Republic. On 27 and 28 September 1990, an Exchange of Notes was executed between the three Western Powers and the Government of the Federal Republic of Germany (the parties to the Settlement Convention) under which that Convention would terminate simultaneously with the entry into force of the Treaty. Whereas that Exchange of Notes terminated the Settlement Convention itself, including Article 5 of Chapter Six (relating to compensation by Germany), it provided that paragraphs 1 and 3 of Article 3, Chapter Six, "shall, however, remain in force".

16. In 1991, a painting by the seventeenth century Dutch artist Pieter van Laer was lent by a museum in Brno (Czechoslovakia) to a museum in Cologne (Germany) for inclusion in an exhibition. This painting had been the property of the family of the Reigning Prince of Liechtenstein since the eighteenth century; it was confiscated in 1945 by Czechoslovakia under the Beneš Decrees. The Administrative Court of Bratislava in 1951 dismissed the appeal by Prince Franz Josef II of Liechtenstein against the measures of confiscation pursuant to which his property, including the Pieter van Laer painting, had been seized (see paragraph 13 above). In 1991, Prince Hans-Adam II of Liechtenstein filed a lawsuit in the German courts in his personal capacity to have the painting sequestered and returned to him as his property (hereinafter referred to as the "*Pieter van Laer Painting case*"). The claim was dismissed by the Cologne Regional Court on 10 October 1995, by the Cologne Court of Appeal on 9 July 1996, by the Federal Court of Justice on 25 September 1997, and by the Federal Constitutional Court on 28 January 1998, on the basis that, under Article 3, Chapter Six, of the Settlement Convention, no claim or action in connection with measures taken against German external assets in the aftermath of the Second World War was admissible in German courts.

17. In 1998 Prince Hans-Adam II of Liechtenstein instituted proceedings before the European Court of Human Rights against Germany, claiming that the above decisions of the German courts violated his rights under Articles 6, paragraph 1, and 14 of the Convention for the Protection of Human Rights and Fundamental Freedoms of the Council of Europe, as well as Article 1 of Protocol No. 1 to that Convention. That Court, on 12 July 2001, held that there had been no violation of the Articles invoked by the Applicant.

18. It is recalled that in the present proceedings, Liechtenstein based the Court's jurisdiction on Article 1 of the European Convention for the Peaceful Settlement of Disputes which provides that:

> "The High Contracting Parties shall submit to the judgement of the International Court of Justice all international legal disputes which may arise between them including, in particular, those concerning:
>
> *(a)* the interpretation of a treaty;
>
> *(b)* any question of international law;
>
> *(c)* the existence of any fact which, if established, would constitute a breach of an international obligation;
>
> *(d)* the nature or extent of the reparation to be made for the breach of an international obligation."

Article 27 *(a)* of the European Convention for the Peaceful Settlement of Disputes reads as follows:

> "The provisions of this Convention shall not apply to:
>
> *(a)* disputes relating to facts or situations prior to the entry into force of this Convention as between the parties to the dispute."

19. Germany has raised six preliminary objections to the jurisdiction of the Court and to the admissibility of Liechtenstein's Application. According to the first objection put forward by Germany, there exists no dispute between Liechtenstein and Germany within the meaning of the Statute of the Court and Article 27 of the European Convention for the Peaceful Settlement of Disputes. In its second objection, Germany argues that all the relevant facts occurred before the entry into force of the European Convention for the Peaceful Settlement of Disputes as between the Parties. Germany contends in its third objection that the European Convention for the Peaceful Settlement of Disputes has no application because the acts on which Liechtenstein bases its claims fall within the domestic jurisdiction of Germany. In its fourth objection, Germany submits that Liechtenstein's claims have not been sufficiently substantiated as required by Article 40, paragraph 1, of the Statute of the Court and Article 38, paragraph 2, of the Rules of Court. Germany argues in its fifth objection that adjudication of Liechtenstein's claims would require the Court to pass judgment on rights and obligations of the successor States of the former Czechoslovakia, in particular the Czech Republic, in their absence and without their consent. Finally, according to Germany's sixth objection, the alleged Liechtenstein victims of the measures of confiscation carried out by Czechoslovakia have failed to exhaust the available local remedies.

In its written observations and final submissions during the oral proceedings, Liechtenstein requested the Court to reject Germany's preliminary objections in their entirety.

20. The Court will now consider Germany's first objection that there is no dispute between itself and Liechtenstein.

21. Germany argues that there is no dispute between the Parties. Germany in particular observes that even though the facts that are at the core of the dispute lie in Czechoslovakia's seizure of certain Liechtenstein property under the Beneš Decrees of 1945, Liechtenstein bases its claims before the Court on an alleged "change of position" by Germany in the 1990s as to the need to apply the Settlement Convention to that property, whilst Germany contends that such a change has never occurred. Germany maintains that a distinction is to be made between the issue of the lawfulness of the Czechoslovak expropri-

ations and that of the jurisdiction of the German courts regarding this matter. Germany contends that on neither issue has it changed its position either before or after 1995: as to the first, it has never accepted the validity of the relevant Czechoslovak measures against Liechtenstein property; as to the second, the German courts have always held that they are barred by the Settlement Convention from adjudicating on the lawfulness of confiscation measures, and for the purposes of the application of Article 3 of Chapter Six of the Settlement Convention, they have always relied on the assessment of the expropriating State.

Germany further claims that it is not German acts related to Czechoslovak confiscations but the lawfulness of the Czechoslovak measures as such and the resulting obligations of compensation on the part of the successor States to the former Czechoslovakia that are in question. Even if all the factual statements by Liechtenstein were correct, they would not justify a claim to compensation against Germany; "[i]ssues of compensation are to be decided between the State confiscating foreign property and the State victim of such measures."

Germany therefore concludes that the only dispute which exists is one between Liechtenstein and the successor States of the former Czechoslovakia.

22. Liechtenstein maintains that its dispute with Germany concerns Germany's position, whereby for the first time in 1995 it began to treat Liechtenstein assets as German external assets for purposes of the Settlement Convention, thus infringing Liechtenstein's neutrality and sovereignty. Liechtenstein also asserts that on numerous occasions since 1995 it has made its legal position known to the German Government, and on each occasion has met with opposition. This opposition, and the opposition of views on the question of whether or not there has been a change of position by the German Government with regard to Liechtenstein property, itself clearly evidences a dispute.

Liechtenstein recognizes the existence of another dispute, one between itself and the Czech Republic, but observes that this does not negate the existence of a separate dispute between itself and Germany, based on Germany's unlawful conduct in relation to Liechtenstein.

23. Liechtenstein contends further that Germany itself acknowledged the existence of the dispute between them. Liechtenstein thus submits that Germany recognized the existence of the Liechtenstein claims and a divergence of legal opinions over these claims, both in the course of bilateral consultations held in July 1998 and June 1999, and in a letter from the German Minister for Foreign Affairs to his Liechtenstein counterpart dated 20 January 2000. This letter stated that "[i]t [was] known that the German Government [did] not share the legal opinion" of the Government of Liechtenstein and "[did] not see a possibility to make compensation payments to the Principality of Liechtenstein for losses of property suffered as a result of post-war expropriations in former Czechoslovakia" as those measures "[could not] be attributed to Germany on a constructive legal basis."

For its part, Germany denies that it acknowledged the existence of a dispute by participating in diplomatic consultations at the request of Liechtenstein. It argues that a discussion of divergent legal opinions should not be considered as evidence of the existence of a dispute in the sense of the Court's Statute "before it reaches a certain threshold."

* * *

24. According to the consistent jurisprudence of the Court and the Permanent Court of International Justice, a dispute is a disagreement on a point of law or fact, a conflict of legal views or interests between parties (see *Mavrommatis Palestine Concessions, Judgment No. 2, 1924, P.C.I.J., Series A, No. 2, p. 11; Northern Cameroons, Judgment, I.C.J.*

Reports 1963, p. 27; Applicability of the Obligation to Arbitrate under Section 21 of the United Nations Headquarters Agreement of 26 June 1947, Advisory Opinion, I.C.J. Reports 1988, p. 27, para. 35; *East Timor, Judgment, I.C.J. Reports 1995*, pp. 99–100, para. 22). Moreover, for the purposes of verifying the existence of a legal dispute it falls to the Court to determine whether "the claim of one party is positively opposed by the other" (*South West Africa, Preliminary Objections, Judgment, I.C.J. Reports* 1962, p. 328).

25. The Court recalls that Liechtenstein has characterized its dispute with Germany as involving the violation of its sovereignty and neutrality by the Respondent, which, for the first time in 1995, treated Liechtenstein property confiscated under the Beneš Decrees as German external assets for the purposes of the Settlement Convention, notwithstanding Liechtenstein's status as a neutral State. Germany for its part denies altogether the existence of a dispute with Liechtenstein. It asserts instead that "the subject-matter of this case" is the confiscation by Czechoslovakia in 1945 of Liechtenstein property without compensation; Germany considers further that, in the case of Liechtenstein, German courts simply applied their consistent case law to what were deemed German external assets under the Settlement Convention. The Court thus finds that in the present proceedings complaints of fact and law formulated by Liechtenstein against Germany are denied by the latter. In conformity with well-established jurisprudence (see paragraph 24 above), the Court concludes that "[b]y virtue of this denial, there is a legal dispute" between Liechtenstein and Germany (*East Timor (Portugal v. Australia), I.C.J. Reports 1995*, p. 100, para. 22; *Application of the Convention on the Prevention and Punishment of the Crime of Genocide, Preliminary Objections, Judgment, I.C.J. Reports 1996*, p. 615, para. 29). The Court further notes that Germany's position taken in the course of bilateral consultations and in the letter by the Minister for Foreign Affairs of 20 January 2000 has evidentiary value in support of the proposition that Liechtenstein's claims were positively opposed by Germany and that this was recognized by the latter.

26. It remains for the Court to identify the subject-matter of the dispute before it. Upon examination of the case file, the Court finds that the subject-matter of the dispute is whether, by applying Article 3, Chapter Six, of the Settlement Convention to Liechtenstein property that had been confiscated in Czechoslovakia under the Beneš Decrees in 1945, Germany was in breach of the international obligations it owed to Liechtenstein and, if so, what is Germany's international responsibility.

27. Having established the existence of a dispute between Liechtenstein and Germany and identified its subject-matter, the Court concludes that the first preliminary objection of Germany must be dismissed.

28. The Court will now examine Germany's second preliminary objection that Liechtenstein's Application should be rejected on the grounds that the Court lacks jurisdiction *ratione temporis* to decide the present dispute.

29. Germany asserts that were the Court to find that there exists a dispute, it would nevertheless fall outside the jurisdiction of the Court by virtue of Article 27 *(a)* of the European Convention for the Peaceful Settlement of Disputes (see paragraph 18 above). In its view, such a dispute would relate to facts or situations prior to 18 February 1980, the date when the European Convention for the Peaceful Settlement of Disputes entered into force between Germany and Liechtenstein. In Germany's view, the Application should therefore be rejected.

30. Germany contends that the key issue for the purpose of applying Article 27 (a) is not the date when this dispute arose, but whether the dispute relates to facts or situations that arose before or after the critical date. Only if these facts or situations took place after

the critical date, that is after 1980, would the Court have jurisdiction *ratione temporis* under Article 27 *(a)*. But since, in Germany's view, this dispute relates to facts and situations that predate 1980, the Court lacks the requisite jurisdiction.

31. Germany claims that the property of Prince Franz Joseph II of Liechtenstein, including the painting by Pieter van Laer, as well as property belonging to other Liechtenstein nationals, was seized in Czechoslovakia pursuant to the Beneš Decrees. The Settlement Convention required Germany to bar any action in its courts that sought to challenge the legality of such confiscations. In Germany's view, the lawsuit brought by Prince Hans-Adam II of Liechtenstein to recover the Pieter van Laer painting was governed by the provisions of the Settlement Convention. The dismissal of the lawsuit by various German courts, beginning with the decision of the Cologne Regional Court in 1995, acting in compliance with the provisions of that Convention, was in conformity with earlier decisions of German courts. According to Germany, its courts have consistently held that they lacked jurisdiction to evaluate the lawfulness of such confiscations. The dispute which arose in the 1990s with regard to the Pieter van Laer painting was directly related to the Settlement Convention and the Beneš Decrees; it had its real source, according to Germany, in facts and situations existing prior to the 1980 critical date.

32. Liechtenstein contends that until the decisions of the German courts in the *Pieter van Laer Painting* case, it was understood between Germany and Liechtenstein that Liechtenstein property confiscated pursuant to the Beneš Decrees could not be deemed to have been covered by the Settlement Convention because of Liechtenstein's neutrality. German courts would therefore not be barred by that Convention from passing on the lawfulness of these confiscations. In Liechtenstein's view, the decisions of the German courts in the 1990s with regard to the painting made clear that Germany no longer adhered to that shared view, and thus amounted to a change of position. It mattered not, according to Liechtenstein, whether the decisions in that case marked a change as such in Germany's position or whether Germany was now applying its earlier case law to a new situation.

33. Liechtenstein maintains, *inter alia*, that, in so far as there was a change of position by Germany, the decisions of the German courts in the *Pieter van Laer Painting* case and the "positions taken by the German Government, in the period after 1995" gave rise to the present dispute. In these decisions and positions, Germany made clear for the first time that it regarded Liechtenstein property as coming within the scope of the reparations régime of the Settlement Convention (see paragraph 14 above). These were the facts with regard to which the dispute arose. Prior thereto there was no dispute between Liechtenstein and Germany. The facts that triggered the present dispute were therefore not the Settlement Convention or the Beneš Decrees, but Germany's decision in 1995 to apply the Settlement Convention to Liechtenstein property.

34. The foregoing conclusion, Liechtenstein argues, accords with the legal test for temporal jurisdiction applied by the Permanent Court of International Justice and by this Court, which is relevant to the interpretation of Article 27 *(a)* of the European Convention for the Peaceful Settlement of Disputes in this case. In Liechtenstein's view, the *Phosphates in Morocco* case makes clear that the limits of temporal jurisdiction are to be construed not by looking at the source of the obligation said to have been violated or at the surrounding factual situation, but by focusing on the fact with regard to which the dispute arose, that is, the "fait générateur" of the dispute. According to Liechtenstein, the Permanent Court of International Justice adopted that same approach in the *Electricity Company of Sofia and Bulgaria* case, where it "distinguish[ed] between the source of the rights relied on by the Claimant and the source of the dispute; what matters is the point at which the rights are denied". Liechtenstein further contends that, as the *Right of Pas-*

sage Case indicates, it is only when the "parties 'adopt clearly-defined legal positions' that the dispute arises, and it arises in relation to the triggering event, not the whole legal and factual matrix against the background of which the event is to be understood."

35. Germany submits that, contrary to Liechtenstein's allegations, there was "no change of position" by Germany because the judicial decisions in the 1990s did not depart from prior German case law on the subject. In Germany's view, there are thus no facts or legal situations that took place subsequent to the entry into force between the parties of the European Convention for the Peaceful Settlement of Disputes to which Liechtenstein can point to establish the jurisdiction of the Court.

36. Germany also suggests that the distinction between the source of the rights claimed by one of the parties and the source of the dispute, referred to by the Permanent Court of International Justice in the *Electricity Company of Sofia and Bulgaria* case and by the International Court of Justice in the *Right of Passage* case, is of no relevance to the present case. This is so, Germany submits, because none of the legal and factual situations "which are the real cause of the alleged dispute" can be attributed to or involve acts or decisions taken after 1980; rather, they relate entirely to the legal situation created in the aftermath of the Second World War and, in particular, to "the confiscation of Liechtenstein property by Czechoslovakia in 1945 and thereafter and possible legal consequences of these confiscations."

37. A further difference, according to Germany, between the Electricity Company of Sofia and Bulgaria and the *Right of Passage case*s, on the one hand, and the present case, on the other, is that in those two cases, the legal situation existing between the parties had been fully recognized by both sides before the act or omission by one party gave rise to the dispute. In the present case, by contrast, there was prior to 1995 no similar recognition of the legal situation existing between the two States. On the contrary, Germany considers that the present case and the *Phosphates in Morocco Case* fall into the same category. In the Phosphates case, "the Court could not look into the matter because the legal situation had been exactly the same since long before the jurisdictional clause applied and no separable facts or legal situations were at issue". According to Germany, that is also the situation in the present case. Here the legal régime applied by "German courts in 1995 and later was a legal régime applicable for Germany since 1955" by virtue of the Settlement Convention.

38. Liechtenstein disagrees with Germany's interpretation of the jurisprudence applicable to this case. It argues that the temporal limitation expressed in Article 27 *(a)* of the European Convention for the Peaceful Settlement of Disputes "refers to the generating fact ... which triggers the dispute." In its view, the dispute was triggered neither by the Settlement Convention nor by the Beneš Decrees because, prior to the 1990s, that Convention had never been applied to neutral assets and thus gave rise to no dispute with neutral Liechtenstein. In Liechtenstein's view, Germany's decisions in the years from 1995 onwards were the origin and are at the heart of the present dispute. They are the facts to which the dispute relates.

39. Germany's second preliminary objection requires the Court to decide whether, applying the provisions of Article 27 *(a)* of the European Convention for the Peaceful Settlement of Disputes, the present dispute relates to facts or situations that arose before or after the 1980 critical date.

40. As recalled by the Parties (see paragraphs 34 and 36 to 38 above), this Court and the Permanent Court of International Justice have dealt with a comparable issue in a number of cases. Thus, in the *Phosphates in Morocco* case, the French declaration ac-

cepting the Permanent Court of International Justice's jurisdiction spoke of "disputes which may arise after the ratification of the present declaration with regard to situations or facts subsequent to this ratification" (*P.C.I.J., Series A/B, No. 74*, p. 22). While the parties in that case agreed that the dispute arose subsequent to the date of the French declaration, the issue that divided them concerned the date of the "situations or facts" with regard to which the dispute arose, that is, whether it was prior or subsequent to the declaration. The Court found that the subject of the dispute was the so-called "monopolization of the Moroccan phosphates" (*ibid.*, p. 25) and the inconsistency of that monopoly régime with earlier French treaty obligations. This régime was established by legislation adopted before the critical date. It was that legislation, the Court ruled, with regard to which the dispute arose.

41. In the *Electricity Company of Sofia and Bulgaria* case, the wording of the Belgian limitation *ratione temporis* was identical to the relevant language of the French declaration in the Phosphates in Morocco case. Here, too, the parties agreed that the dispute arose after the critical date, but they disagreed as to whether the "facts or situations" with regard to which the dispute arose were prior or subsequent to that date. In the *Electricity Company* case, Bulgaria argued that the awards of the Belgo-Bulgarian Mixed Arbitral Tribunal, which predated the critical date, had to be treated as the "situations" that gave rise to the dispute. The Permanent Court of International Justice rejected this argument and held that, while these awards constituted the source of the rights claimed by Belgium, they were not the source of the dispute because the parties had been in agreement throughout regarding their binding character. The Court explained this conclusion as follows:

> "A situation or fact in regard to which a dispute is said to have arisen must be the real cause of the dispute. In the present case it is the subsequent acts with which the Belgian Government reproaches the Bulgarian authorities with regard to a particular application of the formula—which in itself has never been disputed—which form the centre point of the argument and must be regarded as constituting the facts with regard to which the dispute arose." (*P.C.I.J., Series A/B*, No. 77, p. 82.)

Since these facts all took place after the critical date, the Court rejected the Bulgarian preliminary objection to its jurisdiction.

42. In the *Right of Passage* case, this Court had to deal with India's preliminary objection *ratione temporis*. The objection was based on its declaration accepting the Court's jurisdiction "over all disputes arising after 5 February 1930, with regard to situations or facts subsequent to the same date." Here the Court first found that the dispute arose in 1954, when India interfered with Portugal's alleged right of passage over Indian territory to certain Portuguese enclaves. The Court turned next to the question of the date of the situations or facts with regard to which the dispute arose. Relying on the holding of the Permanent Court of International Justice in the *Electricity Company of Sofia and Bulgaria* case, the Court emphasized that in determining the facts or situations with regard to which a dispute has arisen, only those facts or situations are relevant that can be considered as being the source of the dispute, that is, its real cause. It then made the following finding:

> "Up to 1954 the situation of those territories may have given rise to a few minor incidents, but passage had been effected without any controversy as to the title under which it was effected. It was only in 1954 that such a controversy arose and the dispute relates both to the existence of a right of passage to go into the en-

claved territories and to India's failure to comply with obligations which, according to Portugal, were binding upon it in this connection. It was from all of this that the dispute referred to the Court arose; it is with regard to all of this that the dispute exists. This whole, whatever may have been the earlier origin of one of its parts, came into existence only after 5 February 1930." (*I.C.J. Reports 1960*, p. 35.)

43. The text of Article 27 *(a)* of the European Convention for the Peaceful Settlement of Disputes (see paragraph 18 above) does not differ in substance from the temporal jurisdiction limitations dealt with in those cases. In particular, no consequence can be drawn from the use of the expressions "with regard to" or "relating to" which have been employed indifferently in the various texts in question. The Court notes further that in the *Phosphates in Morocco* case, the *Electricity Company in Sofia and Bulgaria* case and the *Right of Passage case*, the Permanent Court of International Justice and this Court were called upon to interpret unilateral declarations accepting the Court's jurisdiction under its Statute, whereas, in the present case, the Court has to interpret a multilateral Convention. Without pronouncing in any more general sense upon the extent to which such instruments are to be treated comparably, the Court finds no reason on this ground to interpret differently the phrase in issue. Nor have the Parties suggested otherwise.

Accordingly, the Court finds its previous jurisprudence on temporal limitations of relevance in the present case.

44. In interpreting the latter *ratione temporis* limitations, this Court and the Permanent Court of International Justice before it emphasized that

> "[t]he facts or situations to which regard must be had ... are those with regard to which the dispute has arisen or, in other words, as was said by the Permanent Court in the case concerning the *Electricity Company of Sofia and Bulgaria*, only 'those which must be considered as being the source of the dispute', those which are its 'real cause'" (*Right of Passage over Indian Territory, Merits, Judgment, I.C.J. Reports 1960*, p. 35).

45. Thus in the *Phosphates in Morocco* case, the facts with regard to which the dispute arose were found to be legislative measures that predated the critical date. The objection *ratione temporis* was accordingly upheld. In the *Electricity Company of Sofia and Bulgaria* and the *Right of Passage cases*, the disputes were found to have had their source in facts or situations subsequent to the critical date and thus the objections *ratione temporis* were rejected.

46. The Court considers that, in so far as it has to determine the facts or situations to which this dispute relates, the foregoing test of finding the source or real cause of the dispute is equally applicable to this case.

47. The Court will now consider whether the present dispute has its source or real cause in the facts or situations which occurred in the 1990s in Germany and, particularly, in the decisions by the German courts in the *Pieter van Laer Painting* case, or whether its source or real cause is the Beneš Decrees under which the painting was confiscated and the Settlement Convention which the German courts invoked as ground for declaring themselves without jurisdiction to hear that case.

48. The Court observes that it is not contested that the present dispute was triggered by the decisions of the German courts in the aforementioned case. This conclusion does not, however, dispose of the question the Court is called upon to decide, for under Article 27 *(a)* of the European Convention for the Peaceful Settlement of Disputes, the crit-

ical issue is not the date when the dispute arose, but the date of the facts or situations in relation to which the dispute arose.

49. In the Court's view, the present dispute could only relate to the events that transpired in the 1990s if, as argued by Liechtenstein, in this period, Germany either departed from a previous common position that the Settlement Convention did not apply to Liechtenstein property, or if German courts, by applying their earlier case law under the Settlement Convention for the first time to Liechtenstein property, applied that Convention "to a new situation" after the critical date.

50. With regard to the first alternative, the Court has no basis for concluding that prior to the decisions of the German courts in the *Pieter van Laer Painting* case, there existed a common understanding or agreement between Liechtenstein and Germany that the Settlement Convention did not apply to the Liechtenstein property seized abroad as "German external assets" for the purpose of reparation or as a result of the war. The issue whether or not the Settlement Convention applied to Liechtenstein property had not previously arisen before German courts, nor had it been dealt with prior thereto in intergovernmental talks between Germany and Liechtenstein. Moreover, German courts have consistently held that the Settlement Convention deprived them of jurisdiction to address the legality of any confiscation of property treated as German property by the confiscating State (see Judgment of the German Federal Court of Justice (*Bundesgerichtshof*) of 11 April 1960, II ZR 64/58; see also Judgment of the German Federal Court of Justice (*Bundesgerichtshof*) of 13 December 1956 (*AKU* case), II ZR 86/54). In the *Pieter van Laer Painting* case, the German courts confined themselves to stating that the Settlement Convention was applicable in cases of confiscation under Decree No. 12, as with the other Beneš Decrees, and that, consequently, it was also applicable to the confiscation of the painting. Liechtenstein's contention regarding the existence of a prior agreement or common understanding and an alleged "change of position" by Germany cannot therefore be upheld.

51. As to Liechtenstein's contention that the dispute relates to the application, for the first time, of pre-1990 German jurisprudence to Liechtenstein property in the 1990s, the Court points out that German courts did not face any "new situation" when dealing for the first time with a case concerning the confiscation of Liechtenstein property as a result of the Second World War. The Court finds that this case, like previous ones on the confiscation of German external assets, was inextricably linked to the Settlement Convention. The Court further finds that the decisions of the German courts in the *Pieter van Laer Painting* case cannot be separated from the Settlement Convention and the Beneš Decrees, and that these decisions cannot consequently be considered as the source or real cause of the dispute between Liechtenstein and Germany.

52. The Court concludes that, although these proceedings were instituted by Liechtenstein as a result of decisions by German courts regarding a painting by Pieter van Laer, these events have their source in specific measures taken by Czechoslovakia in 1945, which led to the confiscation of property owned by some Liechtenstein nationals, including Prince Franz Jozef II of Liechtenstein, as well as in the special régime created by the Settlement Convention. The decisions of the German courts in the 1990s dismissing the claim filed by Prince Hans-Adam II of Liechtenstein for the return of the painting to him were taken on the basis of Article 3, Chapter Six, of the Settlement Convention. While these decisions triggered the dispute between Liechtenstein and Germany, the source or real cause of the dispute is to be found in the Settlement Convention and the Beneš Decrees. In light of the provisions of Article 27 *(a)* of the European Convention for the Peaceful Settlement of Disputes, Germany's second preliminary objection must therefore be upheld.

53. Having dismissed the first preliminary objection of Germany, but upheld its second, the Court finds that it is not required to consider Germany's other objections and that it cannot rule on Liechtenstein's claims on the merits.

54. For these reasons,

THE COURT,

(1)

(a) by fifteen votes to one,

Rejects the preliminary objection that there is no dispute between Liechtenstein and Germany;

IN FAVOUR: *President* Shi; Vice-President Ranjeva; *Judges* Guillaume, Koroma, Vereshchetin, Higgins, Parra-Aranguren, Kooijmans, Rezek, Al-Khasawneh, Buergenthal, Elaraby, Owada, Tomka; *Judge* ad hoc Sir Franklin Berman;

AGAINST: *Judge* ad hoc Fleischhauer;

(b) by twelve votes to four,

Upholds the preliminary objection that Liechtenstein's Application should be rejected on the grounds that the Court lacks jurisdiction *ratione temporis* to decide the dispute;

IN FAVOUR: *President* Shi; *Vice-President* Ranjeva; *Judges* Guillaume, Koroma, Vereshchetin, Higgins, Parra-Aranguren, Rezek, Al-Khasawneh, Buergenthal, Tomka; *Judge* ad hoc Fleischhauer;

AGAINST: *Judges* Kooijmans, Elaraby, Owada; *Judge* ad hoc Sir Franklin Berman;

(2) by twelve votes to four,

Finds that it has no jurisdiction to entertain the Application filed by Liechtenstein on 1 June 2001.

IN FAVOUR: *President* Shi; Vice-President Ranjeva; *Judges* Guillaume, Koroma, Vereshchetin, Higgins, Parra-Aranguren, Rezek, Al-Khasawneh, Buergenthal, Tomka; *Judge* ad hoc Fleischhauer;

AGAINST: *Judges* Kooijmans, Elaraby, Owada; *Judge* ad hoc Sir Franklin Berman.

---

2. Act of State

The act of state doctrine can be viewed as the counterpart to the political question doctrine. While the latter prevents review of a state's behavior in its own court, the act of state doctrine bars judicial review of the behavior of a foreign state.[5] The bar has been applied even when the question is whether the state has violated international law. A U.S. court summarized the policy as follows:

> [T]he policy concerns underlying the doctrine require that the political branches be preeminent in the realm of foreign relations. Accordingly, the Supreme Court has directed that each case be analyzed individually to determine the need for a separation of powers: The less important the implications of an issue are for our

5. Conforti, *supra* note 2, at 20.

foreign relations, the weaker the justification for exclusivity in the political branches.[6]

The earliest record of the act of state doctrine is found in the English case *Blad v. Bamfield*.[7] Today, besides the United Kingdom, the U.S., France, Germany, Greece, Italy, The Netherlands, and Switzerland also employ the doctrine.[8]

Banco Nacional de Cuba v. Sabbatino*

376 U.S. 398 (1964)

Mr. Justice HARLAN delivered the opinion of the Court.

I. In February and July of 1960, respondent Farr, Whitlock & Co., an American commodity broker, contracted to purchase Cuban sugar, free alongside the steamer, from a wholly owned subsidiary of Compania Azucarera Vertientes-Camaguey de Cuba (C.A.V.), a corporation organized under Cuban law whose capital stock was owned principally by United States residents. Farr, Whitlock agreed to pay for the sugar in New York upon presentation of the shipping documents....

Between August 6 and August 9, 1960, the sugar covered by the contract between Farr, Whitlock and C.A.V. was loaded, destined for Morocco, onto the S.S. Hornfels, which was standing offshore at the Cuban port of Jucaro (Santa Maria). On the day loading commenced, the Cuban President and Prime Minister, acting pursuant to Law No. 851, issued Executive Power Resolution No. 1. It provided for the compulsory expropriation of all property and enterprises, and of rights and interests arising therefrom, of certain listed companies, including C.A.V., wholly or principally owned by American nationals. The preamble reiterated the alleged injustice of the American reduction of the Cuban sugar quota and emphasized the importance of Cuba's serving as an example for other countries to follow 'in their struggle to free themselves from the brutal claws of Imperialism.' In consequence of the resolution, the consent of the Cuban Government was necessary before a ship carrying sugar of a named company could leave Cuban waters. In order to obtain this consent, Farr, Whitlock, on August 11, entered into contracts, identical to those it had made with C.A.V., with the Banco Para el Comercio Exterior de Cuba, an instrumentality of the Cuban Government. The S.S. Hornfels sailed for Morocco on August 12.

Banco Exterior assigned the bills of lading to petitioner, also an instrumentality of the Cuban Government, which instructed its agent in New York, Societe Generale, to deliver the bills and a sight draft in the sum of $175,250.69 to Farr, Whitlock in return for payment. Societe Generale's initial tender of the documents was refused by Farr, Whitlock, which on the same day was notified of C.A.V.'s claim that as rightful owner of the sugar it was entitled to the proceeds. In return for a promise not to turn the funds over to pe-

---

6. Banco Nacional de Cuba v. Sabbatino, 376 U.S. 398, 401 (1964), *superseded by statute*, Pub. L. No. 99-8, 99 Stat. 21, *as recognized in* Indus. Inv. Dev. Corp. v. Mitsui & Co., 594 F.2d 48 (5th Cir. 1979). As the *Industrial Development Corp.* court noted, "Although *Sabbatino*'s bar against claims based on the asserted invalidity of Cuban confiscations has been legislatively overruled by the 'Hickenlooper Amendment,' the case is still the leading authority on the act of state doctrine." 594 F.2d at 52 n.7.

7. 3 Swan 604; 36 Eng. Rep. 992 (1674).

8. *See* Ralph H. Folsom et al., International Business Transactions (6th ed. 2000).

* Footnotes omitted.

titioner or its agent, C.A.V. agreed to indemnify Farr, Whitlock for any loss. Farr, Whitlock subsequently accepted the shipping documents, negotiated the bills of lading to its customer, and received payment for the sugar. It refused, however, to hand over the proceeds to Societe Generale. Shortly thereafter, Farr, Whitlock was served with an order of the New York Supreme Court, which had appointed Sabbatino as Temporary Receiver of C.A.V.'s New York assets, enjoining it from taking any action in regard to the money claimed by C.A.V. that might result in its removal from the State. Following this, Farr, Whitlock, pursuant to court order, transferred the funds to Sabbatino, to abide the event of a judicial determination as to their ownership....

We do not believe that [the Act of State] doctrine is compelled either by the inherent nature of sovereign authority, as some of the earlier decision seem to imply, or by some principle of international law. If a transaction takes place in one jurisdiction and the forum is in another, the forum does not by dismissing an action or by applying its own law purport to divest the first jurisdiction of its territorial sovereignty; it merely declines to adjudicate or makes applicable its own law to parties or property before it. The refusal of one country to enforce the penal laws of another is a typical example of an instance when a court will not entertain a cause of action arising in another jurisdiction. While historic notions of sovereign authority do bear upon the wisdom or employing the act of state doctrine, they do not dictate its existence.

That international law does not require application of the doctrine is evidenced by the practice of nations. Most of the countries rendering decisions on the subject fail to follow the rule rigidly. No international arbitral or judicial decision discovered suggests that international law prescribes recognition of sovereign acts of foreign governments, ... and apparently no claim has ever been raised before an international tribunal that failure to apply the act of state doctrine constitutes a breach of international obligation. If international law does not prescribe use of the doctrine, neither does it forbid application of the rule even if it is claimed that the act of state in question violated international law. The traditional view of international law is that it establishes substantive principles for determining whether one country has wronged another. Because of its peculiar nation-to-nation character the usual method for an individual to seek relief is to exhaust local remedies and then repair to the executive authorities of his own state to persuade them to champion his claim in diplomacy or before an international tribunal. Although it is, of course, true that United States courts apply international law as a part of our own in appropriate circumstances, the public law of nations can hardly dictate to a country which is in theory wronged how to treat that wrong within its domestic borders.

Despite the broad statement ... that 'The conduct of the foreign relations of our government is committed by the Constitution to the executive and legislative ... departments,' it cannot of course be thought that 'every case or controversy which touches foreign relations lies beyond judicial cognizance.' The text of the Constitution does not require the act of state doctrine; it does not irrevocably remove from the judiciary the capacity to review the validity of foreign acts of state.

The act of state doctrine does, however, have 'constitutional' underpinnings. It arises out of the basic relationships between branches of government in a system of separation of powers. It concerns the competency of dissimilar institutions to make and implement particular kinds of decisions in the area of international relations. The doctrine as formulated in past decisions expresses the strong sense of the Judicial Branch that its engagement in the task of passing on the validity of foreign acts of state may hinder rather than further this country's pursuit of goals both for itself and for the community of nations as a whole in the international sphere. Many commentators disagree with this view;

they have striven by means of distinguishing and limiting past decisions and by advancing various considerations of policy to stimulate a narrowing of the apparent scope of the rule. Whatever considerations are thought to predominate, it is plain that the problems involved are uniquely federal in nature. If federal authority, in this instance this Court, orders the field of judicial competence in this area for the federal courts, and the state courts are left free to formulate their own rules, the purposes behind the doctrine could be as effectively undermined as if there had been no federal pronouncement on the subject.

...

VI. If the act of state doctrine is a principle of decision binding on federal and state courts alike but compelled by neither international law nor the Constitution, its continuing vitality depends on its capacity to reflect the proper distribution of functions between the judicial and political branches of the Government on matters bearing upon foreign affairs. It should be apparent that the greater the degree of codification or consensus concerning a particular area of international law, the more appropriate it is for the judiciary to render decisions regarding it, since the courts can then focus on the application of an agreed principle to circumstances of fact rather than on the sensitive task of establishing a principle not inconsistent with the national interest or with international justice. It is also evident that some aspects of international law touch much more sharply on national nerves than do others; the less important the implications of an issue are for our foreign relations, the weaker the justification for exclusivity in the political branches. The balance of relevant considerations may also be shifted if the government which perpetrated the challenged act of state is no longer in existence ... for the political interest of this country may, as a result, be measurably altered. Therefore, rather than laying down or reaffirming an inflexible and all-encompassing rule in this case, we decide only that the (Judicial Branch) will not examine the validity of a taking of property within its own territory by a foreign sovereign government, extant and recognized by this country at the time of suit, in the absence of a treaty or other unambiguous agreement regarding controlling legal principles, even if the complaint alleges that the taking violates customary international law.

There are few if any issues in international law today on which opinion seems to be so divided as the limitations on a state's power to expropriate the property of aliens.

There is, of course, authority, in international judicial and arbitral decisions, in the expressions of national governments, and among commentators for the view that a taking is improper under international law if it is not for a public purpose, is discriminatory, or is without provision for prompt, adequate, and effective compensation. However, Communist countries, although they have in fact provided a degree of compensation after diplomatic efforts, commonly recognize no obligation on the part of the taking country. Certain representatives of the newly independent and underdeveloped countries have questioned whether rules of state responsibility toward aliens can bind nations that have not consented to them and it is argued that the traditionally articulated standards governing expropriation of property reflect 'imperialist' interests and are inappropriate to the circumstances of emergent states.

The disagreement as to relevant international law standards reflects an even more basic divergence between the national interests of capital importing and capital exporting nations and between the social ideologies of those countries that favor state control of a considerable portion of the means of production and those that adhere to a free enterprise system. It is difficult to imagine the courts of this country embarking on adjudication in an area which touches more sensitively the practical and ideological goals of the various members of the community of nations....

Following an expropriation of any significance, the Executive engages in diplomacy aimed to assure that United States citizens who are harmed are compensated fairly. Representing all claimants of this country, it will often be able, either by bilateral or multilateral talks, by submission to the United Nations, or by the employment of economic and political sanctions, to achieve some degree of general redress. Judicial determinations of invalidity of title can, on the other hand, have only an occasional impact, since they depend on the fortuitous circumstance of the property in question being brought into this country. Such decisions would, if the acts involved were declared invalid, often be likely to give offense to the expropriating country; since the concept of territorial sovereignty is so deep seated, any state may resent the refusal of the courts of another sovereign to accord validity to acts within its territorial borders. Piecemeal dispositions of this sort involving the probability of affront to another state could seriously interfere with negotiations being carried on by the Executive Branch and might prevent or render less favorable the terms of an agreement that could otherwise be reached. Relations with third countries which have engaged in similar expropriations would not be immune from effect.

The dangers of such adjudication are present regardless of whether the State Department has, as it did in this case, asserted that the relevant act violated international law. If the Executive Branch has undertaken negotiations with an expropriating country, but has refrained from claims of violation of the law of nations, a determination to that effect by a court might be regarded as a serious insult, while a finding of compliance with international law would greatly strengthen the bargaining hand of the other state with consequent detriment to American interests.

Even if the State Department has proclaimed the impropriety of the expropriation, the stamp of approval of its view by a judicial tribunal, however, impartial, might increase any affront and the judicial decision might occur at a time, almost always well after the taking, when such an impact would be contrary to our national interest. Considerably more serious and far-reaching consequences would flow from a judicial finding that international law standards had been met if that determination flew in the face of a State Department proclamation to the contrary. When articulating principles of international law in its relations with other states, the Executive Branch speaks not only as an interpreter of generally accepted and traditional rules, as would the courts, but also as an advocate of standards it believes desirable for the community of nations and protective of national concerns. In short, whatever way the matter is cut, the possibility of conflict between the Judicial and Executive Branches could hardly be avoided.

Respondents contend that, even if there is not agreement regarding general standards for determining the validity of expropriations, the alleged combination of retaliation, discrimination, and inadequate compensation makes it patently clear that this particular expropriation was in violation of international law. If this view is accurate, it would still be unwise for the courts so to determine. Such a decision now would require the drawing of more difficult lines in subsequent cases and these would involve the possibility of conflict with the Executive view. Even if the courts avoided this course, either by presuming the validity of an act of state whenever the international law standard was thought unclear or by following the State Department declaration in such a situation, the very expression of judicial uncertainty might provide embarrassment to the Executive Branch.

Another serious consequence of the exception pressed by respondents would be to render uncertain titles in foreign commerce, with the possible consequence of altering the flow of international trade. If the attitude of the United States courts were unclear, one buying expropriated goods would not know if he could safely import them into this country. Even were takings known to be invalid, one would have difficulty determining after goods had changed hands several times whether the particular articles in question were the product of an ineffective state act....

However offensive to the public policy of this country and its constituent States an expropriation of this kind may be, we conclude that both the national interest and progress toward the goal of establishing the rule of law among nations are best served by maintaining intact the act of state doctrine in this realm of its application....

3. Forum Non Conveniens

Scottish common law developed yet a third prudential or abstention doctrine: *forum non conveniens. Forum non conveniens* is another doctrine used by courts to avoid exercising their jurisdiction over lawsuits. Restatement (Second) of Conflict of Law section 84 defines the doctrine of *forum non conveniens*: as holding that a state's counts will not exercise jurisdiction if they are a seriously inconvenient forum, providing that a more appropriate forum is available. In the area of international law, *forum non conveniens* is a matter of comity. The United States Supreme Court has described the doctrine as applied in U.S. courts:

> The principle of forum non conveniens is simply that a court may resist imposition upon its jurisdiction even when jurisdiction is authorized by the letter of a general venue statute. These statutes are drawn with a necessary generality and usually give a plaintiff a choice of courts, so that he may be quite sure of some place in which to pursue his remedy. But the open door may admit those who seek not simply justice but perhaps justice blended with some harassment. A plaintiff sometimes is under temptation to resort to a strategy of forcing the trial at a most inconvenient place for an adversary, even at some inconvenience to himself.
>
> Many of the states have met misuse of venue by investing courts with a discretion to change the place of trial on various grounds, such as the convenience of witnesses and the ends of justice. The federal law contains no such express criteria to guide the district court in exercising its power. But the problem is a very old one affecting the administration of the courts as well as the rights of litigants, and both in England and in this country the common law worked out techniques and criteria for dealing with it.
>
> Wisely, it has not been attempted to catalogue the circumstances which will justify or require either grant or denial of remedy. The doctrine leaves much to the discretion of the court to which plaintiff resorts, and experience has not shown a judicial tendency to renounce one's own jurisdiction so strong as to result in many abuses.
>
> If the combination and weight of factors requisite to given results are difficult to forecast or state, those to be considered are not difficult to name. An interest to be considered, and the one likely to be most pressed, is the private interest of the litigant. Important considerations are the relative ease of access to sources of proof; availability of compulsory process for attendance of unwilling, and the cost of obtaining attendance of willing, witnesses; possibility of view of premises,

> if view would be appropriate to the action; and all other practical problems that make trial of a case easy, expeditious and inexpensive. There may also be questions as to the enforcibility of a judgment if one is obtained. The court will weigh relative advantages and obstacles to fair trial. It is often said that the plaintiff may not, by choice of an inconvenient forum, 'vex,' 'harass,' or 'oppress' the defendant by inflicting upon him expense or trouble not necessary to his own right to pursue his remedy. But unless the balance is strongly in favor of the defendant, the plaintiff's choice of forum should rarely be disturbed.
>
> Factors of public interest also have place in applying the doctrine. Administrative difficulties follow for courts when litigation is piled up in congested centers instead of being handled at its origin. Jury duty is a burden that ought not to be imposed upon the people of a community which has no relation to the litigation. In cases which touch the affairs of many persons, there is reason for holding the trial in their view and reach rather than in remote parts of the country where they can learn of it by report only. There is a local interest in having localized controversies decided at home. There is an appropriateness, too, in having the trial of a diversity case in a forum that is at home with the state law that must govern the case, rather than having a court in some other forum untangle problems in conflict of laws, and in law foreign to itself.[9]

The doctrine of *forum non conveniens* was applied in the consolidated actions in the wake of the release of methyl isocyanate gas from the Union Carbide plant in Bhopal, India.[10] An interesting aspect of the *Bhopal* case is that the Indian government, as one of the plaintiffs, had originally argued that its own courts were inadequate to adjudicate the claims. The U.S. District Court determined that the Indian legal system was adequate. The private factors considered by the court were that most of the witnesses and evidence were in India, and that many of those involved did not speak English. The public factors taken into account were the large number of local victims in India and the fact that the plaintiff was subject to Indian laws and regulations.[11]

In *Bhatnagar v. Surrendra*, denial of a defendant's *forum non conveniens* argument was upheld because the severe delay in the competing forum's court system rendered it inadequate. Both parties were Indian nationals and the accident in question took place on an "Indian-flagged ship on the high seas."[12] On review, the Third Circuit upheld the trial court's determination that India could not provide an adequate forum because the Indian court system was in a state of "virtual collapse" and it could take "up to a quarter of a century" to resolve the case there.[13] While the Third Circuit recognized that litigation in any court where process is observed suffers delays, the likely delay of fifteen to twenty-five years was "profound and extreme," making the "remedy 'clearly inadequate' under *Piper Aircraft*."[15]

Similarly, in *Nemariam v. Federal Democratic Republic of Ethiopia*, the D.C. Circuit reversed a trial court's dismissal of a case on *forum non conveniens* grounds, instead finding the competing forum inadequate.[16] Nemariam, an Eritrean national, had a claim

---

9. Gulf Oil Corp. v. Gilbert, 330 U.S. 501, 507–09 (1947) (footnotes omitted).

10. Bi v. Union Carbide Chem. & Plastics Corp., 984 F.2d 582 (2d Cir. 1993), *cert. denied*, 510 U.S. 862 (1993).

11. *See id.*; Mark W. Janis, *The Doctrine of Forum Non Conveniens and the Bhopal Case*, 34 Netherlands Int'l L. Rev. 192 (1987).

12. 52 F.3d 1220, 1224 (3d Cir. 1995).

13. *Id.* at 1226–27.

15. *Id.* at 1228.

16. 315 F.3d 390, 392 (D.C. Cir. 2003).

against Ethiopia arising out of the Eritrea-Ethiopia border dispute. She had filed a case in June of 2000 in the District of Columbia; the countries formed the Ethiopia/Eritrea Claims Commission in December of 2000.[17] The D.C. Circuit agreed with the plaintiff that the Commission failed to provide an adequate forum because the Commission had no authority to provide relief directly to her and because the countries may agree to off-set some claims, thereby denying plaintiff relief altogether.[14]

4. Standing

Germany has a reputation for being a strong proponent of international law, yet its courts have been inhospitable to claims against sovereign states alleging violations of international law. A German farmer tried to bring a case against the Soviet Union when his crop was contaminated by radioactive pollution from the Chernobyl nuclear power plant meltdown. The farmer attached Soviet assets in a German bank account to found jurisdiction, but the German court refused to recognize a cause of action.[20]

Mary Ellen O'Connell,
Litigating Enforcement[*]

... In Germany, for example, private parties could not sue the Soviet Union for damage caused by the Chernobyl accident. A non-lawyer, acting *pro se*, tried to bring such a case.[108] In his first attempt he made technical errors and the case was dismissed. He then applied for legal aid. The court also dismissed this request. I stated that the plaintiff might have had a case in tort if he could have shown that the reactor and the Soviet government were legally one and the same. Nevertheless, the court dismissed the request for legal aid because the claimant did not provide enough evidence to show the legal relationship of the Soviet Union to the reactor in order to assure the court that he had a chance of succeeding on the merits.[109] This is a curious conclusion since surely the plaintiff needed legal aid to help establish the case in law of the reactor's legal status.[110]

... [T]he court suggested in [the case that] Germany itself had a claim against the Soviet Union, yet neither Germany nor any other State sued the Soviet Union after Chernobyl despite the clarity of the law and the millions of dollars of lost revenue that it clearly owed.[112] States simply did not wish to put additional pressure on *Mikhail Gorbachev* in the early days of his reform movement.

Moreover, litigation functions best "in a limited context of bilateral compensation for clearly definable losses from specific activities."[113] True, U.S. courts have participated in

17. *Id.*

14. *Id.* at 394.

20. *Garden Contamination Cases*, 80 INT'L LAW RPTS 367 (1989); *see also* Mary Ellen O'Connell, *Enforcing the New International Law of the Environment.* 35 GER. Y.B. INT'L L. 293, 315–316 (1992).

* Mary Ellen O'Connell, *Enforcement and the Success of International Environmental Law*, 3 IND. J. GLOBAL L. Stud. 47 (1995).

108. *Garden Contamination* cases, ILR vol. 80, 1987, 367, 377.

109. *Id.* at 385–87.

110. The Court also made the interesting ruling that if the Soviet Union itself had violated international law, it would not be immune from suit in Germany on grounds of sovereign immunity but that individuals could not raise general international law violations, only a state could do so. This last point is not so well settled, in the U.S. at any rate, that it should not be challenged.

112. *Sands* (note 57).

113. *See Sanford Gaines*, International Principles for Transnational Environmental Liability: Can Developments in Municipal Law Help Break the Impasse?, 30 Harv. Int'l L.J. 311, 311–349 (1989).

a gamut of activities from running school systems to organizing massive tort recovery schemes. Yet most national courts do not perform these tasks and that is doubly true for international courts:

> The optimum conditions that foster a resort to adjudication by the parties embroiled in a dispute and compliance on their part with a judgment are presented when, in addition to the factors previously described, the issue has only restricted implications, and the consequences of a decision one way or the other are easy to foresee.[114]

Note on International Organizations before National Courts

The discussion so far has concerned states before national courts. The excerpt that follows from August Reinisch's book on international institutions reveals that many of the same doctrines relied on by national courts to avoid cases involving sovereign states are also used to avoid cases involving IOs.

August Reinisch, *Avoidance Techniques**

In practice, national courts frequently decline to exercise jurisdiction over disputes involving international organizations either as plaintiffs or defendants, even when the international organizations are only involved peripherally, whether as third parties or as persons whose acts might be decisive for a legal dispute between other parties. Courts may decline to exercise jurisdiction for a number of reasons that could be termed "internal" or "domestic" in so far as their jurisprudential rationale or legal political purpose clearly has roots within the domestic realm. Distribution of powers arguments, underlying the "political questions" doctrine, rank here next to "case" or "controversy" requirements intended to further the efficacy of the administration of justice. Courts may, however, also use "international" reasons or policy arguments that relate to the "external" international relations of a forum state. The most prominent among them is, of course, the grant of immunity to international organizations which is normally perceived as a requirement under international law, conventional or customary. Certain strategies might also involve both internal and external rationales. The US-type act of state doctrine is a good example resting on internal power distribution rationales as well as on external comity considerations.

Apart from official high-level rationales to decline jurisdiction over certain disputes, domestic courts can have considerably more mundane reasons to avoid disputes involving international organizations. Lacking familiarity with the issues involved, ready to seize an opportunity to get rid of another case that awaits decision, courts may have a number of "avoidance" strategies. Much depends upon cultural differences between ju-

---

114. *Milton Katz*, The Relevance of International Adjudication, 33 (1968,). Accordingly to Judge *Jennings*, the British judge on the ICJ: "This of course is one very good reason why governments are rightly cautious before taking a dispute, even a mainly legal dispute, to adjudication or arbitration: the character of the dispute changes rapidly before their eyes and the changes are not wholly within their own control," *Robert Jennings*, International Courts and International Politics, the *Josephine Onoh* Memorial Lecture, 21 January 1986 (Hull University Press).

* INTERNATIONAL ORGANIZATIONS BEFORE NATIONAL COURTS 35–37 (2002) (footnotes omitted).

dicial systems and those involved in the administration of justice. For judges willing to abandon a case, however, the employment of one of the avoidance doctrines discussed below might prove an effective and simple way to free themselves of part of their heavy case load. Considering the rarity of disputes concerning international immunity issues, in particular those involving international organizations, the benefit in numerical terms—might not appear very great. However, the gain of abandoning some of the harder cases—at least from the perspective of the judges confronted with them and not familiar with the issues contained therein—should not be underestimated.

Where the relationship between international organizations and national courts is discussed, attention usually focuses on the problem of their jurisdictional immunity. Immunity is certainly the doctrinal and jurisprudential centrepiece of this relationship. However, judicial practice evidences that the issue of immunity from suit is but one aspect of the sometimes very sophisticated approaches domestic courts take when addressing legal disputes before them that involve international organizations.

One reason for the inherently limited usefulness of the concept of immunity is that, essentially, it works only in suits brought against an international organization and cannot lead to judicial abstention if an international organization chooses to bring suit. Another, probably increasingly important reason for avoiding immunity and replacing it by other avoidance doctrines might lie in the fact that the concept of immunity appears to be regarded as increasingly inappropriate, as a relic of traditional international law favouring its "subjects" improperly *vis-à-vis* individuals. Thus, other avoidance doctrines have resurfaced, in particular those, specific persons. Clearly, immunity for a certain group of persons is not neutral, but rather unilaterally places the burden upon the party seeking judicial redress.

Among those other doctrines may be included "non-recognition" theories, relating to a concept of the legal personality of international organizations or to the legal significance of their activities; procedural law requirements, relating to the ripeness or justiciability of a dispute that might disqualify certain issues from judicial scrutiny; and the "political questions" "act of state" or similar doctrines.

Compared to these broader and not necessarily international-law-related concepts, the issue of immunity is more concrete and will serve as a method of last resort for courts to avoid adjudication of a claim against an international organization.

* * *

Notes and Questions on Issues Arising in National Court Dispute Resolution

1. This chapter features national courts seeking to avoid adjudicating international disputes. Why do you think that is?

2. How do national courts compare as international dispute resolution institutions with the other methods examined in this book? Do you think national courts could play a larger role? Should they?

3. Are any of the barriers to the national court role in dispute resolution required by international law?

4. Is *Medellín* fundamentally a judgment enforcement or treaty enforcement case? Why does this basic characterization make a decisive difference in the case? United States courts

enforce judgments of many foreign and international courts and tribunals as an exercise of their judicial function. Is there some reason why two cases from the ICJ (*Nicaragua* and *Avena*) met resistance in being treated as other judgment enforcement cases? *Medellín* and *Committee of U.S. Citizens* have similar outcomes for the plaintiffs involved, but their treatment of international law and the ICJ seem quite distinct. Point to some differences.

5. The Reuters News Service carried the following story of the aftermath of *Medellín v. Texas* and *Request for Interpretation*:

> Texas defies World Court with execution
> Wed Aug 6, 2008 12:10am EDT
> By Ed Stoddard
>
> DALLAS, Aug 5 (Reuters)—Texas defied the World Court and executed a Mexican national by lethal injection on Tuesday over the objections of the international judicial body and neighboring Mexico.
>
> Jose Medellín, 33, was pronounced dead at 9:57 p.m. CDT (0257 GMT) in the state's death chamber in Huntsville, the Texas Department of Criminal Justice said. He had been condemned for the 1993 rape and murder of 16-year-old Elizabeth Pena in Houston and lost his bid late Tuesday for a last-minute stay from the U.S. Supreme Court.
>
> The World Court last month ordered the U.S. government to "take all measures necessary" to halt the upcoming executions of five Mexicans including Medellín's on the grounds that they had been deprived of their right to consular services after their arrests.
>
> Medellín's execution is sure to anger neighboring Mexico and analysts have said it could make life rough for Americans arrested abroad if other countries decide to evoke the U.S. example and deprive them of their right to consular services. This typically means diplomats will visit and provide legal advice to their nationals being held by authorities....
>
> (Some paragraph breaks omitted.)

6. On July 7, 2011, the Supreme Court refused to order a stay of execution requested by the Obama administration for one of the Mexican nationals named in *Avena*. In the 5–4 decision, *Leal v. Texas*, 546 U.S. ___ (2011) the majority held that an appeal from the president, without enacted implementing legislation from Congress, was insufficient to force Texas to comply with *Avena*. Leal was executed shortly after the decision was handed down.

The *amicus* brief filed by the administration in the case requested a stay of execution for Leal based on legislation recently introduced in Congress, the Consular Notification Compliance Act (CNCA), which would implement *Avena* by providing for review in federal court of alleged violations of the VCCR for individuals sentenced to death. The stay would have postponed Leal's execution until January 2012 while Congress considered whether to enact the legislation. President Obama did not issue an executive order in the case as President Reagan had done in Dames and Moore. Why do you think President Obama did not take a step that had proven effective in an arguably less compelling case, one involving money, versus one involving life and death?

After three years in office, President Obama had not given any indication that the U.S. would return to the dispute settlement protocol of the VCCR.

7. Find the 1928 General Act for the Pacific Settlement of Dispute. Update the Act for re-submission to the international community. Consider what needs to be added to the

Act that will make it a more effective agreement for resolving disputes and what will attract adherence.

8. For further reading on issues arising in national court dispute resolution, see: The Role of Domestic Courts in Treaty Enforcement (David Sloss ed., 2009).

Yuval Shany, Regulating Jurisdictional Relations Between National and International Courts (2007).

The Confiscated Painting Case

The year is 2020 and the United Nations is organizing a retrospective of artworks by Pieter van Laer to be hung in the corridors of the headquarters building in New York. The painting at the heart of the *Certain Property* case (excerpted above) is included in the retrospective and is sent by the Czech Republic by ship. As soon as the ship arrives, Prince Hans Adam V, the current reigning prince of Liechtenstein, has his lawyers file a lawsuit in United States courts claiming title to the painting. The prince argues that the painting is only in the hands of the Czech Republic through an act of illegal confiscation.

The Czech Republic files an answer to the prince's claim. It argues that the International Court of Justice has already ruled on the title question and that U.S. courts should follow the ICJ decision. The Czech Republic also argues that deciding the question of title would violate the Act of State doctrine and, moreover, the Czech Republic will suspend relations with the United States if the painting is transferred to the prince. The Czech Republic maintains that courts have a duty to help maintain the peace. Decisions should be made with an eye to achieving the greater good.

Consider the arguments of the Czech Republic in light of the materials in this chapter and the previous one. What is the duty of a national court in weighing the impact of its decisions? Does the nature of the case make a difference? Would a case involving capital punishment or a criminal case that might undermine peace negotiations have a greater claim for judicial restraint than a property case? If the painting is hung in the UN headquarters building can the prince bring a lawsuit against the UN to get the painting turned over to him? What role should the Secretary General play in this dispute?

Annex

1. United Nations Charter, 1945

Preamble

WE THE PEOPLES OF THE UNITED NATIONS DETERMINED

to save succeeding generations from the scourge of war, which twice in our lifetime has brought untold sorrow to mankind, and

to reaffirm faith in fundamental human rights, in the dignity and worth of the human person, in the equal rights of men and women and of nations large and small, and

to establish conditions under which justice and respect for the obligations arising from treaties and other sources of international law can be maintained, and to promote social progress and better standards of life in larger freedom,

AND FOR THESE ENDS

to practice tolerance and live together in peace with one another as good neighbours, and to unite our strength to maintain international peace and security, and

to ensure, by the acceptance of principles and the institution of methods, that armed force shall not be used, save in the common interest, and

to employ international machinery for the promotion of the economic and social advancement of all peoples,

HAVE RESOLVED TO COMBINE OUR EFFORTS TO ACCOMPLISH THESE AIMS

Accordingly, our respective Governments, through representatives assembled in the city of San Francisco, who have exhibited their full powers found to be in good and due form, have agreed to the present Charter of the United Nations and do hereby establish an international organization to be known as the United Nations.

CHAPTER I: PRINCIPLES AND PURPOSES

Article 1

The Purposes of the United Nations are:

1. To maintain international peace and security, and to that end: to take effective collective measures for the prevention and removal of threats to the peace, and for the suppression of acts of aggression or other breaches of the peace, and to bring about by peaceful means, and in conformity with the principles of justice and international law, adjustment or settlement of international disputes or situations which might lead to a breach of the peace;
2. To develop friendly relations among nations based on respect for the principle of equal rights and self-determination of peoples, and to take other appropriate measures to strengthen universal peace;

3. To achieve international co-operation in solving international problems of an economic, social, cultural, or humanitarian character, and in promoting and encouraging respect for human rights and for fundamental freedoms for all without distinction as to race, sex, language, or religion; and
4. To be a centre for harmonizing the actions of nations in the attainment of these common ends.

Article 2

The Organization and its Members, in pursuit of the Purposes stated in Article 1, shall act in accordance with the following Principles.

1. The Organization is based on the principle of the sovereign equality of all its Members.
2. All Members, in order to ensure to all of them the rights and benefits resulting from membership, shall fulfil in good faith the obligations assumed by them in accordance with the present Charter.
3. All Members shall settle their international disputes by peaceful means in such a manner that international peace and security, and justice, are not endangered.
4. All Members shall refrain in their international relations from the threat or use of force against the territorial integrity or political independence of any state, or in any other manner inconsistent with the Purposes of the United Nations.
5. All Members shall give the United Nations every assistance in any action it takes in accordance with the present Charter, and shall refrain from giving assistance to any state against which the United Nations is taking preventive or enforcement action.
6. The Organization shall ensure that states which are not Members of the United Nations act in accordance with these Principles so far as may be necessary for the maintenance of international peace and security.
7. Nothing contained in the present Charter shall authorize the United Nations to intervene in matters which are essentially within the domestic jurisdiction of any state or shall require the Members to submit such matters to settlement under the present Charter; but this principle shall not prejudice the application of enforcement measures under Chapter VII.

CHAPTER II: MEMBERSHIP

Article 3

The original Members of the United Nations shall be the states which, having participated in the United Nations Conference on International Organization at San Francisco, or having previously signed the Declaration by United Nations of 1 January 1942, sign the present Charter and ratify it in accordance with Article 110.

Article 4

1. Membership in the United Nations is open to all other peace-loving states which accept the obligations contained in the present Charter and, in the judgement of the Organization, are able and willing to carry out these obligations.
2. The admission of any such state to membership in the United Nations will be effected by a decision of the General Assembly upon the recommendation of the Security Council.

Article 5

A Member of the United Nations against which preventive or enforcement action has been taken by the Security Council may be suspended from the exercise of the rights and privileges of membership by the General Assembly upon the recommendation of the Security Council. The exercise of these rights and privileges may be restored by the Security Council.

Article 6

A Member of the United Nations which has persistently violated the Principles contained in the present Charter may be expelled from the Organization by the General Assembly upon the recommendation of the Security Council.

CHAPTER III: ORGANS

Article 7

1. There are established as the principal organs of the United Nations: a General Assembly, a Security Council, an Economic and Social Council, a Trusteeship Council, an International Court of Justice, and a Secretariat.
2. Such subsidiary organs as may be found necessary may be established in accordance with the present Charter.

Article 8

The United Nations shall place no restrictions on the eligibility of men and women to participate in any capacity and under conditions of equality in its principal and subsidiary organs.

CHAPTER IV: THE GENERAL ASSEMBLY

COMPOSITION

Article 9

1. The General Assembly shall consist of all the Members of the United Nations.
2. Each Member shall have not more than five representatives in the General Assembly.

FUNCTIONS AND POWERS

Article 10

The General Assembly may discuss any questions or any matters within the scope of the present Charter or relating to the powers and functions of any organs provided for in the present Charter, and, except as provided in Article 12, may make recommendations to the Members of the United Nations or to the Security Council or to both on any such questions or matters.

Article 11

1. The General Assembly may consider the general principles of co-operation in the maintenance of international peace and security, including the principles governing disarmament and the regulation of armaments, and may make recommendations with regard to such principles to the Members or to the Security Council or to both.
2. The General Assembly may discuss any questions relating to the maintenance of international peace and security brought before it by any Member of the United Nations, or by the Security Council, or by a state which is not a Member of the

United Nations in accordance with Article 35, paragraph 2, and, except as provided in Article 12, may make recommendations with regard to any such questions to the state or states concerned or to the Security Council or to both. Any such question on which action is necessary shall be referred to the Security Council by the General Assembly either before or after discussion.

3. The General Assembly may call the attention of the Security Council to situations which are likely to endanger international peace and security.
4. The powers of the General Assembly set forth in this Article shall not limit the general scope of Article 10.

Article 12

1. While the Security Council is exercising in respect of any dispute or situation the functions assigned to it in the present Charter, the General Assembly shall not make any recommendation with regard to that dispute or situation unless the Security Council so requests.
2. The Secretary-General, with the consent of the Security Council, shall notify the General Assembly at each session of any matters relative to the maintenance of international peace and security which are being dealt with by the Security Council and shall similarly notify the General Assembly, or the Members of the United Nations if the General Assembly is not in session, immediately the Security Council ceases to deal with such matters.

Article 13

1. The General Assembly shall initiate studies and make recommendations for the purpose of:
   a. promoting international co-operation in the political field and encouraging the progressive development of international law and its codification;
   b. promoting international co-operation in the economic, social, cultural, educational, and health fields, and assisting in the realization of human rights and fundamental freedoms for all without distinction as to race, sex, language, or religion.
2. The further responsibilities, functions and powers of the General Assembly with respect to matters mentioned in paragraph 1 (b) above are set forth in Chapters IX and X.

Article 14

Subject to the provisions of Article 12, the General Assembly may recommend measures for the peaceful adjustment of any situation, regardless of origin, which it deems likely to impair the general welfare or friendly relations among nations, including situations resulting from a violation of the provisions of the present Charter setting forth the Purposes and Principles of the United Nations.

Article 15

1. The General Assembly shall receive and consider annual and special reports from the Security Council; these reports shall include an account of the measures that the Security Council has decided upon or taken to maintain international peace and security.
2. The General Assembly shall receive and consider reports from the other organs of the United Nations.

Article 16

The General Assembly shall perform such functions with respect to the international trusteeship system as are assigned to it under Chapters XII and XIII, including the approval of the trusteeship agreements for areas not designated as strategic.

Article 17

1. The General Assembly shall consider and approve the budget of the Organization.
2. The expenses of the Organization shall be borne by the Members as apportioned by the General Assembly.
3. The General Assembly shall consider and approve any financial and budgetary arrangements with specialized agencies referred to in Article 57 and shall examine the administrative budgets of such specialized agencies with a view to making recommendations to the agencies concerned.

VOTING

Article 18

1. Each member of the General Assembly shall have one vote.
2. Decisions of the General Assembly on important questions shall be made by a two-thirds majority of the members present and voting. These questions shall include: recommendations with respect to the maintenance of international peace and security, the election of the non-permanent members of the Security Council, the election of the members of the Economic and Social Council, the election of members of the Trusteeship Council in accordance with paragraph 1 (c) of Article 86, the admission of new Members to the United Nations, the suspension of the rights and privileges of membership, the expulsion of Members, questions relating to the operation of the trusteeship system, and budgetary questions.
3. Decisions on other questions, including the determination of additional categories of questions to be decided by a two-thirds majority, shall be made by a majority of the members present and voting.

Article 19

A Member of the United Nations which is in arrears in the payment of its financial contributions to the Organization shall have no vote in the General Assembly if the amount of its arrears equals or exceeds the amount of the contributions due from it for the preceding two full years. The General Assembly may, nevertheless, permit such a Member to vote if it is satisfied that the failure to pay is due to conditions beyond the control of the Member.

PROCEDURE

Article 20

The General Assembly shall meet in regular annual sessions and in such special sessions as occasion may require. Special sessions shall be convoked by the Secretary-General at the request of the Security Council or of a majority of the Members of the United Nations.

Article 21

The General Assembly shall adopt its own rules of procedure. It shall elect its President for each session.

Article 22

The General Assembly may establish such subsidiary organs as it deems necessary for the performance of its functions.

CHAPTER V: THE SECURITY COUNCIL

COMPOSITION

Article 23

1. The Security Council shall consist of fifteen Members of the United Nations. The Republic of China, France, the Union of Soviet Socialist Republics, the United Kingdom of Great Britain and Northern Ireland, and the United States of America shall be permanent members of the Security Council. The General Assembly shall elect ten other Members of the United Nations to be non-permanent members of the Security Council, due regard being specially paid, in the first instance to the contribution of Members of the United Nations to the maintenance of international peace and security and to the other purposes of the Organization, and also to equitable geographical distribution.
2. The non-permanent members of the Security Council shall be elected for a term of two years. In the first election of the non-permanent members after the increase of the membership of the Security Council from eleven to fifteen, two of the four additional members shall be chosen for a term of one year. A retiring member shall not be eligible for immediate re-election.
3. Each member of the Security Council shall have one representative.

FUNCTIONS AND POWERS

Article 24

1. In order to ensure prompt and effective action by the United Nations, its Members confer on the Security Council primary responsibility for the maintenance of international peace and security, and agree that in carrying out its duties under this responsibility the Security Council acts on their behalf.
2. In discharging these duties the Security Council shall act in accordance with the Purposes and Principles of the United Nations. The specific powers granted to the Security Council for the discharge of these duties are laid down in Chapters VI, VII, VIII, and XII.
3. The Security Council shall submit annual and, when necessary, special reports to the General Assembly for its consideration.

Article 25

The Members of the United Nations agree to accept and carry out the decisions of the Security Council in accordance with the present Charter.

Article 26

In order to promote the establishment and maintenance of international peace and security with the least diversion for armaments of the world's human and economic resources, the Security Council shall be responsible for formulating, with the assistance of the Military Staff Committee referred to in Article 47, plans to be submitted to the Members of the United Nations for the establishment of a system for the regulation of armaments.

VOTING

Article 27

1. Each member of the Security Council shall have one vote.
2. Decisions of the Security Council on procedural matters shall be made by an affirmative vote of nine members.

3. Decisions of the Security Council on all other matters shall be made by an affirmative vote of nine members including the concurring votes of the permanent members; provided that, in decisions under Chapter VI, and under paragraph 3 of Article 52, a party to a dispute shall abstain from voting.

PROCEDURE

Article 28

1. The Security Council shall be so organized as to be able to function continuously. Each member of the Security Council shall for this purpose be represented at all times at the seat of the Organization.
2. The Security Council shall hold periodic meetings at which each of its members may, if it so desires, be represented by a member of the government or by some other specially designated representative.
3. The Security Council may hold meetings at such places other than the seat of the Organization as in its judgement will best facilitate its work.

Article 29

The Security Council may establish such subsidiary organs as it deems necessary for the performance of its functions.

Article 30

The Security Council shall adopt its own rules of procedure, including the method of selecting its President.

Article 31

Any Member of the United Nations which is not a member of the Security Council may participate, without vote, in the discussion of any question brought before the Security Council whenever the latter considers that the interests of that Member are specially affected.

Article 32

Any Member of the United Nations which is not a member of the Security Council or any state which is not a Member of the United Nations, if it is a party to a dispute under consideration by the Security Council, shall be invited to participate, without vote, in the discussion relating to the dispute. The Security Council shall lay down such conditions as it deems just for the participation of a state which is not a Member of the United Nations.

CHAPTER VI: PACIFIC SETTLEMENT OF DISPUTES

Article 33

1. The parties to any dispute, the continuance of which is likely to endanger the maintenance of international peace and security, shall, first of all, seek a solution by negotiation, enquiry, mediation, conciliation, arbitration, judicial settlement, resort to regional agencies or arrangements, or other peaceful means of their own choice.
2. The Security Council shall, when it deems necessary, call upon the parties to settle their dispute by such means.

Article 34

The Security Council may investigate any dispute, or any situation which might lead to international friction or give rise to a dispute, in order to determine whether the continuance of the dispute or situation is likely to endanger the maintenance of international peace and security.

Article 35

1. Any Member of the United Nations may bring any dispute, or any situation of the nature referred to in Article 34, to the attention of the Security Council or of the General Assembly.
2. A state which is not a Member of the United Nations may bring to the attention of the Security Council or of the General Assembly any dispute to which it is a party if it accepts in advance, for the purposes of the dispute, the obligations of pacific settlement provided in the present Charter.
3. The proceedings of the General Assembly in respect of matters brought to its attention under this Article will be subject to the provisions of Articles 11 and 12.

Article 36

1. The Security Council may, at any stage of a dispute of the nature referred to in Article 33 or of a situation of like nature, recommend appropriate procedures or methods of adjustment.
2. The Security Council should take into consideration any procedures for the settlement of the dispute which have already been adopted by the parties.
3. In making recommendations under this Article the Security Council should also take into consideration that legal disputes should as a general rule be referred by the parties to the International Court of Justice in accordance with the provisions of the Statute of the Court.

Article 37

1. Should the parties to a dispute of the nature referred to in Article 33 fail to settle it by the means indicated in that Article, they shall refer it to the Security Council.
2. If the Security Council deems that the continuance of the dispute is in fact likely to endanger the maintenance of international peace and security, it shall decide whether to take action under Article 36 or to recommend such terms of settlement as it may consider appropriate.

Article 38

Without prejudice to the provisions of Articles 33 to 37, the Security Council may, if all the parties to any dispute so request, make recommendations to the parties with a view to a pacific settlement of the dispute.

CHAPTER VII: ACTIONS WITH RESPECT TO THREATS TO THE PEACE, BREACHES OF THE PEACE, AND ACTS OF AGGRESSION

Article 39

The Security Council shall determine the existence of any threat to the peace, breach of the peace, or act of aggression and shall make recommendations, or decide what measures shall be taken in accordance with Articles 41 and 42, to maintain or restore international peace and security.

Article 40

In order to prevent an aggravation of the situation, the Security Council may, before making the recommendations or deciding upon the measures provided for in Article 39, call upon the parties concerned to comply with such provisional measures as it deems necessary or desirable. Such provisional measures shall be without prejudice to the rights, claims, or position of the parties concerned. The Security Council shall duly take account of failure to comply with such provisional measures.

Article 41

The Security Council may decide what measures not involving the use of armed force are to be employed to give effect to its decisions, and it may call upon the Members of the United Nations to apply such measures. These may include complete or partial interruption of economic relations and of rail, sea, air, postal, telegraphic, radio, and other means of communication, and the severance of diplomatic relations.

Article 42

Should the Security Council consider that measures provided for in Article 41 would be inadequate or have proved to be inadequate, it may take such action by air, sea, or land forces as may be necessary to maintain or restore international peace and security. Such action may include demonstrations, blockade, and other operations by air, sea, or land forces of Members of the United Nations.

Article 43

1. All Members of the United Nations, in order to contribute to the maintenance of international peace and security, undertake to make available to the Security Council on its call and in accordance with a special agreement or agreements, armed forces, assistance, and facilities, including rights of passage, necessary for the purpose of maintaining international peace and security.
2. Such agreement or agreements shall govern the numbers and types of forces, their degree of readiness and general location, and the nature of the facilities and assistance to be provided.
3. The agreement or agreements shall be negotiated as soon as possible on the initiative of the Security Council. They shall be concluded between the Security Council and Members or between the Security Council and groups of Members and shall be subject to ratification by the signatory states in accordance with their respective constitutional processes.

Article 44

When the Security Council has decided to use force it shall, before calling upon a Member not represented on it to provide armed forces in fulfilment of the obligations assumed under Article 43, invite that Member, if the Member so desires, to participate in the decisions of the Security Council concerning the employment of contingents of that Member's armed forces.

Article 45

In order to enable the United Nations to take urgent military measures, Members shall hold immediately available national air-force contingents for combined international enforcement action. The strength and degree of readiness of these contingents and plans for their combined action shall be determined within the limits laid down in the special agreement or agreements referred to in Article 43, by the Security Council with the assistance of the Military Staff Committee.

Article 46

Plans for the application of armed force shall be made by the Security Council with the assistance of the Military Staff Committee.

Article 47

1. There shall be established a Military Staff Committee to advise and assist the Security Council on all questions relating to the Security Council's military requirements for the maintenance of international peace and security, the employment and command of forces placed at its disposal, the regulation of armaments, and possible disarmament.
2. The Military Staff Committee shall consist of the Chiefs of Staff of the permanent members of the Security Council or their representatives. Any Member of the United Nations not permanently represented on the Committee shall be invited by the Committee to be associated with it when the efficient discharge of the Committee's responsibilities requires the participation of that Member in its work.
3. The Military Staff Committee shall be responsible under the Security Council for the strategic direction of any armed forces placed at the disposal of the Security Council. Questions relating to the command of such forces shall be worked out subsequently.
4. The Military Staff Committee, with the authorization of the Security Council and after consultation with appropriate regional agencies, may establish regional sub-committees.

Article 48

1. The action required to carry out the decisions of the Security Council for the maintenance of international peace and security shall be taken by all the Members of the United Nations or by some of them, as the Security Council may determine.
2. Such decisions shall be carried out by the Members of the United Nations directly and through their action in the appropriate international agencies of which they remembers.

Article 49

The Members of the United Nations shall join in affording mutual assistance in carrying out the measures decided upon by the Security Council.

Article 50

If preventive or enforcement measures against any state are taken by the Security Council, any other state, whether a Member of the United Nations or not, which finds itself confronted with special economic problems arising from the carrying out of those measures shall have the right to consult the Security Council with regard to a solution of those problems.

Article 51

Nothing in the present Charter shall impair the inherent right of individual or collective self-defence if an armed attack occurs against a Member of the United Nations, until the Security Council has taken measures necessary to maintain international peace and security. Measures taken by Members in the exercise of this right of self-defence shall be immediately reported to the Security Council and shall not in any way affect the authority and responsibility of the Security Council under the present Charter to take at any time such action as it deems necessary in order to maintain or restore international peace and security.

CHAPTER VIII: REGIONAL ARRANGEMENTS

Article 52

1. Nothing in the present Charter precludes the existence of regional arrangements or agencies for dealing with such matters relating to the maintenance of international peace and security as are appropriate for regional action provided that such arrangements or agencies and their activities are consistent with the Purposes and Principles of the United Nations.
2. The Members of the United Nations entering into such arrangements or constituting such agencies shall make every effort to achieve pacific settlement of local disputes through such regional arrangements or by such regional agencies before referring them to the Security Council.
3. The Security Council shall encourage the development of pacific settlement of local disputes through such regional arrangements or by such regional agencies either on the initiative of the states concerned or by reference from the Security Council.
4. This Article in no way impairs the application of Articles 34 and 35.

Article 53

1. The Security Council shall, where appropriate, utilize such regional arrangements or agencies for enforcement action under its authority. But no enforcement action shall be taken under regional arrangements or by regional agencies without the authorization of the Security Council, with the exception of measures against any enemy state, as defined in paragraph 2 of this Article, provided for pursuant to Article 107 or in regional arrangements directed against renewal of aggressive policy on the part of any such state, until such time as the Organization may, on request of the Governments concerned, be charged with the responsibility for preventing further aggression by such a state.
2. The term enemy state as used in paragraph 1 of this Article applies to any state which during the Second World War has been an enemy of any signatory of the present Charter.

Article 54

The Security Council shall at all times be kept fully informed of activities undertaken or in contemplation under regional arrangements or by regional agencies for the maintenance of international peace and security.

CHAPTER IX: INTERNATIONAL ECONOMIC AND SOCIAL COOPERATION

Article 55

With a view to the creation of conditions of stability and well-being which are necessary for peaceful and friendly relations among nations based on respect for the principle of equal rights and self-determination of peoples, the United Nations shall promote:

a. higher standards of living, full employment, and conditions of economic and social progress and development;

b. solutions of international economic, social, health, and related problems; and international cultural and educational cooperation; and

c. universal respect for, and observance of, human rights and fundamental freedoms for all without distinction as to race, sex, language, or religion.

Article 56

All Members pledge themselves to take joint and separate action in co-operation with the Organization for the achievement of the purposes set forth in Article 55.

Article 57

1. The various specialized agencies, established by intergovernmental agreement and having wide international responsibilities, as defined in their basic instruments, in economic, social, cultural, educational, health, and related fields, shall be brought into relationship with the United Nations in accordance with the provisions of Article 63.
2. Such agencies thus brought into relationship with the United Nations are hereinafter referred to as specialized agencies.

Article 58

The Organization shall make recommendations for the co-ordination of the policies and activities of the specialized agencies.

Article 59

The Organization shall, where appropriate, initiate negotiations among the states concerned for the creation of any new specialized agencies required for the accomplishment of the purposes set forth in Article 55.

Article 60

Responsibility for the discharge of the functions of the Organization set forth in this Chapter shall be vested in the General Assembly and, under the authority of the General Assembly, in the Economic and Social Council, which shall have for this purpose the powers set forth in Chapter X.

CHAPTER X: THE ECONOMIC AND SOCIAL COUNCIL

COMPOSITION

Article 61

1. The Economic and Social Council shall consist of fifty-four Members of the United Nations elected by the General Assembly.
2. Subject to the provisions of paragraph 3, eighteen members of the Economic and Social Council shall be elected each year for a term of three years. A retiring member shall be eligible for immediate re-election.
3. At the first election after the increase in the membership of the Economic and Social Council from twenty-seven to fifty-four members, in addition to the members elected in place of the nine members whose term of office expires at the end of that year, twenty-seven additional members shall be elected. Of these twenty-seven additional members, the term of office of nine members so elected shall expire at the end of one year, and of nine other members at the end of two years, in accordance with arrangements made by the General Assembly.
4. Each member of the Economic and Social Council shall have one representative.

FUNCTIONS AND POWERS

Article 62

1. The Economic and Social Council may make or initiate studies and reports with respect to international economic, social, cultural, educational, health, and related matters and may make recommendations with respect to any such matters

to the General Assembly to the Members of the United Nations, and to the specialized agencies concerned.

2. It may make recommendations for the purpose of promoting respect for, and observance of, human rights and fundamental freedoms for all.
3. It may prepare draft conventions for submission to the General Assembly, with respect to matters falling within its competence.
4. It may call, in accordance with the rules prescribed by the United Nations, international conferences on matters falling within its competence.

Article 63

1. The Economic and Social Council may enter into agreements with any of the agencies referred to in Article 57, defining the terms on which the agency concerned shall be brought into relationship with the United Nations. Such agreements shall be subject to approval by the General Assembly.
2. It may co-ordinate the activities of the specialized agencies through consultation with and recommendations to such agencies and through recommendations to the General Assembly and to the Members of the United Nations.

Article 64

1. The Economic and Social Council may take appropriate steps to obtain regular reports from the specialized agencies. It may make arrangements with the Members of the United Nations and with the specialized agencies to obtain reports on the steps taken to give effect to its own recommendations and to recommendations on matters falling within its competence made by the General Assembly.
2. It may communicate its observations on these reports to the General Assembly.

Article 65

The Economic and Social Council may furnish information to the Security Council and shall assist the Security Council upon its request.

Article 66

1. The Economic and Social Council shall perform such functions as fall within its competence in connexion with the carrying out of the recommendations of the General Assembly.
2. It may, with the approval of the General Assembly, perform services at the request of Members of the United Nations and at the request of specialized agencies.
3. It shall perform such other functions as are specified elsewhere in the present Charter or as may be assigned to it by the General Assembly.

VOTING

Article 67

1. Each member of the Economic and Social Council shall have one vote.
2. Decisions of the Economic and Social Council shall be made by a majority of the members present and voting.

PROCEDURE

Article 68

The Economic and Social Council shall set up commissions in economic and social fields and for the promotion of human rights, and such other commissions as may be required for the performance of its functions.

Article 69

The Economic and Social Council shall invite any Member of the United Nations to participate, without vote, in its deliberations on any matter of particular concern to that Member.

Article 70

The Economic and Social Council may make arrangements for representatives of the specialized agencies to participate, without vote, in its deliberations and in those of the commissions established by it, and for its representatives to participate in the deliberations of the specialized agencies.

Article 71

The Economic and Social Council may make suitable arrangements for consultation with non-governmental organizations which are concerned with matters within its competence. Such arrangements may be made with international organizations and, where appropriate, with national organizations after consultation with the Member of the United Nations concerned.

Article 72

1. The Economic and Social Council shall adopt its own rules of procedure, including the method of selecting its President.
2. The Economic and Social Council shall meet as required in accordance with its rules, which shall include provision for the convening of meetings on the request of a majority of its members.

CHAPTER XI: DECLARATION REGARDING NON-SELF GOVERNING TERRITORIES

Article 73

Members of the United Nations which have or assume responsibilities for the administration of territories whose peoples have not yet attained a full measure of self-government recognize the principle that the interests of the inhabitants of these territories are paramount, and accept as a sacred trust the obligation to promote to the utmost, within the system of international peace and security established by the present Charter, the well-being of the inhabitants of these territories, and, to this end:

a. to ensure, with due respect for the culture of the peoples concerned, their political, economic, social, and educational advancement, their just treatment, and their protection against abuses;
b. to develop self-government, to take due account of the political aspirations of the peoples, and to assist them in the progressive development of their free political institutions, according to the particular circumstances of each territory and its peoples and their varying stages of advancement;
c. to further international peace and security;
d. to promote constructive measures of development, to encourage research, and to co-operate with one another and, when and where appropriate, with specialized international bodies with a view to the practical achievement of the social, economic, and scientific purposes set forth in this Article; and
e. to transmit regularly to the Secretary-General for information purposes, subject to such limitation as security and constitutional considerations may require, statistical and other information of a technical nature relating to economic, so-

cial, and educational conditions in the territories for which they are respectively responsible other than those territories to which Chapters XII and XIII apply.

Article 74

Members of the United Nations also agree that their policy in respect of the territories to which this Chapter applies, no less than in respect of their metropolitan areas, must be based on the general principle of good-neighbourliness, due account being taken of the interests and well-being of the rest of the world, in social, economic, and commercial matters.

CHAPTER XII: INTERNATIONAL TRUSTEESHIP SYSTEM

Article 75

The United Nations shall establish under its authority an international trusteeship system for the administration and supervision of such territories as may be placed thereunder by subsequent individual agreements. These territories are hereinafter referred to as trust territories.

Article 76

The basic objectives of the trusteeship system, in accordance with the Purposes of the United Nations laid down in Article 1 of the present Charter, shall be:

a. to further international peace and security;

b. to promote the political, economic, social, and educational advancement of the inhabitants of the trust territories, and their progressive development towards self-government or independence as may be appropriate to the particular circumstances of each territory and its peoples and the freely expressed wishes of the peoples concerned, and as may be provided by the terms of each trusteeship agreement;

c. to encourage respect for human rights and for fundamental freedoms for all without distinction as to race, sex, language, or religion, and to encourage recognition of the interdependence of the peoples of the world; and

d. to ensure equal treatment in social, economic, and commercial matters for all Members of the United Nations and their nationals, and also equal treatment for the latter in the administration of justice, without prejudice to the attainment of the foregoing objectives and subject to the provisions of Article 80.

Article 77

1. The trusteeship system shall apply to such territories in the following categories as may be placed thereunder by means of trusteeship agreements:

    a. territories now held under mandate;

    b. territories which may be detached from enemy states as a result of the Second World War; and

    c. territories voluntarily placed under the system by states responsible for their administration.

2. It will be a matter for subsequent agreement as to which territories in the foregoing categories will be brought under the trusteeship system and upon what terms.

Article 78

The trusteeship system shall not apply to territories which have become Members of the United Nations, relationship among which shall be based on respect for the principle of sovereign equality.

Article 79

The terms of trusteeship for each territory to be placed under the trusteeship system, including any alteration or amendment, shall be agreed upon by the states directly concerned, including the mandatory power in the case of territories held under mandate by a Member of the United Nations, and shall be approved as provided for in Articles 83 and 85.

Article 80

1. Except as may be agreed upon in individual trusteeship agreements, made under Articles 77, 79, and 81, placing each territory under the trusteeship system, and until such agreements have been concluded, nothing in this Chapter shall be construed in or of itself to alter in any manner the rights whatsoever of any states or any peoples or the terms of existing international instruments to which Members of the United Nations may respectively be parties.
2. Paragraph 1 of this Article shall not be interpreted as giving grounds for delay or postponement of the negotiation and conclusion of agreements for placing mandated and other territories under the trusteeship system as provided for in Article 77.

Article 81

The trusteeship agreement shall in each case include the terms under which the trust territory will be administered and designate the authority which will exercise the administration of the trust territory. Such authority, hereinafter called the administering authority, may be one or more states or the Organization itself.

Article 82

There may be designated, in any trusteeship agreement, a strategic area or areas which may include part or all of the trust territory to which the agreement applies, without prejudice to any special agreement or agreements made under Article 43.

Article 83

1. All functions of the United Nations relating to strategic areas, including the approval of the terms of the trusteeship agreements and of their alteration or amendment shall be exercised by the Security Council.
2. The basic objectives set forth in Article 76 shall be applicable to the people of each strategic area.
3. The Security Council shall, subject to the provisions of the trusteeship agreements and without prejudice to security considerations, avail itself of the assistance of the Trusteeship Council to perform those functions of the United Nations under the trusteeship system relating to political, economic, social, and educational matters in the strategic areas.

Article 84

It shall be the duty of the administering authority to ensure that the trust territory shall play its part in the maintenance of international peace and security. To this end the administering authority may make use of volunteer forces, facilities, and assistance from the trust territory in carrying out the obligations towards the Security Council undertaken in this regard by the administering authority, as well as for local defence and the maintenance of law and order within the trust territory.

Article 85

1. The functions of the United Nations with regard to trusteeship agreements for all areas not designated as strategic, including the approval of the terms of the

trusteeship agreements and of their alteration or amendment, shall be exercised by the General Assembly.

2. The Trusteeship Council, operating under the authority of the General Assembly shall assist the General Assembly in carrying out these functions.

CHAPTER XIII: THE TRUSTEESHIP COUNCIL

COMPOSITION

Article 86

1. The Trusteeship Council shall consist of the following Members of the United Nations:
    a. those Members administering trust territories;
    b. such of those Members mentioned by name in Article 23 as are not administering trust territories; and

c. as many other Members elected for three-year terms by the General Assembly as may be necessary to ensure that the total number of members of the Trusteeship Council is equally divided between those Members of the United Nations which administer trust territories and those which do not.

2. Each member of the Trusteeship Council shall designate one specially qualified person to represent it therein.

FUNCTIONS AND POWERS

Article 87

The General Assembly and, under its authority, the Trusteeship Council, in carrying out their functions, may:

a. consider reports submitted by the administering authority;
b. accept petitions and examine them in consultation with the administering authority;
c. provide for periodic visits to the respective trust territories at times agreed upon with the administering authority; and
d. take these and other actions in conformity with the terms of the trusteeship agreements.

Article 88

The Trusteeship Council shall formulate a questionnaire on the political, economic, social, and educational advancement of the inhabitants of each trust territory, and the administering authority for each trust territory within the competence of the General Assembly shall make an annual report to the General Assembly upon the basis of such questionnaire.

VOTING

Article 89

1. Each member of the Trusteeship Council shall have one vote.
2. Decisions of the Trusteeship Council shall be made by a majority of the members present and voting.

PROCEDURE

Article 90

1. The Trusteeship Council shall adopt its own rules of procedure, including the method of selecting its President.

2. The Trusteeship Council shall meet as required in accordance with its rules, which shall include provision for the convening of meetings on the request of a majority of its members.

Article 91

The Trusteeship Council shall, when appropriate, avail itself of the assistance of the Economic and Social Council and of the specialized agencies in regard to matters with which they are respectively concerned.

CHAPTER XIV: THE INTERNATIONAL COURT OF JUSTICE

Article 92

The International Court of Justice shall be the principal judicial organ of the United Nations. It shall function in accordance with the annexed Statute, which is based upon the Statute of the Permanent Court of International Justice and forms an integral part of the present Charter.

Article 93

1. All Members of the United Nations are ipso facto parties to the Statute of the International Court of Justice.
2. A state which is not a Member of the United Nations may become a party to the Statute of the International Court of Justice on conditions to be determined in each case by the General Assembly upon the recommendation of the Security Council.

Article 94

1. Each Member of the United Nations undertakes to comply with the decision of the International Court of Justice in any case to which it is a party.
2. If any party to a case fails to perform the obligations incumbent upon it under a judgement rendered by the Court, the other party may have recourse to the Security Council, which may, if it deems necessary, make recommendations or decide upon measures to be taken to give effect to the judgment.

Article 95

Nothing in the present Charter shall prevent Members of the United Nations from entrusting the solution of their differences to other tribunals by virtue of agreements already in existence or which may be concluded in the future.

Article 96

1. The General Assembly or the Security Council may request the International Court of Justice to give an advisory opinion on any legal question.
2. Other organs of the United Nations and specialized agencies, which may at any time be so authorized by the General Assembly, may also request advisory opinions of the Court on legal questions arising within the scope of their activities.

CHAPTER XV: THE SECRETARIAT

Article 97

The Secretariat shall comprise a Secretary-General and such staff as the Organization may require. The Secretary-General shall be appointed by the General Assembly upon the recommendation of the Security Council. He shall be the chief administrative officer of the Organization.

Article 98

The Secretary-General shall act in that capacity in all meetings of the General Assembly, of the Security Council, of the Economic and Social Council, and of the Trusteeship Council, and shall perform such other functions as are entrusted to him by these organs. The Secretary-General shall make an annual report to the General Assembly on the work of the Organization.

Article 99

The Secretary-General may bring to the attention of the Security Council any matter which in his opinion may threaten the maintenance of international peace and security.

Article 100

1. In the performance of their duties the Secretary-General and the staff shall not seek or receive instructions from any government or from any other authority external to the Organization. They shall refrain from any action which might reflect on their position as international officials responsible only to the Organization.
2. Each Member of the United Nations undertakes to respect the exclusively international character of the responsibilities of the Secretary-General and the staff and not to seek to influence them in the discharge of their responsibilities.

Article 101

1. The staff shall be appointed by the Secretary-General under regulations established by the General Assembly.
2. Appropriate staffs shall be permanently assigned to the Economic and Social Council, the Trusteeship Council, and, as required, to other organs of the United Nations. These staffs shall form a part of the Secretariat.
3. The paramount consideration in the employment of the staff and in the determination of the conditions of service shall be the necessity of securing the highest standards of efficiency, competence, and integrity. Due regard shall be paid to the importance of recruiting the staff on as wide a geographical basis as possible.

CHAPTER XVI: MISCELLANEOUS PROVISION

Article 102

1. Every treaty and every international agreement entered into by any Member of the United Nations after the present Charter comes into force shall as soon as possible be registered with the Secretariat and published by it.
2. No party to any such treaty or international agreement which has not been registered in accordance with the provisions of paragraph 1 of this Article may invoke that treaty or agreement before any organ of the United Nations.

Article 103

In the event of a conflict between the obligations of the Members of the United Nations under the present Charter and their obligations under any other international agreement, their obligations under the present Charter shall prevail.

Article 104

The Organization shall enjoy in the territory of each of its Members such legal capacity as may be necessary for the exercise of its functions and the fulfilment of its purposes.

Article 105

1. The Organization shall enjoy in the territory of each of its Members such privileges and immunities as are necessary for the fulfilment of its purposes.
2. Representatives of the Members of the United Nations and officials of the Organization shall similarly enjoy such privileges and immunities as are necessary for the independent exercise of their functions in connection with the Organization.
3. The General Assembly may make recommendations with a view to determining the details of the application of paragraphs 1 and 2 of this Article or may propose conventions to the Members of the United Nations for this purpose.

CHAPTER XVII: TRANSITIONAL SECURITY ARRANGEMENTS

Article 106

Pending the coming into force of such special agreements referred to in Article 43 as in the opinion of the Security Council enable it to begin the exercise of its responsibilities under Article 42, the parties to the Four-Nation Declaration, signed at Moscow, 30 October 1943, and France, shall, in accordance with the provisions of paragraph 5 of that Declaration, consult with one another and as occasion requires with other Members of the United Nations with a view to such joint action on behalf of the Organization as may be necessary for the purpose of maintaining international peace and security.

Article 107

Nothing in the present Charter shall invalidate or preclude action, in relation to any state which during the Second World War has been an enemy of any signatory to the present Charter, taken or authorized as a result of that war by the Governments having responsibility for such action.

CHAPTER XVIII: AMENDMENTS

Article 108

Amendments to the present Charter shall come into force for all Members of the United Nations when they have been adopted by a vote of two thirds of the members of the General Assembly and ratified in accordance with their respective constitutional processes by two thirds of the Members of the United Nations, including all the permanent members of the Security Council.

Article 109

1. A General Conference of the Members of the United Nations for the purpose of reviewing the present Charter may be held at a date and place to be fixed by a two-thirds vote of the members of the General Assembly and by a vote of any nine members of the Security Council. Each Member of the United Nations shall have one vote in the conference.
2. Any alteration of the present Charter recommended by a two-thirds vote of the conference shall take effect when ratified in accordance with their respective constitutional processes by two thirds of the Members of the United Nations including all the permanent members of the Security Council.
3. If such a conference has not been held before the tenth annual session of the General Assembly following the coming into force of the present Charter, the proposal to call such a conference shall be placed on the agenda of that session of the General Assembly, and the conference shall be held if so decided by a ma-

jority vote of the members of the General Assembly and by a vote of any seven members of the Security Council.

CHAPTER XIX: RATIFICATION AND SIGNATURE

Article 110

1. The present Charter shall be ratified by the signatory states in accordance with their respective constitutional processes.
2. The ratifications shall be deposited with the Government of the United States of America, which shall notify all the signatory states of each deposit as well as the Secretary-General of the Organization when he has been appointed.
3. The present Charter shall come into force upon the deposit of ratifications by the Republic of China, France, the Union of Soviet Socialist Republics, the United Kingdom of Great Britain and Northern Ireland, and the United States of America, and by a majority of the other signatory states. A protocol of the ratifications deposited shall thereupon be drawn up by the Government of the United States of America which shall communicate copies thereof to all the signatory states.
4. The states signatory to the present Charter which ratify it after it has come into force will become original Members of the United Nations on the date of the deposit of their respective ratifications.

Article 111

The present Charter, of which the Chinese, French, Russian, English, and Spanish texts are equally authentic, shall remain deposited in the archives of the Government of the United States of America. Duly certified copies thereof shall be transmitted by that Government to the Governments of the other signatory states.

IN FAITH WHEREOF the representatives of the Governments of the United Nations have signed the present Charter.

DONE at the city of San Francisco the twenty-sixth day of June, one thousand nine hundred and forty-five.

---

2. Statute of the International Court of Justice, June 26, 1945

Article 1

The International Court of Justice established by the Charter of the United Nations as the principal judicial organ of the United Nations shall be constituted and shall function in accordance with the provisions of the present Statute.

CHAPTER I. ORGANIZATION OF THE COURT

Article 2

The Court shall be composed of a body of independent judges, elected regardless of their nationality from among persons of high moral character, who possess the qualifications required In their respective countries for appointment to the highest judicial offices, or are juris-consults of recognized competence in international law.

Article 3

1. The Court shall consist of fifteen members, no two of whom may be nationals of the same state.
2. A person who for the purposes of membership in the Court could be regarded as a national of more than one state shall be deemed to be a national of the one in which he ordinarily exercises civil and political rights.

Article 4

1. The members of the Court shall be elected by the (general Assembly and by the Security Council from a list of persons nominated by the national groups in the Permanent Court of Arbitration, in accordance with the following provisions.
2. In the case of Members of the United Nations not represented in the Permanent Court of Arbitration, candidates shall be nominated by national groups appointed for this purpose by their governments under the same conditions as those prescribed for members of the Permanent Court of Arbitration by Article 44 of the Convention of The Hague of 1907 for the pacific settlement of international disputes.
3. The conditions under which a state which is a party to the present Statute but is not a Member of the United Nations may participate in electing the members of the Court shall, in the absence of a special agreement, be laid down by the General Assembly upon recommendation of the Security Council.

Article 5

1. At least three months before the date of the election, the Secretary-General of the United Nations shall address a written request to the members of the Permanent Court of Arbitration belonging to the states which are parties to the present Statute, and to the members of the national groups appointed under Article 4, paragraph 2, inviting them to undertake, within a given time, by national groups, the nomination of persons in a position to accept the duties of a member of the Court.
2. No group may nominate more than four persons, not more than two of whom shall be of their own nationality. In no case may the nationality. In no case may the number of candidates nominated by a group be more than double the number of seats to be filled.

Article 6

Before making these nominations, each national group is recommended to consult its highest court of justice, its legal faculties and schools of law, and its national academies and national sections of international academies devoted to the study of law.

Article 7

1. The Secretary-General shall prepare a list in alphabetical order of all the persons thus nominated. Save as provided in Article 12, paragraph 2, these shall be the only persons eligible.
2. The Secretary-General shall submit this list to the General Assembly and to the Security Council.

Article 8

The General Assembly and the Security Council shall proceed independently of one another to elect the members of the Court.

Article 9

At every election, the electors shall bear in mind not only that the persons to be elected should individually possess the qualifications required, but also that in the body as a whole the representation of the main forms of civilization and of the principal legal systems of the world should be assured.

Article 10

1. Those candidates who obtain an absolute majority of votes in the General and in the Security Council shall be considered as elected.
2. Any vote of the Security Council, whether for the election of judges or for the appointment of members of the conference envisaged in Article 12, shall be taken without any distinction between permanent and non-permanent members of the Security Council.
3. In the event of more than one national of the same state obtaining an absolute majority of the votes both of the General Assembly and of the Security Council, the eldest of these only shall be considered as elected.

Article 11

If, after the first meeting held for the purpose of the election, one or more seats remain to be filled, a second and, if necessary, a third meeting shall take place.

Article 12

1. If, after the third meeting, one or more seats still remain unfilled, a joint conference consisting of six members, three appointed by the General Assembly and three by the Security Council, may be formed at any time at the request of either the General Assembly or the Security Council, for the purpose of choosing by the vote of an absolute majority one name for each seat still vacant, to submit to the General Assembly and the Security Council for their respective acceptance.
2. If the joint conference is unanimously agreed upon any person who fulfils the required conditions, he may be included in its list, even though he was not included in the list of nominations referred to in Article 7.
3. If the joint conference is satisfied that it will not be successful in procuring an election, those members of the Court who have already been elected shall, within a period to be fixed by the Security Council, proceed to fill the vacant seats by selection from among those candidates who have obtained votes either in the General Assembly or in the Security Council.
4. In the event of an equality of votes among the judges, the eldest judge shall have a casting vote.

Article 13

1. The members of the Court shall be elected for nine years and may be reselected; however, that of the judges elected at the first election, the terms of five judges shall expire at the end of three years and the terms of five more judges shall expire at the end of six years.
2. The judges whose terms are to expire at the end of the abovementioned initial periods of three and six years shall be chosen by lot to be drawn by the Secretary-General immediately after the first election has been completed.

3. The members of the Court shall continue to discharge their duties until their places have been filled. Though replaced, they shall finish any cases which they may have begun.
4. In the case of the resignation of a member of the Court, the resignation shall be addressed to the President of the Court for transmission to the Secretary-General. This last notification makes the place vacant.

Article 14

Vacancies shall be filled by the same method as that laid down for the first election, subject to the following provision: the Secretary-General shall, within one month of the occurrence of the vacancy, proceed to issue the invitations provided for in Article 5, and the date of the election shall be fixed by the Security Council.

Article 15

A member of the Court elected to replace a member whose term of office has not expired shall hold office for the remainder of his predecessor's term.

Article 16

1. No member of the Court may exercise any political or administrative function, or engage in any other occupation of a professional nature.
2. Any doubt on this point shall be settled by the decision of the Court.

Article 17

1. No member of the Court may act as agent, counsel, or advocate in any case.
2. No member may participate in the decision of any case in which he has previously taken part as agent, counsel, or advocate for one of the parties, or as a member of a national or international court, or of a commission of enquiry, or in any other capacity.
3. Any doubt on this point shall be settled by the decision of the Court.

Article 18

1. No member of the Court can be dismissed unless, in the unanimous opinion of the other members, he has ceased to fulfil the required conditions.
2. Formal notification thereof shall be made to the Secretary-General by the Registrar.
3. This notification makes the place vacant.

Article 19

The members of the Court, when engaged on the business of the Court, shall enjoy diplomatic privileges and immunities.

Article 20

Every member of the Court shall, before taking up his duties, make a solemn declaration in open court that he will exercise his powers impartially and conscientiously.

Article 21

1. The Court shall elect its President and Vice-President for three years; they may be reselected.
2. The Court shall appoint its Registrar and may provide for the appointment of such other officers as may be necessary.

Article 22

1. The seat of the Court shall be established at The Hague. This however, shall not prevent the Court from sitting and exercising its functions elsewhere whenever the Court considers it desirable.
2. The President and the Registrar shall reside at the seat of the Court.

Article 23

1. The Court shall remain permanently in session, except during the judicial vacations, the dates and duration of which shall be fixed by the Court.
2. Members of the Court are entitled to periodic leave, the dates and duration of which shall be fixed by the Court, having in mind the distance between The Hague and the home of each judge.
3. Members of the Court shall be bound, unless they are on leave or prevented from attending by illness or other serious reasons duly explained to the President, to hold themselves permanently at the disposal of the Court.

Article 24

1. If, for some special reason, a member of the Court considers that he should not take part in the decision of a particular case, he shall so inform the President.
2. If the President considers that for some special reason one of the members of the Court should not sit in a particular case, he shall give him notice accordingly.
3. If in any such case the member of the Court and the President disagree, the matter shall be settled by the decision of the Court.

Article 25

1. The full Court shall sit except when it is expressly provided otherwise in the present Statute.
2. Subject to the condition that the number of judges available to constitute the Court is not thereby reduced below eleven, the Rules of the Court may provide for allowing one or more judges, according to circumstances and in rotation, to be dispensed from sitting.
3. A quorum of nine judges shall suffice to constitute the Court.

Article 26

1. The Court may from time to time form one or more chambers, composed of three or more judges as the Court may determine, for dealing with particular categories of cases; for example, labor cases and cases relating to transit and communications.
2. The Court may at any time form a chamber for dealing with a particular case. The number of judges to constitute such a chamber shall be determined by the Court with the approval of the parties
3. Cases shall be heard and determined by the chambers provided for in this Article if the parties so request.

Article 27

A judgment given by any of the chambers provided for in Articles 26 and 29 shall be considered as rendered by the Court.

Article 28

The chambers provided for in Articles 26 and 29 may, with the consent of the parties, sit and exercise their functions elsewhere than at The Hague.

Article 29

With a view to the speedy dispatch of business, the Court shall form annually a chamber composed of five judges which, at the request of the parties, may hear and determine cases by summary procedure. In addition, two judges shall be selected for the purpose of replacing judges who find it impossible to sit.

Article 30

1. The Court shall frame rules for carrying out its functions. In particular, it shall lay down rules of procedure.
2. The Rules of the Court may provide for assessors to sit with the Court or with any of its chambers, without the right to vote.

Article 31

1. Judges of the nationality of each of the parties shall retain their right to sit in the case before the Court.
2. If the Court includes upon the Bench a judge of the nationality of one of the parties, any other party may choose a person to sit as judge. Such person shall be chosen preferably from among those persons who have been nominated as candidates as provided in Articles 4 and 5.
3. If the Court includes upon the Bench no judge of the nationality of the parties, each of these parties may proceed to choose a judge as provided in paragraph 2 of this Article.
4. The provisions of this Article shall apply to the case of Articles 26 and 29. In such cases, the President shall request one or, if necessary, two of the members of the Court forming the chamber to give place to the members of the Court of the nationality of the parties concerned, and, failing such, or if they are unable to be present, to the judges specially chosen by the parties.
5. Should there be several parties in the same interest, they shall, for the purpose of the preceding provisions, be reckoned as one party only. Any doubt upon this point shall be settled by the decision of the Court.
6. Judges chosen as laid down in paragraphs 2, 3, and 4 of this Article shall fulfil the conditions required by Articles 2, 17 (paragraph 2), 20, and 24 of the present Statute. They shall take part in the decision on terms of complete equality with their colleagues.

Article 32

1. Each member of the Court shall receive an annual salary.
2. The President shall receive a special annual allowance.
3. The Vice-President shall receive a special allowance for every day on which he acts as President.
4. The judges chosen under Article 31, other than members of the Court, shall receive compensation for each day on which they exercise their functions.
5. These salaries, allowances, and compensation shall be fixed by the General Assembly. They may not be decreased during the term of office.

6. The salary of the Registrar shall be fixed by the General Assembly on the proposal of the Court.
7. Regulations made by the General Assembly shall fix the conditions under which retirement pensions may be given to members of the Court and to the Registrar, and the conditions under which members of the Court and the Registrar shall have their traveling expenses refunded.
8. The above salaries, allowances, and compensation shall be free of all taxation.

Article 33

The expenses of the Court shall be borne by the United Nations in such a manner as shall be decided by the General Assembly.

CHAPTER II. COMPETENCE OF THE COURT

Article 34

1. Only states may be parties in cases before the Court.
2. The Court, subject to and in conformity with its Rules, may request of public international organizations information relevant to cases before it, and shall receive such information presented by such organizations on their own initiative.
3. Wherever the construction of the constituent instrument of a public international organization or of an international convention adopted thereunder is in question in a case before the Court, the Registrar shall so notify the public international organization concerned and shall communicate to it copies of all the written proceedings.

Article 35

1. The Court shall be open to the states parties to the present Statute.
2. The conditions under which the Court shall be open to other states shall, subject to the special provisions contained in treaties in force, be laid down by the Security Council, but in no case shall such conditions place the parties in a position of inequality before the Court.
3. When a state which is not a Member of the United Nations is a party to a case, the Court shall fix the amount which that party is to contribute towards the expenses of the Court. This provision shall not apply if such state is bearing a share of the expenses of the Court.

Article 36

1. The jurisdiction of the Court comprises all cases which the parties refer to it and all matters specially provided for in the Charter of the United Nations or in treaties and conventions in force.
2. The states parties to the present Statute may at any time declare that they recognize as compulsory *ipso facto* and without special agreement, in relation to any other state accepting the same obligation, the jurisdiction of the Court in all legal disputes concerning:
   a. the interpretation of a treaty;
   b. any question of international law;
   c. the existence of any fact which, if established, would constitute a breach of an international obligation;

d. the nature or extent of the reparation to be made for the breach of an international obligation.

3. The declarations referred to above may be made unconditionally or on condition of reciprocity on the part of several or certain states, or for a certain time.
4. Such declarations shall be deposited with the Secretary-General of the United Nations, who shall transmit copies thereof to the parties to the Statute and to the Registrar of the Court.
5. Declarations made under Article 36 of the Statute of the Permanent Court of International Justice and which are still in force shall be deemed, as between the parties to the present Statute, to be acceptances of the compulsory jurisdiction of the International Court of Justice for the period which they still have to run and in accordance with their terms.
6. In the event of a dispute as to whether the Court has jurisdiction, the matter shall be settled by the decision of the Court.

Article 37

Whenever a treaty or convention in force provides for reference of a matter to a tribunal to have been instituted by the League of Nations, or to the Permanent Court of International Justice, the matter shall, as between the parties to the present Statute, be referred to the International Court of Justice.

Article 38

1. The Court, whose function is to decide in accordance with international law such disputes as are submitted to it, shall apply:
   a. international conventions, whether general or particular, establishing rules expressly recognized by the contesting states;
   b. international custom, as evidence of a general practice accepted as law;
   c. the general principles of law recognized Hi civilized nations;
   d. subject to the provisions of Article 5~ judicial decisions and the teachings of the most highly qualified publicists of the various nations, as subsidiary means for the determination of rules of law.
2. This provision shall not prejudice the power of the Court to decide a case *en aequo et bono*, if the parties agree thereto.

CHAPTER III. PROCEDURE

Article 39

1. The official languages of the Court shall be French and English. If the parties agree that the case shall be conducted in French, the judgment shall be delivered in French. If the parties agree that the case shall be conducted in English, the judgment shall be delivered in English.
2. In the absence of an agreement as to which language shall be employed, each party may, m the pleadings, use the language which it prefers; the decision of the Court shall be given in French and English. In this case the Court shall at the same time determine which of the two texts shall be considered as authoritative.
3. The Court shall, at the request of any party, authorize a language other than French or English to be used by that party.

Article 40

1. Cases are brought before the Court, as the case may be, either by the notification of the special agreement or by a written application addressed to the Registrar. In either case the subject of the dispute and the parties shall be indicated.
2. The Registrar shall forthwith communicate the application to all concerned.
3. He shall also notify the Members of the United Nations through the Secretary-General, and also any other states entitled to appear before the Court.

Article 41

1. The Court shall have the power to indicate, if it considers that circumstances so require, any provisional measures which ought to be taken to preserve the respective rights of either party.
2. Pending the final decision, notice of the measures suggested shall forthwith be given to the parties and to the Security Council.

Article 42

1. The parties shall be represented by agents.
2. They may have the assistance of counsel or advocates before the Court.
3. The agents, counsel, and advocates of parties before the Court shall enjoy the privileges and immunities necessary to the independent exercise of their duties.

Article 43

1. The procedure shall consist of two parts: written and oral.
2. The written proceedings shall consist of the communication to the Court and to the parties of memorials, counter-memorials and, if necessary, replies; also all papers and documents in support.
3. These communications shall be made through the Registrar, in the order and within the time fixed by the Court.
4. A certified copy of every document produced by one party shall be communicated to the other party.
5. The oral proceedings shall consist of the hearing by the Court of witnesses, experts, agents, counsel, and advocates.

Article 44

1. For the service of all notices upon persons other than the agents, counsel, and advocates, the Court shall apply direct to the government of the state upon whose territory the notice has to be served.
2. The same provision shall apply whenever steps are to be taken to procure evidence on the spot.

Article 45

The hearing shall be under the control of the President or, if he is unable to preside, of the Vice-President; if neither is able to preside' the senior judge present shall preside.

Article 46

The hearing in Court shall be public, unless the Court shall decide otherwise, or unless the parties demand that the public be not admitted.

Article 47

1. Minutes shall be made at each hearing and signed by the Registrar and the President.
2. These minutes alone shall be authentic.

Article 48

The Court shall make orders for the conduct of the case, shall decide the form and time in which each party must conclude its arguments and make all arrangements connected with the taking of evidence.

Article 49

The Court may, even before the hearing begins, call upon the agents to produce any document or to supply any explanations. Formal note shall be taken of any refusal.

Article 50

The Court may, at any time, entrust any individual, body, bureau, commission, or other organization that it may select, with the task of carrying out an enquiry or giving an expert opinion.

Article 51

During the hearing any relevant questions are to be put to the witnesses and experts under the conditions laid down by the Court in the rules of procedure referred to in Article 30.

Article 52

After the Court has received the proofs and evidence within the time specified for the purpose, it may refuse to accept any further oral or written evidence that one party may desire to present unless the other side consents.

Article 53

1. Whenever one of the parties does not appear before the Court, or fails to defend its case, the other party may call upon the Court to decide in favor of its claim.
2. The Court must, before doing so, satisfy itself, not only that it has jurisdiction in accordance with Articles 36 and 37, but also that the claim is well founded In fact and law.

Article 54

1. When, subject to the control of the Court, the agents, counsel, and advocates have completed their presentation of the case, the President shall declare the hearing closed.
2. The Court shall withdraw to consider the judgment.
3. The deliberations of the Court shall take place in private and remain secret.

Article 55

1. All questions shall be decided by a majority of the judges present.
2. In the event of an equality of votes, the President or the judge who acts in his place shall have a casting vote.

Article 56

1. The judgment shall state the reasons on which it is based.
2. It shall contain the names of the judges who have taken part in the decision.

Article 57

If the judgment does not represent in whole or in part the unanimous opinion of the judges, any judge shall be entitled to deliver a separate opinion.

Article 58

The judgment shall be signed by the President and by the Registrar. It shall be read in open court, due notice having been given to the agents.

Article 59

The decision of the Court has no binding force except between the parties and in respect of that particular case.

Article 60

The judgment is final and without appeal. In the event of dispute as to the meaning or scope of the judgment, the Court shall construe it upon the request of any party.

Article 61

1. An application for revision of a judgment may be made only when it is based upon the discovery of some fact of such a nature as to be a decisive factor, which fact was, when the judgment was given, unknown to the Court and also to the party claiming revision, always provided that such ignorance was not due to negligence.
2. The proceedings for revision shall be opened by a judgment of the Court expressly recording the existence of the new fact, recognizing that it has such a character as to lay the case open to revision, and declaring the application admissible on this Ground.
3. The Court may require previous compliance with the terms of the judgment before it admits proceedings in revision.
4. The application for revision must be made at latest within six months of the discovery of the new fact
5. No application for revision may be made after the lapse of ten years from the date of the judgment.

Article 62

1. Should a state consider that it has an interest of a legal nature which may be affected by the decision in the case, it may submit a request to the Court to be permitted to intervene.
2. It shall be for the Court to decide upon this request.

Article 63

1. Whenever the construction of a convention to which states other than those concerned in the case are parties is in question, the Registrar shall notify all such states forthwith.
2. Every state so notified has the right to intervene in the proceedings; but if it uses this right, the construction given by the judgment will be equally binding upon it.

Article 64

Unless otherwise decided by the Court, each party shall bear its own costs.

CHAPTER IV. ADVISORY OPINIONS

Article 65

1. The Court may give an advisory opinion on any legal question at the request of whatever body may be authorized by or in accordance with the Charter of the United Nations to make such a request.
2. Questions upon which the advisory opinion of the Court is asked shall be laid before the Court by means of a written request containing an exact statement of the question upon which an opinion is required, and accompanied by all documents likely to throw light upon the question.

Article 66

1. The Registrar shall forthwith give notice of the request for an advisory opinion to all states entitled to appear before the Court.
2. The Registrar shall also, by means of a special and direct communication, notify any state entitled to appear before the Court or international organization considered by the Court, or, should it not be sitting, by the President, as likely to be able to furnish information—on the question, that the Court will be prepared to receive, within a time limit to be fixed by the President, written statements, or to hear, at a public sitting to be held for the purpose, oral statements relating to the question.
3. Should any such state entitled to appear before the Court have failed to receive the special communication referred to in paragraph 2 of this Article, such state may express a desire to submit a written statement or to be heard; and the Court will decide.
4. States and organizations having presented written or oral statements or both shall be permitted to comment on the statements made by other states or organizations in the form, to the extent, and within the time limits which the Court, or, should it not be sitting, the President, shall decide in each particular case. Accordingly, the Registrar shall in due time communicate any such written statements to states and organizations having submitted similar statements.

Article 67

The Court shall deliver its advisory opinions in open court, notice having been given to the Secretary-General and to the representatives of Members of the United Nations, of other states and of international organizations immediately concerned.

Article 68

In the exercise of its advisory functions the Court shall further be guided by the provisions of the present Statute which apply in contentious cases to the extent to which it recognizes them to be applicable.

CHAPTER V. AMENDMENT

Article 69

Amendments to the present Statute shall be effected by the same procedure as is provided by the Charter of the United Nations for amendments to that Charter, subject however to any provisions which the General Assembly upon recommendation of the Security Council may adopt concerning the participation of states which are parties to—the present Statute but are not Members of the United Nations.

Article 70

The Court shall have power to propose such amendments to the present Statute as it may deem necessary, through written communications to the Secretary-General, for consideration in conformity with the provisions of Article 69.

---

3. ILC Model Rules on Arbitral Procedure, 1956

Article 1

1. Any undertaking to have recourse to arbitration in order to settle a dispute between States constitutes a legal obligation which must be carried out in good faith.
2. Such an undertaking results from agreement between the parties and may apply to existing disputes (arbitration ad hoc) or to disputes arising in the future (arbitration treaties—arbitration clauses).
3. The undertaking shall result from a written instrument, whatever the form of the instrument may be.
4. The procedures offered to States Parties to a dispute by this draft shall not be compulsory unless the States concerned have agreed, either in the compromis or in some other undertaking, to have recourse thereto.

Article 2

Unless there are earlier agreements which suffice for the purpose, for example in the undertaking to arbitrate itself, the parties having recourse to arbitration shall conclude a compromis which shall specify, as a minimum:

(a) The undertaking to arbitrate under which the dispute shall be submitted to the arbitrators;

(b) The subject-matter of the dispute and, if possible, the points on which the parties are or are not agreed;

(c) The method of constituting the tribunal and the number of arbitrators.

The compromis shall likewise include any other provisions deemed desirable by the Parties, such as:

(1) The rules of law and the principles, to be applied by the tribunal, and the right, if any, conferred on it to decide ex aequo et bono as though it had legislative functions in the matter;

(2) The power, if any, of the tribunal to make recommendations to the parties;

(3) Such power as may be conferred on the tribunal to make its own rules of procedure;

(4) The procedure to be followed by the tribunal, on condition that, once constituted, the tribunal shall remain free to override any provisions of the compromise which may prevent it from rendering its award;

(5) the number of members constituting a quorum for the conduct of the proceedings;

(6) The majority required for the award;

(7) The time-limit within which the award shall be rendered;

(8) The right of members of the tribunal to attach or not to attach dissenting opinions to the award;

(9) The languages to be employed in the proceedings before the tribunal;

(10) The manner in which the costs shall be divided;

(11) The services which the International Court of Justice may be asked to render.

This enumeration is not intended to be exhaustive.

Article 3

1. If, before the constitution of an arbitral tribunal, the parties to an undertaking to arbitrate disagree as to the existence of a dispute, or as to whether the existing dispute is wholly or partly within the scope of the obligation to arbitrate, such preliminary question shall, failing agreement between the parties upon the adoption of another procedure, be brought by them within three months either before the Permanent Court of Arbitration for summary judgement, or, preferably, before the International Court of Justice, likewise for summary judgement or for an advisory opinion.
2. In its decision on the question, either Court may prescribe the provisional measures to be taken for the protection of the respective interests of the parties. The decision shall be final.
3. If the arbitral tribunal has already been constituted, any dispute concerning arbitrability shall be referred to it.

Article 4

1. Immediately after the request made by one of the Governments parties to the dispute for the submission of the dispute to arbitration or after the decision on the arbitrability of the dispute, the parties to an undertaking to arbitrate shall take the necessary steps, either in the compromis or by special agreement, in order to arrive at the constitution of the arbitral tribunal.
2. If the tribunal is not constituted within three months from the date of the request made for the submission of the dispute to arbitration, or from the date of the decision on arbitrability, the President of the International Court of Justice shall at the request of either party appoint the arbitrators not yet designated. If the President is prevented from acting or is a national of one of the parties, the appointments shall be made by the Vice-President. If the Vice-President is prevented from acting or is a national of one of the parties, the appointments shall be made by the oldest member of the Court who is not a national of either party.
3. The appointments referred to in paragraph 2 shall be made in accordance with the provisions of the compromis or of any other instrument pursuant to the undertaking to arbitrate and after consultation with the parties. In so far as these texts contain no rules with regard to the composition of the tribunal, the composition of the tribunals shall be determined, after consultation with the parties, by the President of the International Court of Justice or by the judge acting in his place. It shall be understood that in this event the number of the arbitrators must be uneven and should preferably be five.

4. Where provision is made for the choice of a president of the tribunal by the other arbitrators, the tribunal shall be deemed constituted when the president is selected. If the president has not been chosen within two months of the appointment of the arbitrators, he shall be designated in accordance with the procedure prescribed in paragraph 2.
5. Subject to the special circumstances of the case, the arbitrators shall be chosen from among persons of recognized competence in international law. They may call upon experts.

Article 5

1. Once the tribunal has been constituted, its composition shall remain unchanged until the award has been rendered.
2. A party may, however, replace an arbitrator appointed by it, provided that the tribunal has not yet begun its proceedings. An arbitrator may not be replaced during the proceedings before the tribunal except by agreement between the parties.
3. The proceedings are deemed to have begun when the president of the tribunal or the sole arbitrator has made the first order concerning written or oral proceedings.

Article 6

If a vacancy should occur on account of the death or the incapacity of an arbitrator, the vacancy shall be filled by agreement between the litigants or, if they cannot agree, in accordance with the procedure prescribed for the original appointment.

Article 7

1. Once the proceedings before the tribunal have begun, an arbitrator may withdraw (resign) only with the consent of the tribunal. The resulting vacancy shall be filled by the method laid down for the original appointments.
2. If the withdrawal should take place without the consent of the tribunal, the resulting vacancy shall be filled, at the request of the tribunal, in accordance with the procedure prescribed in Article 4, paragraph 2.

Article 8

1. A party may propose the disqualification of one of the arbitrators on account of a fact arising subsequently to the constitution of the tribunal. It may propose the disqualification of one of the arbitrators on account of a fact arising before the constitution of the tribunal only if it can show that the appointment was made without knowledge of that fact or as a result of fraud. In all cases, and particularly in the case of a sole arbitrator, the decision shall be taken by the International Court of Justice.
2. The resulting vacancies shall be filled in the manner prescribed in Article 4, paragraph 2.

Article 9

1. When the undertaking to arbitrate or any supplementary agreement contains provisions which seem sufficient for the purpose of a compromise and the tribunal has been constituted, either party may submit the dispute to the tribunal by application. If the other party refuses to answer the application on the ground that the provisions above referred to are insufficient, the tribunal shall decide

whether there is already sufficient agreement between the parties on the essential elements of the case as set forth in Article 2 to enable it to proceed. In the case of an affirmative decision the tribunal shall prescribe the necessary measures for the institution or continuation of the proceedings. In the contrary case the tribunal shall order the parties to complete or conclude the compromise within such time limit as it deems reasonable.

2. If the parties fail to agree on or to complete the compromise within the time limit fixed in accordance with the preceding paragraph, the tribunal itself shall draw up the compromis.

3. If the both parties consider that the elements available to the tribunal are insufficient for the purposed of a compromis but are themselves unable to draw up a compromis, the tribunal may do so in their stead, at the request of either party, within three months after they report failure to agree or after the decision, if nay, on the arbitrability of the dispute.

Article 10

The arbitral tribunal, which is the judge of its own competence, possess the widest powers to interpret the compromis.

Article 11

In the absence of any agreement between the parties concerning the law to be applied, the tribunal shall be guided by Article 38, paragraph 1, of the Statute of the International Court of Justice.

Article 12

The tribunal may not bring in a finding of non liquet on the ground of the silence or obscurity of international law or of the compromise.

Article 13

1. In the absence of any agreement between the parties concerning the procedure of the tribunal, or if the tribunal is unable to arrive at an award on the basis of the compromis, the tribunal shall be competent to make its rules of procedure.

2. All questions shall be decided by a majority of the tribunal.

Article 14

The parties shall be equal in any proceedings before the tribunal.

Article 15

When a sovereign is chosen as arbitrator, the arbitral procedure shall be settled by him.

Article 16

If the languages to be employed are not specified in the compromis, this shall be decided by the tribunal.

Article 17

1. The parties shall have the right to appoint special agents to attend the tribunal to act as intermediaries between them and the tribunal.

2. The parties shall also be entitled to retain for the defence of their rights and interests before the tribunal counsel or advocates appointed by them for the purpose.

3. Agents and counsel shall be entitled to submit orally to the tribunal any arguments they may deem expedient in the defence of their case.

4. The agents and counsel shall have the right to raise objections and points of law. The decisions of the tribunal on such objections and points of law shall be final.
5. The members of the tribunal shall have the right to question agents and counsel and to ask them for explanations. Neither the questions put nor the remarks made during the hearing may be regarded as an expression of opinion by the tribunal or by its members.

Article 18

1. The arbitral procedure shall in general comprise two distinct phases: pleadings and hearing.
2. The pleadings shall consist in the communication by the respective agents to the members of the tribunal and to the opposite party of statements, counter-statements and, if necessary, of replies; the parties shall attach all papers and documents referred to in the case.
3. The time fixed by the compromis may be extended by mutual agreement between the parties, or by the tribunal when it deems such extension necessary to enable it to reach a just decision.
4. The hearing shall consist in the oral development of the parties' arguments before the tribunal.
5. A certified true copy of every document produced by either party shall be communicated to the other party.

Article 19

1. The hearing shall be conducted by the president. It shall be public only if the tribunal so decides with the consent of the parties.
2. Records of the hearing shall be kept by secretaries appointed by the president. The records shall be signed by the president and by one of the secretaries; only those so signed shall be authentic.

Article 20

1. After the tribunal has closed the pleadings it shall have the right to reject any new papers and documents which either party may wish to submit to it without the consent of the other party. The tribunal shall, however, remain free to take into consideration any new papers and documents which the agents or counsel for the parties may bring to its notice and to require the production of such papers or documents, provided that they have been made known to the other party.
2. The tribunal may also require the agents and parties to produce all necessary documents and to provide all necessary explanations; it shall take note of any refusal to do so.

Article 21

1. The tribunal shall be the judge of the admissibility and the weight of the evidence presented to it.
2. The parties shall co-operate with the tribunal in the production of evidence and shall comply with the measures ordered by the tribunal for this purpose. The tribunal shall take note of the failure of any party to comply with its obligations under this paragraph.

3. The tribunal shall have the power at any stage of the proceedings to call for such evidence as it may deem necessary.

4. At the request of either party, the tribunal may decide to visit the scene connected with the case before it.

Article 22

1. The tribunal shall decide on any incidental or additional claims or counter-claims arising directly out of the subject-matter of the dispute.

Article 23

1. The tribunal, or in case of urgency its president, subject to confirmation by the tribunal, shall have the power to prescribe, at the request of one of the parties, any provisional measures necessary for the protection of the rights of the parties.

Article 24

1. When, subject to the control of the tribunal, the agents and counsel have completed their presentation of the case, the proceedings shall be formally declared closed.

2. So long as the award has not been rendered, the tribunal shall have the power to reopen the proceedings after their closure on the ground that new evidence is forthcoming of such a nature as to have a decisive influence on its decision.

Article 25

The deliberations of the tribunal, which shall be attended by all of its members, shall remain secret.

Article 26

1. Discontinuance of proceedings by the claimant party, either during the hearing or at the close thereof, shall not be accepted by the tribunal without the consent of the respondent.

2. If the case is discontinued by agreement between the parties, the tribunal shall take note of the fact.

Article 27

The tribunal may, if it thinks fit, take note of a settlement reached by the parties and, at the request of the parties, embody the settlement in an award.

Article 28

The award shall normally be rendered within the period fixed by the compromis, but the tribunal may decide to extend the said period if it would otherwise be unable to render the award.

Article 29

1. Whenever one of the parties has not appeared before the tribunal, or has failed to defend its case, the other party may call upon the tribunal to decide in favour of its claim.

2. The arbitral tribunal may grant the defaulting party a period of grace before rendering the award.

3. On the expiry of this period of grace, the tribunal may render an award after it has satisfied itself that it has jurisdiction and that the claim is well-founded in fact and in law.

Article 30

1. The award shall be drawn up in writing. It shall contain the names of the arbitrators and shall be signed by the president and by the members of the tribunal who have voted for it unless the compromis excludes the expression of separate or dissenting opinions.
2. Unless otherwise provided in the compromis, any member of the tribunal may attach his separate or dissenting opinion to the award.
3. The award shall be deemed to have been rendered when it has been read in open court, the agents of the parties being present or duly summoned to appear.
4. The award shall immediately be communicated to the parties.

Article 31

The award shall state the reasons on which it is based for every point on which it rules.

Article 32

Once rendered, the award shall be binding upon the parties. It shall be carried out in good faith immediately, unless the tribunal has fixed a time limit within which it must be carried out in its entirety or partly.

Article 33

For a period of one month after the award has been rendered and communicated to the parties, the tribunal, either of its own accord or at the request of either party, may rectify any clerical, typographical or arithmetical error or any obvious material error of a similar nature in the award.

Article 34

The arbitral award shall settle the dispute definitively and without appeal.

Article 35

1. Any dispute between the parties as to the meaning and scope of the award shall, at the request of either party and within one month of the rendering of the award, be submitted to the tribunal which rendered the award. A request for interpretation shall stay execution of the award pending the decision of the tribunal on the request.
2. If, for any reason, it is found impossible to submit the dispute to the tribunal which rendered the award, and if within a time limit of three months the parties have not agreed upon another solution, the dispute may be referred to the International Court of Justice at the request of either party.

Article 36

The validity of an award may be challenged by either party on one or more of the following grounds:

(a) That the tribunal has exceeded its powers;

(b) That there was corruption on the part of a member of the tribunal;

(c) That there has been a serious departure from a fundamental rule of procedure, including total or partial failure to state the reasons for the award.

Article 37

1. The International Court of Justice shall be competent, if the parties have not agreed on another court, to declare the nullity of the award on the application of either party.

2. In the cases covered by the Article 36, sub-paragraphs (a) and (c), the application must be made within sixty days of the rendering of the award and in the case covered by sub-paragraph (b) within six month.
3. The application shall stay execution unless otherwise decided by the court to which it is made.

Article 38

If the award is declared invalid by the International Court of Justice, the dispute shall be submitted to a new tribunal constituted by agreement of the parties, or, failing such agreement, in the manner provided in Article 4.

Article 39

1. An application for the revision of the award may be made by either party on the ground of the discovery of some fact of such a nature as to have a decisive influence on the award, provided that when the award was rendered that fact was unknown to the tribunal and to the party requesting revision and that such ignorance was not due to the negligence of the party requesting revision.
2. The application for revision must be made within six months of the discovery of the new fact and in any case within ten years of the rendering of the award.
3. In the proceedings for revision the tribunal shall, in the first instance, make a finding as to the existence of the alleged new fact and rule on the admissibility of the application.
4. If the tribunal finds the application admissible it shall then decide on the merits of the dispute.
5. The application for revision shall, whenever possible, be made to the tribunal which rendered the award.
6. If, for any reason it is not possible to make the application to that tribunal, as reconstituted, the application may, unless the parties agree otherwise, be made by either party either, and preferably, to the International Court of Justice or to the Permanent Court of Arbitration at The Hague.

4. ICSID Convention on the Settlement of Investment Disputes Between States and National of Other States, 1966

Chapter III
Conciliation

Section 1
Request for Conciliation

Article 28

1. Any Contracting State or any national of a Contracting State wishing to institute conciliation proceedings shall address a request to that effect in writing to the Secretary-General who shall send a copy of the request to the other party.

2. The request shall contain information concerning the issues in dispute, the identity of the parties and their consent to conciliation in accordance with the rules of procedure for the institution of conciliation and arbitration proceedings.
3. The Secretary-General shall register the request unless he finds, on the basis of the information contained in the request, that the dispute is manifestly outside the jurisdiction of the Centre. He shall forthwith notify the parties of registration or refusal to register.

Section 2
Constitution of the Conciliation Commission

Article 29

1. The Conciliation Commission (hereinafter called the Commission) shall be constituted as soon as possible after registration of a request pursuant to Article 28.
2.
   (a) The Commission shall consist of a sole conciliator or any uneven number of conciliators appointed as the parties shall agree.
   (b) Where the parties do not agree upon the number of conciliators and the method of their appointment, the Commission shall consist of three conciliators, one conciliator appointed by each party and the third, who shall be the president of the Commission, appointed by agreement of the parties.

Article 30

If the Commission shall not have been constituted within 90 days after notice of registration of the request has been dispatched by the Secretary-General in accordance with paragraph (3) of Article 28, or such other period as the parties may agree, the Chairman shall, at the request of either party and after consulting both parties as far as possible, appoint the conciliator or conciliators not yet appointed.

Article 31

1. Conciliators may be appointed from outside the Panel of Conciliators, except in the case of appointments by the Chairman pursuant to Article 30.
2. Conciliators appointed from outside the Panel of Conciliators shall possess the qualities stated in paragraph (1) of Article 14.

Section 3
Conciliation Proceedings

Article 32

1. The Commission shall be the judge of its own competence.
2. Any objection by a party to the dispute that that dispute is not within the jurisdiction of the Centre, or for other reasons is not within the competence of the Commission, shall be considered by the Commission which shall determine whether to deal with it as a preliminary question or to join it to the merits of the dispute.

Article 33

Any conciliation proceeding shall be conducted in accordance with the provisions of this Section and, except as the parties otherwise agree, in accordance with the Conciliation Rules in effect on the date on which the parties consented to conciliation. If any question of procedure arises which is not covered by this Section or the Conciliation Rules or any rules agreed by the parties, the Commission shall decide the question.

Article 34

1. It shall be the duty of the Commission to clarify the issues in dispute between the parties and to endeavour to bring about agreement between them upon mutually acceptable terms. To that end, the Commission may at any stage of the proceedings and from time to time recommend terms of settlement to the parties. The parties shall cooperate in good faith with the Commission in order to enable the Commission to carry out its functions, and shall give their most serious consideration to its recommendations.
2. If the parties reach agreement, the Commission shall draw up a report noting the issues in dispute and recording that the parties have reached agreement. If, at any stage of the proceedings, it appears to the Commission that there is no likelihood of agreement between the parties, it shall close the proceedings and shall draw up a report noting the submission of the dispute and recording the failure of the parties to reach agreement. If one party fails to appear or participate in the proceedings, the Commission shall close the proceedings and shall draw up a report noting that party's failure to appear or participate.

Article 35

Except as the parties to the dispute shall otherwise agree, neither party to a conciliation proceeding shall be entitled in any other proceeding, whether before arbitrators or in a court of law or otherwise, to invoke or rely on any views expressed or statements or admissions or offers of settlement made by the other party in the conciliation proceedings, or the report or any recommendations made by the Commission.

5. Vienna Convention on the Law of Treaties, 1969

The States Parties to the present Convention,

Considering the fundamental role of treaties in the history of international relations,

Recognizing the ever-increasing importance of treaties as a source of international law and as a means of developing peaceful co-operation among nations, whatever their constitutional and social systems,

Noting that the principles of free consent and of good faith and the *pacta sunt servanda* rule are universally recognized,

Affirming that disputes concerning treaties, like other international disputes, should be settled by peaceful means and in conformity with the principles of justice and international law,

Recalling the determination of the peoples of the United Nations to establish conditions under which justice and respect for the obligations arising from treaties can be maintained,

Having in mind the principles of international law embodied in the Charter of the United Nations, such as the principles of the equal rights and self-determination of peoples, of the sovereign equality and independence of all States, of non-interference in the domestic affairs of States, of the prohibition of the threat or use of force and of universal respect for, and observance of, human rights and fundamental freedoms for all,

Believing that the codification and progressive development of the law of treaties achieved in the present Convention will promote the purposes of the United Nations set forth in the Charter, namely, the maintenance of international peace and security, the development of friendly relations and the achievement of co-operation among nations,

Affirming that the rules of customary international law will continue to govern questions not regulated by the provisions of the present Convention,

Have agreed as follows:

PART I
INTRODUCTION

Article 1
Scope of the present Convention

The present Convention applies to treaties between States.

Article 2
Use of terms

1. For the purposes of the present Convention:
   (a) "treaty" means an international agreement concluded between States in written form and governed by international law, whether embodied in a single instrument or in two or more related instruments and whatever its particular designation;
   (b) "ratification", "acceptance", "approval" and "accession" mean in each case the international act so named whereby a State establishes on the international plane its consent to be bound by a treaty;
   (c) "'full powers"' means a document emanating from the competent authority of a State designating a person or persons to represent the State for negotiating, adopting or authenticating the text of a treaty, for expressing the consent of the State to be bound by a treaty, or for accomplishing any other act with respect to a treaty;
   (d) "'reservation"' means a unilateral statement, however phrased or named, made by a State, when signing, ratifying, accepting, approving or acceding to a treaty, whereby it purports to exclude or to modify the legal effect of certain provisions of the treaty in their application to that State;
   (e) "'negotiating State"' means a State which took part in the drawing up and adoption of the text of the treaty;
   (f) "'contracting State"' means a State which has consented to be bound by the treaty, whether or not the treaty has entered into force;
   (g) "'party"' means a State which has consented to be bound by the treaty and for which the treaty is in force;
   (h) "'third State"' means a State not a party to the treaty;
   (i) "'international organization"' means an intergovernmental organization.
2. The provisions of paragraph 1 regarding the use of terms in the present Convention are without prejudice to the use of those terms or to the meanings which may be given to them in the internal law of any State.

Article 3

International agreements not within the scope of the present Convention

The fact that the present Convention does not apply to international agreements concluded between States and other subjects of international law or between such other subjects of international law, or to international agreements not in written form, shall not affect:

(a) the legal force of such agreements;

(b) the application to them of any of the rules set forth in the present Convention to which they would be subject under international law independently of the Convention;

(c) the application of the Convention to the relations of States as between themselves under international agreements to which other subjects of international law are also parties.

Article 4

Non-retroactivity of the present Convention

Without prejudice to the application of any rules set forth in the present Convention to which treaties would be subject under international law independently of the Convention, the Convention applies only to treaties which are concluded by States after the entry into force of the present Convention with regard to such States.

Article 5

Treaties constituting international organizations and treaties adopted within an international organization

The present Convention applies to any treaty which is the constituent instrument of an international organization and to any treaty adopted within an international organization without prejudice to any relevant rules of the organization.

PART II

CONCLUSION AND ENTRY INTO FORCE OF TREATIES

SECTION 1. CONCLUSION OF TREATIES

Article 6

Capacity of States to conclude treaties

Every State possesses capacity to conclude treaties.

Article 7

Full powers

1. A person is considered as representing a State for the purpose of adopting or authenticating the text of a treaty or for the purpose of expressing the consent of the State to be bound by a treaty if:

   (a) he produces appropriate full powers; or

   (b) it appears from the practice of the States concerned or from other circumstances that their intention was to consider that person as representing the State for such purposes and to dispense with full powers.

2. In virtue of their functions and without having to produce full powers, the following are considered as representing their State:

   (a) Heads of State, Heads of Government and Ministers for Foreign Affairs, for the purpose of performing all acts relating to the conclusion of a treaty;

(b) heads of diplomatic missions, for the purpose of adopting the text of a treaty between the accrediting State and the State to which they are accredited;

(c) representatives accredited by States to an international conference or to an international organization or one of its organs, for the purpose of adopting the text of a treaty in that conference, organization or organ.

Article 8

Subsequent confirmation of an act performed without authorization

An act relating to the conclusion of a treaty performed by a person who cannot be considered under Article 7 as authorized to represent a State for that purpose is without legal effect unless afterwards confirmed by that State.

Article 9

Adoption of the text

1. The adoption of the text of a treaty takes place by the consent of all the States participating in its drawing up except as provided in paragraph 2.
2. The adoption of the text of a treaty at an international conference takes place by the vote of two-thirds of the States present and voting, unless by the same majority they shall decide to apply a different rule.

Article 10

Authentication of the text

The text of a treaty is established as authentic and definitive:

(a) by such procedure as may be provided for in the text or agreed upon by the States participating in its drawing up; or

(b) failing such procedure, by the signature, signature *ad referendum* or initialling by the representatives of those States of the text of the treaty or of the Final Act of a conference incorporating the text.

Article 11

Means of expressing consent to be bound by a treaty

The consent of a State to be bound by a treaty may be expressed by signature, exchange of instruments constituting a treaty, ratification, acceptance, approval or accession, or by any other means if so agreed.

Article 12

Consent to be bound by a treaty expressed by signature

1. The consent of a State to be bound by a treaty is expressed by the signature of its representative when:

   (a) the treaty provides that signature shall have that effect;

   (b) it is otherwise established that the negotiating States were agreed that signature should have that effect; or

   (c) the intention of the State to give that effect to the signature appears from the full powers of its representative or was expressed during the negotiation.

2. For the purposes of paragraph 1:

   (a) the initialling of a text constitutes a signature of the treaty when it is established that the negotiating States so agreed;

   (b) the signature *ad referendum* of a treaty by a representative, if confirmed by his State, constitutes a full signature of the treaty.

Article 13

Consent to be bound by a treaty expressed by an exchange of instruments constituting a treaty

The consent of States to be bound by a treaty constituted by instruments exchanged between them is expressed by that exchange when:

(a) the instruments provide that their exchange shall have that effect; or

(b) it is otherwise established that those States were agreed that the exchange of instruments should have that effect.

Article 14

Consent to be bound by a treaty expressed by ratification, acceptance or approval

1. The consent of a State to be bound by a treaty is expressed by ratification when:

   (a) the treaty provides for such consent to be expressed by means of ratification;

   (b) it is otherwise established that the negotiating States were agreed that ratification should be required;

   (c) the representative of the State has signed the treaty subject to ratification; or

   (d) the intention of the State to sign the treaty subject to ratification appears from the full powers of its representative or was expressed during the negotiation.

2. The consent of a State to be bound by a treaty is expressed by acceptance or approval under conditions similar to those which apply to ratification.

Article 15

Consent to be bound by a treaty expressed by accession

The consent of a State to be bound by a treaty is expressed by accession when:

(a) the treaty provides that such consent may be expressed by that State by means of accession;

(b) it is otherwise established that the negotiating States were agreed that such consent may be expressed by that State by means of accession; or

(c) all the parties have subsequently agreed that such consent may be expressed by that State by means of accession.

Article 16

Exchange or deposit of instruments of ratification, acceptance, approval or accession

Unless the treaty otherwise provides, instruments of ratification, acceptance, approval or accession establish the consent of a State to be bound by a treaty upon:

(a) their exchange between the contracting States;

(b) their deposit with the depositary; or

(c) their notification to the contracting States or to the depositary, if so agreed.

Article 17

Consent to be bound by part of a treaty and choice of differing provisions

1. Without prejudice to Articles 19 to 23, the consent of a State to be bound by part of a treaty is effective only if the treaty so permits or the other contracting States so agree.

2. The consent of a State to be bound by a treaty which permits a choice between differing provisions is effective only if it is made clear to which of the provisions the consent relates.

Article 18
Obligation not to defeat the object and purpose of a treaty prior to its entry into force

A State is obliged to refrain from acts which would defeat the object and purpose of a treaty when:

(a) it has signed the treaty or has exchanged instruments constituting the treaty subject to ratification, acceptance or approval, until it shall have made its intention clear not to become a party to the treaty; or

(b) it has expressed its consent to be bound by the treaty, pending the entry into force of the treaty and provided that such entry into force is not unduly delayed.

SECTION 2. RESERVATIONS

Article 19
Formulation of reservations

A State may, when signing, ratifying, accepting, approving or acceding to a treaty, formulate a reservation unless:

(a) the reservation is prohibited by the treaty;

(b) the treaty provides that only specified reservations, which do not include the reservation in question, may be made; or

(c) in cases not falling under sub-paragraphs (a) and (b), the reservation is incompatible with the object and purpose of the treaty.

Article 20
Acceptance of and objection to reservations

1. A reservation expressly authorized by a treaty does not require any subsequent acceptance by the other contracting States unless the treaty so provides.
2. When it appears from the limited number of the negotiating States and the object and purpose of a treaty that the application of the treaty in its entirety between all the parties is an essential condition of the consent of each one to be bound by the treaty, a reservation requires acceptance by all the parties.
3. When a treaty is a constituent instrument of an international organization and unless it otherwise provides, a reservation requires the acceptance of the competent organ of that organization.
4. In cases not falling under the preceding paragraphs and unless the treaty otherwise provides:

   (a) acceptance by another contracting State of a reservation constitutes the reserving State a party to the treaty in relation to that other State if or when the treaty is in force for those States;

   (b) an objection by another contracting State to a reservation does not preclude the entry into force of the treaty as between the objecting and reserving States unless a contrary intention is definitely expressed by the objecting State;

   (c) an act expressing a State's consent to be bound by the treaty and containing a reservation is effective as soon as at least one other contracting State has accepted the reservation.

5. For the purposes of paragraphs 2 and 4 and unless the treaty otherwise provides, a reservation is considered to have been accepted by a State if it shall have raised

no objection to the reservation by the end of a period of twelve months after it was notified of the reservation or by the date on which it expressed its consent to be bound by the treaty, whichever is later.

Article 21

Legal effects of reservations and of objections to reservations

1. A reservation established with regard to another party in accordance with Articles 19, 20 and 23:
   (a) modifies for the reserving State in its relations with that other party the provisions of the treaty to which the reservation relates to the extent of the reservation; and
   (b) modifies those provisions to the same extent for that other party in its relations with the reserving State.
2. The reservation does not modify the provisions of the treaty for the other parties to the treaty *inter se.*
3. When a State objecting to a reservation has not opposed the entry into force of the treaty between itself and the reserving State, the provisions to which the reservation relates do not apply as between the two States to the extent of the reservation.

Article 22

Withdrawal of reservations and of objections to reservations

1. Unless the treaty otherwise provides, a reservation may be withdrawn at any time and the consent of a State which has accepted the reservation is not required for its withdrawal.
2. Unless the treaty otherwise provides, an objection to a reservation may be withdrawn at any time.
3. Unless the treaty otherwise provides, or it is otherwise agreed:
   (a) the withdrawal of a reservation becomes operative in relation to another contracting State only when notice of it has been received by that State;
   (b) the withdrawal of an objection to a reservation becomes operative only when notice of it has been received by the State which formulated the reservation.

Article 23

Procedure regarding reservations

1. A reservation, an express acceptance of a reservation and an objection to a reservation must be formulated in writing and communicated to the contracting States and other States entitled to become parties to the treaty.
2. If formulated when signing the treaty subject to ratification, acceptance or approval, a reservation must be formally confirmed by the reserving State when expressing its consent to be bound by the treaty. In such a case the reservation shall be considered as having been made on the date of its confirmation.
3. An express acceptance of, or an objection to, a reservation made previously to confirmation of the reservation does not itself require confirmation.
4. The withdrawal of a reservation or of an objection to a reservation must be formulated in writing.

SECTION 3. ENTRY INTO FORCE AND PROVISIONAL APPLICATION OF TREATIES

Article 24
Entry into force

1. A treaty enters into force in such manner and upon such date as it may provide or as the negotiating States may agree.
2. Failing any such provision or agreement, a treaty enters into force as soon as consent to be bound by the treaty has been established for all the negotiating States.
3. When the consent of a State to be bound by a treaty is established on a date after the treaty has come into force, the treaty enters into force for that State on that date, unless the treaty otherwise provides.
4. The provisions of a treaty regulating the authentication of its text, the establishment of the consent of States to be bound by the treaty, the manner or date of its entry into force, reservations, the functions of the depositary and other matters arising necessarily before the entry into force of the treaty apply from the time of the adoption of its text.

Article 25
Provisional application

1. A treaty or a part of a treaty is applied provisionally pending its entry into force if:
   (a) the treaty itself so provides; or
   (b) the negotiating States have in some other manner so agreed.
2. Unless the treaty otherwise provides or the negotiating States have otherwise agreed, the provisional application of a treaty or a part of a treaty with respect to a State shall be terminated if that State notifies the other States between which the treaty is being applied provisionally of its intention not to become a party to the treaty.

PART III
OBSERVANCE, APPLICATION AND INTERPRETATION OF TREATIES

SECTION 1. OBSERVANCE OF TREATIES

Article 26
Pacta sunt servanda

Every treaty in force is binding upon the parties to it and must be performed by them in good faith.

Article 27
Internal law and observance of treaties

A party may not invoke the provisions of its internal law as justification for its failure to perform a treaty. This rule is without prejudice to Article 46.

SECTION 2. APPLICATION OF TREATIES

Article 28
Non-retroactivity of treaties

Unless a different intention appears from the treaty or is otherwise established, its provisions do not bind a party in relation to any act or fact which took place or any situation which ceased to exist before the date of the entry into force of the treaty with respect to that party.

Article 29
Territorial scope of treaties

Unless a different intention appears from the treaty or is otherwise established, a treaty is binding upon each party in respect of its entire territory.

Article 30
Application of successive treaties relating to the same subject-matter

1. Subject to Article 103 of the Charter of the United Nations, the rights and obligations of States parties to successive treaties relating to the same subject-matter shall be determined in accordance with the following paragraphs.
2. When a treaty specifies that it is subject to, or that it is not to be considered as incompatible with, an earlier or later treaty, the provisions of that other treaty prevail.
3. When all the parties to the earlier treaty are parties also to the later treaty but the earlier treaty is not terminated or suspended in operation under Article 59, the earlier treaty applies only to the extent that its provisions are compatible with those of the latter treaty.
4. When the parties to the later treaty do not include all the parties to the earlier one:
   (a) as between States parties to both treaties the same rule applies as in paragraph 3;
   (b) as between a State party to both treaties and a State party to only one of the treaties, the treaty to which both States are parties governs their mutual rights and obligations.
5. Paragraph 4 is without prejudice to Article 41, or to any question of the termination or suspension of the operation of a treaty under Article 60 or to any question of responsibility which may arise for a State from the conclusion or application of a treaty the provisions of which are incompatible with its obligations towards another State under another treaty.

SECTION 3. INTERPRETATION OF TREATIES

Article 31
General rule of interpretation

1. A treaty shall be interpreted in good faith in accordance with the ordinary meaning to be given to the terms of the treaty in their context and in the light of its object and purpose.
2. The context for the purpose of the interpretation of a treaty shall comprise, in addition to the text, including its preamble and annexes:
   (a) any agreement relating to the treaty which was made between all the parties in connection with the conclusion of the treaty;
   (b) any instrument which was made by one or more parties in connection with the conclusion of the treaty and accepted by the other parties as an instrument related to the treaty.
3. There shall be taken into account, together with the context:

(a) any subsequent agreement between the parties regarding the interpretation of the treaty or the application of its provisions;

(b) any subsequent practice in the application of the treaty which establishes the agreement of the parties regarding its interpretation;

(c) any relevant rules of international law applicable in the relations between the parties.

4. A special meaning shall be given to a term if it is established that the parties so intended.

Article 32
Supplementary means of interpretation

Recourse may be had to supplementary means of interpretation, including the preparatory work of the treaty and the circumstances of its conclusion, in order to confirm the meaning resulting from the application of Article 31, or to determine the meaning when the interpretation according to Article 31:

(a) leaves the meaning ambiguous or obscure; or

(b) leads to a result which is manifestly absurd or unreasonable.

Article 33
Interpretation of treaties authenticated in two or more languages

1. When a treaty has been authenticated in two or more languages, the text is equally authoritative in each language, unless the treaty provides or the parties agree that, in case of divergence, a particular text shall prevail.

2. A version of the treaty in a language other than one of those in which the text was authenticated shall be considered an authentic text only if the treaty so provides or the parties so agree.

3. The terms of the treaty are presumed to have the same meaning in each authentic text.

4. Except where a particular text prevails in accordance with paragraph 1, when a comparison of the authentic texts discloses a difference of meaning which the application of Articles 31 and 32 does not remove, the meaning which best reconciles the texts, having regard to the object and purpose of the treaty, shall be adopted.

SECTION 4. TREATIES AND THIRD STATES

Article 34
General rule regarding third States

A treaty does not create either obligations or rights for a third State without its consent.

Article 35
Treaties providing for obligations for third States

An obligation arises for a third State from a provision of a treaty if the parties to the treaty intend the provision to be the means of establishing the obligation and the third State expressly accepts that obligation in writing.

Article 36
Treaties providing for rights for third States

1. A right arises for a third State from a provision of a treaty if the parties to the treaty intend the provision to accord that right either to the third State, or to a

group of States to which it belongs, or to all States, and the third State assents thereto. Its assent shall be presumed so long as the contrary is not indicated, unless the treaty otherwise provides.

2. A State exercising a right in accordance with paragraph 1 shall comply with the conditions for its exercise provided for in the treaty or established in conformity with the treaty.

Article 37
Revocation or modification of obligations or rights of third States

1. When an obligation has arisen for a third State in conformity with Article 35, the obligation may be revoked or modified only with the consent of the parties to the treaty and of the third State, unless it is established that they had otherwise agreed.
2. When a right has arisen for a third State in conformity with Article 36, the right may not be revoked or modified by the parties if it is established that the right was intended not to be revocable or subject to modification without the consent of the third State.

Article 38
Rules in a treaty becoming binding on third States through international custom

Nothing in Articles 34 to 37 precludes a rule set forth in a treaty from becoming binding upon a third State as a customary rule of international law, recognized as such.

PART IV
AMENDMENT AND MODIFICATION OF TREATIES

Article 39
General rule regarding the amendment of treaties

A treaty may be amended by agreement between the parties. The rules laid down in Part II apply to such an agreement except in so far as the treaty may otherwise provide.

Article 40
Amendment of multilateral treaties

1. Unless the treaty otherwise provides, the amendment of multilateral treaties shall be governed by the following paragraphs.
2. Any proposal to amend a multilateral treaty as between all the parties must be notified to all the contracting States, each one of which shall have the right to take part in:
   (a) the decision as to the action to be taken in regard to such proposal;
   (b) the negotiation and conclusion of any agreement for the amendment of the treaty.
3. Every State entitled to become a party to the treaty shall also be entitled to become a party to the treaty as amended.
4. The amending agreement does not bind any State already a party to the treaty which does not become a party to the amending agreement; Article 30, paragraph 4(b), applies in relation to such State.
5. Any State which becomes a party to the treaty after the entry into force of the amending agreement shall, failing an expression of a different intention by that State:
   (a) be considered as a party to the treaty as amended; and

(b) be considered as a party to the unamended treaty in relation to any party to the treaty not bound by the amending agreement.

Article 41

Agreements to modify multilateral treaties between certain of the parties only

1. Two or more of the parties to a multilateral treaty may conclude an agreement to modify the treaty as between themselves alone if:

   (a) the possibility of such a modification is provided for by the treaty; or

   (b) the modification in question is not prohibited by the treaty and:

      (i) does not affect the enjoyment by the other parties of their rights under the treaty or the performance of their obligations;

      (ii) does not relate to a provision, derogation from which is incompatible with the effective execution of the object and purpose of the treaty as a whole.

2. Unless in a case falling under paragraph 1(a) the treaty otherwise provides, the parties in question shall notify the other parties of their intention to conclude the agreement and of the modification to the treaty for which it provides.

PART V

INVALIDITY, TERMINATION AND SUSPENSION OF THE OPERATION OF TREATIES

SECTION 1. GENERAL PROVISIONS

Article 42

Validity and continuance in force of treaties

1. The validity of a treaty or of the consent of a State to be bound by a treaty may be impeached only through the application of the present Convention.

2. The termination of a treaty, its denunciation or the withdrawal of a party, may take place only as a result of the application of the provisions of the treaty or of the present Convention. The same rule applies to suspension of the operation of a treaty.

Article 43

Obligations imposed by international law independently of a treaty

The invalidity, termination or denunciation of a treaty, the withdrawal of a party from it, or the suspension of its operation, as a result of the application of the present Convention or of the provisions of the treaty, shall not in any way impair the duty of any State to fulfil any obligation embodied in the treaty to which it would be subject under international law independently of the treaty.

Article 44

Separability of treaty provisions

1. A right of a party, provided for in a treaty or arising under Article 56, to denounce, withdraw from or suspend the operation of the treaty may be exercised only with respect to the whole treaty unless the treaty otherwise provides or the parties otherwise agree.

2. A ground for invalidating, terminating, withdrawing from or suspending the operation of a treaty recognized in the present Convention may be invoked only with respect to the whole treaty except as provided in the following paragraphs or in Article 60.

3. If the ground relates solely to particular clauses, it may be invoked only with respect to those clauses where:
   (a) the said clauses are separable from the remainder of the treaty with regard to their application;
   (b) it appears from the treaty or is otherwise established that acceptance of those clauses was not an essential basis of the consent of the other party or parties to be bound by the treaty as a whole; and
   (c) continued performance of the remainder of the treaty would not be unjust.
4. In cases falling under Articles 49 and 50 the State entitled to invoke the fraud or corruption may do so with respect either to the whole treaty or, subject to paragraph 3, to the particular clauses alone.
5. In cases falling under Articles 51, 52 and 53, no separation of the provisions of the treaty is permitted.

Article 45
Loss of a right to invoke a ground for invalidating, terminating, withdrawing from or suspending the operation of a treaty

A State may no longer invoke a ground for invalidating, terminating, withdrawing from or suspending the operation of a treaty under Articles 46 to 50 or Articles 60 and 62 if, after becoming aware of the facts:

(a) it shall have expressly agreed that the treaty is valid or remains in force or continues in operation, as the case may be; or
(b) it must by reason of its conduct be considered as having acquiesced in the validity of the treaty or in its maintenance in force or in operation, as the case may be.

SECTION 2. INVALIDITY OF TREATIES

Article 46
Provisions of internal law regarding competence to conclude treaties

1. A State may not invoke the fact that its consent to be bound by a treaty has been expressed in violation of a provision of its internal law regarding competence to conclude treaties as invalidating its consent unless that violation was manifest and concerned a rule of its internal law of fundamental importance.
2. A violation is manifest if it would be objectively evident to any State conducting itself in the matter in accordance with normal practice and in good faith.

Article 47
Specific restrictions on authority to express the consent of a State

If the authority of a representative to express the consent of a State to be bound by a particular treaty has been made subject to a specific restriction, his omission to observe that restriction may not be invoked as invalidating the consent expressed by him unless the restriction was notified to the other negotiating States prior to his expressing such consent.

Article 48
Error

1. A State may invoke an error in a treaty as invalidating its consent to be bound by the treaty if the error relates to a fact or situation which was assumed by that

State to exist at the time when the treaty was concluded and formed an essential basis of its consent to be bound by the treaty.

2. Paragraph 1 shall not apply if the State in question contributed by its own conduct to the error or if the circumstances were such as to put that State on notice of a possible error.

3. An error relating only to the wording of the text of a treaty does not affect its validity; Article 79 then applies.

Article 49
Fraud

If a State has been induced to conclude a treaty by the fraudulent conduct of another negotiating State, the State may invoke the fraud as invalidating its consent to be bound by the treaty.

Article 50
Corruption of a representative of a State

If the expression of a State's consent to be bound by a treaty has been procured through the corruption of its representative directly or indirectly by another negotiating State, the State may invoke such corruption as invalidating its consent to be bound by the treaty.

Article 51
Coercion of a representative of a State

The expression of a State's consent to be bound by a treaty which has been procured by the coercion of its representative through acts or threats directed against him shall be without any legal effect.

Article 52
Coercion of a State by the threat or use of force

A treaty is void if its conclusion has been procured by the threat or use of force in violation of the principles of international law embodied in the Charter of the United Nations.

Article 53
Treaties conflicting with a peremptory norm of general international law (jus cogens)

A treaty is void if, at the time of its conclusion, it conflicts with a peremptory norm of general international law. For the purposes of the present Convention, a peremptory norm of general international law is a norm accepted and recognized by the international community of States as a whole as a norm from which no derogation is permitted and which can be modified only by a subsequent norm of general international law having the same character.

SECTION 3. TERMINATION AND SUSPENSION OF THE OPERATION OF TREATIES

Article 54
Termination of or withdrawal from a treaty under its provisions or by consent of the parties

The termination of a treaty or the withdrawal of a party may take place:

(a) in conformity with the provisions of the treaty; or

(b) at any time by consent of all the parties after consultation with the other contracting States.

Article 55

Reduction of the parties to a multilateral treaty below the number necessary for its entry into force

Unless the treaty otherwise provides, a multilateral treaty does not terminate by reason only of the fact that the number of the parties falls below the number necessary for its entry into force.

Article 56

Denunciation of or withdrawal from a treaty containing no provision regarding termination, denunciation or withdrawal

1. A treaty which contains no provision regarding its termination and which does not provide for denunciation or withdrawal is not subject to denunciation or withdrawal unless:

   (a) it is established that the parties intended to admit the possibility of denunciation or withdrawal; or

   (b) a right of denunciation or withdrawal may be implied by the nature of the treaty.

2. A party shall give not less than twelve months' notice of its intention to denounce or withdraw from a treaty under paragraph 1.

Article 57

Suspension of the operation of a treaty under its provisions or by consent of the parties

The operation of a treaty in regard to all the parties or to a particular party may be suspended:

(a) in conformity with the provisions of the treaty; or

(b) at any time by consent of all the parties after consultation with the other contracting States.

Article 58

Suspension of the operation of a multilateral treaty by agreement between certain of the parties only

1. Two or more parties to a multilateral treaty may conclude an agreement to suspend the operation of provisions of the treaty, temporarily and as between themselves alone, if:

   (a) the possibility of such a suspension is provided for by the treaty; or

   (b) the suspension in question is not prohibited by the treaty and:

      (i) does not affect the enjoyment by the other parties of their rights under the treaty or the performance of their obligations;

      (ii) is not incompatible with the object and purpose of the treaty.

2. Unless in a case falling under paragraph 1(a) the treaty otherwise provides, the parties in question shall notify the other parties of their intention to conclude the agreement and of those provisions of the treaty the operation of which they intend to suspend.

Article 59

Termination or suspension of the operation of a treaty implied by conclusion of a later treaty

1. A treaty shall be considered as terminated if all the parties to it conclude a later treaty relating to the same subject-matter and:

(a) it appears from the later treaty or is otherwise established that the parties intended that the matter should be governed by that treaty; or

(b) the provisions of the later treaty are so far incompatible with those of the earlier one that the two treaties are not capable of being applied at the same time.

2. The earlier treaty shall be considered as only suspended in operation if it appears from the later treaty or is otherwise established that such was the intention of the parties.

Article 60
Termination or suspension of the operation of a treaty as a consequence of its breach

1. A material breach of a bilateral treaty by one of the parties entitles the other to invoke the breach as a ground for terminating the treaty or suspending its operation in whole or in part.

2. A material breach of a multilateral treaty by one of the parties entitles:

(a) the other parties by unanimous agreement to suspend the operation of the treaty in whole or in part or to terminate it either:

(i) in the relations between themselves and the defaulting State, or

(ii) as between all the parties;

(b) a party specially affected by the breach to invoke it as a ground for suspending the operation of the treaty in whole or in part in the relations between itself and the defaulting State;

(c) any party other than the defaulting State to invoke the breach as a ground for suspending the operation of the treaty in whole or in part with respect to itself if the treaty is of such a character that a material breach of its provisions by one party radically changes the position of every party with respect to the further performance of its obligations under the treaty.

3. A material breach of a treaty, for the purposes of this Article, consists in:

(a) a repudiation of the treaty not sanctioned by the present Convention; or

(b) the violation of a provision essential to the accomplishment of the object or purpose of the treaty.

4. The foregoing paragraphs are without prejudice to any provision in the treaty applicable in the event of a breach.

5. Paragraphs 1 to 3 do not apply to provisions relating to the protection of the human person contained in treaties of a humanitarian character, in particular to provisions prohibiting any form of reprisals against persons protected by such treaties.

Article 61
Supervening impossibility of performance

1. A party may invoke the impossibility of performing a treaty as a ground for terminating or withdrawing from it if the impossibility results from the permanent disappearance or destruction of an object indispensable for the execution of the treaty. If the impossibility is temporary, it may be invoked only as a ground for suspending the operation of the treaty.

2. Impossibility of performance may not be invoked by a party as a ground for terminating, withdrawing from or suspending the operation of a treaty if the im-

possibility is the result of a breach by that party either of an obligation under the treaty or of any other international obligation owed to any other party to the treaty.

Article 62

Fundamental change of circumstances

1. A fundamental change of circumstances which has occurred with regard to those existing at the time of the conclusion of a treaty, and which was not foreseen by the parties, may not be invoked as a ground for terminating or withdrawing from the treaty unless:
   (a) the existence of those circumstances constituted an essential basis of the consent of the parties to be bound by the treaty; and
   (b) the effect of the change is radically to transform the extent of obligations still to be performed under the treaty.
2. A fundamental change of circumstances may not be invoked as a ground for terminating or withdrawing from a treaty:
   (a) if the treaty establishes a boundary; or
   (b) if the fundamental change is the result of a breach by the party invoking it either of an obligation under the treaty or of any other international obligation owed to any other party to the treaty.
3. If, under the foregoing paragraphs, a party may invoke a fundamental change of circumstances as a ground for terminating or withdrawing from a treaty it may also invoke the change as a ground for suspending the operation of the treaty.

Article 63

Severance of diplomatic or consular relations

The severance of diplomatic or consular relations between parties to a treaty does not affect the legal relations established between them by the treaty except in so far as the existence of diplomatic or consular relations is indispensable for the application of the treaty.

Article 64

*Emergence of a new peremptory norm of general international law (*jus cogens*)*

If a new peremptory norm of general international law emerges, any existing treaty which is in conflict with that norm becomes void and terminates.

SECTION 4. PROCEDURE

Article 65

Procedure to be followed with respect to invalidity, termination, withdrawal from or suspension of the operation of a treaty

1. A party which, under the provisions of the present Convention, invokes either a defect in its consent to be bound by a treaty or a ground for impeaching the validity of a treaty, terminating it, withdrawing from it or suspending its operation, must notify the other parties of its claim. The notification shall indicate the measure proposed to be taken with respect to the treaty and the reasons therefor.

2. If, after the expiry of a period which, except in cases of special urgency, shall not be less than three months after the receipt of the notification, no party has raised any objection, the party making the notification may carry out in the manner provided in Article 67 the measure which it has proposed.

3. If, however, objection has been raised by any other party, the parties shall seek a solution through the means indicated in Article 33 of the Charter of the United Nations.
4. Nothing in the foregoing paragraphs shall affect the rights or obligations of the parties under any provisions in force binding the parties with regard to the settlement of disputes.
5. Without prejudice to Article 45, the fact that a State has not previously made the notification prescribed in paragraph 1 shall not prevent it from making such notification in answer to another party claiming performance of the treaty or alleging its violation.

Article 66
Procedures for judicial settlement, arbitration and conciliation

If, under paragraph 3 of Article 65, no solution has been reached within a period of 12 months following the date on which the objection was raised, the following procedures shall be followed:

(a) any one of the parties to a dispute concerning the application or the interpretation of Articles 53 or 64 may, by a written application, submit it to the International Court of Justice for a decision unless the parties by common consent agree to submit the dispute to arbitration;

(b) any one of the parties to a dispute concerning the application or the interpretation of any of the other Articles in Part V of the present Convention may set in motion the procedure specified in the Annex to the Convention by submitting a request to that effect to the Secretary-General of the United Nations.

Article 67
Instruments for declaring invalid, terminating, withdrawing from or suspending the operation of a treaty

1. The notification provided for under Article 65 paragraph 1 must be made in writing.
2. Any act declaring invalid, terminating, withdrawing from or suspending the operation of a treaty pursuant to the provisions of the treaty or of paragraphs 2 or 3 of Article 65 shall be carried out through an instrument communicated to the other parties. If the instrument is not signed by the Head of State, Head of Government or Minister for Foreign Affairs, the representative of the State communicating it may be called upon to produce full powers.

Article 68
Revocation of notifications and instruments provided for in Articles 65 and 67

A notification or instrument provided for in Articles 65 or 67 may be revoked at any time before it takes effect.

SECTION 5. CONSEQUENCES OF THE INVALIDITY, TERMINATION OR SUSPENSION OF THE OPERATION OF A TREATY

Article 69
Consequences of the invalidity of a treaty

1. A treaty the invalidity of which is established under the present Convention is void. The provisions of a void treaty have no legal force.
2. If acts have nevertheless been performed in reliance on such a treaty:

(a) each party may require any other party to establish as far as possible in their mutual relations the position that would have existed if the acts had not been performed;

(b) acts performed in good faith before the invalidity was invoked are not rendered unlawful by reason only of the invalidity of the treaty.

3. In cases falling under Articles 49, 50, 51 or 52, paragraph 2 does not apply with respect to the party to which the fraud, the act of corruption or the coercion is imputable.

4. In the case of the invalidity of a particular State's consent to be bound by a multilateral treaty, the foregoing rules apply in the relations between that State and the parties to the treaty.

Article 70
Consequences of the termination of a treaty

1. Unless the treaty otherwise provides or the parties otherwise agree, the termination of a treaty under its provisions or in accordance with the present Convention:

(a) releases the parties from any obligation further to perform the treaty;

(b) does not affect any right, obligation or legal situation of the parties created through the execution of the treaty prior to its termination.

2. If a State denounces or withdraws from a multilateral treaty, paragraph 1 applies in the relations between that State and each of the other parties to the treaty from the date when such denunciation or withdrawal takes effect.

Article 71
Consequences of the invalidity of a treaty which conflict with a peremptory norm of general international law

1. In the case of a treaty which is void under Article 53 the parties shall:

(a) eliminate as far as possible the consequences of any act performed in reliance on any provision which conflicts with the peremptory norm of general international law; and

(b) bring their mutual relations into conformity with the peremptory norm of general international law.

2. In the case of a treaty which becomes void and terminates under Article 64, the termination of the treaty:

(a) releases the parties from any obligation further to perform the treaty;

(b) does not affect any right, obligation or legal situation of the parties created through the execution of the treaty prior to its termination; provided that those rights, obligations or situations may thereafter be maintained only to the extent that their maintenance is not in itself in conflict with the new peremptory norm of general international law.

Article 72
Consequences of the suspension of the operation of a treaty

1. Unless the treaty otherwise provides or the parties otherwise agree, the suspension of the operation of a treaty under its provisions or in accordance with the present Convention:

(a) releases the parties between which the operation of the treaty is suspended from the obligation to perform the treaty in their mutual relations during the period of the suspension;

(b) does not otherwise affect the legal relations between the parties established by the treaty.

2. During the period of the suspension the parties shall refrain from acts tending to obstruct the resumption of the operation of the treaty.

PART VI
MISCELLANEOUS PROVISIONS

Article 73
Cases of State succession, State responsibility and outbreak of hostilities

The provisions of the present Convention shall not prejudge any question that may arise in regard to a treaty from a succession of States or from the international responsibility of a State or from the outbreak of hostilities between States.

Article 74
Diplomatic and consular relations and the conclusion of treaties

The severance or absence of diplomatic or consular relations between two or more States does not prevent the conclusion of treaties between those States. The conclusion of a treaty does not in itself affect the situation in regard to diplomatic or consular relations.

Article 75
Case of an aggressor State

The provisions of the present Convention are without prejudice to any obligation in relation to a treaty which may arise for an aggressor State in consequence of measures taken in conformity with the Charter of the United Nations with reference to that State's aggression.

PART VII
DEPOSITARIES, NOTIFICATIONS, CORRECTIONS AND REGISTRATION

Article 76
Depositaries of treaties

1. The designation of the depositary of a treaty may be made by the negotiating States, either in the treaty itself or in some other manner. The depositary may be one or more States, an international organization or the chief administrative officer of the organization.

2. The functions of the depositary of a treaty are international in character and the depositary is under an obligation to act impartially in their performance. In particular, the fact that a treaty has not entered into force between certain of the parties or that a difference has appeared between a State and a depositary with regard to the performance of the latter's functions shall not affect that obligation.

Article 77
Functions of depositaries

1. The functions of a depositary, unless otherwise provided in the treaty or agreed by the contracting States, comprise in particular:

(a) keeping custody of the original text of the treaty and of any full powers delivered to the depositary;

(b) preparing certified copies of the original text and preparing any further text of the treaty in such additional languages as may be required by the treaty and transmitting them to the parties and to the States entitled to become parties to the treaty;

(c) receiving any signatures to the treaty and receiving and keeping custody of any instruments, notifications and communications relating to it;

(d) examining whether the signature or any instrument, notification or communication relating to the treaty is in due and proper form and, if need be, bringing the matter to the attention of the State in question;

(e) informing the parties and the States entitled to become parties to the treaty of acts, notifications and communications relating to the treaty;

(f) informing the States entitled to become parties to the treaty when the number of signatures or of instruments of ratification, acceptance, approval or accession required for the entry into force of the treaty has been received or deposited;

(g) registering the treaty with the Secretariat of the United Nations;

(h) performing the functions specified in other provisions of the present Convention.

2. In the event of any difference appearing between a State and the depositary as to the performance of the latter's functions, the depositary shall bring the question to the attention of the signatory States and the contracting States or, where appropriate, of the competent organ of the international organization concerned.

Article 78
Notifications and communications

Except as the treaty or the present Convention otherwise provide, any notification or communication to be made by any State under the present Convention shall:

(a) if there is no depositary, be transmitted direct to the States for which it is intended, or if there is a depositary, to the latter;

(b) be considered as having been made by the State in question only upon its receipt by the State to which it was transmitted or, as the case may be, upon its receipt by the depositary;

(c) if transmitted to a depositary, be considered as received by the State for which it was intended only when the latter State has been informed by the depositary in accordance with Article 77, paragraph 1 (e).

Article 79
Correction of errors in texts or in certified copies of treaties

1. Where, after the authentication of the text of a treaty, the signatory States and the contracting States are agreed that it contains an error, the error shall, unless they decide upon some other means of correction, be corrected:

(a) by having the appropriate correction made in the text and causing the correction to be initialled by duly authorized representatives;

(b) by executing or exchanging an instrument or instruments setting out the correction which it has been agreed to make; or

(c) by executing a corrected text of the whole treaty by the same procedure as in the case of the original text.

2. Where the treaty is one for which there is a depositary, the latter shall notify the signatory States and the contracting States of the error and of the proposal to correct it and shall specify an appropriate time-limit within which objection to the proposed correction may be raised. If, on the expiry of the time-limit:

   (a) no objection has been raised, the depositary shall make and initial the correction in the text and shall execute a *procés-verbal* of the rectification of the text and communicate a copy of it to the parties and to the States entitled to become parties to the treaty;

   (b) an objection has been raised, the depositary shall communicate the objection to the signatory States and to the contracting States.

3. The rules in paragraphs 1 and 2 apply also where the text has been authenticated in two or more languages and it appears that there is a lack of concordance which the signatory States and the contracting States agree should be corrected.

4. The corrected text replaces the defective text *ab initio*, unless the signatory States and the contracting States otherwise decide.

5. The correction of the text of a treaty that has been registered shall be notified to the Secretariat of the United Nations.

6. Where an error is discovered in a certified copy of a treaty, the depositary shall execute a *procés-verbal* specifying the rectification and communicate a copy of it to the signatory States and to the contracting States.

Article 80
Registration and publication of treaties

1. Treaties shall, after their entry into force, be transmitted to the Secretariat of the United Nations for registration or filing and recording, as the case may be, and for publication.

2. The designation of a depositary shall constitute authorization for it to perform the acts specified in the preceding paragraph.

PART VIII
FINAL PROVISIONS

Article 81
Signature

The present Convention shall be open for signature by all States Members of the United Nations or of any of the specialized agencies or of the International Atomic Energy Agency or parties to the Statute of the International Court of Justice, and by any other State invited by the General Assembly of the United Nations to become a party to the Convention, as follows: until 30 November 1969, at the Federal Ministry for Foreign Affairs of the Republic of Austria, and subsequently, until 30 April 1970, at United Nations Headquarters, New York.

Article 82
Ratification

The present Convention is subject to ratification. The instruments of ratification shall be deposited with the Secretary-General of the United Nations.

Article 83
Accession

The present Convention shall remain open for accession by any State belonging to any of the categories mentioned in Article 81. The instruments of accession shall be deposited with the Secretary-General of the United Nations.

Article 84
Entry into force

1. The present Convention shall enter into force on the thirtieth day following the date of deposit of the thirty-fifth instrument of ratification or accession.
2. For each State ratifying or acceding to the Convention after the deposit of the thirty-fifth instrument of ratification or accession, the Convention shall enter into force on the thirtieth day after deposit by such State of its instrument of ratification or accession.

Article 85
Authentic texts

The original of the present Convention, of which the Chinese, English, French, Russian and Spanish texts are equally authentic, shall be deposited with the Secretary-General of the United Nations.

IN WITNESS WHEREOF the undersigned Plenipotentiaries, being duly authorized thereto by their respective Governments, have signed the present Convention.

DONE at Vienna, this twenty-third day of May, one thousand nine hundred and sixty-nine.

ANNEX

1. A list of conciliators consisting of qualified jurists shall be drawn up and maintained by the Secretary-General of the United Nations. To this end, every State which is a Member of the United Nations or a party to the present Convention shall be invited to nominate two conciliators, and the names of the persons so nominated shall constitute the list. The term of a conciliator, including that of any conciliator nominated to fill a casual vacancy, shall be five years and may be renewed. A conciliator whose term expires shall continue to fulfil any function for which he shall have been chosen under the following paragraph.
2. When a request has been made to the Secretary-General under Article 66, the Secretary-General shall bring the dispute before a conciliation commission constituted as follows:

The State or States constituting one of the parties to the dispute shall appoint:

(a) one conciliator of the nationality of that State or of one of those States, who may or may not be chosen from the list referred to in paragraph 1; and

(b) one conciliator not of the nationality of that State or of any of those States, who shall be chosen from the list.

The State or States constituting the other party to the dispute shall appoint two conciliators in the same way. The four conciliators chosen by the parties shall be appointed within sixty days following the date on which the Secretary-General receives the request.

The four conciliators shall, within sixty days following the date of the last of their own appointments, appoint a fifth conciliator chosen from the list, who shall be chairman.

If the appointment of the chairman or of any of the other conciliators has not been made within the period prescribed above for such appointment, it shall be made by the Secretary-General within sixty days following the expiry of that period. The appointment of the chairman may be made by the Secretary-General either from the list or from the membership of the International Law Commission. Any of the periods within which appointments must be made may be extended by agreement between the parties to the dispute.

Any vacancy shall be filled in the manner prescribed for the initial appointment.

3. The Conciliation Commission shall decide its own procedure. The Commission, with the consent of the parties to the dispute, may invite any party to the treaty to submit to it its views orally or in writing. Decisions and recommendations of the Commission shall be made by a majority vote of the five members.
4. The Commission may draw the attention of the parties to the dispute to any measures which might facilitate an amicable settlement.
5. The Commission shall hear the parties, examine the claims and objections, and make proposals to the parties with a view to reaching an amicable settlement of the dispute.
6. The Commission shall report within twelve months of its constitution. Its report shall be deposited with the Secretary-General and transmitted to the parties to the dispute. The report of the Commission, including any conclusions stated therein regarding the facts or questions of law, shall not be binding upon the parties and it shall have no other character than that of recommendations submitted for the consideration of the parties in order to facilitate an amicable settlement of the dispute.
7. The Secretary-General shall provide the Commission with such assistance and facilities as it may require. The expenses of the Commission shall be borne by the United Nations.

---

6. Declaration on Principles of International Law Friendly Relations and Co-Operation among States in Accordance with the Charter of the United Nations, UN GA Res. 2625 (XXV), 24 October 1970

The General Assembly,

Recalling its resolutions 1815 (XVII) of 18 December 1962, 1966 (XVIII) of 16 December 1963, 2103 (XX) of 20 December 1965, 2181 (XXI) of 12 December 1966, 2327 (XXII) of 18 December 1967, 2463 (XXIII) of 20 December 1968 and 2533 (XXIV) of 8 December 1969, in which it affirmed the importance of the progressive development and codification of the principles of international law concerning friendly relations and co-operation among States,

Having considered the report of the Special Committee on Principles of International Law concerning Friendly Relations and Co-operation among States, which met in Geneva from 31 March to 1 May 1970,

Emphasizing the paramount importance of the Charter of the United Nations for the maintenance of international peace and security and for the development of Friendly relations and Co-operation among States, Deeply convinced that the adoption of the Declaration on Principles of International Law concerning Friendly Relations and Co-operation among States in accordance with the Charter of the United Nations on the occasion of the twenty-fifth anniversary of the United Nations would contribute to the strengthening of world peace and constitute a landmark in the development of international law and of relations among States, in promoting the rule of law among nations and particularly the universal application of the principles embodied in the Charter,

Considering the desirability of the wide dissemination of the text of the Declaration,

1. Approves the Declaration on Principles of International Law concerning Friendly Relations and Co-operation among States in accordance with the Charter of the United Nations, the text of which is annexed to the present resolution;
2. Expresses its appreciation to the Special Committee on Principles of International Law concerning Friendly Relations and Co-operation among States for its work resulting in the elaboration of the Declaration;
3. Recommends that all efforts be made so that the Declaration becomes generally known.

1883rd plenary meeting, 24 October 1970

ANNEX

DECLARATION ON PRINCIPLES OF INTERNATIONAL LAW CONCERNING FRIENDLY RELATIONS AND CO-OPERATION AMONG STATES IN ACCORDANCE WITH THE CHARTER OF THE UNITED NATIONS

PREAMBLE

The General Assembly,

Reaffirming in the terms of the Charter of the United Nations that the maintenance of international peace and security and the development of friendly relations and co-operation between nations are among the fundamental purposes of the United Nations,

Recalling that the peoples of the United Nations are determined to practise tolerance and live together in peace with one another as good neighbours,

Bearing in mind the importance of maintaining and strengthening international peace founded upon freedom, equality, justice and respect for fundamental human rights and of developing friendly relations among nations irrespective of their political, economic and social systems or the levels of their development,

Bearing in mind also the paramount importance of the Charter of the United Nations in the promotion of the rule of law among nations,

Considering that the faithful observance of the principles of international law concerning friendly relations and co-operation among States and the fulfillment in good faith of the obligations assumed by States, in accordance with the Charter, is of the greatest importance for the maintenance of international peace and security and for the implementation of the other purposes of the United Nations,

Noting that the great political, economic and social changes and scientific progress which have taken place in the world since the adoption of the Charter give increased importance to these principles and to the need for their more effective application in the conduct of States wherever carried on,

Recalling the established principle that outer space, including the Moon and other celestial bodies, is not subject to national appropriation by claim of sovereignty, by means of use or occupation, or by any other means, and mindful of the fact that consideration is being given in the United Nations to the question of establishing other appropriate provisions similarly inspired,

Convinced that the strict observance by States of the obligation not to intervene in the affairs of any other State is an essential condition to ensure that nations live together in peace with one another, since the practice of any form of intervention not only violates the spirit and letter of the Charter, but also leads to the creation of situations which threaten international peace and security,

Recalling the duty of States to refrain in their international relations from military, political, economic or any other form of coercion aimed against the political independence or territorial integrity of any State,

Considering it essential that all States shall refrain in their international relations from the threat or use of force against the territorial integrity or political independence of any State, or in any other manner inconsistent with the purposes of the United Nations,

Considering it equally essential that all States shall settle their international disputes by peaceful means in accordance with the Charter,

Reaffirming, in accordance with the Charter, the basic importance of sovereign equality and stressing that the purposes of the United Nations can be implemented only if States enjoy sovereign equality and comply fully with the requirements of this principle in their international relations,

Convinced that the subjection of peoples to alien subjugation, domination and exploitation constitutes a major obstacle to the promotion of international peace and security, Convinced that the principle of equal rights and self-determination of peoples constitutes a significant contribution to contemporary international law, and that its effective application is of paramount importance for the promotion of friendly relations among States, based on respect for the principle of sovereign equality,

Convinced in consequence that any attempt aimed at the partial or total disruption of the national unity and territorial integrity of a State or country or at its political independence is incompatible with the purposes and principles of the Charter,

Considering the provisions of the Charter as a whole and taking into account the role of relevant resolutions adopted by the competent organs of the United Nations relating to the content of the principles,

Considering that the progressive development and codification of the following principles:

(a) The principle that States shall refrain in their international relations from the threat or use of force against the territorial integrity or political independence of any State, or in any other manner inconsistent with the purposes of the United Nations,

(b) The principle that States shall settle their international disputes by peaceful means in such a manner that international peace and security and justice are not endangered,

(c) The duty not to intervene in matters within the domestic jurisdiction of any State, in accordance with the Charter,

(d) The duty of States to co-operate with one another in accordance with the Charter,

(e) The principle of equal rights and self-determination of peoples,

(f) The principle of sovereign equality of States,

(g) The principle that States shall fulfil in good faith the obligations assumed by them in accordance with the Charter, so as to secure their more effective application within the international community, would promote the realization of the purposes of the United Nations,

Having considered the principles of international law relating to friendly relations and co-operation among States,

1. Solemnly proclaims the following principles:

The principle that States shall refrain in their international ~ relations from the threat or use of force against the territorial integrity or political independence of any State or in any other manner inconsistent with the purposes of the United Nations

Every State has the duty to refrain in its international relations from the threat or use of force against the territorial integrity or political independence of any State, or in any other manner inconsistent with the purposes of the United Nations. Such a threat or use of force constitutes a violation of international law and the Charter of the United Nations and shall never be employed as a means of settling international issues.

A war of aggression constitutes a crime against the peace, for which there is responsibility under international law.

In accordance with the purposes and principles of the United Nations, States have the duty to refrain from propaganda for wars of aggression.

Every State has the duty to refrain from the threat or use of force to violate the existing international boundaries of another State or as a means of solving international disputes, including territorial disputes and problems concerning frontiers of States.

Every State likewise has the duty to refrain from the threat or use of force to violate international lines of demarcation, such as armistice lines, established by or pursuant to an international agreement to which it is a party or which it is otherwise bound to respect. Nothing in the foregoing shall be construed as prejudicing the positions of the parties concerned with regard to the status and effects of such lines under their special regimes or as affecting their temporary character.

States have a duty to refrain from acts of reprisal involving the use of force.

Every State has the duty to refrain from any forcible action which deprives peoples referred to in the elaboration of the principle of equal rights and self-determination of their right to self-determination and freedom and independence.

Every State has the duty to refrain from organizing or encouraging the organization of irregular forces or armed bands including mercenaries, for incursion into the territory of another State.

Every State has the duty to refrain from organizing, instigating, assisting or participating in acts of civil strife or terrorist acts in another State or acquiescing in organized activities within its territory directed towards the commission of such acts, when the acts referred to in the present paragraph involve a threat or use of force.

The territory of a State shall not be the object of military occupation resulting from the use of force in contravention of the provisions of the Charter. The territory of a State shall not be the object of acquisition by another State resulting from the threat or use of force. No territorial acquisition resulting from the threat or use of force shall be recognized as legal. Nothing in the foregoing shall be construed as affecting:

(a) Provisions of the Charter or any international agreement prior to the Charter regime and valid under international law; or

(b) The powers of the Security Council under the Charter.

All States shall pursue in good faith negotiations for the early conclusion of a universal treaty on general and complete disarmament under effective international control and strive to adopt appropriate measures to reduce international tensions and strengthen confidence among States.

All States shall comply in good faith with their obligations under the generally recognized principles and rules of international law with respect to the maintenance of international peace and security, and shall endeavour to make the United Nations security system based on the Charter more effective.

Nothing in the foregoing paragraphs shall be construed as enlarging or diminishing in any way the scope of the provisions of the Charter concerning cases in which the use of force is lawful.

The principle that States shall settle their international disputes by peaceful means in such a manner that international peace and security and justice are not endangered

Every State shall settle its international disputes with other States by peaceful means in such a manner that international peace and security and justice are not endangered.

States shall accordingly seek early and just settlement of their international disputes by negotiation, inquiry, mediation, conciliation, arbitration, judicial settlement, resort to regional agencies or arrangements or other peaceful means of their choice. In seeking such a settlement the parties shall agree upon such peaceful means as may be appropriate to the circumstances and nature of the dispute.

The parties to a dispute have the duty, in the event of failure to reach a solution by any one of the above peaceful means, to continue to seek a settlement of the dispute by other peaceful means agreed upon by them.

States parties to an international dispute, as well as other States shall refrain from any action which may aggravate the Situation so as to endanger the maintenance of international peace and security, and shall act in accordance with the purposes and principles of the United Nations.

International disputes shall be settled on the basis of the Sovereign equality of States and in accordance with the Principle of free choice of means. Recourse to, or acceptance of, a settlement procedure freely agreed to by States with regard to existing or future disputes to which they are parties shall not be regarded as incompatible with sovereign equality.

Nothing in the foregoing paragraphs prejudices or derogates from the applicable provisions of the Charter, in particular those relating to the pacific settlement of international disputes.

The principle concerning the duty not to intervene in matters within the domestic jurisdiction of any State, in accordance with the Charter

No State or group of States has the right to intervene, directly or indirectly, for any reason whatever, in the internal or external affairs of any other State. Consequently, armed intervention and all other forms of interference or attempted threats against the personality of the State or against its political, economic and cultural elements, are in violation of international law.

No State may use or encourage the use of economic political or any other type of measures to coerce another State in order to obtain from it the subordination of the exercise of its sovereign rights and to secure from it advantages of any kind. Also, no State shall organize, assist, foment, finance, incite or tolerate subversive, terrorist or armed activities directed towards the violent overthrow of the regime of another State, or interfere in civil strife in another State.

The use of force to deprive peoples of their national identity constitutes a violation of their inalienable rights and of the principle of non-intervention.

Every State has an inalienable right to choose its political, economic, social and cultural systems, without interference in any form by another State.

Nothing in the foregoing paragraphs shall be construed as reflecting the relevant provisions of the Charter relating to the maintenance of international peace and security.

The duty of States to co-operate with one another in accordance with the Charter

States have the duty to co-operate with one another, irrespective of the differences in their political, economic and social systems, in the various spheres of international relations, in order to maintain international peace and security and to promote international economic stability and progress, the general welfare of nations and international co-operation free from discrimination based on such differences.

To this end:

(a) States shall co-operate with other States in the maintenance of international peace and security;

(b) States shall co-operate in the promotion of universal respect for, and observance of, human rights and fundamental freedoms for all, and in the elimination of all forms of racial discrimination and all forms of religious intolerance;

(c) States shall conduct their international relations in the economic, social, cultural, technical and trade fields in accordance with the principles of sovereign equality and non-intervention;

(d) States Members of the United Nations have the duty to take joint and separate action in co-operation with the United Nations in accordance with the relevant provisions of the Charter.

States should co-operate in the economic, social and cultural fields as well as in the field of science and technology and for the promotion of international cultural and educational progress. States should co-operate in the promotion of economic growth throughout the world, especially that of the developing countries.

The principle of equal rights and self-determination of peoples

By virtue of the principle of equal rights and self-determination of peoples enshrined in the Charter of the United Nations, all peoples have the right freely to determine, without external interference, their political status and to pursue their economic, social and cultural development, and every State has the duty to respect this right in accordance with the provisions of the Charter.

Every State has the duty to promote, through joint and separate action, realization of the principle of equal rights and self-determination of peoples, in accordance with the provisions of the Charter, and to render assistance to the United Nations in carrying out the responsibilities entrusted to it by the Charter regarding the implementation of the principle, in order:

(a) To promote friendly relations and co-operation among States; and

(b) To bring a speedy end to colonialism, having due regard to the freely expressed will of the peoples concerned;

and bearing in mind that subjection of peoples to alien subjugation, domination and exploitation constitutes a violation of the principle, as well as a denial of fundamental human rights, and is contrary to the Charter.

Every State has the duty to promote through joint and separate action universal respect for and observance of human rights and fundamental freedoms in accordance with the Charter.

The establishment of a sovereign and independent State, the free association or integration with an independent State or the emergence into any other political status freely determined by a people constitute modes of implementing the right of self-determination by that people.

Every State has the duty to refrain from any forcible action which deprives peoples referred to above in the elaboration of the present principle of their right to self-determination and freedom and independence. In their actions against, and resistance to, such forcible action in pursuit of the exercise of their right to self-determination, such peoples are entitled to seek and to receive support in accordance with the purposes and principles of the Charter.

The territory of a colony or other Non-Self-Governing Territory has, under the Charter, a status separate and distinct from the territory of the State administering it; and such separate and distinct status under the Charter shall exist until the people of the colony or Non-Self-Governing Territory have exercised their right of self-determination in accordance with the Charter, and particularly its purposes and principles.

Nothing in the foregoing paragraphs shall be construed as authorizing or encouraging any action which would dismember or impair, totally or in part, the territorial integrity or political unity of sovereign and independent States conducting themselves in compliance with the principle of equal rights and self-determination of peoples as described above and thus possessed of a government representing the whole people belonging to the territory without distinction as to race, creed or colour.

Every State shall refrain from any action aimed at the partial or total disruption of the national unity and territorial integrity of any other State or country.

The principle of sovereign equality of States

All States enjoy sovereign equality. They have equal rights and duties and are equal members of the international community, notwithstanding differences of an economic, social, political or other nature.

In particular, sovereign equality includes the following elements:

(a) States are judicially equal;

(b) Each State enjoys the rights inherent in full sovereignty;

(c) Each State has the duty to respect the personality of other States;

(d) The territorial integrity and political independence of the State are inviolable;

(e) Each State has the right freely to choose and develop its political, social, economic and cultural systems;

(f) Each State has the duty to comply fully and in good faith with its international obligations and to live in peace with other States.

The principle that States shall fulfil in good faith the obligations assumed by them in accordance with the Charter—:

Every State has the duty to fulfil in good faith the obligations assumed by it in accordance with the Charter of the United Nations.

Every State has the duty to fulfil in good faith its obligations under the generally recognized principles and rules of international law.

Every State has the duty to fulfil in good faith its obligations under international agreements valid under the generally recognized principles and rules of international law.

Where obligations arising under international agreements are in conflict with the obligations of Members of the United Nations under the Charter of the United Nations, the obligations under the Charter shall prevail.

GENERAL PART

2. Declares that:

In their interpretation and application the above principles are interrelated and each principle should be construed in the context of the other principles. Nothing in this Declaration shall be construed as prejudicing in any manner the provisions of the Charter or the rights and duties of Member States under the Charter or the rights of peoples under the Charter, taking into account the elaboration of these rights in this Declaration.;

3. Declares further that: The principles of the Charter which are embodied in this Declaration constitute basic principles of international law, and consequently appeals to all States to be guided by these principles in their international conduct and to develop their mutual relations on the basis of the strict observance of these principles.

---

7. Rules of the International Court of Justice, 1978

Rules of Court

Article 30 of the Statute of the International Court of Justice provides that "the Court shall frame rules for carrying out its functions". These Rules are intended to supplement the general rules set forth in the Statute and to make detailed provision for the steps to be taken to comply with them.

RULES OF COURT (1978)

ADOPTED ON 14 APRIL 1978 AND ENTERED

INTO FORCE ON 1 JULY 1978[1]

*PREAMBLE**

The Court,

Having regard to Chapter XIV of the Charter of the United Nations;

---

* Amendment entered into force on 14 April 2005.

[1] Any amendments to the Rules of Court, following their adoption by the Court, are now posted on the Court's website, with an indication of the date of their entry into force and a note of any temporal reservations relating to their applicability (for example, whether the application of the amended rule is limited to cases instituted after the date of entry into force of the amendment); they are also

Having regard to the Statute of the Court annexed thereto;

Acting in pursuance of Article 30 of the Statute;

Adopts the following Rules.

PART I

THE COURT

SECTION A. JUDGES AND ASSESSORS

Subsection 1. The Members of the Court

Article 1

1. The Members of the Court are the judges elected in accordance with Articles 2 to 15 of the Statute.
2. For the purposes of a particular case, the Court may also include upon the Bench one or more persons chosen under Article 31 of the Statute to sit as judges ad hoc.
3. In the following Rules, the term "Member of the Court" denotes any elected judge; the term "judge" denotes any Member of the Court, and any judge ad hoc.

Article 2

1. The term of office of Members of the Court elected at a triennial election shall begin to run from the sixth of February[1] in the year in which the vacancies to which they are elected occur.
2. The term of office of a Member of the Court elected to replace a Member whose term of office has not expired shall begin to run from the date of the election.

Article 3

1. The Members of the Court, in the exercise of their functions, are of equal status, irrespective of age, priority of election or length of service.
2. The Members of the Court shall, except as provided in paragraphs 4 and 5 of this Article, take precedence according to the date on which their terms of office respectively began, as provided for by Article 2 of these Rules.
3. Members of the Court whose terms of office began on the same date shall take precedence in relation to one another according to seniority of age.
4. A Member of the Court who is re-elected to a new term of office which is continuous with his previous term shall retain his precedence.
5. The President and the Vice-President of the Court, while holding these offices, shall take precedence before all other Members of the Court.
6. The Member of the Court who, in accordance with the foregoing paragraphs, takes precedence next after the President and the Vice-President is in these Rules designated the "senior judge". If that Member is unable to act, the Member of the Court who is next after him in precedence and able to act is considered as senior judge.

---

published in the Court's *Yearbook*. Articles amended since 1 July 1978 are marked with an asterisk and appear in their amended form.

[1] This is the date on which the terms of office of the Members of the Court elected at the first election began in 1946.

Article 4

1. The declaration to be made by every Member of the Court in accordance with Article 20 of the Statute shall be as follows:

   "I solemnly declare that I will perform my duties and exercise my powers as judge honourably, faithfully, impartially and conscientiously."

2. This declaration shall be made at the first public sitting at which the Member of the Court is present. Such sitting shall be held as soon as practicable after his term of office begins and, if necessary, a special sitting shall be held for the purpose.

3. A Member of the Court who is re-elected shall make a new declaration only if his new term is not continuous with his previous one.

Article 5

1. A Member of the Court deciding to resign shall communicate his decision to the President, and the resignation shall take effect as provided in Article 13, paragraph 4, of the Statute.

2. If the Member of the Court deciding to resign from the Court is the President, he shall communicate his decision to the Court, and the resignation shall take effect as provided in Article 13, paragraph 4, of the Statute.

Article 6

In any case in which the application of Article 18 of the Statute is under consideration, the Member of the Court concerned shall be so informed by the President or, if the circumstances so require, by the Vice-President, in a written statement which shall include the grounds therefor and any relevant evidence. He shall subsequently, at a private meeting of the Court specially convened for the purpose, be afforded an opportunity of making a statement, of furnishing any information or explanations he wishes to give, and of supplying answers, orally or in writing, to any questions put to him. At a further private meeting, at which the Member of the Court concerned shall not be present, the matter shall be discussed; each Member of the Court shall state his opinion, and if requested a vote shall be taken.

Subsection 2. Judges ad hoc

Article 7

1. Judges ad hoc, chosen under Article 31 of the Statute for the purposes of particular cases, shall be admitted to sit on the Bench of the Court in the circumstances and according to the procedure indicated in Article 17, paragraph 2, Articles 35, 36, 37, Article 91, paragraph 2, and Article 102, paragraph 3, of these Rules.

2. They shall participate in the case in which they sit on terms of complete equality with the other judges on the Bench.

3. Judges ad hoc shall take precedence after the Members of the Court and in order of seniority of age.

Article 8

1. The solemn declaration to be made by every judge ad hoc in accordance with Articles 20 and 31, paragraph 6, of the Statute shall be as set out in Article 4, paragraph 1, of these Rules.

2. This declaration shall be made at a public sitting in the case in which the judge ad hoc is participating. If the case is being dealt with by a chamber of the Court, the declaration shall be made in the same manner in that chamber.

3. Judges ad hoc shall make the declaration in relation to any case in which they are participating, even if they have already done so in a previous case, but shall not make a new declaration for a later phase of the same case.

Subsection 3. Assessors

Article 9

1. The Court may, either proprio motu or upon a request made not later than the closure of the written proceedings, decide, for the purpose of a contentious case or request for advisory opinion, to appoint assessors to sit with it without the right to vote.
2. When the Court so decides, the President shall take steps to obtain all the information relevant to the choice of the assessors.
3. The assessors shall be appointed by secret ballot and by a majority of the votes of the judges composing the Court for the case.
4. The same powers shall belong to the chambers provided for by Articles 26 and 29 of the Statute and to the presidents thereof, and may be exercised in the same manner.
5. Before entering upon their duties, assessors shall make the following declaration at a public sitting:

   "I solemnly declare that I will perform my duties as an assessor honourably, impartially and conscientiously, and that I will faithfully observe all the provisions of the Statute and of the Rules of the Court."

SECTION B. THE PRESIDENCY

Article 10

1. The term of office of the President and that of the Vice-President shall begin to run from the date on which the terms of office of the Members of the Court elected at a triennial election begin in accordance with Article 2 of these Rules.
2. The elections to the presidency and vice-presidency shall be held on that date or shortly thereafter. The former President, if still a Member of the Court, shall continue to exercise his functions until the election to the presidency has taken place.

Article 11

1. If, on the date of the election to the presidency, the former President is still a Member of the Court, he shall conduct the election. If he has ceased to be a Member of the Court, or is unable to act, the election shall be conducted by the Member of the Court exercising the functions of the presidency by virtue of Article 13, paragraph 1, of these Rules.
2. The election shall take place by secret ballot, after the presiding Member of the Court has declared the number of affirmative votes necessary for election; there shall be no nominations. The Member of the Court obtaining the votes of a majority of the Members composing it at the time of the election shall be declared elected, and shall enter forthwith upon his functions.
3. The new President shall conduct the election of the Vice-President either at the same or at the following meeting. The provisions of paragraph 2 of this Article shall apply equally to this election.

Article 12

The President shall preside at all meetings of the Court; he shall direct the work and supervise the administration of the Court.

Article 13

1. In the event of a vacancy in the presidency or of the inability of the President to exercise the functions of the presidency, these shall be exercised by the Vice-President, or failing him, by the senior judge.
2. When the President is precluded by a provision of the Statute or of these Rules either from sitting or from presiding in a particular case, he shall continue to exercise the functions of the presidency for all purposes save in respect of that case.
3. The President shall take the measures necessary in order to ensure the continuous exercise of the functions of the presidency at the seat of the Court. In the event of his absence, he may, so far as is compatible with the Statute and these Rules, arrange for these functions to be exercised by the Vice-President, or failing him, by the senior judge.
4. If the President decides to resign the presidency, he shall communicate his decision in writing to the Court through the Vice-President, or failing him, the senior judge. If the Vice-President decides to resign his office, he shall communicate his decision to the President.

Article 14

If a vacancy in the presidency or the vice-presidency occurs before the date when the current term is due to expire under Article 21, paragraph 1, of the Statute and Article 10, paragraph 1, of these Rules, the Court shall decide whether or not the vacancy shall be filled during the remainder of the term.

Section c. The Chambers

Article 15

1. The Chamber of Summary Procedure to be formed annually under Article 29 of the Statute shall be composed of five Members of the Court, comprising the President and Vice-President of the Court, acting ex officio, and three other members elected in accordance with Article 18, paragraph 1, of these Rules. In addition, two Members of the Court shall be elected annually to act as substitutes.
2. The election referred to in paragraph 1 of this Article shall be held as soon as possible after the sixth of February in each year. The members of the Chamber shall enter upon their functions on election and continue to serve until the next election; they may be re-elected.
3. If a member of the Chamber is unable, for whatever reason, to sit in a given case, he shall be replaced for the purposes of that case by the senior in precedence of the two substitutes.
4. If a member of the Chamber resigns or otherwise ceases to be a member, his place shall be taken by the senior in precedence of the two substitutes, who shall thereupon become a full member of the Chamber and be replaced by the election of another substitute. Should vacancies exceed the number of available substitutes, elections shall be held as soon as possible in respect of the vacancies still

existing after the substitutes have assumed full membership and in respect of the vacancies in the substitutes.

Article 16

1. When the Court decides to form one or more of the Chambers provided for in Article 26, paragraph 1, of the Statute, it shall determine the particular category of cases for which each Chamber is formed, the number of its members, the period for which they will serve, and the date at which they will enter upon their duties.
2. The members of the Chamber shall be elected in accordance with Article 18, paragraph 1, of these Rules from among the Members of the Court, having regard to any special knowledge, expertise or previous experience which any of the Members of the Court may have in relation to the category of case the Chamber is being formed to deal with.
3. The Court may decide upon the dissolution of a Chamber, but without prejudice to the duty of the Chamber concerned to finish any cases pending before it.

Article 17

1. A request for the formation of a Chamber to deal with a particular case, as provided for in Article 26, paragraph 2, of the Statute, may be filed at any time until the closure of the written proceedings. Upon receipt of a request made by one party, the President shall ascertain whether the other party assents.
2. When the parties have agreed, the President shall ascertain their views regarding the composition of the Chamber, and shall report to the Court accordingly. He shall also take such steps as may be necessary to give effect to the provisions of Article 31, paragraph 4, of the Statute.
3. When the Court has determined, with the approval of the parties, the number of its Members who are to constitute the Chamber, it shall proceed to their election, in accordance with the provisions of Article 18, paragraph 1, of these Rules. The same procedure shall be followed as regards the filling of any vacancy that may occur on the Chamber.
4. Members of a Chamber formed under this Article who have been replaced, in accordance with Article 13 of the Statute following the expiration of their terms of office, shall continue to sit in all phases of the case, whatever the stage it has then reached.

Article 18

1. Elections to all Chambers shall take place by secret ballot. The Members of the Court obtaining the largest number of votes constituting a majority of the Members of the Court composing it at the time of the election shall be declared elected. If necessary to fill vacancies, more than one ballot shall take place, such ballot being limited to the number of vacancies that remain to be filled.
2. If a Chamber when formed includes the President or Vice-President of the Court, or both of them, the President or Vice-President, as the case may be, shall preside over that Chamber. In any other event, the Chamber shall elect its own president by secret ballot and by a majority of votes of its members. The Member of the Court who, under this paragraph, presides over the Chamber at the time of its formation shall continue to preside so long as he remains a member of that Chamber.

3. The president of a Chamber shall exercise, in relation to cases being dealt with by that Chamber, all the functions of the President of the Court in relation to cases before the Court.

4. If the president of a Chamber is prevented from sitting or from acting as president, the functions of the presidency shall be assumed by the member of the Chamber who is the senior in precedence and able to act.

Section D. Internal Functioning of the Court

Article 19

The internal judicial practice of the Court shall, subject to the provisions of the Statute and these Rules, be governed by any resolutions on the subject adopted by the Court.[1]

Article 20

1. The quorum specified by Article 25, paragraph 3, of the Statute applies to all meetings of the Court.

2. The obligation of Members of the Court under Article 23, paragraph 3, of the Statute, to hold themselves permanently at the disposal of the Court, entails attendance at all such meetings, unless they are prevented from attending by illness or for other serious reasons duly explained to the President, who shall inform the Court.

3. Judges ad hoc are likewise bound to hold themselves at the disposal of the Court and to attend all meetings held in the case in which they are participating. They shall not be taken into account for the calculation of the quorum.

4. The Court shall fix the dates and duration of the judicial vacations and the periods and conditions of leave to be accorded to individual Members of the Court under Article 23, paragraph 2, of the Statute, having regard in both cases to the state of its General List and to the requirements of its current work.

5. Subject to the same considerations, the Court shall observe the public holidays customary at the place where the Court is sitting.

6. In case of urgency the President may convene the Court at any time.

Article 21

1. The deliberations of the Court shall take place in private and remain secret. The Court may however at any time decide in respect of its deliberations on other than judicial matters to publish or allow publication of any part of them.

2. Only judges, and the assessors, if any, take part in the Court's judicial deliberations. The Registrar, or his deputy, and other members of the staff of the Registry as may be required shall be present. No other person shall be present except by permission of the Court.

3. The minutes of the Court's judicial deliberations shall record only the title or nature of the subjects or matters discussed, and the results of any vote taken. They shall not record any details of the discussions nor the views expressed, provided however that any judge is entitled to require that a statement made by him be inserted in the minutes.

---

[1] The resolution now in force was adopted on 12 April 1976.

PART II

THE REGISTRY

Article 22

1. The Court shall elect its Registrar by secret ballot from amongst candidates proposed by Members of the Court. The Registrar shall be elected for a term of seven years. He may be re-elected.
2. The President shall give notice of a vacancy or impending vacancy to Members of the Court, either forthwith upon the vacancy arising, or, where the vacancy will arise on the expiration of the term of office of the Registrar, not less than three months prior thereto. The President shall fix a date for the closure of the list of candidates so as to enable nominations and information concerning the candidates to be received in sufficient time.
3. Nominations shall indicate the relevant information concerning the candidate, and in particular information as to his age, nationality, and present occupation, university qualifications, knowledge of languages, and any previous experience in law, diplomacy or the work of international organizations.
4. The candidate obtaining the votes of the majority of the Members of the Court composing it at the time of the election shall be declared elected.

Article 23

The Court shall elect a Deputy-Registrar: the provisions of Article 22 of these Rules shall apply to his election and term of office.

Article 24

1. Before taking up his duties, the Registrar shall make the following declaration at a meeting of the Court:

   "I solemnly declare that I will perform the duties incumbent upon me as Registrar of the International Court of Justice in all loyalty, discretion and good conscience, and that I will faithfully observe all the provisions of the Statute and of the Rules of the Court."
2. The Deputy-Registrar shall make a similar declaration at a meeting of the Court before taking up his duties.

Article 25

1. The staff-members of the Registry shall be appointed by the Court on proposals submitted by the Registrar. Appointments to such posts as the Court shall determine may however be made by the Registrar with the approval of the President.
2. Before taking up his duties, every staff-member shall make the following declaration before the President, the Registrar being present:

   "I solemnly declare that I will perform the duties incumbent upon me as an official of the International Court of Justice in all loyalty, discretion and good conscience, and that I will faithfully observe all the provisions of the Statute and of the Rules of the Court."

Article 26

1. The Registrar, in the discharge of his functions, shall:

   (a) be the regular channel of communications to and from the Court, and in particular shall effect all communications, notifications and transmission of documents required by the Statute or by these Rules and ensure that the date of despatch and receipt thereof may be readily verified;

(b) keep, under the supervision of the President, and in such form as may be laid down by the Court, a General List of all cases, entered and numbered in the order in which the documents instituting proceedings or requesting an advisory opinion are received in the Registry;

(c) have the custody of the declarations accepting the jurisdiction of the Court made by States not parties to the Statute in accordance with any resolution adopted by the Security Council under Article 35, paragraph 2, of the Statute, and transmit certified copies thereof to all States parties to the Statute, to such other States as shall have deposited declarations, and to the Secretary-General of the United Nations;

(d) transmit to the parties copies of all pleadings and documents annexed upon receipt thereof in the Registry;

(e) communicate to the government of the country in which the Court or a Chamber is sitting, and any other governments which may be concerned, the necessary information as to the persons from time to time entitled, under the Statute and relevant agreements, to privileges, immunities, or facilities;

(f) be present, in person or by his deputy, at meetings of the Court, and of the Chambers, and be responsible for the preparation of minutes of such meetings;

(g) make arrangements for such provision or verification of translations and interpretations into the Court's official languages as the Court may require;

(h) sign all judgments, advisory opinions and orders of the Court, and the minutes referred to in subparagraph (f);

(i) be responsible for the printing and publication of the Court's judgments, advisory opinions and orders, the pleadings and statements, and minutes of public sittings in cases, and of such other documents as the Court may direct to be published;

(j) be responsible for all administrative work and in particular for the accounts and financial administration in accordance with the financial procedures of the United Nations;

(k) deal with enquiries concerning the Court and its work;

(l) assist in maintaining relations between the Court and other organs of the United Nations, the specialized agencies, and international bodies and conferences concerned with the codification and progressive development of international law;

(m) ensure that information concerning the Court and its activities is made accessible to governments, the highest national courts of justice, professional and learned societies, legal faculties and schools of law, and public information media;

(n) have custody of the seals and stamps of the Court, of the archives of the Court, and of such other archives as may be entrusted to the Court.[1]

---

[1] The Registrar also keeps the Archives of the Permanent Court of International Justice, entrusted to the present Court by decision of the Permanent Court of October 1945 (*I.C.J. Yearbook 1946–1947*, p. 26). and the Archives of the Trial of the Major War Criminals before the International

2. The Court may at any time entrust additional functions to the Registrar.
3. In the discharge of his functions the Registrar shall be responsible to the Court.

Article 27

1. The Deputy-Registrar shall assist the Registrar, act as Registrar in the latter's absence and, in the event of the office becoming vacant, exercise the functions of Registrar until the office has been filled.
2. If both the Registrar and the Deputy-Registrar are unable to carry out the duties of Registrar, the President shall appoint an official of the Registry to discharge those duties for such time as may be necessary. If both offices are vacant at the same time, the President, after consulting the Members of the Court, shall appoint an official of the Registry to discharge the duties of Registrar pending an election to that office.

Article 28

1. The Registry shall comprise the Registrar, the Deputy-Registrar, and such other staff as the Registrar shall require for the efficient discharge of his functions.
2. The Court shall prescribe the organization of the Registry, and shall for this purpose request the Registrar to make proposals.
3. Instructions for the Registry shall be drawn up by the Registrar and approved by the Court.
4. The staff of the Registry shall be subject to Staff Regulations drawn up by the Registrar, so far as possible in conformity with the United Nations Staff Regulations and Staff Rules, and approved by the Court.

Article 29

1. The Registrar may be removed from office only if, in the opinion of two-thirds of the Members of the Court, he has either become permanently incapacitated from exercising his functions, or has committed a serious breach of his duties.
2. Before a decision is taken under this Article, the Registrar shall be informed by the President of the action contemplated, in a written statement which shall include the grounds therefor and any relevant evidence. He shall subsequently, at a private meeting of the Court, be afforded an opportunity of making a statement, of furnishing any information or explanations he wishes to give, and of supplying answers, orally or in writing, to any questions put to him.
3. The Deputy-Registrar may be removed from office only on the same grounds and by the same procedure.

Part III

PROCEEDINGS IN CONTENTIOUS CASES

Section A. Communications to the Court and Consultations

Article 30

All communications to the Court under these Rules shall be addressed to the Registrar unless otherwise stated. Any request made by a party shall likewise be addressed to the Registrar unless made in open court in the course of the oral proceedings.

Military Tribunal at Nuremberg (1945–1946), entrusted to the Court by decision of that Tribunal of 1 October 1946; the Court authorized the Registrar to accept the latter Archives by decision of 19 November 1949.

Article 31

In every case submitted to the Court, the President shall ascertain the views of the parties with regard to questions of procedure. For this purpose he shall summon the agents of the parties to meet him as soon as possible after their appointment, and whenever necessary thereafter.

Section B. The Composition of the Court

for Particular Cases

Article 32

1. If the President of the Court is a national of one of the parties in a case he shall not exercise the functions of the presidency in respect of that case. The same rule applies to the Vice-President, or to the senior judge, when called on to act as President.

2. The Member of the Court who is presiding in a case on the date on which the Court convenes for the oral proceedings shall continue to preside in that case until completion of the current phase of the case, notwithstanding the election in the meantime of a new President or Vice-President. If he should become unable to act, the presidency for the case shall be determined in accordance with Article 13 of these Rules, and on the basis of the composition of the Court on the date on which it convened for the oral proceedings.

Article 33

Except as provided in Article 17 of these Rules, Members of the Court who have been replaced, in accordance with Article 13, paragraph 3, of the Statute following the expiration of their terms of office, shall discharge the duty imposed upon them by that paragraph by continuing to sit until the completion of any phase of a case in respect of which the Court convenes for the oral proceedings prior to the date of such replacement.

Article 34

1. In case of any doubt arising as to the application of Article 17, paragraph 2, of the Statute or in case of a disagreement as to the application of Article 24 of the Statute, the President shall inform the Members of the Court, with whom the decision lies.

2. If a party desires to bring to the attention of the Court facts which it considers to be of possible relevance to the application of the provisions of the Statute mentioned in the previous paragraph, but which it believes may not be known to the Court, that party shall communicate confidentially such facts to the President in writing.

Article 35

1. If a party proposes to exercise the power conferred by Article 31 of the Statute to choose a judge ad hoc in a case, it shall notify the Court of its intention as soon as possible. If the name and nationality of the judge selected are not indicated at the same time, the party shall, not later than two months before the time-limit fixed for the filing of the Counter-Memorial, inform the Court of the name and nationality of the person chosen and supply brief biographical details. The judge ad hoc may be of a nationality other than that of the party which chooses him.

2. If a party proposes to abstain from choosing a judge ad hoc, on condition of a like abstention by the other party, it shall so notify the Court which shall inform

the other party. If the other party thereafter gives notice of its intention to choose, or chooses, a judge ad hoc, the time-limit for the party which has previously abstained from choosing a judge may be extended by the President.

3. A copy of any notification relating to the choice of a judge ad hoc shall be communicated by the Registrar to the other party, which shall be requested to furnish, within a time-limit to be fixed by the President, such observations as it may wish to make. If within the said time-limit no objection is raised by the other party, and if none appears to the Court itself, the parties shall be so informed.
4. In the event of any objection or doubt, the matter shall be decided by the Court, if necessary after hearing the parties.
5. A judge ad hoc who has accepted appointment but who becomes unable to sit may be replaced.
6. If and when the reasons for the participation of a judge ad hoc are found no longer to exist, he shall cease to sit on the Bench.

Article 36

1. If the Court finds that two or more parties are in the same interest, and therefore are to be reckoned as one party only, and that there is no Member of the Court of the nationality of any one of those parties upon the Bench, the Court shall fix a time-limit within which they may jointly choose a judge ad hoc.
2. Should any party amongst those found by the Court to be in the same interest allege the existence of a separate interest of its own, or put forward any other objection, the matter shall be decided by the Court, if necessary after hearing the parties.

Article 37

1. If a Member of the Court having the nationality of one of the parties is or becomes unable to sit in any phase of a case, that party shall thereupon become entitled to choose a judge ad hoc within a time-limit to be fixed by the Court, or by the President if the Court is not sitting.
2. Parties in the same interest shall be deemed not to have a judge of one of their nationalities upon the Bench if the Member of the Court having one of their nationalities is or becomes unable to sit in any phase of the case.
3. If the Member of the Court having the nationality of a party becomes able to sit not later than the closure of the written proceedings in that phase of the case, that Member of the Court shall resume his seat on the Bench in the case.

SECTION C. PROCEEDINGS BEFORE THE COURT

Subsection 1. Institution of Proceedings

Article 38

1. When proceedings before the Court are instituted by means of an application addressed as specified in Article 40, paragraph 1, of the Statute, the application shall indicate the party making it, the State against which the claim is brought, and the subject of the dispute.
2. The application shall specify as far as possible the legal grounds upon which the jurisdiction of the Court is said to be based; it shall also specify the precise nature of the claim, together with a succinct statement of the facts and grounds on which the claim is based.

3. The original of the application shall be signed either by the agent of the party submitting it, or by the diplomatic representative of that party in the country in which the Court has its seat, or by some other duly authorized person. If the application bears the signature of someone other than such diplomatic representative, the signature must be authenticated by the latter or by the competent authority of the applicant's foreign ministry.
4. The Registrar shall forthwith transmit to the respondent a certified copy of the application.
5. When the applicant State proposes to found the jurisdiction of the Court upon a consent thereto yet to be given or manifested by the State against which such application is made, the application shall be transmitted to that State. It shall not however be entered in the General List, nor any action be taken in the proceedings, unless and until the State against which such application is made consents to the Court's jurisdiction for the purposes of the case.

Article 39

1. When proceedings are brought before the Court by the notification of a special agreement, in conformity with Article 40, paragraph 1, of the Statute, the notification may be effected by the parties jointly or by any one or more of them. If the notification is not a joint one, a certified copy of it shall forthwith be communicated by the Registrar to the other party.
2. In each case the notification shall be accompanied by an original or certified copy of the special agreement. The notification shall also, in so far as this is not already apparent from the agreement, indicate the precise subject of the dispute and identify the parties to it.

Article 40

1. Except in the circumstances contemplated by Article 38, paragraph 5, of these Rules, all steps on behalf of the parties after proceedings have been instituted shall be taken by agents. Agents shall have an address for service at the seat of the Court to which all communications concerning the case are to be sent. Communications addressed to the agents of the parties shall be considered as having been addressed to the parties themselves.
2. When proceedings are instituted by means of an application, the name of the agent for the applicant shall be stated. The respondent, upon receipt of the certified copy of the application, or as soon as possible thereafter, shall inform the Court of the name of its agent.
3. When proceedings are brought by notification of a special agreement, the party making the notification shall state the name of its agent. Any other party to the special agreement, upon receiving from the Registrar a certified copy of such notification, or as soon as possible thereafter, shall inform the Court of the name of its agent if it has not already done so.

Article 41

The institution of proceedings by a State which is not a party to the Statute but which, under Article 35, paragraph 2, thereof, has accepted the jurisdiction of the Court by a declaration made in accordance with any resolution adopted by the Security Council under that Article,[1] shall be accompanied by a deposit of the declaration in question, un-

[1] The resolution now in force was adopted on 15 October 1946.

less the latter has previously been deposited with the Registrar. If any question of the validity or effect of such declaration arises, the Court shall decide.

Article 42

The Registrar shall transmit copies of any application or notification of a special agreement instituting proceedings before the Court to: *(a)* the Secretary-General of the United Nations; *(b)* the Members of the United Nations; *(c)* other States entitled to appear before the Court.

Article 43*, [1]

1. Whenever the construction of a convention to which States other than those concerned in the case are parties may be in question within the meaning of Article 63, paragraph 1, of the Statute, the Court shall consider what directions shall be given to the Registrar in the matter.
2. Whenever the construction of a convention to which a public international organization is a party may be in question in a case before the Court, the Court shall consider whether the Registrar shall so notify the public international organization concerned. Every public international organization notified by the Registrar may submit its observations on the particular provisions of the convention the construction of which is in question in the case.
3. If a public international organization sees fit to furnish its observations under paragraph 2 of this Article, the procedure to be followed shall be that provided for in Article 69, paragraph 2, of these Rules.

Subsection 2. The Written Proceedings

Article 44

1. In the light of the information obtained by the President under Article 31 of these Rules, the Court shall make the necessary orders to determine, inter alia, the number and the order of filing of the pleadings and the time-limits within which they must be filed.
2. In making an order under paragraph 1 of this Article, any agreement between the parties which does not cause unjustified delay shall be taken into account.
3. The Court may, at the request of the party concerned, extend any time-limit, or decide that any step taken after the expiration of the time-limit fixed therefor shall be considered as valid, if it is satisfied that there is adequate justification for the request. In either case the other party shall be given an opportunity to state its views.
4. If the Court is not sitting, its powers under this Article shall be exercised by the President, but without prejudice to any subsequent decision of the Court. If the consultation referred to in Article 31 reveals persistent disagreement between the parties as to the application of Article 45, paragraph 2, or Article 46, paragraph 2, of these Rules, the Court shall be convened to decide the matter.

Article 45

1. The pleadings in a case begun by means of an application shall consist, in the following order, of: a Memorial by the applicant; a Counter-Memorial by the respondent.

---

* Amendment entered into force on 29 September 2005.

[1] Article 43, paragraph 1, as amended, repeats unchanged the text of Article 43, as adopted on 14 April 1978.

Paragraphs 2 and 3 of the amended Article 43 are new.

2. The Court may authorize or direct that there shall be a Reply by the applicant and a Rejoinder by the respondent if the parties are so agreed, or if the Court decides, proprio motu or at the request of one of the parties, that these pleadings are necessary.

Article 46

1. In a case begun by the notification of a special agreement, the number and order of the pleadings shall be governed by the provisions of the agreement, unless the Court, after ascertaining the views of the parties, decides otherwise.
2. If the special agreement contains no such provision, and if the parties have not subsequently agreed on the number and order of pleadings, they shall each file a Memorial and Counter-Memorial, within the same time-limits. The Court shall not authorize the presentation of Replies unless it finds them to be necessary.

Article 47

The Court may at any time direct that the proceedings in two or more cases be joined. It may also direct that the written or oral proceedings, including the calling of witnesses, be in common; or the Court may, without effecting any formal joinder, direct common action in any of these respects.

Article 48

Time-limits for the completion of steps in the proceedings may be fixed by assigning a specified period but shall always indicate definite dates. Such time-limits shall be as short as the character of the case permits.

Article 49

1. A Memorial shall contain a statement of the relevant facts, a statement of law, and the submissions.
2. A Counter-Memorial shall contain: an admission or denial of the facts stated in the Memorial; any additional facts, if necessary; observations concerning the statement of law in the Memorial; a statement of law in answer thereto; and the submissions.
3. The Reply and Rejoinder, whenever authorized by the Court, shall not merely repeat the parties' contentions, but shall be directed to bringing out the issues that still divide them.
4. Every pleading shall set out the party's submissions at the relevant stage of the case, distinctly from the arguments presented, or shall confirm the submissions previously made.

Article 50

1. There shall be annexed to the original of every pleading certified copies of any relevant documents adduced in support of the contentions contained in the pleading.
2. If only parts of a document are relevant, only such extracts as are necessary for the purpose of the pleading in question need be annexed. A copy of the whole document shall be deposited in the Registry, unless it has been published and is readily available.
3. A list of all documents annexed to a pleading shall be furnished at the time the pleading is filed.

Article 51

1. If the parties are agreed that the written proceedings shall be conducted wholly in one of the two official languages of the Court, the pleadings shall be submitted only in that language. If the parties are not so agreed, any pleading or any part of a pleading shall be submitted in one or other of the official languages.

2. If in pursuance of Article 39, paragraph 3, of the Statute a language other than French or English is used, a translation into French or English certified as accurate by the party submitting it, shall be attached to the original of each pleading.

3. When a document annexed to a pleading is not in one of the official languages of the Court, it shall be accompanied by a translation into one of these languages certified by the party submitting it as accurate. The translation may be confined to part of an annex, or to extracts therefrom, but in this case it must be accompanied by an explanatory note indicating what passages are translated. The Court may however require a more extensive or a complete translation to be furnished.

Article 52[*, 1, 2]

1. The original of every pleading shall be signed by the agent and filed in the Registry. It shall be accompanied by a certified copy of the pleading, documents annexed, and any translations, for communication to the other party in accordance with Article 43, paragraph 4, of the Statute, and by the number of additional copies required by the Registry, but without prejudice to an increase in that number should the need arise later.

2. All pleadings shall be dated. When a pleading has to be filed by a certain date, it is the date of the receipt of the pleading in the Registry which will be regarded by the Court as the material date.

3. The correction of a slip or error in any document which has been filed may be made at any time with the consent of the other party or by leave of the President. Any correction so effected shall be notified to the other party in the same manner as the pleading to which it relates.

Article 53

1. The Court, or the President if the Court is not sitting, may at any time decide, after ascertaining the views of the parties, that copies of the pleadings and documents annexed shall be made available to a State entitled to appear before it which has asked to be furnished with such copies.

2. The Court may, after ascertaining the views of the parties, decide that copies of the pleadings and documents annexed shall be made accessible to the public on or after the opening of the oral proceedings.

Subsection 3. The Oral Proceedings

---

* Amendment entered into force on 14 April 2005.

1. The agents of the parties are requested to ascertain from the Registry the usual format of the pleadings.

2. The text of Article 52, as adopted on 14 April 1978, contained a paragraph 3 concerning the procedure to be followed where the Registrar arranges for the printing of a pleading; this paragraph has been deleted and the footnote to the Article has been amended. Former paragraph 4 has been renumbered and is now paragraph 3.

Article 54

1. Upon the closure of the written proceedings, the case is ready for hearing. The date for the opening of the oral proceedings shall be fixed by the Court, which may also decide, if occasion should arise, that the opening or the continuance of the oral proceedings be postponed.
2. When fixing the date for, or postponing, the opening of the oral proceedings the Court shall have regard to the priority required by Article 74 of these Rules and to any other special circumstances, including the urgency of a particular case.
3. When the Court is not sitting, its powers under this Article shall be exercised by the President.

Article 55

The Court may, if it considers it desirable, decide pursuant to Article 22, paragraph 1, of the Statute that all or part of the further proceedings in a case shall be held at a place other than the seat of the Court. Before so deciding, it shall ascertain the views of the parties.

Article 56

1. After the closure of the written proceedings, no further documents may be submitted to the Court by either party except with the consent of the other party or as provided in paragraph 2 of this Article. The party desiring to produce a new document shall file the original or a certified copy thereof, together with the number of copies required by the Registry, which shall be responsible for communicating it to the other party and shall inform the Court. The other party shall be held to have given its consent if it does not lodge an objection to the production of the document.
2. In the absence of consent, the Court, after hearing the parties, may, if it considers the document necessary, authorize its production.
3. If a new document is produced under paragraph 1 or paragraph 2 of this Article, the other party shall have an opportunity of commenting upon it and of submitting documents in support of its comments.
4. No reference may be made during the oral proceedings to the contents of any document which has not been produced in accordance with Article 43 of the Statute or this Article, unless the document is part of a publication readily available.
5. The application of the provisions of this Article shall not in itself constitute a ground for delaying the opening or the course of the oral proceedings.

Article 57

Without prejudice to the provisions of the Rules concerning the production of documents, each party shall communicate to the Registrar, in sufficient time before the opening of the oral proceedings, information regarding any evidence which it intends to produce or which it intends to request the Court to obtain. This communication shall contain a list of the surnames, first names, nationalities, descriptions and places of residence of the witnesses and experts whom the party intends to call, with indications in general terms of the point or points to which their evidence will be directed. A copy of the communication shall also be furnished for transmission to the other party.

Article 58

1. The Court shall determine whether the parties should present their arguments before or after the production of the evidence; the parties shall, however, retain the right to comment on the evidence given.

2. The order in which the parties will be heard, the method of handling the evidence and of examining any witnesses and experts, and the number of counsel and advocates to be heard on behalf of each party, shall be settled by the Court after the views of the parties have been ascertained in accordance with Article 31 of these Rules.

Article 59

The hearing in Court shall be public, unless the Court shall decide otherwise, or unless the parties demand that the public be not admitted. Such a decision or demand may concern either the whole or part of the hearing, and may be made at any time.

Article 60

1. The oral statements made on behalf of each party shall be as succinct as possible within the limits of what is requisite for the adequate presentation of that party's contentions at the hearing. Accordingly, they shall be directed to the issues that still divide the parties, and shall not go over the whole ground covered by the pleadings, or merely repeat the facts and arguments these contain.
2. At the conclusion of the last statement made by a party at the hearing, its agent, without recapitulation of the arguments, shall read that party's final submissions. A copy of the written text of these, signed by the agent, shall be communicated to the Court and transmitted to the other party.

Article 61

1. The Court may at any time prior to or during the hearing indicate any points or issues to which it would like the parties specially to address themselves, or on which it considers that there has been sufficient argument.
2. The Court may, during the hearing, put questions to the agents, counsel and advocates, and may ask them for explanations.
3. Each judge has a similar right to put questions, but before exercising it he should make his intention known to the President, who is made responsible by Article 45 of the Statute for the control of the hearing.
4. The agents, counsel and advocates may answer either immediately or within a time-limit fixed by the President.

Article 62

1. The Court may at any time call upon the parties to produce such evidence or to give such explanations as the Court may consider to be necessary for the elucidation of any aspect of the matters in issue, or may itself seek other information for this purpose.
2. The Court may, if necessary, arrange for the attendance of a witness or expert to give evidence in the proceedings.

Article 63

1. The parties may call any witnesses or experts appearing on the list communicated to the Court pursuant to Article 57 of these Rules. If at any time during the hearing a party wishes to call a witness or expert whose name was not included in that list, it shall so inform the Court and the other party, and shall supply the information required by Article 57. The witness or expert may be called either if the other party makes no objection or if the Court is satisfied that his evidence seems likely to prove relevant.

2. The Court, or the President if the Court is not sitting, shall, at the request of one of the parties or *proprio motu*, take the necessary steps for the examination of witnesses otherwise than before the Court itself.

Article 64

Unless on account of special circumstances the Court decides on a different form of words,

(*a*) every witness shall make the following declaration before giving any evidence:

"I solemnly declare upon my honour and conscience that I will speak the truth, the whole truth and nothing but the truth";

(*b*) every expert shall make the following declaration before making any statement:

"I solemnly declare upon my honour and conscience that I will speak the truth, the whole truth and nothing but the truth, and that my statement will be in accordance with my sincere belief."

Article 65

Witnesses and experts shall be examined by the agents, counsel or advocates of the parties under the control of the President. Questions may be put to them by the President and by the judges. Before testifying, witnesses shall remain out of court.

Article 66

The Court may at any time decide, either *proprio motu* or at the request of a party, to exercise its functions with regard to the obtaining of evidence at a place or locality to which the case relates, subject to such conditions as the Court may decide upon after ascertaining the views of the parties. The necessary arrangements shall be made in accordance with Article 44 of the Statute.

Article 67

1. If the Court considers it necessary to arrange for an enquiry or an expert opinion, it shall, after hearing the parties, issue an order to this effect, defining the subject of the enquiry or expert opinion, stating the number and mode of appointment of the persons to hold the enquiry or of the experts, and laying down the procedure to be followed. Where appropriate, the Court shall require persons appointed to carry out an enquiry, or to give an expert opinion, to make a solemn declaration.
2. Every report or record of an enquiry and every expert opinion shall be communicated to the parties, which shall be given the opportunity of commenting upon it.

Article 68

Witnesses and experts who appear at the instance of the Court under Article 62, paragraph 2, and persons appointed under Article 67, paragraph 1, of these Rules, to carry out an enquiry or to give an expert opinion, shall, where appropriate, be paid out of the funds of the Court.

Article 69

1. The Court may, at any time prior to the closure of the oral proceedings, either *proprio motu* or at the request of one of the parties communicated as provided in Article 57 of these Rules, request a public international organization, pur-

suant to Article 34 of the Statute, to furnish information relevant to a case before it. The Court, after consulting the chief administrative officer of the organization concerned, shall decide whether such information shall be presented to it orally or in writing, and the time-limits for its presentation.

2. When a public international organization sees fit to furnish, on its own initiative, information relevant to a case before the Court, it shall do so in the form of a Memorial to be filed in the Registry before the closure of the written proceedings. The Court shall retain the right to require such information to be supplemented, either orally or in writing, in the form of answers to any questions which it may see fit to formulate, and also to authorize the parties to comment, either orally or in writing, on the information thus furnished.

3. In the circumstances contemplated by Article 34, paragraph 3, of the Statute, the Registrar, on the instructions of the Court, or of the President if the Court is not sitting, shall proceed as prescribed in that paragraph. The Court, or the President if the Court is not sitting, may, as from the date on which the Registrar has communicated copies of the written proceedings and after consulting the chief administrative officer of the public international organization concerned, fix a time-limit within which the organization may submit to the Court its observations in writing. These observations shall be communicated to the parties and may be discussed by them and by the representative of the said organization during the oral proceedings.

4. In the foregoing paragraph, the term "public international organization" denotes an international organization of States.

Article 70

1. In the absence of any decision to the contrary by the Court, all speeches and statements made and evidence given at the hearing in one of the official languages of the Court shall be interpreted into the other official language. If they are made or given in any other language, they shall be interpreted into the two official languages of the Court.

2. Whenever, in accordance with Article 39, paragraph 3, of the Statute, a language other than French or English is used, the necessary arrangements for interpretation into one of the two official languages shall be made by the party concerned; however, the Registrar shall make arrangements for the verification of the interpretation provided by a party of evidence given on the party's behalf. In the case of witnesses or experts who appear at the instance of the Court, arrangements for interpretation shall be made by the Registry.

3. A party on behalf of which speeches or statements are to be made, or evidence given, in a language which is not one of the official languages of the Court, shall so notify the Registrar in sufficient time for him to make the necessary arrangements.

4. Before first interpreting in the case, interpreters provided by a party shall make the following declaration in open court:

   "I solemnly declare upon my honour and conscience that my interpretation will be faithful and complete."

Article 71

1. A verbatim record shall be made by the Registrar of every hearing, in the official language of the Court which has been used. When the language used is not

one of the two official languages of the Court, the verbatim record shall be prepared in one of the Court's official languages.

2. When speeches or statements are made in a language which is not one of the official languages of the Court, the party on behalf of which they are made shall supply to the Registry in advance a text thereof in one of the official languages, and this text shall constitute the relevant part of the verbatim record.

3. The transcript of the verbatim record shall be preceded by the names of the judges present, and those of the agents, counsel and advocates of the parties.

4. Copies of the transcript shall be circulated to the judges sitting in the case, and to the parties. The latter may, under the supervision of the Court, correct the transcripts of speeches and statements made on their behalf, but in no case may such corrections affect the sense and bearing thereof. The judges may likewise make corrections in the transcript of anything they may have said.

5. Witnesses and experts shall be shown that part of the transcript which relates to the evidence given, or the statements made by them, and may correct it in like manner as the parties.

6. One certified true copy of the eventual corrected transcript, signed by the President and the Registrar, shall constitute the authentic minutes of the sitting for the purpose of Article 47 of the Statute. The minutes of public hearings shall be printed and published by the Court.

Article 72

Any written reply by a party to a question put under Article 61, or any evidence or explanation supplied by a party under Article 62 of these Rules, received by the Court after the closure of the oral proceedings, shall be communicated to the other party, which shall be given the opportunity of commenting upon it. If necessary the oral proceedings may be reopened for that purpose.

Section D. Incidental Proceedings

Subsection 1. Interim Protection

Article 73

1. A written request for the indication of provisional measures may be made by a party at any time during the course of the proceedings in the case in connection with which the request is made.

2. The request shall specify the reasons therefor, the possible consequences if it is not granted, and the measures requested. A certified copy shall forthwith be transmitted by the Registrar to the other party.

Article 74

1. A request for the indication of provisional measures shall have priority over all other cases.

2. The Court, if it is not sitting when the request is made, shall be convened forthwith for the purpose of proceeding to a decision on the request as a matter of urgency.

3. The Court, or the President if the Court is not sitting, shall fix a date for a hearing which will afford the parties an opportunity of being represented at it. The Court shall receive and take into account any observations that may be presented to it before the closure of the oral proceedings.

4. Pending the meeting of the Court, the President may call upon the parties to act in such a way as will enable any order the Court may make on the request for provisional measures to have its appropriate effects.

Article 75

1. The Court may at any time decide to examine proprio motu whether the circumstances of the case require the indication of provisional measures which ought to be taken or complied with by any or all of the parties.
2. When a request for provisional measures has been made, the Court may indicate measures that are in whole or in part other than those requested, or that ought to be taken or complied with by the party which has itself made the request.
3. The rejection of a request for the indication of provisional measures shall not prevent the party which made it from making a fresh request in the same case based on new facts.

Article 76

1. At the request of a party the Court may, at any time before the final judgment in the case, revoke or modify any decision concerning provisional measures if, in its opinion, some change in the situation justifies such revocation or modification.
2. Any application by a party proposing such a revocation or modification shall specify the change in the situation considered to be relevant.
3. Before taking any decision under paragraph 1 of this Article the Court shall afford the parties an opportunity of presenting their observations on the subject.

Article 77

Any measures indicated by the Court under Articles 73 and 75 of these Rules, and any decision taken by the Court under Article 76, paragraph 1, of these Rules, shall forthwith be communicated to the Secretary-General of the United Nations for transmission to the Security Council in pursuance of Article 41, paragraph 2, of the Statute.

Article 78

The Court may request information from the parties on any matter connected with the implementation of any provisional measures it has indicated.

Subsection 2. Preliminary Objections

Article 79*, [1]

1. Any objection by the respondent to the jurisdiction of the Court or to the admissibility of the application, or other objection the decision upon which is requested before any further proceedings on the merits, shall be made in writing as soon as possible, and not later than three months after the delivery of the Memorial. Any such objection made by a party other than the respondent shall be filed within the time-limit fixed for the delivery of that party's first pleading.

---

* Amendment entered into force on 1 February 2001. Article 79 of the Rules of Court as adopted on 14 April 1978 has continued to apply to all cases submitted to the Court prior to 1 February 2001.

[1] In Article 79, paragraph 1, as amended, the words "as soon as possible, and not later than three months after the delivery of the Memorial" have been substituted for the words "within the time-limit fixed for the delivery of the Counter-Memorial" contained in the text of this paragraph as adopted on 14 April 1978.

Paragraphs 2 and 3 of the amended Article 79 are new.

The former paragraphs 2 to 8 have been renumbered, respectively, as paragraphs 4 to 10.

2. Notwithstanding paragraph 1 above, following the submission of the application and after the President has met and consulted with the parties, the Court may decide that any questions of jurisdiction and admissibility shall be determined separately.
3. Where the Court so decides, the parties shall submit any pleadings as to jurisdiction and admissibility within the time-limits fixed by the Court and in the order determined by it, notwithstanding Article 45, paragraph 1.
4. The preliminary objection shall set out the facts and the law on which the objection is based, the submissions and a list of the documents in support; it shall mention any evidence which the party may desire to produce. Copies of the supporting documents shall be attached.
5. Upon receipt by the Registry of a preliminary objection, the proceedings on the merits shall be suspended and the Court, or the President if the Court is not sitting, shall fix the time-limit within which the other party may present a written statement of its observations and submissions; documents in support shall be attached and evidence which it is proposed to produce shall be mentioned.
6. Unless otherwise decided by the Court, the further proceedings shall be oral.
7. The statements of facts and law in the pleadings referred to in paragraphs 4 and 5 of this Article, and the statements and evidence presented at the hearings contemplated by paragraph 6, shall be confined to those matters that are relevant to the objection.
8. In order to enable the Court to determine its jurisdiction at the preliminary stage of the proceedings, the Court, whenever necessary, may request the parties to argue all questions of law and fact, and to adduce all evidence, which bear on the issue.
9. After hearing the parties, the Court shall give its decision in the form of a judgment, by which it shall either uphold the objection, reject it, or declare that the objection does not possess, in the circumstances of the case, an exclusively preliminary character. If the Court rejects the objection or declares that it does not possess an exclusively preliminary character, it shall fix time-limits for the further proceedings.
10. Any agreement between the parties that an objection submitted under paragraph 1 of this Article be heard and determined within the framework of the merits shall be given effect by the Court.

Subsection 3. Counter-Claims

Article 80*, [1]

1. The Court may entertain a counter-claim only if it comes within the jurisdiction of the Court and is directly connected with the subject-matter of the claim of the other party.

---

* Amendment entered into force on 1 February 2001. Article 80 of the Rules of Court as adopted on 14 April 1978 has continued to apply to all cases submitted to the Court prior to 1 February 2001.

[1] Article 80 of the Rules of Court as adopted on 14 April 1978 read as follows:

"*Article 80*

1. A counter-claim may be presented provided that it is directly connected with the subject-matter of the claim of the other party and that it comes within the jurisdiction of the Court.
2. A counter-claim shall be made in the Counter-Memorial of the party presenting it, and shall appear as part of the submissions of that party.
3. In the event of doubt as to the connection between the question presented by way

2. A counter-claim shall be made in the Counter-Memorial and shall appear as part of the submissions contained therein. The right of the other party to present its views in writing on the counter-claim, in an additional pleading, shall be preserved, irrespective of any decision of the Court, in accordance with Article 45, paragraph 2, of these Rules, concerning the filing of further written pleadings.
3. Where an objection is raised concerning the application of paragraph 1 or whenever the Court deems necessary, the Court shall take its decision thereon after hearing the parties.

Subsection 4. Intervention

Article 81

1. An application for permission to intervene under the terms of Article 62 of the Statute, signed in the manner provided for in Article 38, paragraph 3, of these Rules, shall be filed as soon as possible, and not later than the closure of the written proceedings. In exceptional circumstances, an application submitted at a later stage may however be admitted.
2. The application shall state the name of an agent. It shall specify the case to which it relates, and shall set out:
   (a) the interest of a legal nature which the State applying to intervene considers may be affected by the decision in that case;
   (b) the precise object of the intervention;
   (c) any basis of jurisdiction which is claimed to exist as between the State applying to intervene and the parties to the case.
3. The application shall contain a list of the documents in support, which documents shall be attached.

Article 82

1. A State which desires to avail itself of the right of intervention conferred upon it by Article 63 of the Statute shall file a declaration to that effect, signed in the manner provided for in Article 38, paragraph 3, of these Rules. Such a declaration shall be filed as soon as possible, and not later than the date fixed for the opening of the oral proceedings. In exceptional circumstances a declaration submitted at a later stage may however be admitted.
2. The declaration shall state the name of an agent. It shall specify the case and the convention to which it relates and shall contain:
   (a) particulars of the basis on which the declarant State considers itself a party to the convention;
   (b) identification of the particular provisions of the convention the construction of which it considers to be in question;
   (c) a statement of the construction of those provisions for which it contends;
   (d) a list of the documents in support, which documents shall be attached.
3. Such a declaration may be filed by a State that considers itself a party to the convention the construction of which is in question but has not received the notification referred to in Article 63 of the Statute.

---

of counter-claim and the subject-matter of the claim of the other party the Court shall, after hearing the parties, decide whether or not the question thus presented shall be joined to the original proceedings."

Article 83

1. Certified copies of the application for permission to intervene under Article 62 of the Statute, or of the declaration of intervention under Article 63 of the Statute, shall be communicated forthwith to the parties to the case, which shall be invited to furnish their written observations within a time-limit to be fixed by the Court or by the President if the Court is not sitting.
2. The Registrar shall also transmit copies to: (a) the Secretary-General of the United Nations; (b) the Members of the United Nations; (c) other States entitled to appear before the Court; (d) any other States which have been notified under Article 63 of the Statute.

Article 84

1. The Court shall decide whether an application for permission to intervene under Article 62 of the Statute should be granted, and whether an intervention under Article 63 of the Statute is admissible, as a matter of priority unless in view of the circumstances of the case the Court shall otherwise determine.
2. If, within the time-limit fixed under Article 83 of these Rules, an objection is filed to an application for permission to intervene, or to the admissibility of a declaration of intervention, the Court shall hear the State seeking to intervene and the parties before deciding.

Article 85

1. If an application for permission to intervene under Article 62 of the Statute is granted, the intervening State shall be supplied with copies of the pleadings and documents annexed and shall be entitled to submit a written statement within a time-limit to be fixed by the Court. A further time-limit shall be fixed within which the parties may, if they so desire, furnish their written observations on that statement prior to the oral proceedings. If the Court is not sitting, these time-limits shall be fixed by the President.
2. The time-limits fixed according to the preceding paragraph shall, so far as possible, coincide with those already fixed for the pleadings in the case.
3. The intervening State shall be entitled, in the course of the oral proceedings, to submit its observations with respect to the subject-matter of the intervention.

Article 86

1. If an intervention under Article 63 of the Statute is admitted, the intervening State shall be furnished with copies of the pleadings and documents annexed, and shall be entitled, within a time-limit to be fixed by the Court, or by the President if the Court is not sitting, to submit its written observations on the subject-matter of the intervention.
2. These observations shall be communicated to the parties and to any other State admitted to intervene. The intervening State shall be entitled, in the course of the oral proceedings, to submit its observations with respect to the subject-matter of the intervention.

Subsection 5. Special Reference to the Court

Article 87

1. When in accordance with a treaty or convention in force a contentious case is brought before the Court concerning a matter which has been the subject of proceedings

before some other international body, the provisions of the Statute and of the Rules governing contentious cases shall apply.

2. The application instituting proceedings shall identify the decision or other act of the international body concerned and a copy thereof shall be annexed; it shall contain a precise statement of the questions raised in regard to that decision or act, which constitute the subject of the dispute referred to the Court.

Subsection 6. Discontinuance

Article 88

1. If at any time before the final judgment on the merits has been delivered the parties, either jointly or separately, notify the Court in writing that they have agreed to discontinue the proceedings, the Court shall make an order recording the discontinuance and directing that the case be removed from the list.
2. If the parties have agreed to discontinue the proceedings in consequence of having reached a settlement of the dispute and if they so desire, the Court may record this fact in the order for the removal of the case from the list, or indicate in, or annex to, the order, the terms of the settlement.
3. If the Court is not sitting, any order under this Article may be made by the President.

Article 89

1. If in the course of proceedings instituted by means of an application, the applicant informs the Court in writing that it is not going on with the proceedings, and if, at the date on which this communication is received by the Registry, the respondent has not yet taken any step in the proceedings, the Court shall make an order officially recording the discontinuance of the proceedings and directing the removal of the case from the list. A copy of this order shall be sent by the Registrar to the respondent.
2. If, at the time when the notice of discontinuance is received, the respondent has already taken some step in the proceedings, the Court shall fix a time-limit within which the respondent may state whether it opposes the discontinuance of the proceedings. If no objection is made to the discontinuance before the expiration of the time-limit, acquiescence will be presumed and the Court shall make an order officially recording the discontinuance of the proceedings and directing the removal of the case from the list. If objection is made, the proceedings shall continue.
3. If the Court is not sitting, its powers under this Article may be exercised by the President.

Section E. Proceedings before the Chambers

Article 90

Proceedings before the Chambers mentioned in Articles 26 and 29 of the Statute shall, subject to the provisions of the Statute and of these Rules relating specifically to the Chambers, be governed by the provisions of Parts I to III of these Rules applicable in contentious cases before the Court.

Article 91

1. When it is desired that a case should be dealt with by one of the Chambers which has been formed in pursuance of Article 26, paragraph 1, or Article 29 of the

Statute, a request to this effect shall either be made in the document instituting the proceedings or accompany it. Effect will be given to the request if the parties are in agreement.

2. Upon receipt by the Registry of this request, the President of the Court shall communicate it to the members of the Chamber concerned. He shall take such steps as may be necessary to give effect to the provisions of Article 31, paragraph 4, of the Statute.

3. The President of the Court shall convene the Chamber at the earliest date compatible with the requirements of the procedure.

Article 92

1. Written proceedings in a case before a Chamber shall consist of a single pleading by each side. In proceedings begun by means of an application, the pleadings shall be delivered within successive time-limits. In proceedings begun by the notification of a special agreement, the pleadings shall be delivered within the same time-limits, unless the parties have agreed on successive delivery of their pleadings. The time-limits referred to in this paragraph shall be fixed by the Court, or by the President if the Court is not sitting, in consultation with the Chamber concerned if it is already constituted.

2. The Chamber may authorize or direct that further pleadings be filed if the parties are so agreed, or if the Chamber decides, proprio motu or at the request of one of the parties, that such pleadings are necessary.

3. Oral proceedings shall take place unless the parties agree to dispense with them, and the Chamber consents. Even when no oral proceedings take place, the Chamber may call upon the parties to supply information or furnish explanations orally.

Article 93

Judgments given by a Chamber shall be read at a public sitting of that Chamber.

Section F. Judgments, Interpretation and Revision

Subsection 1. Judgments

Article 94

1. When the Court has completed its deliberations and adopted its judgment, the parties shall be notified of the date on which it will be read.

2. The judgment shall be read at a public sitting of the Court and shall become binding on the parties on the day of the reading.

Article 95

1. The judgment, which shall state whether it is given by the Court or by a Chamber, shall contain:

   the date on which it is read;

   the names of the judges participating in it;

   the names of the parties;

   the names of the agents, counsel and advocates of the parties;

   a summary of the proceedings;

   the submissions of the parties;

a statement of the facts;

the reasons in point of law;

the operative provisions of the judgment;

the decision, if any, in regard to costs;

the number and names of the judges constituting the majority;

a statement as to the text of the judgment which is authoritative.

2. Any judge may, if he so desires, attach his individual opinion to the judgment, whether he dissents from the majority or not; a judge who wishes to record his concurrence or dissent without stating his reasons may do so in the form of a declaration. The same shall also apply to orders made by the Court.

3. One copy of the judgment duly signed and sealed, shall be placed in the archives of the Court and another shall be transmitted to each of the parties. Copies shall be sent by the Registrar to: (a) the Secretary-General of the United Nations; (b) the Members of the United Nations; (c) other Sates entitled to appear before the Court.

Article 96

When by reason of an agreement reached between the parties, the written and oral proceedings have been conducted in one of the Court's two official languages, and pursuant to Article 39, paragraph 1, of the Statute the judgment is to be delivered in that language, the text of the judgment in that language shall be the authoritative text.

Article 97

If the Court, under Article 64 of the Statute, decides that all or part of a party's costs shall be paid by the other party, it may make an order for the purpose of giving effect to that decision.

Subsection 2. Requests for the Interpretation or

Revision of a Judgment

Article 98

1. In the event of dispute as to the meaning or scope of a judgment any party may make a request for its interpretation, whether the original proceedings were begun by an application or by the notification of a special agreement.

2. A request for the interpretation of a judgment may be made either by an application or by the notification of a special agreement to that effect between the parties; the precise point or points in dispute as to the meaning or scope of the judgment shall be indicated.

3. If the request for interpretation is made by an application, the requesting party's contentions shall be set out therein, and the other party shall be entitled to file written observations thereon within a time-limit fixed by the Court, or by the President if the Court is not sitting.

4. Whether the request is made by an application or by notification of a special agreement, the Court may, if necessary, afford the parties the opportunity of furnishing further written or oral explanations.

Article 99

1. A request for the revision of a judgment shall be made by an application containing the particulars necessary to show that the conditions specified in Article 61 of the

Statute are fulfilled. Any documents in support of the application shall be annexed to it.

2. The other party shall be entitled to file written observations on the admissibility of the application within a time-limit fixed by the Court, or by the President if the Court is not sitting. These observations shall be communicated to the party making the application.
3. The Court, before giving its judgment on the admissibility of the application may afford the parties a further opportunity of presenting their views thereon.
4. If the Court finds that the application is admissible it shall fix time-limits for such further proceedings on the merits of the application as, after ascertaining the views of the parties, it considers necessary.
5. If the Court decides to make the admission of the proceedings in revision conditional on previous compliance with the judgment, it shall make an order accordingly.

Article 100

1. If the judgment to be revised or to be interpreted was given by the Court, the request for its revision or interpretation shall be dealt with by the Court. If the judgment was given by a Chamber, the request for its revision or interpretation shall be dealt with by that Chamber.
2. The decision of the Court, or of the Chamber, on a request for interpretation or revision of a judgment shall itself be given in the form of a judgment.

SECTION G. MODIFICATIONS PROPOSED BY THE PARTIES

Article 101

The parties to a case may jointly propose particular modifications or additions to the rules contained in the present Part (with the exception of Articles 93 to 97 inclusive), which may be applied by the Court or by a Chamber if the Court or the Chamber considers them appropriate in the circumstances of the case.

PART IV

ADVISORY PROCEEDINGS

Article 102

1. In the exercise of its advisory functions under Article 65 of the Statute, the Court shall apply, in addition to the provisions of Article 96 of the Charter and Chapter IV of the Statute, the provisions of the present Part of the Rules.
2. The Court shall also be guided by the provisions of the Statute and of these Rules which apply in contentious cases to the extent to which it recognizes them to be applicable. For this purpose, it shall above all consider whether the request for the advisory opinion relates to a legal question actually pending between two or more States.
3. When an advisory opinion is requested upon a legal question actually pending between two or more States, Article 31 of the Statute shall apply, as also the provisions of these Rules concerning the application of that Article.

Article 103

When the body authorized by or in accordance with the Charter of the United Nations to request an advisory opinion informs the Court that its request necessitates an urgent answer, or the Court finds that an early answer would be desirable, the Court shall take all necessary steps to accelerate the procedure, and it shall convene as early as possible for the purpose of proceeding to a hearing and deliberation on the request.

Article 104

All requests for advisory opinions shall be transmitted to the Court by the Secretary-General of the United Nations or, as the case may be, the chief administrative officer of the body authorized to make the request. The documents referred to in Article 65, paragraph 2, of the Statute shall be transmitted to the Court at the same time as the request or as soon as possible thereafter, in the number of copies required by the Registry.

Article 105

1. Written statements submitted to the Court shall be communicated by the Registrar to any States and organizations which have submitted such statements.
2. The Court, or the President if the Court is not sitting, shall:
   (a) determine the form in which, and the extent to which, comments permitted under Article 66, paragraph 4, of the Statute shall be received, and fix the time-limit for the submission of any such comments in writing;
   (b) decide whether oral proceedings shall take place at which statements and comments may be submitted to the Court under the provisions of Article 66 of the Statute, and fix the date for the opening of such oral proceedings.

Article 106

The Court, or the President if the Court is not sitting, may decide that the written statements and annexed documents shall be made accessible to the public on or after the opening of the oral proceedings. If the request for advisory opinion relates to a legal question actually pending between two or more States, the views of those States shall first be ascertained.

Article 107

1. When the Court has completed its deliberations and adopted its advisory opinion, the opinion shall be read at a public sitting of the Court.
2. The advisory opinion shall contain:

   the date on which it is delivered;

   the names of the judges participating;

   a summary of the proceedings;

   a statement of the facts;

   the reasons in point of law;

   the reply to the question put to the Court;

   the number and names of the judges constituting the majority;

   a statement as to the text of the opinion which is authoritative.
3. Any judge may, if he so desires, attach his individual opinion to the advisory opinion of the Court, whether he dissents from the majority or not; a judge who wishes to record his concurrence or dissent without stating his reasons may do so in the form of a declaration.

Article 108

The Registrar shall inform the Secretary-General of the United Nations, and, where appropriate, the chief administrative officer of the body which requested the advisory opinion, as to the date and the hour fixed for the public sitting to be held for the reading of the opinion. He shall also inform the representatives of the Members of the United Nations and other States, specialized agencies and public international organizations immediately concerned.

Article 109

One copy of the advisory opinion, duly signed and sealed, shall be placed in the archives of the Court, another shall be sent to the Secretary-General of the United Nations and, where appropriate, a third to the chief administrative officer of the body which requested the opinion of the Court. Copies shall be sent by the Registrar to the Members of the United Nations and to any other States, specialized agencies and public international organizations immediately concerned.

(Signed) Rosalyn Higgins, President.

(Signed) Ph. Couvreur, Registrar.

8. United Nations Convention on the Law of the Sea, Part XV, 1982

Section 1. General Provisions

Article 279
Obligation to settle disputes by peaceful means

States Parties shall settle any dispute between them concerning the interpretation or application of this Convention by peaceful means in accordance with Article 2, paragraph 3, of the Charter of the United Nations and, to this end, shall seek a solution by the means indicated in Article 33, paragraph 1, of the Charter.

Article 280
Settlement of disputes by any peaceful means chosen by the parties

Nothing in this Part impairs the right of any States Parties to agree at any time to settle a dispute between them concerning the interpretation or application of this Convention by any peaceful means of their own choice.

Article 281
Procedure where no settlement has been reached by the parties

1. If the States Parties which are parties to a dispute concerning the interpretation or application of this Convention have agreed to seek settlement of the dispute by a peaceful means of their own choice, the procedures provided for in this Part apply only where no settlement has been reached by recourse to such means and the agreement between the parties does not exclude any further procedure.
2. If the parties have also agreed on a time-limit, paragraph 1 applies only upon the expiration of that time-limit.

Article 282
Obligations under general, regional or bilateral agreements

If the States Parties which are parties to a dispute concerning the interpretation or application of this Convention have agreed, through a general, regional or bilateral agreement or otherwise, that such dispute shall, at the request of any party to the dispute, be submitted to a procedure that entails a binding decision, that procedure shall apply in lieu of the procedures provided for in this Part, unless the parties to the dispute otherwise agree.

Article 283
Obligation to exchange views

1. When a dispute arises between States Parties concerning the interpretation or application of this Convention, the parties to the dispute shall proceed expeditiously to an exchange of views regarding its settlement by negotiation or other peaceful means.
2. The parties shall also proceed expeditiously to an exchange of views where a procedure for the settlement of such a dispute has been terminated without a settlement or where a settlement has been reached and the circumstances require consultation regarding the manner of implementing the settlement.

Article 284
Conciliation

1. A State Party which is a party to a dispute concerning the interpretation or application of this Convention may invite the other party or parties to submit the dispute to conciliation in accordance with the procedure under Annex V, section 1, or another conciliation procedure.
2. If the invitation is accepted and if the parties agree upon the conciliation procedure to be applied, any party may submit the dispute to that procedure.
3. If the invitation is not accepted or the parties do not agree upon the procedure, the conciliation proceedings shall be deemed to be terminated.
4. Unless the parties otherwise agree, when a dispute has been submitted to conciliation, the proceedings may be terminated only in accordance with the agreed conciliation procedure.

Article 285
Application of this section to disputes submitted pursuant to Part XI

This section applies to any dispute which pursuant to Part XI, section 5, is to be settled in accordance with procedures provided for in this Part. If an entity other than a State Party is a party to such a dispute, this section applies mutatis mutandis.

SECTION 2. COMPULSORY PROCEDURES ENTAILING BINDING DECISIONS

Article 286
Application of procedures under this section

Subject to section 3, any dispute concerning the interpretation or application of this Convention shall, where no settlement has been reached by recourse to section 1, be submitted at the request of any party to the dispute to the court or tribunal having jurisdiction under this section.

Article 287
Choice of procedure

1. When signing, ratifying or acceding to this Convention or at any time thereafter, a State shall be free to choose, by means of a written declaration, one or more of the following means for the settlement of disputes concerning the interpretation or application of this Convention:
   (a) the International Tribunal for the Law of the Sea established in accordance with Annex VI;

(b) the International Court of Justice;

(c) an arbitral tribunal constituted in accordance with Annex VII;

(d) a special arbitral tribunal constituted in accordance with Annex VIII for one or more of the categories of disputes specified therein.

2. A declaration made under paragraph 1 shall not affect or be affected by the obligation of a State Party to accept the jurisdiction of the Sea-Bed Disputes Chamber of the International Tribunal for the Law of the Sea to the extent and in the manner provided for in Part XI, section 5.

3. A State Party, which is a party to a dispute not covered by a declaration in force, shall be deemed to have accepted arbitration in accordance with Annex VII.

4. If the parties to a dispute have accepted the same procedure for the settlement of the dispute, it may be submitted only to that procedure, unless the parties otherwise agree.

5. If the parties to a dispute have not accepted the same procedure for the settlement of the dispute, it may be submitted only to arbitration in accordance with Annex VII, unless the parties otherwise agree.

6. A declaration made under paragraph 1 shall remain in force until three months after notice of revocation has been deposited with the Secretary-General of the United Nations.

7. A new declaration, a notice of revocation or the expiry of a declaration does not in any way affect proceedings pending before a court or tribunal having jurisdiction under this Article, unless the parties otherwise agree.

8. Declarations and notices referred to in this Article shall be deposited with the Secretary-General of the United Nations, who shall transmit copies thereof to the States Parties.

Article 288
Jurisdiction

1. A court or tribunal referred to in Article 287 shall have jurisdiction over any dispute concerning the interpretation or application of this Convention which is submitted to it in accordance with this Part.

2. A court or tribunal referred to in Article 287 shall also have jurisdiction over any dispute concerning the interpretation or application of an international agreement related to the purposes of this Convention, which is submitted to it in accordance with the agreement.

3. The Sea-Bed Disputes Chamber of the International Tribunal for the Law of the Sea established in accordance with Annex VI, and any other chamber or arbitral tribunal referred to in Part XI, section 5, shall have jurisdiction in any matter which is submitted to it in accordance therewith.

4. In the event of a dispute as to whether a court or tribunal has jurisdiction, the matter shall be settled by decision of that court or tribunal.

Article 289
Experts

In any dispute involving scientific or technical matters, a court or tribunal exercising jurisdiction under this section may, at the request of a party or proprio motu, select in consultation with the parties no fewer than two scientific or technical experts chosen preferably from the relevant list prepared in accordance with Annex VIII, Article 2, to sit with the court or tribunal but without the right to vote.

Article 290
Provisional measures

1. If a dispute has been duly submitted to a court or tribunal which considers that prima facie it has jurisdiction under this Part or Part XI, section 5, the court or tribunal may prescribe any provisional measures which it considers appropriate under the circumstances to preserve the respective rights of the parties to the dispute or to prevent serious harm to the marine environment, pending the final decision.
2. Provisional measures may be modified or revoked as soon as the circumstances justifying them have changed or ceased to exist.
3. Provisional measures may be prescribed, modified or revoked under this Article only at the request of a party to the dispute and after the parties have been given an opportunity to be heard.
4. The court or tribunal shall forthwith give notice to the parties to the dispute, and to such other States Parties as it considers appropriate, of the prescription, modification or revocation of provisional measures.
5. Pending the constitution of an arbitral tribunal to which a dispute is being submitted under this section, any court or tribunal agreed upon by the parties or, failing such agreement within two weeks from the date of the request for provisional measures, the International Tribunal for the Law of the Sea or, with respect to activities in the Area, the Sea-Bed Disputes Chamber, may prescribe, modify or revoke provisional measures in accordance with this Article if it considers that prima facie the tribunal which is to be constituted would have jurisdiction and that the urgency of the situation so requires. Once constituted, the tribunal to which the dispute has been submitted may modify, revoke or affirm those provisional measures, acting in conformity with paragraphs 1 to 4.
6. The parties to the dispute shall comply promptly with any provisional measures prescribed under this Article.

Article 291
Access

1. All the dispute settlement procedures specified in this Part shall be open to States Parties.
2. The dispute settlement procedures specified in this Part shall be open to entities other than States Parties only as specifically provided for in this Convention.

Article 292
Prompt release of vessels and crews

1. Where the authorities of a State Party have detained a vessel flying the flag of another State Party and it is alleged that the detaining State has not complied with the provisions of this Convention for the prompt release of the vessel or its crew upon the posting of a reasonable bond or other financial security, the question of release from detention may be submitted to any court or tribunal agreed upon by the parties or, failing such agreement within 10 days from the time of detention, to a court or tribunal accepted by the detaining State under Article 287

or to the International Tribunal for the Law of the Sea, unless the parties otherwise agree.

2. The application for release may be made only by or on behalf of the Flag State of the vessel.

3. The court or tribunal shall deal without delay with the application for release and shall deal only with the question of release, without prejudice to the merits of any case before the appropriate domestic forum against the vessel, its owner or its crew. The authorities of the detaining State remain competent to release the vessel or its crew at any time.

4. Upon the posting of the bond or other financial security determined by the court or tribunal, the authorities of the detaining State shall comply promptly with the decision of the court or tribunal concerning the release of the vessel or its crew.

Article 293
Applicable law

1. A court or tribunal having jurisdiction under this section shall apply this Convention and other rules of international law not incompatible with this Convention.

2. Paragraph 1 does not prejudice the power of the court or tribunal having jurisdiction under this section to decide a case ex aequo et bono, if the parties so agree.

Article 294
Preliminary proceedings

1. A court or tribunal provided for in Article 287 to which an application is made in respect of a dispute referred to in Article 297 shall determine at the request of a party, or may determine proprio motu, whether the claim constitutes an abuse of legal process or whether prima facie it is well founded. If the court or tribunal determines that the claim constitutes an abuse of legal process or is prima facie unfounded, it shall take no further action in the case.

2. Upon receipt of the application, the court or tribunal shall immediately notify the other party or parties of the application, and shall fix a reasonable time-limit within which they may request it to make a determination in accordance with paragraph 1.

3. Nothing in this Article affects the right of any party to a dispute to make preliminary objections in accordance with the applicable rules of procedure.

Article 295
Exhaustion of local remedies

Any dispute between States Parties concerning the interpretation or application of this Convention may be submitted to the procedures provided for in this section only after local remedies have been exhausted where this is required by international law.

Article 296
Finality and binding force of decisions

1. Any decision rendered by a court or tribunal having jurisdiction under this section shall be final and shall be complied with by all the parties to the dispute.

2. Any such decision shall have no binding force except between the parties and in respect of that particular dispute.

SECTION 3. LIMITATIONS AND EXCEPTIONS TO APPLICABILITY OF SECTION 2

Article 297
Limitations on applicability of section 2

1. Disputes concerning the interpretation or application of this Convention with regard to the exercise by a coastal State of its sovereign rights or jurisdiction provided for in this Convention shall be subject to the procedures provided for in section 2 in the following cases:

   (a) when it is alleged that a coastal State has acted in contravention of the provisions of this Convention in regard to the freedoms and rights of navigation, overflight or the laying of submarine. cables or pipelines.

ANNEX VII. ARBITRATION

Article 1
Institution of proceedings

Subject to the provisions of Part XV, any party to a dispute may submit the dispute to the arbitral procedure provided for in this Annex by written notification addressed to the other party or parties to the dispute. The notification shall be accompanied by a statement of the claim and the grounds on which it is based.

Article 2
List of arbitrators

1. A list of arbitrators shall be drawn up and maintained by the Secretary-General of the United Nations. Every State Party shall be entitled to nominate four arbitrators, each of whom shall be a person experienced in maritime affairs and enjoying the highest reputation for fairness, competence and integrity. The names of the persons so nominated shall constitute the list.
2. If at any time the arbitrators nominated by a State Party in the list so constituted shall be fewer than four, that State Party shall be entitled to make further nominations as necessary.
3. The name of an arbitrator shall remain on the list until withdrawn by the State Party which made the nomination, provided that such arbitrator shall continue to serve on any arbitral tribunal to which that arbitrator has been appointed until the completion of the proceedings before that arbitral tribunal.

Article 3
Constitution of arbitral tribunal

For the purpose of proceedings under this Annex, the arbitral tribunal shall, unless the parties otherwise agree, be constituted as follows:

(a) Subject to subparagraph (g), the arbitral tribunal shall consist of five members.

(b) The party instituting the proceedings shall appoint one member to be chosen preferably from the list referred to in Article 2 of this Annex, who may be its national. The appointment shall be included in the notification referred to in Article 1 of this Annex.

(c) The other party to the dispute shall, within 30 days of receipt of the notification referred to in Article 1 of this Annex, appoint one member to be chosen preferably from the list, who may be its national. If the appointment is not made within that period, the party instituting the proceedings may, within two weeks of the expiration of that period, request that the appointment be made in accordance with subparagraph (e).

(d) The other three members shall be appointed by agreement between the parties. They shall be chosen preferably from the list and shall be nationals of third States unless the parties otherwise agree. The parties to the dispute shall appoint the President of the arbitral tribunal from among those three members. If, within 60 days of receipt of the notification referred to in Article 1 of this Annex, the parties are unable to reach agreement on the appointment of one or more of the members of the tribunal to be appointed by agreement, or on the appointment of the President, the remaining appointment or appointments shall be made in accordance with subparagraph (e), at the request of a party to the dispute. Such request shall be made within two weeks of the expiration of the aforementioned 60-day period.

(e) Unless the parties agree that any appointment under subparagraphs (c) and (d) be made by a person or a third State chosen by the parties, the President of the International Tribunal for the Law of the Sea shall make the necessary appointments. If the President is unable to act under this subparagraph or is a national of one of the parties to the dispute, the appointment shall be made by the next senior member of the International Tribunal for the Law of the Sea who is available and is not a national of one of the parties. The appointments referred to in this subparagraph shall be made from the list referred to in Article 2 of this Annex within a period of 30 days of the receipt of the request and in consultation with the parties. The members so appointed shall be of different nationalities and may not be in the service of, ordinarily resident in the territory of, or nationals of, any of the parties to the dispute.

(f) Any vacancy shall be filled in the manner prescribed for the initial appointment.

(g) Parties in the same interest shall appoint one member of the tribunal jointly by agreement. Where there are several parties having separate interests or where there is disagreement as to whether they are of the same interest, each of them shall appoint one member of the tribunal. The number of members of the tribunal appointed separately by the parties shall always be smaller by one than the number of members of the tribunal to be appointed jointly by the parties.

(h) In disputes involving more than two parties, the provisions of subparagraphs (a) to (f) shall apply to the maximum extent possible.

Article 4
Functions of arbitral tribunal

An arbitral tribunal constituted under Article 3 of this Annex shall function in accordance with this Annex and the other provisions of this Convention.

Article 5
Procedure

Unless the parties to the dispute otherwise agree, the arbitral tribunal shall determine its own procedure, assuring to each party a full opportunity to be heard and to present its case.

Article 6
Duties of parties to a dispute

The parties to the dispute shall facilitate the work of the arbitral tribunal and, in particular, in accordance with their law and using all means at their disposal, shall:

(a) provide it with all relevant documents, facilities and information; and

(b) enable it when necessary to call witnesses or experts and receive their evidence and to visit the localities to which the case relates.

Article 7
Expenses

Unless the arbitral tribunal decides otherwise because of the particular circumstances of the case, the expenses of the tribunal, including the remuneration of its members, shall be borne by the parties to the dispute in equal shares.

Article 8
Required majority for decisions

Decisions of the arbitral tribunal shall be taken by a majority vote of its members. The absence or abstention of less than half of the members shall not constitute a bar to the tribunal reaching a decision. In the event of an equality of votes, the President shall have a casting vote.

Article 9
Default of appearance

If one of the parties to the dispute does not appear before the arbitral tribunal or fails to defend its case, the other party may request the tribunal to continue the proceedings and to make its award. Absence of a party or failure of a party to defend its case shall not constitute a bar to the proceedings. Before making its award, the arbitral tribunal must satisfy itself not only that it has jurisdiction over the dispute but also that the claim is well founded in fact and law.

Article 10
Award

The award of the arbitral tribunal shall be confined to the subject-matter of the dispute and state the reasons on which it is based. It shall contain the names of the members who have participated and the date of the award. Any member of the tribunal may attach a separate or dissenting opinion to the award.

Article 11
Finality of award

The award shall be final and without appeal, unless the parties to the dispute have agreed in advance to an appellate procedure. It shall be complied with by the parties to the dispute.

Article 12
Interpretation or implementation of award

1. Any controversy which may arise between the parties to the dispute as regards the interpretation or manner of implementation of the award may be submitted by either party for decision to the arbitral tribunal which made the award. For this purpose, any vacancy in the tribunal shall be filled in the manner provided for in the original appointments of the members of the tribunal.
2. Any such controversy may be submitted to another court or tribunal under Article 287 by agreement of all the parties to the dispute.

Article 13
Application to entities other than states parties

The provisions of this Annex shall apply *mutatis mutandis* to any dispute involving entities other than States Parties.

Annex VI. Statute of the International Tribunal For the Law of the Sea

Article 1
General provisions

1. The International Tribunal for the Law of the Sea is constituted and shall function in accordance with the provisions of this Convention and this Statute.
2. The seat of the Tribunal shall be in the Free and Hanseatic City of Hamburg in the Federal Republic of Germany.
3. The Tribunal may sit and exercise its functions elsewhere whenever it considers this desirable.
4. A reference of a dispute to the Tribunal shall be governed by the provisions of Parts XI and XV.

SECTION 1. ORGANIZATION OF THE TRIBUNAL

Article 2
Composition

1. The Tribunal shall be composed of a body of 21 independent members, elected from among persons enjoying the highest reputation for fairness and integrity and of recognized competence in the field of the law of the sea.
2. In the Tribunal as a whole the representation of the principal legal systems of the world and equitable geographical distribution shall be assured.

Article 3
Membership

1. No two members of the Tribunal may be nationals of the same State. A person who for the purposes of membership in the Tribunal could be regarded as a national of more than one State shall be deemed to be a national of the one in which he ordinarily exercises civil and political rights.
2. There shall be no fewer than three members from each geographical group as established by the General Assembly of the United Nations.

Article 4
Nominations and elections

1. Each State Party may nominate not more than two persons having the qualifications prescribed in Article 2 of this Annex. The members of the Tribunal shall be elected from the list of persons thus nominated.
2. At least three months before the date of the election, the Secretary-General of the United Nations in the case of the first election and the Registrar of the Tribunal in the case of subsequent elections shall address a written invitation to the States Parties to submit their nominations for members of the Tribunal within two months. He shall prepare a list in alphabetical order of all the persons thus nominated, with an indication of the States Parties which have nominated them, and shall submit it to the States Parties before the seventh day of the last month before the date of each election.

3. The first election shall be held within six months of the date of entry into force of this Convention.
4. The members of the Tribunal shall be elected by secret ballot. Elections shall be held at a meeting of the States Parties convened by the Secretary-General of the United Nations in the case of the first election and by a procedure agreed to by the States Parties in the case of subsequent elections. Two thirds of the States Parties shall constitute a quorum at that meeting. The persons elected to the Tribunal shall be those nominees who obtain the largest number of votes and a two-thirds majority of the States Parties present and voting, provided that such majority includes a majority of the States Parties.

Article 5
Term of office

1. The members of the Tribunal shall be elected for nine years and may be re-elected; provided, however, that of the members elected at the first election, the terms of seven members shall expire at the end of three years and the terms of seven more members shall expire at the end of six years.
2. The members of the Tribunal whose terms are to expire at the end of the above-mentioned initial periods of three and six years shall be chosen by lot to be drawn by the Secretary-General of the United Nations immediately after the first election.
3. The members of the Tribunal shall continue to discharge their duties until their places have been filled. Though replaced, they shall finish any proceedings which they may have begun before the date of their replacement.
4. In the case of the resignation of a member of the Tribunal, the letter of resignation shall be addressed to the President of the Tribunal. The place becomes vacant on the receipt of that letter.

Article 6
Vacancies

1. Vacancies shall be filled by the same method as that laid down for the first election, subject to the following provision: the Registrar shall, within one month of the occurrence of the vacancy, proceed to issue the invitations provided for in Article 4 of this Annex, and the date of the election shall be fixed by the President of the Tribunal after consultation with the States Parties.
2. A member of the Tribunal elected to replace a member whose term of office has not expired shall hold office for the remainder of his predecessor's term.

Article 7
Incompatible activities

1. No member of the Tribunal may exercise any political or administrative function, or associate actively with or be financially interested in any of the operations of any enterprise concerned with the exploration for or exploitation of the resources of the sea or the seabed or other commercial use of the sea or the seabed.
2. No member of the Tribunal may act as agent, counsel or advocate in any case.
3. Any doubt on these points shall be resolved by decision of the majority of the other members of the Tribunal present.

Article 8
Conditions relating to participation of members in a particular case

1. No member of the Tribunal may participate in the decision of any case in which he has previously taken part as agent, counsel or advocate for one of the parties, or as a member of a national or international court or tribunal, or in any other capacity.
2. If, for some special reason, a member of the Tribunal considers that he should not take part in the decision of a particular case, he shall so inform the President of the Tribunal.
3. If the President considers that for some special reason one of the members of the Tribunal should not sit in a particular case, he shall give him notice accordingly.
4. Any doubt on these points shall be resolved by decision of the majority of the other members of the Tribunal present.

Article 9
Consequence of ceasing to fulfil required conditions

If, in the unanimous opinion of the other members of the Tribunal, a member has ceased to fulfil the required conditions, the President of the Tribunal shall declare the seat vacant.

Article 10
Privileges and immunities

The members of the Tribunal, when engaged on the business of the Tribunal, shall enjoy diplomatic privileges and immunities.

Article 11
Solemn declaration by members

Every member of the Tribunal shall, before taking up his duties, make a solemn declaration in open session that he will exercise his powers impartially and conscientiously.

Article 12
President, Vice-President and Registrar

1. The Tribunal shall elect its President and Vice-President for three years; they may be re-elected.
2. The Tribunal shall appoint its Registrar and may provide for the appointment of such other officers as may be necessary.
3. The President and the Registrar shall reside at the seat of the Tribunal.

Article 13
Quorum

1. All available members of the Tribunal shall sit; a quorum of 11 elected members shall be required to constitute the Tribunal.
2. Subject to Article 17 of this Annex, the Tribunal shall determine which members are available to constitute the Tribunal for the consideration of a particular dispute, having regard to the effective functioning of the chambers as provided for in Articles 14 and 15 of this Annex.
3. All disputes and applications submitted to the Tribunal shall be heard and determined by the Tribunal, unless Article 14 of this Annex applies, or the parties request that it shall be dealt with in accordance with Article 15 of this Annex.

Article 14
Seabed Disputes Chamber

A Seabed Disputes Chamber shall be established in accordance with the provisions of section 4 of this Annex. Its jurisdiction, powers and functions shall be as provided for in Part XI, section 5.

Article 15
Special chambers

1. The Tribunal may form such chambers, composed of three or more of its elected members, as it considers necessary for dealing with particular categories of disputes.
2. The Tribunal shall form a chamber for dealing with a particular dispute submitted to it if the parties so request. The composition of such a chamber shall be determined by the Tribunal with the approval of the parties.
3. With a view to the speedy dispatch of business, the Tribunal shall form annually a chamber composed of five of its elected members which may hear and determine disputes by summary procedure. Two alternative members shall be selected for the purpose of replacing members who are unable to participate in a particular proceeding.
4. Disputes shall be heard and determined by the chambers provided for in this Article if the parties so request.
5. A judgment given by any of the chambers provided for in this Article and in Article 14 of this Annex shall be considered as rendered by the Tribunal.

Article 16
Rules of the Tribunal

The Tribunal shall frame rules for carrying out its functions. In particular it shall lay down rules of procedure.

Article 17
Nationality of members

1. Members of the Tribunal of the nationality of any of the parties to a dispute shall retain their right to participate as members of the Tribunal.
2. If the Tribunal, when hearing a dispute, includes upon the bench a member of the nationality of one of the parties, any other party may choose a person to participate as a member of the Tribunal.
3. If the Tribunal, when hearing a dispute, does not include upon the bench a member of the nationality of the parties, each of those parties may choose a person to participate as a member of the Tribunal.
4. This Article applies to the chambers referred to in Articles 14 and 15 of this Annex. In such cases, the President, in consultation with the parties, shall request specified members of the Tribunal forming the chamber, as many as necessary, to give place to the members of the Tribunal of the nationality of the parties concerned, and, failing such, or if they are unable to be present, to the members specially chosen by the parties.
5. Should there be several parties in the same interest, they shall, for the purpose of the preceding provisions, be considered as one party only. Any doubt on this point shall be settled by the decision of the Tribunal.
6. Members chosen in accordance with paragraphs 2, 3 and 4 shall fulfil the conditions required by Articles 2, 8 and 11 of this Annex. They shall participate in the decision on terms of complete equality with their colleagues.

Article 18
Remuneration of members

1. Each elected member of the Tribunal shall receive an annual allowance and, for each day on which he exercises his functions, a special allowance, provided that in any year the total sum payable to any member as special allowance shall not exceed the amount of the annual allowance.
2. The President shall receive a special annual allowance.
3. The Vice-President shall receive a special allowance for each day on which he acts as President.
4. The members chosen under Article 17 of this Annex, other than elected members of the Tribunal, shall receive compensation for each day on which they exercise their functions.
5. The salaries, allowances and compensation shall be determined from time to time at meetings of the States Parties, taking into account the workload of the Tribunal. They may not be decreased during the term of office.
6. The salary of the Registrar shall be determined at meetings of the States Parties, on the proposal of the Tribunal.
7. Regulations adopted at meetings of the States Parties shall determine the conditions under which retirement pensions may be given to members of the Tribunal and to the Registrar, and the conditions under which members of the Tribunal and Registrar shall have their travelling expenses refunded.
8. The salaries, allowances, and compensation shall be free of all taxation.

Article 19
Expenses of the Tribunal

1. The expenses of the Tribunal shall be borne by the States Parties and by the Authority on such terms and in such a manner as shall be decided at meetings of the States Parties.
2. When an entity other than a State Party or the Authority is a party to a case submitted to it, the Tribunal shall fix the amount which that party is to contribute towards the expenses of the Tribunal.

SECTION 2. COMPETENCE

Article 20
Access to the Tribunal

1. The Tribunal shall be open to States Parties.
2. The Tribunal shall be open to entities other than States Parties in any case expressly provided for in Part XI or in any case submitted pursuant to any other agreement conferring jurisdiction on the Tribunal which is accepted by all the parties to that case.

Article 21
Jurisdiction

The jurisdiction of the Tribunal comprises all disputes and all applications submitted to it in accordance with this Convention and all matters specifically provided for in any other agreement which confers jurisdiction on the Tribunal.

Article 22
Reference of disputes subject to other agreements

If all the parties to a treaty or convention already in force and concerning the subject-matter covered by this Convention so agree, any disputes concerning the interpretation or application of such treaty or convention may, in accordance with such agreement, be submitted to the Tribunal.

Article 23
Applicable law

The Tribunal shall decide all disputes and applications in accordance with Article 293.

SECTION 3. PROCEDURE

Article 24
Institution of proceedings

1. Disputes are submitted to the Tribunal, as the case may be, either by notification of a special agreement or by written application, addressed to the Registrar. In either case, the subject of the dispute and the parties shall be indicated.
2. The Registrar shall forthwith notify the special agreement or the application to all concerned.
3. The Registrar shall also notify all States Parties.

Article 25
Provisional measures

1. In accordance with Article 290, the Tribunal and its Seabed Disputes Chamber shall have the power to prescribe provisional measures.
2. If the Tribunal is not in session or a sufficient number of members is not available to constitute a quorum, the provisional measures shall be prescribed by the chamber of summary procedure formed under Article 15, paragraph 3, of this Annex. Notwithstanding Article 15, paragraph 4, of this Annex, such provisional measures may be adopted at the request of any party to the dispute. They shall be subject to review and revision by the Tribunal.

Article 26
Hearing

1. The hearing shall be under the control of the President or, if he is unable to preside, of the Vice-President. If neither is able to preside, the senior judge present of the Tribunal shall preside.
2. The hearing shall be public, unless the Tribunal decides otherwise or unless the parties demand that the public be not admitted

Article 27
Conduct of case

The Tribunal shall make orders for the conduct of the case, decide the form and time in which each party must conclude its arguments, and make all arrangements connected with the taking of evidence.

Article 28
Default

When one of the parties does not appear before the Tribunal or fails to defend its case, the other party may request the Tribunal to continue the proceedings and make its decision. Absence of a party or failure of a party to defend its case shall not constitute a bar to the proceedings. Before making its decision, the Tribunal must satisfy itself not only that it has jurisdiction over the dispute, but also that the claim is well founded in fact and law.

Article 29
Majority for decision

1. All questions shall be decided by a majority of the members of the Tribunal who are present.
2. In the event of an equality of votes, the President or the member of the Tribunal who acts in his place shall have a casting vote.

Article 30
Judgment

1. The judgment shall state the reasons on which it is based.
2. It shall contain the names of the members of the Tribunal who have taken part in the decision.
3. If the judgment does not represent in whole or in part the unanimous opinion of the members of the Tribunal, any member shall be entitled to deliver a separate opinion.
4. The judgment shall be signed by the President and by the Registrar. It shall be read in open court, due notice having been given to the parties to the dispute.

Article 31
Request to intervene

1. Should a State Party consider that it has an interest of a legal nature which may be affected by the decision in any dispute, it may submit a request to the Tribunal to be permitted to intervene.
2. It shall be for the Tribunal to decide upon this request.
3. If a request to intervene is granted, the decision of the Tribunal in respect of the dispute shall be binding upon the intervening State Party in so far as it relates to matters in respect of which that State Party intervened.

Article 32
Right to intervene in cases of interpretation or application

1. Whenever the interpretation or application of this Convention is in question, the Registrar shall notify all States Parties forthwith.
2. Whenever pursuant to Article 21 or 22 of this Annex the interpretation or application of an international agreement is in question, the Registrar shall notify all the parties to the agreement.
3. Every party referred to in paragraphs 1 and 2 has the right to intervene in the proceedings; if it uses this right, the interpretation given by the judgment will be equally binding upon it.

Article 33
Finality and binding force of decisions

1. The decision of the Tribunal is final and shall be complied with by all the parties to the dispute.

2. The decision shall have no binding force except between the parties in respect of that particular dispute.

3. In the event of dispute as to the meaning or scope of the decision, the Tribunal shall construe it upon the request of any party.

Article 34
Costs

Unless otherwise decided by the Tribunal, each party shall bear its own costs.

SECTION 4. SEABED DISPUTES CHAMBER

Article 35
Composition

1. The Seabed Disputes Chamber referred to in Article 14 of this Annex shall be composed of 11 members, selected by a majority of the elected members of the Tribunal from among them.

2. In the selection of the members of the Chamber, the representation of the principal legal systems of the world and equitable geographical distribution shall be assured. The Assembly of the Authority may adopt recommendations of a general nature relating to such representation and distribution.

3. The members of the Chamber shall be selected every three years and may be selected for a second term.

4. The Chamber shall elect its President from among its members, who shall serve for the term for which the Chamber has been selected.

5. If any proceedings are still pending at the end of any three-year period for which the Chamber has been selected, the Chamber shall complete the proceedings in its original composition.

6. If a vacancy occurs in the Chamber, the Tribunal shall select a successor from among its elected members, who shall hold office for the remainder of his predecessor's term.

7. A quorum of seven of the members selected by the Tribunal shall be required to constitute the Chamber.

Article 36
Ad hoc chambers

1. The Seabed Disputes Chamber shall form an *ad hoc* chamber, composed of three of its members, for dealing with a particular dispute submitted to it in accordance with Article 188, paragraph 1(b). The composition of such a chamber shall be determined by the Seabed Disputes Chamber with the approval of the parties.

2. If the parties do not agree on the composition of an *ad hoc* chamber, each party to the dispute shall appoint one member, and the third member shall be appointed by them in agreement. If they disagree, or if any party fails to make an appointment, the President of the Seabed Disputes Chamber shall promptly make the appointment or appointments from among its members, after consultation with the parties.

3. Members of the *ad hoc* chamber must not be in the service of, or nationals of, any of the parties to the dispute.

Article 37
Access

The Chamber shall be open to the States Parties, the Authority and the other entities referred to in Part XI, section 5.

Article 38
Applicable law

In addition to the provisions of Article 293, the Chamber shall apply:

(a) the rules, regulations and procedures of the Authority adopted in accordance with this Convention; and

(b) the terms of contracts concerning activities in the Area in matters relating to those contracts.

Article 39
Enforcement of decisions of the Chamber

The decisions of the Chamber shall be enforceable in the territories of the States Parties in the same manner as judgments or orders of the highest court of the State Party in whose territory the enforcement is sought.

Article 40
Applicability of other sections of this Annex

1. The other sections of this Annex which are not incompatible with this section apply to the Chamber.
2. In the exercise of its functions relating to advisory opinions, the Chamber shall be guided by the provisions of this Annex relating to procedure before the Tribunal to the extent to which it recognizes them to be applicable.

Annex VII. Arbitration

Article 1
Institution of proceedings

Subject to the provisions of Part XV, any party to a dispute may submit the dispute to the arbitral procedure provided for in this Annex by written notification addressed to the other party or parties to the dispute. The notification shall be accompanied by a statement of the claim and the grounds on which it is based.

Article 2
List of arbitrators

1. A list of arbitrators shall be drawn up and maintained by the Secretary-General of the United Nations. Every State Party shall be entitled to nominate four arbitrators, each of whom shall be a person experienced in maritime affairs and enjoying the highest reputation for fairness, competence and integrity. The names of the persons so nominated shall constitute the list.
2. If at any time the arbitrators nominated by a State Party in the list so constituted shall be fewer than four, that State Party shall be entitled to make further nominations as necessary.
3. The name of an arbitrator shall remain on the list until withdrawn by the State Party which made the nomination, provided that such arbitrator shall continue to serve on any arbitral tribunal to which that arbitrator has been appointed until the completion of the proceedings before that arbitral tribunal.

Article 3
Constitution of arbitral tribunal

For the purpose of proceedings under this Annex, the arbitral tribunal shall, unless the parties otherwise agree, be constituted as follows:

(a) Subject to subparagraph (g), the arbitral tribunal shall consist of five members.

(b) The party instituting the proceedings shall appoint one member to be chosen preferably from the list referred to in Article 2 of this Annex, who may be its national. The appointment shall be included in the notification referred to in Article 1 of this Annex.

(c) The other party to the dispute shall, within 30 days of receipt of the notification referred to in Article 1 of this Annex, appoint one member to be chosen preferably from the list, who may be its national. If the appointment is not made within that period, the party instituting the proceedings may, within two weeks of the expiration of that period, request that the appointment be made in accordance with subparagraph (e).

(d) The other three members shall be appointed by agreement between the parties. They shall be chosen preferably from the list and shall be nationals of third States unless the parties otherwise agree. The parties to the dispute shall appoint the President of the arbitral tribunal from among those three members. If, within 60 days of receipt of the notification referred to in Article 1 of this Annex, the parties are unable to reach agreement on the appointment of one or more of the members of the tribunal to be appointed by agreement, or on the appointment of the President, the remaining appointment or appointments shall be made in accordance with subparagraph (e), at the request of a party to the dispute. Such request shall be made within two weeks of the expiration of the aforementioned 60-day period.

(e) Unless the parties agree that any appointment under subparagraphs (c) and (d) be made by a person or a third State chosen by the parties, the President of the International Tribunal for the Law of the Sea shall make the necessary appointments. If the President is unable to act under this subparagraph or is a national of one of the parties to the dispute, the appointment shall be made by the next senior member of the International Tribunal for the Law of the Sea who is available and is not a national of one of the parties. The appointments referred to in this subparagraph shall be made from the list referred to in Article 2 of this Annex within a period of 30 days of the receipt of the request and in consultation with the parties. The members so appointed shall be of different nationalities and may not be in the service of, ordinarily resident in the territory of, or nationals of, any of the parties to the dispute.

(f) Any vacancy shall be filled in the manner prescribed for the initial appointment.

(g) Parties in the same interest shall appoint one member of the tribunal jointly by agreement. Where there are several parties having separate interests or where there is disagreement as to whether they are of the same interest, each of them shall appoint one member of the tribunal. The number of members of the tribunal appointed separately by the parties shall always be smaller by one than the number of members of the tribunal to be appointed jointly by the parties.

(h) In disputes involving more than two parties, the provisions of subparagraphs (a) to (f) shall apply to the maximum extent possible.

Article 4
Functions of arbitral tribunal

An arbitral tribunal constituted under Article 3 of this Annex shall function in accordance with this Annex and the other provisions of this Convention.

Article 5
Procedure

Unless the parties to the dispute otherwise agree, the arbitral tribunal shall determine its own procedure, assuring to each party a full opportunity to be heard and to present its case.

Article 6
Duties of parties to a dispute

The parties to the dispute shall facilitate the work of the arbitral tribunal and, in particular, in accordance with their law and using all means at their disposal, shall:

(a) provide it with all relevant documents, facilities and information; and

(b) enable it when necessary to call witnesses or experts and receive their evidence and to visit the localities to which the case relates.

Article 7
Expenses

Unless the arbitral tribunal decides otherwise because of the particular circumstances of the case, the expenses of the tribunal, including the remuneration of its members, shall be borne by the parties to the dispute in equal shares.

Article 8
Required majority for decisions

Decisions of the arbitral tribunal shall be taken by a majority vote of its members. The absence or abstention of less than half of the members shall not constitute a bar to the tribunal reaching a decision. In the event of an equality of votes, the President shall have a casting vote.

Article 9
Default of appearance

If one of the parties to the dispute does not appear before the arbitral tribunal or fails to defend its case, the other party may request the tribunal to continue the proceedings and to make its award. Absence of a party or failure of a party to defend its case shall not constitute a bar to the proceedings. Before making its award, the arbitral tribunal must satisfy itself not only that it has jurisdiction over the dispute but also that the claim is well founded in fact and law.

Article 10
Award

The award of the arbitral tribunal shall be confined to the subject-matter of the dispute and state the reasons on which it is based. It shall contain the names of the members who have participated and the date of the award. Any member of the tribunal may attach a separate or dissenting opinion to the award.

Article 11
Finality of award

The award shall be final and without appeal, unless the parties to the dispute have agreed in advance to an appellate procedure. It shall be complied with by the parties to the dispute.

Article 12
Interpretation or implementation of award

1. Any controversy which may arise between the parties to the dispute as regards the interpretation or manner of implementation of the award may be submitted by either party for decision to the arbitral tribunal which made the award. For this purpose, any vacancy in the tribunal shall be filled in the manner provided for in the original appointments of the members of the tribunal.
2. Any such controversy may be submitted to another court or tribunal under Article 287 by agreement of all the parties to the dispute.

Article 13
Application to entities other than States Parties

The provisions of this Annex shall apply *mutatis mutandis* to any dispute involving entities other than States Parties.

---

9. IBA Model Rules on Ethics for International Arbitrators, 1987

Introductory Note

International arbitrators should be impartial, independent, competent, diligent and discreet. These rules seek to establish the manner in which these abstract qualities may be assessed in practice. Rather than rigid rules, they reflect internationally acceptable guidelines developed by practising lawyers from all continents. They will attain their objectives only if they are applied in good faith.

The rules cannot be directly binding either on arbitrators, or on the parties themselves, unless they are adopted by agreement. Whilst the International Bar Association hopes that they will be taken into account in the context of challenges to arbitrators, it is emphasised that these guidelines are not intended to create grounds for the setting aside of awards by national courts.

If parties wish to adopt the rules they may add the following to their arbitration clause or arbitration agreement:

> 'The parties agree that the Rules of Ethics for International Arbitrators established by the International Bar Association, in force at the date of the commencement of any arbitration under this clause, shall be applicable to the arbitrators appointed in respect of such arbitration.'

The International Bar Association takes the position that (whatever may be the case in domestic arbitration) international arbitrators should in principle be granted immunity from suit under national laws, except in extreme cases of wilful or reckless disregard of their legal obligations. Accordingly, the International Bar Association wishes to make it clear that it is not the intention of these rules to create opportunities for aggrieved parties to sue international arbitrators in national courts. The normal sanction for breach of an ethical duty is removal from office, with consequent loss of entitlement to remuneration. The International Bar Association also emphasises that these rules do not affect, and are intended to be consistent with,the International Code of Ethics for lawyers, adopted at Oslo on 25 July 1956, and amended by the General Meeting of the International Bar Association at Mexico City on 24 July 1964.

1. Fundamental Rule

Arbitrators shall proceed diligently and efficiently to provide the parties with a just and effective resolution of their disputes, and shall be and shall remain free from bias.

2. Acceptance of Appointment

2.1 A prospective arbitrator shall accept an appointment only if he is fully satisfied that he is able to discharge his duties without bias.

2.2 A prospective arbitrator shall accept an appointment only if he is fully satisfied that he is competent to determine the issues in dispute, and has an adequate knowledge of the language of the arbitration.

2.3 A prospective arbitrator should accept an appointment only if he is able to give to the arbitration the time and attention which the parties are reasonably entitled to expect.

2.4 It is inappropriate to contact parties in order to solicit appointment as arbitrator.

3. Elements of Bias

3.1 The criteria for assessing questions relating to bias are impartiality and independence. Partiality arises when an arbitrator favours one of the parties, or where he is prejudiced in relation to the subject,matter of the dispute. Dependence arises from relationships between an arbitrator and one of the parties, or with someone closely connected with one of the parties.

3.2 Facts which might lead a reasonable person, not knowing the arbitrator's true state of mind, to consider that he is dependent on a party create an appearance of bias. The same is true if an arbitrator has a material interest in the outcome of the dispute, or if he has already taken a position in relation toit. The appearance of bias is best overcome by full disclosure as described in Article 4 below.

3.3 Any current direct or indirect business relationship between an arbitrator and a party, or with a person who is known to be a potentially important witness, will normally give rise to justifiable doubts as to a prospective arbitrator's impartiality or independence. He should decline to accept an appointment in such circumstances unless the parties agree in writing that he may proceed. Examples of indirect relationships are where a member of the prospective arbitrator's family, his firm, or any business partner has a business relationship with one of the parties.

3.4 Past business relationships will not operate as an absolute bar to acceptance of appointment, unless they are of such magnitude or nature as to be likely to affect a prospective arbitrator's judgment.

3.5 Continuous and substantial social or professional relationships between a prospective arbitrator and a party, or with a person who is known to be a potentially important witness in the arbitration, will normally give rise to justifiable doubts as to the impartiality or independence of a prospective arbitrator.

4. Duty of Disclosure

4.1 A prospective arbitrator should disclose all facts or circumstances that may give rise to justifiable doubts as to his impartiality or independence. Failure to make such disclosure creates an appearance of bias, and may of itself be a ground for disqualification even though he non-disclosed facts or circumstances would not of themselves justify disqualification.

4.2 A prospective arbitrator should disclose:

(a) any past or present business relationship, whether direct or indirect as illustrated in Article 3.3, including prior appointment as arbitrator, with any party to the dispute, or any representative of a party, or any person known to be a potentially important witness in the arbitration. With regard to present relationships, the duty of disclosure applies irrespective of their magnitude, but with regard to past relationships only if they were of more than a trivial nature in relation to the arbitrator's professional or business affairs. Non-disclosure of an indirect relationship unknown to a prospective arbitrator will not be a ground for disqualification unless it could have been ascertained by making reasonable enquiries;

(b) the nature and duration of any substantial social relationships with any party or any person known to be likely to be an important witness in the arbitration;

(c) the nature of any previous relationship with any fellow arbitrator (including prior joint service as an arbitrator);

(d) the extent of any prior knowledge he may have of the dispute;

(e) the extent of any commitments which may affect his availability to perform his duties as arbitrator as may be reasonably anticipated.

4.3 The duty of disclosure continues throughout the arbitral proceedings as regards new facts or circumstances.

4.4 Disclosure should be made in writing and communicated to an parties and arbitrators. When an arbitrator has been appointed, any previous disclosure made to the parties should be communicated to the other arbitrators.

5. Communications with Parties

5.1 When approached with a view to appointment, a prospective arbitrator should make sufficient enquiries in order to inform himself whether there may be any justifiable doubts regarding his impartiality or independence; whether he is competent to determine the issues in dispute; and whether he is able to give the arbitration the time and attention required. He may also respond to enquiries from those approaching him, provided that such enquiries are designed to determine his suitability and availability for the appointment and provided that the merits of the case are not discussed. In the event that a prospective sole arbitrator or presiding arbitrator is approached by one party alone, or by one arbitrator chosen unilaterally by a party (a 'party, nominated' arbitrator), he should ascertain that the other party or parties, or the other arbitrator, has consented to the manner in which he has been approached. In such circumstances he should, in writing or orally, inform the other party or parties, or the other arbitrator, of the substance of the initial conversation.

5.2 If a party-nominated arbitrator is required to participate in the selection of a third or presiding arbitrator, it is acceptable for him (although he is not so required) to obtain the views of the party who nominated him as to the acceptability of candidates being considered.

5.3 Throughout the arbitral proceedings, an arbitrator should avoid any unilateral communications regarding the case with any party, or its representatives. If such communication should occur, the arbitrator should inform the other party or parties and arbitrators of its substance.

5.4 If an arbitrator becomes aware that a fellow arbitrator has been in improper communication with a party, he may inform the remaining arbitrators and they should together determine what action should be taken. Normally, the appropriate initial course of action is for the offending arbitrator to be requested to refrain from making any further improper communications with the party. Where the offending arbitrator fails or refuses to refrain from improper communications, the remaining arbitrators may inform the innocent party in order that he may consider what action he should take. An arbitrator may act unilaterally to inform a party of the conduct of another arbitrator in order to allow the said party to consider a challenge of the offending arbitrator only in extreme circumstances, and after communicating his intention to his fellow arbitrators in writing.

5.5 No arbitrator should accept any gift or substantial. hospitality, directly or indirectly, from any party to the arbitration. Sole arbitrators and presiding arbitrators should be particularly meticulous in avoiding significant social or professional contacts with any party to the arbitration other than in the presence of the other parties.

6. Fees

Unless the parties agree otherwise or a party defaults, an arbitrator shall make no unilateral arrangements for fees or expenses.

7. Duty of Diligence

All arbitrators should devote such time and attention as the parties may reasonably require having regard to all the circumstances of the case, and shall do their best to conduct the arbitration in such a manner that costs do not rise to an unreasonable proportion of the interests at stake.

8. Involvement in Settlement Proposals

Where the parties have so requested, or consented to a suggestion to this effect by the arbitral tribunal, the tribunal as a whole (or the presiding arbitrator where appropriate), may make proposals for settlement to both parties simultaneously, and preferably in the presence of each other. Although any procedure is possible with the agreement of the parties, the arbitral tribunal should point out to the parties that it is undesirable that any arbitrator should discuss settlement terms with a party in the absence of the other parties since this will normally have the result that any arbitrator involved in such discussions will become disqualified from any future participation in the arbitration.

9. Confidentiality of the Deliberations

The deliberations of the arbitral tribunal, and the contents of the award itself, remain confidential in perpetuity unless the parties release the arbitrators from this obligation. An arbitrator should not participate in, or give any information for the purpose of assistance in, any proceedings to consider the award unless, exceptionally, he considers it his duty to disclose any material misconduct or fraud on the part of his fellow arbitrators.

10. World Trade Organization, Understanding on Rules and Procedures Governing the Settlement of Disputes, 1994

Members hereby *agree* as follows:

Article 1
Coverage and Application

1. The rules and procedures of this Understanding shall apply to disputes brought pursuant to the consultation and dispute settlement provisions of the agreements listed in Appendix 1 to this Understanding (referred to in this Understanding as the "covered agreements"). The rules and procedures of this Understanding shall also apply to consultations and the settlement of disputes between Members concerning their rights and obligations under the provisions of the Agreement Establishing the World Trade Organization (referred to in this Understanding as the "WTO Agreement") and of this Understanding taken in isolation or in combination with any other covered agreement.
2. The rules and procedures of this Understanding shall apply subject to such special or additional rules and procedures on dispute settlement contained in the covered agreements as are identified in Appendix 2 to this Understanding. To the extent that there is a difference between the rules and procedures of this Understanding and the special or additional rules and procedures set forth in Appendix 2, the special or additional rules and procedures in Appendix 2 shall prevail. In disputes involving rules and procedures under more than one covered agreement, if there is a conflict between special or additional rules and procedures of such agreements under review, and where the parties to the dispute cannot agree on rules and procedures within 20 days of the establishment of the panel, the Chairman of the Dispute Settlement Body provided for in paragraph 1 of Article 2 (referred to in this Understanding as the "DSB"), in consultation with the parties to the dispute, shall determine the rules and procedures to be followed within 10 days after a request by either Member. The Chairman shall be guided by the principle that special or additional rules and procedures should be used where possible, and the rules and procedures set out in this Understanding should be used to the extent necessary to avoid conflict.

Article 2
Administration

1. The Dispute Settlement Body is hereby established to administer these rules and procedures and, except as otherwise provided in a covered agreement, the consultation and dispute settlement provisions of the covered agreements. Accordingly, the DSB shall have the authority to establish panels, adopt panel and Appellate Body reports, maintain surveillance of implementation of rulings and recommendations, and authorize suspension of concessions and other obligations under the covered agreements. With respect to disputes arising under a covered agreement which is a Plurilateral Trade Agreement, the term "Member" as used

herein shall refer only to those Members that are parties to the relevant Plurilateral Trade Agreement. Where the DSB administers the dispute settlement provisions of a Plurilateral Trade Agreement, only those Members that are parties to that Agreement may participate in decisions or actions taken by the DSB with respect to that dispute.

2. The DSB shall inform the relevant WTO Councils and Committees of any developments in disputes related to provisions of the respective covered agreements.

3. The DSB shall meet as often as necessary to carry out its functions within the time-frames provided in this Understanding.

4. Where the rules and procedures of this Understanding provide for the DSB to take a decision, it shall do so by consensus.[1]

Article 3
General Provisions

1. Members affirm their adherence to the principles for the management of disputes heretofore applied under Articles XXII and XXIII of GATT 1947, and the rules and procedures as further elaborated and modified herein.

2. The dispute settlement system of the WTO is a central element in providing security and predictability to the multilateral trading system. The Members recognize that it serves to preserve the rights and obligations of Members under the covered agreements, and to clarify the existing provisions of those agreements in accordance with customary rules of interpretation of public international law. Recommendations and rulings of the DSB cannot add to or diminish the rights and obligations provided in the covered agreements.

3. The prompt settlement of situations in which a Member considers that any benefits accruing to it directly or indirectly under the covered agreements are being impaired by measures taken by another Member is essential to the effective functioning of the WTO and the maintenance of a proper balance between the rights and obligations of Members.

4. Recommendations or rulings made by the DSB shall be aimed at achieving a satisfactory settlement of the matter in accordance with the rights and obligations under this Understanding and under the covered agreements.

5. All solutions to matters formally raised under the consultation and dispute settlement provisions of the covered agreements, including arbitration awards, shall be consistent with those agreements and shall not nullify or impair benefits accruing to any Member under those agreements, nor impede the attainment of any objective of those agreements.

6. Mutually agreed solutions to matters formally raised under the consultation and dispute settlement provisions of the covered agreements shall be notified to the DSB and the relevant Councils and Committees, where any Member may raise any point relating thereto.

7. Before bringing a case, a Member shall exercise its judgement as to whether action under these procedures would be fruitful. The aim of the dispute settle-

1. The DSB shall be deemed to have decided by consensus on a matter submitted for its consideration, if no Member, present at the meeting of the DSB when the decision is taken, formally objects to the proposed decision.

ment mechanism is to secure a positive solution to a dispute. A solution mutually acceptable to the parties to a dispute and consistent with the covered agreements is clearly to be preferred. In the absence of a mutually agreed solution, the first objective of the dispute settlement mechanism is usually to secure the withdrawal of the measures concerned if these are found to be inconsistent with the provisions of any of the covered agreements. The provision of compensation should be resorted to only if the immediate withdrawal of the measure is impracticable and as a temporary measure pending the withdrawal of the measure which is inconsistent with a covered agreement. The last resort which this Understanding provides to the Member invoking the dispute settlement procedures is the possibility of suspending the application of concessions or other obligations under the covered agreements on a discriminatory basis vis-à-vis the other Member, subject to authorization by the DSB of such measures.

8. In cases where there is an infringement of the obligations assumed under a covered agreement, the action is considered *prima facie* to constitute a case of nullification or impairment. This means that there is normally a presumption that a breach of the rules has an adverse impact on other Members parties to that covered agreement, and in such cases, it shall be up to the Member against whom the complaint has been brought to rebut the charge.

9. The provisions of this Understanding are without prejudice to the rights of Members to seek authoritative interpretation of provisions of a covered agreement through decision-making under the WTO Agreement or a covered agreement which is a Plurilateral Trade Agreement.

10. It is understood that requests for conciliation and the use of the dispute settlement procedures should not be intended or considered as contentious acts and that, if a dispute arises, all Members will engage in these procedures in good faith in an effort to resolve the dispute. It is also understood that complaints and counter-complaints in regard to distinct matters should not be linked.

11. This Understanding shall be applied only with respect to new requests for consultations under the consultation provisions of the covered agreements made on or after the date of entry into force of the WTO Agreement. With respect to disputes for which the request for consultations was made under GATT 1947 or under any other predecessor agreement to the covered agreements before the date of entry into force of the WTO Agreement, the relevant dispute settlement rules and procedures in effect immediately prior to the date of entry into force of the WTO Agreement shall continue to apply.[2]

12. Notwithstanding paragraph 11, if a complaint based on any of the covered agreements is brought by a developing country Member against a developed country Member, the complaining party shall have the right to invoke, as an alternative to the provisions contained in Articles 4, 5, 6 and 12 of this Understanding, the corresponding provisions of the Decision of 5 April 1966 (BISD 14S/18), except that where the Panel considers that the time-frame provided for in paragraph 7 of that Decision is insufficient to provide its report and with the agreement of the complaining party, that time-frame may be extended. To the extent that there

2. This paragraph shall also be applied to disputes on which panel reports have not been adopted or fully implemented.

is a difference between the rules and procedures of Articles 4, 5, 6 and 12 and the corresponding rules and procedures of the Decision, the latter shall prevail.

Article 4
Consultations

1. Members affirm their resolve to strengthen and improve the effectiveness of the consultation procedures employed by Members.
2. Each Member undertakes to accord sympathetic consideration to and afford adequate opportunity for consultation regarding any representations made by another Member concerning measures affecting the operation of any covered agreement taken within the territory of the former.[3]
3. If a request for consultations is made pursuant to a covered agreement, the Member to which the request is made shall, unless otherwise mutually agreed, reply to the request within 10 days after the date of its receipt and shall enter into consultations in good faith within a period of no more than 30 days after the date of receipt of the request, with a view to reaching a mutually satisfactory solution. If the Member does not respond within 10 days after the date of receipt of the request, or does not enter into consultations within a period of no more than 30 days, or a period otherwise mutually agreed, after the date of receipt of the request, then the Member that requested the holding of consultations may proceed directly to request the establishment of a panel.
4. All such requests for consultations shall be notified to the DSB and the relevant Councils and Committees by the Member which requests consultations. Any request for consultations shall be submitted in writing and shall give the reasons for the request, including identification of the measures at issue and an indication of the legal basis for the complaint.
5. In the course of consultations in accordance with the provisions of a covered agreement, before resorting to further action under this Understanding, Members should attempt to obtain satisfactory adjustment of the matter.
6. Consultations shall be confidential, and without prejudice to the rights of any Member in any further proceedings.
7. If the consultations fail to settle a dispute within 60 days after the date of receipt of the request for consultations, the complaining party may request the establishment of a panel. The complaining party may request a panel during the 60-day period if the consulting parties jointly consider that consultations have failed to settle the dispute.
8. In cases of urgency, including those which concern perishable goods, Members shall enter into consultations within a period of no more than 10 days after the date of receipt of the request. If the consultations have failed to settle the dispute within a period of 20 days after the date of receipt of the request, the complaining party may request the establishment of a panel.
9. In cases of urgency, including those which concern perishable goods, the parties to the dispute, panels and the Appellate Body shall make every effort to accelerate the proceedings to the greatest extent possible.

3. Where the provisions of any other covered agreement concerning measures taken by regional or local governments or authorities within the territory of a Member contain provisions different from the provisions of this paragraph, the provisions of such other covered agreement shall prevail.

10. During consultations Members should give special attention to the particular problems and interests of developing country Members.

11. Whenever a Member other than the consulting Members considers that it has a substantial trade interest in consultations being held pursuant to paragraph 1 of Article XXII of GATT 1994, paragraph 1 of Article XXII of GATS, or the corresponding provisions in other covered agreements,[4] such Member may notify the consulting Members and the DSB, within 10 days after the date of the circulation of the request for consultations under said Article, of its desire to be joined in the consultations. Such Member shall be joined in the consultations, provided that the Member to which the request for consultations was addressed agrees that the claim of substantial interest is well-founded. In that event they shall so inform the DSB. If the request to be joined in the consultations is not accepted, the applicant Member shall be free to request consultations under paragraph 1 of Article XXII or paragraph 1 of Article XXIII of GATT 1994, paragraph 1 of Article XXII or paragraph 1 of Article XXIII of GATS, or the corresponding provisions in other covered agreements.

Article 5
Good Offices, Conciliation and Mediation

1. Good offices, conciliation and mediation are procedures that are undertaken voluntarily if the parties to the dispute so agree.

2. Proceedings involving good offices, conciliation and mediation, and in particular positions taken by the parties to the dispute during these proceedings, shall be confidential, and without prejudice to the rights of either party in any further proceedings under these procedures.

3. Good offices, conciliation or mediation may be requested at any time by any party to a dispute. They may begin at any time and be terminated at any time. Once procedures for good offices, conciliation or mediation are terminated, a complaining party may then proceed with a request for the establishment of a panel.

4. When good offices, conciliation or mediation are entered into within 60 days after the date of receipt of a request for consultations, the complaining party must allow a period of 60 days after the date of receipt of the request for consultations before requesting the establishment of a panel. The complaining party may request the establishment of a panel during the 60-day period if the parties to the dispute jointly consider that the good offices, conciliation or mediation process has failed to settle the dispute.

---

4. The corresponding consultation provisions in the covered agreements are listed hereunder: Agreement on Agriculture, Article 19; Agreement on the Application of Sanitary and Phytosanitary Measures, paragraph 1 of Article 11; Agreement on Textiles and Clothing, paragraph 4 of Article 8; Agreement on Technical Barriers to Trade, paragraph 1 of Article 14; Agreement on Trade-Related Investment Measures, Article 8; Agreement on Implementation of Article VI of GATT 1994, paragraph 2 of Article 17; Agreement on Implementation of Article VII of GATT 1994, paragraph 2 of Article 19; Agreement on Preshipment Inspection, Article 7; Agreement on Rules of Origin, Article 7; Agreement on Import Licensing Procedures, Article 6; Agreement on Subsidies and Countervailing Measures, Article 30; Agreement on Safeguards, Article 14; Agreement on Trade-Related Aspects of Intellectual Property Rights, Article 64.1; and any corresponding consultation provisions in Plurilateral Trade Agreements as determined by the competent bodies of each Agreement and as notified to the DSB.

5. If the parties to a dispute agree, procedures for good offices, conciliation or mediation may continue while the panel process proceeds.

6. The Director-General may, acting in an *ex officio* capacity, offer good offices, conciliation or mediation with the view to assisting Members to settle a dispute.

Article 6
Establishment of Panels

1. If the complaining party so requests, a panel shall be established at the latest at the DSB meeting following that at which the request first appears as an item on the DSB's agenda, unless at that meeting the DSB decides by consensus not to establish a panel.[5]

2. The request for the establishment of a panel shall be made in writing. It shall indicate whether consultations were held, identify the specific measures at issue and provide a brief summary of the legal basis of the complaint sufficient to present the problem clearly. In case the applicant requests the establishment of a panel with other than standard terms of reference, the written request shall include the proposed text of special terms of reference.

Article 7
Terms of Reference of Panels

1. Panels shall have the following terms of reference unless the parties to the dispute agree otherwise within 20 days from the establishment of the panel:

"To examine, in the light of the relevant provisions in (name of the covered agreement(s) cited by the parties to the dispute), the matter referred to the DSB by (name of party) in document ... and to make such findings as will assist the DSB in making the recommendations or in giving the rulings provided for in that/those agreement(s)."

2. Panels shall address the relevant provisions in any covered agreement or agreements cited by the parties to the dispute.

3. In establishing a panel, the DSB may authorize its Chairman to draw up the terms of reference of the panel in consultation with the parties to the dispute, subject to the provisions of paragraph 1. The terms of reference thus drawn up shall be circulated to all Members. If other than standard terms of reference are agreed upon, any Member may raise any point relating thereto in the DSB.

Article 8
Composition of Panels

1. Panels shall be composed of well-qualified governmental and/or non-governmental individuals, including persons who have served on or presented a case to a panel, served as a representative of a Member or of a contracting party to GATT 1947 or as a representative to the Council or Committee of any covered agreement or its predecessor agreement, or in the Secretariat, taught or published on international trade law or policy, or served as a senior trade policy official of a Member.

2. Panel members should be selected with a view to ensuring the independence of the members, a sufficiently diverse background and a wide spectrum of experience.

---

5. If the complaining party so requests, a meeting of the DSB shall be convened for this purpose within 15 days of the request, provided that at least 10 days' advance notice of the meeting is given.

3. Citizens of Members whose governments[6] are parties to the dispute or third parties as defined in paragraph 2 of Article 10 shall not serve on a panel concerned with that dispute, unless the parties to the dispute agree otherwise.

4. To assist in the selection of panelists, the Secretariat shall maintain an indicative list of governmental and non-governmental individuals possessing the qualifications outlined in paragraph 1, from which panelists may be drawn as appropriate. That list shall include the roster of non-governmental panelists established on 30 November 1984 (BISD 31S/9), and other rosters and indicative lists established under any of the covered agreements, and shall retain the names of persons on those rosters and indicative lists at the time of entry into force of the WTO Agreement. Members may periodically suggest names of governmental and non-governmental individuals for inclusion on the indicative list, providing relevant information on their knowledge of international trade and of the sectors or subject matter of the covered agreements, and those names shall be added to the list upon approval by the DSB. For each of the individuals on the list, the list shall indicate specific areas of experience or expertise of the individuals in the sectors or subject matter of the covered agreements.

5. Panels shall be composed of three panelists unless the parties to the dispute agree, within 10 days from the establishment of the panel, to a panel composed of five panelists. Members shall be informed promptly of the composition of the panel.

6. The Secretariat shall propose nominations for the panel to the parties to the dispute. The parties to the dispute shall not oppose nominations except for compelling reasons.

7. If there is no agreement on the panelists within 20 days after the date of the establishment of a panel, at the request of either party, the Director-General, in consultation with the Chairman of the DSB and the Chairman of the relevant Council or Committee, shall determine the composition of the panel by appointing the panelists whom the Director-General considers most appropriate in accordance with any relevant special or additional rules or procedures of the covered agreement or covered agreements which are at issue in the dispute, after consulting with the parties to the dispute. The Chairman of the DSB shall inform the Members of the composition of the panel thus formed no later than 10 days after the date the Chairman receives such a request.

8. Members shall undertake, as a general rule, to permit their officials to serve as panelists.

9. Panelists shall serve in their individual capacities and not as government representatives, nor as representatives of any organization. Members shall therefore not give them instructions nor seek to influence them as individuals with regard to matters before a panel.

10. When a dispute is between a developing country Member and a developed country Member the panel shall, if the developing country Member so requests, include at least one panelist from a developing country Member.

11. Panelists' expenses, including travel and subsistence allowance, shall be met from the WTO budget in accordance with criteria to be adopted by the General Coun-

---

6. In the case where customs unions or common markets are parties to a dispute, this provision applies to citizens of all member countries of the customs unions or common markets.

cil, based on recommendations of the Committee on Budget, Finance and Administration.

Article 9
Procedures for Multiple Complainants

1. Where more than one Member requests the establishment of a panel related to the same matter, a single panel may be established to examine these complaints taking into account the rights of all Members concerned. A single panel should be established to examine such complaints whenever feasible.
2. The single panel shall organize its examination and present its findings to the DSB in such a manner that the rights which the parties to the dispute would have enjoyed had separate panels examined the complaints are in no way impaired. If one of the parties to the dispute so requests, the panel shall submit separate reports on the dispute concerned. The written submissions by each of the complainants shall be made available to the other complainants, and each complainant shall have the right to be present when any one of the other complainants presents its views to the panel.
3. If more than one panel is established to examine the complaints related to the same matter, to the greatest extent possible the same persons shall serve as panelists on each of the separate panels and the timetable for the panel process in such disputes shall be harmonized.

Article 10
Third Parties

1. The interests of the parties to a dispute and those of other Members under a covered agreement at issue in the dispute shall be fully taken into account during the panel process.
2. Any Member having a substantial interest in a matter before a panel and having notified its interest to the DSB (referred to in this Understanding as a "third party") shall have an opportunity to be heard by the panel and to make written submissions to the panel. These submissions shall also be given to the parties to the dispute and shall be reflected in the panel report.
3. Third parties shall receive the submissions of the parties to the dispute to the first meeting of the panel.
4. If a third party considers that a measure already the subject of a panel proceeding nullifies or impairs benefits accruing to it under any covered agreement, that Member may have recourse to normal dispute settlement procedures under this Understanding. Such a dispute shall be referred to the original panel wherever possible.

Article 11
Function of Panels

The function of panels is to assist the DSB in discharging its responsibilities under this Understanding and the covered agreements. Accordingly, a panel should make an objective assessment of the matter before it, including an objective assessment of the facts of the case and the applicability of and conformity with the relevant covered agreements, and make such other findings as will assist the DSB in making the recommendations or in giving the rulings provided for in the covered agreements. Panels should consult regularly with the parties to the dispute and give them adequate opportunity to develop a mutually satisfactory solution.

Article 12
Panel Procedures

1. Panels shall follow the Working Procedures in Appendix 3 unless the panel decides otherwise after consulting the parties to the dispute.
2. Panel procedures should provide sufficient flexibility so as to ensure high-quality panel reports, while not unduly delaying the panel process.
3. After consulting the parties to the dispute, the panelists shall, as soon as practicable and whenever possible within one week after the composition and terms of reference of the panel have been agreed upon, fix the timetable for the panel process, taking into account the provisions of paragraph 9 of Article 4, if relevant.
4. In determining the timetable for the panel process, the panel shall provide sufficient time for the parties to the dispute to prepare their submissions.
5. Panels should set precise deadlines for written submissions by the parties and the parties should respect those deadlines.
6. Each party to the dispute shall deposit its written submissions with the Secretariat for immediate transmission to the panel and to the other party or parties to the dispute. The complaining party shall submit its first submission in advance of the responding party's first submission unless the panel decides, in fixing the timetable referred to in paragraph 3 and after consultations with the parties to the dispute, that the parties should submit their first submissions simultaneously. When there are sequential arrangements for the deposit of first submissions, the panel shall establish a firm time-period for receipt of the responding party's submission. Any subsequent written submissions shall be submitted simultaneously.
7. Where the parties to the dispute have failed to develop a mutually satisfactory solution, the panel shall submit its findings in the form of a written report to the DSB. In such cases, the report of a panel shall set out the findings of fact, the applicability of relevant provisions and the basic rationale behind any findings and recommendations that it makes. Where a settlement of the matter among the parties to the dispute has been found, the report of the panel shall be confined to a brief description of the case and to reporting that a solution has been reached.
8. In order to make the procedures more efficient, the period in which the panel shall conduct its examination, from the date that the composition and terms of reference of the panel have been agreed upon until the date the final report is issued to the parties to the dispute, shall, as a general rule, not exceed six months. In cases of urgency, including those relating to perishable goods, the panel shall aim to issue its report to the parties to the dispute within three months.
9. When the panel considers that it cannot issue its report within six months, or within three months in cases of urgency, it shall inform the DSB in writing of the reasons for the delay together with an estimate of the period within which it will issue its report. In no case should the period from the establishment of the panel to the circulation of the report to the Members exceed nine months.
10. In the context of consultations involving a measure taken by a developing country Member, the parties may agree to extend the periods established in paragraphs 7 and 8 of Article 4. If, after the relevant period has elapsed, the consulting parties cannot agree that the consultations have concluded, the Chairman of the DSB shall decide, after consultation with the parties, whether to extend the rel-

evant period and, if so, for how long. In addition, in examining a complaint against a developing country Member, the panel shall accord sufficient time for the developing country Member to prepare and present its argumentation. The provisions of paragraph 1 of Article 20 and paragraph 4 of Article 21 are not affected by any action pursuant to this paragraph.

11. Where one or more of the parties is a developing country Member, the panel's report shall explicitly indicate the form in which account has been taken of relevant provisions on differential and more-favourable treatment for developing country Members that form part of the covered agreements which have been raised by the developing country Member in the course of the dispute settlement procedures.

12. The panel may suspend its work at any time at the request of the complaining party for a period not to exceed 12 months. In the event of such a suspension, the time-frames set out in paragraphs 8 and 9 of this Article, paragraph 1 of Article 20, and paragraph 4 of Article 21 shall be extended by the amount of time that the work was suspended. If the work of the panel has been suspended for more than 12 months, the authority for establishment of the panel shall lapse.

Article 13
Right to Seek Information

1. Each panel shall have the right to seek information and technical advice from any individual or body which it deems appropriate. However, before a panel seeks such information or advice from any individual or body within the jurisdiction of a Member it shall inform the authorities of that Member. A Member should respond promptly and fully to any request by a panel for such information as the panel considers necessary and appropriate. Confidential information which is provided shall not be revealed without formal authorization from the individual, body, or authorities of the Member providing the information.

2. Panels may seek information from any relevant source and may consult experts to obtain their opinion on certain aspects of the matter. With respect to a factual issue concerning a scientific or other technical matter raised by a party to a dispute, a panel may request an advisory report in writing from an expert review group. Rules for the establishment of such a group and its procedures are set forth in Appendix 4.

Article 14
Confidentiality

1. Panel deliberations shall be confidential.

2. The reports of panels shall be drafted without the presence of the parties to the dispute in the light of the information provided and the statements made.

3. Opinions expressed in the panel report by individual panelists shall be anonymous.

Article 15
Interim Review Stage

1. Following the consideration of rebuttal submissions and oral arguments, the panel shall issue the descriptive (factual and argument) sections of its draft report to the parties to the dispute. Within a period of time set by the panel, the parties shall submit their comments in writing.

2. Following the expiration of the set period of time for receipt of comments from the parties to the dispute, the panel shall issue an interim report to the parties,

including both the descriptive sections and the panel's findings and conclusions. Within a period of time set by the panel, a party may submit a written request for the panel to review precise aspects of the interim report prior to circulation of the final report to the Members. At the request of a party, the panel shall hold a further meeting with the parties on the issues identified in the written comments. If no comments are received from any party within the comment period, the interim report shall be considered the final panel report and circulated promptly to the Members.

3. The findings of the final panel report shall include a discussion of the arguments made at the interim review stage. The interim review stage shall be conducted within the time-period set out in paragraph 8 of Article 12.

Article 16
Adoption of Panel Reports

1. In order to provide sufficient time for the Members to consider panel reports, the reports shall not be considered for adoption by the DSB until 20 days after the date they have been circulated to the Members.
2. Members having objections to a panel report shall give written reasons to explain their objections for circulation at least 10 days prior to the DSB meeting at which the panel report will be considered.
3. The parties to a dispute shall have the right to participate fully in the consideration of the panel report by the DSB, and their views shall be fully recorded.
4. Within 60 days after the date of circulation of a panel report to the Members, the report shall be adopted at a DSB meeting[7] unless a party to the dispute formally notifies the DSB of its decision to appeal or the DSB decides by consensus not to adopt the report. If a party has notified its decision to appeal, the report by the panel shall not be considered for adoption by the DSB until after completion of the appeal. This adoption procedure is without prejudice to the right of Members to express their views on a panel report.

Article 17
Appellate Review

Standing Appellate Body

1. A standing Appellate Body shall be established by the DSB. The Appellate Body shall hear appeals from panel cases. It shall be composed of seven persons, three of whom shall serve on any one case. Persons serving on the Appellate Body shall serve in rotation. Such rotation shall be determined in the working procedures of the Appellate Body.
2. The DSB shall appoint persons to serve on the Appellate Body for a four-year term, and each person may be reappointed once. However, the terms of three of the seven persons appointed immediately after the entry into force of the WTO Agreement shall expire at the end of two years, to be determined by lot. Vacancies shall be filled as they arise. A person appointed to replace a person whose term of office has not expired shall hold office for the remainder of the predecessor's term.

---

7. If a meeting of the DSB is not scheduled within this period at a time that enables the requirements of paragraphs 1 and 4 of Article 16 to be met, a meeting of the DSB shall be held for this purpose.

3. The Appellate Body shall comprise persons of recognized authority, with demonstrated expertise in law, international trade and the subject matter of the covered agreements generally. They shall be unaffiliated with any government. The Appellate Body membership shall be broadly representative of membership in the WTO. All persons serving on the Appellate Body shall be available at all times and on short notice, and shall stay abreast of dispute settlement activities and other relevant activities of the WTO. They shall not participate in the consideration of any disputes that would create a direct or indirect conflict of interest.

4. Only parties to the dispute, not third parties, may appeal a panel report. Third parties which have notified the DSB of a substantial interest in the matter pursuant to paragraph 2 of Article 10 may make written submissions to, and be given an opportunity to be heard by, the Appellate Body.

5. As a general rule, the proceedings shall not exceed 60 days from the date a party to the dispute formally notifies its decision to appeal to the date the Appellate Body circulates its report. In fixing its timetable the Appellate Body shall take into account the provisions of paragraph 9 of Article 4, if relevant. When the Appellate Body considers that it cannot provide its report within 60 days, it shall inform the DSB in writing of the reasons for the delay together with an estimate of the period within which it will submit its report. In no case shall the proceedings exceed 90 days.

6. An appeal shall be limited to issues of law covered in the panel report and legal interpretations developed by the panel.

7. The Appellate Body shall be provided with appropriate administrative and legal support as it requires.

8. The expenses of persons serving on the Appellate Body, including travel and subsistence allowance, shall be met from the WTO budget in accordance with criteria to be adopted by the General Council, based on recommendations of the Committee on Budget, Finance and Administration.

Procedures for Appellate Review

9. Working procedures shall be drawn up by the Appellate Body in consultation with the Chairman of the DSB and the Director-General, and communicated to the Members for their information.

10. The proceedings of the Appellate Body shall be confidential. The reports of the Appellate Body shall be drafted without the presence of the parties to the dispute and in the light of the information provided and the statements made.

11. Opinions expressed in the Appellate Body report by individuals serving on the Appellate Body shall be anonymous.

12. The Appellate Body shall address each of the issues raised in accordance with paragraph 6 during the appellate proceeding.

13. The Appellate Body may uphold, modify or reverse the legal findings and conclusions of the panel.

Adoption of Appellate Body Reports

14. An Appellate Body report shall be adopted by the DSB and unconditionally accepted by the parties to the dispute unless the DSB decides by consensus not to adopt the Appellate Body report within 30 days following its circulation to the

Members.[8] This adoption procedure is without prejudice to the right of Members to express their views on an Appellate Body report.

Article 18
Communications with the Panel or Appellate Body

1. There shall be no *ex parte* communications with the panel or Appellate Body concerning matters under consideration by the panel or Appellate Body.
2. Written submissions to the panel or the Appellate Body shall be treated as confidential, but shall be made available to the parties to the dispute. Nothing in this Understanding shall preclude a party to a dispute from disclosing statements of its own positions to the public. Members shall treat as confidential information submitted by another Member to the panel or the Appellate Body which that Member has designated as confidential. A party to a dispute shall also, upon request of a Member, provide a non-confidential summary of the information contained in its written submissions that could be disclosed to the public.

Article 19
Panel and Appellate Body Recommendations

1. Where a panel or the Appellate Body concludes that a measure is inconsistent with a covered agreement, it shall recommend that the Member concerned[9] bring the measure into conformity with that agreement.[10] In addition to its recommendations, the panel or Appellate Body may suggest ways in which the Member concerned could implement the recommendations.
2. In accordance with paragraph 2 of Article 3, in their findings and recommendations, the panel and Appellate Body cannot add to or diminish the rights and obligations provided in the covered agreements.

Article 20
Time-frame for DSB Decisions

Unless otherwise agreed to by the parties to the dispute, the period from the date of establishment of the panel by the DSB until the date the DSB considers the panel or appellate report for adoption shall as a general rule not exceed nine months where the panel report is not appealed or 12 months where the report is appealed. Where either the panel or the Appellate Body has acted, pursuant to paragraph 9 of Article 12 or paragraph 5 of Article 17, to extend the time for providing its report, the additional time taken shall be added to the above periods.

Article 21
Surveillance of Implementation of Recommendations and Rulings

1. Prompt compliance with recommendations or rulings of the DSB is essential in order to ensure effective resolution of disputes to the benefit of all Members.
2. Particular attention should be paid to matters affecting the interests of developing country Members with respect to measures which have been subject to dispute settlement.

---

8. If a meeting of the DSB is not scheduled during this period, such a meeting of the DSB shall be held for this purpose.

9. The "Member concerned" is the party to the dispute to which the panel or Appellate Body recommendations are directed.

10. With respect to recommendations in cases not involving a violation of GATT 1994 or any other covered agreement, see Article 26.

3. At a DSB meeting held within 30 days[11] after the date of adoption of the panel or Appellate Body report, the Member concerned shall inform the DSB of its intentions in respect of implementation of the recommendations and rulings of the DSB. If it is impracticable to comply immediately with the recommendations and rulings, the Member concerned shall have a reasonable period of time in which to do so. The reasonable period of time shall be:
   (a) the period of time proposed by the Member concerned, provided that such period is approved by the DSB; or, in the absence of such approval,
   (b) a period of time mutually agreed by the parties to the dispute within 45 days after the date of adoption of the recommendations and rulings; or, in the absence of such agreement,
   (c) a period of time determined through binding arbitration within 90 days after the date of adoption of the recommendations and rulings.[12] In such arbitration, a guideline for the arbitrator[13] should be that the reasonable period of time to implement panel or Appellate Body recommendations should not exceed 15 months from the date of adoption of a panel or Appellate Body report. However, that time may be shorter or longer, depending upon the particular circumstances.

4. Except where the panel or the Appellate Body has extended, pursuant to paragraph 9 of Article 12 or paragraph 5 of Article 17, the time of providing its report, the period from the date of establishment of the panel by the DSB until the date of determination of the reasonable period of time shall not exceed 15 months unless the parties to the dispute agree otherwise. Where either the panel or the Appellate Body has acted to extend the time of providing its report, the additional time taken shall be added to the 15-month period; provided that unless the parties to the dispute agree that there are exceptional circumstances, the total time shall not exceed 18 months.

5. Where there is disagreement as to the existence or consistency with a covered agreement of measures taken to comply with the recommendations and rulings such dispute shall be decided through recourse to these dispute settlement procedures, including wherever possible resort to the original panel. The panel shall circulate its report within 90 days after the date of referral of the matter to it. When the panel considers that it cannot provide its report within this time frame, it shall inform the DSB in writing of the reasons for the delay together with an estimate of the period within which it will submit its report.

6. The DSB shall keep under surveillance the implementation of adopted recommendations or rulings. The issue of implementation of the recommendations or rulings may be raised at the DSB by any Member at any time following their adoption. Unless the DSB decides otherwise, the issue of implementation of the recommendations or rulings shall be placed on the agenda of the DSB meeting after six months following the date of establishment of the reasonable period of time pursuant to paragraph 3 and shall remain on the DSB's agenda until the

---

11. If a meeting of the DSB is not scheduled during this period, such a meeting of the DSB shall be held for this purpose.

12. If the parties cannot agree on an arbitrator within ten days after referring the matter to arbitration, the arbitrator shall be appointed by the Director-General within ten days, after consulting the parties.

13. The expression "arbitrator" shall be interpreted as referring either to an individual or a group.

issue is resolved. At least 10 days prior to each such DSB meeting, the Member concerned shall provide the DSB with a status report in writing of its progress in the implementation of the recommendations or rulings.

7. If the matter is one which has been raised by a developing country Member, the DSB shall consider what further action it might take which would be appropriate to the circumstances.

8. If the case is one brought by a developing country Member, in considering what appropriate action might be taken, the DSB shall take into account not only the trade coverage of measures complained of, but also their impact on the economy of developing country Members concerned.

Article 22
Compensation and the Suspension of Concessions

1. Compensation and the suspension of concessions or other obligations are temporary measures available in the event that the recommendations and rulings are not implemented within a reasonable period of time. However, neither compensation nor the suspension of concessions or other obligations is preferred to full implementation of a recommendation to bring a measure into conformity with the covered agreements. Compensation is voluntary and, if granted, shall be consistent with the covered agreements.

2. If the Member concerned fails to bring the measure found to be inconsistent with a covered agreement into compliance therewith or otherwise comply with the recommendations and rulings within the reasonable period of time determined pursuant to paragraph 3 of Article 21, such Member shall, if so requested, and no later than the expiry of the reasonable period of time, enter into negotiations with any party having invoked the dispute settlement procedures, with a view to developing mutually acceptable compensation. If no satisfactory compensation has been agreed within 20 days after the date of expiry of the reasonable period of time, any party having invoked the dispute settlement procedures may request authorization from the DSB to suspend the application to the Member concerned of concessions or other obligations under the covered agreements.

3. In considering what concessions or other obligations to suspend, the complaining party shall apply the following principles and procedures:

   (a) the general principle is that the complaining party should first seek to suspend concessions or other obligations with respect to the same sector(s) as that in which the panel or Appellate Body has found a violation or other nullification or impairment;

   (b) if that party considers that it is not practicable or effective to suspend concessions or other obligations with respect to the same sector(s), it may seek to suspend concessions or other obligations in other sectors under the same agreement;

   (c) if that party considers that it is not practicable or effective to suspend concessions or other obligations with respect to other sectors under the same agreement, and that the circumstances are serious enough, it may seek to suspend concessions or other obligations under another covered agreement;

   (d) in applying the above principles, that party shall take into account:

(i) the trade in the sector or under the agreement under which the panel or Appellate Body has found a violation or other nullification or impairment, and the importance of such trade to that party;

(ii) the broader economic elements related to the nullification or impairment and the broader economic consequences of the suspension of concessions or other obligations;

(e) if that party decides to request authorization to suspend concessions or other obligations pursuant to subparagraphs (b) or (c), it shall state the reasons therefor in its request. At the same time as the request is forwarded to the DSB, it also shall be forwarded to the relevant Councils and also, in the case of a request pursuant to subparagraph (b), the relevant sectoral bodies;

(f) for purposes of this paragraph, "sector" means:

(i) with respect to goods, all goods;

(ii) with respect to services, a principal sector as identified in the current "Services Sectoral Classification List" which identifies such sectors;[14]

(iii) with respect to trade-related intellectual property rights, each of the categories of intellectual property rights covered in Section 1, or Section 2, or Section 3, or Section 4, or Section 5, or Section 6, or Section 7 of Part II, or the obligations under Part III, or Part IV of the Agreement on TRIPS;

(g) for purposes of this paragraph, "agreement" means:

(i) with respect to goods, the agreements listed in Annex 1A of the WTO Agreement, taken as a whole as well as the Plurilateral Trade Agreements in so far as the relevant parties to the dispute are parties to these agreements;

(ii) with respect to services, the GATS;

(iii) with respect to intellectual property rights, the Agreement on TRIPS.

4. The level of the suspension of concessions or other obligations authorized by the DSB shall be equivalent to the level of the nullification or impairment.

5. The DSB shall not authorize suspension of concessions or other obligations if a covered agreement prohibits such suspension.

6. When the situation described in paragraph 2 occurs, the DSB, upon request, shall grant authorization to suspend concessions or other obligations within 30 days of the expiry of the reasonable period of time unless the DSB decides by consensus to reject the request. However, if the Member concerned objects to the level of suspension proposed, or claims that the principles and procedures set forth in paragraph 3 have not been followed where a complaining party has requested authorization to suspend concessions or other obligations pursuant to paragraph 3(b) or (c), the matter shall be referred to arbitration. Such arbitration shall be carried out by the original panel, if members are available, or by an arbitrator[15] appointed by the Director-General and shall be completed within 60 days after the date of expiry of the reasonable period of time. Concessions or other obligations shall not be suspended during the course of the arbitration.

---

14. The list in document MTN.GNS/W/120 identifies eleven sectors.
15. The expression "arbitrator" shall be interpreted as referring either to an individual or a group.

7. The arbitrator[16] acting pursuant to paragraph 6 shall not examine the nature of the concessions or other obligations to be suspended but shall determine whether the level of such suspension is equivalent to the level of nullification or impairment. The arbitrator may also determine if the proposed suspension of concessions or other obligations is allowed under the covered agreement. However, if the matter referred to arbitration includes a claim that the principles and procedures set forth in paragraph 3 have not been followed, the arbitrator shall examine that claim. In the event the arbitrator determines that those principles and procedures have not been followed, the complaining party shall apply them consistent with paragraph 3. The parties shall accept the arbitrator's decision as final and the parties concerned shall not seek a second arbitration. The DSB shall be informed promptly of the decision of the arbitrator and shall upon request, grant authorization to suspend concessions or other obligations where the request is consistent with the decision of the arbitrator, unless the DSB decides by consensus to reject the request.

8. The suspension of concessions or other obligations shall be temporary and shall only be applied until such time as the measure found to be inconsistent with a covered agreement has been removed, or the Member that must implement recommendations or rulings provides a solution to the nullification or impairment of benefits, or a mutually satisfactory solution is reached. In accordance with paragraph 6 of Article 21, the DSB shall continue to keep under surveillance the implementation of adopted recommendations or rulings, including those cases where compensation has been provided or concessions or other obligations have been suspended but the recommendations to bring a measure into conformity with the covered agreements have not been implemented.

9. The dispute settlement provisions of the covered agreements may be invoked in respect of measures affecting their observance taken by regional or local governments or authorities within the territory of a Member. When the DSB has ruled that a provision of a covered agreement has not been observed, the responsible Member shall take such reasonable measures as may be available to it to ensure its observance. The provisions of the covered agreements and this Understanding relating to compensation and suspension of concessions or other obligations apply in cases where it has not been possible to secure such observance.[17]

Article 23
Strengthening of the Multilateral System

1. When Members seek the redress of a violation of obligations or other nullification or impairment of benefits under the covered agreements or an impediment to the attainment of any objective of the covered agreements, they shall have recourse to, and abide by, the rules and procedures of this Understanding.

2. In such cases, Members shall:

   (a) not make a determination to the effect that a violation has occurred, that benefits have been nullified or impaired or that the attainment of any objective

---

16. The expression "arbitrator" shall be interpreted as referring either to an individual or a group or to the members of the original panel when serving in the capacity of arbitrator.

17. Where the provisions of any covered agreement concerning measures taken by regional or local governments or authorities within the territory of a Member contain provisions different from the provisions of this paragraph, the provisions of such covered agreement shall prevail.

of the covered agreements has been impeded, except through recourse to dispute settlement in accordance with the rules and procedures of this Understanding, and shall make any such determination consistent with the findings contained in the panel or Appellate Body report adopted by the DSB or an arbitration award rendered under this Understanding;

(b) follow the procedures set forth in Article 21 to determine the reasonable period of time for the Member concerned to implement the recommendations and rulings; and

(c) follow the procedures set forth in Article 22 to determine the level of suspension of concessions or other obligations and obtain DSB authorization in accordance with those procedures before suspending concessions or other obligations under the covered agreements in response to the failure of the Member concerned to implement the recommendations and rulings within that reasonable period of time.

Article 24
Special Procedures Involving Least-Developed Country Members

1. At all stages of the determination of the causes of a dispute and of dispute settlement procedures involving a least-developed country Member, particular consideration shall be given to the special situation of least-developed country Members. In this regard, Members shall exercise due restraint in raising matters under these procedures involving a least-developed country Member. If nullification or impairment is found to result from a measure taken by a least-developed country Member, complaining parties shall exercise due restraint in asking for compensation or seeking authorization to suspend the application of concessions or other obligations pursuant to these procedures.

2. In dispute settlement cases involving a least-developed country Member, where a satisfactory solution has not been found in the course of consultations the Director-General or the Chairman of the DSB shall, upon request by a least-developed country Member offer their good offices, conciliation and mediation with a view to assisting the parties to settle the dispute, before a request for a panel is made. The Director-General or the Chairman of the DSB, in providing the above assistance, may consult any source which either deems appropriate.

Article 25
Arbitration

1. Expeditious arbitration within the WTO as an alternative means of dispute settlement can facilitate the solution of certain disputes that concern issues that are clearly defined by both parties.

2. Except as otherwise provided in this Understanding, resort to arbitration shall be subject to mutual agreement of the parties which shall agree on the procedures to be followed. Agreements to resort to arbitration shall be notified to all Members sufficiently in advance of the actual commencement of the arbitration process.

3. Other Members may become party to an arbitration proceeding only upon the agreement of the parties which have agreed to have recourse to arbitration. The parties to the proceeding shall agree to abide by the arbitration award. Arbitration awards shall be notified to the DSB and the Council or Committee of any relevant agreement where any Member may raise any point relating thereto.

4. Articles 21 and 22 of this Understanding shall apply *mutatis mutandis* to arbitration awards.

Article 26

1. *Non-Violation Complaints of the Type Described in Paragraph 1(b) of Article XXIII of GATT 1994*

Where the provisions of paragraph 1(b) of Article XXIII of GATT 1994 are applicable to a covered agreement, a panel or the Appellate Body may only make rulings and recommendations where a party to the dispute considers that any benefit accruing to it directly or indirectly under the relevant covered agreement is being nullified or impaired or the attainment of any objective of that Agreement is being impeded as a result of the application by a Member of any measure, whether or not it conflicts with the provisions of that Agreement. Where and to the extent that such party considers and a panel or the Appellate Body determines that a case concerns a measure that does not conflict with the provisions of a covered agreement to which the provisions of paragraph 1(b) of Article XXIII of GATT 1994 are applicable, the procedures in this Understanding shall apply, subject to the following:

(a) the complaining party shall present a detailed justification in support of any complaint relating to a measure which does not conflict with the relevant covered agreement;

(b) where a measure has been found to nullify or impair benefits under, or impede the attainment of objectives, of the relevant covered agreement without violation thereof, there is no obligation to withdraw the measure. However, in such cases, the panel or the Appellate Body shall recommend that the Member concerned make a mutually satisfactory adjustment;

(c) notwithstanding the provisions of Article 21, the arbitration provided for in paragraph 3 of Article 21, upon request of either party, may include a determination of the level of benefits which have been nullified or impaired, and may also suggest ways and means of reaching a mutually satisfactory adjustment; such suggestions shall not be binding upon the parties to the dispute;

(d) notwithstanding the provisions of paragraph 1 of Article 22, compensation may be part of a mutually satisfactory adjustment as final settlement of the dispute.

2. *Complaints of the Type Described in Paragraph 1(c) of Article XXIII of GATT 1994*

Where the provisions of paragraph 1(c) of Article XXIII of GATT 1994 are applicable to a covered agreement, a panel may only make rulings and recommendations where a party considers that any benefit accruing to it directly or indirectly under the relevant covered agreement is being nullified or impaired or the attainment of any objective of that Agreement is being impeded as a result of the existence of any situation other than those to which the provisions of paragraphs 1(a) and 1(b) of Article XXIII of GATT 1994 are applicable. Where and to the extent that such party considers and a panel determines that the matter is covered by this paragraph, the procedures of this Understanding shall apply only up to and including the point in the proceedings where the panel report has been circulated to the Members. The dispute settlement rules and procedures contained in the Decision of 12 April

1989 (BISD 36S/61-67) shall apply to consideration for adoption, and surveillance and implementation of recommendations and rulings. The following shall also apply:

(a) the complaining party shall present a detailed justification in support of any argument made with respect to issues covered under this paragraph;

(b) in cases involving matters covered by this paragraph, if a panel finds that cases also involve dispute settlement matters other than those covered by this paragraph, the panel shall circulate a report to the DSB addressing any such matters and a separate report on matters falling under this paragraph.

Article 27
Responsibilities of the Secretariat

1. The Secretariat shall have the responsibility of assisting panels, especially on the legal, historical and procedural aspects of the matters dealt with, and of providing secretarial and technical support.
2. While the Secretariat assists Members in respect of dispute settlement at their request, there may also be a need to provide additional legal advice and assistance in respect of dispute settlement to developing country Members. To this end, the Secretariat shall make available a qualified legal expert from the WTO technical cooperation services to any developing country Member which so requests. This expert shall assist the developing country Member in a manner ensuring the continued impartiality of the Secretariat.
3. The Secretariat shall conduct special training courses for interested Members concerning these dispute settlement procedures and practices so as to enable Members' experts to be better informed in this regard.

APPENDIX 1
AGREEMENTS COVERED BY THE UNDERSTANDING

(A) Agreement Establishing the World Trade Organization

(B) Multilateral Trade Agreements

Annex 1A: Multilateral Agreements on Trade in Goods

Annex 1B: General Agreement on Trade in Services

Annex 1C: Agreement on Trade-Related Aspects of Intellectual Property Rights

Annex 2: Understanding on Rules and Procedures Governing the Settlement of Disputes

(C) Plurilateral Trade Agreements

Annex 4: Agreement on Trade in Civil Aircraft

Agreement on Government Procurement

International Dairy Agreement

International Bovine Meat Agreement

The applicability of this Understanding to the Plurilateral Trade Agreements shall be subject to the adoption of a decision by the parties to each agreement setting out the terms for the application of the Understanding to the individual agreement, including any special or additional rules or procedures for inclusion in Appendix 2, as notified to the DSB.

11. United Nations Model Rules for the Conciliation of Disputes between States, 1995

CHAPTER I
APPLICATION OF THE RULES

Article 1

1. These rules apply to the conciliation of disputes between States where those States have expressly agreed in writing to their application.

2. The States which agree to apply these rules may at any time, through mutual agreement, exclude or amend any of their provisions.

CHAPTER II
INITIATION OF THE CONCILIATION PROCEEDINGS

Article 2

1. The conciliation proceedings shall begin as soon as the States concerned (henceforth: the parties) have agreed in writing to the application of the present rules, with or without amendments, as well as on a definition of the subject of the dispute, the number and emoluments of members of the conciliation commission, its seat and the maximum duration of the proceedings, as provided in article 24. If necessary, the agreement shall contain provisions concerning the language or languages in which the proceedings are to be conducted and the linguistic services required.

2. If the States cannot reach agreement on the definition of the subject of the dispute, they may by mutual agreement request the assistance of the Secretary-General of the United Nations to resolve the difficulty. They may also by mutual agreement request his assistance to resolve any other difficulty that they may encounter in reaching an agreement on the modalities of the conciliation proceedings.

CHAPTER III
NUMBER AND APPOINTMENT OF CONCILIATORS

Article 3

There may be three conciliators or five conciliators. In either case the conciliators shall form a commission.

Article 4

If the parties have agreed that three conciliators shall be appointed, each one of them shall appoint a conciliator, who may not be of its own nationality. The parties shall appoint by mutual agreement the third conciliator, who may not be of the nationality of any of the parties or of the other conciliators. The third conciliator shall act as president of the commission. If he is not appointed within two months of the appointment of the conciliators appointed individually by the parties, the third conciliator shall be appointed by the Government of a third State chosen by agreement between the parties or, if such agreement is not obtained within two months, by the President of the International Court of Justice. If the President is a national of one of the parties, the appointment shall be made by the Vice-President or the next member of the Court in order of seniority who is not a national of the parties. The third conciliator shall not reside habitually in the territory of the parties or be or have been in their service.

Article 5

1. If the parties have agreed that five conciliators should be appointed, each one of them shall appoint a conciliator who may be of its own nationality. The other three conciliators, one of whom shall be chosen with a view to his acting as president, shall be appointed by agreement between the parties from among nationals of third States and shall be of different nationalities. None of them shall reside habitually in the territory of the parties or be or have been in their service. None of them shall have the same nationality as that of the other two conciliators.

2. If the appointment of the conciliators whom the parties are to appoint jointly has not been effected within three months, they shall be appointed by the Government of a third State chosen by agreement between the parties or, if such an agreement is not reached within three months, by the President of the International Court of Justice. If the President is a national of one of the parties, the appointment shall be made by the Vice-President or the next judge in order of seniority who is not a national of the parties. The Government or member of the International Court of Justice making the appointment shall also decide which of the three conciliators shall act as president.

3. If, at the end of the three-month period referred to in the preceding paragraph, the parties have been able to appoint only one or two conciliators, the two conciliators or the conciliator still required shall be appointed in the manner described in the preceding paragraph. If the parties have not agreed that the conciliator or one of the two conciliators whom they have appointed shall act as president, the Government or member of the International Court of Justice appointing the two conciliators or the conciliator still required shall also decide which of the three conciliators shall act as president.

4. If, at the end of the three-month period referred to in paragraph 2 of this article, the parties have appointed three conciliators but have not been able to agree which of them shall act as president, the president shall be chosen in the manner described in that paragraph.

Article 6

Vacancies which may occur in the commission as a result of death, resignation or any other cause shall be filled as soon as possible by the method established for appointing the members to be replaced.

CHAPTER IV

FUNDAMENTAL PRINCIPLES

Article 7

The commission, acting independently and impartially, shall endeavour to assist the parties in reaching an amicable settlement of the dispute. If no settlement is reached during the consideration of the dispute, the commission may draw up and submit appropriate recommendations to the parties for consideration.

CHAPTER V

PROCEDURES AND POWERS OF THE COMMISSION

Article 8

The commission shall adopt its own procedure.

Article 9

1. Before the commission begins its work, the parties shall designate their agents and shall communicate the names of such agents to the president of the commission. The

president shall determine, in agreement with the parties, the date of the commission's first meeting, to which the members of the commission and the agents shall be invited.

2. The agents of the parties may be assisted before the commission by counsel and experts appointed by the parties.

3. Before the first meeting of the commission, its members may meet informally with the agents of the parties, if necessary, accompanied by the appointed counsel and experts to deal with administrative and procedural matters.

Article 10

1. At its first meeting, the commission shall appoint a secretary.

2. The secretary of the commission shall not have the nationality of any of the parties, shall not reside habitually in their territory and shall not be or have been in the service of any of them. He may be a United Nations official if the parties agree with the Secretary-General on the conditions under which the official will exercise these functions.

Article 11

1. As soon as the information provided by the parties so permits, the commission, having regard, in particular, to the time-limit laid down in article 24, shall decide in consultation with the parties whether the parties should be invited to submit written pleadings and, if so, in what order and within what time-limits, as well as the dates when, if necessary, the agents and counsel will be heard. The decisions taken by the commission in this regard may be amended at any later stage of the proceedings.

2. Subject to the provisions of article 20, paragraph 1, the commission shall not allow the agent or counsel of one party to attend a meeting without having also given the other party the opportunity to be represented at the same meeting.

Article 12

The parties, acting in good faith, shall facilitate the commission's work and, in particular, shall provide it to the greatest possible extent with whatever documents, information and explanations may be relevant.

Article 13

1. The commission may ask the parties for whatever relevant information or documents, as well as explanations, it deems necessary or useful. It may also make comments on the arguments advanced as well as the statements or proposals made by the parties.

2. The commission may accede to any request by a party that persons whose testimony it considers necessary or useful be heard, or that experts be consulted.

Article 14

In cases where the parties disagree on issues of fact, the commission may use all means at its disposal, such as the joint expert advisers mentioned in article 15, or consultation with experts, to ascertain the facts.

Article 15

The commission may propose to the parties that they jointly appoint expert advisers to assist it in the consideration of technical aspects of the dispute. If the proposal is accepted, its implementation shall be conditional upon the expert advisers being appointed by the parties by mutual agreement and accepted by the commission and upon the parties fixing their emoluments.

Article 16

Each party may at any time, at its own initiative or at the initiative of the commission, make proposals for the settlement of the dispute. Any proposal made in accordance with this article shall be communicated immediately to the other party by the president, who may, in so doing, transmit any comment the commission may wish to make thereon.

Article 17

At any stage of the proceedings, the commission may, at its own initiative or at the initiative of one of the parties, draw the attention of the parties to any measures which in its opinion might be advisable or facilitate a settlement.

Article 18

The commission shall endeavour to take its decisions unanimously but, if unanimity proves impossible, it may take them by a majority of votes of its members. Abstentions are not allowed. Except in matters of procedure, the presence of all members shall be required in order for a decision to be valid.

Article 19

The commission may, at any time, ask the Secretary-General of the United Nations for advice or assistance with regard to the administrative or procedural aspects of its work.

CHAPTER VI

CONCLUSION OF THE CONCILIATION PROCEEDINGS

Article 20

1. On concluding its consideration of the dispute, the commission may, if full settlement has not been reached, draw up and submit appropriate recommendations to the parties for consideration. To that end, it may hold an exchange of views with the agents of the parties, who may be heard jointly or separately.

2. The recommendations adopted by the commission shall be set forth in a report communicated by the president of the commission to the agents of the parties, with a request that the agents inform the commission, within a given period, whether the parties accept them. The president may include in the report the reasons which, in the commission's view, might prompt the parties to accept the recommendations submitted. The commission shall refrain from presenting in its report any final conclusions with regard to facts or from ruling formally on issues of law, unless the parties have jointly asked it to do so.

3. If the parties accept the recommendations submitted by the commission, a proces-verbal shall be drawn up setting forth the conditions of acceptance. The proces-verbal shall be signed by the president and the secretary. A copy thereof signed by the secretary shall be provided to each party. This shall conclude the proceedings.

4. Should the commission decide not to submit recommendations to the parties, its decision to that effect shall be recorded in a proces-verbal signed by the president and the secretary. A copy thereof signed by the secretary shall be provided to each party. This shall conclude the proceedings.

Article 21

1. The recommendations of the commission will be submitted to the parties for consideration in order to facilitate an amicable settlement of the dispute. The parties undertake to study them in good faith, carefully and objectively.

2. If one of the parties does not accept the recommendations and the other party does, it shall inform the latter, in writing, of the reasons why it could not accept them.

Article 22

1. If the recommendations are not accepted by both parties but the latter wish efforts to continue in order to reach agreement on different terms, the proceedings shall be resumed. Article 24 shall apply to the resumed proceedings, with the relevant time limit, which the parties may, by mutual agreement, shorten or extend, running from the commission's first meeting after resumption of the proceedings.

2. If the recommendations are not accepted by both parties and the latter do not wish further efforts to be made to reach agreement on different terms, a proces-verbal signed by the president and the secretary of the commission shall be drawn up, omitting the proposed terms and indicating that the parties were unable to accept them and do not wish further efforts to be made to reach agreement on different terms. The proceedings shall be concluded when each party has received a copy of the proces-verbal signed by the secretary.

Article 23

Upon conclusion of the proceedings, the president of the commission shall, with the prior agreement of the parties, deliver the documents in the possession of the secretariat of the commission either to the Secretary-General of the United Nations or to another person or entity agreed upon by the parties. Without prejudice to the possible application of article 26, paragraph 2, the confidentiality of the documents shall be preserved.

Article 24

The commission shall conclude its work within the period agreed upon by the parties. Any extension of this period shall be agreed upon by the parties.

CHAPTER VII

CONFIDENTIALITY OF THE COMMISSION'S WORK AND DOCUMENTS

Article 25

1. The commission's meetings shall be closed. The parties and the members and expert advisers of the commission, the agents and counsel of the parties, and the secretary and the secretariat staff, shall maintain strictly the confidentiality of any documents or statements, or any communication concerning the progress of the proceedings unless their disclosure has been approved by both parties in advance.

2. Each party shall receive, through the secretary, certified copies of any minutes of the meetings at which it was represented.

3. Each party shall receive, through the secretary, certified copies of any documentary evidence received and of experts' reports, records of investigations and statements by witnesses.

Article 26

1. Except with regard to certified copies referred to in article 25, paragraph 3, the obligation to respect the confidentiality of the proceedings and of the deliberations shall remain in effect for the parties and for members of the commission, expert advisers and secretariat staff after the proceedings are concluded and shall extend to recommendations and proposals which have not been accepted.

2. Notwithstanding the foregoing, the parties may, upon conclusion of the proceedings and by mutual agreement, make available to the public all or some of the documents that

in accordance with the preceding paragraph are to remain confidential, or authorize the publication of all or some of those documents.

CHAPTER VIII

OBLIGATION NOT TO ACT IN A MANNER WHICH MIGHT HAVE AN ADVERSE EFFECT ON THE CONCILIATION

Article 27

The parties shall refrain during the conciliation proceedings from any measure which might aggravate or widen the dispute. They shall, in particular, refrain from any measures which might have an adverse effect on the recommendations submitted by the commission, so long as those recommendations have not been explicitly rejected by either of the parties.

CHAPTER IX

PRESERVATION OF THE LEGAL POSITION OF THE PARTIES

Article 28

1. Except as the parties may otherwise agree, neither party shall be entitled in any other proceedings, whether in a court of law or before arbitrators or before any other body, entity or person, to invoke any views expressed or statements, admissions or proposals made by the other party in the conciliation proceedings, but not accepted, or the report of the commission, the recommendations submitted by the commission or any proposal made by the commission, unless agreed to by both parties.

2. Acceptance by a party of recommendations submitted by the commission in no way implies any admission by it of the considerations of law or of fact which may have inspired the recommendations.

CHAPTER X

COSTS

Article 29

The costs of the conciliation proceedings and the emoluments of expert advisers appointed in accordance with article 15, shall be borne by the parties in equal shares.

---

12. Rome Statute of the International Criminal Court, 1998

Part 1. Establishment of the Court

Article 1.
The Court

An International Criminal Court ("the Court") is hereby established. It shall be a permanent institution and shall have the power to exercise its jurisdiction over persons for the most serious crimes of international concern, as referred to in this Statute, and shall be complementary to national criminal jurisdictions. The jurisdiction and functioning of the Court shall be governed by the provisions of this Statute.

Part 2. Jurisdiction, Admissibility and Applicable Law

. . .

Article 5.
Crimes within the Jurisdiction of the Court

1. The jurisdiction of the Court shall be limited to the most serious crimes of concern to the international community as a whole. The Court has jurisdiction in accordance with this Statute with respect to the following crimes:
   (a) The crime of genocide;
   (b) Crimes against humanity;
   (c) War crimes;
   (d) The crime of aggression.
2. The Court shall exercise jurisdiction over the crime of aggression once a provision is adopted in accordance with Articles 121 and 123 defining the crime and setting out the conditions under which the Court shall exercise jurisdiction with respect to this crime. Such a provision shall be consistent with the relevant provisions of the Charter of the United Nations.

Article 6.
Genocide

For the purpose of this Statute, "genocide" means any of the following acts committed with intent to destroy, in whole or in part, a national, ethnical, racial or religious group, as such:

(a) Killing members of the group;
(b) Causing serious bodily or mental harm to members of the group;
(c) Deliberately inflicting on the group conditions of life calculated to bring about its physical destruction in whole or in part;
(d) Imposing measures intended to prevent births within the group;
(e) Forcibly transferring children of the group to another group.

Article 7
Crimes Against Humanity

1. For the purpose of this Statute, "crime against humanity" means any of the following acts when committed as part of a widespread or systematic attack directed against any civilian population, with knowledge of the attack;
   (a) Murder;
   (b) Extermination;
   (c) Enslavement;
   (d) Deportation or forcible transfer of population;
   (e) Imprisonment or other severe deprivation of physical liberty in violation of fundamental rules of international law;
   (f) Torture;
   (g) Rape, sexual slavery, enforced prostitution, forced pregnancy, enforced sterilization, or any other form of sexual violence of comparable gravity;
   (h) Persecution against any identifiable group or collectivity on political, racial, national, ethnic, cultural, religious, gender as defined in paragraph 3, or other grounds that are universally recognized as impermissible under in-

ternational law, in connection with any act referred to in this paragraph or any crime within the jurisdiction of the Court;

(i) Enforced disappearance of persons;

(j) The crime of apartheid;

(k) Other inhumane acts of a similar character intentionally causing great suffering, or serious injury to body or to mental or physical health.

....

Article 8
War Crimes

1. The Court shall have jurisdiction in respect of war crimes in particular when committed as part of a plan or policy or as part of a large-scale commission of such crimes.

2. For the purpose of this Statute, "war crimes" means:

(a) Grave breaches of the Geneva Conventions of 12 August 1949, namely, any of the following acts against persons or property protected under the provisions of the relevant Geneva Convention:

(i) Wilful killing;

(ii) Torture or inhuman treatment, including biological experiments;

(iii) Wilfully causing great suffering, or serious injury to body or health;

(iv) Extensive destruction and appropriation of property, not justified by military necessity and carried out unlawfully and wantonly;

(v) Compelling a prisoner of war or other protected person to serve in the forces of a hostile Power;

(vi) Wilfully depriving a prisoner of war or other protected person of the rights of fair and regular trial;

(vii) Unlawful deportation or transfer or unlawful confinement;

(viii) Taking of hostages.

(b) Other serious violations of the laws and customs applicable in international armed conflict, within the established framework of international law, namely, any of the following acts:

(i) Intentionally directing attacks against the civilian population as such or against individual civilians not taking direct part in hostilities;

(ii) Intentionally directing attacks against civilian objects, that is, objects which are not military objectives; ...

....

Article 8 *bis*[3]
Crime of aggression

1. For the purpose of this Statute, "crime of aggression" means the planning, preparation, initiation or execution, by a person in a position effectively to exercise control over or to direct the political or military action of a State, of an act of

3. Inserted by resolution RC/Res.6 of 11 June 2010.

aggression which, by its character, gravity and scale, constitutes a manifest violation of the Charter of the United Nations.

2. For the purpose of paragraph 1, "act of aggression" means the use of armed force by a State against the sovereignty, territorial integrity or political independence of another State, or in any other manner inconsistent with the Charter of the United Nations. Any of the following acts, regardless of a declaration of war, shall, in accordance with United Nations General Assembly resolution 3314 (XXIX) of 14 December 1974, qualify as an act of aggression:

   (a) The invasion or attack by the armed forces of a State of the territory of another State, or any military occupation, however temporary, resulting from such invasion or attack, or any annexation by the use of force of the territory of another State or part thereof;

   (b) Bombardment by the armed forces of a State against the territory of another State or the use of any weapons by a State against the territory of another State;

   (c) The blockade of the ports or coasts of a State by the armed forces of another State;

   (d) An attack by the armed forces of a State on the land, sea or air forces, or marine and air fleets of another State;

   (e) The use of armed forces of one State which are within the territory of another State with the agreement of the receiving State, in contravention of the conditions provided for in the agreement or any extension of their presence in such territory beyond the termination of the agreement;

   (f) The action of a State in allowing its territory, which it has placed at the disposal of another State, to be used by that other State for perpetrating an act of aggression against a third State;

   (g) The sending by or on behalf of a State of armed bands, groups, irregulars or mercenaries, which carry out acts of armed force against another State of such gravity as to amount to the acts listed above, or its substantial involvement therein.

....

Article 11
Jurisdiction Ratione Temporis

1. The Court has jurisdiction only with respect to crimes committed after the entry into force of this Statute.

2. If a State becomes a y to this Statute after its entry into force, the Court may exercise its jurisdiction only with respect to crimes committed after the entry into force of this Statute for that State, unless that State has made a declaration under Article 12, paragraph 3.

Article 12
Preconditions to the Exercise of Jurisdiction

1. A State which becomes a Party to this Statute thereby accepts the jurisdiction of the Court with respect to the crimes referred to in Article 5.

2. In the case of Article 13, paragraph (a) or (c), the Court may exercise its jurisdiction if one or more of the following States are Parties to this Statute or have accepted the jurisdiction of the Court in accordance with paragraph 3:

(a) The State on the territory of which the conduct in question occurred or, if the crime was committed on board a vessel or aircraft, the State Of registration of that vessel or aircraft;

(b) The State of which the person accused of the crime is a national.

3. If the acceptance of a State which is not a Party to this Statute is required under paragraph 2, that State may, by declaration lodged with the Registrar, accept the exercise of jurisdiction by the Court with respect to the crime in question. The accepting State shall cooperate with the Court without any delay or exception in accordance with Part 9.

Article 13
Exercise of Jurisdiction

The Court may exercise its jurisdiction with respect to a crime referred to in Article 5 in accordance with the provisions of this Statute if:

(a) A situation in which one or more of such crimes appears to have been committed is referred to the Prosecutor by a State Party in accordance with Article 14;

(b) A situation in which one or more of such crimes appears to have been committed is referred to the Prosecutor by the Security Council acting under Chapter VII of the Charter of the United Nations; or

(c) The Prosecutor has initiated an investigation in respect of such a crime in accordance with Article 15.

Article 14
Referral of a Situation by a State Party

1. A State Party may refer to the Prosecutor a situation in which one or more crimes within the jurisdiction of the Court appear to have been committed requesting the Prosecutor to investigate the situation for the purpose of determining whether one or more specific persons should be charged with the commission of such crimes.

2. As far as possible, a referral shall specify the relevant circumstances and be accompanied by such supporting documentation as is available to the State referring the situation.

Article 15
Prosecutor

1. The Prosecutor may initiate investigations *proprio motu* on the basis of information on crimes within the jurisdiction of the Court.

2. The Prosecutor shall analyse the seriousness of the information received. For this purpose, he or she may seek additional information from States, organs of the United Nations, intergovernmental or non-governmental organizations, or other reliable sources that he or she deems appropriate, and may receive written or oral testimony at the seat of the Court.

3. If the Prosecutor concludes that there is a reasonable basis to proceed with an investigation, he or she shall submit to the Pre-Trial Chamber a request for authorization of an investigation, together with any supporting material collected. Victims may make representations to the Pre-Trial Chamber, in accordance with the Rules of Procedure and Evidence.

4. If the Pre-Trial Chamber, upon examination of the request and the supporting material, considers that there is a reasonable basis to proceed with an investigation, and that the case appears to fall within the jurisdiction of the Court, it shall authorize the commencement of the investigation, without prejudice to subsequent determinations by the Court with regard to the jurisdiction and admissibility of a case.
5. The refusal of the Pre-Trial Chamber to authorize the investigation shall not preclude the presentation of a subsequent request by the Prosecutor based on new facts or evidence regarding the same situation.
6. If, after the preliminary examination referred to in paragraphs 1 and 2, the Prosecutor concludes that the information provided does not constitute a reasonable basis for an investigation, he or she shall inform those who provided the information. This shall not preclude the Prosecutor from considering further information submitted to him or her regarding the same situation in the light of new facts or evidence.

Article 16
Deferral of Investigation or Prosecution

No investigation or prosecution may be commenced or proceeded with under this Statute for a period of 12 months after the Security Council, in a resolution adopted under Chapter VII of the Charter of the United Nations, has requested the Court to that effect; that request may be renewed by the Council under the same conditions.

Article 17
Issues of Admissibility

1. Having regard to paragraph 10 of the Preamble and Article 1, the Court shall determine that a case is inadmissible where:
   (a) The case is being investigated or prosecuted by a State which has jurisdiction over it, unless the State is unwilling or unable genuinely to carry out the investigation or prosecution;
   (b) The case has been investigated by a State which has jurisdiction over it and the State has decided not to prosecute the person concerned, unless the decision resulted from the unwillingness or inability of the State genuinely to prosecute;
   (c) The person concerned has already been tried for conduct which is the subject of the complaint, and a trial by the Court is not permitted under Article 20, paragraph 3;
   (d) The case is not of sufficient gravity to justify further action by the Court.
2. In order to determine unwillingness in a particular case, the Court shall consider, having regard to the principles of due process recognized by international law, whether one or more of the following exist, as applicable:
   (a) The proceedings were or are being undertaken or the national decision was made for the purpose of shielding the person concerned from criminal responsibility for crimes within the jurisdiction of the Court referred to in Article 5;
   (b) There has been an unjustified delay in the proceedings which in the circumstances is inconsistent with an intent to bring the person concerned to justice;

(c) The proceedings were not or are not being conducted independently or impartially, and they were or are being conducted in a manner which, in the circumstances, is inconsistent with an intent to bring the person concerned to justice.

3. In order to determine inability in a particular case, the Court shall consider whether, due to a total or substantial collapse or unavailability of its national judicial system, the State is unable to obtain the accused or the necessary evidence and testimony or otherwise unable to carry out its proceedings.

Article 18
Preliminary Rulings Regarding Admissibility

1. When a situation has been referred to the Court pursuant to Article 13 (a) and the Prosecutor has determined that there would be a reasonable basis to commence an investigation, or the Prosecutor initiates an investigation pursuant to Articles 13 (c) and 15, the Prosecutor shall notify all States Parties and those States which, taking into account the information available, would normally exercise jurisdiction over the crimes concerned. The Prosecutor may notify such States on a confidential basis and, where the Prosecutor believes it necessary to protect persons, prevent destruction of evidence or prevent the absconding of persons, may limit the scope of the information provided to States.

2. Within one month of receipt of that notification, a State may inform the Court that it is investigating or has investigated its nationals or others within its jurisdiction with respect to criminal acts which may constitute crimes referred to in Article 5 and which relate to the information provided in the notification to States. At the request of that State, the Prosecutor shall defer to the State's investigation of those persons unless the Pre-Trial Chamber, on the application of the Prosecutor, decides to authorize the investigation.

3. The Prosecutor-s deferral to a State-s investigation shall be open to review by the Prosecutor six months after the date of deferral or at any time when there has been a significant change of circumstances based on the State's unwillingness or inability genuinely to carry out the investigation.

4. The State concerned or the Prosecutor may appeal to the Appeals Chamber against a ruling of the Pre-Trial Chamber, in accordance with Article 82. The appeal may be heard on an expedited basis.

5. When the Prosecutor has deferred an investigation in accordance with paragraph 2, the Prosecutor may request that the State concerned periodically inform the Prosecutor of the progress of its investigations and any subsequent prosecutions. States Parties shall respond to such requests without undue delay.

6. Pending a ruling by the Pre-Trial Chamber, or at any time when the Prosecutor has deferred an investigation under this Article, the Prosecutor may, on an exceptional basis, seek authority from the Pre-Trial Chamber to pursue necessary investigative steps for the purpose of preserving evidence where there is a unique opportunity to obtain important evidence or there is a significant risk that such evidence may not be subsequently available.

7. A State which has challenged a ruling of the Pre-Trial Chamber under this Article may challenge the admissibility of a case under Article 19 on the grounds of additional significant facts or significant change of circumstances.

Article 19.
Challenges to the Jurisdiction of the Court or the Admissibility of a Case

1. The Court shall satisfy itself that it has jurisdiction in any case brought before it. The Court may, on its own motion, determine the admissibility of a case in accordance with Article 17.
2. Challenges to the admissibility of a case on the grounds referred to in Article 17 or challenges to the jurisdiction of the Court may be made by:
   (a) An accused or a person for whom a warrant of arrest or a summons to ap pear has been issued under Article 58;
   (b) A State which has jurisdiction over a case, on the ground that it is investigating or prosecuting the case or has investigated or prosecuted; or
   (c) A State from which acceptance of jurisdiction is required under Article 12.
3. The Prosecutor may seek a ruling from the Court regarding a question of jurisdiction or admissibility. In proceedings with respect to jurisdiction or admissibility, those who have referred the situation under Article 13, as well as victims, may also submit observations to the Court.
4. The admissibility of a case or the jurisdiction of the Court may be challenged only once by any person or State referred to in paragraph 2. The challenge shall take place prior to or at the commencement of the trial. In exceptional circumstances, the Court may grant leave for a challenge to be brought more than once or at a time later than the commencement of the trial.

   Challenges to the admissibility of a case, at the commencement of a trial, or subsequently with the leave of the Court, may be based only an Article 17, paragraph 1 (c),
5. A State referred to in paragraph 2 (b) and (c) shall make a challenge at the earliest opportunity.
6. Prior to the confirmation of the charges, challenges to the admissibility of a case or challenges to the jurisdiction of the Court shall be referred to the Pre-Trial Chamber. After confirmation of the charges, they shall be referred to the Trial Chamber. Decisions with respect to jurisdiction or admissibility may be appealed to the Appeals Chamber in accordance with Article 82.
7. If a challenge is made by a State referred to in paragraph 2 (b) or (c), the Prosecutor shall suspend the investigation until such time as the Court makes a determination in accordance with Article 17.
8. Pending a ruling by the Court, the Prosecutor may seek authority from the Court:
   (a) To pursue necessary investigative steps of the kind referred to in Article 18, paragraph 6;
   (b) To take a statement or testimony from a witness or complete the collection and examination of evidence which had begun prior to the making of the challenge; and
   (c) in cooperation with the relevant States, to prevent the absconding of persons in respect of whom the Prosecutor has already requested a warrant of arrest under Article 58.
9. The making of a challenge shall not affect the validity of any act performed by the Prosecutor or any order or warrant issued by the Court prior to the making of the challenge.

10. If the Court has decided that a case is inadmissible under Article 17, the Prosecutor may submit a request for a review of the decision when he or she is fully satisfied that new facts have arisen which negate the basis on which the case had previously been found inadmissible under Article 17.
11. If the Prosecutor, having regard to the matters referred to in Article 17, defers an investigation, the Prosecutor may request that the relevant State make available to the Prosecutor information on the proceedings. That information shall, at the request of the State concerned, be confidential. If the Prosecutor thereafter decides to proceed with an investigation, he or she shall notify the State to which deferral of the proceedings has taken place.

....

Article 21
Applicable law

1. The Court shall apply:
   (a) In the first place, this Statute, Elements of Crimes and its Rules of Procedure and Evidence;
   (b) In the second place, where appropriate, applicable treaties and the principles and rules of international law, including the established principles of the international law of armed conflict;
   (c) Failing that, general principles of law derived by the Court from national laws of legal systems of the world including, as appropriate, the national laws of States that would normally exercise jurisdiction over the crime, provided that those principles are not inconsistent with this statute and with international law and internationally recognized norms and standards.
2. The Court may apply principles and rules of law as interpreted in its previous decisions.
3. The application and interpretation of law pursuant to this Article must be consistent with internationally recognized human rights, and be without any adverse distinction founded on grounds such as gender as defined in Article 7, paragraph 3, age, race, colour, language, religion or belief, political or other opinion, national, ethnic or social origin, wealth, birth or other status.

....

Part 3. General Principles of Criminal Law ...

....

Article 27
Irrelevance of Official Capacity

1. This Statute shall apply equally to all persons without any distinction based on official capacity. In particular, official capacity as a Head of State or Government, a member of a Government or parliament, an elected representative or a government official shall in no case exempt a person from criminal responsibility under this Statute, nor shall it, in and of itself, constitute a ground for reduction of sentence.
2. Immunities or special procedural rules which may attach to the official capacity of a person, whether under national or international law, shall not bar the Court from exercising its jurisdiction over such a person.

....

Article 35
Service of Judges

1. All judges shall be elected as full-time members of the Court and shall be available to serve on that basis from the commencement of their terms of office.
2. The judges composing the Presidency shall serve on a full-time basis as soon as they are elected.
3. The Presidency may, on the basis of the workload of the Court and in consultation with its members, decide from time to time to what extent the remaining judges shall be required to serve on a full-time basis. Any such arrangement shall be without prejudice to the provisions of Article 40.
4. The financial arrangements for judges not required to serve on a full-time basis shall be made in accordance with Article 49.

Article 36.
Qualifications, Nomination and Election of Judges

1. Subject to the provisions of paragraph 2, there shall be 18 judges of the Court.

. . . .

3.
   (a) The judges shall be chosen from among persons of high moral character, impartiality and integrity who possess the qualifications required in their respective States for appointment to the highest judicial offices.
   (b) Every candidate for election to the Court shall:
      (i) Have established competence in criminal law and procedure, and the necessary relevant experience, whether as judge, prosecutor, advocate or in other similar capacity, in criminal proceedings; or
      (ii) Have established competence in relevant areas of international law such as international humanitarian law and the law of human rights, and extensive experience in a professional legal capacity which is of relevance to the judicial work of the Court;
   (c) Every candidate for election to the Court shall have an excellent knowledge of and be fluent in at least one of the working languages of the Court.

4.
   (a) Nominations of candidates for election to the Court may be made by any State Party to this Statute, and shall be made either:
      (i) By the procedure for the nomination of candidates for appointment to the highest judicial offices in the State in question; or
      (ii) By the procedure provided for the nomination of candidates for the International Court of Justice in the Statute of that Court. Nominations shall be accompanied by a statement in the necessary detail specifying how the candidate fulfils the requirements of paragraph 3.
   (b) Each State Party may put forward one candidate for any given election who need not necessarily be a national of that State Party but shall in any case be a national of a State Party.
   (c) The Assembly of States Parties may decide to establish, if appropriate, an Advisory Committee on nominations. In that event, the Committee's composition and mandate shall be established by the Assembly of States Parties.

5. For the purposes of the election, there shall be two lists of candidates: List A containing the names of candidates with the qualifications specified in paragraph 3 (b) (i); and List B containing the names of candidates with the qualifications specified in paragraph 3 (b) (ii). A candidate with sufficient qualifications for both lists may choose on which list to appear. At the first election to the Court, at least nine judges shall be elected from list A and at least five judges from list B. Subsequent elections shall be so organized as to maintain the equivalent proportion on the Court of judges qualified on the two lists.

6.

(a) The judges shall be elected by secret ballot at a meeting of the Assembly of States Parties convened for that purpose under Article 112. Subject to paragraph 7, the persons elected to the Court shall be the 18 candidates who obtain the highest number of votes and a two-thirds majority of the States Parties present and voting.

(b) In the event that a sufficient number of judges is not elected on the first ballot, successive ballots shall be held in accordance with the procedures laid down in subparagraph (a) until the remaining places have been filled.

7. No two judges may be nationals of the same State. A person who, for the purposes of membership of the Court, could be regarded as a national of more than one State shall be deemed to be a national of the State in which that person ordinarily exercises civil and political rights.

8.

(a) The States Parties shall, in the selection of judges, take into account the need, within the membership of the Court, for:

(i) The representation of the principal legal systems of the world;

(ii) Equitable geographical representation; and

(iii) A fair representation of female and male judges.

(b) States Parties shall also take into account the need to include judges with legal expertise on specific issues, including, but not limited to, violence against women or children.

9.

(a) Subject to subparagraph (b), judges shall hold office for a term of nine years and, subject to subparagraph (c) and to Article 37, paragraph 2, shall not be eligible for reelection.

(b) At the first election, one third of the judges elected shall be selected by lot to serve for a term of three years; one third of the judges elected shall be selected by lot to serve for a term of six years; and the remainder shall serve for a term of nine years.

(c) A judge who is selected to serve for a term of three years under subparagraph (b) shall be eligible for re-election for a full term.

10. Notwithstanding paragraph 9, a judge assigned to a Trial or Appeals Chamber in accordance with Article 39 shall continue in office to complete any trial or appeal the hearing of which has already commenced before that Chamber.

....

Article 39
Chambers

1. As soon as possible after the election of the judges, the Court shall organize itself into the divisions specified in Article 34, paragraph (b). The Appeals Division shall be composed of the President and four other judges, the Trial Division of not less than six judges and the Pre-Trial Division of not less than six judges. The assignment of judges to divisions shall be based on the nature of the functions to be performed by each division and the qualifications and experience of the judges elected to the Court, in such a way that each division shall contain an appropriate combination of expertise in criminal law and procedure and in international law. The Trial and Pre-Trial Divisions shall be composed predominantly of judges with criminal trial experience.

2.
   (a) The judicial functions of the Court shall be carried out in each division by Chambers.

   (b)
      (i) The Appeals Chamber shall be composed of all the judges of the Appeals Division;

      (ii) The functions of the Trial Chamber shall be carried out by three judges of the Trial Division;

      (iii) The functions of the Pre-Trial Chamber shall be carried out either by three judges of the Pre-Trial Division or by a single judge of that division in accordance with this Statute and the Rules of Procedure and Evidence;

   (c) Nothing in this paragraph shall preclude the simultaneous constitution of more than one Trial Chamber or Pre-Trial Chamber when the efficient management of the Court's workload so requires.

3.
   (a) Judges assigned to the Trial and Pre-Trial Divisions shall serve in those divisions for a period of three years, and thereafter until the completion of any case the hearing of which has already commenced in the division concerned.

   (b) Judges assigned to the Appeals Division shall serve in that division for their entire term of office.

4. Judges assigned to the Appeals Division shall serve only in that division. Nothing in this Article shall, however, preclude the temporary attachment of judges from the Trial Division to the Pre-Trial Division or vice versa, if the Presidency considers that the efficient management of the Court's workload so requires, provided that under no circumstances shall a judge who has participated in the pre-trial phase of a case be eligible to sit on the Trial Chamber hearing that case.

Article 40
Independence of the Judges

1. The judges shall be independent in the performance of their functions.

2. Judges shall not engage in any activity which is likely to interfere with their judicial functions or to affect confidence in their independence.

3. Judges required to serve on a full-time basis at the seat of the Court shall not engage in any other occupation of a professional nature.
4. Any question regarding the application of paragraphs 2 and 3 shall be decided by an absolute majority of the judges. Where any such question concerns an individual judge, that judge shall not take part in the decision.

Article 41.
Excusing and Disqualification of Judges

1. The Presidency may, at the request of a judge, excuse that judge from the exercise of a function under this Statute, in accordance with the Rules of Procedure and Evidence.
2.
   (a) A judge shall not participate in any case in which his or her impartiality might reasonably be doubted on any ground. A judge shall be disqualified from a case in accordance with this paragraph if, inter alia, that judge has previously been involved in any capacity in that case before the Court or in a related criminal case at the national level involving the person being investigated or prosecuted. A judge shall also be disqualified on such other grounds as may be provided for in the Rules of Procedure and Evidence.
   (b) The Prosecutor or the person being investigated or prosecuted may request the disqualification of a judge under this paragraph.
   (c) Any question as to the disqualification of a judge shall be decided by an absolute majority of the judges. The challenged judge shall be entitled to present his or her comments on the matter, but shall not take part in the decision.

Article 42
The Office of the Prosecutor

1. The Office of the Prosecutor shall act independently as a separate organ of the Court. It shall be responsible for receiving referrals and any substantiated information on crimes within the jurisdiction of the Court, for examining them and for conducting investigations and prosecutions before the Court. A member of the office shall not seek or act on instructions from any external source....

....

Part 6. The Trial

Article 63
Trial in the Presence of the Accused

1. The accused shall be present during the trial.
2. If the accused, being present before the Court, continues to disrupt the trial, the Trial Chamber may remove the accused and shall make provision for him or her to observe the trial and instruct counsel from outside the courtroom, through the use of communications technology, it required. Such measures shall be taken only in exceptional circumstances after other reasonable alternatives have proved inadequate, and only for such duration as is strictly required.

....

Article 66
Presumption of Innocence

1. Everyone shall be presumed innocent until proved guilty before the Court in accordance with the applicable law.
2. The onus is on the Prosecutor to prove the quilt of the accused.
3. In order to convict the accused, the Court must be convinced of the guilt of the accused beyond reasonable doubt.

Article 67
Rights of the Accused

1. In the determination of any charge, the accused shall be entitled to a public hearing, having regard to the provisions of this statute, to a fair hearing conducted impartially, and to the following minimum guarantees, in full equality:
   (a) To be informed promptly and in detail of the nature, cause and content of the charge, in a language which the accused fully understands and speaks;
   (b) To have adequate time and facilities for the preparation of the defence and to communicate freely with counsel of the accused's choosing in confidence;
   (c) To be tried without undue delay;
   (d) Subject to Article 63, paragraph 2, to be present at the trial, to conduct the defence in person or through legal assistance of the accused's choosing, to be informed, if the accused does not have legal assistance, of this right and to have legal assistance assigned by the Court in any case where the interests of justice so require, and without payment if the accused lacks sufficient means to pay for it;
   (e) To examine, or have examined, the witnesses against him or her and to obtain the attendance and examination of witnesses on his or her behalf under the same conditions as witnesses against him or her. The accused shall also be entitled to raise defences and to present other evidence admissible under this Statute;
   (f) To have, free of any cost, the assistance of a competent interpreter and such translations as are necessary to meet the requirements of fairness, if any of the proceedings of or documents presented to the Court are not in a language which the accused fully understands and speaks;
   (g) Not to be compelled to testify or to confess guilt and to remain silent, without such silence being a consideration in the determination of guilt or innocence;
   (h) To make an unsworn oral or written statement in his or her defence; and
   (i) Not to have imposed on him or her any reversal of the burden of proof or any onus of rebuttal.
2. In addition to any other disclosure provided for in this Statute, the Prosecutor shall, as soon as practicable, disclose to the defence evidence in the Prosecutor's possession or control which he or she believes shows or tends to show the innocence of the accused, or to mitigate the guilt of the accused, or which may affect the credibility of prosecution evidence. In case of doubt as to the application of this paragraph, the Court shall decide.

13. UN Articles on the Responsibility of States for Internationally Wrongful Acts, UN A/RES/56/83, 28 January 2002

The General Assembly,

Having considered chapter IV of the report of the International Law Commission on the work of its fifty-third session, which contains the draft Articles on responsibility of States for internationally wrongful acts,

Noting that the International Law Commission decided to recommend to the General Assembly that it should take note of the draft Articles on responsibility of States for internationally wrongful acts in a resolution and annex the draft Articles to that resolution, and that it should consider at a later stage, in the light of the importance of the topic, the possibility of convening an international conference of plenipotentiaries to examine the draft Articles with a view to concluding a convention on the topic,

Emphasizing the continuing importance of the codification and progressive development of international law, as referred to in Article 13, paragraph 1 (*a*), of the Charter of the United Nations,

Noting that the subject of responsibility of States for internationally wrongful acts is of major importance in the relations of States,

1. *Welcomes* the conclusion of the work of the International Law Commission on responsibility of States for internationally wrongful acts and its adoption of the draft Articles and a detailed commentary on the subject;
2. *Expresses its appreciation* to the International Law Commission for its continuing contribution to the codification and progressive development of international law;
3. *Takes note* of the Articles on responsibility of States for internationally wrongful acts, presented by the International Law Commission, the text of which is annexed to the present resolution, and commends them to the attention of Governments without prejudice to the question of their future adoption or other appropriate action;
4. *Decides* to include in the provisional agenda of its fifty-ninth session an item entitled "Responsibility of States for internationally wrongful acts".

PART ONE
THE INTERNATIONALLY WRONGFUL ACT OF A STATE

Chapter I
General principles

Article 1
Responsibility of a State for its internationally wrongful acts

Every internationally wrongful act of a State entails the international responsibility of that State.

Article 2
Elements of an internationally wrongful act of a State

There is an internationally wrongful act of a State when conduct consisting of an action or omission:

(a) Is attributable to the State under international law; and

(b) Constitutes a breach of an international obligation of the State.

Article 3
Characterization of an act of a State as internationally wrongful

The characterization of an act of a State as internationally wrongful is governed by international law. Such characterization is not affected by the characterization of the same act as lawful by internal law.

Chapter II
Attribution of conduct to a State

Article 4
Conduct of organs of a State

1. The conduct of any State organ shall be considered an act of that State under international law, whether the organ exercises legislative, executive, judicial or any other functions, whatever position it holds in the organization of the State, and whatever its character as an organ of the central government or of a territorial unit of the State.
2. An organ includes any person or entity which has that status in accordance with the internal law of the State.

Article 5
Conduct of persons or entities exercising elements of governmental authority

The conduct of a person or entity which is not an organ of the State under Article 4 but which is empowered by the law of that State to exercise elements of the governmental authority shall be considered an act of the State under international law, provided the person or entity is acting in that capacity in the particular instance.

Article 6
Conduct of organs placed at the disposal of a State by another State

The conduct of an organ placed at the disposal of a State by another State shall be considered an act of the former State under international law if the organ is acting in the exercise of elements of the governmental authority of the State at whose disposal it is placed.

Article 7
Excess of authority or contravention of instructions

The conduct of an organ of a State or of a person or entity empowered to exercise elements of the governmental authority shall be considered an act of the State under international law if the organ, person or entity acts in that capacity, even if it exceeds its authority or contravenes instructions.

Article 8
Conduct directed or controlled by a State

The conduct of a person or group of persons shall be considered an act of a State under international law if the person or group of persons is in fact acting on the instructions of, or under the direction or control of, that State in carrying out the conduct.

Article 9

Conduct carried out in the absence or default of the official authorities

The conduct of a person or group of persons shall be considered an act of a State under international law if the person or group of persons is in fact exercising elements of the governmental authority in the absence or default of the official authorities and in circumstances such as to call for the exercise of those elements of authority.

Article 10

Conduct of an insurrectional or other movement

1. The conduct of an insurrectional movement which becomes the new government of a State shall be considered an act of that State under international law.
2. The conduct of a movement, insurrectional or other, which succeeds in establishing a new State in part of the territory of a pre-existing State or in a territory under its administration shall be considered an act of the new State under international law.
3. This Article is without prejudice to the attribution to a State of any conduct, however related to that of the movement concerned, which is to be considered an act of that State by virtue of Articles 4 to 9.

Article 11

Conduct acknowledged and adopted by a State as its own

Conduct which is not attributable to a State under the preceding Articles shall nevertheless be considered an act of that State under international law if and to the extent that the State acknowledges and adopts the conduct in question as its own.

Chapter III

Breach of an international obligation

Article 12

Existence of a breach of an international obligation

There is a breach of an international obligation by a State when an act of that State is not in conformity with what is required of it by that obligation, regardless of its origin or character.

Article 13

International obligation in force for a State

An act of a State does not constitute a breach of an international obligation unless the State is bound by the obligation in question at the time the act occurs.

Article 14

Extension in time of the breach of an international obligation

1. The breach of an international obligation by an act of a State not having a continuing character occurs at the moment when the act is performed, even if its effects continue.
2. The breach of an international obligation by an act of a State having a continuing character extends over the entire period during which the act continues and remains not in conformity with the international obligation.
3. The breach of an international obligation requiring a State to prevent a given event occurs when the event occurs and extends over the entire period during which the event continues and remains not in conformity with that obligation.

Article 15
Breach consisting of a composite act

1. The breach of an international obligation by a State through a series of actions or omissions defined in aggregate as wrongful occurs when the action or omission occurs which, taken with the other actions or omissions, is sufficient to constitute the wrongful act.
2. In such a case, the breach extends over the entire period starting with the first of the actions or omissions of the series and lasts for as long as these actions or omissions are repeated and remain not in conformity with the international obligation.

Chapter IV
Responsibility of a State in connection with the act of another State

Article 16
Aid or assistance in the commission of an internationally wrongful act

A State which aids or assists another State in the commission of an internationally wrongful act by the latter is internationally responsible for doing so if:

(a) That State does so with knowledge of the circumstances of the internationally wrongful act; and

(b) The act would be internationally wrongful if committed by that State.

Article 17
Direction and control exercised over the commission of an internationally wrongful act

A State which directs and controls another State in the commission of an internationally wrongful act by the latter is internationally responsible for that act if:

(a) That State does so with knowledge of the circumstances of the internationally wrongful act; and

(b) The act would be internationally wrongful if committed by that State.

Article 18
Coercion of another State

A State which coerces another State to commit an act is internationally responsible for that act if:

(a) The act would, but for the coercion, be an internationally wrongful act of the coerced State; and

(b) The coercing State does so with knowledge of the circumstances of the act.

Article 19
Effect of this chapter

This chapter is without prejudice to the international responsibility, under other provisions of these Articles, of the State which commits the act in question, or of any other State.

Chapter V
Circumstances precluding wrongfulness

Article 20
Consent

Valid consent by a State to the commission of a given act by another State precludes the wrongfulness of that act in relation to the former State to the extent that the act remains within the limits of that consent.

Article 21
Self-defence

The wrongfulness of an act of a State is precluded if the act constitutes a lawful measure of self-defence taken in conformity with the Charter of the United Nations.

Article 22
Countermeasures in respect of an internationally wrongful act

The wrongfulness of an act of a State not in conformity with an international obligation towards another State is precluded if and to the extent that the act constitutes a countermeasure taken against the latter State in accordance with chapter II of part three.

Article 23
Force majeure

1. The wrongfulness of an act of a State not in conformity with an international obligation of that State is precluded if the act is due to force majeure, that is the occurrence of an irresistible force or of an unforeseen event, beyond the control of the State, making it materially impossible in the circumstances to perform the obligation.
2. Paragraph 1 does not apply if:
   (a) The situation of force majeure is due, either alone or in combination with other factors, to the conduct of the State invoking it; or
   (b) The State has assumed the risk of that situation occurring.

Article 24
Distress

1. The wrongfulness of an act of a State not in conformity with an international obligation of that State is precluded if the author of the act in question has no other reasonable way, in a situation of distress, of saving the author's life or the lives of other persons entrusted to the author's care.
2. Paragraph 1 does not apply if:
   (a) The situation of distress is due, either alone or in combination with other factors, to the conduct of the State invoking it; or
   (b) The act in question is likely to create a comparable or greater peril.

Article 25
Necessity

1. Necessity may not be invoked by a State as a ground for precluding the wrongfulness of an act not in conformity with an international obligation of that State unless the act:
   (a) Is the only way for the State to safeguard an essential interest against a grave and imminent peril; and
   (b) Does not seriously impair an essential interest of the State or States towards which the obligation exists, or of the international community as a whole.
2. In any case, necessity may not be invoked by a State as a ground for precluding wrongfulness if:
   (a) The international obligation in question excludes the possibility of invoking necessity; or
   (b) The State has contributed to the situation of necessity.

Article 26
Compliance with peremptory norms

Nothing in this chapter precludes the wrongfulness of any act of a State which is not in conformity with an obligation arising under a peremptory norm of general international law.

Article 27
Consequences of invoking a circumstance precluding wrongfulness

The invocation of a circumstance precluding wrongfulness in accordance with this chapter is without prejudice to:

(a) Compliance with the obligation in question, if and to the extent that the circumstance precluding wrongfulness no longer exists;

(b) The question of compensation for any material loss caused by the act in question.

PART TWO
CONTENT OF THE INTERNATIONAL RESPONSIBILITY OF A STATE

Chapter I
General principles

Article 28
Legal consequences of an internationally wrongful act

The international responsibility of a State which is entailed by an internationally wrongful act in accordance with the provisions of part one involves legal consequences as set out in this part.

Article 29
Continued duty of performance

The legal consequences of an internationally wrongful act under this part do not affect the continued duty of the responsible State to perform the obligation breached.

Article 30
Cessation and non-repetition

The State responsible for the internationally wrongful act is under an obligation:

(a) To cease that act, if it is continuing;

(b) To offer appropriate assurances and guarantees of non-repetition, if circumstances so require.

Article 31
Reparation

1. The responsible State is under an obligation to make full reparation for the injury caused by the internationally wrongful act.
2. Injury includes any damage, whether material or moral, caused by the internationally wrongful act of a State.

Article 32
Irrelevance of internal law

The responsible State may not rely on the provisions of its internal law as justification for failure to comply with its obligations under this part.

Article 33
Scope of international obligations set out in this part

1. The obligations of the responsible State set out in this part may be owed to another State, to several States, or to the international community as a whole, depending in particular on the character and content of the international obligation and on the circumstances of the breach.
2. This part is without prejudice to any right, arising from the international responsibility of a State, which may accrue directly to any person or entity other than a State.

Chapter II
Reparation for injury

Article 34
Forms of reparation

Full reparation for the injury caused by the internationally wrongful act shall take the form of restitution, compensation and satisfaction, either singly or in combination, in accordance with the provisions of this chapter.

Article 35
Restitution

A State responsible for an internationally wrongful act is under an obligation to make restitution, that is, to re-establish the situation which existed before the wrongful act was committed, provided and to the extent that restitution:

(a) Is not materially impossible;

(b) Does not involve a burden out of all proportion to the benefit deriving from restitution instead of compensation.

Article 36
Compensation

1. The State responsible for an internationally wrongful act is under an obligation to compensate for the damage caused thereby, insofar as such damage is not made good by restitution.
2. The compensation shall cover any financially assessable damage including loss of profits insofar as it is established.

Article 37
Satisfaction

1. The State responsible for an internationally wrongful act is under an obligation to give satisfaction for the injury caused by that act insofar as it cannot be made good by restitution or compensation.
2. Satisfaction may consist in an acknowledgement of the breach, an expression of regret, a formal apology or another appropriate modality.
3. Satisfaction shall not be out of proportion to the injury and may not take a form humiliating to the responsible State.

Article 38
Interest

1. Interest on any principal sum due under this chapter shall be payable when necessary in order to ensure full reparation. The interest rate and mode of calculation shall be set so as to achieve that result.

2. Interest runs from the date when the principal sum should have been paid until the date the obligation to pay is fulfilled.

Article 39

Contribution to the injury

In the determination of reparation, account shall be taken of the contribution to the injury by wilful or negligent action or omission of the injured State or any person or entity in relation to whom reparation is sought.

Chapter III

Serious breaches of obligations under peremptory norms of general international law

Article 40

Application of this chapter

1. This chapter applies to the international responsibility which is entailed by a serious breach by a State of an obligation arising under a peremptory norm of general international law.
2. A breach of such an obligation is serious if it involves a gross or systematic failure by the responsible State to fulfil the obligation.

Article 41

Particular consequences of a serious breach of an obligation under this chapter

1. States shall cooperate to bring to an end through lawful means any serious breach within the meaning of Article 40.
2. No State shall recognize as lawful a situation created by a serious breach within the meaning of Article 40, nor render aid or assistance in maintaining that situation.
3. This Article is without prejudice to the other consequences referred to in this part and to such further consequences that a breach to which this chapter applies may entail under international law.

PART THREE

THE IMPLEMENTATION OF THE INTERNATIONAL RESPONSIBILITY OF A STATE

Chapter I

Invocation of the responsibility of a State

Article 42

Invocation of responsibility by an injured State

A State is entitled as an injured State to invoke the responsibility of another State if the obligation breached is owed to:

(a) That State individually; or

(b) A group of States including that State, or the international community as a whole, and the breach of the obligation:

  (i) Specially affects that State; or

  (ii) Is of such a character as radically to change the position of all the other States to which the obligation is owed with respect to the further performance of the obligation.

Article 43

Notice of claim by an injured State

1. An injured State which invokes the responsibility of another State shall give notice of its claim to that State.

2. The injured State may specify in particular:

   (a) The conduct that the responsible State should take in order to cease the wrongful act, if it is continuing;

   (b) What form reparation should take in accordance with the provisions of part two.

Article 44
Admissibility of claims

The responsibility of a State may not be invoked if:

(a) The claim is not brought in accordance with any applicable rule relating to the nationality of claims;

(b) The claim is one to which the rule of exhaustion of local remedies applies and any available and effective local remedy has not been exhausted.

Article 45
Loss of the right to invoke responsibility

The responsibility of a State may not be invoked if:

(a) The injured State has validly waived the claim;

(b) The injured State is to be considered as having, by reason of its conduct, validly acquiesced in the lapse of the claim.

Article 46
Plurality of injured States

Where several States are injured by the same internationally wrongful act, each injured State may separately invoke the responsibility of the State which has committed the internationally wrongful act.

Article 47
Plurality of responsible States

1. Where several States are responsible for the same internationally wrongful act, the responsibility of each State may be invoked in relation to that act.

2. Paragraph 1:

   (a) Does not permit any injured State to recover, by way of compensation, more than the damage it has suffered;

   (b) Is without prejudice to any right of recourse against the other responsible States.

Article 48
Invocation of responsibility by a State other than an injured State

1. Any State other than an injured State is entitled to invoke the responsibility of another State in accordance with paragraph 2 if:

   (a) The obligation breached is owed to a group of States including that State, and is established for the protection of a collective interest of the group; or

   (b) The obligation breached is owed to the international community as a whole.

2. Any State entitled to invoke responsibility under paragraph 1 may claim from the responsible State:

   (*a*) Cessation of the internationally wrongful act, and assurances and guarantees of non-repetition in accordance with Article 30; and (*b*) Performance of the obligation of reparation in accordance with the preceding Articles, in the interest of the injured State or of the beneficiaries of the obligation breached.

3. The requirements for the invocation of responsibility by an injured State under Articles 43, 44 and 45 apply to an invocation of responsibility by a State entitled to do so under paragraph 1.

Chapter II
Countermeasures

Article 49
Object and limits of countermeasures

1. An injured State may only take countermeasures against a State which is responsible for an internationally wrongful act in order to induce that State to comply with its obligations under part two.
2. Countermeasures are limited to the non-performance for the time being of international obligations of the State taking the measures towards the responsible State.
3. Countermeasures shall, as far as possible, be taken in such a way as to permit the resumption of performance of the obligations in question.

Article 50
Obligations not affected by countermeasures

1. Countermeasures shall not affect:

(*a*) The obligation to refrain from the threat or use of force as embodied in the Charter of the United Nations;

(*b*) Obligations for the protection of fundamental human rights;

(*c*) Obligations of a humanitarian character prohibiting reprisals;

(*d*) Other obligations under peremptory norms of general international law.

2. A State taking countermeasures is not relieved from fulfilling its obligations:

(a) Under any dispute settlement procedure applicable between it and the responsible State;

(b) To respect the inviolability of diplomatic or consular agents, premises, archives and documents.

Article 51
Proportionality

Countermeasures must be commensurate with the injury suffered, taking into account the gravity of the internationally wrongful act and the rights in question.

Article 52
Conditions relating to resort to countermeasures

1. Before taking countermeasures, an injured State shall:

(*a*) Call upon the responsible State, in accordance with Article 43, to fulfil its obligations under part two;

(*b*) Notify the responsible State of any decision to take countermeasures and offer to negotiate with that State.

2. Notwithstanding paragraph 1 (*b*), the injured State may take such urgent countermeasures as are necessary to preserve its rights.

3. Countermeasures may not be taken, and if already taken must be suspended without undue delay if:
   (*a*) The internationally wrongful act has ceased; and
   (*b*) The dispute is pending before a court or tribunal which has the authority to make decisions binding on the parties.
4. Paragraph 3 does not apply if the responsible State fails to implement the dispute settlement procedures in good faith.

Article 53
Termination of countermeasures

Countermeasures shall be terminated as soon as the responsible State has complied with its obligations under part two in relation to the internationally wrongful act.

Article 54
Measures taken by States other than an injured State

This chapter does not prejudice the right of any State, entitled under Article 48, paragraph 1, to invoke the responsibility of another State, to take lawful measures against that State to ensure cessation of the breach and reparation in the interest of the injured State or of the beneficiaries of the obligation breached.

PART FOUR
GENERAL PROVISIONS

Article 55
Lex specialis

These Articles do not apply where and to the extent that the conditions for the existence of an internationally wrongful act or the content or implementation of the international responsibility of a State are governed by special rules of international law.

Article 56
Questions of State responsibility not regulated by these Articles

The applicable rules of international law continue to govern questions concerning the responsibility of a State for an internationally wrongful act to the extent that they are not regulated by these Articles.

Article 57
Responsibility of an international organization

These Articles are without prejudice to any question of the responsibility under international law of an international organization, or of any State for the conduct of an international organization.

Article 58
Individual responsibility

These Articles are without prejudice to any question of the individual responsibility under international law of any person acting on behalf of a State.

Article 59
Charter of the United Nations

These Articles are without prejudice to the Charter of the United Nations.

Index